Lecture Notes in Computer Science

Lecture Notes in Computer Science

Vol. 88: Mathematical Foundations of Computer Science 1980. Proceedings, 1980. Edited by P. Dembiński. VIII, 723 pages. 1980.

Vol. 89: Computer Aided Design - Modelling, Systems Engineering, CAD-Systems. Proceedings, 1980. Edited by J. Encarnacao. XIV, 461 pages. 1980.

Vol. 90: D. M. Sandford, Using Sophisticated Models in Resolution Theorem Proving.
XI, 239 pages. 1980

Vol. 91: D. Wood, Grammar and L Forms: An Introduction. IX, 314 pages. 1980.

Vol. 92: R. Milner, A Calculus of Communication Systems. VI, 171 pages. 1980.

Vol. 93: A. Nijholt, Context-Free Grammars: Covers, Normal Forms, and Parsing. VII, 253 pages. 1980.

Vol. 94: Semantics-Directed Compiler Generation. Proceedings, 1980. Edited by N. D. Jones. V, 489 pages. 1980.

Vol. 95: Ch. D. Marlin, Coroutines. XII, 246 pages. 1980.

Vol. 96: J. L. Peterson, Computer Programs for Spelling Correction: VI, 213 pages. 1980.

Vol. 97: S. Osaki and T. Nishio, Reliability Evaluation of Some Fault-Tolerant Computer Architectures. VI, 129 pages. 1980.

Vol. 98: Towards a Formal Description of Ada. Edited by D. Bjørner and O. N. Oest. XIV, 630 pages. 1980.

Vol. 99: I. Guessarian, Algebraic Semantics. XI, 158 pages. 1981.

Vol. 100: Graphtheoretic Concepts in Computer Science. Edited by H. Noltemeier. X, 403 pages. 1981.

Vol. 101: A. Thayse, Boolean Calculus of Differences. VII, 144 pages. 1981.

Vol. 102: J. H. Davenport, On the Integration of Algebraic Functions. 1–197 pages. 1981.

Vol. 103: H. Ledgard, A. Singer, J. Whiteside, Directions in Human Factors of Interactive Systems. VI, 190 pages. 1981.

Vol. 104: Theoretical Computer Science. Ed. by P. Deussen. VII, 261 pages. 1981.

Vol. 105: B. W. Lampson, M. Paul, H. J. Siegert, Distributed Systems – Architecture and Implementation. XIII, 510 pages. 1981.

Vol. 106: The Programming Language Ada. Reference Manual. X, 243 pages. 1981.

Vol. 107: International Colloquium on Formalization of Programming Concepts. Proceedings. Edited by J. Diaz and I. Ramos. VII, 478 pages. 1981.

Vol. 108: Graph Theory and Algorithms. Edited by N. Saito and T. Nishizeki. VI, 216 pages. 1981.

Vol. 109: Digital Image Processing Systems. Edited by L. Bolc and Zenon Kulpa. V, 353 pages. 1981.

Vol. 110: W. Dehning, H. Essig, S. Maass, The Adaptation of Virtual Man-Computer Interfaces to User Requirements in Dialogs. X, 142 pages. 1981.

Vol. 111: CONPAR 81. Edited by W. Händler. XI, 508 pages. 1981.

Vol. 112: CAAP '81. Proceedings. Edited by G. Astesiano and C. Böhm. VI, 364 pages. 1981.

Vol. 113: E.-E. Doberkat, Stochastic Automata: Stability, Nondeterminism, and Prediction. IX, 135 pages. 1981.

Vol. 114: B. Liskov, CLU, Reference Manual. VIII, 190 pages. 1981.

Vol. 115: Automata, Languages and Programming. Edited by S. Even and O. Kariv. VIII, 552 pages. 1981.

Vol. 116: M. A. Casanova, The Concurrency Control Problem for Database Systems. VII, 175 pages. 1981.

Vol. 117: Fundamentals of Computation Theory. Proceedings, 1981. Edited by F. Gécseg. XI, 471 pages. 1981.

Vol. 118: Mathematical Foundations of Computer Science 1981. Proceedings, 1981. Edited by J. Gruska and M. Chytil. XI, 589 pages. 1981.

Vol. 119: G. Hirst, Anaphora in Natural Language Understanding: A Survey. XIII, 128 pages. 1981.

Vol. 120: L. B. Rall, Automatic Differentiation: Techniques and Applications. VIII, 165 pages. 1981.

Vol. 121: Z. Zlatev, J. Wasniewski, and K. Schaumburg, Y12M Solution of Large and Sparse Systems of Linear Algebraic Equations. IX, 128 pages. 1981.

Vol. 122: Algorithms in Modern Mathematics and Computer Science. Proceedings, 1979. Edited by A. P. Ershov and D. E. Knuth. XI, 487 pages. 1981.

Vol. 123: Trends in Information Processing Systems. Proceedings, 1981. Edited by A. J. W. Duijvestijn and P. C. Lockemann. XI, 349 pages. 1981.

Vol. 124: W. Polak, Compiler Specification and Verification. XIII, 269 pages. 1981.

Vol. 125: Logic of Programs. Proceedings, 1979. Edited by E. Engeler. V, 245 pages. 1981.

Vol. 126: Microcomputer System Design. Proceedings, 1981. Edited by M. J. Flynn, N. R. Harris, and D. P. McCarthy. VII, 397 pages. 1982.

Voll. 127: Y. Wallach, Alternating Sequential/Parallel Processing. X, 329 pages. 1982.

Vol. 128: P. Branquart, G. Louis, P. Wodon, An Analytical Description of CHILL, the CCITT High Level Language. VI, 277 pages. 1982.

Vol. 129: B. T. Hailpern, Verifying Concurrent Processes Using Temporal Logic. VIII, 208 pages. 1982.

Vol. 130: R. Goldblatt, Axiomatising the Logic of Computer Programming. XI, 304 pages. 1982.

Vol. 131: Logics of Programs. Proceedings, 1981. Edited by D. Kozen. VI, 429 pages. 1982.

Vol. 132: Data Base Design Techniques I: Requirements and Logical Structures. Proceedings, 1978. Edited by S.B. Yao, S.B. Navathe, J.L. Weldon, and T.L. Kunii. V, 227 pages. 1982.

Vol. 133: Data Base Design Techniques II: Proceedings, 1979. Edited by S.B. Yao and T.L. Kunii. V, 229–399 pages. 1982.

Vol. 134: Program Specification. Proceedings, 1981. Edited by J. Staunstrup. IV, 426 pages. 1982.

Vol. 135: R.L. Constable, S.D. Johnson, and C.D. Eichenlaub, An Introduction to the PL/CV2 Programming Logic. X, 292 pages. 1982.

Vol. 136: Ch. M. Hoffmann, Group-Theoretic Algorithms and Graph Isomorphism. VIII, 311 pages. 1982.

Vol. 137: International Symposium on Programming. Proceedings, 1982. Edited by M. Dezani-Ciancaglini and M. Montanari. VI, 406 pages. 1982.

Vol. 138: 6th Conference on Automated Deduction. Proceedings, 1982. Edited by D.W. Loveland. VII, 389 pages. 1982.

Vol. 139: J. Uhl, S. Drossopoulou, G. Persch, G. Goos, M. Dausmann, G. Winterstein, W. Kirchgässner, An Attribute Grammar for the Semantic Analysis of Ada. IX, 511 pages. 1982.

Vol. 140: Automata, Languages and programming. Edited by M. Nielsen and E.M. Schmidt. VII, 614 pages. 1982.

Vol. 141: U. Kastens, B. Hutt, E. Zimmermann, GAG: A Practical Compiler Generator. IV, 156 pages. 1982.

Lecture Notes in Computer Science

Edited by G. Goos and J. Hartmanis

188

Advances in Petri Nets 1984

APN

84

Edited by G. Rozenberg
with the cooperation of H. Genrich and G. Roucairol

Springer-Verlag
Berlin Heidelberg New York Tokyo

Editor

G. Rozenberg
University of Leiden, Dept. of Mathematics and Computer Science
Postbus 9512, 2300 RA Leiden, The Netherlands

CR Subject Classification (1982): 4.29, 4.39, 4.6, 5.23, 5.29, 5.9, 3.89

ISBN 3-540-15204-0 Springer-Verlag Berlin Heidelberg New York Tokyo
ISBN 0-387-15204-0 Springer-Verlag New York Heidelberg Berlin Tokyo

Printed in Germany

Printing and binding: Beltz Offsetdruck, Hemsbach/Bergstr.
2145/3140-543210

PREFACE

Petri nets (invented by Carl Adam Petri in his renowned dissertation of 1962) have developed over the years as a major model for the representation and analysis of concurrent systems. In particular, they have attracted widespread interest in computer science where in recent years problems of concurrency in systems and computations became of paramount importance.

Although an active research in the area of Petri nets concerning both its practical applications and theoretical properties has been going on for a very long time, in its initial stage this research has been conducted in a number of (rather isolated) groups around the world without the acclaim it deserved and hence was not known to the wide community of computer scientists. The situation has changed significantly since the "Advanced Course on General Net Theory of Processes and Systems" was organized (by W. Brauer, C.A. Petri and B. Randell) in Hamburg in 1979. This course not only helped to systematize and organize the main body of knowledge concerning Petri nets, but it also resulted in the increase of the number of computer scientists actively interested in Petri nets. Moreover, this course has also stimulated more cooperation within the Petri net research community and as a result of this cooperation the "European Workshop on Applications and Theory of Petri Nets" emerged (1980). This series of workshops is organized on regular (annual) basis and has become an established forum for presenting recent results on Petri nets.

The idea of the series of volumes called "Advances in Petri Nets" has originated during these workshops. The main thought behind this series was to present to the general computer science community recent advances in Petri nets - it is the recent results which are the most significant for the development of the area. Thus in particular the "best" papers from the past workshops are considered for the series (but they go through yet another, independent, refereeing process and often appear in "Advances" in a quite revised and extended form) as well as various papers not presented at the workshops.

It is hoped that this series will serve at least two aims:
(1) present to the "outside" scientific community a fair picture of recent advances in the area of Petri nets, and
(2) stimulate those interested in the field of applications and theory of concurrent systems to look more closely at Petri nets and then join the group of researchers working in this fascinating and challenging area.

The present (first) volume of "Advances" covers the last two years which include the workshop 1983 in Toulouse and the workshop 1984 in Aarhus. I would like to thank the chairmen of these workshops, H. Genrich and G. Roucairol, for their cooperation in preparing this volume. I am also indebted to the following individuals who have helped in refereeing papers for this volume:

IJ.J. Aalbersberg, E. Best, M. Diaz, F. Feldbrugge, C. Fernandez, H. Genrich, L. Groenewegen, H.J. Hoogeboom, C. Hopmann, K. Jensen, H.J. Kreowski, K. Lautenbach, M. Nielsen, A. Pagnoni, W. Reisig, P. Starke, P.S. Thiagarajan, R. Valk, K. Voss.

G. Rozenberg

Leiden, December 1984

TABLE OF CONTENTS

PSI: A PETRI NET BASED SIMULATOR FOR FLEXIBLE MANUFACTURING SYSTEMS

P. Alanche[+], K. Benzakour[++], F. Dollé[+], P. Gillet[+++],
P. Rodrigues[+], R. Valette[++]

[+] DAST/RNUR 9,11 Ave. du 18 juin 1940, F-92500 RUEIL MALMAISON
[++] LAAS/CNRS 7 Ave. du Colonel Roche, F-31400 TOULOUSE
[+++] SERAM 151 Bd de l'Hopital, F-75013 PARIS

1. INTRODUCTION

Design and implementation of flexible manufacturing systems is a complex task. Performance evaluation is necessary as early as the first specification step and this evaluation has generally to be done by simulation [DO1]. It is the reason why a comparison of the existing packages utilized in this domain has been done [DO2].

Petri nets and related specification tools such as the Grafcet are more and more used to express the operation constraints (i.e. the synchronisation mechanisms imposed by the mechanical part of the system), however no Petri net based discrete event simulator was available. So PSI, a prototype of such a package, has been realized [VA] in order to complement the comparison of the existing packages by an evaluation of such an approach.

In the following section, PSI (Petri net based SImulator) is presented, then in section 3 the utilization of PSI in the case of an actual system is shown. Finally, the advantages and the limitation of PSI are discussed.

2. THE PSI SIMULATOR

2.1. Outlines

The general definition of Petri nets assumes that the firing of transitions are instantaneous, therefore it seems more natural to associate time durations with places. When a token is put into a timed place, it remains thus non-disposible during a certain amount of time. Then, it becomes disposible that means: it can be used to enable and fire some transitions. Clearly, time durations could be associated with transitions. As a matter of fact, the two approaches are equivalent. A place timed net can be transformed into a transition timed net by replacing each timed place by the sequence "place, timed transition, place", and conversely a transition timed net can be transformed into a place timed net by replacing each timed transition by the sequence "transition, timed place, transition".

Discrete event simulation systems can be classified into three main families: event driven, activity based and communicating process based systems [BE]. In the case of event driven simulators, the modeling of the system to be evaluated is uniquely done by describing events and their consequences i.e. the production of futur events stored into a calendar. They are efficient but the modeling is very poorly structured. On the contrary, activity based simulators keep the calendar transparent, modeling is done by describing activities with their durations and their activation conditions. They are generally badly efficient because all activation conditions have to be evaluated at each step. Communicating process based simulators have been realized in order to combine the advantages of the two first classes, but interprocess synchronization can only be introduced at the input and output points of the processes. Consequently, the modeling of complex synchronization problems is not very easy.

If the notion of timed nets described above is used, transitions correspond to events and places to activities. A token player algorithm can then be considered as a way of scanning all the activities in order to detect if they can initiate. The events corresponding to the transformation of a non-disposible token into a disposible one (activity termination) can be easily implemented by means of a calendar. Moreover, as transitions (events) are known at the designer level and as the designer can introduce into the calendar events corresponding to the firing of input transitions, a discrete event simulation based upon timed Petri nets can be considered as an approach mixing event driving and activities.

Consequently, PSI is made up of:

- a token player for interpreted Petri net that searches for fireable transitions and fires them (pure synchronization or initiation of an activity),
- a calendar used to store transparent events (a token becomes disposible) or events on the responsability of the designer (firing of input transitions or boolean variables becoming true or false),
- statistical functions concerning the markings of some places and the number of times transitions have been fired.

The notion of interpreted Petri net utilized here is as follows. With each transition of the Petri net an extra firing condition involving boolean variables and integers can be associated. These variables can be manipulated by elementary procedures also associated with the transitions and executed each time the corresponding transition is fired. These variables are particularly useful to express priorities rules in case of conflicts.

2.2. Input Language

A given simulation is determined by the description of the model together with the specification of the simulation conditions. In our case, it is necessary to depict the interpreted Petri net, and then to describe activity durations and the part of the calendar on the responsability of the designer. Consequently two languages have been defined.

The specification of the interpreted Petri net is a mere sequence of declarations. Each identifier has to be declared with an associated type (place, transition, boolean variable or integer). The program control is structured by means of four kinds of composed instructions (node, arc or variable declaration and interpretation).

Simulation conditions are specified in a separate program, all the identifiers utilized have to have been declared during the preceding step. The program control is also structured by means of four kinds of initialisation composed instructions (place, boolean variable, integer and calendar).

The program describing the interpreted Petri net is firstly analysed and tables are produced. This is done by a syntactical and semantical analyser/translator. These tables correspond, as a matter of fact, to the data structure on which the token player will play. Afterwards, the second program is analysed and the initialization of the data structure is done.

In the following section, these two input languages will be illustrated. It must be pointed out that if the model building is Petri net based, the statement model (coding) is performed very easily.

2.3. Statistical aspects

The first version of PSI did not allow the use of random variables. Only fixed constant time could be associated with the places. The statistics done between two dates (beginning of statistics and simulation termination) are the following ones:

- number of times a transition has been fired,
- maximum and mean value of the token load of a place,
- maximum and mean value of the time a token have been disposible in a place.

2.4. Implementation and performance considerations

PSI has been written in PASCAL and develloped on a microsystem based on a Z80 8 bits microcomputer under the operating system CP/M. With 64K bytes of memory the maximum size of the Petri net is 150 places, 150 transitions, 50 boolean variables, 50 integers. However, PSI has been compiled with the PASCAL/Z compiler and is presently relatively slow. A version compiled by an INTEL PASCAL compiler seems much more efficient.

3. EXAMPLE: A TRANSPORT SYSTEM

3.1. Description of the transport system

Parts and tools are frequently transported by self-propelling trucks in flexible manufacturing systems. These trucks called "Automated Guided Vehicle" or "Unmanned Carriers" are wire guided. In fact there is a wire net in the floor of the shop. Contacts are used as sensors in order to determine the position of the trucks. When a truck is crossing a contact, a dialogue between the control system and the truck allows to stop it or to route it. Each portion of wire has a different frequency and so the trucks can identify them at a switching.

In order to avoid collision the transport network is divided into cells and the control is such that at any time at most one truck can circulate in a given cell.

The troughput of such a system depends on many variables (for instance the routes, the layout of the cells, the number of the trucks, etc...). Bottlenecks, generally, cannot be obtained analytically and simulation is necessary. Packages (SLAM for example) allowing the simulation of such system exists. However the logical constraints, such as the mutual exclusion with respect to cells, are not easy to specify and to verify. On the other hand Petri net are particularly well suited for the description and the analysis of these logical constraints. It is why we have chosen to develop a Petri net based simulator: PSI.

An example of a real transport network for self-propelling trucks is represented in figure 1. It is being built in a french car factory and PSI has been used in order to evaluate its performance. It is used for the feeding of 3 test workbench from 3 loading stations. As many as 20 trucks can circulate at a given time 'GI'.

3.2. Petri net modelling

The direct drawing of a Petri net representing the transport system with its operation rules would be a hard work. It is necessary to have a structured approach [MA] [GI] using the

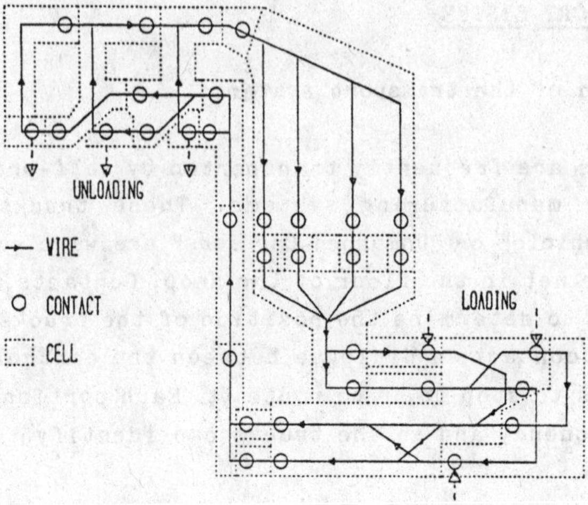

FIGURE 1 : transport network

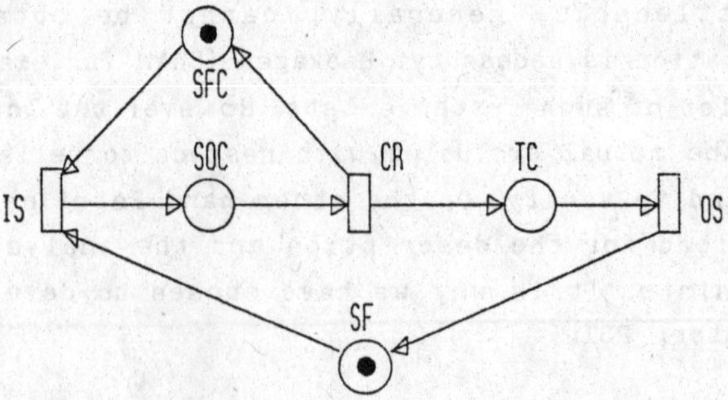

FIGURE 2 : Petri net of a section

decomposition of the network into cells. As it can be seen in figure 1, there exists a large number of cells of different kinds. It is why cells are also decomposed into a more elementary unit: the section. As a matter of fact, the notion of section results from the fact that as soon as a truck has left a contact it cannot be controlled until the next contact is reached. A section is the part of the network bounded by two contacts including the second contact [GI].

A Petri net representing a section can be found in figure 2. Transition IS is fired when the truck enter the section (preceding contact is left). The meaning of the places is shown below:

- SFC the section can be crossed by a truck following an other section (this is only necessary when the section belongs to a switching or a crossing),
- SOC a truck is moving along the section,
- TC a truck is passing over the contact or is stopping,
- SF the whole section is free.

When the truck leaves the section, transition OS is fired.

A cell is a set of supperposed sections. A Petri net representing a cell is easily obtained by composing the nets describing the sections. Corresponding SFC places are merged in order to express the operation rules "only one truck is moving in a cell at a given time". Some particular cases exists, for instance a junction cell correspond to two sections terminating with a unique contact. In this case, the two places SF and the two places TC have to be merged also. After the merging of the places, it is sometimes possible to reduce the net. For example in the case of the junction cell places SFC can be omitted.

An example of a crossing cell is given in figure 3. The cell is represented in a) and the correponding Petri net in b).

Finally the global net is obtained by the composition of the cells. This is done by merging the corresponding input (IS) and output (OS) transitions of the Petri nets representing the cells.

It must be pointed out that by construction the global net contains place invariants (involving places SFC and SOC of various sections) proving the main synchronization constraint: "only one truck moving within a cell". The behavioural equivalence [AN] can be used in order to obtain a strongly reduced net for the analysis with respect to "good" properties.

The Petri net obtained represents the so called operation rules, i.e. the synchronization constraints resulting of the mechanical system. A full description of the transport system implies also some decision rules, i.e. the complementary information necessary to solve the conflicts (choices) in the Petri net. In some complex cases it is also necessary to specify which object will be removed from a queue, in the transport system considered here only FIFO are employed.

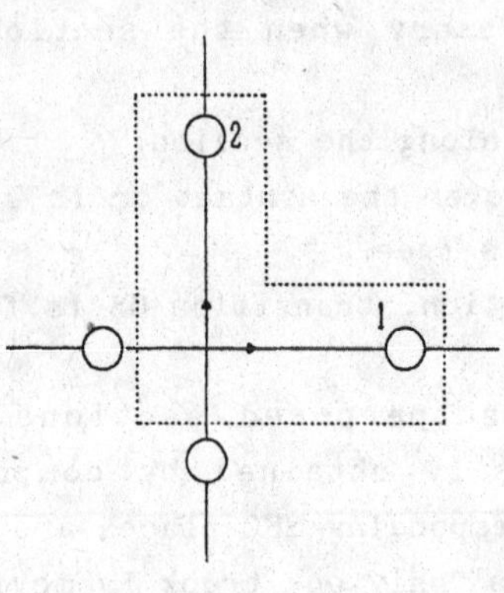

a) Cell

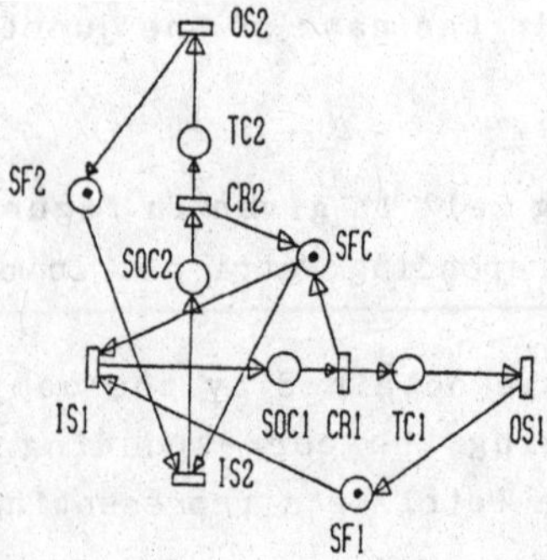

b) Petri net

<u>FIGURE 3</u> : Crossing cell

The decision rules imply an interpretation of the net. In PSI only a simple interpretation based on the use of Boolean variables and integers is possible. For a first approximation it is only necessary to associate with each bifurcation cell a predicate determining the routes respecting the proportions of truck for each branch of the bifurcation. A more precise description would imply the use of colored bifurcation cells.

3.3. Statement model

Let us consider a bifurcation cell. It results from the merging of two sections where only the output transitions OS are different. As this cell contains only one contact, the place SF implements the mutual exclusion and place SFC is useless (redondant). The place TC can be merged with place SOC and transition CR is useless. Let us suppose that only one truck out of ten will follow the branch OS2, the description of the decision rule implies the use of the integer X. The corresponding interpreted Petri net is represented in figure 4.

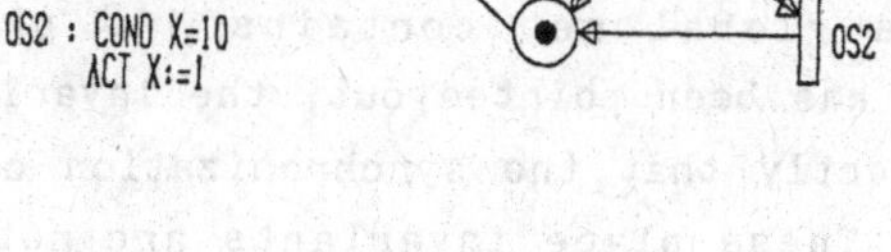

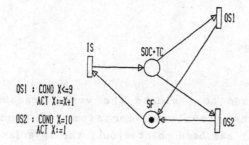

FIGURE 4 : Petri net representing a bifurcation cell

The program describing this cell is as follows.

```
NODES
  IS,OS1,OS2 : TRANSITION ;
  SOC_TC,SF : PLACE ;
ARCS
  PATH = (IS,SOC_TC,OS1,SF,IS) ;
  PATH = (SOC_TC,OS2,SF) ;
VAR
  X : INTEGER ;
INTERPRETATION
  ACTION OS1 = X := X+1 ;
  ACTION OS2 = X := 1   ;
  COND   OS1 = X <= 9   ;
  COND   OS2 = X  = 10  ;
END.
```

3.4. Simulation

In order to simulate the transport system, durations (for transport) are associated with the SOC place of each segment. In the case of the segments representing loading or unloading operations, time is also attached to the TC place.

Consequently, the simulation conditions for the bifurcation cell are as follows:

```
PLACE TIME SOC_TC := 25 ;
      MARKING SF := 1 ;
```

PSI has been used to evaluate the whole transport system described above. The global net contains 118 places and 83 transitions 'GI'. As it has been pointed out, the invariants existing in each cell prove directly that the synchronization contraints are verified at any time. These place invariants are not affected by transition merging and therefore it is guaranteed that no collision is possible in the transport system. This proof is important because collisions would not be detected by means of the analysis of the simulation results (number of part transported during the simulation).

On the contrary dealock or starvation will produce a heavy

performance degradation and therefore they will be easily detected. Consequently analysis with respect to these properties is not so essential.

The results of the simulation have allowed an optimisation of the system and an improvement of the throughput by minor modifications concerning the contact lay-out.

4. LIMITATIONS OF PSI

The simulation of the example in section 3 has been done with constant durations. A new version of the package allows now the use of random variables. This allows a better performance analysis and also enable to resolve conflicts on a stochastic basis.

The strongest limitation of PSI is that no list of attributes can be associated with tokens. In fact, a more correct description of the transport system would have implied the definition of routes associated with trucks (i.e. associated with some tokens). Consequently, conflicts would have been solved by the execution of procedure involving the token attributes.

A Petri net with attributes attached to tokens can be seen as a colored Petri net. However, it must be pointed out that operation contraints are generally expressed without involving the attributes. As for the decision rules, they involves the attributes but they are described in the interpretation of the net. Consequently, the power of description of colored net is not completely utilized, the attributes being employed uniquely in the interpretation when complex decision rules are concerned.

This limitation of the present version of PSI is the reason why a new project (SEDRIC) is under development [TH]. This package will offer the possibility of attaching attributes to tokens and of employing Fortran procedures to express complex decision rules. The required memory for data storage go beyond the capacity of 8 bits microsystems, so the aim machines are 16 bits or 32 bits systems. Project SEDRIC is presently under specification by means of PDL package.

Another limitation is that PSI seems relatively slow in comparison with other packages such as SLAM. Clearly, it is a little hazardous to compare a package running on a 8 bits micro-system with one running on a 32 bits computer. Anyhow, some principles used to implement PSI may be responsible for this slowness.

In fact, activity based discrete event simulator may be not very efficient because it is necessary to scan systematically all the activities to detect if they can initiate, and this after each event. The token algorithm used in PSI only checks transitions that have at least one input marked. This is very efficient in the case of programmable logic controllers because very few places are simultaneously marked. On the contrary, in the case of Petri nets modelling flexible systems it is not the case because tokens represent trucks, parts, tools etc...

On the other hand, the utilization of a token player is essential to ensure that any transition that can be fired is immediately fired, otherwise, Petri net validation will not guarantee correct simulation. Fortunately some optimization of the token player remains possible, for example by considering only those transitions for which the marking of an input place have just been changed.

5. CONCLUSION

Our feeling is that there is a need for Petri net based discrete event simulators for the design of flexible manufacturing systems. In fact, the limit of the present discrete event simulators is that they do not allow an analysis of complex synchronization problems. Either they are not based upon a formal mathematical tool, or this tool (queuing theory) is oriented to the solution of other kind of problems.

One reason is that when flexible transport systems are concerned, the operation rules imply synchronization mechanisms that are not straightforward. A Petri net based simulation is more reliable because these mechanisms are clearly specified and because they can be proved correct by a mere analysis.

Another reason is that graphical tools such as Petri nets and Grafcet are more and more utilized for the programmation of control systems [DO1]. If the same tools are used for the design, the evaluation and the implementation of the control system, a better understanding within the project team will result. The modelling effort done for the simulation will be the first step of the modelling effort for the implementation. For example, the global net representing the transport system in figure 1 contains some information necessary to decide whether its control will be centralized, distributed or hierarchical.

REFERENCES

AN C. André: "Use of the behaviour equivalence in place-transition analysis", Application and Theory of Petri nets, Informatik-Fachberichte, N52, Spinger-Verlag, 1982.

BE G. Bel: "Méthodes et langages de simulation pour la production automatisée: principes, choix, utilisation", Congrès AFCET Productique et Robotique Intelligente", Besançon, 15-17 nov. 1983, p.41-52.

DO1 F. Dollé, M. Moalla, P. Rodrigues: "Concevoir des systèmes automatisés", Le Nouvel Automatisme, N36, mars 1983, p.33-38.

DO2 F. Dollé, P. Alanche, B. Ancelin, C. Catsoyannis, C. Muller, P. Rodrigues: "Méthodes de conception des systèmes automatiques pour la production discontinue, Action de Recherche ADI No 81/543, mai 1983.

GI P. Gillet: "Système flexible de transport", Dossier Seram/Regienov No 11.641, 21 oct. 1983.

MA D. Mayeux: "Modélisation et validation de la synchronisation des tâches du logiciel de commande d'un système de transport dans un atelier flexible", Rapport partiel GIS Ateliers Flexibles, Note Interne LAAS 82.0.16, mars 1982.

TH V. Thomas, R. Valette: "Simulateur à événements discrets

utilisant les réseaux de Petri colorés", Rapport de recherche LAAS 83059, 3 oct. 1983.

VA R. Valette: "Ecriture d'un simulateur à événements discrets basé sur l'utilisation des réseaux de Petri", Rapport final du contrat 03.03.021/LAAS11 avec le G.I.E. Renault Recherche Innovation, juillet 1982.

MODELLING AND VALIDATION OF COMPLEX SYSTEMS BY COLOURED PETRI NETS

APPLICATION TO A FLEXIBLE MANUFACTURING SYSTEM

H. Alla [+] P. Ladet [+] J. Martinez [++] M. Silva-Suarez [++]

+ Laboratoire d'Automatique de Grenoble
(Associé au C.N.R.S. L.A. n°228)

B.P. 46, 38402 - Saint-Martin-d'Hères
France

++ Depto Automatica - Escuela Tecnica Superior de
Ingenieros Industriales
Zaragoza - Spain

====================

INTRODUCTION

Faced with the growing complexity of data processing and industrial control systems, Petri nets represent an interesting compromise between expressive power and analysis capacity on the built models. Nevertheless in many cases, the complexity of a PN model may be important even for systems functionnally not very complex. In this way, the representation of a FIFO with n elements and p message types requires a binary PN of (p+1).n places.

Under these conditions, coloured Petri nets [JEN 81a] may bring an important contribution. The association with tokens and with transitions of colour sets and the definition of functions associated with the nets arcs, allow a very concise and readable representation of the described mechanisms. There is a simplification of the net structure through the transfer of information on the markings (colours) and on the transformations (functions) made on these markings. As it will be shown (§ 2.3) a FIFO queue may be modelled by means of a coloured Petri Net with only two places.

In this paper we introduce a subclass of CPN and a technique for the calculation of p-invariants (and t-invariants) based on commutativity of certain functions. If commutativity conditions are verified, then for general CPN it is possible to calculate invariants by using a decomposition/composition strategy. Also in this paper it is presented a CPN model of a complex flexible manufacturing system. Finally this model is proved to be deadlock-free and bounded.

2. COLOURED PETRI NETS. DEFINITIONS.

2.1. Definition given by Jensen [JEN 81a]

A coloured Petri net (CPN) is a 6-tuple

CPN = (P,T,C,Pre, Post,M_o) where

1) P = (P1,P2,...,Pn) is a finite set of places
2) T = (t1,t2,...,tm) is a finite set of transitions ($P \cap T = \emptyset$)
3) C is the colour function defined from PxT into non-empty sets
4) Pre and Post are respectively the input function and the output function defined on Pxt such that :

   $Pre(p,t)$ and $Post(p,t) : C(t) \rightarrow (C(p) \rightarrow N)\ \forall (p,t) \in Pxt$

5) M_o, initial marking, is a function defined on P such that :

   $M_o(p) : C(p) \rightarrow N\ \forall\ p \in P$

   A marking of CPN is a function M defined on P such that :

   $M(p) : C(p) \rightarrow N\ \forall\ p \in P$

   Elements of C(p) and C(t) are called colours.

   M(p) and $M_o(p)$ give respectively the number of tokens of each colour in the place p for the current and initial markings.

   A CPN can be represented as a directed graph.

The function Pre(p,t) gives the weight of the arc joining a place with a transition (Pre(p,t) is equal to zero if there is no arc). The function Post(p,t) gives the weight of the arc joining a transition with a place (Post(p,t) is equal to zero if there is no arc). Pre(p,t) and Post(p,t) are linear functions $\forall(p,t) \in Pxt$ and can be represented by matrices with Card (C(p)) rows and Card (C(t)) columns ; the general term of Pre(p,t) is $\alpha'ij = Pre(p,t)(C')(C'')$ and of Post(p,t) is $\alpha''ij = Post(p,t)(C')(C'')\ \forall\ C' \in C(t)$ and $\forall\ C'' \in C(p)$, $\alpha'ij$ and $\alpha''ij \in N$.

A positive weighted set of transitions is a function S defined on T, such that $S(t) : C(t) \rightarrow N$

S is enabled in a marking M iff $M > Pre \circ S$

M and S are respectively vectors of dimension n and m

Pre, Post and W are matrices of dimensions n x m.

Operator "$\circ$" is the generalization of matrix multiplication sustituting each product on a function composition. When S is enabled, it may fire. If S fires, a new marking $M' = M + W \circ S$ (1) is reached, with W = Post - Pre : incidence matrix.

This relation is very interesting because it allows the determination of linear relations between the markings of the net [LAU 74]

Let us consider the equations system $X^T \circ W = 0$.

If X = U is a solution and if we multiply relation (1) on the left by U^T, we have for all reachable markings M and M'.

$$U^T \circ M' = U^T \circ M + U^T \circ W \circ S$$

$$U^T \circ M' = U^T \circ M \qquad \text{because} \qquad U^T \circ W = 0$$

So for all marking M, we have $U^T \circ M = U^T \circ M_o$.

This relation is called a linear invariant of markings.

The exploitation of these relations allows us to verify specific properties of the net and particularly allows us to show that the net is bounded and deadlock-free.

Until to day, in the case of matrix W defined above there was no mathematical method to resolve the system $X^T \circ W = 0$. We are going to answer this problem by defining a sub-class of CPN.

2.2. Definition 2.

It only differs from the definition given before by the fourth point :

$$\begin{aligned} Pre/Pre(p,t) &= a'(p,t).f_p \circ g_t & a',a'' \in N \\ Post/Post(p,t) &= a''(p,t).f_p \circ g_t & \forall(p,t) \in PXT \\ W/\ W(p,t) &= a(p,t).f_p \circ g_t & \end{aligned}$$

with $f_p : \bigcup_{t/a(p,t) \neq 0} C(t) \to [C(p) \to N]$

and $g_t : C(t) \to [C(t) \to N]$

Then W has the following form :

$$W = (a_{ij}\ f_i \circ g_j) \quad i \in [1,n] \quad j \in [1,m] \quad a_{ij} \in Z$$

$$W = F \circ A \circ G \quad \text{with}$$

$$F = \begin{bmatrix} f_1 & & 0 \\ & \ddots & \\ 0 & & f_n \end{bmatrix} \qquad A = (a_{ij}.id) \qquad G = \begin{bmatrix} g_1 & & 0 \\ & \ddots & \\ 0 & & g_m \end{bmatrix}$$

id is the identity function.

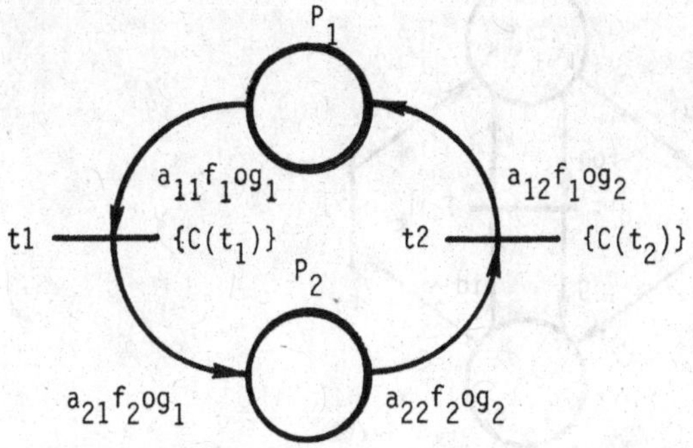

Figure 1. Example of a CPN belonging to our subclass

In most cases, functions g_t are equal to function id.

With our definition, we can notice that with each place and transition are respectively associated the same functions f_p and g_t.

2.3. Example 1 : FIFO queue.

A queue delivers messages in the same order it receives them (FIFO : first in, first out). Above the queue, we have a multi-producer system (p different types of messages). Below, we have a multi-consumer system of these messages. The type specifies the producer-consumer relation. This queue has a capacity of n messages and can transfer simultaneously the p different types messages $m_\ell (\ell \in [1,p])$. FIFO queue is modelled by the CPN of figure 2. This CPN does not represent the producer and the consumer system.

The set of colours is $C = \{ <m_\ell> \cup <e_k> \cup <m_\ell , e_k> \ ; \ \ell \in [1,n], \ \ell \in [1,p] \}$

A token e_k in the place E means that the queue element k is empty and a token $<m_\ell , e_k>$ in the place Q means that there is a message m_ℓ in the queue element k.

$$u : \{m_\ell\} \rightarrow \{<m_\ell , e_1>\} \ / \ u(m_\ell) = <m_\ell , e_1>$$

$$v : \{m_\ell\} \rightarrow \{<m_\ell , e_n>\} \ / \ v(m_\ell) = <m_\ell , e_n>$$

$$f : \{<m_\ell , e_k>\} \rightarrow \{e_k\} \ / \ f(<m_\ell , e_k>) = e_k \ , \ k \in [1,n] \qquad \ell \in [1,p]$$

$$g : \{<m_\ell , e_k>\} \rightarrow \{<m_\ell , e_k>\} \ / \ g(<m_\ell , e_k>) = <m_\ell , e_{k+1}> \ , \ k \in [1,n-1]$$

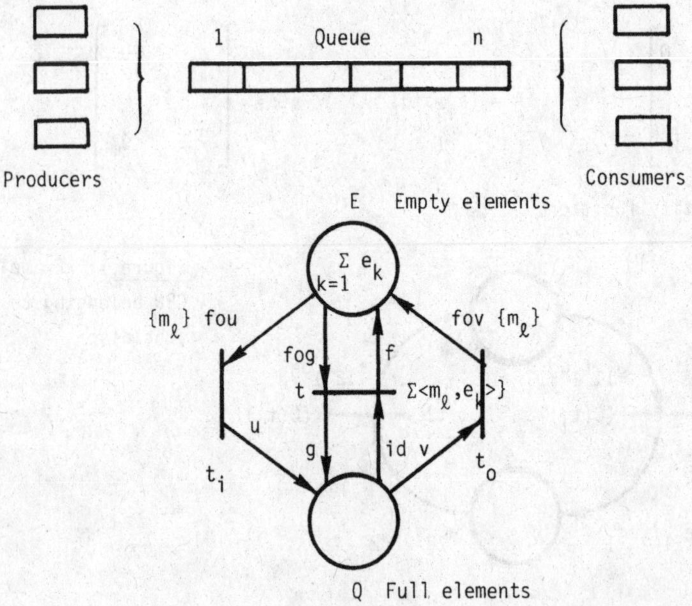

Figure 2 : Modeling of a FIFO queue with n elements.

The set associated with places may be deduced from the functions range . With Q is associated the set $(<m_\ell,e_k>)$ and with E, the set (e_k).

The initial marking M_0 is

$$M_0(Q) = 0 \qquad \text{and} \quad M_0(E) = \sum_{k=1}^{n} e_k$$

What means the queue is empty.

Transition t_i is enabled with regard to colour m_ℓ if the place E contains a token with the colour $fou(m_\ell) = e_1$, i.e. the queue element 1 is empty. Firing of t_i deposits a token with a colour $u(m_\ell) = <m_\ell,e_1>$ in the place Q, element 1 contains a message of type ℓ. This message will then be transfered from an element to the following one by firing transition t. Let us assume that the place Q contains a token $<m_\ell,e_k>$, transition t will be enabled according to colour $<m_\ell,e_k>$ if the place E contains a token with a colour $fog(<m_\ell,e_k>) = e_{k+1}$, i.e. the queue element k+1 must be empty. Firing of t deposits a token with a colour $f(<m_\ell,e_k>) = e_k$ in the place E (element k is empty) and a token $g(<m_\ell,e_k>) = <m_\ell,e_{k+1}>$ in place Q (element k+1 is occupied). This transfer goes on as long as there is some space in the queue until the message arrives to element n. Then it is evacuated from the queue by firing t_0 which releases the last element.

3. SOLUTIONS OF THE SYSTEM $X^T \circ W = 0$

In this section, we shall show how to find mathematical solutions for our subclass of CPN.

We have seen that finding place is equivalent to solve the system $X^T \circ W = 0$ and then to characterize Ker(W). Ker(W) is the kernel at left of matrix W, that is $Ker(W) = \{X/X^T \circ W = 0\}$, X is a vector which has n components, each one is a linear function.

$$W = (a_{ij}\ f_i \circ g_j) \qquad \forall i \in [1,n] \ ; \quad \forall j \in [1,n] \ ; \ a_{ij} \in Z$$

$$W = F \circ A \circ G$$

We proceed the calculation of Ker(W) in two steps.

3.1. Characterization of Ker(F $\circ$ A).

Let A' be the matrix built from A

$$A = (a_{ij}.id) \quad \text{and} \quad A' = (a_{ij}) \quad \text{where} \quad a_{ij} \in Z$$

It can be considered that A' is a linear mapping from Z^n into Z^m such that $\forall\ V \in Z^n \ \exists\ U \in Z^m /\ U^T = V^T . A'$.

Z^n is a module over Z and has a basis. Since Z is a principal ring thenthe kernel of A', Ker(A') is a sub-module of Z^n and admits a basis of dimension q such that [CHA 66] $q = n - \text{rank}(A')$

A basis may be found by classical algebra (see [SIL 80] in the context of PN theory and application). The set of all minimal support non negative invariants may be calculated by the algorithms presented in [MAR 82].

Let $\{V_r\}$, $r \in [1,q]$ be a basis of Ker A', $V_r = (v_{ir})$ $i \in [1,n]$

We have $Vr \,.\, A' = 0 \rightarrow (v_{ir}) \cdot (a_{ij}) = 0 \qquad \forall j \in [1,m]$

$$\rightarrow \sum_{i=1}^{n} v_{ir} \cdot a_{ij} = 0 \qquad \forall r \in [1,q]$$

Let us consider the following product of functions associated with each vector Vr : $\pi_r = \prod_{k \in FS_r} f'_k$ (product of functions means composition of functions). To make this product possible, f'_k will be any extension of f_k when it is necessary. The extension is such that $f'_k = f_k$ over the domain of f_k. FSr is the set of index k such that $v_{kr} \neq 0$ and all the functions f_k should be different to each other. If several functions are equal, we shall take the representative function which has the least index.

Let us multiply the relation $\sum_{i=1}^{n} V_{ir} \cdot a_{ij} = 0$ on the left by π_r, then we get

$$[\prod_{k \in FS_r} f'_k] \,.\, \sum_{i=1}^{n} v_{ir} \cdot a_{ij} = 0 = \sum_{i=1}^{n} [\prod_{k \in FS_r} f'_k] \,.\, v_{ir} \cdot a_{ij}$$

For each index i corresponding to a function included in the product π_r, let us assume that

$$\prod_{k \in FS_r} f'_k = (\prod_{\substack{k \in FS_r \\ k \neq i}} f'_k) \circ f'_i \qquad \underline{\text{(commutativity)}}$$

Then $\sum_{i=1}^{n} [\prod_{\substack{k \in FS_r \\ k \neq i}} f'_k] \, o v_{ir} \, a_{ij} \cdot f_i = 0 \qquad \forall j \in [1,m]$

If we define a vector $U_r = (u_{ir})$ $i \in [1,n]$, $r \in [1,q]$

with $u_{ir} = [\prod_{\substack{k \in FS_r \\ k \neq i}} f'_k] . v_{ir}$ we have

$$\sum_{i=1}^{n} u_{ir} \cdot a_{ij} \cdot f_i = 0$$

$$U_r^T \circ F \circ A = 0 \quad \text{and} \quad \underline{U_r \in \text{Ker}(F \circ A)}$$

In conclusion, solutions can be found if one can find extensions of the functions

f_k which fulfill the condition of commutativity. In this sense, our method presents sufficient conditions, particularly we don't know if all the solutions are obtained.

When this extension is necessary, according to our experience, a simple one which may preserve the commutativity is such that $f'_k(x) = x$, $x \notin$ Domain (f_k).

3.2. Characterization of Ker (W).

$$W = F \circledcirc A \circledcirc G$$

$\forall X \in \text{Ker}(F \circledcirc A)$, we have $X^T \circledcirc F \circledcirc A = 0$

Then $X^T \circledcirc F \circledcirc A \circledcirc G = 0$ and $\text{Ker}(F \circledcirc A) \subseteq \text{Ker}(F \circledcirc A \circledcirc G)$

Moreover if g_j is bijective $\forall j \in [1,m]$

then $\text{Ker}(F \circledcirc A) = \text{Ker}\ W$.

4. USEFUL METHOD.

The set of solutions is built in the following way :

- We choose a basis $\{V_r\}$, $r \in [1,q]$ of Ker A' such that the non-null components (v_{ir}), $i \in [1,n]$ correspond to a minimum number of different functions in a way that the condition of commutativity is less constrained.
- We build $U_r \,/\, u_{ir} = [\prod_{\substack{k \in FS_r \\ k \neq i}} f'_k] \cdot v_{ir}$

f'_k is the extension of f_k . Every function f'_i in the product π must verify the property of commutativity : $\prod_{k \in FS_r} f'_k = (\prod_{\substack{k \in FS_r \\ k \neq i}} f'_k) \circ f'_i$ (sufficient condition).

Let us take again the example of the FIFO queue. The incidence matrix is :

$$W = \begin{array}{c} \\ Q \\ E \end{array} \begin{array}{c} \begin{array}{ccc} t_i & t & t_o \end{array} \\ \begin{bmatrix} u & g-id & -v \\ -fou & f-fog & fov \end{bmatrix} \end{array} = \underbrace{\begin{bmatrix} id & 0 \\ 0 & f \end{bmatrix}}_{F} \circledcirc \underbrace{\begin{bmatrix} id & id & -id \\ -id & -id & id \end{bmatrix}}_{A} \circledcirc \underbrace{\begin{bmatrix} u & 0 & 0 \\ 0 & g-id & 0 \\ 0 & 0 & v \end{bmatrix}}_{G}$$

As the function u and v are bijective then $\text{Ker}\ W = \text{Ker}\ (F \circledcirc A)$

$$A' = \begin{bmatrix} 1 & 1 & -1 \\ -1 & -1 & 1 \end{bmatrix}$$ and a basis of Ker A' is the vector (1 1)

Then the vector $U = (f\ id') \in$ Ker W, with $id'/id'(e_k) = e_k$ and

$id' = id$ over $\{<m_\ell, e_k>\}$

It is clear that $f \circ id' = id' \circ f$.

Let us calculate the expression $U^T \circledcirc M = U^T \circledcirc M_o$.

$$(f\ id') \circledcirc \begin{bmatrix} M(Q) \\ M(E) \end{bmatrix} = (f\ id') \circledcirc \begin{bmatrix} 0 \\ \sum_{k=1}^{n} e_k \end{bmatrix}$$

$$F\ (M(Q)) + M(E) = \sum_{k=1}^{n} e_k$$

We can interprete this invariant in two ways :

- If the place E contains a token e_k, that means there is no token $<m_\ell, e_k>$, $\forall \ell$ in the place Q. Hence the element k is empty, which is consistent with the signification of place E (empty elements).
- The element k can contain only one token of index k. If not, this place could contain for example two tokens $<m_\ell, e_k>$ and $<m_{\ell'}, e_k>$. The transformation by f would give $2.e_k$ which is impossible in comparison with the second member.

Moreover, we can prove that :

- The net is bounded since $M(E) \leqslant \sum_{k=1}^{n} e_k$ and $M(Q) \leqslant \sum_{k=1}^{n} <m_\ell, e_k>$
- The net cannot deadlock.

Let us assume that M is reachable from the initial marking. From the invariant, we deduce :

- $M(E) = \sum_{k=1}^{n} e_k$ then t_i is enabled.
- $M(E) = 0$ then $M(Q) = \sum_{k=1}^{n} <m_\ell, e_k>$ and t_o is enabled.
- $M(E) = e_{k1} + e_{k2} + \dots + e_{kj}$ $j \in [1, n-1]$

a) $\forall r \in [1,j]$, $k_r \neq n$ then Q contains $<m_\ell, e_n>$ and t_o is enabled.

b) $r \in [1,j] /\ k_r = n$ then $\exists k \in [1, n-1]$ such that Q contains $<m_\ell, e_k>$ and does not contain $<m_\ell, e_{k+1}>$ and t is enabled.

Then the CPN is deadlock-free.

5. EXAMPLE 2. A FLEXIBLE MANUFACTURING SYSTEM [CAV 81], [VAL 82].

As a more complicated example, let us consider a production workshop which is shown in figure 3. It is a workshop of puttying cars bodies designed and operated by the "Régie RENAULT". The puttying operation is making tight the joints between the various parts, before painting.

This workshop has 12 working posts divided in two groups of 6. Only the right side group is detailed in figure 3. Each station is autonomous and supplied with a conveyor consisting of modules called roller-tables. Each table can contain only one car-body. Among these tables, the tables TT allow a simple conveyance towards the following tables, the tables TP allow either a conveyance or a pivoting so as to load or unload a station. Table TR allows a distribution between the two groups of stations. A multiplexing table TM allows the production flow in two directions. This cross flow occurs either to evacuate the production from the right side stations, or to supply the left side stations. Tables TD (distribution table) and TE (evacuation table) facilitate the production flow through the workshop.

Each station is composed of a working post P and a transfer bench (T1 and T2 tables). T1 is designed for unloading (the bench is in right side position), T2 is designed for loading (the bench is in left side position).

We shall concentrate here on the right side part of the workshop (6 stations), the conveyance system included between TP1 and TP6. The loading and unloading of stations as well as the operation of the six stations will be modelled. The conveyance system from the workshop entrance to the table TD will not be described, it consists of a common conveyance line with switching in TR.

5.1. Definition of the colours sets and functions.

$$C = \{ RP_i, RE_i, e_i, C_i, \ < RP_i, e_j >, < RE_i, e_j > \ ; \forall\ i,j \in [1,6] \}$$

RP_i and RE_i indicate respectively the body to be puttied (P) in station i and to be evacuated (E) after puttying in station i of the right level of the workshop.

The couple $<RP_i,e_j>$ or $<RE_i,e_j>$ means that there is a body to be puttied or to be evacuated occupying the table TP_j.

e_i and C_i are intermediate colours to specify special constraints of the workshop.

- All the functions are defined $\forall_i \in [1,6]$

$f : f(<RP_i,e_j>) = f(<RE_i,e_j>) = e_j \quad \forall_j \in [1,6]$

function f allows to check the presence of bodies in tables TP_j.

$g : g(<RP_i, e_j>) = <RP_i, e_{j+1}>$; $g(<RE_i, e_j>) = <RE_i, e_{j+1}>$ $\forall j \in [1,5]$

function g describes the body's transfer from a table TP_j to a table TP_{j+1}.

$h : h(RP_i) = RE_i$

function h changes the puttying state to the evacuating state.

$h' : h'(RP_i) = h'(RE_i) = C_i$

function h' permits to specify a constraint which we shall see later.

$u : u(RP_i) = <RP_i, e_1>$

$v : v(RE_i) = <RE_i, e_6>$

$v' : v'(RP_i) = <RP_i, e_i>$ and $v'(RE_i) = <RE_i, e_i>$

The three functions u, v and v' model the loading and unloading operations of the tables TP.

5.2. Specification of the workshop.

The model of the workshop is shown in figure 4. Two places have an important part with regard to physical constraints. The place P1 is initialized at the value $\sum_{i=1}^{6} 2.C_i$ because on each station we can have, at the utmost, 2 bodies (i.e. 12 on the whole). The place P3 represents the stations j vacant, it has no body). In this case there are tokens e_j in P3.

Each one of the other places represents a state of the workshop and each transition represents a transfer operation explained in figure 4.

Suppose a body which is positionned before table TP1 has to be sent to the station n°3. The loading of table TP1 will occur by firing transition T2. The latter may fire with respect to colour $<RP_3>$ if :

. TP1 is empty (i.e. the place P3 contains a token f o $u(RP_3) = e_1$).

. There is less than 2 bodies concerning the station 3 in the set of the six stations and the tables TP (i.e. the place P1 contains at least one token $h'(RP_i) = C_i$). As a consequence of firing T2, table TP1 is loaded. By firing t1, the body is removed from table TP1 to table TP2 and then to TP3 according the occupation of these tables (functions f and g). Then the body is recognized by the station 3. It is loaded in this station by firing one of the following transitions according to the station state :

. t4 : if the station is vacant (i.e. place P4 contains a token RP3). After firing, there is now one body into the station.

. t6 : if the station in left position has one body when P is loaded (i.e. place

P5 contains a token RP_3). There are now two bodies into the station (2 id).

. t7 : if the station in right position has one body when T1 is loaded (i.e. place P6 contains a token RP_3).

We notice that there is no conflict between transitions t1 and t4, t6 and t7, because the set of colours associated with the transition t1 does not include the colour $<RP_3,e_3>$.

Other transitions are explained in Figure 4.

After the puttying work a change happens in colour from RP_3 to RE_3 (function h) and the body resumes its place in the line of tables TP by firing the transitions t9 or t10. The body is then evacuated from the right side of the workshop by firing t3 and the place P1 gets a token $h'(RE_3) = C_3$, it becomes possible to load a new body for station 3.

This case was considered in [VAL 82] using PTN. The conclusion of this study was that it was impossible to carry out a complete model of the workshop. That is to say, the different parts of the workshop were specified independently by using the classical PTN. Therefore the coordination and the control of the workshop as a whole wasn't possible. It has been necessary to use a coordinator written in advanced language, this asks the problem of the multiplicity of the tools used which makes each validation impossible.

Whereas in our study, we achieved a global control of the workshop, i.e. complete model, with the same tool CPN which gives a concise graph and a net easily validated.

5.3. Validation of the model.

Let W be the incidence matrix associated with the CPN shown in figure 3.

This matrix has not the form of our sub-class, we are going to use an algorithm of decomposition of matrix W given in [SIL 84].

We choose a sub-matrix W_1 of W such that W_1 has the good form and the maximum rank.

Then we calculate a set of solution B_1 of $X^t \odot W_1 = 0$

We have $B_1^t \odot W_1 = 0$ and $B_1^t \odot W = [||| \quad 0 \quad ||]$

We choose a new matrix W_2 with the same conditions as W_1, which gives a second set of solution B_2 of $X^t \odot W_2 = 0$, then $B_2^t \odot W_2 = 0$. $B_2^t \odot B_1^t \odot W$ must be again decomposed until the ith iteration where $B^t_i \odot B^t_{i-1} \dots \odot B^t_1 \odot W = 0$. The set $B_i^t \odot B_{i-1}^t \odot \dots \odot B_1^t$ is the final solution.

Let u' and h" be the extensions of u and h' such that

. $u' = u$ over $\{ RP_i \}$ and $u'(C_i) = C_i$

. $h'' = h'$ over $\{ RP_i \}$ and $h''(<RP_i,e_j>) = C_i$

W =

p \ t	1	2	3	4	5	6	7	8	9	10
1		-h'	h'							
2	g-id	u	-v	-v'		-v'	-v'		v'oh	v'oh
3	(f-fog)	-fou	fov	fov'		fov'	fov'		(-fov'oh)	(-fov'oh)
4				-id					id	
5				id	-id	-id				id
6					id		-id		-id	
7						2id		-2id		
8							2id	2id		-2id

Rows 2–3: TP line; rows 4–8: 6 Stations. Columns 4–8: W1

A_1' =

p_1 \ t	4	5	6	7	8
2	-1		-1	-1	
3	1		1	1	
4	-1				
5	1	-1	-1		
6		1		-1	
7			2		-2
8				2	2

$$\dim \operatorname{Ker} A_1' = 8 - \operatorname{rank}(A') = 8 - 4 = 4$$

then we obtain 4 solutions :

$$V_1^t = (0\ 1\ 1\ 0\ 0\ 0\ 0\ 0)$$
$$V_2^t = (0\ 1\ 0\ 0\ 1\ 1\ 1\ 1)$$
$$V_3^t = (0\ 0\ 0\ 2\ 2\ 2\ 1\ 1)$$
$$V_4^t = (1\ 0\ 0\ 0\ 0\ 0\ 0\ 0)$$

$$\text{Then } B_1^t = \begin{bmatrix} 0 & f & id & 0 & 0 & 0 & 0 & 0 \\ 0 & id & 0 & 0 & v' & v' & v' & v' \\ 0 & 0 & 0 & 2id & 2id & 2id & id & id \\ id & 0 & 0 & 0 & 0 & 0 & 0 & 0 \end{bmatrix}$$

Every function commute with function identity.

then $B_1^t \otimes W$ =

t1	t2	t3	t9	t10
0	0	0	0	0
g-id	u	-v	(v'oh-v')	(v'oh-v')
0	0	0	0	0
0	-h'	h'	0	0

$h'' \circ u' = u' \circ h''$ over $\{\bar{R}P_i\}$

and $$B_2^t = \begin{bmatrix} id & 0 & 0 & 0 \\ 0 & 0 & id & 0 \\ 0 & h'' & 0 & u' \end{bmatrix}$$

as $B_2^t \circ B_1^t \circ W = 0$, the final set of solution is

$$B_t^2 \circ B_1^t = \begin{bmatrix} 0 & f & id & 0 & 0 & 0 & 0 & 0 \\ 0 & 0 & 0 & 2id & 2id & 2id & id & id \\ u' & h'' & 0 & 0 & h''ov' & h''ov' & h''ov' & h''ov' \end{bmatrix}$$

We can notice that $h''ov' = h'$

5.4. Interpretation of the invariants.

I_1 : $f[M(P2)] + M(P3) = \sum_{j=1}^{6} e_j$

Which can be interpreted in the same way as the FIFO queue, a table TP being replaced by an element.

I_2 : $2\,M(P4) + 2\,M(P5) + 2\,M(P6) + M(P7) + M(P8) = \sum_{i=1}^{6} 2\,RP_i$

At any time, one and only one place among the places P4, P5 and P6 contains a token RP_i. The places P7 and P8 contain two tokens in the same colour when they are marked. This implies that never two tasks concerning the station are executed simultaneously.

I_3 : $u'[M(P1)] + h''[M(P2)] + h'[M(P5)] + h'[M(P6)] + h'[M(P7)] + h'[M(P8)]$
$= \sum_{i=1}^{6} 2.\,C_i$

Then at most

- two bodies can be transfered to station i
- there are a total of 12 bodies between the TP line and the stations.

The two invariants I_1 and I_2 were expected because the two systems constituted by the TP line and the 6 stations are independant (they have no shared places).

All the net places intervene, at least in one invariant and each place has a bound (for example I_2 implies $|M(P6)| < 6$) ; then the net is bounded.

We may also show by exploiting all these invariants that the net cannot deadlock.

Let us assume that M is reachable from the initial marking

$$. M(P3) = \sum_{i=1}^{6} e_j$$

From I_1, we have $M(P2) = 0$, if $M(P1) \neq 0$ then t_2 is enabled

if $M(P1) = 0$ then from I_2 and I_3,

we deduce that, at least one place among P5, P6, P7 and P8 is marked and at least one transition among t5, t6, t7, t8, t9 and t10 is enabled.

$$. M(P3) \neq \sum_{i=1}^{6} e_j$$

In this case, we have the same proof as for the FIFO queue.

6. CONCLUSIONS

Two are the main points considered in this paper : the calculation of invariants for a given CPN and the modelling and validation of a complex manufacturing system [CAV 81] [VAL 82].

The importance of analysis techniques for CPN derived from the invariant method is recognized from the beginning [JEN 81a]. Nevertheless, there is no elaborate method for invariants calculation [JEN 81b]. The method proposed in this paper may be applied directly to : (1) the CPN sub-class defined in § 2.2. (for a place all functions associated to its input and output arcs are the same) and (2) when the functions appearing in the CPN shows certain commutativities (§ 3.1.).

Unfortunately it seems that in the context of the theory and applications of CPN there is not any immediate physical interpretation of a mathematical property as interesting as the commutativity is.

When a CPN belongs to the sub-class constitued, then W = F.A and it follows that t-invariants of the PN which incidence matrix is A are also t-invariants of the CPN.

If a CPN does not verify the condition 1, it is always possible to decompose it in several sub-sets that hold the property. This technic is presented in detail in [SIL 84] where the utilization of generalised inverses matrices provide a very powerfull method for the calculation of invariants.

REFERENCES

[CAV 81] CAVANNA B., DOLLE F., MOALLA H. : "Outils CAO pour l'Analyse, la Spécification et la Réalisation de l'Automatisation d'Equipements de Production Mécanique". 3ème Journées Scientifiques et Techniques de la Production Automatisée. TOULOUSE.

[CHA 66] CHAMBADAL L, OVAERT J. : "Notions Fondamentales d'Algèbre et d'Analyse". Ed. GAUTHIER - VILLARS - PARIS.

[JEN 81a] JENSEN K. : "Coloured Petri Nets and the Invariant Method". Theoretical Computer Science 14. North Holland Publ. Co., pp. 317-336.

[JEN 81b] JENSEN K. : "How to Find Invariants for Coloured Petri Nets". Mathematical Foundations of Computer Science. Lecture Notes in Computer Science 118. Springer Verlag, BERLIN.

[LAU 74] LAUTENBACH K., SCHMID H.A. : "Use of Petri Nets for Proving Correctness of Concurrent Process Systems". IFIP 74. North Holland Pub. Co. pp. 187-191.

[MAR 82] MARTINEZ J., SILVA M. : "A Simple and Fast Algorithm to obtain all Invariants of a Generalised Petri Net". 2nd European Workshop on Petri Nets Theory and Applications (Bad Honnef, September 1981). Informatik Fachbeichte 52, Springer Verlag, BERLIN, pp. 301-310.

[SIL 80] SILVA M. : "Simplification des Réseaux de Petri par Elimination de Places Implicites". Digital Processes, Vol. 6, n°4, pp. 245-256.

[SIL 84] SILVA M., MARTINEZ J., LADET P., ALLA H. : "Generalised Inverses and the Calculation of Symbolic Invariants for Coloured Petri Nets". To be published in Technique et Science Informatique (TSI).

[VAL 82] VALETTE R., COURVOISIER M., MAYEUX D. : "Control of Flexible Production Systems and Petri Nets". 3th European Workshop on Applications and Theory of Petri Nets. VARENNA, September, 1982.

=:=:=:=:=:=:=:=:=

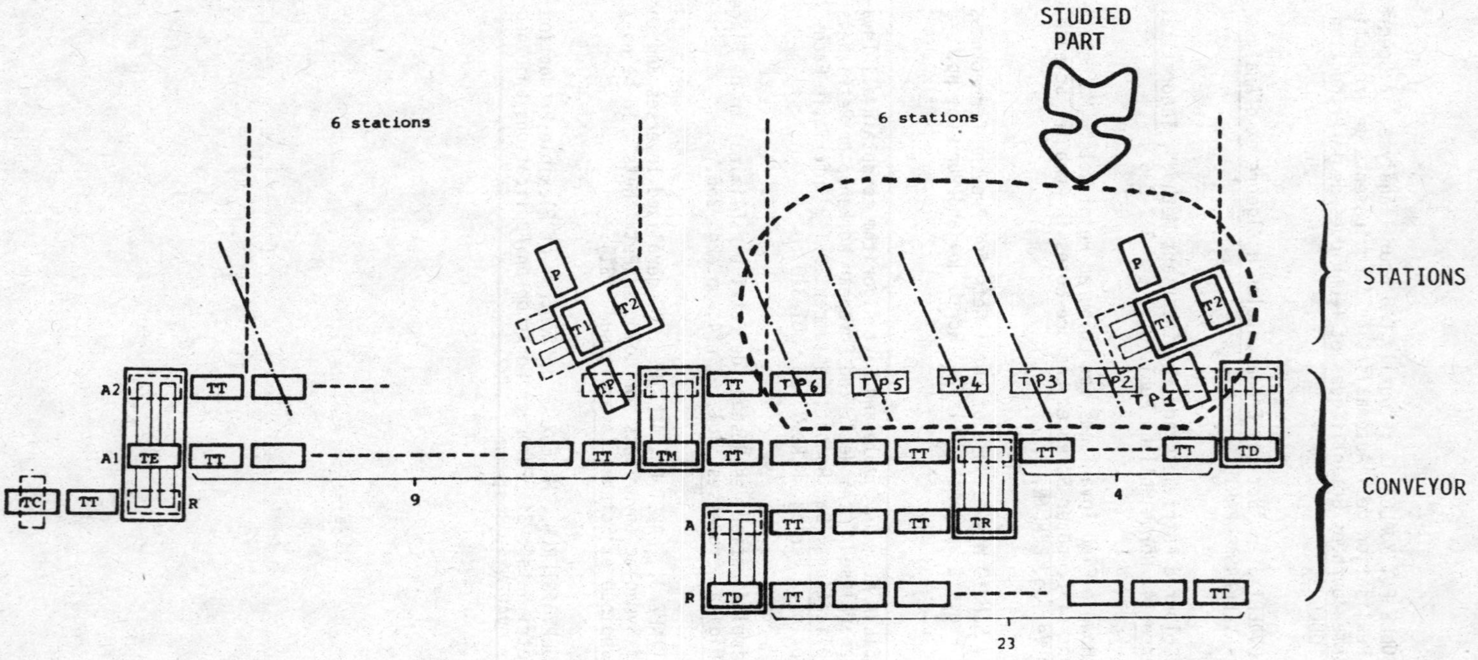

Figure 3. Lay-out of the workshop.

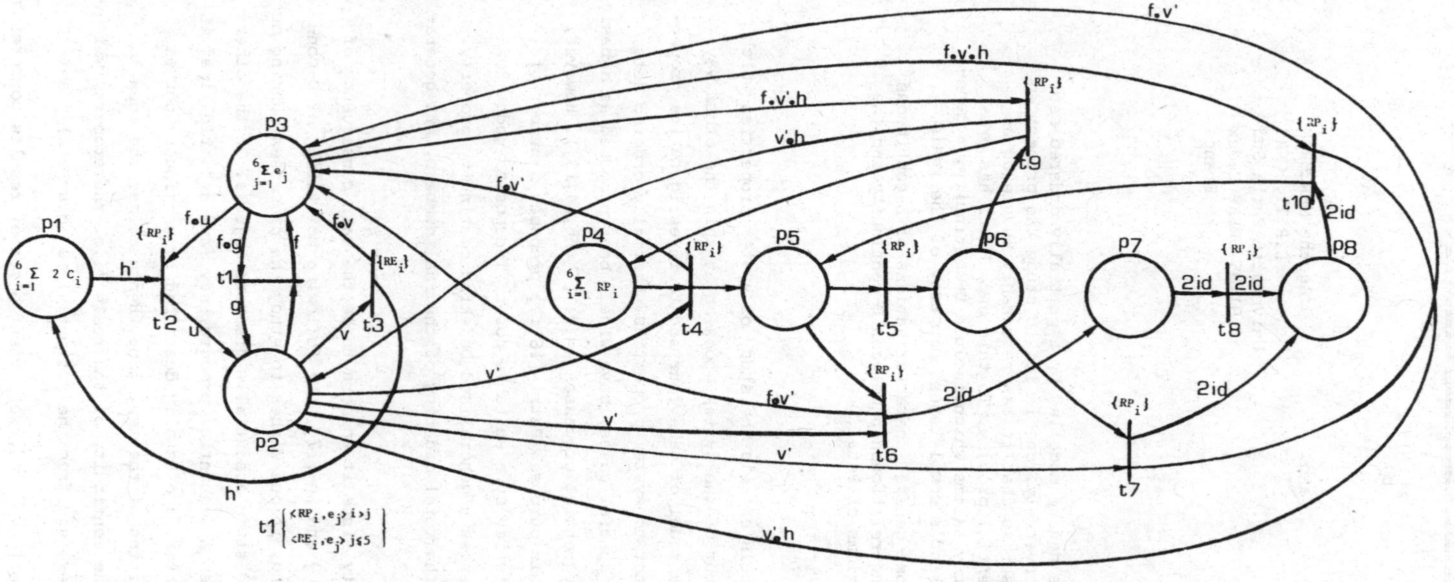

P2 : TP_i is occupied.

P3 : TP_i is vacant.

P4 : Station i is vacant and in left position.

P5 : P is loaded, station is in left position.

P6 : T1 is loaded, station is in right position.

P7 : P and T2 are loaded, station is in right position.

P8 : P and T1 are loaded, station is in left position.

t1 : TP_{j+1} loading.

t2 : TP loading.

t3 : Evacuation.

t4 : Transfer from TP to T2 then from T2 to P.

t5 : Transfer from P to T1.

t6 : Transfer from TP to T2.

t7 : Transfer from TP to T2 then from T2 to P.

t8 : Transfer from P to T1 then from T2 to P.

t9 : Transfer from T1 to TP.

t10 : Transfer from T1 to TP.

Figure 4. CPN modelling the flexible manufacturing system.

CONCURRENCY AXIOMS AND D-CONTINUOUS POSETS

by

Eike BEST
GMD-F1P
Schloß Birlinghoven
5205 St. AUGUSTIN 1
Fed. Rep. Germany

and

Agathe MERCERON
L.R.I., CNRS
Université Paris-Sud
91405 ORSAY Cedex
France

ABSTRACT

A non-sequential process can be modelled by a partially ordered set of basic occurrences. Conversely, one is led to study the properties to be fulfilled by a poset so that it can reasonably be viewed as the model of a non-sequential process. To this end, Petri has proposed a set of concurrency axioms which include D-continuity, a generalised version of Dedekind's completeness property of the reals.

In this paper we give some general characterisations of D-continuous posets. We also study the relationship between D-continuity and the remaining concurrency axioms of Petri.

1. INTRODUCTION

The study of concurrent system models entails the study of system properties which give information about the behaviour of the system. Looking at this the other way round, it is possible to propose a model of behaviour and to investigate its properties, eventually relating the latter to system properties. Partially ordered sets, of which occurrence nets [12] are special cases, have widely been proposed as a basis for constructing a model of non-sequential processes (e.g. [7 , 9 ,14,15]). However, not all posets are suitable for this purpose. Petri [16,17] proposes a number of "axioms of concurrency" to be satisfied by a suitable poset. The posets under consideration there are stated to possess a generalised Dedekind continuity property, "the kind of continuity found in the total ordering of the real numbers, but generalised to partial orders" [17].

In this paper we study D-continuity since it appears to be the main consequence of Petri's concurrency axioms. In [9] and in [17], the following motivation of D-continuity is implied. On the one hand, if one wishes to study the processes running on a digital computer then one should study essentially discrete objects. On the other hand, there is some analogy between a sequential process, say, and a "world line" in Physics [15,17]; world lines, however, are usually described by continuous curves with properties akin to the properties of the real line. Hence arises the idea to generalise Dedekind's notion of the continuity of the reals (i.e. the property which distinguishes them from the integers and from the rationals) to (discrete) posets.

In this paper which is a sequel to [3 , 4 , 9], we present a set of results concerning

D-continuity in general, without regard to its relation to system properties. In a companion paper found in this Volume [6], we apply these results in order to show that D-continuity corresponds to a particularly "nice" system property. The present paper is organised as follows: In section 2, D-continuity is defined and D-continuous posets are then characterised in terms of other (it is hoped: simpler) properties. Using this characterisation, we show in section 3 how Petri's concurrency axioms might be used to imply the D-continuity property. In the conclusion (section 4) we sum up our results and we briefly discuss the significance of the D-continuity axiom.

2. DEFINITION AND CHARACTERISATION OF D-CONTINUOUS POSETS

2.1 Definition.

$(X,\leq)$ is a poset iff X is a (non-empty) set and $\leq\ \subseteq X\times X$ is a relation satisfying

(i) $\leq\cap\leq^{-1} = id$, where id is the identity relation on X (reflexivity and antisymmetry)

(ii) $\leq^2\ \subseteq\ \leq$ (transitivity).

If a poset is considered as a model of a non-sequential process then two kinds of subsets are of interest: linearly ordered subsets (corresponding to the relation of sequentiality) and unordered subsets (corresponding to the relation of concurrency). Throughout the remainder of this paper, we assume $(X,\leq)$ to be a poset.

2.2 Definition.

(i) $< \ = \ \leq\backslash id$, $\lessdot\ =\ <\backslash<^2$, $co = X\times X\backslash(<\cup>)$, $li = \leq\cup\geq$;

(ii) $c\subseteq X$ is a co-set iff $\forall x,y\in c$: x co y;

c is a cut iff c is a co-set and $\forall z\in X\backslash c\ \exists x\in c$: **z li x** (i.e. **c** is **maximal**);

the set of cuts of $(X,\leq)$ will be denoted by C;

(iii) $l\subseteq X$ is a li-set iff $\forall x,y\in l$: x li y;

l is a line iff l is a **li-set** and $\forall z\in X\backslash l\ \exists x\in l$: z co **x**;

the set of lines of $(X,\leq)$ will be denoted by L.

We assume the axiom of choice to hold. As a consequence, for every co-set (li-set) there exists a cut (line, respectively) containing it.

The idea behind D-continuity is to generalise Dedekind's construction of the real numbers to posets. The set of reals, $\mathbb{R}$, with the usual ordering is a linear order (i.e. co=id); it has one line, $\mathbb{R}$ itself, and each real number forms a singleton cut. Any partitioning of $\mathbb{R}$ into two disjoint sets $\mathbb{R}_1$ and $\mathbb{R}_2 = \mathbb{R}\backslash\mathbb{R}_1$ such that no number in $\mathbb{R}_2$ is smaller than any number in $\mathbb{R}_1$ gives exactly one real number separating $\mathbb{R}_1$ and $\mathbb{R}_2$. [16] transports this idea to posets.

2.3 Definition and Notation.

(i) For $A\subseteq X$ we define $\overline{A} = X\backslash A$;

(ii) For $A\subseteq X$, $\downarrow A = \{z\in X \mid \exists x\in A: z\leq x\}$, $\uparrow A = \{y\in X \mid \exists x\in A: x\leq y\}$;

for $x\in X$, $\downarrow x = \downarrow\{x\}$, $\uparrow x = \uparrow\{x\}$;

(iii) $A\subseteq X$ is a Dedekind cut (D-cut) iff $A\neq\emptyset\neq\overline{A}$ and $A=\downarrow A$;

The set of all D-cuts of $(X,\leq)$ will be denoted by D;

(iv) For $A\subseteq X$, $\quad Max(A) = \{x\in A \mid \underline{\text{not}}\ \exists z\in A\colon x<z\}$,

$Min(\overline{A}) = \{x\in\overline{A} \mid \underline{\text{not}}\ \exists z\in\overline{A}\colon z<x\}$,

$M(A) = Max(A) \cup Min(\overline{A})$;

(v) For $x,y\in X$, the interval between x and y will be denoted by

$[x,y] = \{z\in X \mid x\leq z\leq y\}$.

An immediate generalisation of the Dedekind construction would be to call a poset D-continuous if $|M(A)\cap l|=1$ for every D-cut A and every line l, because A and $\overline{A}$ correspond to $\mathbb{R}_1$ and $\mathbb{R}_2$ above and $M(A)$ "separates" them. Let us investigate this definition.

<u>2.4 Definition.</u>

(i) $(X,\leq)$ is D'-continuous iff $\forall A\in D\ \forall l\in L\colon |M(A)\cap l|=1$;

(ii) $(X,\leq)$ is dense iff $\lessdot = \emptyset$.

<u>2.5 Proposition.</u>

If $(X,\leq)$ is D'-continuous then $(X,\leq)$ is dense.

<u>Proof:</u> Suppose otherwise, then $\exists x,y\in X\colon x \lessdot y$.

Define $A = {\downarrow}y\setminus\{y\}$; it is easy to show that $x\in Max(A)$, $y\in Min(\overline{A})$ and $A\in D$.

Let l be any line containing x and y.

Then $|M(A)\cap l|=2$, contradicting D'-continuity. □2.5

Because of 2.5, D'-continuity is not suited as a generalisation of the Dedekind construction to discrete (i.e. non-dense) posets. One possibility is to narrow down the set $M(A)$, as has been advocated in [16]:

<u>2.6 Definition.</u>

(i) For $A\in D$, $\quad Obmax(A) = \{x\in Max(A) \mid \forall A'\in D\ \forall l\in L\colon x\in Max(A'\cap l) \Rightarrow x\in Max(A')\}$;

$Obmin(\overline{A}) = \{x\in Min(\overline{A}) \mid \forall A'\in D\ \forall l\in L\colon x\in Min(\overline{A'}\cap l) \Rightarrow x\in Min(\overline{A'})\}$;

$c(A) = Obmax(A) \cup Obmin(\overline{A})$;

(ii) $(X,\leq)$ is D-continuous iff $\forall A\in D\ \forall l\in L\colon |c(A)\cap l|=1$.

The idea behind the Obmax definition is that of an element being "objectively maximal" in the sense that "all lines (all observers) agree on its maximality"; and similarly for Obmin. The following proposition gives a characterisation of Obmax and Obmin:

<u>2.7 Proposition.</u>

Let $A\in D$ and $x\in Max(A)$, $y\in Min(\overline{A})$.

(i) $x\in Obmax(A) \;\Leftrightarrow\; \underline{\text{not}}\ \exists z>x,\ l\in L\colon l\cap[x,z] = \{x\}$;

(ii) $y\in Obmin(\overline{A}) \;\Leftrightarrow\; \underline{\text{not}}\ \exists z<y,\ l\in L\colon l\cap[z,y] = \{y\}$.

<u>Proof:</u>

(i$\Rightarrow$): Suppose $\exists z>x,\ l\in L\colon l\cap[x,z] = \{x\}$.

Define $A'={\downarrow}z$.

A' is a D-cut, and we have $x\in Max(A'\cap l)$ (otherwise $\exists w\in l\colon x<w\leq z$),

and furthermore, $x\notin Max(A')$ (since $z\in A'$ and $x<z$).

Hence $x\notin Obmax(A)$ by definition 2.6(i).

(i$\Leftarrow$): Suppose $x\notin Obmax(A)$.

Then $x \in Max(A' \cap l)$, $x \notin Max(A')$ for some $A' \in D$, $l \in L$.

Since $x \notin Max(A')$, $x<z$ for some $z \in A'$.

Suppose $x<w\leq z$ for some $w \in l$; this contradicts $x \in Max(A' \cap l)$.

Hence $l \cap [x,z] = \{x\}$.

(ii): Similar. □2.7

In order to obtain a characterisation of D-continuity, it is meaningful to distinguish the two cases $|c(A) \cap l| \neq 0$ and $|c(A) \cap l| \neq 2$. For totally ordered sets, it is easy to see that these two cases reduce to $|M(A)| \neq 0$ and $|M(A)| \neq 2$, respectively. For example, in the set of rationals Q with the usual ordering we have $|M(Q\_ \cup \{x \in Q \mid x^2<2\})| = 0$. This may be expressed by saying that Q contains "gaps". On the other hand, in the set $\mathbb{Z}$ of integers we have $|M(\{x \in \mathbb{Z} \mid x \leq 0\})| = |\{0,1\}| = 2$. This may be called a "jump". This justifies the following definition.

2.8 Definition.

(i) $(X,\leq)$ is gap-free iff $\forall A \in D\ \forall l \in L$: $|c(A) \cap l| \neq 0$;

(ii) $(X,\leq)$ is jump-free iff $\forall A \in D\ \forall l \in L$: $|c(A) \cap l| \neq 2$.

Clearly, $(X,\leq)$ is D-continuous iff it is both gap-free and jump-free. We characterise the latter properties separately. In case $|c(A) \cap l|=2$, there must be $x,y \in c(A)$ such that not only $x \lessdot y$ but also no line through x can bypass y and no line through y can bypass x. By requiring the contrary, the case $|c(A) \cap l|=2$ can be prohibited:

2.9 Definition.

$(X,\leq)$ is nsd (for "non-single degree"; this term is explained in section 4 of [6]) iff $\forall x,y \in X$: $x \lessdot y \Rightarrow \exists z \in X, x \neq z \neq y$: $(x < z \text{ co } y) \vee (x \text{ co } z < y)$.

2.10 Theorem.

$(X,\leq)$ is jump-free iff it satisfies the nsd property.

Proof:

(⇒): Suppose $(X,\leq)$ is not nsd; then $\exists x,y \in X$ with the following properties:

(i) $x \lessdot y$, (ii) not $\exists z \in X$: $(x < z \text{ co } y) \vee (x \text{ co } z < y)$.

Consider any D-cut A with $x \in A$, $y \in \bar{A}$ (such D-cuts exist), and define a line l such that $x \in l$ and $y \in l$.

To show $|c(A) \cap l|=2$, it suffices to show that $x,y \in c(A)$.

We show only $x \in c(A)$, the proof of $y \in c(A)$ being analogous.

First we show $x \in Max(A)$.

Suppose not, then $x<z$ for some $z \in A$; but $z<y$ contradicts (i), z co y contradicts (ii), and $z>y$ contradicts $z \in A$.

We complete the proof by showing $x \in Obmax(A)$.

Suppose $l \cap [x,z] = \{x\}$ for some $l \in L$, $z>x$.

If $y \in l$ then z co y, contradicting (ii).

If $y \notin l$ then $\exists z'$: z' co y; clearly, $z'>x$, again contradicting (ii).

Hence, by 2.7(i), $x \in Obmax(A)$.

(⇐): By contradiction.

Suppose $(X,\leq)$ is not jump-free; then $|c(A)\cap l|=2$ for some $A\in D$ and $l\in L$.

Say, $c(A)\cap l = \{x,y\}$; clearly, $x\in Obmax(A)$, $y\in Obmin(\overline{A})$ and $x \lessdot y$.

By the nsd property, $\exists z\neq y$: $x<z$ co y or $\exists z\neq x$: x co $z<y$; suppose the former (the latter case can be handled analogously).

Define $l\in L$ such that $x\in l$ and $y\in l$.

We have $l\cap[x,z] = \{x\}$, and by 2.7(i), $x\notin Obmax(A)$, contradiction. □2.10

It remains to characterise the case that $c(A)\cap l \neq \emptyset$. To this end we make a connection to the well known property of K-density [1 ,15,18].

2.11 Definition.

$(X,\leq)$ is K-dense iff $\forall c\in C\ \forall l\in L$: $c\cap l \neq \emptyset$.

Note first that if $c(A)$ contains a cut then K-density implies $c(A)\cap l \neq \emptyset$. Conversely, it is easy to see (and has been noted in [9 ,16]) that gap-freeness implies K-density. Hence we need an appropriate condition to ensure that $c(A)$ contains a cut. This is achieved by the next definition.

2.12 Definition.

$(X,\leq)$ is strongly cut-bounded iff $\forall A\in D$: $A\subseteq\downarrow c(A) \wedge \overline{A}\subseteq\uparrow c(A)$.

2.13 Theorem.

$(X,\leq)$ is gap-free iff it is K-dense and strongly cut-bounded.

Proof:

($\Rightarrow$): We start by showing that gap-freeness implies K-density.

Let $c\in C$ and $l\in L$ be arbitrary.

If $c = \downarrow c = \uparrow c$ then $|l|=1$ and the result is trivially true.

Otherwise, suppose $c \neq \uparrow c$ (the case $c \neq \downarrow c$ is symmetrical).

Define $A = \downarrow c$, $\overline{A} = \uparrow c\setminus c$; clearly, $A\in D$ and $Max(A) = c$.

By gap-freeness, $\exists y$: $y\in c(A)\cap l$.

If $y\in Obmax(A)$ then $y\in Max(A) = c$.

If $y\in Obmin(\overline{A})$ then $\exists z\in c$: $z<y$; from 2.7(ii) we derive $z\in l$.

We proceed by showing that gap-freeness implies strong cut-boundedness.

We prove $A\subseteq\downarrow c(A)$, the proof of $\overline{A}\subseteq\uparrow c(A)$ being dual.

Let $x\in A$ and pick any line l such that $x\in l$.

By gap-freeness, $\exists z\in l$: $z\in c(A)$.

$z\in l \Rightarrow x\leq z$ and $z\in c(A) \Rightarrow x\in\downarrow c(A)$.

($\Leftarrow$): We first show that $c(A)$ contains a cut, provided $(X,\leq)$ is strongly cut-bounded.

To this end, let c be any subset of $c(A)$ such that c is a co-set and $\forall z\in c(A)\setminus c\ \exists x\in c$: z li x (i.e. c is co-maximal in $c(A)$).

We show that $c\in C$.

Suppose $\exists z\in X\setminus c\ \forall x\in c$: z co x; we derive a contradiction.

Assume first $z\in A\setminus c(A)$.

By strong cut-boundedness, $\exists z'\in c(A)$: $z < z'$.

By the choice of c, z' li x for some $x\in c$.

However, $z' \leq x$ implies $z < x$, contradicting the choice of z.

Hence $x < z'$ and $x \in \text{Obmax}(A)$, $z' \in \text{Obmin}(\bar{A})$.

Because x co z, $[x,z'] \cap l = \{z'\}$ for any line l through z and z', which contradicts $z' \in \text{Obmin}(\bar{A})$ on account of 2.7(ii).

The case $z \in \bar{A} \setminus c(A)$ can be brought to an analogous contradiction.

Hence c is a cut in c(A), and the desired result follows with K-density. □2.13

2.14 Theorem.

$(X,\leq)$ is D-continuous iff $(X,\leq)$ is nsd, K-dense and strongly cut-bounded.

Proof: 2.10, 2.13 and the fact that D-continuous ⇔ gap-free ∧ jump-free. □2.14

In the characterisation 2.14 of D-continuity, K-density and the nsd property are reasonably "nice" (K-density can be further characterised using the results of [1 ,18]). However, strong cut-boundedness remains a rather "awkward" property, relying as it does on the complicated definition of c(A). The next set of results is designed to replace strong cut-boundedness by two (hopefully) simpler properties.

2.15 Definition.

(i) $(X,\leq)$ is cut-bounded iff $\forall A \in D$: $A \subseteq {\downarrow}M(A) \wedge \bar{A} \subseteq {\uparrow}M(A)$;

(ii) $(X,\leq)$ will be said to have the up-fork property iff
$\forall x,y \in X,\ x < y\ \forall l \in L$: $l \cap [x,y] = \{x\} \Rightarrow (\exists y' > x$: ${\downarrow}y' = {\downarrow}x \cup \{y'\})$

(iii) $(X,\leq)$ will be said to have the low-fork property iff
$\forall x,y \in X,\ x < y\ \forall l \in L$: $l \cap [x,y] = \{y\} \Rightarrow (\exists x' < y$: ${\uparrow}x' = {\uparrow}y \cup \{x'\})$

(iv) $(X,\leq)$ will be said to have the fork property iff both (ii) and (iii) hold.

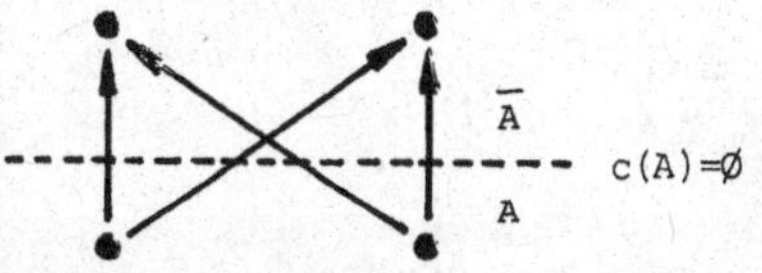

The Figure on the left shows a poset which is cut-bounded but not strongly cut-bounded.(Pictorially, we respresent a poset by a directed graph, such that X corresponds to the vertex set of the graph and ≤ corresponds to the transitive closure of the edge relation given by the graph.)

The picture for the up-fork property 2.15(ii) looks as follows:

If x,y and l stand in the relationship shown in the Figure on the right then the up-fork property requires some $y' > x$ with ${\downarrow}y' = {\downarrow}x \cup \{y'\}$ to exist. This not only means that $x < y'$ but also that if $z < y'$ then also $z \leq x$ (see the Figure). This implies a restriction on concurrency in the sense that an "up-forking" element x must be immediately below some "non-low-forking" element y'. The existence of such a y' becomes important in connection with 2.7: If x is not in Obmax(A) then the properties of y' ensure that y' is in $\text{Obmin}(\bar{A})$.

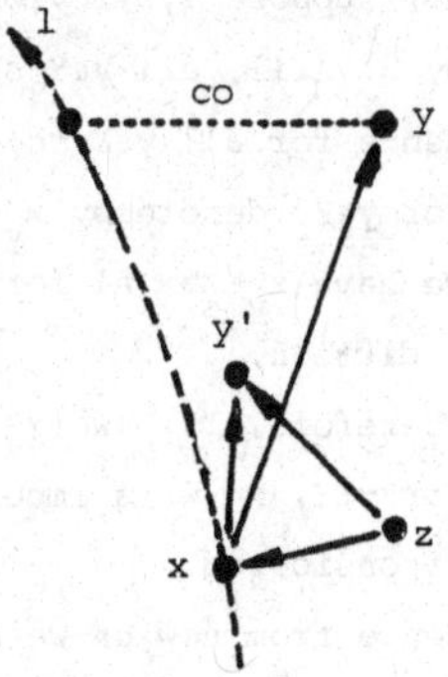

2.16 Theorem.

$(X,\leq)$ is strongly cut-bounded iff it is cut-bounded and has the fork property.

Proof:

($\Rightarrow$): Strong cut-boundedness implies cut-boundedness because $c(A) \subseteq M(A)$.

We prove that strong cut-boundedness implies the fork property by contradiction.

Suppose $l \cap [x,y] = \{x\}$ and $\forall y'>x\ \exists z \in X: z<y' \wedge z \nleq x,\quad x<y$.

Define $A = {\downarrow}x$.

By 2.7(i) we have $x \notin \mathrm{Obmax}(A)$.

Also, not $\exists y'>x: y' \in \mathrm{Obmin}(\overline{A})$. (Otherwise, $x < y'$ and, by assumption, $z<y' \wedge z \nleq x$ for some z; with $l' \in L$ such that $z \in l'$, $y' \in l'$, we obtain $l' \cap [x,y'] = \{y'\}$, whence by 2.7(ii), $y' \notin \mathrm{Obmin}(\overline{A})$, contradiction.)

Therefore, $x \notin {\downarrow}c(A)$.

Hence the up-fork property can be derived from $A \subseteq {\downarrow}c(A)$; similarly, the low-fork property can be derived from $\overline{A} \subseteq {\uparrow}c(A)$.

($\Leftarrow$): Assume that $A \in D$ and $w \in A$; we wish to prove that $w \in {\downarrow}c(A)$.

By cut-boundedness, either $w \leq x$ for $x \in \mathrm{Max}(A)$ or $w \leq y$ for $y \in \mathrm{Min}(\overline{A})$.

We distinguish these two cases and we reduce the latter to the former.

Case 1: $w \leq x$ and $x \in \mathrm{Max}(A)$.

If $x \in \mathrm{Obmax}(A)$ then the result is proved.

If $x \notin \mathrm{Obmax}(A)$ then, by 2.7(i), $\exists y>x,\ l \in L: l \cap [x,y] = \{x\}$.

By the up-fork property, $\exists y'>x\ \forall z \in X: z<y' \Rightarrow z \leq x$.

We claim $y' \in \mathrm{Obmin}(\overline{A})$.

First, $y' \in \mathrm{Min}(\overline{A})$ because if $z<y'$ then $z \in \overline{A}$ and $z \leq x$ give a contradiction.

Next, suppose $l' \in L$ and $x'<y'$ such that $l' \cap [x',y'] = \{y'\}$.

If $x \in l'$ then $x \text{ co } x' < y'$, contradicting $\forall z<y': z \leq x$.

If $x \notin l'$ then $\exists z \in l': x \text{ co } z < y'$, again a contradiction.

By 2.7(ii), therefore, $y' \in \mathrm{Obmin}(\overline{A})$, and $w \leq y'$.

Case 2: $w \leq y$ and $y \in \mathrm{Min}(\overline{A})$.

By using the lemma of Appendix A.1 we shall reduce Case 2 to Case 1.

We need to consider all elements in $\mathrm{Min}(\overline{A})$ which are above w.

Therefore, define $Y = \{y \in \mathrm{Min}(\overline{A}) \mid w \leq y\}$; from our assumption we know that $Y \neq \emptyset$.

If $Y \cap \mathrm{Obmin}(\overline{A}) \neq \emptyset$ then the result is proved.

So, suppose $\forall y \in Y: y \notin \mathrm{Obmin}(\overline{A})$.

By 2.7(ii), all $y \in Y$ satisfy the low-fork property 2.15(iii).

Hence for all $y \in Y$ there is at least one $x < y$ with $\forall z \in X: x<z \Rightarrow y \leq z$.

For $y \in Y$, denote by x_y some x associated in this way to y.

We have $x_y \in \mathrm{Max}(A)$ for all $y \in Y$, for suppose $x_y<z$ then $z \in A$ and $y \leq z$ give a contradiction.

Therefore, if ${\uparrow}w \cap \{x_y \mid y \in Y\} \neq \emptyset$ then we have a reduction to Case 1.

For $y \in Y$, $x_y<w$ is impossible because $x_y \in \mathrm{Max}(A)$, and the case $w \leq x_y$ has just been considered.

Hence from now on we may suppose the following:

(i) $\forall y\in Y$: $x_y \neq w$ and x_y co w.

The set $X_o = \{x_y \mid y\in Y\}$ satisfies the conditions of the lemma of Appendix A.1, and we define a new set B as follows: $B = A\setminus X_o$, $\bar{B} = X\setminus B$.

The lemma gives:

(ii) $B\in D$, i.e. B is a D-cut;

(iii) $M(A)\setminus\{y'\in\bar{A} \mid \exists y\in Y: x_y \lessdot y'\} = M(B)\setminus\{x'\in A \mid \exists y\in Y: x' \lessdot x_y\}$.

By the cut-boundedness property applied to B, $w\leq x$ for some $x\in M(B)$.

If $x\lessdot x_y$ for some $y\in Y$ then this contradicts (i).

Hence $x\in M(B)\setminus\{x'\in A \mid \exists y\in Y: x'\lessdot x_y\}$.

By (iii), $x\in M(A)\setminus\{y'\in\bar{A} \mid \exists y\in Y: x_y\lessdot y'\}$.

Also, because $x_y\lessdot y$ for all $y\in Y$, we have $Y\subseteq\{y'\in\bar{A} \mid \exists y\in Y: x_y\lessdot y'\}$.

By the definition of Y, $w<x\in \mathrm{Min}(\bar{A})\setminus Y$ is impossible, and a fortiori, $x\notin \mathrm{Min}(\bar{A})\setminus\{y'\in\bar{A} \mid \exists y\in Y: x_y\lessdot y'\}$.

The case $x\in \mathrm{Max}(A)$ remains, and the reduction to Case 1 is complete. □2.16

Combining the results so far we get the following consequence:

2.17 Theorem.

$(X,\leq)$ is D-continuous iff it is nsd, K-dense, cut-bounded and satisfies the fork property. □2.17

This ends our general investigation of D-continuity in posets. We mention that a similar investigation can be done if the set c(A) is replaced by M(A), and we hope to describe the relevant results in a future report. If 2.17 is applied to the special case of occurrence nets [12], it turns out that the fork property is always satisfied and that a simpler characterisation of D-continuity can therefore be obtained. For this, we refer the reader to section 4 of the companion paper which also contains some examples to illustrate the meaning of the properties used in 2.17 [6].

3. D-CONTINUITY AND PETRI'S AXIOMS OF CONCURRENCY

The concurrency axioms of [16,17] are applicable to structures (X,co) where co is a reflexive and symmetric relation over X. Hence they are also applicable to posets $(X,\leq)$, with (X,co) being a derived structure. In this section, our aim will be to show how the properties used in 2.17 which characterise D-continuity follow from the concurrency axioms. The axioms make heavy use of a "proximity relation" $P\subseteq X\times X$ which describes how the elements of X are locally related to each other.

3.1 Definition.

Let $x,y\in X$.

(i) $\mathrm{Co}(x)=\{z\in X \mid z \text{ co } x\}$; $\mathrm{Li}(x)=\{z\in X \mid z \text{ li } x\}$;

(ii) $(x,y)\in P$ iff $\mathrm{Li}(x)\subseteq \mathrm{Li}(y)$ and $x\neq y$;

(iii) $p(x) = \{z\in X \mid (x,z)\in P \text{ or } (z,x)\in P\}$;

(iv) $F\subseteq X\times X$ is called consistent orientation on $(X,\leq)$ iff

(a) $F\cap F^{-1}=\emptyset$, (b) $F\cup F^{-1} = P\cup P^{-1}$, (c) $F\circ F\subseteq \text{li}$, (d) $F\circ F^{-1}\subseteq \text{co}$ and $F^{-1}\circ F\subseteq \text{co}$.

We consider the concurrency axioms essentially as they appear in [17]:

P1: $(X,\leq)$ is K-dense

P2a: $(X,\leq)$ is co-reduced: $\forall x,y\in X$: $Co(x)=Co(y) \Rightarrow x=y$.

P2b: $(X,\leq)$ is li-reduced: $\forall x,y\in X$: $Li(x)=Li(y) \Rightarrow x=y$.

P3: $(X,\leq)$ is coherent: $co^* = X\times X = li^*$.

P4a: $P^2 = \emptyset$.

P4b: $(P\cup P^{-1})^* = X\times X$.

P5: A consistent orientation exists on $(X,\leq)$.

P6a: $\forall x\in X$: $\emptyset \neq (\overline{co}\cap(p(x)\times p(x)))^2$, where $\overline{co} = X\times X\backslash co$ by definition.

P6b: $\forall x\in X$: $(\overline{co}\cap(p(x)\times p(x)))^2 \subseteq co$.

P6c: $\forall x\in X$: $(co\cap(p(x)\times p(x)))^2 \subseteq co$.

P7: $(X,\leq)$ has the cone property: $\forall x,y\in X$: $\downarrow x\cap\downarrow y \neq \emptyset \neq \uparrow x\cap\uparrow y$.

P7 has been proposed in [9,10] because it has been found that P1-P5 alone do not imply D-continuity.

We are now ready to deduce the four characterising properties of 2.17, i.e. K-density, the nsd property, the fork property and cut-boundedness, from the above axioms. Since K-density is P1 we need not worry about it. The nsd property can equally easily be taken care of as follows:

<u>3.2 Proposition.</u>

Let $(X,\leq)$ be li-reduced. Then it satisfies the nsd property.

<u>Proof:</u> Suppose not.

Then $\exists x,y\in X$: $x \lessdot y$ and $\forall z\in X\backslash\{x,y\}$: <u>not</u> $(x < z \text{ co } y)$ and <u>not</u> $(x \text{ co } z < y)$.

Hence $\forall z\in X$: $z>x \Rightarrow z \text{ li } y$ and $z<y \Rightarrow z \text{ li } x$.

Thus $Li(x)=Li(y)$, contradicting li-reducedness. □3.2

The reverse of 3.2 does not hold true in general.

We now tackle the fork property and cut-boundedness. First we need the following result.

<u>3.3 Theorem.</u>

Suppose that $(X,\leq)$ satisfies P1, P2a, P4a and P6b.

Then $(P\cup P^{-1}) \subseteq (\lessdot \cup \lessdot^{-1})$.

<u>Proof:</u> Suppose $x<z<y$ and $(x,y)\in P$; we construct a contradiction.

xPy implies that also zPy.

By $P^2=\emptyset$ (axiom P4a), $\exists z'\neq z$: $x < z' \text{ co } z$; by xPy, $z' < y$.

By co-reducedness (axiom P2a), $Co(z)\neq Co(z')$.

W.l.o.g., we can assume $\exists w\neq z$: $z \text{ li } w \text{ co } z'$.

If $z<w$ then by zPy, $w<y$.

If $w<z$ then either $x<w$ or $x \text{ co } w$; in the latter case, by K-density (axiom P1), $\exists w'$: $x<w'<w$, $w' \text{ co } z'$. (Take a cut through w,z' and a line through x,z.)

In all, $\exists z_1,z_2$: $x<z_1<z_2<y$ and z_1Py, z_2Py.

But by axiom P6b, $x\ \overline{co}\ z_1\ \overline{co}\ z_2 \Rightarrow x \text{ co } z_2$, contradiction. □3.3

Theorem 3.3 means that from xPy one can always deduce either $x \lessdot y$ or $y \lessdot x$. However, this is not enough to derive the fork property: [5] shows an example which satisfies the premiss of theorem 3.3 but not the fork property. (We do not reproduce this example here because it is slightly complicated; essentially, the idea is to consider the smallest poset which does not satisfy the up-fork property and to augment it so that all axioms except P6a are satisfied.) Axiom P6a turns out to be crucial in the derivation of the fork property, in a way which will be shown next.

3.4 Definition.

For $x \in X$, $\;{}^{\bullet}x = \{y \in X \mid y \lessdot x\}$, $\;x^{\bullet} = \{y \in X \mid x \lessdot y\}$.

3.5 Proposition.

Suppose that $(X,\le)$ satisfies P1, P2a, P4a and P6a,b.

Then $\forall x \in X$: ${}^{\bullet}x \cap p(x) \neq \emptyset \neq x^{\bullet} \cap p(x)$.

Proof: By P6a, $\emptyset \neq (\overline{co} \cap (p(x) \times p(x)))^2$.

This means $\exists y,z \in X$: $(y,z) \in (\overline{co} \cap (p(x) \times p(x)))^2$.

Further, $\exists w$: $(y,w) \in \overline{co} \cap (p(x) \times p(x))$, $(w,z) \in \overline{co} \cap (p(x) \times p(x))$.

In all, $\exists y,z,w \in p(x)$: $y \;\overline{co}\; w \;\overline{co}\; z$.

By theorem 3.3, either $y \lessdot x$ or $x \lessdot y$.

Suppose $y \lessdot x$, then it easily follows that $z \lessdot x$ and $x \lessdot w$; if $x \lessdot y$, on the other hand, then $x \lessdot z$ and $w \lessdot x$.

In both cases, ${}^{\bullet}x \cap p(x) \neq \emptyset \neq x^{\bullet} \cap p(x)$. □3.5

3.6 Proposition.

Suppose that $(X,\le)$ satisfies P1, P2a, P4a and P6a,b.

Then $(X,\le)$ satisfies the fork property.

Proof: We prove the up-fork property, the proof of 2.15(iii) being symmetrical.

Suppose we have $x<y$ and $l \cap [x,y] = \{x\}$.

By proposition 3.5 there is some $y' \gtrdot x$ with $y' \in p(x)$.

Either $y' \neq y$ and y' co y, or $y' \neq y''$ and y' co y'' for some $y'' \in l$.

Hence not xPy' and, instead, $y'Px$.

Suppose $z<y'$; $x<z$ contradicts $x \lessdot y'$;

x co z and $x \neq z$ contradicts $y'Px$;

so $z \le x$ remains which was to be proved. □3.6

Thus, P6a is needed in order to derive the fork property. Conversely, the fork property implies P6a if the poset is endless (see definition 3.7 below).

It remains to take care of the cut-boundedness property. A result that can be found in [3, 4] can easily be generalised to give an equivalence between cut-boundedness and the cone property P7 for a subclass of posets. We list this result next.

3.7 Definition.

(i) $(X,\le)$ is combinatorial iff $\le\, = (\lessdot)^*$;

(ii) $(X,\le)$ is endless iff $\forall x \in X$: $\downarrow x \neq \{x\} \neq \uparrow x$.

Note that posets satisfying P6a are endless.

3.8 Proposition.

(i) If $(X,\leq)$ is K-dense, combinatorial and satisfies P7, then it is cut-bounded.

(ii) If $(X,\leq)$ is endless and cut-bounded then it satisfies P7.

Proof:

(i): Let $A\in D$ and $x\in A$; we wish to prove $x\leq x'$ for some $x'\in Max(A)\cup Min(\overline{A})$.

Because $\overline{A}\neq\emptyset$, $\exists y\in\overline{A}$: $x\nleq y$.

By P7, $\exists z\in\overline{A}$: $z\geq y$ and $z\geq x$.

By combinatorialness, $x=x_0 \lessdot x_1 \lessdot \ldots \lessdot x_n=z$ for some $n>0$.

Since $x\in A$, $z\in\overline{A}$, $\exists i$: $x_i \lessdot x_{i+1}$ for $x_i\in A$ and $x_{i+1}\in\overline{A}$.

We prove that $x_i\notin Max(A) \wedge x_{i+1}\notin Min(\overline{A})$ is impossible.

For suppose so, then $\exists u\in A$: $u>x_i$ and $\exists v\in\overline{A}$: $v<x_{i+1}$.

$u\leq v$ is impossible since $x_i \lessdot x_{i+1}$, and $v<u$ contradicts $A\in D$.

Hence u co v, but then a cut containing u,v and a line containing x_i,x_{i+1} do not intersect, contradicting K-density.

Hence either $x_i\in Max(A)$ or $x_{i+1}\in Min(\overline{A})$ (or both), which proves the result.

(ii): Omitted since this is not needed to derive D-continuity. □3.8

Proposition 3.8(i) shows that cut-boundedness (and therefore, by 2.17, D-continuity as a whole) can be derived from P1-P7, provided that P1-P7 can be shown to imply combinatorialness. Unfortunately this is not true. Appendix A.2 shows a counterexample of a poset satisfying P1-P7 but not the cut-boundedness property. By 2.17 the poset also fails to be D-continuous.

We end this section by giving, without proof, a few additional results which may be of interest to readers wishing to explore the connections between the concurrency axioms. In particular, it can be shown that $\lessdot$ and $\lessdot^{-1}$ are the only consistent orientations. The proof of 3.9 can be found in the original version of this paper [5].

3.9 Theorem.

(i) Suppose P1, P2a, P4a and P6a,b.

Then: $(\lessdot\cup\lessdot^{-1}) \subseteq (P\cup P^{-1})$;

$\lessdot$ and $\lessdot^{-1}$ are consistent orientations;

$\forall x\in X$: $p(x) = {}^{\bullet}x\cup x^{\bullet}$;

$\forall x\in dom(P)$: $|{}^{\bullet}x| = 1 = |x^{\bullet}|$.

(ii) Suppose P1, P2a, P4a,b and P6a,b.

Then: If F is a consistent orientation then $F = \lessdot$ or $F = \lessdot^{-1}$. □3.9

Conversely, the property P5 can be used in place of P6b in the proof of theorem 3.3. All other proofs go through as a consequence, and therefore, P1-P5 imply P6b and P6a (the proof being analogous to the proof of proposition 3.5). Also, it can be shown that the posets satisfying P1-P7 are "almost" occurrence nets (an exception being given by the poset shown in Appendix A.2). If combinatorialness is added to the list of axioms then one gets occurrence nets by putting B=dom(P), E=cod(P) and $F=\lessdot$.

4. CONCLUDING REMARKS

In the first part of this paper, we have proved a characterisation of D-continuity in terms of two global properties (K-density and cut-boundedness) and two local properties (the non-single degree property and the fork property).

K-density has been introduced in [15] as an axiom of concurrency and studied more closely in [1,4,18]. It is motivated by the intuitive idea that all sequential subprocesses (lines) of a process should always (i.e. for every cut) be in a well-defined state. For example, K-density excludes

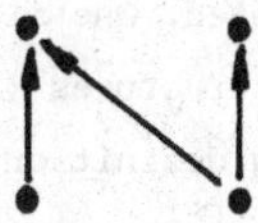

and requires

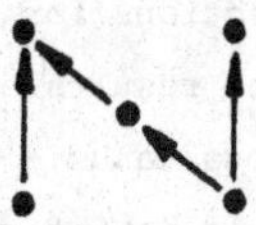

For the special case of occurrence nets, only infinite occurrence nets can violate K-density.

Cut-boundedness excludes subprocesses which are, in a sense, independent of each other. For example, the following is excluded:

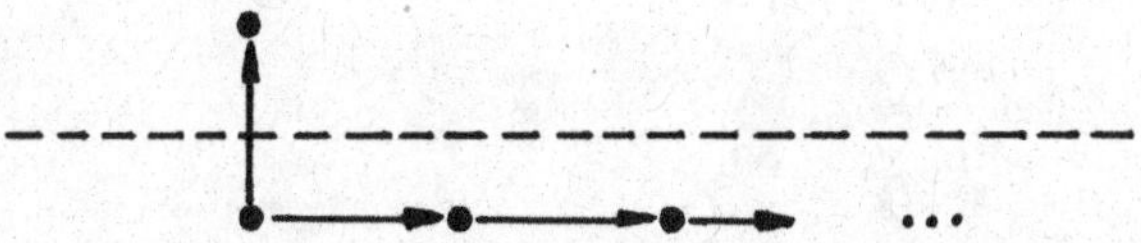

The non-single degree property requires that two immediately neighbouring elements do not have the same Li-sets. Thus, for example, non-dense lines such as the following are excluded:

The fork property is closely related to Petri's definition of c(A) (definition 2.6) and also to his axiom P6a. It guarantees that if, for some D-cut A, some element x is in Max(A) but not in Obmax(A) then an element above x can be found which is in Obmin($\overline{A}$), and vice versa.

In the second part of the paper we have shown that D-continuity does not follow from the concurrency axioms as they stand. We have also proved a series of results which show that it is possible to derive D-continuity provided combinatorialness is added to the list of axioms (for example, as a slightly stronger form of axiom P4b).

We have not aimed at a complete understanding of all axioms, and we refer the reader to [9,19] for further reading.

Using the Petri net model of concurrent systems, the question may be asked what are the conditions for a Petri net to have only D-continuous processes? [6] shows that such nets are strongly well-behaved in the sense that they have no "frozen tokens". By definition, a token is frozen if it stays unused on some place during some infinite process (this is related to cut-boundedness). There are interesting classes of nets which have only gap-free processes, for example the class of well-behaved bp schemes [11,13]. On the other hand, there are also interesting classes of nets which do have frozen tokens, and hence we conclude that more work is required to settle the question of whether or not to adopt D-continuity (or any set of axioms implying it) as an a priori postulate.

Several possible directions for future research may be suggested. One might be interested in extending the results of this paper to concurrency structures (X,co); however, it is not obvious to us how some of the order-depending definitions can be generalised. Also, it could be interesting to know the system equivalents of axioms P2-P7 (aiming, perhaps, at transporting the results by which the characterising properties of D-continuity can be derived from the axioms, as well as 2.17, to the system level). Also, D-continuity and K-density are related to other meaningful process properties [2, 8]; these connections can well be further explored. Finally, it should be interesting to do more work on the frozen token property which seems also to be related to fairness properties.

ACKNOWLEDGEMENTS

Theorem 2.14 took shape during a discussion with César Fernández on how our previous results on D-continuity [4 ,9] could be generalised. There have been helpful discussions with Cornelius Hopmann about the question whether or not combinatorialness is implied by the set of axioms. Helmut Plünnecke has helped us in verifying that the poset shown in Appendix A.2 satisfies the axioms.

REFERENCES (LNCS = Lecture Notes in Computer Science, Springer Verlag)

1. E.Best: A Theorem on the Characteristics of Non-sequential Processes. Fundamenta Informaticae Vol. 3(1), 77-94 (1980).

2. E.Best: Concurrent Behaviour: Sequences, Processes and Axioms. Arbeitspapiere der GMD No.118 (1984), also in Proc. of CMU Workshop on Concurrency (1984).

3. E.Best and A.Merceron: Some Properties of Non-sequential Processes. GMD-ISF Report 82.07 (1982).

4. E.Best and A.Merceron: Discreteness, K-density and D-continuity of Occurrence Nets. LNCS Vol.145, 73-83 (1982).

5. E.Best and A.Merceron: Concurrency Axioms and D-continuous Posets. 4th Petri Net Workshop, Toulouse (1983).

6. E.Best and A.Merceron: Frozen Tokens and D-continuity: A Study in Relating System Properties to Process Properties. In this Volume.

7. E.Best and B.Randell: A Formal Model of Atomicity in Asynchronous Systems. Acta Informatica Vol.16, 93-124 (1981).

8. C.Fernândez, M.Nielsen and P.S.Thiagarajan: A Note on Observable Occurrence Nets. 5th Petri Net Workshop, Århus (1984). Also to appear in this Volume.

9. C.Fernândez and P.S.Thiagarajan: D-Continuous Causal Nets: A Model of Non-sequential Processes. TCS Vol.28, 171-196 (1984).

10. C.Fernândez and P.S.Thiagarajan: A Note D-continuous Causal Nets. 3rd Petri Net Workshop, Varenna (1982).

11. H.J.Genrich and P.S.Thiagarajan: A Theory of Bipolar Synchronisation Schemes. TCS Vol.30, 241-318 (1984).

12. H.J.Genrich and E.Stankiewicz-Wiechno: A Dictionary of some Basic Notions of Net Theory. LNCS Vol.84, 519-535 (1980).

13. W.M.Lu and A.Merceron: The Equivalence between the Well Behaved Bipolar Schemes and the Live and Safe Free Choice Nets without Frozen Tokens. 5th Petri Net Workshop, Århus (1984).

14. M.Nielsen, G.Plotkin and G.Winskel: Petri Nets, Event Structures and Domains. TCS Vol.13, 85-108 (1981).

15. C.A.Petri: Non-Sequential Processes. GMD-ISF Report 77.05 (1977).

16. C.A.Petri: Concurrency. LNCS Vol.84, 251-260 (1980).

17. C.A.Petri: State Transition Structures in Physics and in Computation. International Journal on Theoretical Physics, Vol.21(12), 979-992 (1982).

18. H.Plünnecke: Schnitte in Halbordnungen. GMD-ISF Report 81.09 (1981). Shorter version also to appear in this Volume.

19. H.Plünnecke: Partial Orders. Arbeitspapiere der GMD No.93 (1984).

A.1 APPENDIX: A Technical Lemma about D-cuts.

Let $(X,\leq)$ be a poset.

Let $A\in D$ and $X_0 \subseteq Max(A)$, $X_0 \neq A$.

Define $B=A\setminus X_0$, $\overline{B}=X\setminus B$.

Then,

(i) $B\in D$, i.e. $B\neq\emptyset\neq\overline{B}$ and $\downarrow B=B$;

(ii) $X_0 \subseteq Min(\overline{B})$, $X_0 \neq \overline{B}$.

Furthermore, with $Y_1 = \{y\in A \mid \exists x\in X_0: y \lessdot x\}$

and $Y_2 = \{y\in \overline{A} \mid \exists x\in X_0: x \lessdot y\}$, we have:

(iii) $M(A)\setminus Y_2 = M(B)\setminus Y_1$.

Proof:

(i): $B\neq\emptyset$ because of $X_0\neq A$, $\overline{B}\neq\emptyset$ because of $\emptyset\neq\overline{A}\subseteq\overline{B}$.

It remains to be proved that $\downarrow B\subseteq B$.

Suppose $z\in\downarrow B$; then $\exists x\in A\setminus X_0$: $z\leq x$.

If $z\in\overline{A}$ then $z<x\in A$ contradicts $\downarrow A=A$; hence $z\in A$.

If $z\in X_0$ then $z<x\in A$ contradicts $z\in X_0\subseteq Max(A)$; hence $z\notin X_0$.

Hence $z\in B$ by the definition of B.

(ii): Suppose $x\in X_0$ and assume $y<x$ for $y\in\overline{B}=\overline{A}\cup X_0$;

if $y\in\overline{A}$ then $y<x\in A$ contradicts $\uparrow\overline{A}=\overline{A}$;

if $y\in X_0$ then $y<x\in A$ contradicts $y\in X_0\subseteq Max(A)$.

Hence no such y exists, and $x\in Min(\overline{B})$.

$X_0\neq\overline{B}$ because $\overline{B}=\overline{A}\cup X_0$ and $\overline{A}\neq\emptyset$.

(iii): We prove the following two statements separately:

(a) $y \in Max(A)\backslash X_o \Leftrightarrow y \in Max(B)\backslash Y_1$;

(b) $y \in Min(\overline{B})\backslash X_o \Leftrightarrow y \in Min(\overline{A})\backslash Y_2$.

(a): Suppose $y \in Max(A)\backslash X_o$; then $y \in B$ by definition of B.

Suppose $y<z$, $z \in B$; this contradicts $y \in Max(A)$ since $B \subseteq A$.

Hence $y \in Max(B)$.

Suppose $y \lessdot x$ for some $x \in X_o$; this contradicts $y \in Max(A)$ because $X_o \subseteq Max(A)$.

Hence $y \notin Y_1$, i.e. $y \in Max(B)\backslash Y_1$.

Conversely, suppose $y \in Max(B)\backslash Y_1$; then $y \in A$ since $B \subseteq A$.

Suppose $y<z$, $z \in A$;

if $z \in X_o$ then $y \lessdot z$ because $y \in Max(B)$, contradicting $y \notin Y_1$;

if $z \notin X_o$ then $z \in B$ by definition of B, again contradicting $y \in Max(B)$.

Hence $y \in Max(A)$.

Also, $y \notin X_o$ because $y \in B$; so, $y \in Max(A)\backslash X_o$.

(b): The proof is analogous and is omitted.

Having established (a) and (b) we now return to (iii).

By definition of M(A) and M(B) we have:

$y \in M(A)\backslash Y_2 \Leftrightarrow y \in Max(A)\backslash X_o \vee y \in X_o \vee y \in Min(\overline{A})\backslash Y_2$;

$y \in M(B)\backslash Y_1 \Leftrightarrow y \in Min(\overline{B})\backslash X_o \vee y \in X_o \vee y \in Max(B)\backslash Y_1$.

The result finally follows from an application of (a) and (b) to this pair of equivalences. □A.1

A.2 APPENDIX: A Worked Example

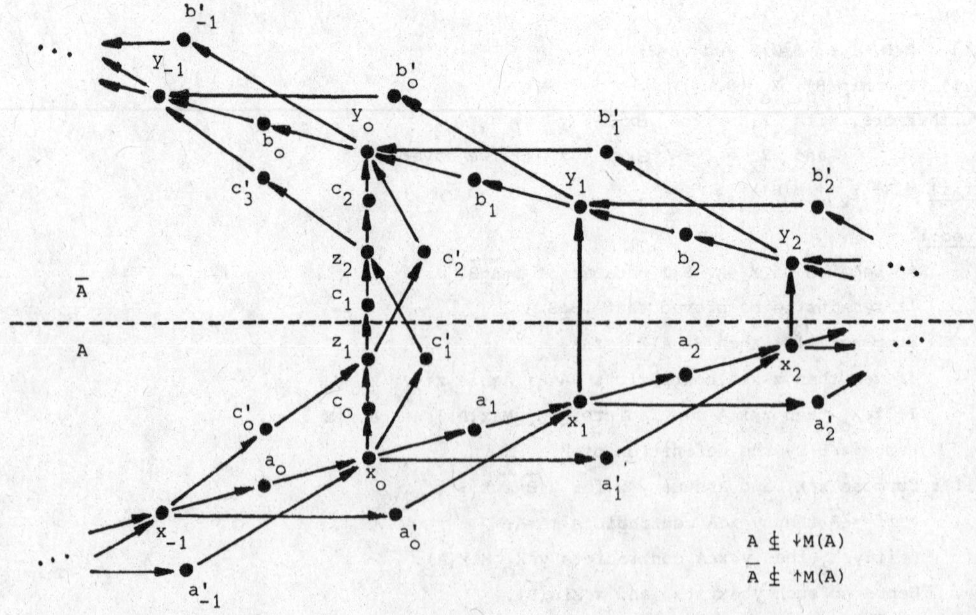

The poset shown on the previous page satisfies the axioms P1-P7 but fails to be combinatorial and cut-bounded; consequently it is also not D-continuous due to 2.17.

In order to verify the axioms we list the Co-sets of some elements of X:

$$\begin{aligned}
Co(x_{-1}) &= \{x_{-1}, a'_{-1}\}\\
Co(a'_{-1}) &= \{a'_{-1}, x_{-1}, a'_{-2}, a'_{0}, a_{-1}, a_{0}, c'_{0}\}\\
Co(x_{0}) &= \{x_{0}, a'_{0}, c'_{0}\}\\
Co(a_{0}) &= \{a_{0}, a'_{0}, a'_{-1}, c'_{0}\}\\
Co(a_{1}) &= \{a_{1}, a'_{1}, a'_{0}\} \cup X_{0} \quad \text{where } X_{0} = \{z_1, z_2, c_0, c_1, c_2, c'_0, c'_1, c'_2, c'_3\}\\
Co(x_{1}) &= \{x_{1}, a'_{1}\} \cup X_{0}\\
Co(a'_{1}) &= \{a'_{1}, x_{1}, a'_{0}, a'_{2}, a_{1}, a_{2}\} \cup X_{0}\\
Co(c'_{0}) &= \{c'_{0}, c_{0}, c'_{1}, a_{0}, a'_{-1}, x_{0}\} \cup X_{1} \cup Y_{1} \quad \text{where}\\
X_1 &= \{x_i, a_i \mid i\geq 1\} \cup \{a'_i \mid i\geq 0\}\\
Y_1 &= \{y_i, b_i \mid i\geq 1\} \cup \{b'_i \mid i\geq 0\}\\
Co(c_{0}) &= \{c_{0}, c'_{0}, c'_{1}\} \cup X_{1} \cup Y_{1}\\
Co(z_{1}) &= \{z_{1}, c'_{1}\} \cup X_{1} \cup Y_{1}, \quad \text{etc.}
\end{aligned}$$

P1 - The poset is K-dense. Any cut goes either through x_i, a_i, a'_i $(i<0)$ or through X_1 and an element of X_0, or symmetrically for the upper part, while any line goes through $\{x_i, a_i, a'_i, y_i, b_i, b'_i \mid i<0\}$ and crosses either X_0 or $X_1 \cup Y_1$.

P2 - The poset is co-reduced and li-reduced because of the a'_i and the b'_i.

P3 - The poset is coherent since it is li-connected and co-connected.

P4 - We have $cod(P) = \{x_i, y_i\} \cup \{z_1, z_2\}$

$dom(P) = \{a_i, a'_i, b_i, b'_i\} \cup \{c_0, c_1, c_2, c'_0, c'_1, c'_2, c'_3\}$.

Hence $P^2=\emptyset$ follows.

To check P4b, it is easy to see that any two elements of X can be reached from each other by a finite number of P-steps using the "bridge" X_0.

P5 - $F=\lessdot$ is a consistent orientation (note that $\lessdot$ excludes (x_i, y_i), $i\geq 1$!)

P6 and P7: Easily checked. For example, check P6a for $x=x_0$:

We claim $(a_0, a_0) \in (\overline{co}np(x) \times p(x))^2$; this holds because $(a_0, a_1), (a_1, a_0) \in \overline{co}np(x) \times p(x)$.

D-property: The D axioms (mentioned in [16] but not in [17]) are also easily checked. With xDy iff $Co(x) \subseteq Co(y) \wedge x \neq y$, the axioms are $D^2=\emptyset$ and $(D \cup D^{-1})^* = X \times X$.

Natural order: [16] defines $(X,\leq)$ to be a natural order iff

for all posets $(X',\leq')$: $(X'=X \wedge co'=co) \Rightarrow (\leq' = \leq \vee \leq' = \leq^{-1})$.

To show that the poset shown on the previous page is a natural order, an argument due to Plünnecke [19] may usefully be employed. Call a set of three distinct elements $x,y,z \in X$ a "V" iff x li y li z and x co z. The result states that $(X,\leq)$ is a natural order provided it is V-connected, that is, by definition, a sequence of V's can be found which connects any two-element li-set with any other two-element li-set.

□A.2

FROZEN TOKENS AND D-CONTINUITY:

A STUDY IN RELATING SYSTEM PROPERTIES TO PROCESS PROPERTIES

by

Eike BEST
GMD-F1P
Schloß Birlinghoven
5205 St. Augustin 1
Fed. Rep. Germany

Agathe MERCERON
L.R.I., CNRS
Université Paris-Sud
91405 Orsay Cedex
France

ABSTRACT

This paper is based on the notion that there is a formal relationship between a system and the set of its processes. Both the system and its processes are described in terms of Petri nets. We prove a theorem which gives a correspondence between a property of the processes called D-continuity and a set of properties of the system. D-continuity has first been introduced as a generalisation of the Dedekind completeness properties of the real numbers. Our main result shows that a system has only D-continuous processes iff it is safe (in the sense that its capacities are finite), behaviourally connected (in the sense that its infinite processes use all parts of the system) and satisfies another (minor) property.

1. INTRODUCTION

Petri nets have widely been proposed as models of concurrent systems [5,6]. Net theory is uniform in the sense that if a system is given by a net then the processes running on the system may also be modelled by special kinds of nets, viz. occurrence nets [6, 9].

Many investigations have aimed at studying the properties of either Petri nets in general (see [5,6,15] for a selection of textbooks) or occurrence nets in particular [1,2,7]. More specifically, the properties of K-density [1,2,13] and D-continuity [4,7,14] of occurrence nets have been studied and are by now well understood.

By contrast, relatively little has been done in relating the properties of occurrence nets to properties of the system net of which they represent executions. A result of this flavour is described in [9] where it is shown that the safeness (boundedness) of a Petri net essentially corresponds to its processes being K-dense in the sense of [2,13].

In this paper we present a similar result for D-continuity. D-continuity, first defined in [14], is a generalisation to posets of Dedekind's completeness properties of the real numbers and is stronger than K-density. Our main result will show that the imposition of D-continuity means that all system parts must interact infinitely often with each other in every infinite execution; i.e. that, in some sense, the system is behaviourally connected.

Before being able to state the result we first have to define the notion of a process and to study some properties of processes. To this end we use ideas from [9]. We will also make use of the characterisation of the D-continuity property given in a companion paper [4].

This paper is organised as follows. In section 2 we introduce system nets (P/T-nets) and occurrence nets. In section 3 we define the processes of a P/T-net. We also prove a few properties needed later. In section 4 we recall the definitions of D-continuity and K-density, and we recall the concomitant result from [4]. Section 5 contains the proof of the main result of this paper. It essentially states that D-continuity requires the absence of "frozen tokens" in the given system net. A token is frozen on some place of the net if it may stay put there during some infinite execution. Finally, section 6 offers some concluding remarks.

2. MARKED NETS AND OCCURRENCE NETS

In our definition of a net we deviate slightly from the standard definition [5,6].

2.1 Definition.

$N=(S,T,F)$ is called a net iff

(i) S is a set of places,

(ii) T is a set of transitions, $S \cap T = \emptyset$,

(iii) F is the flow relation: $F \subseteq (S \times T) \cup (T \times S)$,

(iv) $T \subseteq cod(F)$.

Graphically we represent places by circles , transitions by boxes , and F by arrows ⟶, as usual. We write

$${}^{\bullet}x = \{y \in S \cup T \mid (y,x) \in F\}, \quad x^{\bullet} = \{y \in S \cup T \mid (x,y) \in F\}$$

for the pre-set and the post-set, respectively, of $x \in S \cup T$.

With a view to the process definition (section 3), we find it convenient (as do [9]) to relax the definition of a net slightly by allowing isolated places; hence the requirement $S \cup T = dom(F) \cup cod(F)$ of [6] is replaced by 2.1(iv). Also, 2.1(iv) disallows proper input transitions, i.e. we require ${}^{\bullet}t \neq \emptyset$ for all $t \in T$. We consider this to be a weak and rather appropriate restriction since, in a sense, it means that one cannot put infinitely many tokens on a place. Neither the results of [9] nor the results of this paper would be true without this restriction.

2.2 Definition.

M is called a marking of $N=(S,T,F)$ iff $M: S \to \mathbb{N}_o$ (where $\mathbb{N}_o$ is the set of non-negative integers)

M is represented by placing M(s) "tokens" on each $s \in S$, thus $M(s)=3$ gives .

2.3 Definition.

(S,T,F,M_o) is called a (finite) marked net iff:

(i) $N=(S,T,F)$ is a net with $|S|<\infty$ and $|T|<\infty$,

(ii) $M_o: S \to \mathbb{N}_o$ is the initial marking.

2.4 Definition.

Let M be a marking of $N=(S,T,F)$.

(i) A transition $t \in T$ is enabled by M iff $\forall s \in {}^\cdot t$: $M(s) \geq 1$.

(ii) A transition which is enabled by M may "fire" to yield a follower marking M' defined as follows:

$$M'(s) = \begin{cases} M(s)-1 & \text{if } s \in {}^\cdot t \setminus t^\cdot \\ M(s)+1 & \text{if } s \in t^\cdot \setminus {}^\cdot t \\ M(s) & \text{otherwise} \end{cases}$$

We write $M'=M[t>$ or $M[t>M'$.

(iii) A finite sequence $M_1 t_1 M_2 \ldots t_{m-1} M_m$ $(m \geq 1)$ (an infinite sequence $M_1 t_1 M_2 \ldots$) will be called a firing sequence from M iff

$M_1=M$ and $M_i[t_i>M_{i+1}$ for $1 \leq i \leq m$ $(1 \leq i$, respectively);

in the finite case, M_m is called the marking reached from M by the sequence.

(iv) $[M>$ is the set of markings reachable from M by finite sequences.

Next we give the definition of occurrence nets, based on which the notion of a process will be defined in section 3.

2.5 Definition.

$N'=(B,E,F')$ will be called an occurrence net iff

(i) N' satisfies the net axioms 2.1;

(ii) $\forall x,y \in B \cup E$: $(x,y) \in F'^*$ and $(y,x) \in F'^*$ implies $x=y$ (F'^* denotes the transitive closure of F');

(iii) $\forall b \in B$: $|{}^\cdot b| \leq 1 \wedge |b^\cdot| \leq 1$.

In an occurrence net (B,E,F') we call B the set of conditions and E the set of events. 2.5(ii) requires that there are no "loops". 2.5(iii) requires that there is no "conflict". Because of 2.5(ii), F'^* is a partial order on the set $X=B \cup E$. We sometimes write B(N'), E(N'), X(N'), etc., to indicate the net in question.

2.6 Definition.

Let $N'=(B,E,F')$ be an occurrence net and let $X=B \cup E$.

(i) $\leq \; = F'^*$, $< \; = F'^+ = F'^* \setminus id_X$;

(ii) $li = \leq \cup \geq$, $co = \overline{li} \cup id_X$ $(\overline{li} = (X \times X) \setminus li)$;

(iii) $l \subseteq X$ is a li-set (chain) iff $\forall x,y \in l$: x li y;

$l \subseteq X$ is a line iff it is a maximal li-set ("maximal" means $\forall z \in X \setminus l \; \exists y \in l$: z co y);

the set of lines of N' will be denoted by L (or L(N'));

(iv) $c \subseteq X$ is a co-set (anti-chain) iff $\forall x,y \in c$: x co y;

c is a cut iff it is a maximal co-set ("maximal" means $\forall z \in X \setminus c \; \exists y \in c$: z li y);

the set of cuts of N' will be denoted by $C = C(N')$;

a cut c containing only elements of B (i.e. $c \subseteq B$) will be called a B-cut;

the set of B-cuts of N' will be denoted by $BC = BC(N')$.

We assume the axiom of choice to hold. Consequently, for every li-set (co-set) there is a line (a cut) containing it.

The next definition introduces some notation.

2.7 Definition.

Let $N'=(B,E,F')$ be an occurrence net and let $X=B\cup E$.

(i) $^{\circ}N' = \{x\in X \mid {}^{\bullet}x=\emptyset\}$, $N'^{\circ} = \{x\in X \mid x^{\bullet}=\emptyset\}$;

(ii) For $A\subseteq X$, $\downarrow A = \{y\in X \mid \exists x\in A\colon y\leq x\}$, $\uparrow A = \{y\in X \mid \exists x\in A\colon x\leq y\}$;
for $x\in X$, $\downarrow x = \downarrow\{x\}$, $\uparrow x = \uparrow\{x\}$.

Next (and finally in this section) we need the notion of an occurrence net N' being approximable by a sequence of subnets.

2.8 Definition.

Let $N_1'=(B_1,E_1,F_1')$ and $N_2'=(B_2,E_2,F_2')$ be two occurrence nets.

(i) $N_1' \leq N_2'$ (N_1' is an initial subnet of N_2') iff
$\exists A\in BC(N_2')\colon B_1 = B_2\cap\downarrow A$, $E_1 = E_2\cap\downarrow A$ and $F_1 = F_2\cap(\downarrow A\times\downarrow A)$;

(ii) For chains $N_0' \leq N_1' \leq N_2' \leq \ldots$ we define

$$\bigsqcup_{i=0}^{\infty} N_i' = \Big(\bigcup_{i=0}^{\infty} B_i,\ \bigcup_{i=0}^{\infty} E_i,\ \bigcup_{i=0}^{\infty} F_i'\Big).$$

Definition 2.8(i) of an initial subnet differs from the corresponding definition given in [9]. However, for the purposes of this paper, the two definitions are interchangeable. As in [9] we have:

2.9 Proposition.

$\leq$ is a partial order with lubs $\bigsqcup N_i'$.

Proof: Easy; we omit it because the result is not needed in the sequel. □2.9

3. PROCESSES OF MARKED NETS AND SOME OF THEIR PROPERTIES

In this section we first recall the process definition of [9], giving also a few additional results. The idea is to use labelled occurrence nets, where the labelling provides the link back to the system net.

3.1 Definition.

Let $(N,M_0)=(S,T,F,M_0)$ be a marked net and let (N',p) be a pair such that $N'=(B,E,F')$ is an occurrence net and $p\colon B\cup E\rightarrow S\cup T$ is a labelling function.

Then (N',p) is a process of (N,M_0) iff

(i) $p(B)\subseteq S$, $p(E)\subseteq T$;

(ii) $^{\circ}N'\in BC(N')$ and $\forall s\in S\colon M_0(s) = |p^{-1}(s)\cap{}^{\circ}N'|$;

(iii) $\forall e\in E\colon p({}^{\bullet}e)={}^{\bullet}p(e)$, $p(e^{\bullet})=p(e)^{\bullet}$, $|{}^{\bullet}e|=|{}^{\bullet}p(e)|$ and $|e^{\bullet}|=|p(e)^{\bullet}|$;

(iv) $N' = \bigsqcup_{i=0}^{\infty} N_i$ for some finite occurrence nets N_i with $N_i\leq N_{i+1}$ for $0\leq i$.

We will sometimes express the condition of 3.1(ii) by saying that the marking M_0 "corresponds to" the B-cut $^{\circ}N'$.

Actually, the definition given in [9] requires only (i)-(iii), but (iv) is suggested as an additional requirement in the last section of [9]. We use this requirement because, as will be stated next, the objects defined in 3.1 correspond exactly to what one would expect when relating the process notion to the notion of a firing sequence defined in 2.4(iii). To this end, the next definition gives a construction by which a process (N',p) can be associated to a given firing sequence of (N,M_o).

3.2 Construction.

Let $(N,M_o)=(S,T,F,M_o)$ be a marked net and let $\sigma = M_o t_o M_1 \ldots$ be a firing sequence of (N,M_o) starting with M_o.

To σ we associate a process (N',p) as follows.

First we construct processes $(N_i,p_i)=(B_i,E_i,F_i,p_i)$ by induction on $i \geq 0$.

i=0. Define $E_o=F_o=\emptyset$, and B_o as containing, for each $s \in S$, $M_o(s)$ new conditions b with $p_o(b)=s$ (this defines p_o as well).

i→i+1. Suppose (N_i,p_i) to be constructed up to M_i.

By construction, N_i^o is a finite B-cut corresponding to M_i (i.e. $\forall s \in S$: $M_i(s)=|p_i^{-1}(s) \cap N_i^o|$).

Suppose ${}^\bullet t_i=\{s_1,\ldots,s_q\}$ and $t_i^\bullet=\{s_1',\ldots,s_r'\}$.

Since M_i enables t_i, N_i^o contains conditions $b_1,\ldots,b_q$ with $p_i(b_j)=s_j$ for $1 \leq j \leq q$; of course, $b_j^\bullet=\emptyset$ by the definition of N_i^o.

We choose one such set $\{b_1,\ldots,b_q\}$ and add a new event e_i such that $b_j F_{i+1} e_i$; also we put $p_{i+1}(e_i)=t_i$.

Further, we add new conditions $b_1',\ldots,b_r'$ such that $e_i F_{i+1} b_j'$ and $p_{i+1}(b_j')=s_j'$ for $1 \leq j \leq r$.

If σ is finite, say $\sigma = M_o \ldots M_m$ then the construction stops at i=m, and we may put $(N',p) = (N_m,p_m)$.

Otherwise put $N' = \bigsqcup_{i=0}^{\infty} N_i$ and $p = \bigcup_{i=0}^{\infty} p_i$.

It is important to note that the construction given in 3.2 is non-deterministic in the sense that there may be several different sets $\{b_1,\ldots,b_q\}$ to which a new event e_i can be added. We will exploit this non-determinacy later when constructing a non-D-continuous process in the proof of theorem 5.6.

The next theorem states that the process axioms 3.1 are consistent and complete with respect to the construction 3.2. Theorem 3.3(ii) (as, indeed, does construction 3.2) relies on the finiteness of (N,M_o). In [3], it is shown that this assumption can be weakened, but also that 3.3(ii) is not true in general. For the proof of 3.3, the reader is referred to [3]; it is not reproduced here because it is slightly lengthy.

3.3 Theorem.

(i) Any pair (N',p) constructed by 3.2 satisfies the process axioms 3.1.

(ii) Conversely, for every (N',p) that satisfies 3.1 there is a firing sequence σ such that (N',p) can be derived from σ using 3.2. □3.3

As an illustration, we may use the following example. Note that in this example, N' is infinite but that it is, indeed, generable as the lub of a ≤-chain of finite nets. Note also that N' contains an infinite B-cut (namely, $p^{-1}(s_1)$) which is, of course, not contained in any of the finite approximations of N'.

<u>A system (N,M_0):</u>

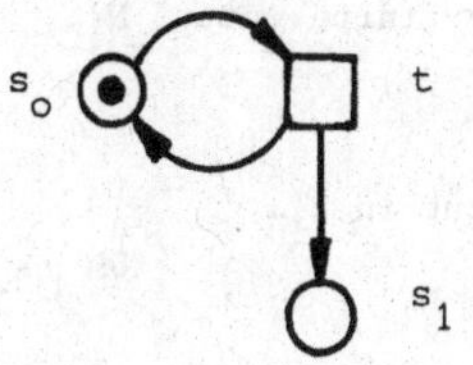

<u>A firing sequence σ:</u>

$$\binom{1}{0}\ t\ \binom{1}{1}\ t\ \binom{1}{2}\ \ldots$$

<u>A process (N',p) derivable from σ:</u>

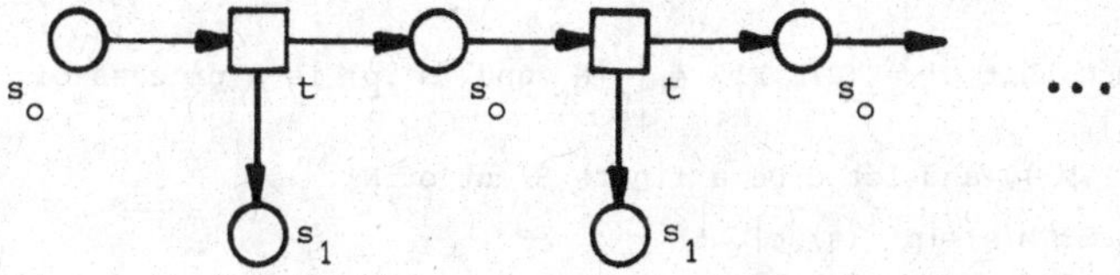

<u>Figure 1</u>

Our next aim is to show that, however, the <u>finite</u> cuts of N' are exactly the cuts of its finite approximations.

<u>3.4 Proposition.</u>

Suppose $N_i=(B_i,E_i,F_i) \le N_{i+1}=(B_{i+1},E_{i+1},F_{i+1})$.
Then $C(N_i) \subseteq C(N_{i+1})$.

<u>Proof:</u> Define $X_i=B_i \cup E_i$, $X_{i+1}=B_{i+1} \cup E_{i+1}$.

Assume $c \in C(N_i)$ and suppose $x \in X_{i+1} \setminus X_i$ s.t. x co y for all $y \in c$; we derive a contradiction.

By definition of ≤, $\exists A \in BC(N_{i+1})$: $X_i = X_{i+1} \cap {\downarrow}A$.

Hence $x \notin A$, and $\exists z \in A$: $x<z$ or $z<x$ (in N_{i+1}).

$x<z$ is impossible by $x \notin X_i$.

Hence $z<x$.

Now consider N_i and any line through z in N_i (clearly, $z \in X_i$ by definition).

From previous theory (see e.g. [2]) we know that $|c \cap l|=1$, since N_i is finite.

Say, $y \in c \cap l$.

We have either $y \le z$ or $z<y$; the latter is impossible since A is a cut.

Hence $y \le z < x$, which gives the desired contradiction. □3.4

<u>3.5 Proposition.</u>

Let $N' = \bigsqcup_{i=0}^{\infty} N_i$, $N_i \le N_{i+1}$. Then $\{c \in C(N') \mid c \text{ is finite}\} = \bigcup_{i=0}^{\infty} C(N_i)$.

Proof:

($\subseteq$): Let c be a finite cut of N'. Then clearly for some i, $c \in C(N_i)$.

($\supseteq$): Let c be a cut of some N_i.

If $x \in X(N')$ such that x could be added to c then $x \in X(N_k)$ for some k>i, and the argument given in 3.4 can be repeated to derive a contradiction. □3.5

3.6 Proposition.

Every finite co-set in $N' = \bigcup_{i=0}^{\infty} N_i$ is contained in some finite cut of N'.

Proof: Let c_o be a finite co-set in N'.

Then c_o is a co-set in some N_i, hence contained in a cut in N_i.

By 3.5, the result follows. □3.6

Next, we prove that every finite B-cut in a process (N',p) corresponds to some reachable marking of (N,M_o).

3.7 Proposition.

Let (N',p) be such that $N' = (B,E,F') = \bigcup_{i=0}^{\infty} N_i$ and (N',p) is a process of $(N,M_o) = (S,T,F,M_o)$, and let c be a finite B-cut of N'.

Then $\exists M \in [M_o\rangle\colon \forall s \in S\colon M(s)=|p^{-1}(s) \cap c|$.

Proof: We consider the initial subnet of N' below c, i.e. $N_c = (B_c,E_c,F_c)$ with $B_c = B \cap {\downarrow}c$, $E_c = E \cap {\downarrow}c$, $F_c = F \cap ({\downarrow}c \times {\downarrow}c)$.

Clearly, ${}^{o}N' = {}^{o}N_c$ and $N_c^{o} = c$.

Since M_o corresponds to ${}^{o}N_c$ and N_c is finite, it is possible to serialise the events in E_c in such a way that one obtains a firing sequence $M_o t_o \ldots t_{n-1} M_n$ (where $n=|E_c|$) such that $M=M_n$. (This argument is in full in [3].)

Hence $M \in [M_o\rangle$; it can be proved that $\forall s \in S\colon M(s)=|p^{-1}(s) \cap c|$ as required. □3.7

Lastly, we prove that every infinite N' contains an infinite line.

3.8 Proposition.

Let (N',p) be an infinite process of (N,M_o).

Then (N',p) contains an infinite line.

Proof: ${}^{o}N'$ is finite, whence $\exists b_o \in {}^{o}N'\colon |{\uparrow}b_o|=\infty$.

Thus $\exists e_o \in b_o^{\bullet}\colon |{\uparrow}e_o|=\infty$.

Since N is finite and because of 3.1(iii), $|e_o^{\bullet}|<\infty$; hence $\exists b_1 \in e_o^{\bullet}\colon |{\uparrow}b_1|=\infty$.

Continuing in this way, an infinite line may be constructed. □3.8

4. D-CONTINUITY

D-continuity has been introduced in [12] with the aim of transporting Dedekind's completeness properties of the real numbers to posets. Its definition involves the division of a poset into a lower part and an upper part, and the consideration of the "border" between them. A characterisation of D-continuity for general posets can be found in the companion paper [4] of the present paper. In this section we restrict our attention to (the posets derivable from) occurrence nets, and we therefore restrict the characterisation of D-continuity to this case. First, however, we repeat the relevant definitions.

4.1 Definition.

Let $N'=(B,E,F')$ be an occurrence net. Let $X=B\cup E$ and $A\subseteq X$. We write $\overline{A}=X\setminus A$.

(i) A is called a D-cut iff $\emptyset\neq A\neq X$ and $\downarrow A=A$;

(ii) D denotes the set of all D-cuts of N';

(iii) $Max(A) = \{x\in A \mid \underline{not}\ \exists y\in A: y>x\}$, $Min(\overline{A}) = \{x\in \overline{A} \mid \underline{not}\ \exists y\in \overline{A}: y<x\}$,
$M(A) = Max(A)\cup Min(\overline{A})$;

(iv) $Obmax(A) = \{x\in Max(A) \mid \forall A'\in D\ \forall l\in L: x\in Max(A'\cap l) \Rightarrow x\in Max(A')\}$,
$Obmin(\overline{A}) = \{x\in Min(\overline{A}) \mid \forall A'\in D\ \forall l\in L: x\in Min(\overline{A'}\cap l) \Rightarrow x\in Min(\overline{A'})\}$,
$c(A) = Obmax(A)\cup Obmin(\overline{A})$;

(v) N' is D-continuous iff $\forall A\in D\ \forall l\in L: |c(A)\cap l| = 1$.

The idea behind the Obmax definition is that of an element being "objectively maximal" (i.e. all lines "agree on its maximality"). To aid the reader we specialise the characterisation of the sets Obmax and Obmin given in [4, proposition 2.7] to the case of occurrence nets:

4.2 Proposition.

Let $A\in D$, $x\in Max(A)$ and $y\in Min(\overline{A})$.

(i) $x\in Obmax(A)$ iff $|x^{\bullet}|\leq 1$;

(ii) $y\in Obmin(\overline{A})$ iff $|{}^{\bullet}y|\leq 1$.

Proof: This follows easily from proposition 2.7 of [4], together with the occurrence net properties. □4.2

We give the following examples:

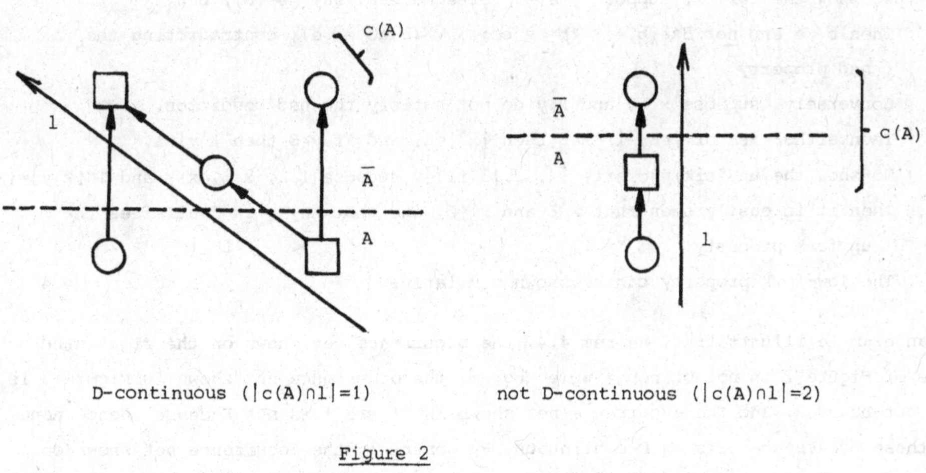

D-continuous ($|c(A)\cap l|=1$)   not D-continuous ($|c(A)\cap l|=2$)

Figure 2

The occurrence net shown in Figure 3 below indicates that the case $c(A)\cap l=\emptyset$ is also possible:

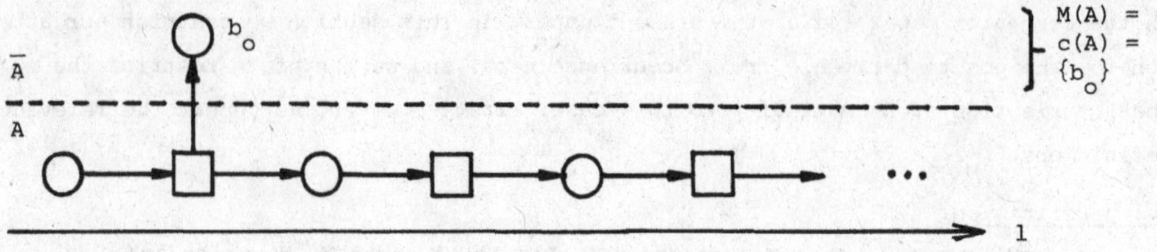

not D-continuous ($c(A) \cap l = \emptyset$)

Figure 3

We now specialise the characterisation of D-continuous posets given in [4, theorem 2.17] to occurrence nets. We need the following three properties:

4.3 Definition.

Let $N' = (B,E,F')$ be an occurrence net.

(i) N' is called K-dense iff $\forall l \in L\ \forall c \in C$: $|c \cap l| = 1$;

(ii) N' is called of non-single degree iff $\forall e \in E$: $|{}^{\bullet}e| \neq 1 \neq |e^{\bullet}|$;

(iii) N' is called cut-bounded from above iff $\forall A \in D$: $A \subseteq \downarrow M(A)$;

N' is called cut-bounded from below iff $\forall A \in D$: $\bar{A} \subseteq \uparrow M(A)$;

N' is called cut-bounded iff it is cut-bounded from above and cut-bounded from below.

4.4 Theorem.

N' is D-continuous iff it is K-dense, cut-bounded, and has the non-single degree property.

Proof: Using theorem 2.17 of [4], all we have to do is to show that the nsd property defined in [4, 2.9] reduces to the non-single degree property 4.3(ii), and that the fork property is always satisfied for occurrence nets.

To show the former, suppose $|{}^{\bullet}e|=1$ for some $e \in E$, say ${}^{\bullet}e=\{b\}$, $b \in B$.

Then $b \lessdot e$ and not $\exists z \notin \{b,e\}$: $(b < z \text{ co } e) \vee (b \text{ co } z < e)$, contradicting the nsd property.

Conversely, suppose $x \lessdot y$ and x,y do not satisfy the nsd condition.

Then either $x \in E$ or $y \in E$; if $x \in E$ then $|x^{\bullet}|=1$, and if $y \in E$ then $|{}^{\bullet}y|=1$.

To show the up-fork property [4, 2.15(ii)], suppose $l \in L$, $x \in l$, $x<y$ and $l \cap [x,y]=\{x\}$.

Then it is easily seen that $x \in E$ and $x^{\bullet} \neq \emptyset$, and that any $y' \in x^{\bullet}$ satisfies the up-fork property.

The low-fork property can be shown similarly. □4.4

As an example illustrating theorem 4.4, the occurrence net shown on the right hand side of Figure 2 is not of non-single degree; the occurrence net shown in Figure 3 is not cut-bounded; and the occurrence net shown in Figure 1 is not K-dense. Hence none of these occurrence nets is D-continuous. By contrast, the occurrence net shown on the left hand side of Figure 2 satisfies all properties required in theorem 4.4.

5. NECESSARY AND SUFFICIENT CONDITIONS FOR A NET TO HAVE ONLY D-CONTINUOUS PROCESSES

In this section we prove the main result of this paper which shows that the three characterising properties of D-continuity, i.e. K-density, the non-single degree property and cut-boundedness, all correspond to certain system properties. As shown in [9], K-density corresponds to the safeness of a system (as defined below in 5.1). The non-single degree property can be translated directly. The main result (theorem 5.6) gives a correspondence between cut-boundedness and the absence of any "frozen" tokens. A token will be called frozen if there is some infinite execution of the system which does not move it. The absence of frozen tokens means that all tokens interact infinitely often with each other in every infinite execution.

5.1 Definition.

Let (N,M_o) be a marked net.

(i) (N,M_o) is called safe iff $\exists n\in\mathbb{N}\ \forall M\in[M_o>\ \forall s\in S$: $M(s)\le n$;

(ii) (N,M_o) is called of non-single degree iff

$\forall t\in T$: $(\exists M\in[M_o>$: M enables t) $\Rightarrow |{}^\bullet t| \neq 1 \neq |t^\bullet|$;

(iii) (N,M_o) will be said to contain a frozen token iff

$\exists s\in S$ $\exists$infinite firing sequence $M_1t_1M_2t_2\ldots$, $M_1\in[M_o>$, such that

$$\forall i\ge 1:\ M_i(s) \ge \begin{cases} 1 & \text{if } s\notin {}^\bullet t_i \\ 2 & \text{if } s\in {}^\bullet t_i \end{cases}$$

The requirement in 5.1(iii) means that there is always one token in excess on s which is never moved away. In the absence of side-conditions (i.e. places s with $s\in{}^\bullet t\cap t^\bullet$ for some $t\in T$), (iii) can be simplified to "...$\forall i\ge 1$: $M_i(s)\ge 1$.".

Figure 3 indicates the connection between D-continuity and the frozen token property defined in 5.1(iii). The line l represents some infinite activity which never changes condition b_o (i.e. leaves the token represented by b_o on its place).

5.2 Theorem. [9]

All processes of (N,M_o) are K-dense iff (N,M_o) is safe. □5.2

5.3 Proposition.

All processes of (N,M_o) are of non-single degree iff (N,M_o) is of non-single degree.

Proof: Immediate by the property 3.1(iii) of processes.

The more complicated form of 5.1(ii) (as compared to 4.3(ii)) just excludes transitions that are dead in the initial marking. □5.3

5.4 Proposition.

Let (N,M_o) be non-safe.

Then (N,M_o) contains a frozen token.

Proof: Since (N,M_o) is not safe, there is a finite firing sequence σ and a marking $M\in[M_o>$ such that σ transforms M into M' with M<M'.

Of course, σ transforms M' into M" with M'<M", and so on.

Let m be the length of σ and consider $M_m \in [M\rangle$ s.t. $M_m(s) > m+2$ for some $s \in S$.
Then for the infinite firing sequence $\sigma\sigma\sigma\ldots$, starting from M_m, there is a frozen token on s. □5.4

5.5 Proposition.

All processes of (N,M_o) are cut-bounded from below.

Proof: Let (N',p) be a process of (N,M_o) and let $A \in D$.

We have to prove that $\bar{A} \subseteq \uparrow M(A)$.

Let $x \in \bar{A}$ and let N_i be one of the approximations of N' which contains x (i.e. $x \in X(N_i)$).

Consider $A_i = A \cap X(N_i)$, $\bar{A}_i = \bar{A} \cap X(N_i) = X(N_i) \setminus A_i$.

Since N_i is finite, $x \geq y$ for some $y \in M(A_i)$ in N_i.

W.l.o.g. we can take $y \in B$.

It is easily seen that $B \cap M(A_i) \subseteq B \cap M(A)$, which implies that $y \in M(A)$. □5.5

5.6 Theorem.

Let (N,M_o) be safe.

Then all processes are cut-bounded from above iff (N,M_o) has no frozen tokens.

Proof:

($\Rightarrow$): Suppose that (N,M_o) has frozen tokens.

Then there is a firing sequence $\sigma = M_o t_o \ldots M_1 t_1 M_2 t_2 \ldots$ and a place $s \in S$ such that for all $i \geq 1$: $M_i(s) \geq 1$ if $s \notin {}^\bullet t_i$ and $M_i(s) \geq 2$ if $s \in {}^\bullet t_i$.

Using the construction 3.2 we define a process associated to σ as follows.

First note that $\sigma = \sigma_1 \sigma_2$ where σ_1 leads from M_o to M_1 and σ_2 starts with M_1.

For σ_1 we take any of the processes which may be a result of an application of construction 3.2; say this is (N_1,p_1).

We know that N_1 is finite and that N_1^o corresponds to M_1.

We now construct a process (N',p) by induction on $i \geq 1$.

For i=1 let (N_1,p_1) be given as above.

Since $M_1(s) \geq 1$, we can fix some $b_o \in N_1^o$ such that $p_1(b_o) = s$ and $b_o^\bullet = \emptyset$.

Suppose (N_i,p_i) to be given; we construct (N_{i+1},p_{i+1}).

If $s \in {}^\bullet t_i$ then $M_i(s) \geq 2$, and there exists a $b_o' \neq b_o$ with $p_i(b_o') = s$.

We use b_o' (rather than b_o!) in the construction 3.2 when adding a new event e_i to N_i, so that in N_{i+1} we still have $b_o^\bullet = \emptyset$.

If, on the other hand, $s \notin {}^\bullet t_i$, then b_o need not be used in this construction, whence again $b_o^\bullet = \emptyset$ in N_{i+1}.

Finally put $N' = \bigsqcup N_i$ and $p = \cup p_i$ as before.

Having constructed $N' = (B,E,F')$ and p we now consider the set A s.t. $\bar{A} = N'^o$.

We know that $\bar{A} \neq \emptyset$ since $b_o \in \bar{A}$.

Of course, also $A \neq \emptyset$ and $A = \downarrow A$; hence $A \in D$.

It is also clear that $\bar{A}$ is a co-set and that $\bar{A} = Min(\bar{A})$.

By proposition 3.8, N' contains an infinite li-set, say, w.l.o.g., $x_1 < x_2 < \ldots$, $x_i \in E$; clearly, $x_i \in A$.

Suppose that $\forall x_i\ \exists y \in \bar{A}: x_i < y$.

Then a line containing $x_1, x_2, \ldots$ does not meet a cut containing $\bar{A}$, contradicting safeness on account of 5.2.

Hence $\exists x_i\ \forall y \in \bar{A}: x_i$ co y.

Fix such an x_i.

By the definition of x_i, $x_i \notin \downarrow Min(\bar{A})$.

But also $x_i \notin \downarrow Max(A)$ because if $x_i \le z$ for some $z \in Max(A)$ then $z^{\bullet} \neq \emptyset$ (by the definition of A) and for $y \in z^{\bullet}$, $x_i < y \in \bar{A}$, contradiction to the choice of x_i.

Thus, $x_i \in A$ and $x_i \notin \downarrow M(A)$, which means that N' is not cut-bounded from above.

This proves the direction (⇒) of theorem 5.6.

Figure 1 shows that safeness is needed for the proof of 5.6(⇒). The processes of the net shown in Figure 1 are cut-bounded from above and yet, there is a frozen token on s_1. In general, 5.4 shows that an unsafe net always contains a frozen token on one of its unsafe places.

(⇐): We proceed with the proof of 5.6(⇐).

Suppose that there is a process $(N',p) = (B,E,F',p)$ which is not cut-bounded from above.

That is, $A \not\subseteq \downarrow M(A)$ for some $A \in D$.

Then $\exists x_1 \in A: x_1 \notin \downarrow M(A)$.

W.l.o.g. we can take $x_1 \in B$; define $b_1 = x_1$.

Since $\bar{A} \neq \emptyset$ and ${}^{\bullet}e \neq \emptyset$ for all $e \in E$ we can choose $z \in B \cap \bar{A}$ or $z \in {}^{\bullet}e$ for $e \in E \cap \bar{A}$.

Put $s = p(z)$.

We have b_1 co z since otherwise, $b_1 < z$ implies $b_1 \le y$ for some $y \in M(A)$.

Starting with b_1 we construct an infinite execution which is "co to z".

Since $\{b_1, z\}$ is a co-set, by proposition 3.6 we find a finite B-cut c_1 which contains b_1 and z, i.e. $\{b_1, z\} \subseteq c_1$.

We claim that $\exists e_1 \in A \cap E: {}^{\bullet}e_1 \subseteq c_1$.

Since $b_1 \notin Max(A)$, $b_1^{\bullet} \neq \emptyset$.

Hence there is some $e_1 \in b_1^{\bullet}$; of course $e_1 \in A$ because $b_1 \notin Max(A)$.

If ${}^{\bullet}e_1 \subseteq c_1$ then the proof is done.

If ${}^{\bullet}e_1 \not\subseteq c_1$ then there is some $b_1' \neq b_1$, $b_1' \in c_1$ and $b_1' < e_1$ but $b_1' \notin {}^{\bullet}e_1$.

Then b_1' has an output event $e_1' \neq e_1$ for which the argument just given can be repeated; of course both $b_1' \in A$ and $e_1' \in A$.

By the finiteness of c_1 we eventually find some $e_1 \in E \cap A$ with ${}^{\bullet}e_1 \subseteq c_1$.

Define $c_2 = (c_1 \setminus {}^{\bullet}e_1) \cup e_1^{\bullet}$; again, c_2 is finite and contains z.

In this way we may define B-cuts $c_1, c_2, \ldots$ and events $e_1, e_2, \ldots$ such that $c_{i+1} = (c_i \setminus {}^{\bullet}e_i) \cup e_i^{\bullet}$ for $i \ge 1$.

Let M_i correspond to c_i (proposition 3.7) and put $t_i = p(e_i)$.

Clearly, $M_1 \in [M_0\rangle$, and $M_1 t_1 M_2 t_2 \ldots$ is a firing sequence from M_1 which satisfies the desired properties with a frozen token on s. □5.6

Combining the results of this section with theorem 4.4 of the previous section we get:

5.7 Theorem.

All processes of (N,M_o) are D-continuous iff (N,M_o) is of non-single degree and has no frozen tokens.

Proof:

(⇒): By 5.3(⇒), (N,M_o) is of non-single degree.
By 5.2(⇒), and because D-continuity implies K-density, (N,M_o) is safe.
Hence 5.6(⇒) is applicable to show that (N,M_o) has no frozen tokens.

(⇐): By 5.4, (N,M_o) is safe.
Hence the result follows from 5.6(⇐), 5.3(⇐) and 5.2(⇐). □5.7

6. CONCLUSION

The main result of this paper establishes a relationship between a property of the processes of a system (i.e. D-continuity) and a set of properties of the system itself (i.e. the non-single degree property and the absence of frozen tokens). We consider that this achieves two things: first, a further clarification of the D-continuity property, and second, a further insight into the formal connections between a system and its processes.

The frozen token property seems particularly relevant since it represents the main distinction between D-continuity and K-density. The absence of frozen tokens means that any system execution will eventually either stop or involve all parts of the system. This is quite a general concept since there may be a variety of reasons for a token to be frozen, ranging from its complete uselessness to the fact that for some infinite firing sequence it is not necessary or not used because of unfairness [11]. Properties related to the absence of frozen tokens are also known elsewhere in the literature; for example, in the theory of path expressions one is led to consider a property called "very connectedness" [16] which expresses a rather similar requirement. Also, P.S.Thiagarajan has made the interesting conjecture, which has meanwhile been proved in [12], that the absence of frozen tokens might just be the property which distinguishes the bipolar schemata [8] from live and safe free choice nets.

ACKNOWLEDGEMENTS

The meaning of D-continuity in terms of system nets was first studied by the second author who, in [10], has studied a set of, at first, unrelated properties. An approximation of the freeze property defined in 5.1(iii) has been identified as their common denominator, in an afternoon's discussion involving also César Fernândez and P.S.Thiagarajan who thus have had a direct influence on the production of this paper.

REFERENCES (LNCS denotes Springer Lecture Notes in Computer Science)

1. E.Best: A Theorem on the Characteristics of Non-sequential Processes. Fundamenta Informaticae Vol. 3(1), 77-94 (1980).

2. E.Best: The Relative Strength of K-density. In [6].

3. E.Best: Concurrent Behaviour: Sequences, Processes and Axioms. Arbeitspapiere der GMD No.118 (1984), also in Proc. of CMU Workshop on Concurrency (1984).

4. E.Best and A.Merceron: Concurrency Axioms and D-continuous Posets. In this Volume.

5. G.W.Brams: Réseaux de Petri: Théorie & Pratique, Masson-Paris (1982).

6. W.Brauer (ed.): Net Theory and Applications. LNCS Vol.84 (1980).

7. C.Fernândez and P.S.Thiagarajan: D-continuous Causal Nets: A Model of Non-sequential Processes. TCS Vol.28, 171-196 (1984).

8. H.J.Genrich and P.S.Thiagarajan: A Theory of Bipolar Synchronisation Schemes. TCS Vol.30, 241-318 (1984).

9. U.Goltz and W.Reisig: The Non-sequential Behaviour of Place/Transition Nets. Information and Control, Vol.57(2-3), 125-147 (1983).

10. A. Merceron: A Study of some Dependencies between a Concurrent System and its Processes, applied to Petri Nets. 1st International Conference on Computers and Applications, Bei-Jing (Peking) (1984).

11. W.M.Lu and A.Merceron: On the Meaning of Frozen Tokens. Report in preparation.

12. W.M.Lu and A.Merceron: The Equivalence between the Well Behaved Bipolar Schemes and the Live and Safe Free Choice Nets without Frozen Tokens. 5th Petri Net Workshop, Århus (1984).

13. C.A.Petri: Non-sequential Processes. GMD-ISF Report 77.05 (1977).

14. C.A.Petri: Concurrency. In [6].
Also: C.A.Petri: State/Transition Structures in Physics and in Computation. Int. Journal on Theoretical Physics, Vol.21(12), 979-992 (1982).

15. W.Reisig: Petrinetze. Springer Verlag (1982).

16. M.W.Shields: Some Theorems on Adequacy-Preserving Substitutions. ASM/51, Computing Laboratory, University of Newcastle upon Tyne (1978).

MODELLING SCHEDULING PROBLEMS WITH TIMED PETRI NETS

J.CARLIER, Ph.CHRETIENNE and C.GIRAULT
Institut de Programmation
Université Pierre et Marie Curie (Paris VI)
C.N.R.S. - E.R.A. 592

ABSTRACT

In this paper, we show how to model with a timed Petri net, tasks, resources and constraints of a scheduling problem.

This model has the significant advantage, over the classical one, to represent with a single formalism, succession constraints as well as resource ones.

This model allows us to extend the scheduling field and to propose solutions to new problems.

I - INTRODUCTION

Until now, time has been introduced in the Petri net model under the two following ways :

- the time Petri net model [15] further studied in [2] ;
- the timed Petri net model [17] for which a more general theory has been rebuilt [8] .

In this paper, we use the timed Petri nets to model scheduling problems ; so we first briefly present the two essential concepts of this model : feasible controlled execution and instantaneous state.

The main quantitative results have been got for the particular case of timed event-graphs. They concern the reachability problem [10] , the existence and building of K-periodic controlled executions and the analysis of the earliest controlled execution [8].

In the classical model of scheduling problems, tasks, resources and constraints are represented independently : a valued graph describes tasks and their relations ; for each resource, one specifies on the one hand if it is renewable or non-renewable, on the other hand its availability and the amount required by each task. In this paper, we simultaneously model with a timed Petri net tasks and resources and we show that Petri nets provide new results to scheduling theory.

We show how to model scheduling problems with potential constraints by timed event-graphs and general scheduling problems with limitations on resources and possibility of preemption by timed Petri nets.

Scheduling problems use simple subsets of Petri nets such as event-graphs and state-machines. But additional constraints bring up new problems ; some of them are still open.

We show that the results obtained on timed event-graphs allow us to solve the scheduling problem with recycling. Until now, this problem could'nt be studied by the classical scheduling methods. Conversely, it is shown that the solution of the payments of debts scheduling problem solves the existence problem of a feasible firing sequence of a state-machine when the number of firings of each transition is given.

II - TIMED PETRI NETS

A marked Petri net [3][4] [16] is a pair R = (G,M) where :

- $G = (P \cup T, U, a)$ is a bipartite valued graph (the set of nodes is divided in two disjoint subsets P and T ; P is the set of places, T is the set of transitions, U is the set of edges and a an integer valuation of the edge set U),

- and M is a function ($M : P \to N$) giving the marking of each place (on figure 1, M = (2,0,4)).

In a timed Petri net, time is introduced by the following manner : a processing time p_i is associated with transition T_i . If transition T_i is fired at time t :

a. - a_{ji} is substracted to the marking of P_j for each input place P_j of T_i ,at time t ;

b. - a_{ik} is added to the marking of P_k for each output place P_k of T_i , at time $t + p_i$.

t is called starting firing time and $t+p_i$, ending firing time. Transition T_i is said to be processed between t and $t+p_i$.

If one associates with each transition the sequence of its successive starting firing times, the family of these sequences is called a controlled execution when the marking of the net remains positive or null.

At time t , the timed Petri net is not completely described by its marking M(t) because some transitions are currently processed at that time. By convention, the firings started at time t are not taken into account in M(t).

$\rho(t)$ is the residual processing times vector. This notion has not been introduced before.

The chart of figure 2 reports a controlled execution of the previous net when the processing times of transitions T_1 and T_2 are respectively 3 and 1 .

A <u>controlled execution</u> is said to be <u>complete</u> if each transition is fired at least once ; it is said to be <u>finite</u> if each transition is fired a finite number of times. This notion allows transitions to be processed simultaneously.

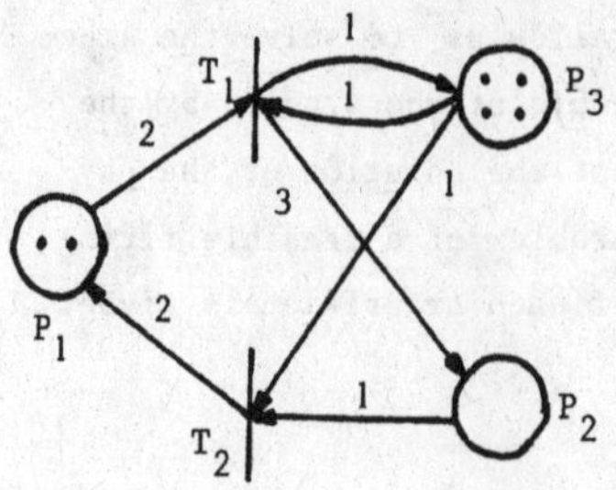

Figure 1

A marked Petri net

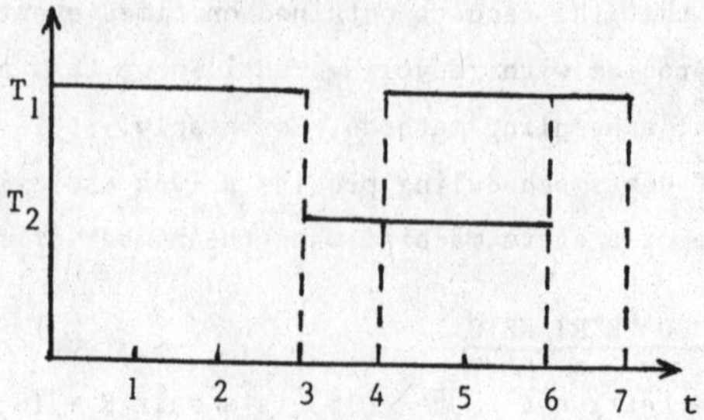

Figure 2

A controlled execution

$M(0) = (2,0,4)$ $\rho(0) = (0,0)$; $M(1) = (0,0,3)$ $\rho(1) = (2,0)$

$M(2) = (0,0,3)$ $\rho(2) = (1,0)$; $M(3) = (0,3,4)$ $\rho(3) = (0,0)$

$M(4) = (2,2,3)$ $\rho(4) = (0,0)$; $M(5) = (2,1,1)$ $\rho(5) = (2,0)$

$M(6) = (4,0,0)$ $\rho(6) = (1,0)$; $M(7) = (4,3,1)$ $\rho(7) = (0,0)$

States of the timed Petri net.

General results have been established in [8] and [9] on timed Petri nets. They mainly concern :

- the links between the time reachability relation among states on a timed Petri net and the usual reachability one among markings on the underlying Petri net;
- the lattice structure of the set of initial states (M(0),0) feasible for a given controlled execution ;
- a sufficiency condition for the existence of a periodic controlled execution.

III - TIMED EVENT-GRAPHS

Classical scheduling problems are easily modelled by a particular class of Petri net : timed event-graphs.

An event-graph is a Petri net within which every place has exactly one pre-transition and exactly one post-transition (figure 3).

In order to have a simpler presentation of the following results, the valuations of the edges of an event-graph will be equal to one. In an event-graph, two transitions do not share the same input place. So, there is no conflict to simultaneously process several enabled transitions.

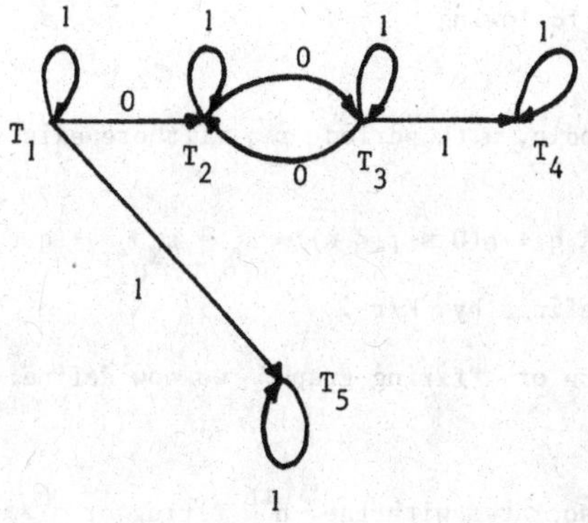

Figure 3 : an event-graph

Transitions can be fired as soon as they are enabled and the so defined controlled execution is called the earliest one.

Our purpose is to study the earliest controlled execution. We shall see that its main feature is based on a new concept of periodicity ; we call it : K-periodicity. In 1974 , RAMCHANDANI studied the usual case of periodicity (K=1) for strongly connected nets but this notion is not sufficient to explain the periodic behaviour of the earliest controlled execution in the most general case, even when the net is strongly connected.

Intuitively, a sequence is K-periodic if , from one rank N_0 , the K succesive occurences repeat periodically (see figure 4).

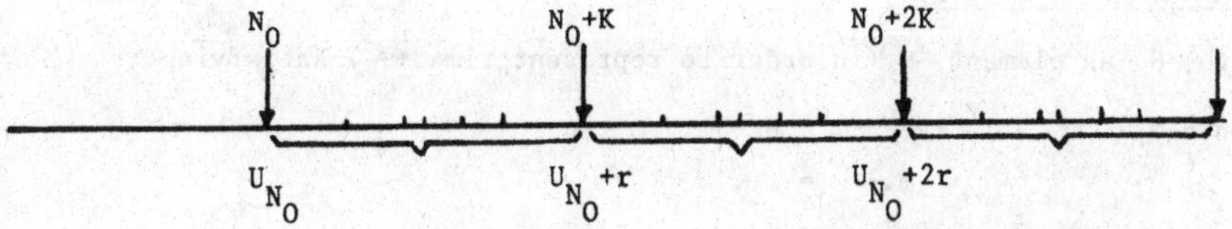

Figure 4 : a K-periodic sequence

More formally, we have the following

Definition

A sequence s_n is K-periodic, with period r, if there exists an integer N_0 such that :

$$\forall n \geq N_0 \qquad n - N_0 = K\,q + \rho(0 \leq \rho < K) \Rightarrow s_n = s_{N_0+\rho} + q\,r\,.$$

The frequency of s_n is defined by K/r .

We shall also use the notion of "firing graph" we now define.

Firing graph

We denote T_i^n the task associated with the nth firing of T_i and t_i^n the starting time of this firing.

We associate with the timed event-graph R the valued graph $g(R) = (\tau, E, v)$ where τ, E, v are defined by :

$$\tau = \{T_i^n \;/\; T_i \in T \text{ and } n \in N^*\} \quad , \quad \tau \text{ is the set of vertices;}$$

$$E = \{(T_i^n \,,\, T_j^{n+M_{ij}}) \;/\; (T_i,T_j) \in P \text{ and } n \in N^*\}, \text{ E is the set of edges;}$$

$$\forall n \geq 1, \forall (T_i,T_j) \in P \quad , \quad v(T_i^n, T_j^{n+M_{ij}}) = p_i \quad , \quad v \text{ is the valuation function.}$$

M_{ij} is the initial marking of place (T_i,T_j) (we suppose here : $\rho(0) = (0,0,\ldots,0)$).

An edge of the firing graph is connected with the feasibility of the $(n + M_{ij})^{th}$ firing of transition T_j.

The firing graph of the timed event-graph drawn on figure 3 is shown on figure 5 ; the processing times of the transitions are :

$$p_1 = 1 \;,\; p_2 = 1 \;,\; p_3 = 1 \;,\; p_4 = 1 \;,\; p_5 = 2\,.$$

Starting times set on g(R)

We add to N an element ω (in order to represent time $+\infty$) satisfying :

$$\forall n \in N \qquad \omega + n = \omega - n = \omega \;;\; \omega > n \;;$$

$$\omega - \omega = \omega\,.$$

Let us denote: $\overline{N} = N \cup \{\omega\}$.

$\{t_i^n \;/\; T_i \in T$ and $n \geq 1\}$ is a starting times set if and only if :

$$\forall T_i \in T, \forall n \geq 1 : t_i^n \in \overline{N}\;;$$

$$\forall (T_i,T_j) \in P, \forall\, n \geq 1 \quad t_j^{n+M_{ij}} - t_i^n \geq p_i\,.$$

We have proved the following results [8] :

Proposition 1

There is a one to one correspondence between the starting times sets on g(R) and the feasible controlled executions of R .

Proposition 2

The set of starting times sets on $g(R)$ is a lattice ; it has a minimum element denoted $s = \{s_i^n \mid T_i \in T , n \geq 1 \}$; s_i^n is the starting time of the nth firing of transition T_i in the earliest controlled execution.

An algorithm is given in [8] to compute the value of s . It is based on the fact that s_i^n is the maximal value of a path on $g(R)$ whose ending node is T_i^n .

On figure 5 , the values associated with each node are the s_i^n $(1 \leq n \leq 5)$.

Results on the earliest controlled execution

The essential problem is to answer the question : does the net remain bounded for the earliest controlled execution ? The following theorems give the answer. The first two ones deal with strongly connected nets and the third one with the general case. Their proofs can be found in [8].

To obtain these results, a new optimization problem in the Operations Research field has to be defined and solved. We call it "Maximal paths values on a bi-valued graph".

This problem and the associated main results are presented in the ANNEX.

If we associate with each place P_{ij} of a timed event graph an height equal to its initial marking M_{ij} and a value equal to the processing time p_i , we define a bi-valued graph from which the following two theorems can be derived.

THEOREM 1

If R is a strongly connected event-graph , the sequence s_i^n is K-periodic with frequency f (f is independent of i).
That frequency f can be computed using

THEOREM 2

The firing frequency of each transition of R is equal to :

$$f = 1 \Big/ \max_{\Psi \in CE(R)} \left\{\frac{v(\Psi)}{m(\Psi)}\right\}$$

where $CE(R)$ is the set of simple cycles of R , $v(\Psi)$ the sum of processing times of transitions belonging to Ψ and $m(\Psi)$ the sum of the marks of the places belonging to Ψ .

If the graph is not strongly connected, we have to compute the frequency of each strongly connected component and the following theorem solves the main problem.

THEOREM 3

Let f_i be the frequency of the strongly connected component R ; R remains bounded, for its earliest controlled execution, if and only if :

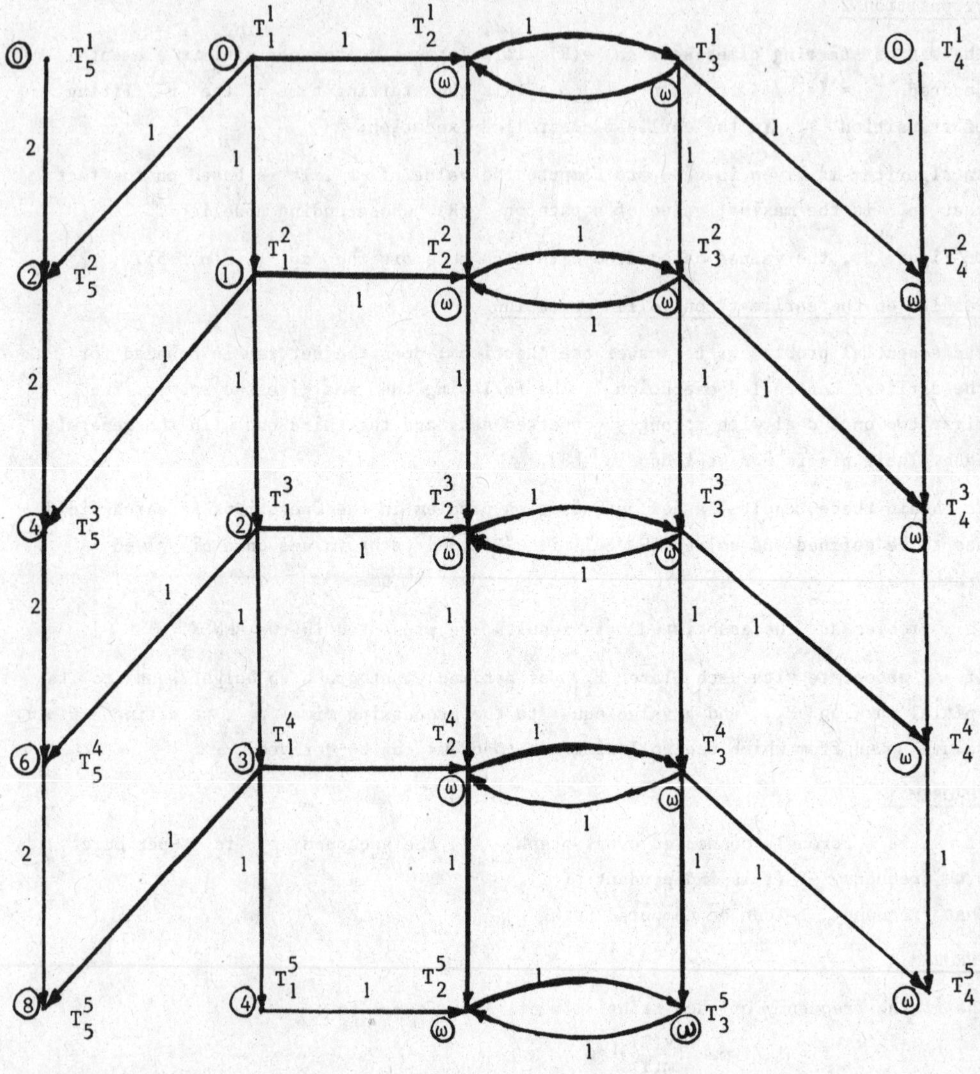

Figure 5 : A firing graph

1\. - for each R_i , input node of the reducted graph : $f_i = f$;

2\. - for the other components R_i : $f_i \geq f$.

IV - SCHEDULING PROBLEMS WITH POTENTIAL CONSTRAINTS

We associate an event-graph with a succession constrained scheduling problem and we show how these event-graphs introduce new scheduling problems : repetitive problems (tasks have to be executed more that once), recycling problems (each task has to be executed an infinite number of times).

IV.1. - Modelling succession constraints

In the potential method [18] , a valued graph is associated with the scheduling problem ; the nodes are associated with tasks, edges with succession constraints.

In the timed event-graph, a transition T_i is associated with task i (with the same processing time). If task i has to be executed before task j begins, a place P_{ij} (output-place for T_i and input-place for T_j) is introduced. Moreover, transitions T_o and T_* are introduced with null processing times; they represent beginning and ending fictitious tasks. At last, place P_{*o} with mark 1 is created ; all the other marks are 0 . A schedule is a controlled execution where each transition is fired exactly once. t_i is the firing time of T_i ; we suppose that $t_o = 0$.

Example :

Four tasks 1, 2, 3, 4 with processing times 6, 7, 4, 5 have to be scheduled such that task 1 precedes tasks 2 and 4 , and task 3 precedes task 4 .

A graph and an event-graph (figure 6) is associated with that problem.

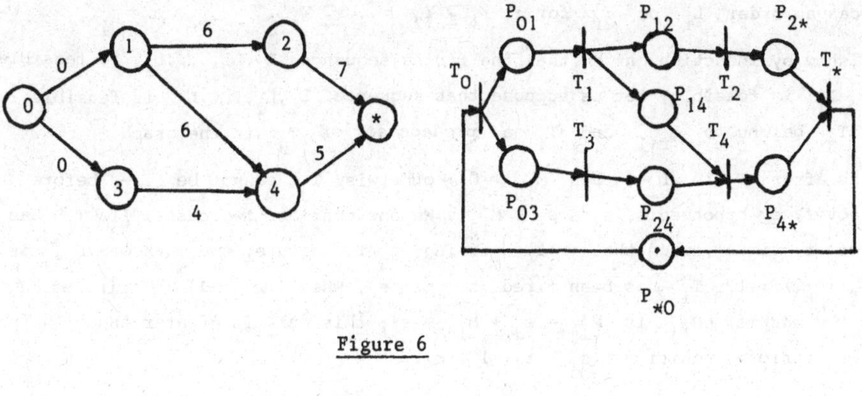

Figure 6

IV.2. - Existence conditions of a controlled execution

The number of times s_i that task i has to be executed is specified in the data of a scheduling problem. A controlled execution will be a solution if transition T_i is fired s_i times. Previous works of Holt and Pnueli have brought necessary and sufficient conditions for the existence of a sequence in the case of a (not timed) event-graph. We propose a new proof the advantage of which is to be constructive and we state conditions for the timed case.

PROPERTY 1 [14]

Each transition can be fired exactly once if and only if the graph $H = (T,V)$ is without cycles where T is the set of transitions and V is the set of null marked places.

PROPERTY 2 [14]

Each transition T_i can be fired exactly s_i (≥ 1) times if and only if :

(i) each transition can be fired exactly once ;

(ii) for each place P_{ij} : $s_j \leq s_i + M_{ij}$.

Proof

These conditions are necessary.

(i) is necessary because places are not shared ;

(ii) is necessary because the final marking must be positive or null.

These conditions are sufficient (constructive method).

Let $(T_{i_1},T_{i_2},\ldots,T_{i_p})$ be a firing sequence such that each transition is fired exactly once.

Such a sequence exists (i).

Let us denote $Y_r = \{T_i \ / \ s_i \geq r\}$ and consider the order $L_1 = (T_{i_1},T_{i_2},\ldots,T_{i_p})$;

L_1 induces an order L_r on Y_r for : $Y_1 \supseteq Y_2 \supseteq \ldots \supseteq Y_r$.

We shall show by induction on r that the firing sequence $L_1,L_2,\ldots,L_r$ is feasible. Sequence L_1 is feasible; let us suppose that sequence $L_1,L_2,\ldots,L_r$ is feasible; and let T_j belong to L_{r+1} and T_i a predecessor of T_j in the graph.

If T_i is after T_j in L_1 , then $M_{ij} > 0$; otherwise T_j cannot be fired before T_i . Moreover, by hypothesis, $s_j \leq s_i + M_{ij}$. We now consider two cases. If T_i has been fired r times , when the $(r+1)^{th}$ firing of T_j occurs, the mark of P_{ij} is $M'_{ij} = M_{ij}$ (> 0). If T_i has been fired s_i times , when the $(r+1)^{th}$ firing of T_j occurs , the mark of P_{ij} is $M'_{ij} = s_i + M_{ij} - r$; this mark is greater than $s_j - r$, so strictly positive ($s_j \geq r + 1 > r$).

If T_i is before T_j in L_1, we also consider two cases. If T_i has been fired r+1 times when the $(r+1)^{th}$ firing of T_j occurs, the mark of P_{ij} is strictly positive ; if T_i has been fired s_i times , the mark of P_{ij} is $M'_{ij} = s_i + M_{ij} - r$; it is greater than $s_j - r$, so strictly positive ($s_j \geq r + 1 > r$).

When the valuations of the edges of the event-graph are not restricted to be equal to one, and for a timed Petri net, the following property gives the method to obtain the schedule :

PROPERTY 3 [8]

A controlled execution is feasible if and only if the set of nodes $A = \{T_i^p \ / \ T_i \in T, 1 \leq p \leq s_i\}$ is initial in the firing graph and if the subgraph generated by A is without cycle (A subset of nodes is initial if it contains all its predecessors).

IV.3. - An application : a scheduling problem which recycling

Problem definition

We consider the mass production of an equipment E. The manufacturing of one item of E can be splitted in a set of tasks $\mathcal{C} = \{T_1, T_2, \ldots, T_n\}$ linked by succession constraints

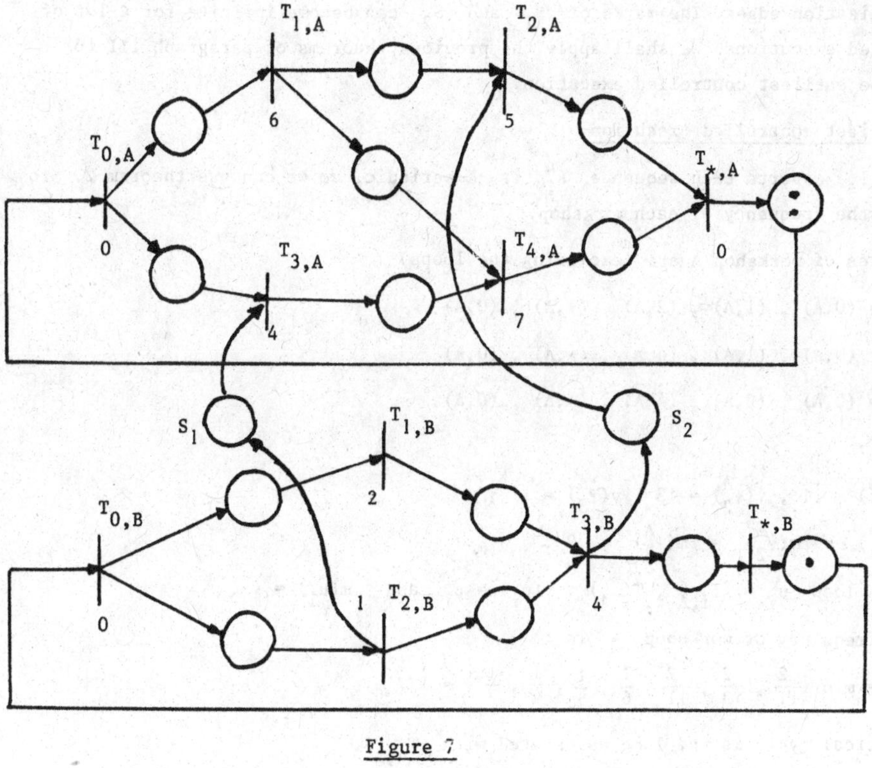

Figure 7

(The loops associated with each node are not drawn)

represented by a valued graph $G = (\mathcal{C},U,a)$. Tasks are executed in r distinct workshops ; so , the set of tasks is divided in r subsets $\mathcal{C}_1,\mathcal{C}_2,\ldots,\mathcal{C}_r$ where $\mathcal{C}_k$ is the set of tasks executed in workshop k . Moreover , in workshop k , the maximum number of items is limited to C_k . For each workshop, the scheduling problem is modelled by a timed event-graph ; the items limitation is modelled by a special place Π_k with marking C_k (place Π_k replaces place P_{*0}).

Figure 7 reports one example we shall deal with.

Problem analysis

The event-graph associated with workshop k is strongly connected ; Π_k is included in any cycle of the event-graph , so the marking is live [12] .

The entire net, denoted R , is also an event-graph ; it is composed of local subnets associated with workshops and of synchronization edges. We aggregate the workshops contained in the same strongly connected class.Each edge of a strongly connected class R_k belongs to one cycle , so the mark of each place in R_k is bounded. Consequently,if a place is not bounded, it corresponds to a synchronization edge. In our example, the event-graph contains two strongly connected components and two synchronization edges. The marks of S_1 and S_2 can become infinite for a lot of controlled executions. We shall apply the previous theorems of paragraph III to study the earliest controlled execution.

The earliest controlled execution

Theorem 1. asserts each sequence s_i^n is K-periodic, so we can use theorem 2. to compute the frequency of each workshop.

The cycles of workshop A are (excluding the loops) :

$$\Psi_1^A = (0,A)\ ,\ (1,A)\ ,\ (2,A)\ ,\ (*,A)\ ,\ (0,A)$$

$$\Psi_2^A = (0,A)\ ,\ (1,A)\ ,\ (4,A)\ ,\ (*,A)\ ,\ (0,A)$$

$$\Psi_3^A = (0,A)\ ,\ (3,A)\ ,\ (4,A)\ ,\ (*,A)\ ,\ (0,A).$$

We have :

$$v(\Psi_1^A) = 11\ ,\ v(\Psi_2^A) = 13\ ,\ v(\Psi_3^A) = 11\ ;$$

$$m(\Psi_1^A) = m(\Psi_2^A) = m(\Psi_3^A) = 2\ .$$

For each loop $\mu_i = (T_{i,A}\ ,\ T_{i,A}) : v(\mu_i) = p_i$ and $m(\mu_i) = 1$.

So the frequency of workshop A is :

$$f_A = \min\left\{\frac{2}{11}, \frac{2}{13}, \frac{2}{11}, \frac{1}{6}, \frac{1}{5}, \frac{1}{4}, \frac{1}{7}\right\} = 1/7\ .$$

The critical cycle is the loop associated with $T_{4,A}$.

In the same way , we can compute the frequency f_B of workshop B : $f_B = 1/6$.

In order to apply theorem 3. , we have to construct the reduced graph (figure 8).

$B \longrightarrow A$

Figure 8

We have $f_B > f_A$, so the second condition is not satisfied and the mark of places S_1 and S_2 will increase and become infinite for the earliest controlled execution. To avoid this fact , we can for instance :

- create an arc $(T_{2,B}, T_{1,B})$ in order to decrease the frequency of workshop B so that it becomes less or equal than f_A ;
- or to decrease the processing time of task $T_{4,A}$ from 7 to 6 .

V - RESOURCE CONSTRAINED SCHEDULING PROBLEMS

In a general scheduling problem , tasks are not only linked by succession constraints but require resources : processors, memory, workforce, money ... When two tasks use one resource the availability of which is equal to one, they cannot be simultaneously executed.

More generally the availability limitations introduce cumulative constraints.

Moreover, preemption is sometimes allowed (for instance in a time shared system).

In order to model a scheduling problem, we associate a transition with each task and a place with each resource. A schedule will be a finite controlled execution. The usual objective functions are functions of starting times of tasks (makespan : $\max \{t_i + p_i\}$, flow-time : $\Sigma\, t_i$, weighted flow time $\Sigma\, w_i\, t_i$ ...) ; they will be functions of the firing times of the associated transitions.

V.1. - Resource modelling

In the general case, the execution of task i requires an amount α_r of resource r and returns an amount β_r at the end of its execution.

Renewable resources are the most studied case : resources are returned to the system when a task is achieved $(\alpha_r = \beta_r)$: for instance, processors, memory and workforce are renewable.

Non-renewable resources are actually consumed by the tasks using them $(\beta_r = 0)$; for instance, money and raw material are non-renewable resources. The most general case has not been widely studied though it is useful : β_r represents an electricity production, or $\beta_r - \alpha_r$ an added value ; when $\alpha_r = 0$, β_r can be a number of pieces made by one machine.

We shall illustrate this model with some examples in paragraphs V.3. and V.4.

V.2. - Preemption modelling

In order to model preemption, we associate with every premptive job of processing time p_i a transition T_i of processing time 1 and a place P_i of mark 1 ; P_i is an input and output place for T_i .

A controlled execution is a schedule if transition T_i is fired p_i times ; P_i avoids parallel execution of distinct parts of job i .

V.3. - A problem with processors

m identical processors are available to execute n independent* jobs $J_1, J_2, \ldots, J_n$ the processing times of which are $p_1, p_2, \ldots, p_n$; the objective function is the makespan. Some jobs can be preemptive.

Example 1

n=6 ; m=3 ; processing times are respectively 2, 7, 3, 5, 8, 4 and preemption is not allowed. Figure 9 reports the Petri-net and the Gantt chart associated with a solution of value 11 (the optimal makespan is 10).

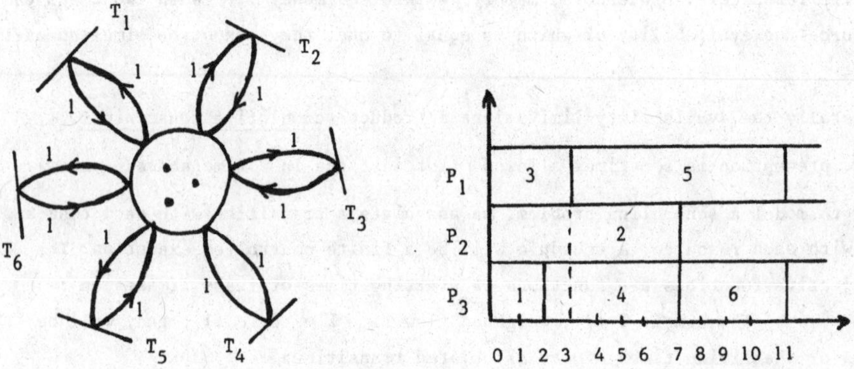

Figure 9

Example 2

n=4 ; m=2 ; processing times are respectively 2, 6, 9, 3 . Preemption is allowed only for jobs J_1 and J_4. A controlled execution is a schedule if T_1 and T_4 are respectively fired 2 and 3 times, T_2 and T_3 once. Figure 10 reports the Petri net and the Gantt chart associated with an optimal solution.

* When no succession constraints are imposed, jobs are said independent.

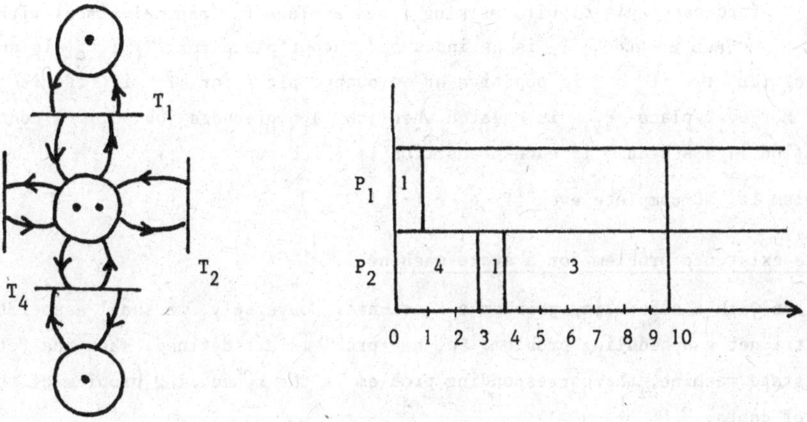

Figure 10

V.4. - The financing problem solution existence

One processor is available to execute n jobs $J_1, J_2, \ldots, J_n$ (not independent). A job J_i either costs money or brings in money ; we denote c_i the algebraic cost of job J_i and C the initial capital. The processing times are equal to one. The Petri net of figure 11 is associated with this problem.

c_i is positive

c_j is negative

and i precedes j

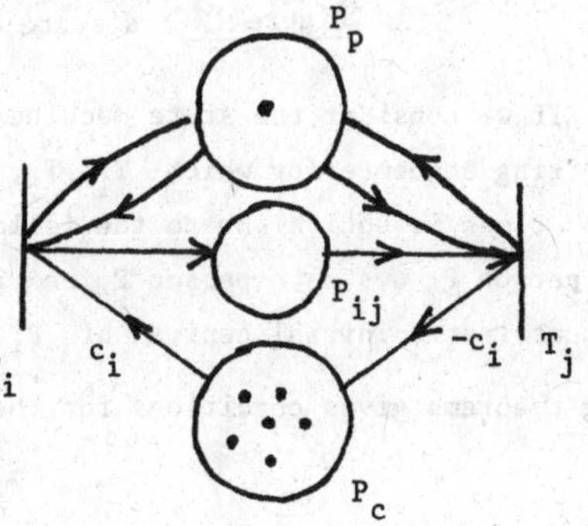

Figure 11

A place P_p (processor place) with marking 1 and a place P_c (capital place) with marking C have been created ; P_p is an input and output place for T_i ; P_c is an input place for T_i if c_i is positive or an output place for T_i if c_i is negative. Moreover place P_{ij} is created when job J_i precedes job J_j . A controlled execution is a schedule if each transition is fired once.

This problem is NP-complete even if $c_i \in \{-1,1\}$ [1] .

V.5. - The existence problem for a state machine

We associate with a scheduling problem a Petri-net. Conversely, we shall associate with a Petri-net a scheduling problem. So, new problems are defined. When the Petri-net is a state machine, the corresponding problem is the scheduling problem of the payments of debts.

Let us recall that a state machine is a Petri net obtained by associating with each node of a graph a place, and, with each edge, a transition (figure 12).

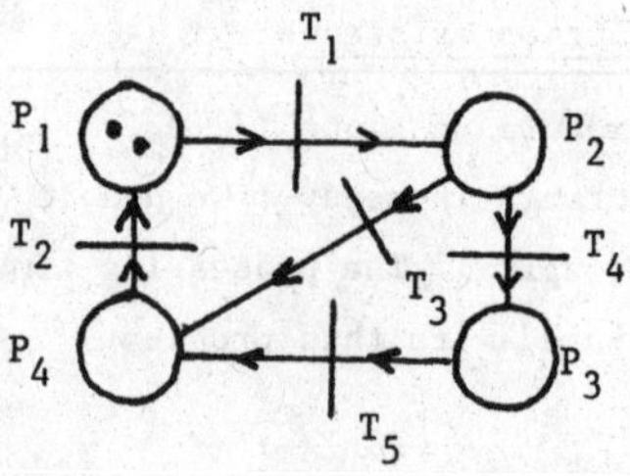

Figure 12 : a state machine

For instance, if we consider the state machine of figure 12, the problem of the search of a firing sequence for which T_1, T_2, T_3, T_4 , T_5 are respectively fired 5, 3, 3, 3, 2 times is equivalent to the following problem : person P_1 ows 5 to person P_2 ; person P_2 ows 3 to person P_4 and 2 to person P_3 ; P_3 ows 2 to P_4 , P_4 ows 3 to P_1 ; at last , initial capital of P_1 is 2 and the other ones are null.

The following theorems gives conditions for the feasibility problem for a connected graph.

THEOREM

The feasibility problem has a solution if and only if for each place P_i

(a) $\sum_j s_{ij} \leq a_i + \sum_k s_{ki}$

(a_i is the marking of place P_i and s_{ij} the debt amount from P_i to P_j)

(b) there exists a path ending at P_i and beginning at a strictly positive capital node.

(a) is necessary : $a_i + \sum_k s_{ki} - \sum_j s_{ij}$ is the final marking of node P_i .

(b) is necessary : otherwise, it will be impossible to fire a transition with input place P_i .

These conditions are fulfilled for our example. To build a solution, we associate with the problem a flow on a graph obtained by adding a root s and a sink p (figure 13).

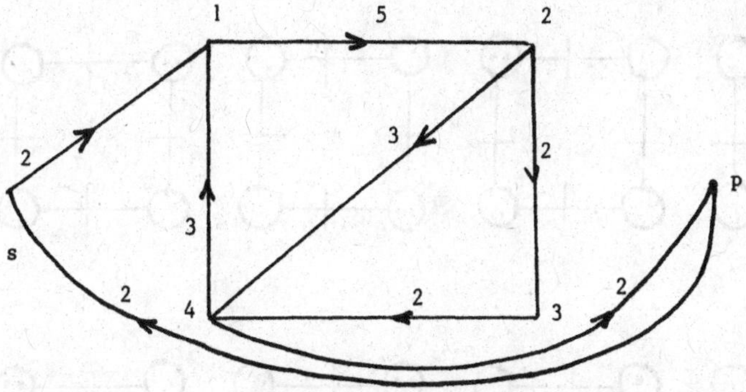

Figure 13 : the flow

Then we break up the flow as a sum of cycles (figure 14).

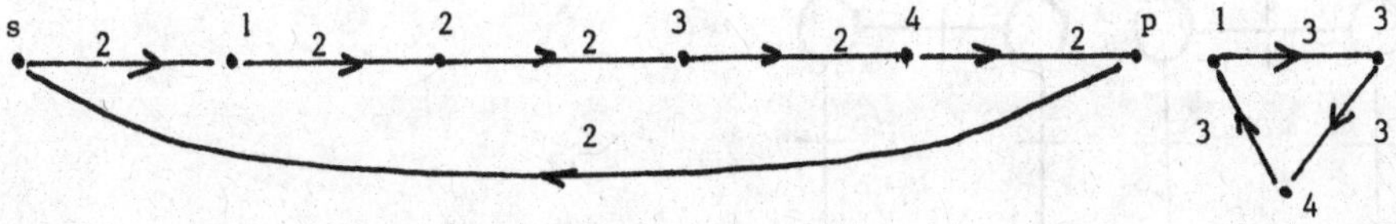

Figure 14 : the cycles

With each cycle running through (p,s) is associated a sequence of firings. Other cycles can be sticked to the former ones to obtain generalized cycles (figure 15) . With each generalized cycle is associated a sequence of firings (figure 16).

The problem is NP complete when the valuations of the edges are not restricted to be equal to one or when each debt cannot be splitted ([7]).

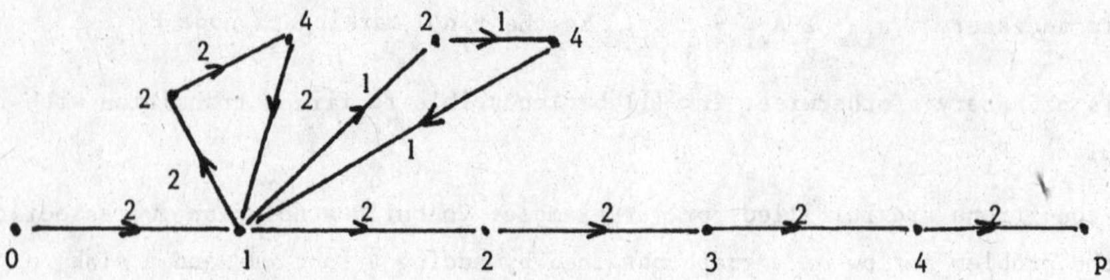

Figure 15 : a generalized cycle

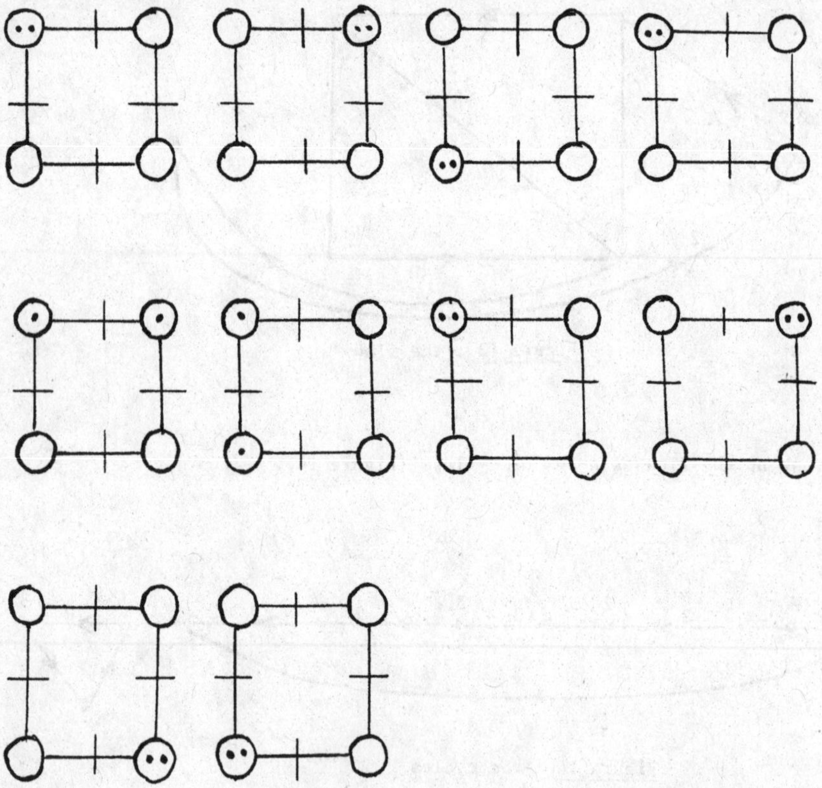

Figure 16 : a solution

CONCLUSION

During the last decade, a lot of research has been done simultaneously on Petri nets and scheduling problems. It is due to the realistic origin of these problems and to the necessity to have a better understanding of complex parallel systems.

We have shown in this paper that both theories model similar problems and are enriched by one another.

Petri nets allow to smartly model scheduling problems and to bring new ones : repetitive and recycling problems. We have shown how to solve them.

The time dimensions of scheduling problems is naturally transmitted to Petri nets by the controlled execution notion.

We have solved two open problems : a method to calculate the earliest controlled execution of an event graph and a method to find a feasible firing sequence the characteristic vector of which is given, for a state machine.

We now work on other classes of Petri nets.

ANNEX

MAXIMAL PATH VALUES ON A BI-VALUED GRAPH

A - Problem definition

Let $G = (X,U)$ be a strongly connected graph. Each edge u of U is valued both by an integer $h(u)$ (its height) and a real $v(u)$ (its value).

The height (resp value) of a path is the sum of the heights (resp values) of its edges , the height (resp value) of one edge being taken in the sum as many times as this edge is runned through in the path.

The two following problems are solved :

- computing $a_n(i,j)$, the maximal value of a path with height n between vertices i and j ;
- studying the limiting behaviour of the sequence $a_n(i,j)$ when n increases.

In order finite solutions exist for these problems , we assume :

1. - there is a loop with height one at every node ;
2. - there is no cycle with a null height and a strictly positive value.

B - First problem solution

We denote $C_n(i,j)$ the set of the paths from i to j with height n .

In order to compute $a_n(i,j)$, an associated expanded graph $\gamma(G,h,v)$ is built as follows :

- a node T_i^n is associated with each pair (i,n) of $X \times N$;
- an edge $(T_i^n, T_j^{n+h(i,j)})$, valued by v_{ij} is associated with each pair of $U \times N$.

The expanded graph corresponding to the bi-valued graph of figure 1.a. is shown on figure 1.b.

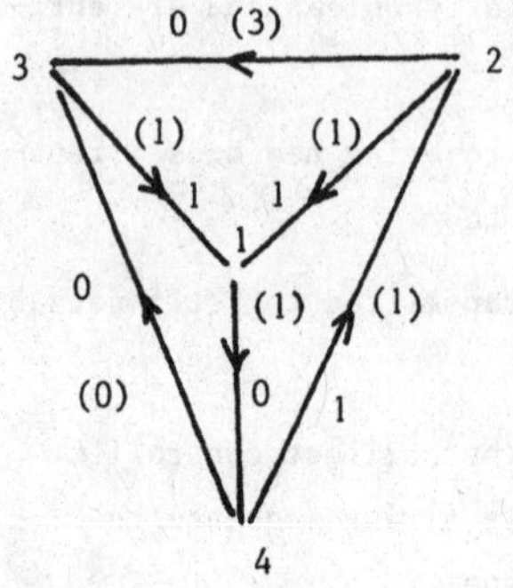

G

(heights are between parentheses)

Figure 1.a.

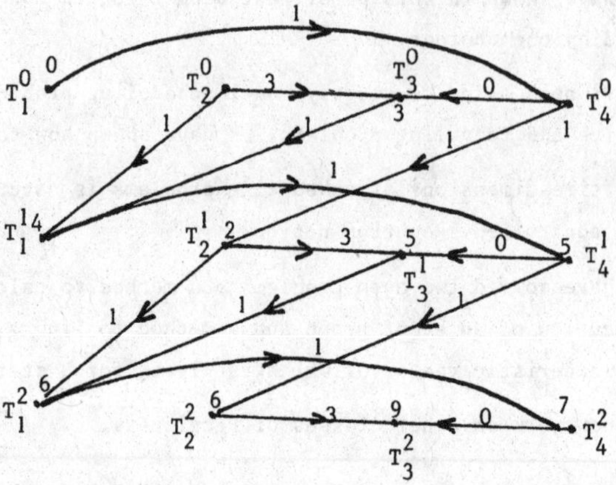

the expanded graph $\gamma(G,h,v)$

Figure 1.b.

The set $C_n(i,j)$ is in one to one correspondence with the sets of paths from T_i^o to T_j^n in the expanded graph. Further, two corresponding paths have the same value. So $a_n(i,j)$ is the maximal value of a path from T_i^o to T_j^n in the expanded graph. $a_n(i,j)$ can be computed (i.e. : $a_n(i,j) < \infty$) by the means of classical extremal paths algorithms because assumption 2. implies that there is no strictly positive values cycle in the expanded graph.

On our example of figure 1.a. , we find that $a_2(1,3) = 9$, the corresponding optimal path being (1,4,3,1,4,2,3).

C - Second problem solution

In order to study the limiting behaviour of $a_n(i,j)$ as n increases, we introduce the critical cycle notion. A cycle is critical if the ratio of its value to its height is maximal.

Any critical cycle can be splitted in a set of simple critical cycles. Then, we shall be only concerned by simple critical cycles and we denote α the maximal ratio.

First we consider the case when only a critical cycle denoted μ , exists ; $H(\mu)$ is its height , $V(\mu)$ is its value and $\alpha = V(\mu) / H(\mu)$. It has been proved in [8] that for n large enough :

- the maximal valued path of $C_n(i,j)$ runs through μ one time at least ;
- a maximal valued path of $C_{n+H(\mu)}(i,j)$ can be obtained from one of $C_n(i,j)$ by running through μ one time more.

These two results allow to conclude that $a_n(i,j)$ is K-periodic with K equal to $H(\mu)$ and a frequency equal to $1/\alpha$.

Then we extend these results to the general case when more than one critical cycle exists . We prove that $a_n(i,j)$ is still K-periodic , with K equal to the product of the critical cycles heights and a frequency equal to $1/\alpha$.

On the example of figure 1.a. , we have three simple cycles μ_1 , μ_2 , μ_3 .

$\mu_1 = (2,1,4,2)$ $V(\mu_1) = 3$ $H(\mu_1) = 2$;

$\mu_2 = (3,1,4,3)$ $V(\mu_2) = 2$ $H(\mu_2) = 1$;

$\mu_3 = (3,1,4,2,3)$ $V(\mu_3) = 6$ $H(\mu_3) = 2$.

μ_3 is the only critical cycle and α equals 3 .

The sequence $a_n(1,3)$ is 2-periodic with frequency equal to 1/3 . We have $a_0(1,3)=3$ and $a_1(1,3)=5$; the following values are easily verified :

$$a_{2p} = 3 + 6\ p\ ,\ a_{2p+1} = 5 + 6\ p.$$

BIBLIOGRAPHY

[1] ABDEL-WAHAB, H.M., KAMEDA, T.
"Scheduling to minimize maximum cumulative cost subject to series-parallel precedence constraints"
Operations Res. 26, 141-158, 1978.

[2] BERTHOMIEU, B., MENASCHE, M.
"A state enumeration approach for analyzing time Petri nets"
3rd european workshop on application and theory of Petri nets,
VARENNA, sept. 1982.

[3] BRAMS, G.W.
"Réseaux de Petri : théorie et pratique"
Tome 1 : Théorie et Analyse (Masson 1981).

[4] BRAUER, W. (Editor)
"Advanced course on general net theory of processes and systems,
HAMBURG, october 1979
Lecture notes in Computer Science, n°84, Springer Verlag, 1980.

[5] CARLIER, J., CHRETIENNE, Ph.
"Un domaine très ouvert : les problèmes d'ordonnancement"
RAIRO, recherche opérationnelle, n°3, août 1982.

[6] CARLIER, J., RINNOOY-KAN, A.H.G.
"Financing and scheduling"
Operations Research Letters, 1, 1982.

[7] CARLIER, J.
"Le problème de l'ordonnancement des paiements de dettes"
RAIRO, série verte, n°1, février 1984.

[8] CHRETIENNE, Ph.
"Thèse d'Etat : Les réseaux de Petri temporisés"
Université Paris VI, juin 1983.

[9] CHRETIENNE, Ph.
"Some results on the control of timed Petri nets"
2nd european workshop on theory and application of Petri-nets.
BAD-HONNEF, septembre 1981.

[10] CHRETIENNE, Ph.
"Timed event graphs : behaviour analysis and a study of the reachability relation"
C.I.S.S. 83 , John Hopkins University, BALTIMORE, mars 1983.

[11] COFFMAN, E.G.
"Computer and job-shop scheduling theory"
John Wiley and Sons, 1976.

[12] GAREY, M.R., JOHNSON, D.S.
"Computers and intractability"
W.H. Freeman and Company, 1978.

[13] GRAHAM, R.L., LAWLER, E.L., LENSTRA, J.K., RINNOOY KAN, A.H.G.
"Optimization and approximation in deterministic sequencing and scheduling : a survey"
Ann Discrete Math., 1979.

[14] HOLT, A., COMMONER ,F., EVEN, S., PNUELI, A.
"Marked directed graphs"
Journal of computer and system sciences, vol.5, n°5, oct. 1971.

[15] MERLIN, P.
"A study of the recoverability of computer systems"
Ph. D. thesis, University of California, IRVINE Computer Science.

[16] PETERSON, J.
"Petri-net theory and the modelling of systems"
Prentice-Hall, 1981.

[17] RAMCHANDANI, C.
"Analysis of asynchronous concurrent systems by timed Petri nets"
Ph. D. thesis, M.I.T., CAMBRIDGE, Mass. Projet MAC. MAC-TR120, Feb. 1974.

[18] ROY, B.
"Algèbre moderne et théorie des graphes"
Tome 2, Dunod, 1970.

[19] SIFAKIS, J.
"Le contrôle des systèmes asynchrones : concepts, priorités, analyse statique"
Thèse d'Etat, Université scientifique et médicale de Grenoble, juin 1979.

INFINITE BEHAVIOUR AND FAIRNESS IN PETRI NETS

HEINO CARSTENSEN and RÜDIGER VALK

Universität Hamburg, Fachbereich Informatik
Rothenbaumchaussee 67/69, D-2000 Hamburg 13

Abstract

Several classes of ω-languages of labelled Petri nets are defined and related to each other. Since such nets can be interpreted to behave fair, these notions are compared with explicit definitions of fairness for nets.

1. Introduction

Concurrent systems often appear as discrete time continuous dynamical processes. Therefore it is natural to represent the behaviour of a Petri net by the set of all infinite sequences of transitions that can occur. Infinite sequences have been used to study traditional problems of deadlocks and starvation [Nivat].

The subject of this paper is the notion of fairness in Petri nets. There are many opinions about the meaning of fairness in concurrent systems. In general,fairness expresses the observance of certain rules for the actors.

For Petri nets we first give such rules as specifications on markings and in the same manner for transitions. By this only those sequences are allowed (behave fair) which repeat some markings (or transitions) infinitely often. As an example we mention Dijkstra's problem of the dining five philosophers. They will behave fair, if every philosopher is infinitely often in a state (marking), in which he is eating. Another approach to fairness in Petri nets is to demand that the selection of transitions, enabled at the same time, will be "fair".

For the first approach we adopt definitions for ω-languages, which were developed by [Landweber] for ω-languages of finite automata. He introduced some definitions of the acceptance of infinite sequences and called them i-successful for $i \in \{1,1',2,2',3\}$. To give an example, 3-successful means that exactly every state of a designated "anchor set" is visited infinitely often. Investigations of such i-successful ω-languages were also made for push down automata and turing machines by [Cohen, Gold] and [Hossley].

For Petri nets we define i-successful ω-languages in three different ways. First we consider markings of the net as anchor states, then only markings on some bounded places, and at last the fired transitions. The three behaviours of Petri nets are called i-behaviour, bounded i-behaviour, and transitional i-behaviour.

In sections three and four we define thoses classes of i-accepting languages for nets and compare the expressional power of these classes with each other.

The second approach to fairness in Petri nets is that every transition has a kind of finite delay property. This means that the firing rule is extended so that no transition is infinitely long (or often) enabled without firing. In section five we will define ω-languages of Petri nets with such firing rules and compare their expressional power with the clases of languages investigated before.

In this paper we have not drawn out all proofs perfectly. Most of them are described in [Valk] and [Carstensen1] in detail.

2. Basic Definitions and Notations

This section recalls some definitions about ω-languages, infinite words and Petri net languages. It defines also the infinite behaviour of Petri nets.

a) Basic definitions on ω-languages:

The symbol for *infinitely many* is $\omega := |\mathbb{N}|$ (the cardinality of the nonnegative integers). The arithmetic operations on $\mathbb{N}$ are extended to $\mathbb{N} \cup \{\omega\}$ by $\forall n \in \mathbb{N}$: $n < \omega$ and $n + \omega = \omega + n = \omega + \omega = \omega$.

The quantor *there are infinitely many* is defined by

$\exists_{\infty} x : P(x) :\Leftrightarrow |\{x \mid P(x)\}| = \omega$.

We now give some definitions of languages. Let X be always an arbitrary but finite set (alphabet).

A mapping $v: M \to X$, where $M = \{1,\dots,k\}$ $(k \in \mathbb{N}^+)$ or $M = \mathbb{N}^+$, is called *sequence* over X, v(i) denotes the i-th element $(i \in \mathbb{N})$ of v. The cardinality of M is the *length* of v, i.e. $|v| := |M|$. If $|v| \neq \omega$ v is called *finite* otherwise *infinite* sequence. The set of all finite sequences over X is denoted by X^*, the set of all infinite sequences by X^ω, and $X^\infty := X^* \cup X^\omega$. We often use the notation *word* instead of sequence for elements of languages.

For a sequence v over X, v[i] denotes the *prefix* with the length i of v, for $i \le |v|$, $v[i] : \{1,\dots,i\} \to X$ with $v[i](j) = v(j)$ for all $j \le i$. v[0] is defined as the empty word λ.

For an infinite sequence $v \in X^\omega$ we define the *infinity set* of v:

$In(v) := \{x \in X \mid \exists_{\infty} i \in \mathbb{N}^+ : v(i) = x\}$.

b) Basic definitions on Petri nets and their ω-behaviour:

A sixtupel $N = (S,T,F,W,h,m_o)$ is called *λ-free (labelled) Petri net*, if (S,T,F) is a directed net, the set of places S and the set of transitions T are finite and disjoint sets, $F \subseteq (S \times T) \cup (T \times S)$ is called the flow relation; $W: F \to \mathbb{N}^+$

is the multiplicity function, $h: T \to X$ the labelling function, and $m_0: S \to \mathbb{N}$ the initial marking.
The well-known firing rule and token game are assumed, for more details see [Genrich, Stankiewics-Wichno].
Beside this definition we will also use a vector representation of the flow relation and the markings.
For a Petri net we define the *backward incidence matrix* $U: S\times T \to \mathbb{N}$ by

$U(s,t) = \begin{cases} W(s,t) & \text{if } (s,t) \in F \\ 0 & \text{otherwise} \end{cases}$, the *foreward incidence matrix* $V: S\times T \to \mathbb{N}$ by

$V(s,t) = \begin{cases} W(t,s) & \text{if } (t,s) \in F \\ 0 & \text{otherwise} \end{cases}$, and the *incidence matrix* $C: S\times T \to \mathbb{Z}$ by

$C := V - U$. A marking is treated as a one-column-matrix (or a vector) and a column of the matrix C is denoted by $C(-,t)$.

A sequence of transitions is called *firing sequence* of N, if the successively firing of the transitions is allowed by the firing rule; an infinite sequence of transitions is an *infinite firing sequence* if every prefix is a firing sequence.
The set of all (infinite) firing sequences of N is denoted by $F(N)$ ($F_\omega(N)$). The sets $F(N)$ and $F_\omega(N)$ are languages over the transitions, the corresponding classes of languages are $\mathcal{F}$ and $\mathcal{F}_\omega$, respectively.
For a Petri net N we call $M(N) := \mathbb{N}^{|S|}$ the marking set of N. Let $v \in T^*$ ($v \in T^\omega$) be a firing sequence, we call $\delta_0(v): \{0,\dots,|v|\} \to M(N)$ ($\mathbb{N} \to M(N)$) the *marking sequence* of v, if
$\forall i \in \mathbb{N}, i \leq |v| : \delta_0(v)(i) = m_0 + \sum_{j=1}^{i} C(-,v(j))$. The set of all *reachable markings* from m_0 is defined as $(m_0> := \{m \mid \exists v \in F(N) \exists i \in \{1,\dots,|v|\} : \delta_0(v)(i) = m\}$.

We extend the labelling function $h: T \to X$ to $h: T^\infty \to X^\infty$ by $h(v)(i) = h(v(i))$ for all $v \in T^\infty$ and $i \leq |v|$. Now we define the *language* (or the *behaviour*) of a labelled Petri net by
$L(N) := \{h(v) \in X^* \mid v \in F(N)\}$ and $L_\omega(N) := \{h(v) \in X^\omega \mid v \in F_\omega(N)\}$.
The corresponding classes of languages are denoted by $\mathcal{L}$ and $\mathcal{L}_\omega$, respectively.
Let $\mathcal{L}_a$ and $\mathcal{L}_b$ be classes of languages of finite words and $\mathcal{L}_c$ a class of ω-languages. Then we define:
For $L \in \mathcal{L}_a$, $L^\omega := \{ w \in X^\omega \mid w = \prod_{i=1}^{\infty} w_i \text{ and } \forall i \in \mathbb{N}^+ : w_i \in L\}$;

$\mathcal{L}_a \circ \mathcal{L}_c := \{ \biguplus_{i=1}^{k} A_i B_i \mid A_i \in \mathcal{L}_a, B_i \in \mathcal{L}_c, k \in \mathbb{N}\}$;

$\mathcal{L}_a \overset{\circ}{\omega} \mathcal{L}_b := \{ \biguplus_{i=1}^{k} A_i (B_i)^\omega \mid A_i \in \mathcal{L}_a, B_i \in \mathcal{L}_b, k \in \mathbb{N}\}$; and

$KC_\omega(\mathcal{L}_a) := \mathcal{L}_a \overset{\circ}{\omega} \mathcal{L}_a$ (the ω-Kleene-closure of $\mathcal{L}_a$).

Let N be a labelled Petri net and $D \subseteq M(N)$ a finite set of markings, then $L(N,D) := \{h(v) \in X^* \mid v \in F(N) \text{ and } \delta_0(v)(|v|) \in D\}$ is the *terminal language* of (N,D) and the *cyclic language* of N is $L_{cyc}(N) := L(N,\{m_0\})$. The corresponding classes of languages are denoted by $\mathcal{L}_0$ and $\mathcal{L}_{cyc}$.

3. Specification of Fairness by Anchor Sets of Markings

Finite languages of finite automata or push-down automata are defined by all possible sequences reaching certain final states. For ω-languages this definition makes no sense. In the theory of ω-languages it is usual to mark sets of states so that all sequences allowed must hold certain conditions with respect to these states. Such conditions were introduced by Landweber and the accepted infinite sequences were called i-successful [Landweber]. (Originally this definition was made for $i \in \{1,1',2,2',3\}$, we extend it to the case of $i = 3'$).

We will transform these definitions from automata to Petri nets. In the same manner as terminal languages of nets were defined, we will consider all possible markings of a net as its set of states in this section.

Let Y be a finite or infinite set, $\mathcal{A} \subseteq \mathcal{P}(Y)$ a finite set of finite non-empty subsets of Y, and $u \in Y^\omega$ an infinite sequence over Y. u is called

1 -successful or *touching* for $\mathcal{A}$, if $\exists A \in \mathcal{A}\ \exists i \in \mathbb{N}^+ : u(i) \in A$

1'-successful or *completely enclosed* for $\mathcal{A}$, if $\exists A \in \mathcal{A}\ \forall i \in \mathbb{N}^+ : u(i) \in A$

2 -successful or *repeatedly successful* for $\mathcal{A}$, if $\exists A \in \mathcal{A} : \emptyset \neq In(u) \cap A$

2'-successful or *eventually enclosed* for $\mathcal{A}$, if $\exists A \in \mathcal{A} : \emptyset \neq In(u) \subseteq A$

3 -successful or *eventually terminal* for $\mathcal{A}$, if $\exists A \in \mathcal{A} : In(u) = A$

3'-successful or *continual* for $\mathcal{A}$, if $\exists A \in \mathcal{A} : A \subseteq In(u)$.

Let N be a λ-free Petri net, $\mathcal{D} \subseteq \mathcal{P}(M(N))$ a finite set of finite non-empty sets of markings, then we define the *i-behaviour* of $(N,\mathcal{D})$ for $i \in \{1,1',2,2',3,3'\}$ by $L^i_\omega(N,\mathcal{D}) := \{h(v) \mid v \in F_\omega(N)$ and $\delta_0(v)$ is i-successful for $\mathcal{D}\}$.
The corresponding classes of all such i-behaviours are denoted by $\mathcal{L}^i_\omega$.
In this definition we introduce some restrictions for the empty set which are usually not considered. The definitions were made for infinite words in finite automata, so that every word must visit at least one state infinitely often. In a Petri net this must not be the case, e.g. a net which counts the number of firings on one place never reaches a marking twice. For this reason we only allow non-empty sets to be member of $\mathcal{A}$ and $\emptyset \neq In(u)$ for 2'-successful. In our papers [Valk] and [Carstensen 1] we had this restriction in mind but forgot to mention it.

To improve the understanding of these definitions and their relations to fairness the reader is invited to look at the example at the end of section 4.

In the same manner as we defined i-successful words for Petri nets, it was done for finite automata and push-down automata. The resulting classes of ω-languages are denoted by $\mathcal{R}^i_\omega$ and $\mathcal{PD}^i_\omega$, respectively.

<u>Observation:</u> $\mathcal{R}^i_\omega \subseteq \mathcal{L}^i_\omega$ (since every finite automaton can be seen as a labelled Petri net)

<u>Lemma</u> 3.1: Each class $\mathcal{L}^i_\omega$, for $i \in \{1,1',2,2',3,3'\}$, is closed under finite union.

The proof of this lemma is very similar to the corresponding proofs for final net languages [Hack]. We will omit it in this paper.

Since the closure under finite union holds for all classes of ω-languages mentioned in this paper (with the exception of $\mathcal{F}_\omega$), the inclusion between an i-successful language and an ω-language must only be proved for behaviours with a singleton anchor set $\mathcal{A} = \{A\}$ instead of the general case $\mathcal{A} = \{A_1,\dots,A_K\}$.

For a labelled Petri net $N = (S,T,F,W,h,m_o)$ and a marking $d \in M(N)$ we define N_d to be the net N with the new initial marking d , i.e. $N_d := (S,T,F,W,h,d)$.

<u>Theorem</u> 3.1: a) $\mathcal{L}^1_\omega = \mathcal{L}_o \circ \mathcal{L}_\omega$,

b) $\mathcal{L}^{1'}_\omega = \mathcal{R}^{1'}_\omega$,

c) $\mathcal{L}^2_\omega = \mathcal{L}_o \overset{o}{\omega} \mathcal{L}_{cyc} \subseteq \mathcal{L}^{3'}_\omega$,

d) $\mathcal{L}^{2'}_\omega = \mathcal{L}_o \circ \mathcal{L}^{1'}_\omega$, and

e) $\mathcal{L}^3_\omega = \mathcal{L}_o \circ \mathcal{R}^3_\omega$.

<u>Proof:</u>

1. Let be $L = L^i_\omega(N, \{D\})$.
For the case $i = 1'$ there are only finitely many markings allowed, thus the behaviour can also be realized by a finite automaton, i.e. the marking graph only with the markings of D .

2. In the other cases every successful firing sequence must consist of two parts. The first part will lead to a marking in D , i.e. a word from a language in $\mathcal{L}_o$. We refer to the definition of i-successful: it is excluded that an anchor set is empty and in the case of i=2' that there is no marking visited infinitely often. In the case of finite automaca these restrictions are not necessary, since the set of states if finite. In the case of Petri nets, however, the set of reachable markings is not necessarily finite.

The second part will start in that marking (there are only finitely many) and have the following properties:

For i = 1 : there is no restriction for the firing sequence.

For i = 2 : the marking from which it starts must be reached infinitely often.

For i = 2': only markings of D may be used.

For i = 3 : exactly the markings of D must be reached infinitely often.

3. For the other direction of the inclusions there are similar methods used as in the case of concatenations of net languages.

4. To show $\mathcal{L}_\omega^2 \subseteq \mathcal{L}_\omega^{3'}$:
Let $L = L_\omega^2(N, \{D\})$. We define $\mathcal{D}' := \{D' \mid \emptyset \neq D' \subseteq D\}$, then $L = L_\omega^{3'}(N, \mathcal{D}')$.

We are now able to give a hierarchy of theses classes of languages.

<u>Theorem</u> 3.2:

$$\begin{array}{ccccccccccc} \mathcal{L}_\omega & \subsetneq & \mathcal{L}_\omega^1 & & & & & & & & \\ \cup\!\!\!\!\!\not\;\; & & \cup\!\!\!\!\!\not\;\; & & & & & & & & \\ \mathcal{L}_\omega^{1'} & \subsetneq & \mathcal{L}_\omega^{2'} & \subsetneq & \mathcal{L}_\omega^3 & \subsetneq & \mathcal{L}_\omega^2 & \subsetneq & \mathcal{L}_\omega^{3'} & \subsetneq & KC_\omega(\mathcal{L}_0) \end{array}$$

<u>Proof:</u> We will show that the inclusions are valid and that these are the only inclusions between the mentioned classes.

a) $\mathcal{L}_\omega \subseteq \mathcal{L}_\omega^1$ since $\mathcal{L}_\omega^1 = \mathcal{L}_0 \circ \mathcal{L}_\omega$ and $\{\lambda\} \in \mathcal{L}_0$.

b) $\mathcal{L}_\omega^{1'} \subseteq \mathcal{L}_\omega$ since $\mathcal{L}_\omega^{1'}$ can be seen as the behaviour of a finite automaton and hence as the ω-behaviour of a Petri net.

c) $\mathcal{L}_\omega^{1'} \subseteq \mathcal{L}_\omega^{2'}$ since $\mathcal{L}_\omega^{1'} = \mathcal{R}_\omega^{1'}$, $\mathcal{L}_\omega^{2'} = \mathcal{L}_0 \circ \mathcal{R}_\omega^{1'}$ and $\{\lambda\} \in \mathcal{L}_0$.

d) $\mathcal{L}_\omega^{2'} \subseteq \mathcal{L}_\omega^1$ since $\mathcal{L}_\omega^{2'} = \mathcal{L}_0 \circ \mathcal{R}_\omega^{1'} = \mathcal{L}_0 \circ \mathcal{L}_\omega^{1'} \subseteq \mathcal{L}_0 \circ \mathcal{L}_\omega = \mathcal{L}_\omega^1$.

e) $\mathcal{L}_\omega^{2'} \subseteq \mathcal{L}_\omega^3$ since $\mathcal{L}_\omega^{2'} = \mathcal{L}_0 \circ \mathcal{R}_\omega^{1'} \subseteq \mathcal{L}_0 \circ \mathcal{R}_\omega^3 = \mathcal{L}_\omega^3$.

f) $\mathcal{L}_\omega^3 \subseteq \mathcal{L}_\omega^2$: It holds: $\mathcal{R}_\omega^3 = KC_\omega(\mathcal{R}) = \mathcal{R} \overset{\circ}{\omega} \mathcal{R}$ [Eilenberg]

and $C \in \mathcal{R} \Rightarrow \exists D \in \mathcal{L}_{cyc} : C^\omega = D^\omega$.

Let be $L \in \mathcal{L}_\omega^3 = \mathcal{L}_0 \circ \mathcal{R}_\omega^3 = \mathcal{L}_0 \circ (\mathcal{R} \overset{\circ}{\omega} \mathcal{R})$, thus L is a finite union of languages $A_i B_i C_i^\omega$, where $A_i \in \mathcal{L}_0$, B_i, $C_i \in \mathcal{R}$. A terminal net language concatenated with a regular language is also a terminal net language, hence $A_i B_i \in \mathcal{L}_0$. And there is a cyclic net language $D \in \mathcal{L}_{cyc}$ with $C^\omega = D^\omega$, hence $L \in \mathcal{L}_0 \overset{\circ}{\omega} \mathcal{L}_{cyc} = \mathcal{L}_\omega^2$.

g) $\mathcal{L}_\omega^2 \subseteq \mathcal{L}_\omega^{3'}$ (see Theorem 3.1)

h) $\mathcal{L}_\omega^{3'} \subseteq KC_\omega(\mathcal{L}_0)$: Let be $L = L_\omega^{3'}(N,\{D\}) \in \mathcal{L}_\omega^{3'}$, $D = \{d_1,\ldots,d_k\}$, then we can write L as the concatenation of terminal net languages $L = L(N,\{d_1\}) \,.\, [L(N_{d_1},\{d_2\}) \,.\, \ldots \,.\, L(N_{d_k},\{d_1\})]^\omega$. The class $\mathcal{L}_0$ is closed under finite concatenation [Hack], thus $\exists\, L2 \in \mathcal{L}_0 : L = L(N,\{d_1\}) \,.\, L2^\omega \in \mathcal{L}_0 \overset{\circ}{\omega} \mathcal{L}_0 = KC_\omega(\mathcal{L}_0)$.

The following parts of the proof show that there are no more inclusions.

i) $\mathcal{L}_\omega^{2'} \not\subseteq \mathcal{L}_\omega$: Let $L = a^* b c^\omega \in \mathcal{R}_\omega^{2'} \subseteq \mathcal{L}_\omega^{2'}$, $L \notin \mathcal{L}_\omega$. Suppose there is a net N so that $L = L_\omega(N)$, then there is a firing sequence u in N with $h(u) = a^\omega$, but $a^\omega \notin L$.

j) $\mathcal{L}_\omega \not\subseteq KC_\omega(\mathcal{L}_0)$: Consider the net in figure 3.1 . N is a net with a language L(N) which has a not semilinear Parikh image. $v \in L(N) \Rightarrow |v|_a < 2^{|v|_d + 1}$
For the language $L = L_\omega(N)$ it holds that $L \notin KC_\omega(\mathcal{F})$ for any family of languages $\mathcal{F} \subseteq \mathcal{P}(X^*)$.

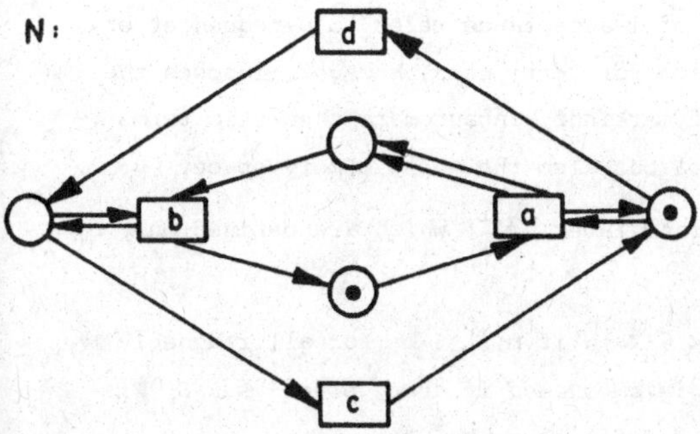

Figure 3.1

k) $\mathcal{L}_\omega^3 \not\subseteq \mathcal{L}_\omega^1$: $L = (a^* b)^\omega \in \mathcal{R}_\omega^3 \subseteq \mathcal{L}_\omega^3$, but $L \notin \mathcal{L}_\omega^1$.

l) $\mathcal{L}_\omega^2 \not\subseteq \mathcal{L}_\omega^3$: Consider the net N:

and $D = \{(\underline{0})\}$. $L_\omega^2(N,\{D\}) \notin \mathcal{L}_\omega^3$.

m) $\mathcal{L}_\omega^{3'} \not\subseteq \mathcal{L}_\omega^2$: Consider the net in figure 3.2 . It can be shown that $L_\omega^{3'}(N,\{D\}) \notin \mathcal{L}_\omega^2$.

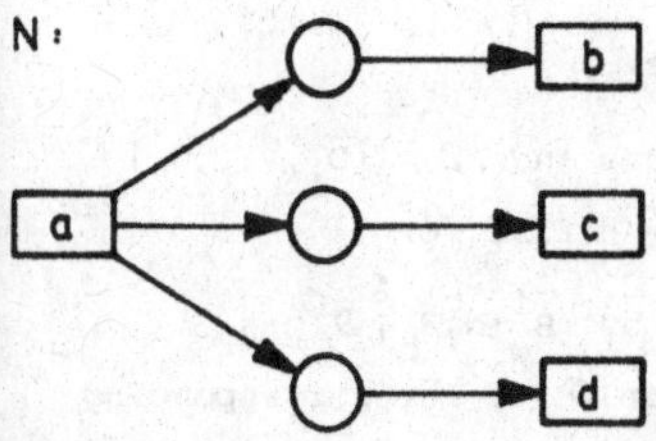

$$D = \left\{ \begin{pmatrix}1\\0\\0\end{pmatrix}, \begin{pmatrix}0\\1\\0\end{pmatrix}, \begin{pmatrix}0\\0\\1\end{pmatrix} \right\}$$

Figure 3.2

n) $KC_\omega(\mathcal{L}_0) \not\subseteq \mathcal{L}_\omega^{3'}$: Consider the net N in figure 3.3. Let $L = [L(N,D)]^\omega$, i.e. $L = A^\omega$ with $A = \{a^n b^n \mid n \geq 1\}$, then $L \notin \mathcal{L}_\omega^{3'}$. (In [Valk] the proof was made for $\mathcal{L}_\omega^2$, but it remains unchanged for $\mathcal{L}_\omega^{3'}$.)

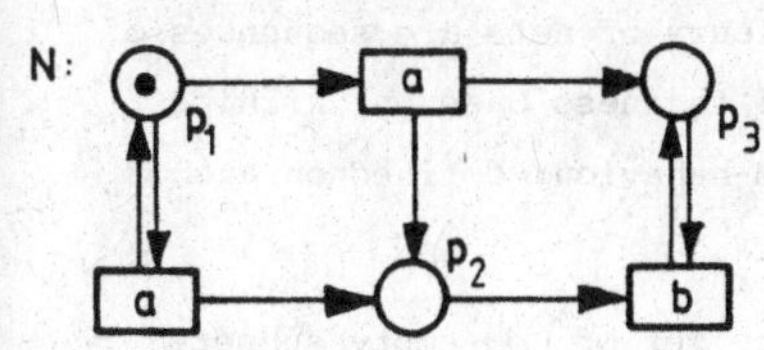

$$D = \left\{ \begin{pmatrix}0\\0\\1\end{pmatrix} \right\}$$

Figure 3.3

4. Specifications of Fairness by Anchor Sets of Markings on Bounded Places and of Transitions

The hierarchy of ω-languages $\mathcal{L}_\omega^i$ in theorem 3.2 differs from the corresponding hierarchies of nondeterministic finite automata and of nondeterministic push-down automata. ($\mathcal{P}D_\omega^{1'} \subseteq \mathcal{P}D_\omega^1 = \mathcal{P}D_\omega^{2'} \subseteq \mathcal{P}D_\omega^2 = \mathcal{P}D_\omega^3$ [Cohen,Gold], $\mathcal{P}D_\omega^{3'}$ was not investigated but it seems to be easy to show that $\mathcal{P}D_\omega^3 = \mathcal{P}D_\omega^{3'}$.) Having a closer look to the reasons for this difference, we observe a fundamental difference in the definition of ω-languages. For automata the definitions of i-acceptance refer to ω-sequences of states in the finite control. Our definition for Petri nets, however, imposes the corresponding definition on ω-sequences of markings. In automata theoretic terms we did not only restrict the finite control but also the whole memory space. Therefore we now define the classes $\mathcal{B}^i_\omega$ (and later $\mathcal{K}^i_\omega$) which are defined only by some finite control for the net.

A place $s \in S$ of a net N is *k-bounded* ($k \in \mathbb{N}$), if $m(s) \leq k$ for all reachable markings $m \in (m_0\rangle$. A set of places S_b is *k-bounded* if every place $s \in S_b$ is k-bounded, S_b is *bounded*, if it is k-bounded for some $k \in \mathbb{N}$.

We mention that it is decidable whether a set S_b is bounded nor not [Karp,Miller]. An arbitrary set of bounded places can be seen as the finite control of the net. Therefore we restrict the definition of an i-successful sequence to the markings of a fixed set of places.

If $S_b = \{s_{i_1},\ldots,s_{i_k}\}$ is a subset of $S = \{s_1,\ldots,s_n\}$, then the *projection* $pr_{S_b} : (S \to \mathbb{N}) \to (S_b \to \mathbb{N})$ gives for every marking $m \in M(N)$ the restriction to the places of S_b, i.e. for all $s \in S_b$: $pr_{S_b}(m)(s) = m(s)$.

Let N be a λ-free Petri net, $S_b \subseteq S$ a bounded set of places and $\mathcal{D} = \{D_1,\ldots,D_k\}$ a finite set of non-empty subsets $D_i \subseteq pr_{S_b}(M(N))$. Then we define for $i \in \{1,1',2,2',3,3'\}$ the *bounded i-behaviour* of $(N,S_b,\mathcal{D})$ by $B^i_\omega(N,S_b,\mathcal{D}) :=$ $\{h(v) \in X^\omega \mid v \in F_\omega(N)$ and $pr_{S_b}(\delta_0(v))$ is i-successful for $\mathcal{D}\}$. The corresponding classes of bounded i-behaviour are denoted by $\mathcal{B}^i_\omega$.

<u>Lemma</u> 4.1: Each class $\mathcal{B}^i_\omega$, for $i \in \{1,1',2,2',3,3'\}$, is closed under finite union.

Often it is easier to state conditions on the sequence of transitions instead of the sequence of markings, because the elements of ω-behaviours of nets are sequences of labels of transitions. Also traditional definitions of fairness base on infinite sequences of transitions. Hence we will introduce an ω-behaviour defined on anchor sets of transitions.

Let N be a λ-free Petri net, $\mathcal{E} = \{E_1,\ldots,E_k\}$ a finite set of non-empty subsets $E_i \subseteq T$, then we define the *transitional i-behaviour* of $(N,\mathcal{E})$ by $K^i_\omega(N,\mathcal{E}) :=$ $\{h(v) \in X^\omega \mid v \in F_\omega(N)$ and v is i-successful for $\mathcal{E}\}$. The corresponding classes of transitional i-behaviour are denoted by $\mathcal{K}^i_\omega$.

<u>Lemma</u> 4.2: Each class $\mathcal{K}^i_\omega$, for $i \in \{1,1',2,2',3,3'\}$, is closed under finite union.

<u>Theorem</u> 4.1: $\mathcal{K}^i_\omega = \mathcal{B}^i_\omega$, for each $i \in \{1,1',1,1',3,3'\}$.

Proof:

1) ($\mathcal{K}^i_\omega \subseteq \mathcal{B}^i_\omega$) Let be $L = K^i_\omega(N, E) \in \mathcal{K}^i_\omega$, with $N = (S,T,F,W,h,m_o)$, $T = \{t_1,\ldots,t_n\}$ and $E = \{t_1,\ldots,t_k\}$, $k \leq n$.
We will construct a net N' (Figure 4.1) which has the bounded i-behaviour L .
- We introduce k+2 new places called $p_o,p_1,\ldots,p_k,p_{k+1}$ which will become the set of bounded (safe) places.
- We build k+2 copies of the set of transitions called $T^o,\ldots,T^{k+1}$, let $T^j = \{t^j_1,\ldots,t^j_n\}$.
- The transition $t^j_i \in T^j$, $1 \leq i \leq n$, $0 \leq j \leq k+1$, has the same arcs with the places of S as t_i in the original net N , additionally t^j_i removes a token from p_j and fires a token on p_i if $i \leq k$ and on p_{k+1} if $i > k$.
- For the new initial marking there is the marking m_o on the places of S and one token on the place p_o .

It is easy to see that this new net N' has the same behaviour as N . A token on the place p_i , $i \leq i \leq k$, indicates that a copy of $t_i \in E$ was the last fired transition and a token on p_{k+1} that it was a copy of a transition of T/E .

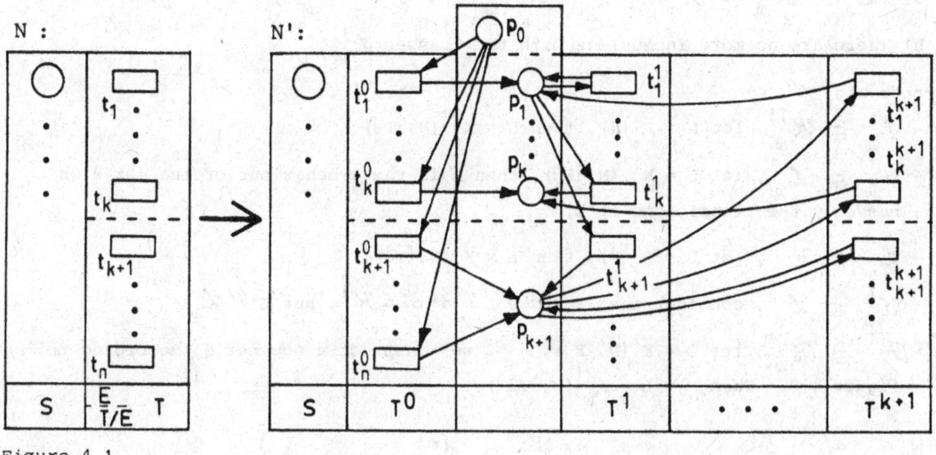

Figure 4.1

Let be $S_b = \{p_0,\ldots,p_{k+1}\}$ and m_{pi} , $0 \leq i \leq k$, the marking where only the place p_i contains a token, i.e. $m_{pi}(p_i) = 1$ and $j \neq i$ $m_{pi}(p_j) = 0$.
Let be $D := \{m_{pi} \mid t_i \in E\}$.
Then $L = B^i_\omega(N',S_b,\{D\})$ for $i \in \{1,2,2',3,3'\}$ or $L = B^i_\omega(N'S_b,\{D \cup \{m_{p0}\}\})$ for $i = 1'$.

2) ($\mathcal{B}^i_\omega \subseteq \mathcal{K}^i_\omega$) Let be $L = B^i_\omega(N,S_b,\{D\})$.
We first construct the coverability-graph $G = (V,E,v_o)$ of N as defined in [Jantzen, Valk] (also described in [Valk]). The finite set of vertices V is a

subset of $\mathbb{N}_\omega^{|S|}$ ($\mathbb{N}_\omega := \mathbb{N} \cup \{\omega\}$), the set of edges a subset of $V \times T \times V$.
We build a new net from the coverability-graph G and the original net N in the following way:

- The coverability-graph is transformed into a Petri net (a state machine). The vertices become places, v_o contains a token in the initial marking. Every edge $e = (v_1, t, v_2)$ becomes a transition t_e with $h(t_e) = h(t)$, and arcs (v_1, t_e) and (v_2, t_e).
- This new net will allow more firing sequences than N. Thus the original places of N are added and for every t_e, $e = (v_1, t, v_2)$, the arcs of t in N (it would be sufficient to add only the unbounded places).

Different markings on the bounded places in N have different vertices in G. For every $d \in D$ let T_d be the set of all transitions which have a vertex v, $pr_{S_b}(v) = d$, as an input place.
Define $\mathcal{E}'$ as the set of all sets E' of transitions so that there is at least one transition of every T_d, $d \in D$, in E' . E' is a subset of the union of all sets T_d, $d \in D$. Then $L = K^i(N', \mathcal{E}')$.

Theorem 4.2 :

a) $\mathcal{L}_\omega = \mathcal{K}_\omega^{1'} \subsetneq \mathcal{K}_\omega^{1} = \mathcal{K}_\omega^{2'} \subsetneq \mathcal{K}_\omega^{2} = \mathcal{K}_\omega^{3} = \mathcal{K}_\omega^{3'}$,

b) There are no more inclusions with the classes $\mathcal{L}_\omega^i$.

Proof: a)

- $\mathcal{L}_\omega \subseteq \mathcal{K}_\omega^{1'}$, let $L = L_\omega(N)$, then $L = K_\omega^{1'}(N, \{T\})$.
- $\mathcal{K}_\omega^{1'} \subseteq \mathcal{L}_\omega$, let $L = K_\omega^{1'}(N, \{E\})$, then L is the ω-behaviour of the net N which has only the transitions of E.
- $\mathcal{L}_\omega \subseteq \mathcal{K}_\omega^{1}$, let $L = L_\omega(N)$, then $L = K_\omega^1(N, \{T\})$.
- $\mathcal{K}_\omega^{1} \not\subseteq \mathcal{L}_\omega$, consider the language $L = a^* b^\omega \in \mathcal{K}_\omega^1$, but $L \notin \mathcal{L}_\omega$.
- $\mathcal{K}_\omega^{1} \subseteq \mathcal{K}_\omega^{2'}$, let $L = K_\omega^1(N, \{E\})$, we construct a new net N' according to figure 4.2. Then $L = K_\omega^{2'}(N, \{T2\})$.

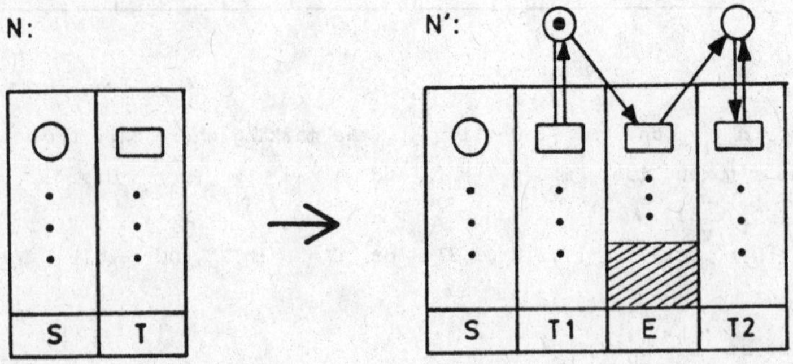

Figure 4.2

- $\mathcal{K}_\omega^{2'} \subseteq \mathcal{K}_\omega^1$, let $L = K_\omega^{2'}(N,\{E\})$, we construct a new net N' according to figure 4.3. Then $L = K_\omega^1(N,\{T2\})$.

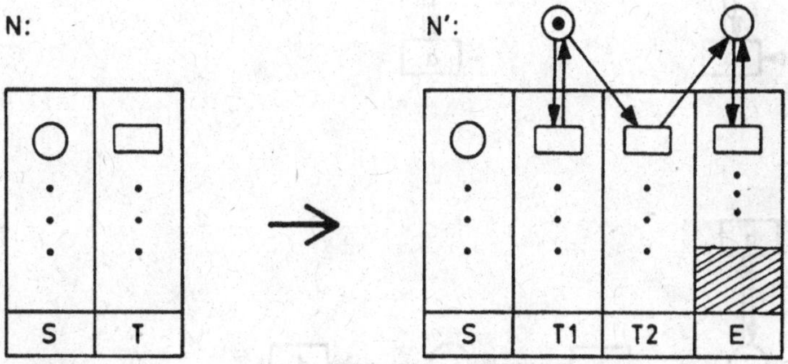

Figure 4.3

- $\mathcal{K}_\omega^{2'} \subseteq \mathcal{K}_\omega^3$, let $L = K_\omega^{2'}(N,\{E\})$, we define $\mathcal{E}' := \{E' \mid \emptyset \neq E' \subseteq E\}$, then $L = K_\omega^3(N,\mathcal{E}')$.
- $\mathcal{K}_\omega^2 \not\subseteq \mathcal{K}_\omega^{2'}$, consider the language $L = (a^*b)^\omega \in \mathcal{K}_\omega^2$, but $L \notin \mathcal{K}_\omega^{2'}$.
- $\mathcal{K}_\omega^2 \subseteq \mathcal{K}_\omega^{3'}$, let $L = K_\omega^2(N,\{E\})$, we define $\mathcal{E}' := \{\{t\} \mid t \in E\}$, then $L = K_\omega^{3'}(N,\mathcal{E}')$.
- $\mathcal{K}_\omega^{3'} \subseteq \mathcal{K}_\omega^3$, let $L = K_\omega^{3'}(N,\{E\})$, we define $\mathcal{E}' := \{E' \mid E \subseteq E' \subseteq T\}$, then $L = K_\omega^3(N,\mathcal{E}')$.
- $\mathcal{K}_\omega^3 \subseteq \mathcal{K}_\omega^2$, let $L = K_\omega^3(N,\{E\})$, we construct a new net N' according to figure 4.4, then $L = K_\omega^2(N,\{T2\})$.

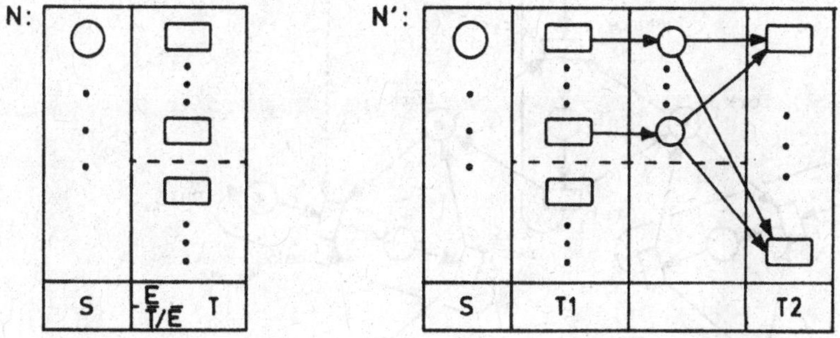

Figure 4.4

b) - $\mathcal{L}_\omega^{2'} \not\subseteq \mathcal{K}_\omega^2$, consider the net N in figure 4.5, then $L := L_\omega^2(N,\{D\}) = \{a^i b^i a^\omega \mid i \geq 1\}$, and $L \notin \mathcal{K}_\omega^2$.

- $\mathcal{K}_\omega^1 \not\subseteq \mathcal{L}_\omega^1$, consider the net N in figure 4.6 with $E := \{t_2\}$, then $L = K_\omega^1(N,\{E\}) \notin \mathcal{L}_\omega^1$.

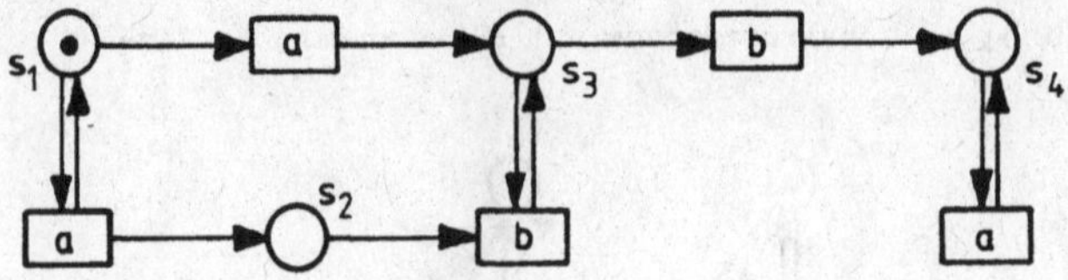

Figure 4.5

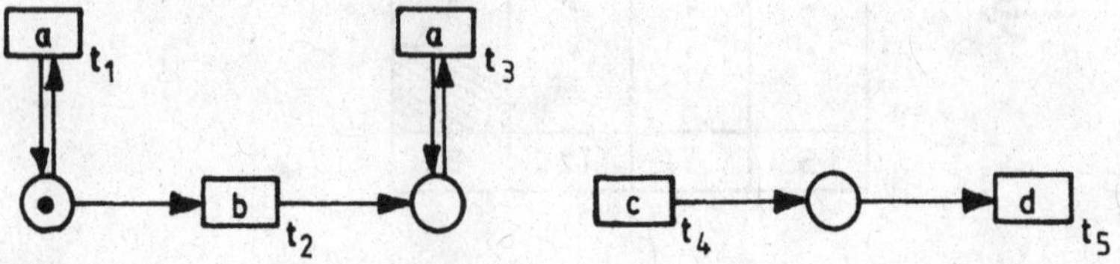

Figure 4.6

To describe fairness by i-behaviour we will look at Dijkstra's well-known problem of the dining five philosophers as an example. A Petri net solution of that problem is shown in figure 4.7. Let N be the net without the dotted part. A fair schedule is obviously a sequence in which every philosopher will eat infinitely often. We may express it by the 3-behaviour of $(N, \mathcal{D})$, where $\mathcal{D} := \{ D \mid \forall j \in \{1,\dots,5\} \; \exists m \in D: m(eat_j) = 1 \}$. Another problem is shown by the net N', where N' is the net in figure 4.7 including the dotted place 'diff'. This net only allows sequences in which

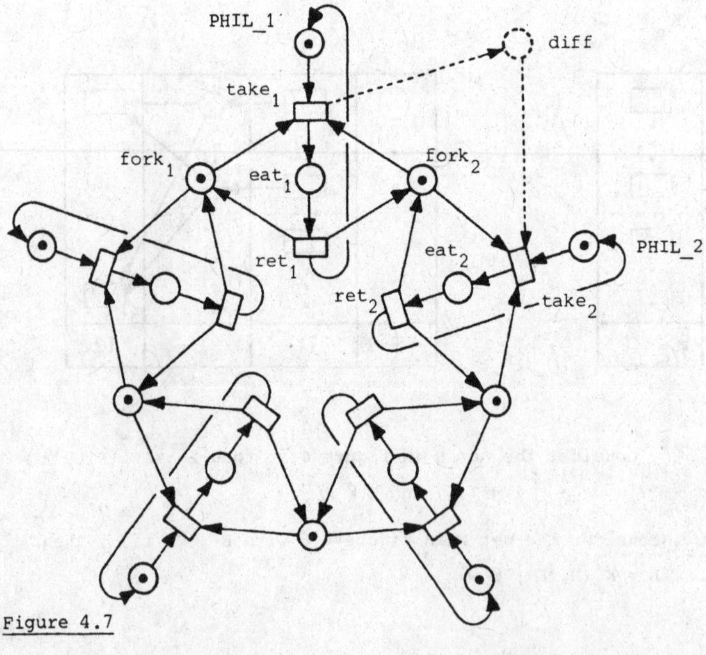

Figure 4.7

'PHIL_1' eats at least as often as 'PHIL_2'. It is not possible to describe the fair behaviour of N' by an i-behaviour. But it is still possible by a bounded 3-behaviour, if we only look at the old places. The same behaviour can be described, however, by a transitional 3'-behaviour. To do this, it is sufficent to consider the singleton anchor set $\mathcal{E} = \{E\}$, where $E = \{take_1, \ldots, take_5\}$.

5. A Fair Selection Rule

In the previous sections we introduced some possibilities to describe fair behaviour of a Petri net. We did not investigate how to find a control which forces the net to behave fair.

Now we will look at fairness in the selection of enabled transitions to fire. We will prohibit that enabled transitions are always neglected by introducing a kind of finite delay property for Petri nets. The notations are derived from papers about parallel programming, e.g. [Lehmann,Pnueli,Stavi].

Let N be a λ-free Petri net, then we define an *enabling counter* for an infinite firing sequence and a transition: $en : F_\omega(N) \times T \rightarrow \mathbb{N} \cup \{\omega\}$, where
$en(v,t) := |\{i \in \mathbb{N}^+ \mid \delta_0(v)(i) \geq U(-,t)\}|$, and a *continuality predicate:*
$con(v,t) := \exists\, i \in \mathbb{N}^+\ \forall\, j \in \mathbb{N}^+, j \geq i : \delta_0(v)(j) \geq U(-,t)$.

Informally, 'en' gives the number of times a transition is enabled and 'con' is true, if the transition is continuously enabled from some time on.

Now we are able to define languages with fairness in the selection of transitions for the firing rule. We will introduce two new classes of languages.

Let N be a λ-free Petri net, then we define the *just language* of N by
$L_\omega^{just}(N) := \{h(v) \in X^\omega \mid v \in F_\omega(N) \text{ and } \forall\, t \in T : con(v,t) \Rightarrow t \in In(v)\}$, and the *fair language* of N by
$L_\omega^{fair}(N) := \{h(v) \in X^\omega \mid v \in F_\omega(N) \text{ and } en(v,t) = \omega \Rightarrow t \in In(v)\}$. The corresponding classes of languages are denoted by $\mathcal{L}_\omega^{just}$ and $\mathcal{L}_\omega^{fair}$, respectively.

Note however, that the net N describing the five philosophers' problem in figure 4.7 $L_\omega^{fair}(N)$ is not the fair behaviour as specified in the previous section. In fact there is an infinite firing sequence w where two philosophers, say PHIL_1 and PHIL_3, take their forks in such way that PHIL_2 never has two free forks, i.e. transition $take_2$ is never enabled. Hence w satisfies the definition of the fair language: $w \in L^{fair}(N)$, but PHIL_1 and PHIL_3 behave unfair to PHIL_2. If the net is changed in such a way that the philosophers take their forks one after the other, and avoiding a deadlock by allowing at most four philosophers simultaneously at the table, the fair language of that net will describe a behaviour deserving the name fair.

There are only infinite sequences allowed for $\mathcal{L}_\omega^{just}$ and $\mathcal{L}_\omega^{fair}$. To show the significance of this restriction by an example we mention the net N in figure 5.1.

Figure 5.1

It holds $L_\omega^{just}(N) = \emptyset$ because transition 'b' is always enabled and its firing will lead the net into a deadlock.

Lemma 5.1 : The classes $\mathcal{L}_\omega^{just}$ and $\mathcal{L}_\omega^{fair}$ are each closed under finite union.

We will compare these new classes of Petri net languages with the classes already investigated.

Theorem 5.1 : $\mathcal{K}_\omega^{2} \subseteq \mathcal{L}_\omega^{just}$.

Proof: Let $L = K_\omega^2(N,\{E\})$. We construct a new net N' in the same manner as in theorem 4.1 1). Then we add a new place s_{run} as a side condition for every transition, s_{run} contains a token in the initial marking. We also add a new transition which removes a token from s_{run} and p_{k+1}. A firing of this new transition will cause a deadlock. Hence there must be infinitely many situations where it is not enabled, i.e. p_{k+1} does not contain a token. p_{k+1} contains no token iff a transition of E has fired.

Lemma 5.2 : $L1 \in \mathcal{L}_0$ and $L2 \in \mathcal{L}_\omega^{just} \Rightarrow L1 . L2 \in \mathcal{L}_\omega^{just}$.

The proof of this lemma is similar to the proof of theorem 5.1, but in this case we have to ensure that the first net has reached a terminal marking.

Theorem 5.2 : $\mathcal{L}_\omega^{3'} \subseteq \mathcal{L}_\omega^{just}$.

Proof: Let $L = L_\omega^{3'}(N,\{D\})$ with $D = \{d_1,\dots,d_k\}$ for some $k \geq 1$. We construct a net N' according to the sketch in figure 5.2. We give a short description of the behaviour of the net N':

On the place p_{sumi} there is always one token more than the sum of tokens on the places of S, with the exception that a transition of T_{di} has fired.

For every firing sequence in N' it is possible to find a firing sequence in N with the same word (and vice versa). (Transitions in T_{di} and T_{di}^j may only fire if a corresponding transition in T would be enabled if only the places of S are looked at.)

In N' infinite firing sequences are only possible if no transition $t_{\emptyset i}$ must fire. Hence there must be infinitely often no token on each place p_{sumi}.

Then a transition of T_{di} has fired and there was the marking d_i on the places of S.

$$\Sigma_0 := \sum_{s \in S} m_0(s) \qquad\qquad \alpha(t) := \sum_{s \in S} U(s,t)$$

$$\Sigma_{di} := \sum_{s \in S} di(s) \qquad\qquad \beta(t) := \sum_{s \in S} V(s,t)$$

$$\delta(t) := \beta(t) - \alpha(t)$$

$$T_{d1} := \{ t_j' \mid t_j \in T \text{ and } pr_S(U(-,t_j)) \le d1 \}$$

$$T_{d1}^i := \{ t_j^i \mid t_j \in T \}$$

For every d1, ... , dk

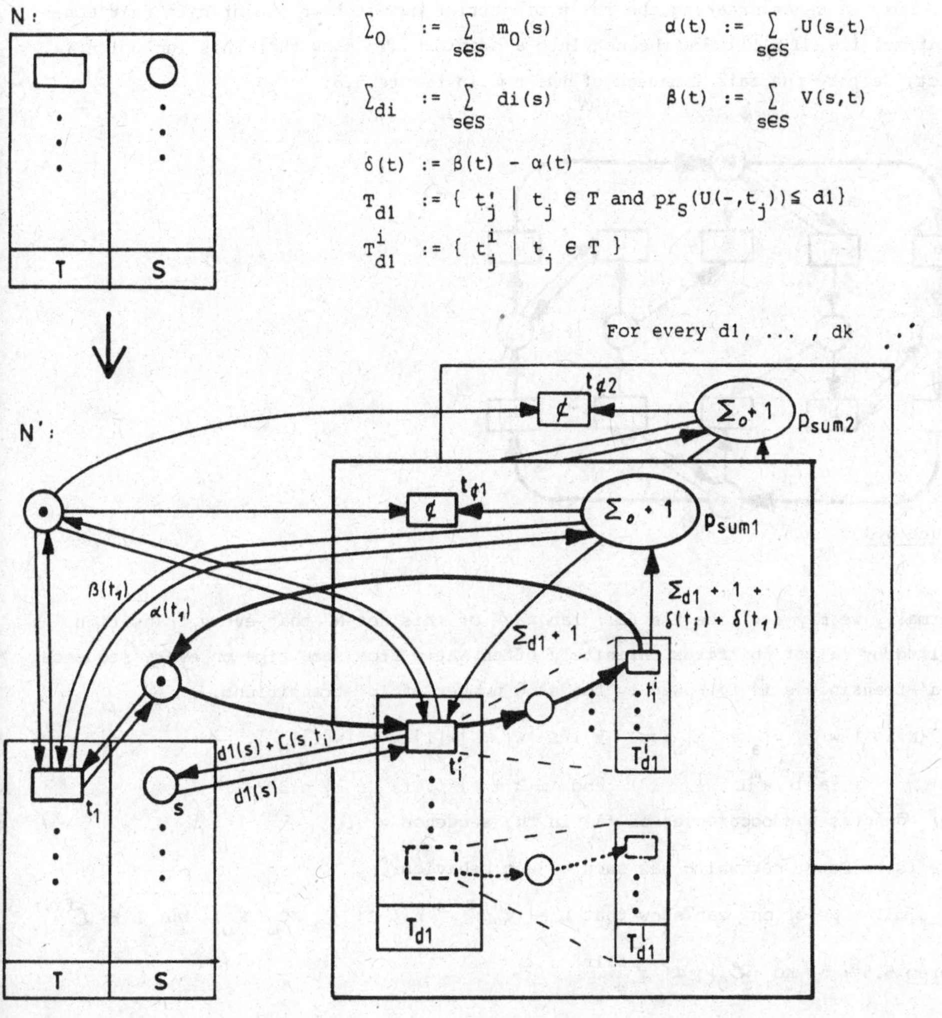

Figure 5.2

Theorem 5.3 : $\mathcal{L}_\omega^1 \subseteq \mathcal{L}_\omega^{just}$.

Proof: $\mathcal{L}_\omega^1 = \mathcal{L}_0 \circ \mathcal{L}_\omega$ (Theorem 3.1) and $\mathcal{L}_\omega \subseteq \mathcal{L}_\omega^{just}$ (Theorem 5.1 and Theorem 4.2). By lemma 5.2 follows the proposition.

A comparison between the classes of fair and of just behaviours of Petri nets gives the following result.

Theorem 5.4 $\mathcal{L}_\omega^{just} \subsetneqq \mathcal{L}_\omega^{fair}$.

To prove the inclusion it is shown that a net N can be transformed into a net N' so that $L_\omega^{just}(N) = L_\omega^{fair}(N')$. The transformation is rather long, it also uses the idea, that every sequence breaking the rules of justice cannot have an infinite fair continuation, i.e. it will bring the net into a deadlock. To show that this inclusion is strict, we take the fair language of the net in figure 5.3.

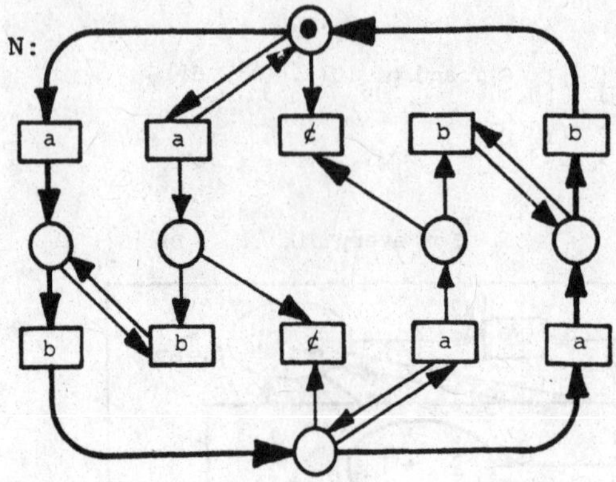

Figure 5.3

Informally we may describe the fair language of this net N that every transition labelled by 'a' or 'b' fires infinitely often where from some time on every sequence of 'a'-transitions is followed by the same number of 'b'-transitions.

$L_\omega^{fair}(N) = \{ w \mid |w|_a = |w|_b$ and $\forall i \leq |w| : |w[i]|_a \geq |w[i]|_b \}$.

$(\{a^n b^n a^m b^m \mid n \geq 1$ and $m \geq 1 \}^* . \{a^n b^n \mid n \geq 2\})^\omega$

($|w|_a$ denotes the occurences of 'a' in the sequence w) .

There is no Petri net which has such a just behaviour.

In a similar proof one can show that $L = \{a^n b^n \mid n \geq 1\}^\omega \in KC_\omega(\mathcal{L}_0)$, but $L \notin \mathcal{L}_\omega^{fair}$.

Theorem 5.5 : $KC_\omega(\mathcal{L}_0) \not\subseteq \mathcal{L}_\omega^{fair}$.

In the final figure 5.4 we show all inclusions between classes of languages proved in this paper. It was also shown that there are no further inclusions between these classes.

As some concluding remarks we want to mention that for the classes $\mathcal{K}_\omega^i$ [Valk,Jantzen] showed that the emptiness problem is decidable. (That paper also contains additional results on infinite firing sequences, that are continual for some $E \subseteq T$.) For the other classes the emptiness problem is at least as difficult as the reachability problem for Petri nets.

6. Conclusions

In this paper we investigated the inclusions between several classes of ω-behaviour of Petri nets dealing with fairness.

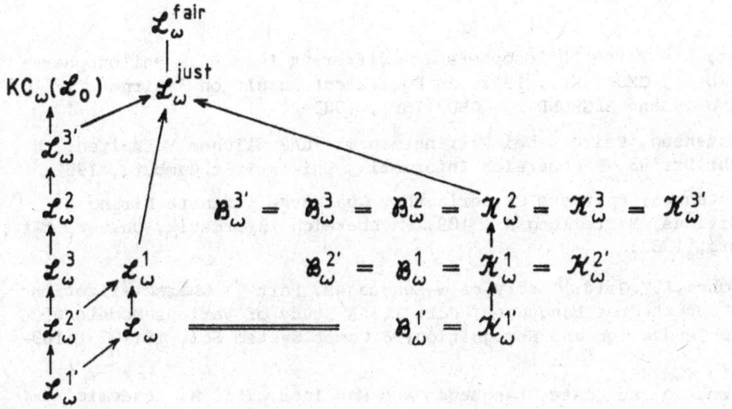

Figure 5.4

An aim for further research will be the relation between the specification of fairness (e.g. markings or transitions which must appear infinitely often) and fairness criteria in the selection of transitions to fire.

An idea is that a specification of fairness can be implemented by nets with some fair selection rule for the transitions.

For an implementation one needs nets which are free of deadlocks. Therefore one question is: what must be changed if we allow only deadlock-free Petri nets? (Certainly a different hierarchy of classes of net languages will follow).

Perhaps it is also more adequate to look at deterministic Petri net languages, as defined in [Vidal-Naquet].

We have investigated two criteria of a fair selection: justice and fairness. Are there other more useful criteria?

For liveness in Petri nets there are many fine results for restriced classes of nets, e.g. for state machine and for free choice nets. Are there also classes of Petri nets in which the problem for fairness becomes much easier as in the general case? Some ideas in that direction are made in [Best] and [Carstensen2]. One such question is : is there a fairness criterion in the selection of transitions for a restricted class of nets which guarantees the infinite firing of certain transitions?

Most of the proofs in this paper are valid for labelled Petri nets only. In these constructions two or more transitions with a same label are used to simulate one transition in the original net. So it would be interesting to see similar results for unlabelled nets.

Acknowledgements : We thank the referees for their hints to improvements and DFG (German Research Community) for supporting a related project.

7. References

[Best] E.Best; Why Three Philosophers are different from Five Philosophers; BEGRUND-11, GMD (ISF), 1982. An Equivalent Result on 'Fairness'; BEGRUND-19 and BEGRUND-20, GMD (ISF), 1983

[Carstensen1] H.Carstensen; Fairneß bei Petrinetzen mit unendlichem Verhalten; Bericht Nr. 93, Fachbereich Informatik, Universität Hamburg, 1982

[Carstensen2] H.Carstensen; Fairness Criteria that Guarantee Infinite Firing of Transitions; Mitteilung Nr. 109, Fachbereich Informatik, Universität Hamburg, 1983.

[Cohen,Gold] R.S.Cohen,A.Y.Gold; Theory of ω-Languages, Part I: Characterization of ω-Context-Free Languages, Part II: A Study of Various Models of ω-Type Generation and Recognition; J.Compt.System Sci. 15(1977) 169-208.

[Eilenberg] S.Eilenberg; Automata, Languages and Machines, Vol. A, Academic Press, New York, 1974.

[Genrich, Stankiewics-Wichno] H.J.Genrich,E.Stankiewics-Wichno; A Dictionary of some Basic Notations of Net Theory; in Brauer (ed.) Net Theory and Applications, LNCS Vol. 84, 198o.

[Hack] R.M.Hack;Petri Net Languages; MIT, Project MAC, Computer Structure Group, Memo 124, 1975.

[Hossley] R.Hossley; Finite Tree Automata and ω-automata; MIT,MAC, Tech.Rep. 102, Cambridge Mass., 1972.

[Jantzen,Valk] M.Jantzen,R.Valk; Formal Properties of Place/Transition Nets; in Brauer (ed.), Net Theory and Applications, LNCS Vol. 84, 1980.

[Karp,Miller] R.M.Karp,R.E.Miller; Parallel Program Schemata; J.Compt.System Sci. 3(1969) 147-195.

[Landweber] L.H.Landweber; Decision Problems for ω-automata; Math.Syst. Theory 3(1969) 376-384.

[Lehmann,Pnueli, Stavi] D.Lehmann,A.Pnueli,J.Stavi; Impartiality, Justice, Fairness: The Ethics of Concurrent Termination; Automata, Languages, Programming, 8th Colloquium, LNCS Vol. 115, 1981.

[Nivat] M.Nivat; On the Synchronisation of Processes; INRIA, Rap.Rech. No 3 1980.

[Valk] R.Valk; Infinite Behaviour of Petri Nets; Theor.Comp.Sci. 25(1983) 311-341.

[Valk,Jantzen] R.Valk,M.Jantzen; The Residue of Vector Sets with Applications to Decidability Problems in Petri Nets, in this volume. also Bericht Nr. 101, Fachbereich Informatik, Univ. Hamburg.

[Vidal-Naquet] G.Vidal-Naquet; Réseaux de Petri Dêterministes,Thèse d'Etat, Univ. Paris VI, 1981.

PETRI NET BASED MODELS FOR THE SPECIFICATION AND VALIDATION OF PROTOCOLS

Michel DIAZ - Pierre AZEMA

LABORATOIRE d'AUTOMATIQUE
et d'Analyse des Systèmes du C.N.R.S.
7, avenue du Colonel Roche
31077 TOULOUSE CEDEX - France

I. INTRODUCTION

Lot of processors exist and will be integrated together to build different and dedicated functional units. As a consequence, any sophisticated system is to be based upon sets of interconnected computers that have to communicate and cooperate. If the system is complex and contains, because of its behavior, different parts -machines having different purposes- characteristics from different producers- manufacturers, then, interconnecting the resulting subsystems will be quite difficult : in order to tackle these difficulties at the design stage, it is mandatory to define and realize OPEN systems, i.e. systems that are designed in such a way that they allow any kind of processor to be easily interconnected. It is now of great evidence that interactions in open distributed systems are complex and difficult to specify, implement and test. This is why formal approaches are of interest and needed to derive correct and robust mechanisms, whatever the field of application, including networks for office automation and flexible automatized production.

A complex system will be constituted of two parts : one part describes the set of the functional units, functional machines, functional processors ; the other part explicits by which way those functional subsystems communicate and cooperate, i.e. explicits the set of the communication functions which are needed. Thus, the whole system, including functional elements and communication elements has to be explicitely defined.

It appears that the interaction functions are of fundamental importance although they are frequently not well described. Usually those interactions are called protocols and are defined as the set of rules followed by the different processors in order to communicate and cooperate, i.e. receiving messages, analyzing their meaning and taking the correct related actions (computing, sending others messages,...).

Due to their complexity and importance computer networks have led to the first studies in formal specification, validation and implementation of protocols /SUN/-/BOC,SUN/ before the present general recognition of their interests. Various approaches are presently developed including state approaches, data types, temporal ordering and languages. After indicating the general problems and underlining the necessity of models to support the design of protocols in distributed systems, approaches which use Petri nets based models will be presented , because of their interests and potentialities.

II. WHY ARE FORMAL MODELING AND DESCRIPTION TECHNIQUES OF FUNDAMENTAL IMPORTANCE

In the general case, the design of the interactions between computers will need to deal with the communication between a number n of sequential processor activities. The activities, say Ai, Figure 1, are located in different computers, in different locations, possibly in different countries ; as a consequence, managing the -interacting- software of the global system appears to be very difficult and a four steps methodology (specification - validation - implementation - testing) is needed.

The first step, specification, which is the starting point of the design can be divided into two parts :

a) defining the set of sequential processes that SEND and RECEIVE messages,
b) defining the kinds of interactions that exist between the senders and receivers.

Formal validation, conducted off-line, will allow to check some nice properties of the system, starting as soon as possible, ending as close as possible of the implementation. Testing and on-line verification (during run time checking), due to the geographical distribution, are of very high importance and must also be supported by formal approaches.

The interactions, and, as a consequence the global distributed architecture, may be described in an informal way, by using a pseudo-language or a natural language. But it becomes quite difficult to express sophisticated cooperation mechanisms and leads to incomplete or ambiguous specifications which in turn contains potentialities of implementation errors. This possibility is clearly unacceptable for the realization of OPEN systems for which quite different implementations -by different manufacturers- must lead to totally compatible behaviour, whatever the area of application.

As a consequence, formal description has to be used because it is mandatory to have in open systems :

- a unambiguous description, because separate (and different) implementations will be derived from it and these implementations must be fully compatible ; note that this point is specific for protocols in open distributed systems ;
- a high level specification, without containing any implementation constraints, for it to be realized as efficiently as possible on different target systems by different people ;
- an off-line validation, before implementation, because it is actually very difficult to debug distributed systems when all the processors are running in parallel, sending lot of wrong messages on listings ;
- a starting support to derive a preliminary set of functional test sequences with respect to a given reference and without accounting for implementation choices.

All of these goals aim to help the designer to understand, discuss, design and implement in his environment. The main benefits are to avoid different and not compatible implementations, not to give unnecessary constraints to the implementors, to help the designers by allowing off-line validation and on-line debugging.

III. THE CONCEPTUAL ARCHITECTURE

When systems are complex, people must have a certain knowledge before dealing with them. In open distributed systems, a very important conceptual model which has been proved of high interest is the OSI -Open System Interconnection- reference model of the ISO-CCITT international standardization organisms /ZIM/.

One of the basic concepts of the model is the concept of layering which means that the architecture to be dealt with is structured as a set of adjacent layers, numbered in the OSI model from 1 to 7 (Figure 2).

The important point is that those layers can be more or less complex -or some of them unnecessary- in given architectures and applications ; but, anyway, the structure should follow a defined layering approach - layered architecture.

It is argued by OSI users that such a layering approach is to be used to manage the architecture of complex systems and solve the implementation problems resulting from the complexity. Of course, the layers can be the ones of the OSI model or different from them, but they must support a layered design of the intended functionalities.

In such a case, the ISO-CCITT model defines the global design as the architecture which interconnect different systems, those systems being the actual nodes (computers) that are interconnected : so a layer of the architecture appears in each of the systems that are interconnected. When a layer is designed, the systems that are involved in this layer have to cooperate ; protocols to realize the functionalities implemented at that layer have to be defined. When the considered layer, say N, is not the lowest one, then there is another layer under it, say (N-1) : then the N-layer uses the functions delivered by the (N-1) layer. As these functions are distributed and complex, they are called "services" in the OSI terminology.

So, in the general case, each layer uses services from its lower layer and offers services to its upper layer. At a given layer say N, the N-services are provided by using N-protocols (protocols inside that layer) designed on top of (N-1) services (Figure 3).

In the general case, p processors or p systems, in p geographically distinct nodes, are interconnected to provide the users a set of application services which are designed as a set of layers of protocols and services, the uppest services being the ones that are given to the users.

Then, a <u>protocol</u> is a set of rules between distant processes-processors that defines the messages and their sequencing: it is a possible implementation of a service ; a <u>service</u> is the set of functions to be realized by the protocol (it is the purpose of the exchange of the messages) which are given to the users.

IV. <u>MODELING DISTRIBUTED SYSTEMS</u>

As a consequence of the previous comments, it appears that each of the layers of the architecture has to be formally described in two steps ; it is needed :

- first, to define the sequential functions that have to cooperate,
- second, to define the actual way those functions interact, i.e. which lower layer service is used to support the resulting interactions ; note that this step is fundamental to construct the global architecture.

Then, obviously, two formal descriptions will be necessary : one formal description has to define the (N-1)-Services which are used to support the N-protocols ; another formal description must define the designed N-protocols.

Once the support services and designed protocols are specified, they must be interconnected to define the global architecture which can be formally handled.

In fact, the situation is more complex. A service in the OSI model is accessed through a SAP-Service Access Point-which is used to address the service. SAPs need a functional support which, in the OSI model, is called an entity. Then it will be necessary to define a set of models for the entities with respect to the SAPs to represent the global architecture.

Different modelling approaches exist, e.g. state transition systems, abstract data types, temporal sequences of events, value or buffer histories. This paper will deal with a very important one, namely based on Petri net models.

As it will be seen, the model of the distributed N-entities will be derived by :

1. For each of the N-level processes, defining a model, a state machine, which SENDS and RECEIVES messages.
2. For each of the SEND-RECEIVE interaction, defining an explicit model of the interaction.
3. Connecting together the state machines and the interaction models in order to obtain the global net - the one which has to be valided.

Two main possibilities exist :

a) in Data Communications, the global model is very often obtained by using Extended State Machines which communicate through FIFO queues ; this model is well adapted to important protocols and used for instance by the ISO/WG6/FDT/Subgroup B Community ;
b) in the general case, it seems quite interesting (state machines are subclasses of Petri nets) to obtain the model by using Extended Petri Nets which communicate through Extended Petri Nets ; those different nets are connected together to give the global model, giving more flexibility by allowing to connect very different nets.

Differents classes of nets (sometimes also called states/ transitions systems) are being used to represent protocols, the most important ones being state machines and extensions, Place-Transition (Pe-Tr) nets (Petri nets), Predicate-Transition (Pr-Tr) nets, Predicate-Actions (Pr-Ac) nets and Numerical Petri nets.

How they are used will be given now.

V. THE PRINCIPLE OF MODELING

V.1. Approaches

A. Extended State Machines

Using a state machine to represent the states of entities of protocols has been the first formal approach to describe their behavior and is still of a widespread use.

The machine is defined by a set $\{I, O, S, \delta, \omega, So\}$ where : I is the input set, O the output set, S the set of states, δ the next state function, ω the output function and So the initial state.

Two comments are needed :

1. The representation by states, for complex protocols, limits the number of the represented states ; it is necessary to extend state machines by including how the input message is processed -for instance receiving the message, checking its contents, doing actions, sending messages- before going to the next state. So transition functions include predicates and procedures and the state of the machine is the concate-nation of the control state and of the existing variables states.
2. The state machine representation does not explicit the interactions that exist between machines. In protocols, it is very often assumed that machines interact through FIFO queues.

Such approaches are frequently encountered in protocol design and modeling, for instance in /LEMO/ /BOCH/ /SUN-DAL/ /BOC1/ /DAN/ /POS/ /WES/.

B. Petri nets

The basic improvement coming from the use of Petri nets is to allow an explicit specification of the synchronization constraints between different state machines. Furthermore they can serve as a basis for modular graphical representation and for efficient analyses.

Petri nets are used since a few years now to design protocols /DAN - DIA/ and many classes are used such as Places/ Transitions nets /PETR/ Predicates/Transitions nets /GEN-LAU/,Predicates/Actions nets /KEL/, Time Petri nets /MER-FAR/,Numerical Petri nets /SYM/;,...

B.1. Classes of nets

Places/Transitions nets are commonly referred to as Petri nets ; they are constituted of places, transitions, arcs with weights having non negative values.

Those nets, although of interest for medium scale protocols, have some limitations because they can become very complex ; furthermore they cannot specify every type of behaviour.

Then Predicate/Transition nets have been considered because: first, each token has an identity -sometimes called a colour- and, second, firing a Transition occurs when :

- the transition is enabled,
- the right types of tokens are avalaible,
- its associated predicate -which deals with a relation on the types of the tokens in the input places- is true.

In Predicate/Actions nets, the extension is that predicates and actions can handle not only tokens but (classical) program variables.

Numerical Petri nets are defined as extensions of Predicate-Action nets and Predicate/Actions nets ; they allow to handle program variables, tokens with identity and for an input place of a Transition, the enabling condition may be different from the removing of the tokens in that place.

Another quite important aspect of Petri nets is their ability to handle time. Two time values can be associated to each transition of the net /MER - FAR/. The first one, tmin, defines the minimal time the transition must wait, after being enabled, before being fired ; the second one, tmax, defines the maximal time the transition will wait, after being and staying enabled, before firing (an enabled transition will fire in any case at tmax, which is the definition of a time-out behaviour).

The previous models are different in inherent information and complexity ; they give trade-offs between power of specification and efficiency of validation. The latter point is of fundamental interest.

B.2. Analyses

Analyses algorithms allow to show whether nets fulfil different properties :

- general properties, such as boundedness, and liveness, which must be true whatever the considered net,
- specific properties, such as mutual exclusion, depending on the net, defined as invariants.

In particular, it must be emphasized that for time Petri nets, reachability analysis has recently being developed /BER-MEN/.

C. Tools and applications

Some software tools exist, such as GALIGEO /VID/, SARA /RA - ES/ for simulation, OGIVE/OVIDE for validation and proof. Those tools are general purpose tools ; specific and efficient tools dedicated to protocols have also being developed, as the duologue matrix approach at IBM /WES - ZAF/, a NPN simulator at Telecom Australia /SYM/ and VADILOC at ADI/RHIN /RAF - ANS/.

As an example, VADILOC is based on a combination "automaton and algorithms" which is dedicated towards handling protocols ; the consequence is that VADILOC is a quite efficient package which has been applied to HDLC, File Transfer, ISO Tranport/Session /ANS 1-3/. On another hand, OVIDE/OGIVE is based on a combination of Petri nets and related analysis algorithms which are dedicated to validate the behaviour of nets, whatever their applications ; the consequence is that OVIDE/ OGIVE is a quite powerfull, easy to use package for handling Petri nets ; OVIDE/OGIVE has been applied to connexion handling, virtual rings, ISO Transport /JUA/ /AYA-COU-DIA/ /ALG/.

V.2. Some models

The general approach for modeling communicating entities in distributed architectures is derived when : each node is represented by state machines, and the communicating processes are explicitly connected together, leading to Petri nets. When two transitions send and receive one message, they can be connected :

- either directly by merging (rendez-vous), shared place, request acknowledge,
- either indirectly through a FIFO queue or a service of any complexity.

Figure 4 gives some simple possibilities of interconnexion between two communicating actions.

To stress the problems that can result from inadequate modeling, let us consider, from /DIA/, the following example : two processes exchange messages ; Process P1 sends A to Process P2 ; Process P2 sends B to Process P1 (Figure 5.a.). These two cyclic processes communicate and an interaction mechanism has to be selected for their interconnection.

Let us first consider merging. If processes P1 and P2 are connected by merging the send-receive transitions, then the global net (Figure 5.b.) is safe and live. Now, if processes P1 and P2 are connected by a shared place between the related transitions, then the global net (Figure 5.c.) is unbounded. Last, when processes P1 and P2 are connected by the request-acknowledge mechanism, the global net is bounded but not live.

Note that the problems may be subtle. Let us select the rendez-vous mechanism as an interaction mechanism. The model resulting from one implementation is given in Figure 6 /DIA/. Then interconnecting processes P1 and P2 by the net given in Figure 6 leads to a global net which is not live (compare with merging : there exist two states which respectively correspond to the end of the processing of the SEND primitive and of the RECEIVE primitive and they are possible deadlock states).

This example emphasizes the main problem of the modeling : there is a direct relationship between the selected interaction model and the actual behavior of the lower layers of the protocol : the model must represent the actual (N-1) service, the one which is actually implemented.

Note that one very simple model, a shared place model, is often selected to interconnect the different state machines. Its conceptual characteristics must be clearly understood.

Sequential machines and Petri nets based models have been applied in protocols /DAN/-/DIA/, for instance to the alternating bit /BOC-GEC/ /POS/, opening - closing connections /DAN1/ /SYM/ /JUA/, CCITT number 7 /AYA-DIA-KON/, X21 /WES-ZAF/ /RAZ-EST/, blocking channels /DEV-DIA/, virtual rings /AYA-COU-DIA/ /AZE-ROL-SED/-/EST-GIR/, Transport layer /BIL/ /BER-TER/ /JUA/ /ALG/, concurrent acces and distributed data bases /AZE-BER-DEC/-/VOS/.

In order to understand how nets can be used, let us consider first a very simple protocol, the alternating bit protocol. Two processes, a sender and a receiver, exchange messages. The sender sends data together with a control bit, 0 or 1. There are two phases in the transfer : during the first phase, the sender sends the data with the 0, then wait for an ack ; during the second phase, the same behavior occurs with the control bit set to 1. Figure 7 gives the representation of the behavior of the protocol by considering that the emission and the reception of a message are connected by using a shared place. In order to understand the interest of the control bit, let us now consider that messages can be lost. The new protocol is given by Figure 8 in which the loss of a message together with a value of the control bit results in a new emission of the message together with the same value of the control bit. Note that D-0 can be received more than once but it is saved only once during the first reception. In order to again send D, the loss must be detected : this is modelled by the places "D or A" which, in fact, mean that there is a way to detect that the message has been lost, this by receiving a logical event. Obviously, such a model is an approximation of the actual behavior because there is no way for the sender to logically know that the message has been lost. The actual implementations use a time-out, independantly of the state of the message once it has been sent. Figure 9 gives the resulting model which now uses a timed Petri net in order to account for the explicit value of the time-out. Note that there is no more direct relationship between the loss of the message and the re-emission resulting from the firing of the "time-out" transition.

Of course, this is a simple example. Real protocol are much more complex and, furthermore, as it has been seen, there is a hierarchy of protocols. As a consequence of this point, the general model of a protocol inside a hierarchy will consist of different submodels, each of them being for instance defined as given in Figure 10. The seven sub-models, which are either state machines or Petri nets represent the entities, the system interfaces or SAPs and the underlying service. The global model of the protocol results from the interconnection of those seven sub-models. One can realize the possible resulting complexity and the interest of tools.

V.3. The OBSERVER concept

From the previous design step, a model exists that represents the protocol behavior ; this model must be translated into code in a given language. As there is no automatic way to derive the target implementation, errors can occur, which are very difficult to show and locate.

It has been proposed in /AYA-AZE-DIA/ to use a Petri net model to observe the behavior of communicating systems by using the observer concept. This leads to build the system as a pair : a worker and an observer.

The observer implements the Petri net-based model of a high level control. The worker is composed of a set of processes which are implemented for example by the methodology previously described. The resulting redundancy constitutes the basis of an on-line verification during the functionning of the protocol.

The basic checking principle consists of running in parallel, possibly on different hardware, the observer and the worker. Then this allows comparison, during run-time, of the concurrent control states of both worker and observer.

For instance, in local networks, the protocols are written on the network processors and the observer can be located on a specific processor, connected to the bus, and only dedicated to testing debugging and measurement purposes /AYA-COU-DIA1/. This observer posseses all the models of the protocols that have to be tested.

Then, its purpose is to confirm that every computation sequence of the worker corresponds exactly to a valid firing sequence of the associated Petri net. If an invalid sequence occurs, the observer delivers an error message or signal which can be used to give adequate traces,stop the process, initiate recovery actions, etc. This approach allows the definition, from all the invalid firing sequences, of the set of detected errors.

It must be noted that the model which constitutes the observation reference, is not always the same than the global model Therefore, the observer model can be computed from the global one through a projection as it has been done to derive the service model.

Two main interests appear. First, the programming effort is reduced in the sense that this approach takes the advantage of the formal modelling, which is already required for the design specification and validation. Secondly, the observer represents a secure way to the valid sequence checking problem ; the reliability attained by the observer results from the two following points :

a) the net used as the basis for the observer can be proved correct by its analysis ;
b) the implementation of the observer is in fact a Petri net simulator ; this means that the corresponding software is extremely simple, the same whatever the net and, in consequence,can reach a high degree of reliability.

This possibility of defining a debugging tool in accordance with the design methodology looks of high interest.

VI. RELATION WITH OTHERS MODELS

Data types, temporal logic and dedicated languages have also been used to describe protocols.

Data types consider not the data but the functions that are related to them. Two classes exist, abstract and axiomatic /GUT/. Abstract data types use a lower level representation for defining the behavior of the functions and axiomatic data types define functions with respect to the others by axioms. Then, a protocol is defined as a set of data, including FIFO queues, on which are defined selectors (giving values) and constructors (modifying values) for instance /BERTHO/.

Temporal logic /PNU/ uses a higher level logic than first order logic in which is it possible to explicit the definition of some properties such as reachability, liveness,... in order to simplify their statements and their proofs. Some attempts have been made to relate temporal logic and Petri nets /GEN-LAU-THI/ /QUE-SIF/ /DIA-GUI/.

Whatever the specification method, its final aim is to lead to an implementation and, as a consequence, it has to be supported by an adequate language.

Many possibilities exist, for instant PASCAL and ADA, but it looks sound to build a dedicated language on top of a specification model, as state machines in PDIL /ANS-RAF-CHA/ Petri nets in LC/1 /AYA-COU/, abstract data types in AFFIRM /GER-ET AL/, buffer histories in GYPSY /GOO-COH-KEE/.

Two approaches seem to be followed to define languages for protocols : either people start from concepts of classical distributed languages or they consider protocol architectures and protocol models, for instance by considering the one which is widely used, state/transition machines. In the latter case /ANS-RAF-CHA/ /BLU-TEN/ /BOC-ETAL/, a machine is for instance an entity and the actual realization of the interactions is left as an implementation choice ; this leads to specifications independent of the operating systems but there is no abstract machines, no processes and very few structuring concepts. In the former case, structuring processes and interprocesses communication are explicit and gives the bases of the language /AYA-COU/ /DIV/. Petri nets based models appear to be good candidates to define the semantical support of such languages ; one possibility is given in /AYA-COU/. Others attempts have also to be developed.

VII. CONCLUSION

The main interest which comes from the use of state based approaches is their easy acceptance by users. People understand and become able to use them in a rather short time, beginning with problems or parts of protocols of a given simplicity and then going to use more complex nets.

Furthermore, state approaches give implementations that can be derived in a semi-automatic way from the design. They can serve as a basis for the design, validation, implementation and testing steps. This is why using Petri net based models as semantical supports prove to be of high theoretical and practical interests in protocols.

ACKNOWLEDGEMENTS

The authors should like to thank the members of the team Software and Communication of the LAAS, particularly MM. J.M.AYACHE, B. BERTHOMIEU, J.P. COURTIAT, G. JUANOLE and Mme B. PRADIN. They have greatly contributed to develop and understand numerous points which have been presented here.

REFERENCES

ALG B. ALGAYRES, "Sur la modélisation, la validation et l'implémentation d'un protocole de transport", Thèse de Docteur-Ingénieur, INSA, Toulouse, December 1982.

ANS-ETAL J.P. ANSART et al, "PDIL, un langage pour la description et l'implémentation de protocoles", Journées ADI/RHIN, Paris, 27-28 April 1983.

AYA-AZE-DIA J.M. AYACHE, P. AZEMA, M. DIAZ, "Observer : a concept for on-line detection of control errors in concurrent systems", IEEE Int. Symp. on Fault-Tolerant Computing, Madison, USA, June 1979.

AYA-ET-AL J.M. AYACHE, P. AZEMA, J.P. COURTIAT, M.DIAZ, G.JUANOLE "On the applicability of Petri net based models in protocol design and verification", Protocol Testing Workshop, NPL, Teddington, G.B., May 1981 ; Europ. Workshop on Application and Theory of Petri nets, Bad Honnef, RFA, Sept.1981.

AYA-COU J.M. AYACHE, J.P. COURTIAT, "LC/1, un langage pour la description, l'analyse et l'implémentation de protocoles", Journées ADI/RHIN, Paris, 27-28 April 1983.

AYA-COU-DIA J.M. AYACHE, J.P. COURTIAT, M. DIAZ, "REBUS : a fault-tolerant distributed system for industrial real time control", IEEE T. on Computers Special Issue on Fault-Tolerant Computing, July 1982.

AYA-COU-DIA1 J.M. AYACHE, J.P. COURTIAT, M. DIAZ, "Self-checking software in distributed systems", 3rd Conf. on Distributed Computing Systems, Miami, Nov. 1982.

AYA-DIA-KON J.M. AYACHE, M. DIAZ, H. KONBER, "Specification and verification of signalling protocols", Int. Switching Symp., ISS 81, Montreal, Sept. 1981.

AZE-BER-DEC P. AZEMA, B. BERTHOMIEU, P. DECITRE, "The design and validation by Petri nets of a mechanism for the invocation of remote servers", Proc. of IFIP Congress, Melbourne Oct. 1980.

AZE-ROL-SED P. AZEMA, P. ROLIN, S. SEDILLOT, "Virtual ring protection in distributed systems", IEEE Int. Symp. on Fault-Tolerant Computing, Portland, Maine, USA, June 1981.

BER-MEN B. BERTHOMIEU, M. MENASCHE, "A state enumeration approach for analyzing time Petri nets", 3rd Europ

Workshop on Applications and Theory of Petri nets, Varenna, Italie, Sept. 1982.

BER-MEN1 B. BERTHOMIEU, M. MENASCHE, "An enumerative ap-proach for analyzing time Petri nets", Proc. of the IFIP Congress, Paris, Sept. 1983.

BER-ROU-VAL G. BERTHELOT, G. ROUCAIROL, R. VALK, "Reduction of nets and parallel programs", Net Theory and Applications, Lect. Notes in Computer Science, 45, Springer Verlag, 1977.

BER-TER G. BERTHELOT, R. TERRAT, "Petri nets theory for the correctness of protocols", 2nd Europ. Workshop on Appl. & Theory of Petri nets, Bad Honnef, RFA, Sept. 1981, pp.31-58 ; also 2nd Int. Workshop on Protocol Specification Testing and Verification, Idyllwild Los Angeles, May 1982, North-Holland, 1982, C.Sunshine Ed.

BERTHO B. BERTHOMIEU, "Algebraic specification of communication protocols", research Report ISI-RR-81-98, also Technical Report LAAS-CNRS, 81.T.26, Oct.1981.

BIL J. BILLINGTON, "Specification of the transport service using numerical Petri nets", 2nd Int. Worshop on Protocol Specification, testing and Verification, Idyllwild Los Angeles, May 1982, North-Holland, 1982, C. Sunshine Ed.

BLU-TEN T.P. BLUMER, R.L. TENNEY, "A formal specification technique and implementation method for protocols", Computer Networks 6, 1982, pp.201-217.

BOC G. BOCHMAN et al, "Some experience with the use of formal specifications", Proc. IFIP WG 6.1, 2nd Int. Workshop on Protocol Specification Testing and Verification, Idyllwild, May 1982.

BOC1 G.V. BOCHMANN, "Finite state description of communication protocols", Conf.Computer Network Protocols,Liège 1978, also in Computer Networks 2, 1978, pp.361-372.

BOC2 G.V. BOCHMANN, "A general transition model for protocols and communication services", IEEE Trans. on Communications, vol.COM-28, n°4, April 1980, pp.643-650.

BOC-GEC G.V. BOCHMANN, J. GECSEI, "A unified method for the specification and verification of protocols", IFIP Proceedings, North-Holland, 1977.

BOC-SUN G.V. BOCHMANN, C.A. SUNSHINE, "Formal methods in communication protocol design", IEEE Trans. on Com-munications, vol.COM-28, n°4, April 1980, pp.624-631.

BRA-ZAF D. BRAND, P. ZAFIROPOULO, "Synthesis of protocols for an unlimited number of processes", Proc. of the Trends and Applications Symp., NBS, USA, May 1980.

CHE-PRA B. CHEZALVIEL-PRADIN, "Un outil graphique interactif pour la validation des systèmes à évolution parallèle décrits par réseaux de Petri (OGIVE)", Thèse de Docteur-Ingénieur, Université Paul Sabatier, Toulouse, Dec. 1979.

DAN A. DANTHINE, "Protocol representation with finite-state models", IEEE Trans. on Communications, vol.COM-28, n°4 April 1980, pp.632-643.

DAN1 A. DANTHINE, "Petri nets for protocols modeling and verification", IFIP-TC6, COMNET Symp., Budapest, Hong. Oct. 1977.

DEV-DIA M. DEVY, M. DIAZ, "Multilevel specification and validation of the control in communication systems", 1st Int. Conf. on Distributed Computing Systems, Hunstville Alabama, Oct. 1-4,1979.

DIA M. DIAZ, "Modeling and analysis of communication and cooperation protocols using Petri net based models", Tutorial paper, Proc. of the IFIP WG 6.1 Second Int. Workshop on Protocol Specification, Testing and Verification, Idyllwid, CA, May 1982, C. Sunshine, Ed. North-Holland 1982 ; also Computer Networks, vol.6, n°6, Dec. 1982.

DIA ET AL M. DIAZ, J.P. COURTIAT, B. BERTHOMIEU, J.M. AYACHE, "Status of Petri net based models for protocols", IEEE Int. Conf. on Communications, ICC 83, Boston, June 1983.

DIA-GUI M. DIAZ, G. GUIDACCI DA SILVEIRA, "On the specification and validation of protocols by temporal logic and nets", Proceedings of the IFIP 83 Congress, Paris, Sept. 1983.

DIV B.L. DIVITO, "Verification of communications protocols and abstract process models", University of Texas at Austin, Technical Report 25, Aug. 1982.

EST-GIR P. ESTRAILLIER, C. GIRAULT, "Petri nets specification of virtual ring protocols", Proc. on the Applications and Theory of Petri nets, A. Pagnoni, G. Rozenberg Editors, IFB66, Springer Verlag, 1983, pp.74-85.

GEN-LAU H.J. GENRICH, K. LAUTENBACH, "The analysis of distributed systems by means of predicate/transition nets", Semantics of Concurrent Computation, Evian, 1979, G. Kahn ed., Lect. Notes in Computer Sciences vol.70, Springer Verlag 1979, pp.123-146.

GEN-LAU-THI H.J. GENRICH, K. LAUTENBACH, P.S. THIAGARAJAN, "Elements of nets theory", lect. Notes in Computer Science 84, 1980, pp.21-163.

GER-ET-AL S.L. GERHART et al, "An overview of AFFIRM : a specification and verification system", Proc. of the IFIP Congress, Oct. 1980, PP.343-348.

GOO-COH D.I. GOOD, R.M. COHEN, "Verifiable communications processing in GYPSY", Proc. of COMPCON 78, IEEE, Sept.78.

GUT J. GUTTAG, "Notes on type abstraction", Proc. of the Conf. on Reliable Software, 1979, pp.170-189.

GUI-DIA G. GUIDACCI DA SILVEIRA, M. DIAZ, "Une logique temporelle pour les systèmes distribués", Journées AFCET "Protocoles et Systèmes Distribués", Paris, June 1981.

HAI-OWI B.T. HAILPERN, S.S. OWICKI, "Modular verification of computer communication protocols", IEEE T. on Communications, vol.COM-31, n°1, January 1983, pp.56-68.

ISO-B ISO/TC 97/SC 16/WG-FDT/SG-B, "ESTELLE Language for the specification of protocols".

ISO-C ISO/TC 97/SC 16/WG-FDT/SG-C, "LOTOS Temporal ordering specification".

JUA G. JUANOLE, "A data transfert protocol. Informal specification and modeling by Petri nets", 2nd Europ. Workshop on the Theory and Applications of Petri nets, Bad Honnef, RFA, Sept. 1981, pp.347-364.

KEL R.M. KELLER, "Formal verification of parallel programs" Com. ACM 19-7, vol.19, n°7, July 1976, pp.371-384.

LAM L. LAMPORT, "Sometimes is sometimes not never", Proc. POPL, 1980, ACM, Las Vegas, Jan. 1980.

LEMO G. LE MOLI, "A theory of colloquies", Proc. of the 1st Europ. Workshop on Computer Network, Arles, April 1973.

LOP I. LOPEZ, "The use of GALILEO to represent and analyse telecommunication protocols", 2nd Eur. Workshop on the Theory and Application of Petri nets, Bad Honnef, FRG,

September 1981, PP.397-410.

MERL P.M. MERLIN, "A study of the recoverability of computing systems", Univ. of California, Irvine, 1974, Ph.D. Thesis.

MER-FAR P.M. MERLIN, D.J. FARBER, "Recoverability of communication protocols - implication of a theoritical study", IEEE Trans.on Communications, Sept.1976, pp.1036-1043.

OVI OVIDE, Petri net validation tool, SYSECA, Jan. 1983.

PNU A. PNUELLI, "The temporal logic of programs", IEEE 18th Symp. on Foundations of Computer Science, 1977.

POS J.B. POSTEL, "A graph model analysis of computer communications protocols", Ph.D. Thesis, Research Report UCLA, ENG/7410, Jan. 1974.

POS-FAR J.B. POSTEL, D. FARBER, "Graph modeling of computer communications protocols", Proc. 5th Texas Conf. on Computing Systems, Austin, 1976.

QUE-SIF J.P. QUEILLE, J. SIFAKIS, "Specification and verification of concurrent systems in CESAR, an example", 2nd Europ. Workshop on the Theory and Application of Petri nets, Bad Honnef, FRG, Sept. 1981, pp.483-517.

RAM C. RAMCHANDANI, "Analysis of asynchronous concurrent systems by timed Petri nets", Research Report, Project MAC-TR 120, MIT, Feb. 1974.

RAZ R. RAZOUK, "Modelling X.25 using the graph model of behaviour", 2nd Int.Workshop on Protocol Specification, Testing and Verification, Idyllwild Los Angeles, May 1982, North-Holland, 1982, C. Sunshine Ed.

RAZ-EST R.R. RAZOUK, G. ESTRIN, "Modelling and verification of communication protocols in SARA : the X.21 interface", IEEE Trans. on Computers, vol.C-29, n°12, Dec. 1980, pp.1038-1051.

RIC-AGR G. RICART, A.K. AGRAWALA, "An optimal algorithm for mutual exclusion in computers networks", Comm. of the ACM, 24, n°1, Jan. 1981.

SCH D. SCHWABE, "Formal specification and verification of a connection - establishment protocol", Report ISI/RR 81-91, USC/ISI, April 1981.

SCH-MEL R.L. SCHWARTZ, P.M. MELLIAR-SMITH, "Temporal logic specification of distributed systems", 2nd Conf. Distributed Computing Systems, Paris, April 1981, pp.446-454.

SCH-MEL1 R.L. SCHWARTZ, P.M. MELLIAR-SMITH, "From state machine to temporal logic : specification methods for protocol standards", Tutorial Paper, 2nd Workshop on Protocol Specification, Testing and Verification, Idyllwild Los Angeles, May 1982, North-Holland, 1982, C. Sunshine Ed., also IEEE Trans. on Communications, COM-30, n°12, Dec. 1982, pp.2486-2496.

SUN-DAL C.A. SUNSHINE, Y.K. DALAL, "Connection management in transport protocols", Computer Networks 2, Dec. 1978, pp.454-473.

SUN C.A. SUNSHINE, "Survey of protocol definition and verification techniques", Computer Networks, 2, 1978, pp.346-350.

SUN1 C.A. SUNSHINE, "Formal modelling of communication protocols", ISI-USC report RR-81-89, March 1981 ; 1st Workshop on Protocol Testing, NPL, Teddington, GB, May 1981.

SYM F.J.W. SYMONS, "Modelling and analysis of communication protocols using numerical Petri nets", Ph.D. Thesis, University of Essex, Being Dept. of Elect. Eng. Sc.

Telecomm. Syst. Group Report n°152, May 1978.

SYM1 F.J.W. SYMONS, "Representation, analysis and verification of communication protocols", Research Report 7380, Telecom., Australia, 1980.

THO-ET-AL D.T. THOMPSON, C.A. SUNSHINE, R.W. ERICKSON, S.L. GERHART, D. SCHWABE, "Specification and verification of communication protocols in AFFIRM using state transition models", Research Report ISI-RR-81-88, USC, Inf. Sc. Institute, March 1981.

VID F. VIDONDO, "GALILEO, experiences in the design of a Petri net based language for real-time systems", 2nd Eur. Workshop on the Theory and Application of Petri nets, Bad Honnef, FRG, Sept. 1981, pp.541-550.

VOS K. VOSS, "Using predicate/transition-nets to model and analyze distributed database systems", IEEE Trans. on Software Eng., vol.6, n°6, Nov.1980, pp.539-544.

WES C.H. WEST, "General technique for communications protocols validation", IBM J. Research Develop., vol.22, July 1978, pp.393-404.

WES-ZAF C. WEST, P. ZAFIROPOULO, "Automated validation of a communication protocol : the CCITT X.21 recommendation",IBM J.R. and Develop., vol.22, Jan.1978, pp.60-71

ZAF-ET-AL P. ZAFIROPOULO et al, "Towards analyzing and synthesizing protocols", IEEE Trans. on Communications, COM-28, April 1980, pp.651-661.

ZIM H. ZIMMERMAN, "OSI reference model. The ISO model of architecture for open systems interconnection", IEEE Trans. on Communications, vol.COM-28, April 1980.

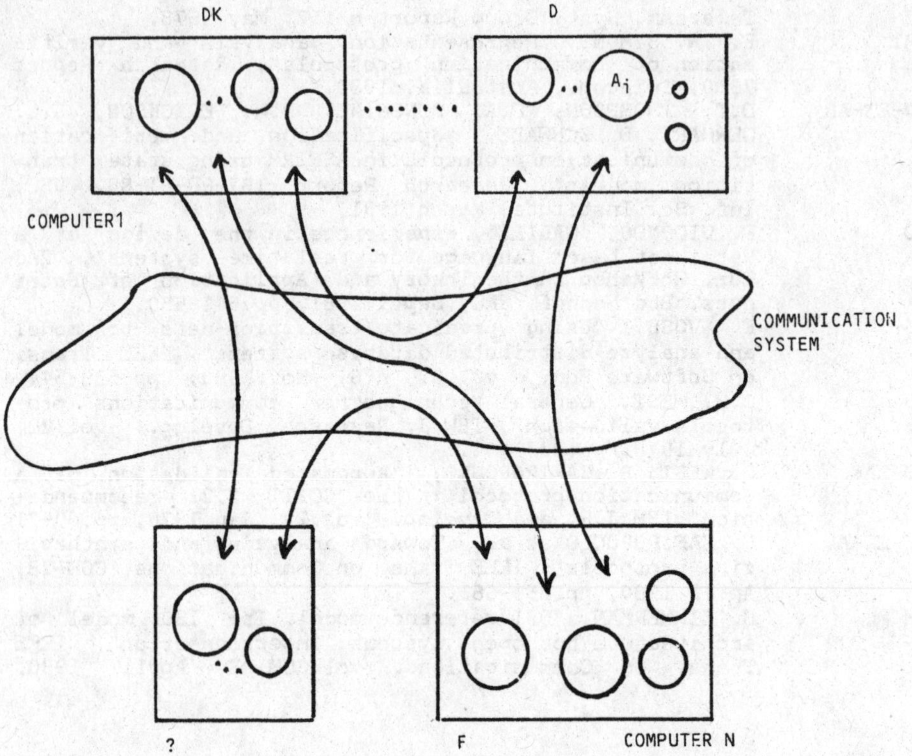

FIGURE 1

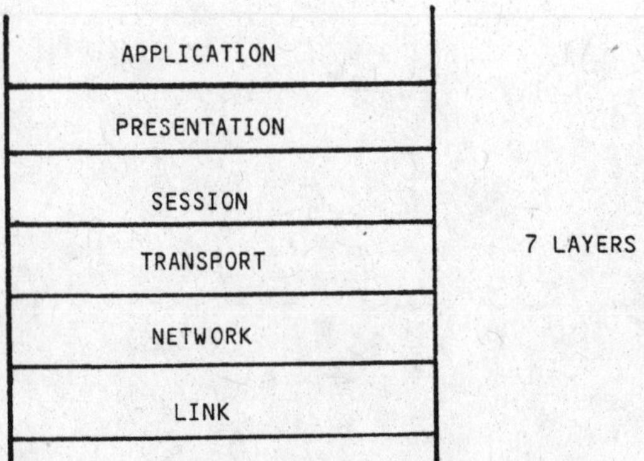

FIGURE 2

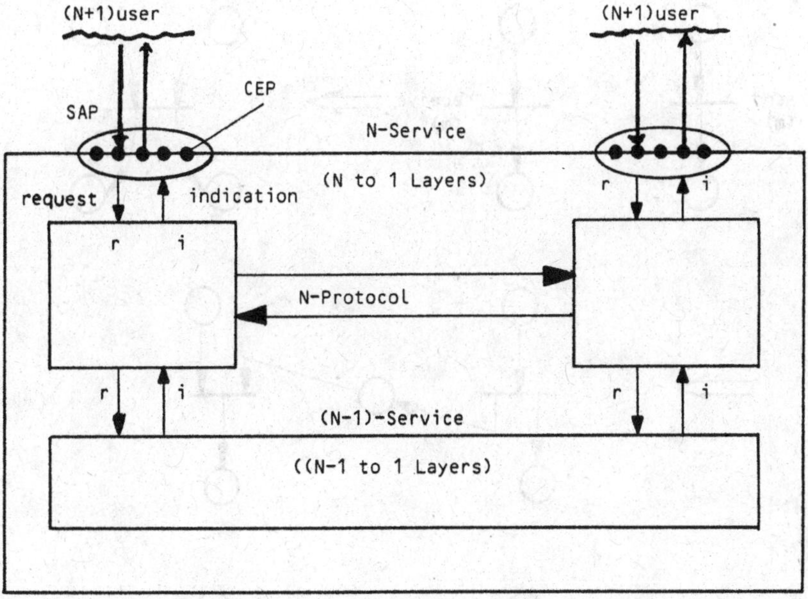

FIGURE 3

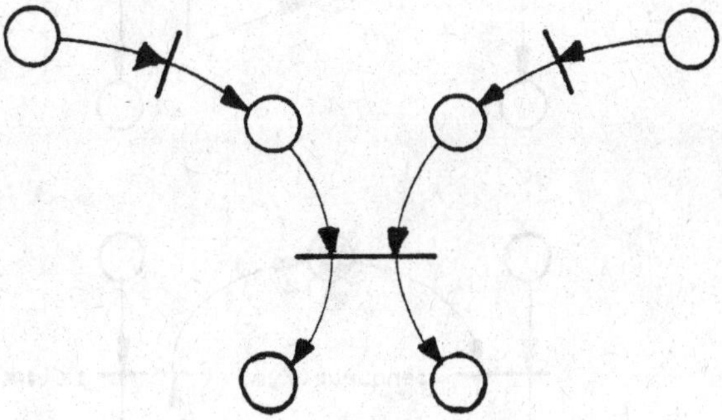

FIGURE 6

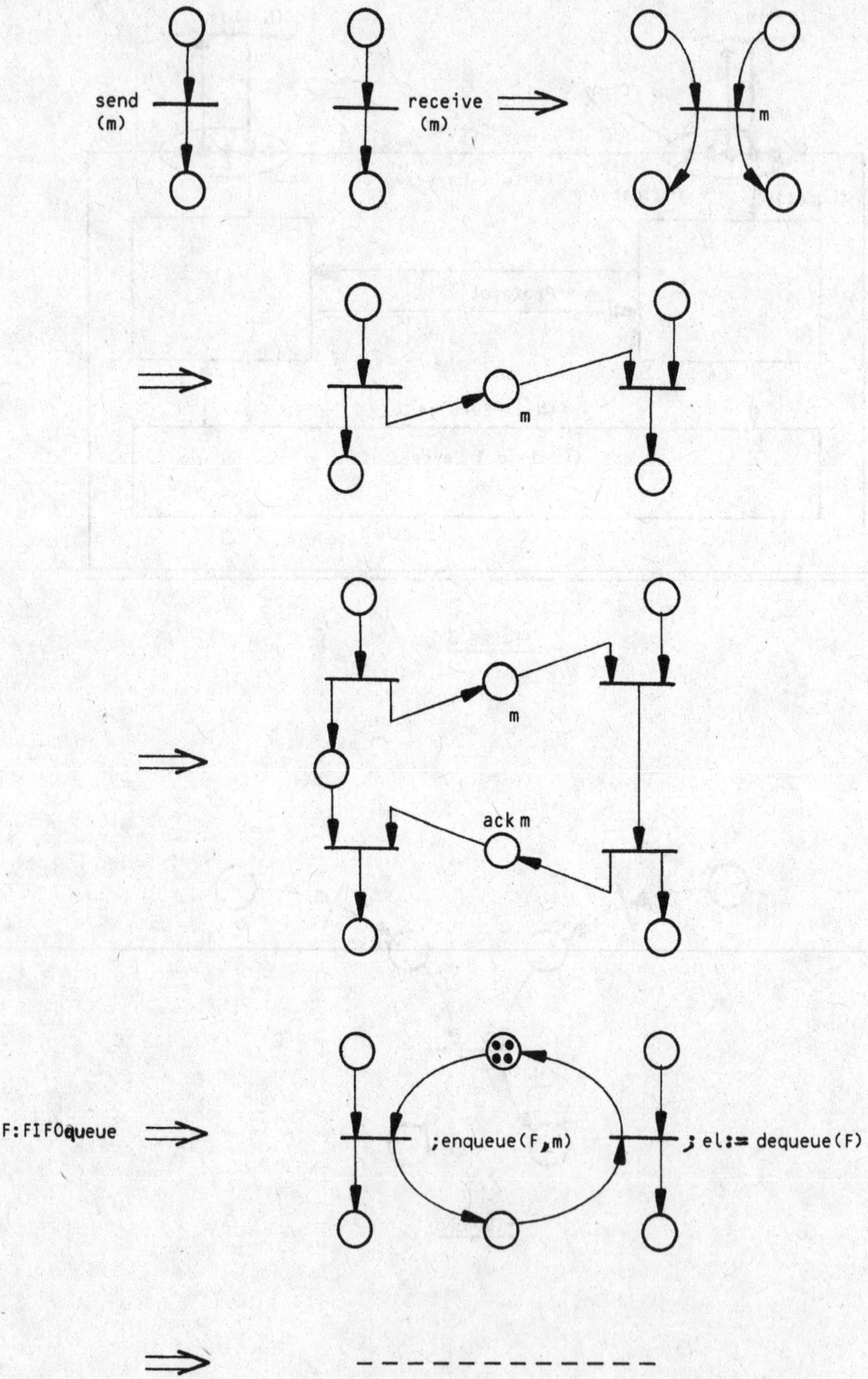

FIGURE 4

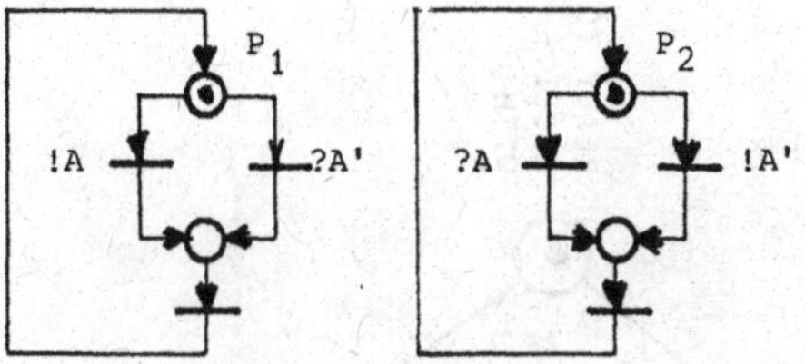

a)

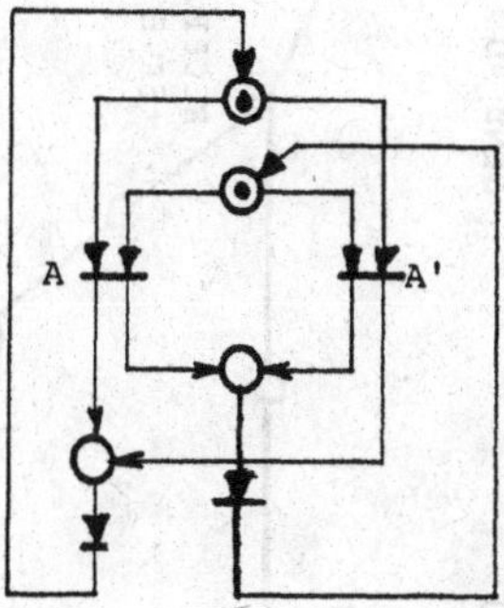

b)

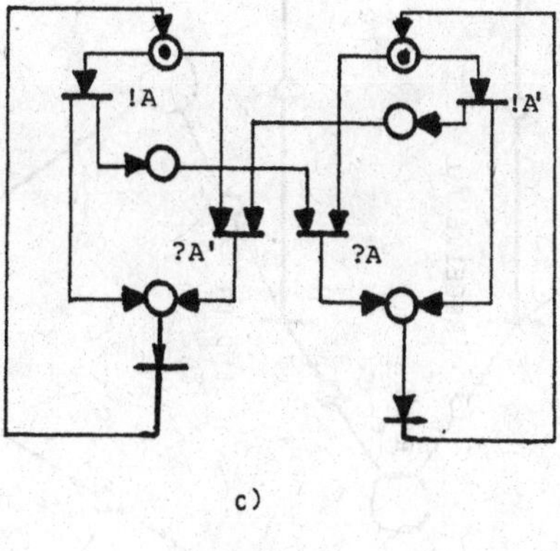

c)

FIGURE 5

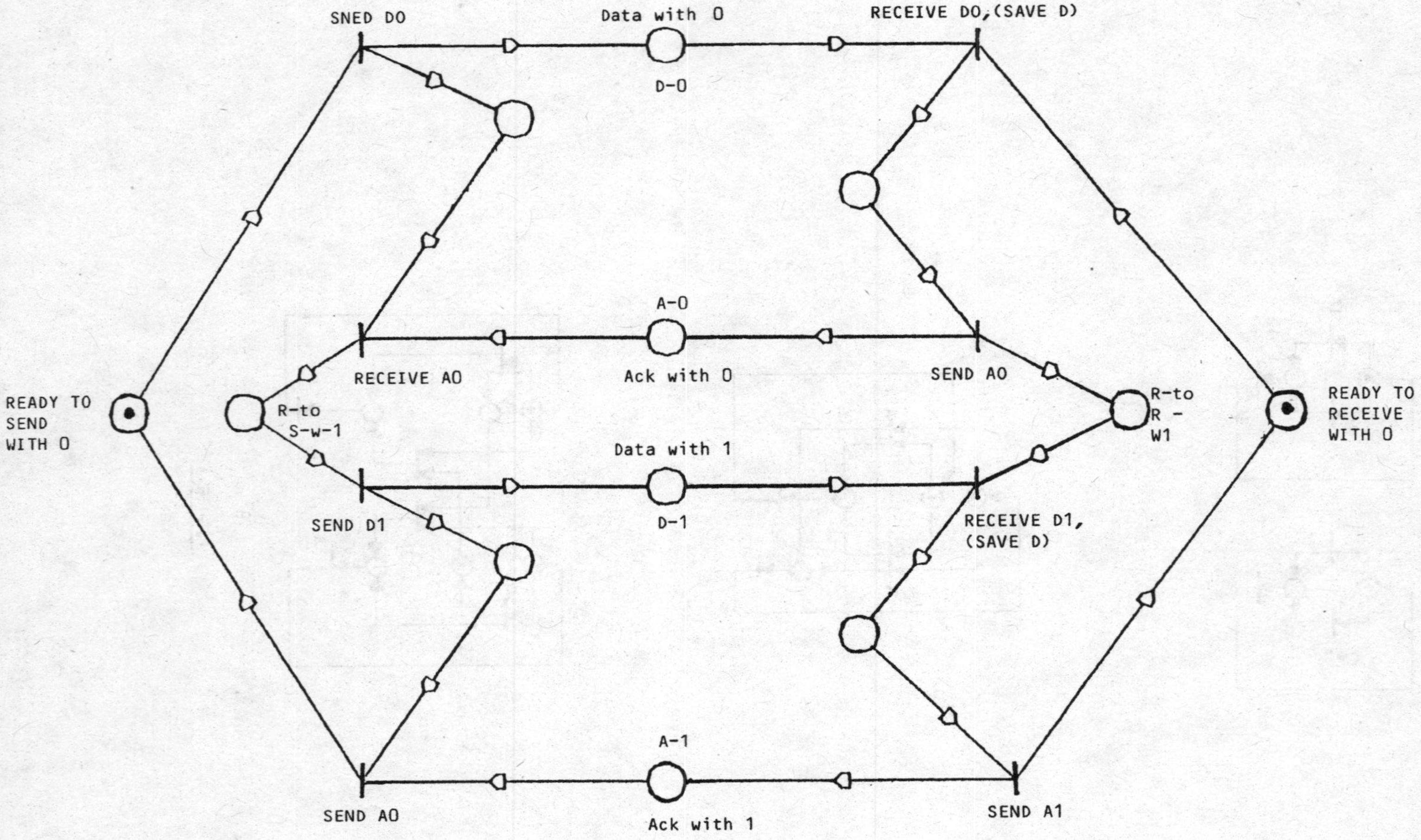
SNED DO
Data with 0
RECEIVE DO,(SAVE D)
D-0
A-0
RECEIVE AO
Ack with 0
SEND AO
READY TO
SEND
WITH 0
R-to
S-w-1
R-to
R -
W1
READY TO
RECEIVE
WITH 0
Data with 1
SEND D1
D-1
RECEIVE D1,
(SAVE D)
A-1
SEND AO
Ack with 1
SEND A1

FIGURE 7

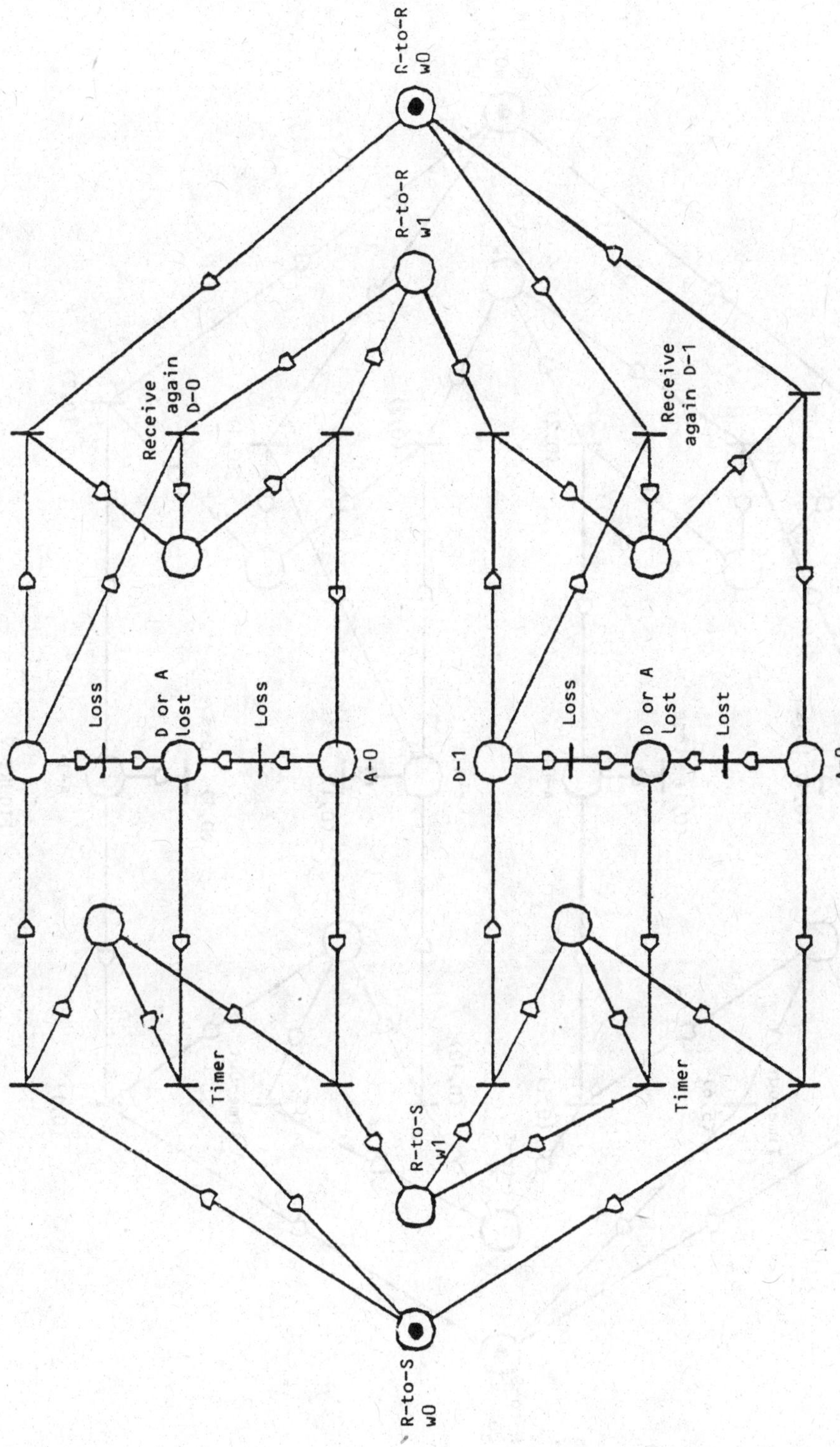
R-to-S
w0
R-to-S
w1
R-to-R
w0
R-to-R
w1
D-0
Loss
D or A
lost
Loss
A-0
D-1
Loss
D or A
lost
Lost
A-0
Receive
again
D-0
Receive
again D-1
Timer
Timer

FIGURE 8

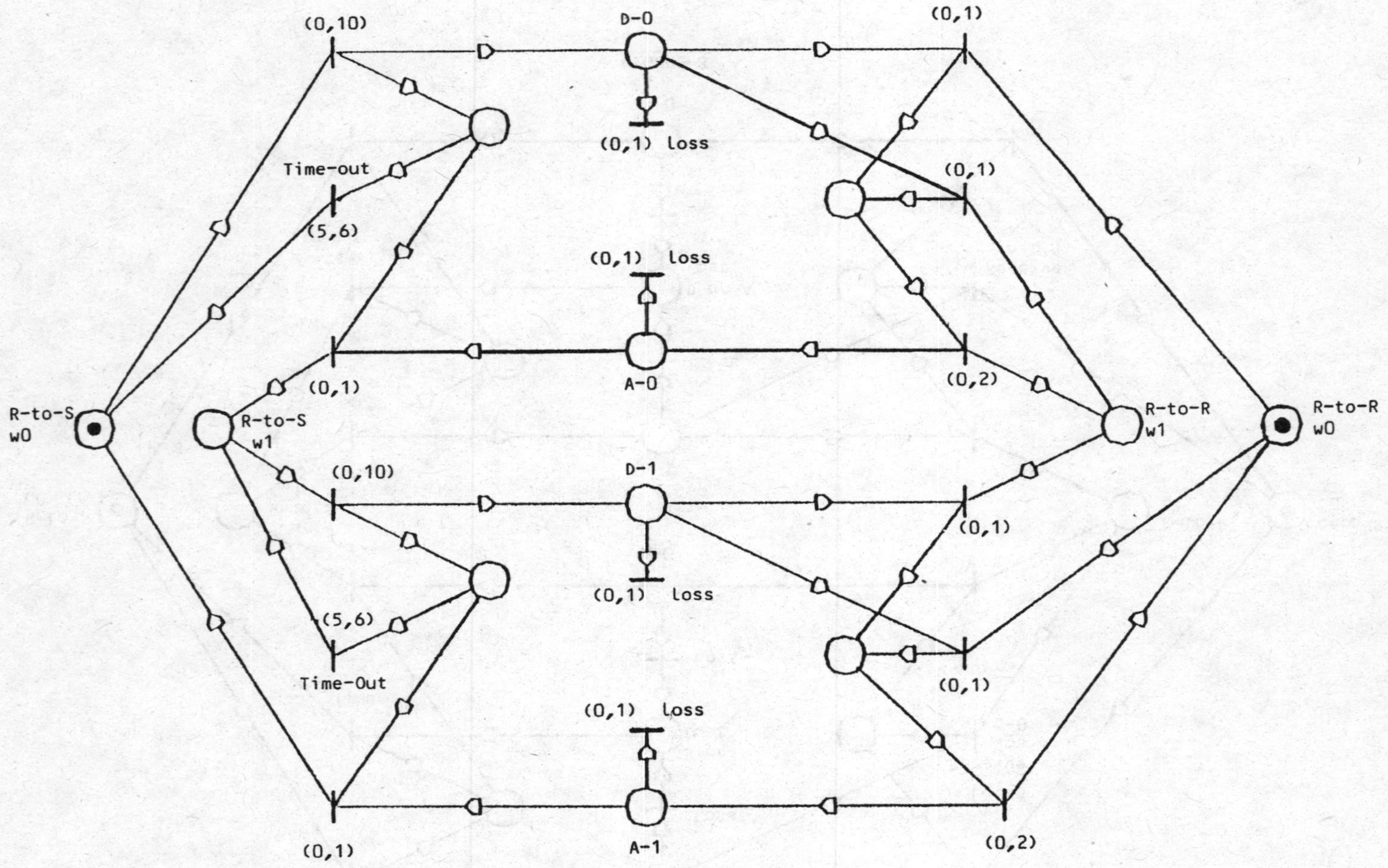
(0,10)
D-0
(0,1)
(0,1) loss
Time-out
(0,1)
(5,6)
(0,1) loss
(0,1)
A-0
(0,2)
R-to-S
w0
R-to-S
w1
R-to-R
w1
R-to-R
w0
(0,10)
D-1
(0,1)
(0,1) loss
(5,6)
Time-Out
(0,1)
(0,1) loss
(0,1)
A-1
(0,2)

FIGURE 9

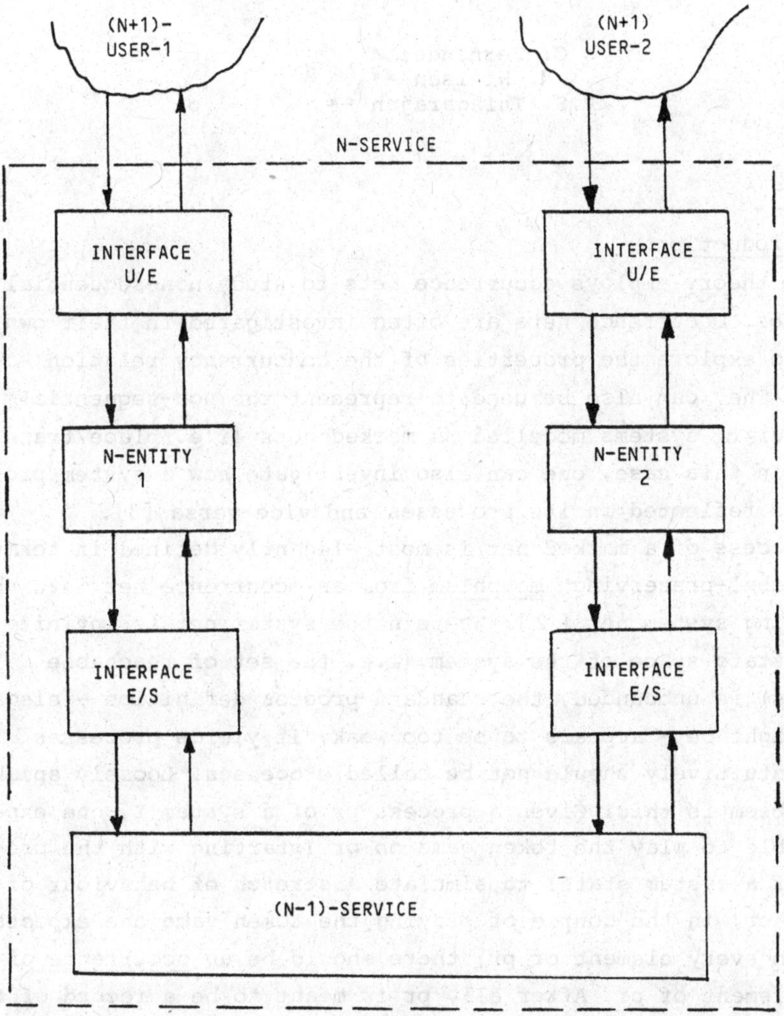
(N+1)-
USER-1
(N+1)
USER-2
N-SERVICE
INTERFACE
U/E
INTERFACE
U/E
N-ENTITY
1
N-ENTITY
2
INTERFACE
E/S
INTERFACE
E/S
(N-1)-SERVICE

FIGURE 10

A NOTE ON OBSERVABLE OCCURRENCE NETS

C. Fernandez *
M. Nielsen **
P.S. Thiagarajan **

0. Introduction

Net theory employs occurrence nets to study non-sequential processes. Occurrence nets are often investigated in their own right to explore the properties of the concurrency relation [1, 4]. They can also be used to represent the non-sequential behaviours of systems modelled as marked nets (i.e. place/transition nets). In this case, one can also investigate how a system property is reflected in its processes and vice-versa [3].

A process of a marked net is most elegantly defined in terms of a 'label-preserving' morphism from an occurrence net into the underlying system net [2]. Wherein the system net is infinite or the state space of the system (i.e. the set of reachable markings) is unbounded, the standard process definition - elegant as it might be - appears to be too weak; it yields processes which intuitively should not be called processes. Loosely speaking, the problem is this: Given a process pr of a system Σ, one expects to be able to play the token game on pr (starting with the pre-image of a system state) to simulate a stretch of behaviour of Σ. Further, in the course of playing the token game one expects to reach every element of pr; there should be an occurrence of every element of pr. After all, pr is meant to be a record of the condition-holdings and event-occurrences in Σ. Well, the standard process definition in general yields processes for which this is not the case. Below we show, without any additional explanation, an example to illustrate the difficulty. Actually the problem was first identified by Goltz and Reisig [3] at the level of place/transition nets.

---

* GMD, St. Augustin, W. Germany
** Computer Science Department, Aarhus University, Denmark

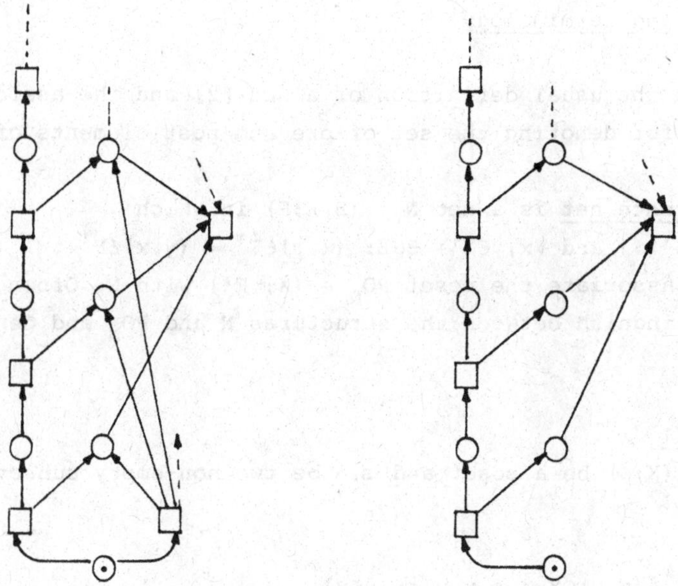

A C/E system Σ   A process of Σ!

Figure 1.

One way to get around this problem would be to restrict the domain of process morphisms. The aim of this paper is to offer one such restriction and characterise the resulting sub-class of occurrence nets. We introduce the notion of 'full state space' and study those occurrence nets that have full state spaces.

We show the slightly surprising result that our notion is equivalent to the notion of observability due to Winskel [5]. Our second result is motivated by a suggestion made in [3]. There it is suggested that one should restrict the domain of process morphisms to those occurrence nets that can be 'built up' using <u>finite</u> occurrence nets. We show that occurrence nets that have full state spaces are precisely those that can be built up using - not necessarily finite but - <u>chain-bounded</u> occurrence nets.

In the next section we introduce the required notations and terminology. The two succeeding sections contain the two characterisations of the sub-class of occurrence nets identified in the paper. The concluding section contains a more detailed review of related work.

1. Notations and terminology

We assume the usual definition of a net [2] and the associated dot notation for denoting the set of pre and post elements of a net element.

An occurrence net is a net $N = (B,E;F)$ in which $\forall b \in B: |{}^{\bullet}b|, |b^{\bullet}| \leq 1$ and $\forall x,y \in X = B \cup E: (x,y) \in F^+ \Rightarrow (y,x) \notin F^+$. Hence we can associate the poset $PO_N = (X; F^*)$ with N. Often we will not distinguish between the structures N and PO_N and denote F^* as $\leq$.

Definition 1.1

Let $PO = (X;\leq)$ be a poset and s,l be two non-empty subsets of X. Then

a) $li = \{(x,y) \in X \times X \mid x \leq y \text{ or } y \leq x\}$.

b) l is a chain (li-set) iff $\forall x,y \in l$: x li y. $|l|$ is the length of l.

c) $co = \{(x,y) \in X \times X \mid x \not< y \text{ and } y \not< x\}$.

d) s is a co-set iff $\forall x,y \in s$: x co y.

e) s is a slice iff s is a maximal co-set.

f) The set of slices of PO is denoted as SL_{PO} or just SL, where PO is clear from the context.

g) $\uparrow s = \{y \in X \mid \exists x \in s \text{ with } x \leq y\}$.

h) $\downarrow s = \{y \in X \mid \exists x \in s \text{ with } y \leq x\}$.

i) If $s = \{x\}$ is a singleton then we write $\uparrow x$ ($\downarrow x$) instead of $\uparrow\{x\}$ ($\downarrow\{x\}$) .

□

Next we consider the state space generated by a slice of an occurrence net. Let s be a slice of the occurrence net $N = (B,E;F)$. Then $act(s) = \{x \in s \mid x^{\bullet} \neq \emptyset \wedge {}^{\bullet}(x^{\bullet}) \subseteq s\}$. For $s_1, s_2 \in SL$, $s_1 \rightarrow s_2$ iff $\exists X' \subseteq act(s_1)$ such that $s_2 = (s_1 \setminus X') \cup (X')^{\bullet}$. Clearly for the slice s and $X' \subseteq act(s)$, $(s \setminus X') \cup (X')^{\bullet}$ is also a slice (see [6]).

Now let $\sigma = s_0, s_1, \ldots, s_n$ be a sequence of slices. Then σ is a permissable sequence iff for $0 \leq i < n$, either $s_i \rightarrow s_{i+1}$ or $s_{i+1} \rightarrow s_i$.

Definition 1.2

Let $N = (B,E;F)$ be an occurrence net, $s \in SL$ and $SL' \subseteq SL$. Then,

a) $[s]$, the state space generated by s is the least sub-set of SL given by

a1) $s \in [s]$

a2) If $s' \in [s]$ and $s'' \in SL$ such that $s' \rightarrow s''$ or $s'' \rightarrow s'$ then $s'' \in [s]$.

b) SL' is a state space of N iff for some slice s', $SL' = [s']$.

c) The state space SL' is a full state space of N iff $X = \bigcup\{s' \mid s' \in SL'\}$. □

Note that the $\rightarrow$-relation captures the "obvious" token game one can play on an occurrence net. If [s] is a full state space, then starting from s we can reach every element of N within a finite number (forwards and backwards) of steps (a permissable sequence).

Our first characterisation of occurrence nets that have full state spaces is in terms of observability. In what follows $\mathbb{N}$ is the set of non-negative integers and $\mathbb{Z}$ is the set of integers.

Definition 1.3

Let $N = (B,E;F)$ be an occurrence net and $O: X \rightarrow \mathbb{Z}$. Then O is said to be an observer for N iff $\forall x,y \in X: x<y \Rightarrow O(x)<O(y)$. N is said to be observable iff it has an observer.

□

Our second characterisation of occurrence nets that have full state spaces is in terms of chain-bounded convex subnets.

The net $N_1 = (B_1,E_1;F_1)$ is a <u>sub-net</u> of the net $N_2 = (B_2,E_2;F_2)$ iff $B_1 \subseteq B_2$, $E_1 \subseteq E_2$ and $F_1 = F_2 \mid X_1$ ($X_1 = B_1 \cup E_1$ and $X_2 = B_2 \cup E_2$). The occurrence net N_1 is a <u>convex sub-net</u> of the occurrence net N_2 iff N_1 is a sub-net of N_2 and

$$\forall x,y \in X_1 \ \forall z \in X_2: x \leq_2 z \leq_2 y \Rightarrow z \in X_1 \quad (\leq_2 = F_2^*).$$

Finally the occurrence net $N = (B,E;F)$ is <u>chain-bounded</u> iff there is an integer k such that for every chain $l \subseteq X$, $|l| \leq k$.

Nets can be summed up as follows. Let $\{N_i = (B_i,E_i;F_i) \mid i \geq 1\}$ be a set of nets. Then $\bigsqcup_{i\geq 1} N_i = (B',E';F')$ where

$$B' = \bigcup_{i\geq 1} B_i,\ E' = \bigcup_{i\geq 1} E_i \text{ and } F' = \bigcup_{i\geq 1} F_i.$$

We conclude this section with a minor but - as it will turn out - useful result.

First let us agree that $\mathbb{N}$ is augmented with the special element ∞ and the standard ordering over $\mathbb{N}$ is extended to $\mathbb{N} \cup \{\infty\}$ in the obvious way. Next we need the following.

<u>Definition 1.4</u>

Let s be a slice of the occurrence net $N = (B,E;F)$ and $x \in X$. Then,

$$d_F(x,s) = \begin{cases} \sup\{n \mid y \in s \ \wedge \ yF^n x\}, \text{ if } x \in \uparrow s \\ \sup\{n \mid y \in s \ \wedge \ xF^n y\}, \text{ if } x \in \downarrow s \end{cases}$$

□

Since s is a slice and F^0 is the identity relation over X by convention, we have that d_F is a well-defined mapping $X \times SL \to \mathbb{N} \cup \{\infty\}$.

<u>Proposition 1.5</u>

Let s be a slice of the occurrence net $N = (B,E;F)$. Then $[s]$ is a full state space of N iff $\forall x \in X: d_F(x,s) < \infty$.

Proof

⇒) It follows from the assumption that for every $x \in X$ there exists a permissable sequence $s = s_0, s_1, \ldots, s_k$ such that $x \in s_k$. Assume that $y\ F^n\ x$ for some $y \in s$ - we want to prove that $n \leq k$ (the proof for the case $x\ F^n\ y$ being completely symmetrical). So we have $y = x_0\, F\, x_1\, F\, x_2 \ldots F\, x_n = x$ for some x_i's in X. It follows from the definition of permissable sequences that each x_i belongs to some s_j. Assume $n>k$. Using the pidgeon hole principle gives you that at least two different x_i's belong to the same s_j - a contradiction to the fact that all s_j's are slices.

⇐) We want to prove the following

$\forall x \in X.\quad \exists s = s_0, s_1, \ldots, s_k$ permissable sequence such that $x \in s_k$.
The proof is by induction on $d_F(x,s) = n$.

n = 0 $\quad d_F(x,s) = 0$ implies $x \in s$ and the result follows immediately.

n > 0 $\quad$ We only consider the case $x \in \uparrow s$, the other - $(x \in \downarrow s)$ - being completely symmetrical.

Define $a \subseteq s$ by

$$a = \{y \in s \mid y\ F^n\ x\}$$

a is by definition a nonempty subset of s, and we claim that $a \subseteq act(s)$. Assume $y \in a$, and ${}^\bullet(y^\bullet) \not\subseteq s$. From the definition of occurrence nets $y \in B$, and there exists another B-element $y' \in {}^\bullet(y^\bullet)$ not in s

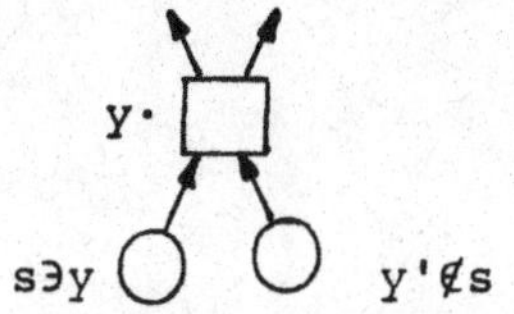

Since s is a slice, either $y' < z$ or $z < y'$ for some $z \in s$.

First possibility implies $y<z$ which contradicts s being a slice, and the second possibility implies $z\ F^m\ x$, $m>n$, which contradicts $d_F(x,s) = n$.

So, $a \subseteq act(s)$. Define $s_1 = (s \setminus a) \cup a^{\bullet}$. We then have $s \to s_1$, and $d(x,s_1)<n$. The result now follows from the induction hypothesis.

□

2. First characterisation of occurrence nets with full state spaces

The aim of this section is to prove that the class of occurrence nets with full state spaces coincides with the class of observable occurrence nets. This result is proved in the next three lemmas, but first we need the following definition.

Definition 2.1

Given an occurrence net with observer O and a slice, s, we say that <u>O is synchronized on s</u> iff $s = \{x \in X \mid O(x) = 0\}$.

□

Lemma 2.2

Let N be an occurence net with ([s] as) a full state space. Then N has an observer (which is synchronized on s).

Proof

Define $O: X \to \mathbb{Z}$ as follows

$$\forall x \in X . \quad O(x) = \begin{cases} d_F(x,s) & \text{if } x \in \uparrow s \\ -d_F(x,s) & \text{if } x \in \downarrow s \end{cases}$$

It follows from Prop. 1.5 that O is a well defined mapping. And it follows from the definition of d_F that O is an observer which is synchronized on s.

□

Lemma 2.3

Let N be an observable occurrence net. Then N has an observer which is synchronized on some slice of N.

Proof

Let O be an observer for N. We first modify O as follows. Define

$$\forall x \in X. \quad \eta(x) = \begin{cases} 2\times O(x) & \text{if } O(x) \geq 0 \\ 2\times O(x)+1 & \text{if } O(x) < 0 \end{cases}$$

It is clear that η is an observer for N, with the property that all positive values are even and all negative values odd. From this it follows that all sets

$$\{x \in X \mid |\eta(x)| = i\} \qquad i \geq 0$$

($|k|$ is the absolute value of the integer k) are co-sets. This property is used in the following.

Now define inductively

$$X_0 = \{x \in X \mid \eta(x) = 0\}$$

<u>i>0</u>: $X_i = \{x \in X \mid |\eta(x)| = i \text{ and } x \text{ co } X_j,\ 0 \leq j < i\}$ (x co X_j iff $\forall y \in X_j$: x co y)

We claim that $s = \bigcup_{i \geq 0} X_i$ is a slice. It is straightforward to see that s is a nonempty co-set. All we have to prove is that it is maximal. Assume $x \notin s$. For some i, $|\eta(x)| = i$ and $x \notin X_i$, which means that x li y for some $y \in X_j$, $j<i$ (and hence $y \in s$).

Now define

$$\tau(x) = \begin{cases} 0 & \text{if } x \in s \\ \eta(x) & \text{otherwise.} \end{cases}$$

We claim that τ is an observer - which is then obviously synchronized on s. So, let $x<y$. We know that $\eta(x)<\eta(y)$, and we want to prove that $\tau(x)<\tau(y)$.

This is obviously the case if $\eta(x) = \tau(x)$ and $\eta(y) = \tau(y)$. Both values $\tau(x)$ and $\tau(y)$ cannot be changed (to 0) since s is a slice and x<y. So, the following two cases represent all that "could go wrong".

$\tau(x) \neq \eta(x) < \eta(y) = \tau(y)$

If $\eta(y)$ is positive nothing can go wrong. Clearly $\eta(y) \neq 0$. Suppose $\eta(y) < 0$. Since $\eta(y) = \tau(y)$ we have (from construction) that $y<z$ for some $z \in X_j$, $0 \leq j < |\eta(y)|$. But then also $x<z$ which contradicts $\eta(x) \neq \tau(x)$ since $|\eta(y)|<|\eta(x)|$ in this case.

$\tau(x) = \eta(x) < \eta(y) \neq \tau(y)$

Once again we just have to consider $\eta(x) > 0$. Since $\eta(x) = \tau(x)$ we have (from construction) that $x>z$ for some $z \in X_j$, $0 \leq j < |\eta(x)|$. But then also $y>z$ which contradicts $\eta(y) \neq \tau(y)$ since $|\eta(x)| < |\eta(y)|$ in this case.

□

Lemma 2.4

Let N be an occurrence net with an observer which is synchronized on a slice s. Then [s] is a full state space.

Proof

Let O be an observer which is synchronized on s. It follows from definitions that

$$\forall x \in X. \quad d_F(x,s) \leq |O(x)|,$$

and the desired result follows immediately from Prop. 1.5.

□

To sum up, we have

Theorem 2.5

An occurrence net is observable iff it has a full state space.

□

3. Second characterisation of occurrence nets with full state space

Our next goal is to obtain another characterisation of the class of occurrence nets we are considering, namely that it is exactly the class of occurrence nets which can be approximated by chain-bounded occurrence nets in the following technical sense.

Definition 3.1

An occurrence net N is said to be approximated by $N_1, N_2, \ldots$ iff

1) Each N_i is a convex subnet of N_{i+1}

2) $\bigsqcup_{i \geq 1} N_i = N$

Lemma 3.2

Let N be an occurrence net which is approximated by a sequence of chain-bounded occurrence nets $N_1, N_2, \ldots$. Then N is observable.

Proof

Let us start by defining an observer for N_1. First, note that for any chain-bounded occurrence net N, the set of maximal elements, max_N, constitutes a slice, with the property that for all $x \in X$, $d_F(x, max_N) \leq k$, where k is the bound of all chain lengths.

Assume that all chain lengths of N_1 are bounded by k_1. Define

$$\forall x \in X_1 . \quad O_1(x) = k_1 - d_{F_1}(x, max_{N_1})$$

It is easy to verify that O_1 is an observer for N_1 with the property that $|O_1(x)| \leq k_1$ for all $x \in X_1$.

We now define observers for N_i inductively. Assume chain lengths in N_i are bounded by k_i. First we define a 'partial' observer, τ_i for N_i.

$$\forall i>1:\quad \forall x\in X_i.\quad \tau_i(x) = \begin{cases} O_{i-1}(x), & \text{if } x\in X_{i-1} \\ \sum_{j=1}^{i} k_j, & \text{if } x\in \max_{N_i} \setminus X_{i-1} \\ \text{undefined, otherwise} \end{cases}$$

Intuitively, O_{i-1} is just extended with some large value for possibly new maximal elements in X_i (part of the induction hypothesis is that $|O_{i-1}(x)| \leq \sum_{j=1}^{i-1} k_j$).

Now τ_i is extended to what will turn out to be a full observer for N_i.

$$\forall x\in X_i.\quad O_i(x) = \begin{cases} \tau_i(x), & \text{if } \tau_i(x) \text{ is defined} \\ \min\{\tau_i(y)-n \mid x\ F^n\ y,\ \tau_i(y) \text{ defined}\}, & \text{otherwise} \end{cases}$$

First of all it follows from the fact that $\max_{N_i}$ is a slice and that N_i is chain bounded that O_i is a well defined mapping $X_i \to \mathbb{Z}$. Furthermore, from the hypothesis that $|O_{i-1}(x)| \leq \sum_{j=1}^{i-1} k_j$ it follows that all values for O_i are numerically less than or equal to $\sum_{j=1}^{i} k_j$.

So all we have to prove is that $O_i(x)<O_i(y)$ for all $x,y\in X_i$ for which $x<y$.

If $\tau_i(x)$ is undefined the desired property follows immediately from definition. If $\tau_i(x)$ is defined then $x\in X_{i-1}$ and if also $y\in X_{i-1}$ the property follows for the fact that O_{i-1} is an observer for N_{i-1}. If $x\in X_{i-1}$ and $y\notin X_{i-1}$, then it follows from the fact that N_{i-1} is a convex subset of N_i that for no $z\in X_{i-1}$, $y\ F^n\ z$, and hence from definition $O_i(y) > \sum_{j=0}^{i-1} k_j$. But $x\in X_{i-1}$, and from the induction hypothesis we have that

$O_i(x) = O_{i-1}(x) \leq \sum_{j=1}^{i-1} k_j$, and so $O_i(x) < O_i(y)$.

Finally define $O: X \rightarrow \mathbb{Z}$ as

$$\forall x \in X. \quad O(x) = O_i(x) \text{ where } x \in X_i.$$

It is straightforward from the above to verify that O is an observer for N.

□

Lemma 3.3

Let N be an observable occurrence net. Then N is approximated by a sequence of chain-bounded occurrence nets.

Proof

It follows from Lemma 2.3 that there exists an observer O and a slice s for N such that O is synchronized on s. Furthermore, it is easy to see that we can assume without loss of generality that there exists at least one $x \in X$ such that $|O(x)| = 1$.

Now define inductively for $i \geq 1$

$$Y_i = \{y \in X \mid 0 < |O(y)| \leq i\}$$

$$Z_i = \{z \in s \mid \exists y \in Y_i.\ z \text{ li } y\}$$

$$X_i = Y_i \cup Z_i$$

$$N_i = (X_i \cap B,\ X_i \cap E,\ F|X_i).$$

We claim that the N_i's constitute an approximating sequence of chain-bounded occurrence nets. So, we have to prove

Claim 1 Each N_i is a chain-bounded occurrence net.
Claim 2 Each N_i is a convex subnet of N_{i+1}.
Claim 3 $\bigcup X_i = X$.

Proof of Claim 1

To see that N_i is an occurrence net is merely an observation. The only part which is not completely trivial is to verify that $dom(F_i) \cup codom(F_i) = X_i$. If $y \in Y_i$, then from definition there exists $z \in Z_i$ such that z li y, and hence there must exist an $x \in X_i$ such that $x F y$ if $O(y)>0$ or $y F x$ if $O(y)<0$. For $z \in Z_i$ the argument is similar.

The fact that N_i is chain-bounded follows immediately from the observation that all O-values on X_i are numerically bounded by i.

Proof of Claim 2

N_i is a subnet of N_{i+1} from definition, so all we have to prove is convexity. It is sufficient to prove that each N_i is a convex subnet of N.

So, assume $x,y \in X_i$ and $x<z<y$ for some $z \in X$. If $O(z) = 0$ then $z \in s$ and $z \in Z_i \subseteq X_i$ from definition. If $O(z) \neq 0$ then $|O(z)| < \max(|O(x)|, |O(y)|)$, and hence $z \in Y_i \subseteq X_i$.

Proof of Claim 3

We want to prove that each $x \in X$ is a member of some X_i. If $O(x) \neq 0$ then obviously $x \in Y_{|O(x)|} \subseteq X_{|O(x)|}$. If $O(x) = 0$, then $x \in s$, and since N is an occurrence net there exists a $y \in X$ such that either $x F y$ or $y F x$ and $O(y) \neq 0$. In both cases $x \in Z_{|O(y)|} \subseteq X_{|O(y)|}$.

□

To sum up, we now have from Theorem 2.5, Lemma 3.2 and Lemma 3.3

Theorem 3.4

The following are equivalent characterisations of a class of occurrence nets

1. N has a full state space.
2. N is observable.
3. N is approximated by chain-bounded occurrence nets.

□

Discussion

In the introduction we outlined our motivation for considering occurrence nets with full state space.

Our first characterisation result states the equivalence of this net-theoretic notion and the more mathematical notion of observability due to Winskel [5]. Winskel already considered the relationship between observability and a concept termed b-discreteness in net theory.

Definition

An occurrence net N is said to be b-discrete iff for every $x,y \in X$ there exists a natural number $d_{x,y}$ such that the length of any chain from x to y is bounded by $d_{x,y}$.

□

Theorem (Winskel)

1) All observable occurrence nets are b-discrete.
2) There exist b-discrete occurrence nets which are not observable.
3) All countable, b-discrete occurrence nets are observable.

□

Now, it turns out that there is a nice characterisation in terms of state spaces of all b-discrete occurrence nets. We shall merely state the result here. The proof will appear elsewhere.

Theorem

An occurrence net is b-discrete iff any finite subset of X is covered by some state space ([s] covers $X' \subseteq X$ iff $X' \subseteq \bigcup\{s' \mid s' \in [s]\}$).

□

From these two results, we get the following "compactness" result as a corollary.

Corollary

Let N be a countable occurrence net. Then

any subset of X is covered by a state space

$\Updownarrow$

any finite subset of X is covered by a state space.

This is not true for any (noncountable) occurrence net.

□

Now turning to the other characterisation result, Goltz and Reisig [3] made the proposal that one should consider only those occurrence nets that can be built up by using finite occurrence nets. In building they start with an initial marking of a finite marked net, and build up only forward processes, and this way of building agrees completely with ours. The main difference is, of course, that we use (in our characterisation result) chain-bounded nets as building blocks, rather than finite nets. One might ask what kind of nets one gets using the more restricted finite nets as building blocks. One answer is given in the following theorem, whose proof will also appear elsewhere.

Definition

An occurrence net is said to be interval-finite iff

$$\forall x,y \in X. \quad \{z \in X \mid x<z<y\} \text{ is finite.}$$

□

Theorem

An occurrence net is approximated by finite occurrence nets iff it is countable and interval-finite.

□

[1] C. Fernandez and P.S. Thiagarajan: D-continuous Causal Nets: A Model of Non-Sequential Processes. TCS 28 (1984), 171-196.

[2] H.J. Genrich and E. Stankiewicz-Wiechno: A Dictionary of Some Basic Notions of Net Theory. Lecture Notes in Computer Science, Vol. 84, Springer-Verlag, Berlin, Heidelberg, New York (1980), 519-531.

[3] U. Goltz and W. Reisig: The Non-Sequential Behaviour of Petri Nets To appear in Information and Control.

[4] C.A. Petri: Concurrency. Lecture Notes in Computer Science, Vol. 84, Springer-Verlag, Berlin, Heidelberg, New York (1980), 251-261.

[5] G. Winskel: Events in Computation. Ph.D. Thesis, University of Edinburgh, Edinburgh, Great Britain (1980).

[6] C. Fernández and P.S. Thiagarajan: A Lattice Theoretic View of K-Density. Arbeitspapiere der GMD Nr. 76 (1983). GMD-F1, 5205 St. Augustin 1, Postfach 1240, W. Germany.

A LATTICE THEORETIC VIEW OF K-DENSITY

C. Fernández and P.S. Thiagarajan
Gesellschaft für Mathematik und Datenverarbeitung
Postfach 1240, Schloß Birlinghoven, 5205 St. Augustin 1, W. Germany

0. Introduction

A variety of properties of non-sequential processes can be formulated and studied using occurrence nets as evidenced in the literature [6,1, 7,3,2]. As is known, an occurrence net is basically a partially ordered set of condition holdings and event occurrences. Thus a poset can be associated with an occurrence net in an obvious way. The maximal chains of such a poset - called lines - represent the life histories of the sequential components participating in the process; the maximal anti-chains - called slices - correspond to "time points" or the distributed states of the process.

Our first aim here is to study the structure of the set of slices of an occurrence net. We show that the slices under the obvious ordering form a lattice which is "almost" a complete lattice. "Almost" in the sense, the lattice might, at worst, lack a least or greatest element.

Our next aim is to determine how the various density properties that have been defined for processes are reflected in the corresponding lattices of slices. In this paper we concentrate on just one of these density properties, namely K-density. This property captures the intuitive demand that in every distributed state of the process, every sequential component taking part in this process should be in a well-defined state. The main result of the paper is that an occurrence net is K-dense iff the associated lattice of slices does not have any "dense" elements. To be honest, our result holds only for a sub-class of occurrence nets. However, through an example we shall try to convince the reader that one can not hope to do very much better.

In the next section three standard orderings that can be imposed over the subsets of a poset are first mentioned. It turns out however that all the three orderings collapse together when one starts to deal with slices. Section 2 contains the result that the set of slices of an occurrence net is - more or less - a complete lattice. Comparable results in this direction have been obtained by A.W. Holt et al. [4] and J. Winkowski [8]. What is new here is that our result applies to all occurrence nets. More importantly our proof idea let us construct slices which have certain desired properties.

In section 3 we consider well-founded occurrence nets in which each event has a finite number of pre- and post-conditions. We characterise the K-density of such nets in terms of the associated lattice of slices. We impose well-foundedness basically (though not quite) for convenience. The finiteness restriction however is crucial as brought out through an example. The last section presents a more elaborate motivation of the work initiated in this paper.

1. Orderings Associated with a Poset

First we shall put down, without any explanations some definitions. Unexplained terms and notations are defined in [3].

An <u>occurrence net</u> is a net $N = (B,E;F)$ in which:

1) $\forall b \in B : |{}^{\cdot}b|, |b^{\cdot}| \leq 1$
2) $\forall x,y \in B \cup E : (x,y) \in F^{+} \Rightarrow (y,x) \notin F^{+}$

$X = B \cup E$ is the set of elements of N; $\leq = F^{*}$, the associated (partial) ordering relation; $PO_N = (X;\leq)$ is the associated poset. Where N is clear from the context we write PO instead of PO_N. We shall often, for convenience, not distinguish between the structures N and PO_N.

<u>Definition 1.1</u> Let $PO = (X;\leq)$ be a poset, l and s be two <u>non-empty</u> subsets of X.

a) $li = \{(x,y) \in X \times X \mid x \leq y \text{ or } y < x\}$
b) l is a <u>li-set</u> iff $\forall x,y \in l$: x li y.
c) l is a <u>line</u> iff l is a maximal li-set.
d) The set of lines of PO is denoted by L_{PO} (or a simply L, when PO is clear from the context).
e) $co = \{(x,y) \in X \times X \mid x \nleq y \text{ and } y \nleq x\}$.
f) s is a <u>co-set</u> iff $\forall x,y \in s$: x co y.
g) s is a <u>slice</u> iff it is a maximal co-set.

h) The set of slices of PO is denoted by SL_{PO} (or as simply SL when PO is clear from the context).

In what follows we assume the axiom of choice. This will enable us to extend, whenever necessary, a li-set to a line and a co-set to a slice.

Definition 1.2 Let PO = $(X;\leq)$ be a poset and $X_1, X_2 \subseteq X$. Then:

a) $X_1 \sqsubseteq_1 X_2$ iff $\forall x \in X_1\ \exists y \in X_2$ such that $x \leq y$

b) $X_1 \sqsubseteq_2 X_2$ iff $\forall y \in X_2\ \exists x \in X_1$ such that $x \leq y$

c) $X_1 \sqsubseteq_3 X_2$ iff $X_1 \sqsubseteq_1 X_2$ and $X_1 \sqsubseteq_2 X_2$.

$\sqsubseteq_1$ is the Egli-ordering; $\sqsubseteq_2$, the Milner-ordering and $\sqsubseteq_3$ is the Egli-Milner ordering. A related, and for our purposes very useful, idea is:

Let PO = $(X;\leq)$ be a poset and $X_1 \subseteq X$. Then $\downarrow X_1 = \{x \in X \mid \exists y \in X_1: x \leq y\}$ and $\uparrow X_1 = \{x \in X \mid \exists y \in X_1: y \leq x\}$. X_1 is a lower set iff $\downarrow X_1 = X_1$ and X_1 is an upper set iff $\uparrow X_1 = X_1$. We note that if s is a slice of PO, then $Max(\downarrow s) = s = Min(\uparrow s)$. We first observe:

Proposition 1.1 Let PO = $(X;\leq)$ be a poset and $X_1, X_2 \subseteq X$. Then:

a) $X_1 \sqsubseteq_1 X_2$ iff $\downarrow X_1 \subseteq \downarrow X_2$

b) $X_1 \sqsubseteq_2 X_2$ iff $\uparrow X_2 \subseteq \uparrow X_1$

Proof. Trivial. □

A less trivial observation is:

Proposition 1.2 Let PO = $(X;\leq)$ be a poset and s_1, s_2 two slices of PO. Then: $s_1 \sqsubseteq_1 s_2$ iff $s_1 \sqsubseteq_2 s_2$ iff $s_1 \sqsubseteq_3 s_2$.

Proof: Assume $s_1 \sqsubseteq_1 s_2$. To show $s_1 \sqsubseteq_2 s_2$, let $x \in s_2$. If $x \in s_1$ we are done. If not, s_1 being a maximal co-set, we can find $y \in s_1$ such that y li x. Since $s_1 \sqsubseteq_1 s_2$, for some $x' \in s_2$ we must have $y \leq x'$. Now $x < y$ would lead to the contradiction $x < x'$ (because we know that x co x'). Thus $y < x$. The rest of the proof is routine and we omit it. □

Thus in dealing with the slices of an occurrence net, we can - and shall - collapse the three ordering relations $\sqsubseteq_1$, $\sqsubseteq_2$, and $\sqsubseteq_3$ into the single relation $\sqsubseteq$.

2. The Lattice of Slices of an Occurrence Net

The title of this section is justified by our first result.

Theorem 2.1 Let $N = (B,E;F)$ be an occurrence net. Then $(SL;\sqsubseteq)$ is a lattice.

Before proving this result it will be convenient to prove a lemma.

Lemma 2.2 Let $N = (B,E;F)$ be an occurrence net, $SL' \subseteq SL$, $A_1 = \cap\{{\downarrow}s' \mid s' \in SL'\}$ and $A_2 = \cup\{{\downarrow}s' \mid s' \in SL'\}$.

a) Let $x \in A_1$ and $y \in \bar{A}_1 = X - A_1$ such that $x < y$. Then $\exists z \in Max(A_1)$ such that $x \leq z < y$.

b) Let $x \in A_2$ and $y \in \bar{A}_2 = X - A_2$ such that $x < y$. Then $\exists z \in Max(A_2)$ such that $x \leq z < y$.

Proof. To prove a), we first construct a finite sequence of the form $u_0, u_1, \ldots, u_n$ such that $x = u_0$, $u_n = y$ and for $0 \leq i < n$, $(u_i, u_{i+1}) \in F$. Let $j \in \{0,1,\ldots,n-1\}$ be such that $u_j \in A_1$ and $u_{j+1} \in \bar{A}_1$. We claim that $u_j \in Max(A_1)$.
If not, $\exists u \in A_1$ with $u_j < u$. It is now easy to verify that $u_j \in E$ and $u_{j+1} \in B$. Let $s' \in SL'$ such that $u_{j+1} \notin {\downarrow}s'$. Then $\exists u' \in s'$ such that $u' < u_{j+1}$. But this implies that $u' \leq u_j < u$. This is a contradiction because $u \in {\downarrow}s'$ (note $u \in A_1$) and $Max({\downarrow}s') = s'$. Thus $u_j \in Max(A_1)$ and we have at once $x \leq u_j < y$.
The proof of b) is symmetric and we omit it. □

<u>Proof of theorem 2.1</u> Let $s_1, s_2 \in SL$ and $A_1 = (\downarrow s_1) \cap (\downarrow s_2)$. We shall first show that $s_1 \sqcap s_2$, the greatest lower bound of $\{s_1,s_2\}$ is $Max(A_1)$.

To this end, we first note that $A_1 \neq \emptyset$. Secondly if $A_1 = X$, then $s_1 = s_2$ so that $s_1 \sqcap s_2 = s_1 = Max(A_1)$. So assume that $A_1 \neq X$. Then $\exists y \in \bar{A}_1 = X - A_1$ and hence $y \notin \downarrow s_1$ or $y \notin \downarrow s_2$. Without loss of generality, assume that $y \notin s_1$. Then $\exists x_1 \in s_1$ such that $x_1 < y$. If $x_1 \in A_1$ then by lemma 2.2, we have at once that $Max(A_1) \neq \emptyset$.

But then $x_1 \notin A_1$ implies that $x_1 \notin \downarrow s_2$ so that for some $x \in s_2$, $x < x_1$. Clearly $x \in A_1$ and again by lemma 2.2, we have $Max(A_1) \neq \emptyset$.

At this stage we have that $Max(A_1) = s$ is a co-set.

To see that s is a slice first consider $x \in A_1$. Then there exists $y_1 \in s_1$ such that $x \leq y_1$. If $y_1 \notin A_1$ then by lemma 2.2, for some $y \in s$, $x \leq y$. If $y_1 \in A_1$, then for some $y_2 \in \downarrow s_2$, $y_1 \leq y_2$ so that $x \leq y_2$. Clearly $y_2 \in Max(A_1) = s$. So that for every $x \in A_1$, $\exists y \in s$ such that $x \leq y$.

Now consider $y \in \bar{A}_1$. Let $x_1 \in s_1$ such that $x_1 < y$. If $x_1 \in A_1$ then by lemma 2.2, $\exists z \in s$ such that $z < y$. If $x_1 \notin A_1$ then for some $x_2 \in s_2$, $x_2 < x_1$ so that $x_2 < y$. It is routine to check that $x_2 \in s = Max(A_1)$. Hence s is indeed a slice.

Since $\downarrow s \subseteq \downarrow s_1$ and $\downarrow s \subseteq \downarrow s_2$ we at once have that s is a lower bound of $\{s_1,s_2\}$.

Now suppose that s' is also a lower bound of $\{s_1,s_2\}$. Let $x \in s'$. We need to show that for some $y \in s$, $x \leq y$. If $x \in s$ we are done at once. If not for some $y \in s$, x li y. If $x > y$, then $x \notin A_1$. But this implies that $\downarrow s' \nsubseteq \downarrow s_1$ or $\downarrow s' \nsubseteq \downarrow s_2$ which contradicts the assumption that s' is also a lower bound of $\{s_1,s_2\}$. Thus indeed s is the greatest lower bound of $\{s_1,s_2\}$.

If we consider now $A_2 = (\downarrow s_1) \cup (\downarrow s_2)$, then the proof of the fact that $Max(A_2)$ is the least upper bound of $\{s_1,s_2\}$ is completely symmetric and we shall omit it. □

Theorem 2.1 can be strengthened considerably as follows:

<u>Theorem 2.3</u> Let $N = (B,E;F)$ be an occurrence net and $\emptyset \neq SL' \subseteq SL$. Then:

a) If SL' has a lower bound in SL then $\sqcap SL'$, the greatest lower bound of SL' exists and is given by

$$\sqcap SL' = Max[\cap\{\downarrow s' \mid s' \in SL'\}]$$

b) If SL' has an upper bound in SL then $\bigsqcup$ SL', the least upper bound of SL' exists and is given by
$\bigsqcup SL' = Max[\cup\{\downarrow s' | s' \in SL'\}]$

<u>Proof.</u> To prove a), let $A_1 = \cap\{\downarrow s' | s' \in SL'\}$ and let $\hat{s}$ be a lower bound of SL', i.e. $\forall s' \in SL'$: $\hat{s} \sqsubseteq s'$. Since $SL' \neq \emptyset$, $A_1 \neq \emptyset$. If $A_1 = X$ then $\forall s' \in SL'$: $\downarrow s' = X$ so that $SL' = \{s'\}$ where $s' = Max(X) \in SL$. Clearly $\bigsqcap\{s'\} = s' = Max(A_1)$. So assume that $A_1 \neq X$. We first show that $Max(A_1) \neq \emptyset$.
Now let $y \in \bar{A}_1 = X - A_1$. Then, because $\hat{s}$ is a slice, $\exists x \in \hat{s}$ with $x < y$. By lemma 2.2, $\exists z \in Max(A_1)$ with $x \leq z < y$. Thus $s = Max(A_1)$ is a co-set.
To show that s is a slice, consider $x \in A_1$ and $s' \in SL'$. Then $x \in \downarrow s'$ so that for some $y \in s'$, $x \leq y$. If $y \in \bar{A}_1$, then $x < y$ and by lemma 2.2 we have that for some $z \in s$, $x \leq z$. So assume that $y \in A_1$. We claim that $y \in s = Max(A_1)$.
If not, $\exists y' \in A_1$ such that $y < y'$. But clearly $y < y'$ and $y \in s'$ implies that $y' \notin \downarrow s'$ so that $y' \notin A_1$, a contradiction.
So indeed $y \in s$. Thus at this stage we have that $\forall x \in A_1$: $\exists y \in s$ such that $x \leq y$.
Now consider $x \in \bar{A}_1$. Then for some $y \in \hat{s}$, the given lower bound of SL', $y < x$(note that $\downarrow\hat{s} \subseteq A_1$). Once more, by lemma 2.2, $\exists z \in s$ such that $z < x$. Thus indeed s is a slice.
That s is a lower bound of SL' is trivial.
Let $\tilde{s}$ be also a lower bound of SL' and $x \in \tilde{s}$. We must show that for some $y \in s$, $x \leq y$. If $x \in s$ we are done at once. So assume that $x \notin s$ so that for some $y \in s$, x li y.
Suppose that $x > y$. Since $y \in s = Max(A_1)$, we then have $x \in \bar{A}_1$. Thus for some $s' \in SL'$: $x \notin \downarrow s'$. But this at once implies that $\tilde{s}$ is <u>not</u> a lower bound of SL', a contradiction. Hence s is the greatest lower bound of SL'.
The proof of b) is similar and hence we omit it. □

As a consequence, the lattice of slices of an occurrence net can fail to be a complete lattice only due to the absence of a maximum or minimum element. Formally,

<u>Corollary 2.4</u> Let N = (B,E;F) be an occurrence net. Then (SL;$\sqsubseteq$), the associated lattice of slices is complete iff SL has a greatest and least element.

<u>Proof.</u> Follows easily from theorem 2.3. □

Anticipating the contents of the next section we shall conclude by introducing the notion of well-foundedness.

<u>Definition 2.1</u> Let N = (B,E;F) be an occurrence net. N is said to be <u>well-founded</u> iff $\forall l \in L : l \cap Min(X) \neq \emptyset$.

A well-founded occurrence net is a convenient object to work with. This will become clear in the next section. Now we shall content ourselves with the following observation.

<u>Proposition 2.5</u> Let N = (B,E;F) be a well-founded occurrence net and (SL;$\sqsubseteq$) the associated lattice of slices. Then $\bot = Min(X)$ is the least element of SL (under $\sqsubseteq$).

<u>Proof.</u> Follows easily from the definitions. □

As done in the statement of prop. 2.5, from now on we shall let $\bot_N$ denote the least slice of the well-founded occurrence net N. As usual we write $\bot$ instead of $\bot_N$ whenever N is clear from the context.

3. A Characterisation of K-density

To start with we recall the notion of K-density and the related notion of discreteness.

The poset PO = (X;≤) is <u>K-dense</u> iff for every line l and every slice s of PO, $l \cap s \neq \emptyset$. Let $x,y \in X$, then $[x,y] = \{z \in X | x \leq z \leq y\}$. Let $x,y \in X$ and l be a line. Then $[x,y;l] = [x,y] \cap l$. PO is <u>discrete</u> iff

$\forall x,y \in X$, $\forall l \in L$, the set of lines of PO, $|[x,y;l]| < \infty$. The relationship between K-density and discreteness for occurrence nets is that:

Theorem 3.1 Let N = (B,E;F) be an occurrence net. If N is K-dense (i.e. PO is K-dense) then N is also discrete.

Proof. See [1]. □

Our characterisation of K-density works only for occurrence nets of finite degree. We say that the occurrence net N = (B,E;F) is of *finite degree* iff $\forall e \in E : |{}^{\bullet}e|, |e^{\bullet}| < \infty$. We can now introduce the key idea of this section.

Definition 3.1 Let PO = (SL;$\sqsubseteq$) be a poset and $s \in SL$. The ordering relation $\sqsubseteq$ is said to be *dense below* s iff
$\forall s' \in SL : s' \sqsubset s \Rightarrow \exists s'' \in SL : s' \sqsubset s'' \sqsubset s$.

For occurrence nets, two related ideas are:

Definition 3.2 Let N = (B,E;F) be an occurrence net, (SL; $\sqsubseteq$) the associated lattice of slices and $s, s' \in SL$. Then:

a) $s' \sqsubset\!\!\cdot\; s$ iff $s' \sqsubset s$ and $\forall s'' \in SL$: $s' \sqsubseteq s'' \sqsubseteq s \Rightarrow s' = s''$ or $s'' = s$.
b) $act(s) := \{x \in s \mid {}^{\bullet}x \neq \emptyset \wedge ({}^{\bullet}x)^{\bullet} \subseteq s\}$.

Two simple but useful observations are:

Proposition 3.2 Let N = (B,E;F) be an occurrence net and $s \in SL$. Then:

a) $\forall e \in E : {}^{\bullet}e \neq \emptyset$ and $e \in s \Rightarrow e \in act(s)$
b) If $X_1 \subseteq act(s)$, then $[s - ({}^{\bullet}X_1)^{\bullet}] \cup {}^{\bullet}X_1$ is also a slice.

Proof. Follows easily from the definitions. □

<u>Proposition 3.3</u> Let $N = (B,E;F)$ be an occurrence net and $(SL;\sqsubseteq)$ the associated lattice of slices. Let $s \in SL$ be such that $s \neq \bot$ where $\bot$ is the least element of SL, if it exists. Then the following statements are equivalent:

a) $\sqsubseteq$ is dense below s.

b) $\{s' \in SL \mid s' \sqsubset\!\cdot\, s\} = \emptyset$.

c) $act(s) = \emptyset$.

<u>Proof.</u> Follows at once from prop. 3.2 and the definitions. □

One half of our main result is:

<u>Theorem 3.4</u> Let $N = (B,E;F)$ be an occurrence net, $(SL;\sqsubseteq)$ the associated lattice of slices and $\bot$, the least element of SL if it exists. If N is K-dense then $\forall s \in SL$: $s \neq \bot \Rightarrow \sqsubseteq$ is <u>not</u> dense below s.

<u>Proof.</u> (Indirect) Assume $s \neq \bot$ is a slice below which $\sqsubseteq$ is dense. By prop. 3.3, $act(s) = \emptyset$. Hence by prop. 3.2, $[s - Min(X)] \cap E = \emptyset$. Clearly $s - Min(X) \neq \emptyset$ because $s \neq \bot$ so we can pick $b^0 \in s - Min(X) \subseteq B$. Then for some $e_0 \in E$, ${}^\bullet b^0 = \{e_0\}$. We first note that $|e_0{}^\bullet| > 1$. Otherwise $({}^\bullet b^0)^\bullet \subseteq s$ which implies $b^0 \in act(s)$ and this contradicts the hypothesis $act(s) = \emptyset$. If $e_0^\bullet \subseteq s$ then we would once again have the contradiction $b^0 \in act(s)$. Hence we can pick $b_0 \in e_0^\bullet$ such that $b_0 \notin s$ so that $b_0 \neq b^0$ (see fig. 1)

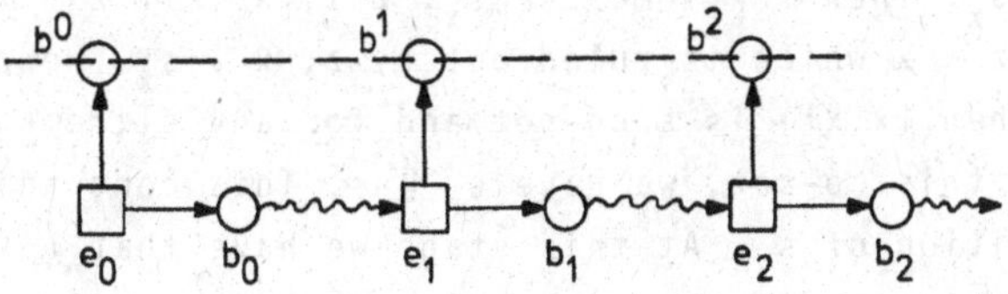

Fig.1

Now $b_0 \notin s$ implies that for some $b^1 \in s - Min(X)$, b_0 li b^1. If $b^1 < b_0$ then $b^1 < b^0$ which is impossible because $b^1, b^0 \in s$. Hence $b^0 < b^1$. Now we can apply to b^1 the argument presented above for b^0 to find $e_1 \in {}^{\cdot}b^1$ and $b_1 \in e_1^{\cdot} - s$. Iterating this argument, we can construct the infinite set $A = \{e_0, b_0, e_1, b_1, \ldots,\}$ which satisfies: $\forall i \in \mathbb{N}$: $e_i < b_i < e_{i+1}$, $e_i, b_i \notin s$ and $b^i \in (e_i)^{\cdot} \cap s$. A is a li-set and we can pick $l \in L$ such that $A \subseteq l$. If $l \cap s = \emptyset$ we at once have that N is not K-dense and we are done. So assume that $x \in l \cap s$. Then $\forall i \geq 0$, $x > e_i$ because $x \leq e_i$ would imply $x < b^i$ and we know that x co b^i. But then $x > e_i$ for every $i \geq 0$ implies that $|[e_0, x; l]| = \infty$. Thus N is not discrete from which it follows (theorem 3.1) that N is not K-dense either. □

The converse of the above result is true only for occurrence nets of finite degree. We will present an example to justify this claim towards the end of this section. For now, we shall show that the converse of theorem 3.4 is indeed true for well-founded occurrence nets of finite degree.

Before proceeding to the main proof we shall adopt a notation and establish a lemma. Let N = (B,E;F) be a well-founded occurrence net and $x \in X$. Then s_x denotes the least slice containing x. In other words, $s_x = \sqcap \{s \in SL \mid x \in s\}$

<u>Lemma 3.5</u> Let N = (B,E;F) be a well-founded occurrence net and $x, y \in X$. Then:

a) $act(s_x) = ({}^{\cdot}x)^{\cdot}$

b) $x \leq y \Rightarrow s_x \sqsubseteq s_y$.

<u>Proof.</u> a) If ${}^{\cdot}x = \emptyset$ then $\emptyset^{\cdot} = \emptyset \subseteq act(s_x)$. So assume that ${}^{\cdot}x \neq \emptyset$. If $x \in E$ then by prop. 3.2, $({}^{\cdot}x)^{\cdot} = \{x\} \subseteq act(s_x)$. Suppose that $x \in B$, ${}^{\cdot}x = \{e\}$ and for some $x' \in e^{\cdot}$ with $x \neq x'$, we have $x' \notin s_x$. Then for some $z \in s_x$, z li x'. If $z < x'$ we would have $z < x$ which is ruled out by $z, x \in s_x$. Hence $z > x'$. But then $\{x, x'\}$ is a co-set and for any slice s which contains this co-set, we have $s_x \not\sqsubseteq s$. This contradicts the definition of s_x. At this stage we have that $({}^{\cdot}x)^{\cdot} \subseteq act(s_x)$. The inclusion in the other direction is easily obtained by appealing to the definition of s_x.

b) We observe that $\forall x' \in s_x - \mathrm{Min}(X)$ if $x' \neq x$ then $x' \in B$ and moreover $e' < x$ where $^{\cdot}x' = \{e'\}$. This follows from part a). Now assume $x \leq y$ and that $z \in s_y$. We will have to show that for some $z' \in s_x$, $z' \leq z$. If $z \in s_x$ we are done at once. So suppose that $z \notin s_x$. Then for some $z' \in s_x$, z' li z. We claim that $z' < z$. If not, $z < z'$. Then $z' \in s_x - \mathrm{Min}(X)$ so that by the observation that we started with, $z \leq e'$ where $^{\cdot}z' = \{e'\}$ and $e' < x$. But this would imply that $z < x \leq y$ which contradicts z co y. Thus indeed $z' < z$ and we are done. □

<u>Theorem 3.6</u> Let $N = (B,E;F)$ be a well-founded occurrence net of finite degree and $(SL; \sqsubseteq)$ the associated lattice of slices. N is K-dense iff $\forall s \in SL - \{\bot\}$, $\sqsubseteq$ is <u>not</u> dense below s.

<u>Proof.</u> Assume that $\forall s \in SL - \{\bot\}$, $\sqsubseteq$ is not dense below s. Let $s \in SL$ and $l \in L$. We shall show that $s \cap l \neq \emptyset$. If $s = \bot$ then by the well-foundedness of N, it follows that $s \cap l \neq \emptyset$. So assume that $s \neq \bot$.
Set $A = {\downarrow}s$ and $SL' = \{s_x \mid x \in A \cap l\}$. Once again from the well-foundedness of N it follows that $A \cap l \neq \emptyset$ so that $SL' \neq \emptyset$. We shall now show that s is an upper bound of SL'. To see this, let $x \in A \cap l$. Then $\exists y \in s$ such that $x \leq y$. By the previous lemma, $s_x \sqsubseteq s_y$ and clearly $s_y \sqsubseteq s$ and thus s is an upper bound of SL'. From theorem 2.3 it follows that $\bigsqcup SL'$, the least upper bound of SL' exists. Let $\tilde{s} = \bigsqcup SL'$. By hypothesis, act $(\tilde{s}) \neq \emptyset$. Let $x \in \mathrm{act}(\tilde{s})$. We shall prove that $(^{\cdot}x)^{\cdot} \subseteq s = \mathrm{Max}(A)$ and $(^{\cdot}x)^{\cdot} \cap l \neq \emptyset$. This would establish the required result. From a notational standpoint, it is convenient to consider two cases.

<u>Case 1.</u> $x \in E$
Since $x \in \mathrm{act}(\tilde{s})$, $^{\cdot}x \neq \emptyset$. Suppose $x \notin l$, then $\hat{s} = [\tilde{s} - (^{\cdot}x)^{\cdot}] \cup {}^{\cdot}x$ is an upper bound of SL' and we have the contradiction $\tilde{s} \not\sqsubseteq \hat{s}$.
Hence $x \in l$. We just need to show that $x \in s$.
First note that $x \in \tilde{s}$ implies that for some $s' \in SL'$, $x \in {\downarrow}s'$ (theorem 2.3). While s is an upper bound of SL' we are assured that $x \in A = {\downarrow}s$. Suppose that $x^{\cdot} = \emptyset$. Then it is easy to veri-

fy that $x \in Max(A) = s$. So assume that $x^\bullet \neq \emptyset$. Then from $|x^\bullet| < \infty$ it follows easily that for some $y \in x^\bullet$, $y \in l$ also (see [3] for instance). $y \notin A$ because if $y \in A$ then $y \in A \cap l$ so that $s_y \in SL'$ and we know already that $s_y \not\sqsubseteq \tilde{s}$ (recall that we started with $x \in \tilde{s}$). Now $x \in A$ and $y \notin A$ with $x < y$. Hence by lemma 2.2, $x \in Max(A) = s$ and we have proved $l \cap s \neq \emptyset$.

Case 2. $x \in B$

Once again $^\bullet x \neq \emptyset$. So let $^\bullet x = \{e\}$, $e^\bullet = B_1$. If $B_1 \cap l = \emptyset$ then $[\tilde{s} - (^\bullet B_1)^\bullet] \cup {}^\bullet B_1$ would also be an upper bound of SL'. So $B_1 \cap l \neq \emptyset$. Assume without loss of generality that $x \in B_1 \cap l$. By repeating the argument for the previous case it is easy to verify that $x \in Max(A) = s$ and thus $s \cap L \neq \emptyset$. The second half of the result follows from theorem 3.4. □

The result stated above depends crucially on the well-foundedness assumption and also on the finite degree restriction. This is brought out by the examples shown in fig. 2 (a) and 2(b).

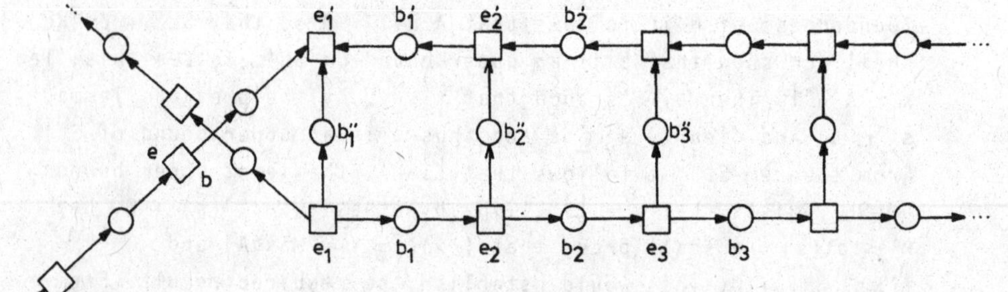

Fig.2(a)

In fig. 2(a), we have that for every slice $s \in SL - \{\bot\}$, $\sqsubseteq$ is not dense below s. However the net is not K-dense since the line $l = \{e_i, b_i, e_i', b_i' \mid i \geq 1\}$ and the slice $s = \{e, b, b_1'', b_2'', \ldots\}$ have an empty intersection.

Here, the theorem fails because the net is not well-founded. (This example was pointed out to us by E. Best).

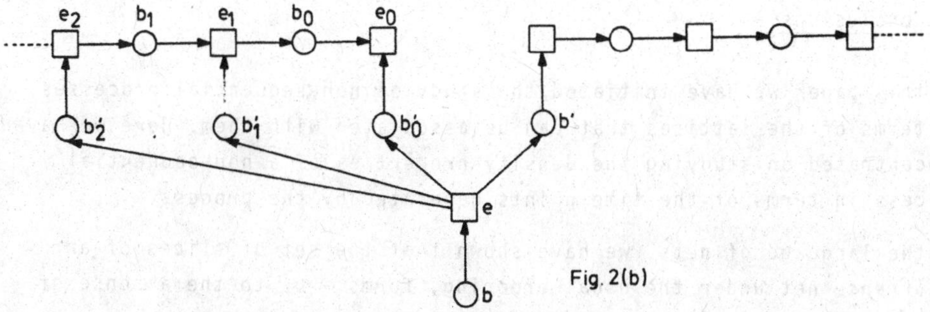

Fig. 2(b)

In fig 2(b), we have $l = \{b, e, e_0, b_0, e_1, b_1, \ldots\}$ is a line and $s = \{b', b'_0, b'_1, b'_2, \ldots\}$ is a slice and $l \cap s = \emptyset$. The net is not K-dense. In SL however there is no element below which $\sqsubseteq$ is dense.

We conclude this section by pointing that the structure (SL; $\sqsubseteq$) is too coarse for recognising the stronger density properties of <u>gap-freeness</u> and <u>D-continuity</u> (for definitions, see [3]).

In Fig. 3, N_1 is not gap-free, N_2 is gap-free but not D-continuous and N_3 is D-continuous. The corresponding lattices of slices will be isomorphic to each other.

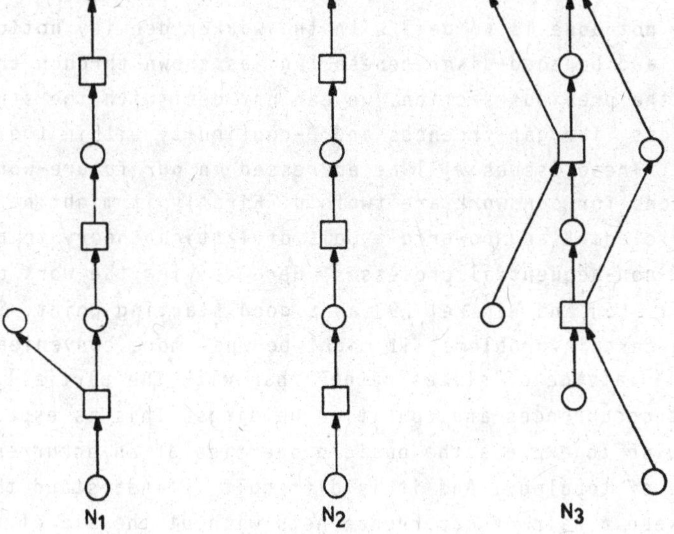

Fig. 3

4. Conclusions.

In this paper we have initiated the study of non-sequential processes in terms of the lattices that can be associated with them. Here we have concentrated on studying the density properties of a non-sequential process in terms of the time points generated by the process.

In the language of nets, we have shown that the set of slices of an occurrence net under the usual ordering, forms - up to the absense of a least and greatest element - a complete lattice. In doing so, we have characterised least upper bounds and greatest lower bounds, whenever they exist, in terms of the intersection or union of a set of lower sets. Consequently we can now explicitly construct and work with slices having desired properties. We have in mind notions like s_x, the least slice containing the net element x and $\tilde{s}$ as defined in the proof of the main result. We also feel hopeful that using this idea we can prove that the lattice of slices of an occurrence net is in fact algebraic.

The main result is that the well-known K-density notion at the process level can be expressed in terms of the normal density notion at the level of slices. As pointed out in the previous section our result holds only for occurrence nets of finite degree. In a way this is good because we find events with infinite number of pre-conditions or post-conditions very bizarre. And now there is yet another reason for throwing them out.

What we have not done is to deal with the weaker density notions like discreteness and bounded-discreteness. And as shown through the three examples in the previous section, we can not deal with the stronger density notions like gap-freeness and D-continuity within the structure $(SL;\sqsubseteq)$. These issues will be addressed in our future-work.

The motivations for our work are twofold. Firstly it might be useful to bring the elegant and powerful tools of lattice theory to bear upon the study of non-sequential processes. Here we view the work of Nielson et al. [5] and Winskel [9] as a good starting point. Secondly, for studying certain problems, it might be much more convenient to work with the lattice of slices rather than with the partially ordered set of event occurrences and condition holdings. This is especially true if we wish to express the basic properties of an occurrence net in the language of topology. And it is difficult to understand the relationship between a pair of occurrence nets without the aid of topology.

References.

[1] E. Best, A Theorem on the Characteristics of Non-sequential Processes.
Fundamenta Informaticae, Vol. 3, (1980), 77-94.

[2] E. Best and A. Merceron, Some Properties of Non-sequential Processes.
GMD-ISF report 82.07, Schloß Birlinghoven, 5205 St. Augustin W. Germany (1982).

[3] C. Fernandez and P.S. Thiagarajan, D-continuous Causal Nets: A Model of Non-sequential Processes.
GMD-ISF report 82.05, Schloß Birlinghoven, 5205 St.Augustin W. Germany (1982). Also to appear in TCS.

[4] A.W. Holt et al., Information System Theory Project.
Final Report, RADC-TR-G8-305, Applied Data Research Inc., Princeton, New Jersey, USA (1968).

[5] M. Nielson, G. Plotkin and G. Winskel, Petri Nets, Event Structures and Domains, Part I,
Theoretical Computer Science 13 (1981), 85-108.

[6] C.A. Petri, Non-sequential Processes,
Interner Bericht ISF-77-5, GMD, Schloß Birlinghoven, 5205 St. Augustin, W. Germany (1977).

[7] C.A. Petri, Concurrency.
Lecture Notes in Computer Science, Ed. W. Brauer, Vol. 84, 251-260, Springer Verlag (1980).

[8] J. Winkowski, Behaviours of Concurrent Systems,
Theoretical Computer Science 12 (1980), 39-60.

[9] G. Winskel, Events in Computation,
Ph.D. Thesis, University of Edinburgh, Edinburgh, Great Britain (1980).

FAIR SERIALIZABILITY OF ITERATED TRANSACTIONS USING FIFO-NETS

M.P. Flé and G. Roucairol
Laboratoire de Recherche en Informatique
Unité Associée 410 du CNRS
Bâtiment 490
Université de Paris-Sud
91405 Orsay Cedex (France)

ABSTRACT: The serializability condition is usually considered in order to maintain the consistency of a Database in the presence of conflicting accesses to the Database performed by concurrent transactions. The transactions considered in this paper may be infinitely often repeated and a synchronization algorithm is proposed which controls the serializability condition for such transactions. This algorithm, based upon the use of FIFO-Nets, provides the maximal amount of parallelism among the transactions and guaranties fairness, i.e., every transaction is actually performed infinitely often. As an application, the synchronization algorithm is shown to give also a fair solution to the classical dining philosophers problem. The size of the memory needed by the algorithm cannot be bounded, however a particular case is pointed out for which memory boundedness can be achieved. This particular case covers the problem of updating multiple copies of a Database.

KEY WORDS: concurrency, maximal serializability, fair, Petri-nets (FIFO-Nets).

1. INTRODUCTION

The *serializability problem* is a synchronization problem which has been mainly studied in the framework of *concurrent accesses to a Data Base* (see [1],[3],[10]). Being given a so-called consistency predicate over the content of a Data Base and a set of *transactions* (finite sequence of operations), each one preserving individually the consistency predicate, the serializability problem consists of *synchronizing* the transactions in order to allow only concurrent behaviours which are equivalent to some serial composition of the transactions. Hence, these *behaviours* preserve also the consistency predicate. We shall call such behaviours *correct* behaviours. In this paper, we consider that a transaction can be infinitely often iterated as might behave for instance a preexisting service process in an operating system. In [5], we have shown that serializability can be controlled by a finite automaton. However, there are behaviours allowed by this automaton which are not *fair* i.e. not every transaction is repeated infinitely often. Here, we detail a synchronization algorithm which allows every correct and fair behaviour. This algorithm, which achieves maximal serializability, is based upon the use of *FIFO-nets*, nets in which places behave as

FIFO-queues instead of counters. As an example, we use this algorithm in order to provide a maximally concurrent and fair solution to the well-known dining philosophers problem [2].
However, the length of the queues employed by this algorithm cannot be bounded. We conclude this paper by pointing out a condition over the transactions for which boundedness of the queues can be achieved. In this case, the synchronization algorithm could be simulated by an ordinary Petri-net. The use of this second algorithm is illustrated in order to provide a fair and correct solution of the problem of updating multiple copies of a Data Base.

2. NOTATIONS AND BASIC DEFINITIONS

Notations: Let X be an alphabet; X^* denotes the free monoid generated by X; e is the empty word; X^ω is the set of infinite words over X; let u be in $X^*\backslash\{e\}$; u^ω is the infinite word obtained by catenating u infinitely often with itself; let x be in $X^* \cup X^\omega$, Y be a subset of X; $proj_Y(x)$ is the erasing homomorphism which suppresses from x the symbols not in Y; $u \leq x$ means that u is a prefix of x; let W be a subset of X^*; W^* is the set of words obtained by catenating items of W; W^ω is the set of infinite words whose every prefix is a prefix of an item of W^*.

2.1 Definition of a transaction system

Definition 2.1 (*Transaction System*):
A *transaction system* is a couple TS= $<\mathcal{T},R>$, where:
- $\mathcal{T} = \{T_1,\ldots,T_n\}$ is a finite set of *transactions*, each transaction T_i being considered as a finite sequence of distinct operations: $T_i = a_{i,1}\ldots a_{i,m_i}$; let A_i be the set of operations occurring in transaction T_i, and $A = \bigcup_{i=1,n} A_i$; in the sequel, we shall assume that the sets of operations of different transactions are disjoint i.e. $\forall i,j \in [1,n],\ A_i \cap A_j \neq \emptyset \iff i=j$.
- $R \subseteq A \times A$ is a symmetric relation so-called "conflict relation" among the operations of different transactions i.e. $\forall i \in [1,n],\ R \cap (A_i \times A_i) = \emptyset$. (This relation is generally deduced from the way operations may access to shared data; read-write conflict, write-write conflict). □

In the sequel, TS will denote a transaction system $<\mathcal{T},R>$ as it is defined in definition 2.1.

Definition 2.2 (*Behaviour*):
A *behaviour* or a *computation* of a transaction system is an infinite word over A obtained by shuffling possibly infinite loops of the transactions. We note PB(TS) the set of all the possible behaviours of TS i.e.
$PB(TS) = \{x \in A^\omega \mid \forall i \in [1,n],\ proj_{A_i}(x) \in \{T_i\}^* \cup \{T_i^\omega\}\}$. □

Example 2.1: Let us consider two transactions T_1 and T_2 performing the following sequences of instructions on two variables A and B satisfying the consistency predicate "A = B":

T_1 : A:=A*2; B:=B*2 T_2 : A:=A+10; B:=B+10

Calling a (resp.a') the first operation of T_1 (resp.T_2) and b (resp.b') the second operation of T_1 (resp. T_2), an instance of transaction system could be:

$<\{T_1, T_2\}, R>$ where $R = \{(a,a'), (a',a), (b,b'), (b',b)\}$.

$(ab)^\omega$, $(aa'bb')^\omega$, $(a'ab'b)^\omega$ are examples of behaviours of this transaction system.

Remark: We consider each operation performed by a transaction as atomic. This assumption is not too restrictive as far as we are concerned in this paper only by the relative ordering of conflicting operations.

Parallelism among transactions is represented in behaviours by the fact that some occurrence of transactions can start while some others are not finished. For instance, in $(aa'bb')^\omega$, T_2 begins before T_1 is finished.

As a matter of fact, the concept of concurrency we shall use is basically the same as the one defined by R. Keller [7] or A. Mazurkiewicz [9].

2.2 Maximal serializability

In order to define maximal serializability, we introduce first the notion of correct behaviour. A behaviour of a transaction system is said correct if it is equivalent to a sequential behaviour (behaviour obtained only by catenation of transactions). The equivalence which is mainly used in the literature on serializability can be formalized by an equivalence defined by R. Keller [7]. It concerns the comparison of occurrences of conflicting operations.

Definition 2.3 (*Equivalence of behaviours*):
Let x and y be two behaviours of a transaction system. x is said *equivalent* to $y (x \simeq y)$ if and only if:

(i) $\forall a \in A$, $proj_{\{a\}}x = proj_{\{a\}}y$ (identical occurrences of operations).

(ii) $\forall (a,b) \in R$, $proj_{\{a,b\}}x = proj_{\{a,b\}}y$ (identical ordering of occurrence of conflicting operations). □

Example 2.2: The following behaviours taken from Example 2.1 are equivalent:
$x = (aa'bb')^\omega$, $y = (aba'b')^\omega$.

Definition 2.4 (*Correct behaviour*):
A behaviour x of a transaction system is *correct* if and only if there exists a sequential computation equivalent to x i.e. $\exists\, y \in T^\omega$, $x \simeq y$. □

Example 2.3: In Example 2.1, behaviour $(aa'bb')^\omega$ is correct and behaviour $(aa'b'b)^\omega$ is not.

We note Cor(TS) the set of correct behaviours of the transaction system TS.

We shall say informally that a *synchronization algorithm allows maximal serializability* for the transaction system TS if the set of behaviours allowed by such an algorithm is exactly Cor(TS), (an infinite behaviour allowed by a synchronization algorithm being a word whose every prefix is computed by it).
Let us remark that concurrency is represented in our formalism by the possibility of shuffling sequences of operations. Therefore, the more behaviours a synchronization algorithm allows, the more possibilities of shuffling the transaction sequences exists, so more concurrency (or serializability) by this synchronization algorithm is allowed.

3. FAIR SERIALIZABILITY

In this paper, we describe and prove the correctness of a fair synchronization algorithm allowing maximal serializability for a transaction system. In order to define what we mean by fair synchronization algorithm, we need some remarks and definitions.

Definition 3.1 (*Fair behaviour*):
A *fair* behaviour x of a transaction system is a behaviour in which every transaction is infinitely often repeated i.e. $\forall i \in [1,n]$, $\text{proj}_{A_i}(x) = T_i^{\omega}$. □

Generally, a correct behaviour is not necessarily fair. In [5], we gave an important result that says that maximal serializability can be controlled by a finite automaton. But let us consider the infinite words whose prefixes are accepted by such an automaton; counter examples show that even some behaviour (in a sense, realistic [8]) satisfying the finite delay property may be not fair. (The finite delay property of a behaviour means that whenever an operation becomes persistently enabled at each step of this behaviour, it is not delayed forever [6] (see section 3.2.2, definition 3.6).

Example 3.1: Consider the transaction system composed by the transactions T_1=ab, T_2= cd and the conflict relation R={(a,d), (d,a), (b,c), (c,b)}.

The automaton accepting the prefixes of correct behaviours is (q_0 is the initial state):

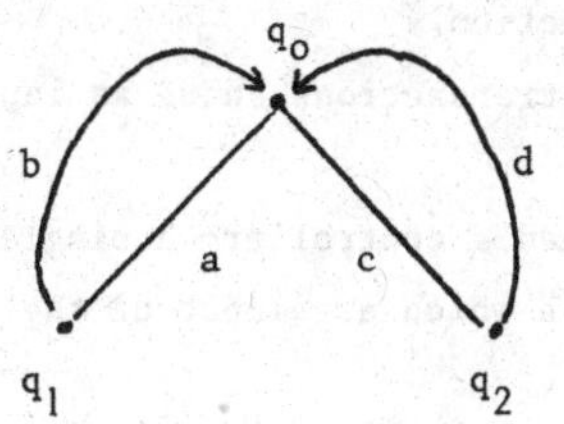

- Figure 3.1 -

Behabiour $(ab)^{\omega}$ satisfies the finite delay property since c and d are not persistently enabled at each step of this behaviour, and it is unfair.

In the sequel, we describe what we call a *fair* synchronization algorithm in the sense that every behaviour it allows and which satisfies the finite delay property is fair and every prefix of behaviour can be extended into a behaviour satisfying the finite delay property.

3.1 Description of a fair synchronization algorithm for a transaction system

The synchronization algorithm we are going to describe is based upon the use of FIFO-nets [4] i.e. a Petri-net in which places are considered as FIFO-queues and whose edges are labelled by words which are removed from the head of a queue or appended to the end of a queue under a transition firing.

Definition 3.2 (*FIFO-net)*:

A *FIFO-net* is a 6-tuple $N = \langle P,T,Pre,Post,Q,M_0\rangle$, where:

- P is the set of queues.
- T is the set of transitions ($P \cap T = \emptyset$).
- Q is a queue alphabet.
- $Pre: P \times T \to Q^*$ and $Post: P \times T \to Q^*$ are the backward and forward incidence mappings.
- $M_0 : P \to Q^*$ is the initial marking.

We say that the transition t is *fireable* for the marking M (M(t>) if and only if $\forall p \in P$, $Pre(p,t) \leq M(p)$.

The marking M' obtained by the *firing* of a transition t under the marking M (M (t>M') is such that:

$Pre(p,t)M'(p) = M(p)\, Post(p,t)$ holds for every place p.

We note M_{ut}, $u \in T^*$, the marking M' such that M_u(t>M' holds. If $M = M_0$ then ut is a *firing sequence* of N. □

Let us now give an informal description of a fair synchronization algorithm based upon the use of FIFO queues (let us recall that every transaction is of the form: $T_i = a_{i,1}\, a_{i,2} \dots a_{i,m_i}$ (definition 2.1)).

- Each transaction is described by a Petri-net (a FIFO-net whose places will contain at most one letter) forming an elementary circuit and whose transitions are labelled by the operations of the transaction.
- Two transitions of different transactions share an input queue if and only if there labels are conflicting.
- To each transaction is attached a controller: a single loop which adds simultaneously a symbol to all the queues which are input of the transitions of this transaction.

An edge like (c_i, c_i, f) means that symbol c_i is appended to the queue f whenever c_i fires.

An edge like $(f, c_i, a_{i,r})$ means that $a_{i,r}$ cannot be fireable while symbol c_i is not the head of f; this symbol is removed when $a_{i,r}$ fires.

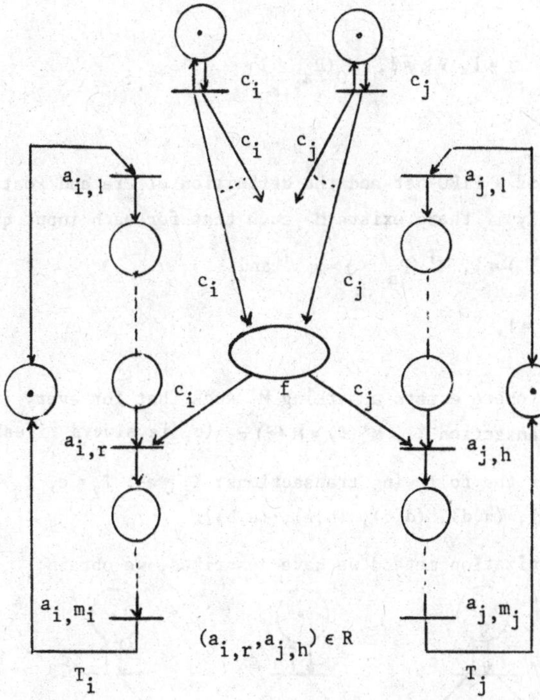

- Figure 3.2 -

More precisely, the FIFO-net Q_{TS} which controls the transaction system TS is built as follows.

Definition 3.3:

$Q_{TS} = \langle P \cup F,\ A \cup C,\ Pre,\ Post,\ C \cup \{1\},\ M_0 \rangle$ where:

(i) $C = \{c_i,\ i \in [1,n]\}$ is the set of controllers.

(ii) $P = \{P_t,\ t \in A \cup C\}$ where P_t is called the input place of t.

(iii) $F = \{F_{\{a,a'\}},\ (a,a') \in R\}$ and for every b in A, $\{F_{\{b,a'\}},\ (b,a') \in R\}$ is called the set of input queues of b.

(iv) $\forall\ i \in [1,n],\ k \in [1,m_i],\ \forall$ b such that $(a_{i,k}, b) \in R$,

$Post(P_{c_i}, c_i) = 1$, $Pre(P_{c_i}, c_i) = 1$,

$Post(F_{\{a_{i,k},b\}}, c_i) = c_i$, $Pre(F_{\{a_{i,k},b\}}, a_{i,k}) = c_i$,

$Pre(P_{a_{i,k}}, a_{i,k}) = 1$, $Post(P_{a_{i,k(\text{mod } m_i)+1}}, a_{i,k}) = 1$.

(v) $M_0\ (P_{c_i}) = 1$,

$\forall\, i \in [1,n], M_0(P_{a_{i,1}}) = 1$, $\forall k \neq 1$, $M_0(P_{a_{i,k}}) = e$,

$\forall f \in F$, $M_0\ (f) = e$. □

From the definition of a FIFO-net and the definition of Pre and Post, part (iv) means:
- $M(a_{i,k}>$ if and only if there exists M' such that for each input queue f of $a_{i,k}$,

$c_i M'(f) = M(f)$, $M(P_{a_{i,k}}) = 1$, $M'\ (P_{a_{i,k}}) = e$ and

$M'\ (P_{a_{i,k+1(\text{mod } m_i)}}) = 1$,

- for every c_i of C, there exists a marking M' such that for every input queue f of the operations of transaction T_i, $M'(f) = M\ (f)\ c_i$ (c_i is always fireable).

<u>Example 3.2</u>: Consider the following transactions: $T_1 = ab$, $T_2 = c$, $T_3 = de$ with $R = \{(a,c), (c,a), (c,d), (d,c), (b,e), (e,b)\}$.

Applying the synchronization method we have described, we obtain:

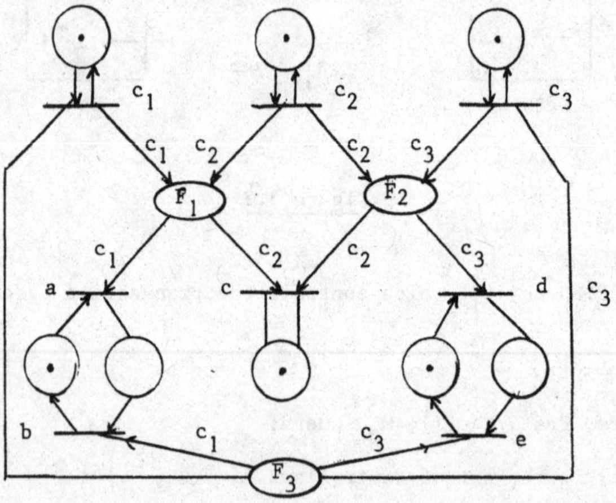

- <u>Figure 3.3</u> -

Due to the possibility to insert some occurrences of c between a and d, queues F_1 and F_3 (resp. F_2 and F_3) must *indivisibly* receive symbol c_1 (resp. c_3). (Consider for instance the word acd, which is a prefix of a correct behaviour, and its possible extensions with symbols b and e). This indivisibility is achieved by the fact that there is only one controller per transaction.

Let us remark that the conflicts between controllers in order to fill shared output-queues can be viewed also as a serializability problem. This latter problem is solved by assuming the indivisibility of a transaction firing.

Now, let us discuss the fact that a controller must run independently from the transaction it controls.

In example 3.2, consider a prefix of the form $a(de)^pb$. For every integer p, this word is a prefix of a correct behaviour. The only way of controlling such a prefix is to append a symbol c_1 to the queue F_1 before firing transition a. But, indivisibly, queue F_3 also receives a symbol c_1. So, in order to execute the sequence "de" p times before executing b, queue F_3 must have been filled up with p symbols c_3 before having received symbol c_1. That yields the word $(c_3)^pc_1a(de)^pb$. So controller c_3 must run independently from the transaction T_3.

3.2 Correctness of the synchronization algorithm Q_{TS}

We mean by correctness of the synchronization algorithm Q_{TS} the fact that Q_{TS} is fair and allows maximal serializability.

3.2.1 Maximal serializability

The firing sequences of Q_{TS} are words over the alphabet $A \cup C$. So, in order to prove that it allows maximal serializability, we shall prove that the projection of the firing sequences over the alphabet A are exactly the prefixes of correct behaviours.

In order to characterize prefixes of correct behaviours, we introduced in [5] a precedence relation among the occurrences of transactions in prefixes of behaviours. This relation is based upon the notion of precedence relation among the occurrences of conflicting operations in prefixes of behaviours.

Definition 3.4 (*predecence relation between occurrences of symbols in a word*):
Let u be a word over an alphabet X, a and b be distinct symbols of X and h and k be integers. We say that the hth occurrence of a *precedes* in u the kth occurrence of b and we write: $(a,h) \to_u (b,k)$, if and only if operation a occurs h times in u and this occurrence appears before the kth occurrence of b if it exists in u, i.e., $u \in \{v_1\ a\ v_2,\ v_1\ a\ v_2\ b\ v_3\}$ for some v_1, v_2, v_3 in X^* such that $|v_1|_a = h-1$, $|v_1\ a\ v_2|_b = k-1$. □

Definition 3.5 (*precedence relation between occurrences of transaction in a prefix of a behaviour*):
Let u be a prefix of a behaviour of TS, h and k be integers, T_i and T_j be transactions. We say that the hth occurrence of T_i *precedes* in u the kth occurrence of T_j and we write $(T_i,h) <_u (T_j,k)$ if and only if:

- either i=j, h < k and T_i occurs at least k-1 times in u i.e. $proj_{A_i}\ u = T_i^{k-1}v$ for some v in Pref (T_i^*),

- or i≠j and there exists one operation a in A_i, conflicting with one operation b in A_j, such that the hth occurrence of a precedes in u the kth occurrence of b, i.e.,

$\exists$ $(a,b) \in R \cap A_i \times A_j$, $(a,h) \to_u (b,k)$. □

We proved in [5] that a word u is a prefix of a correct behaviour if and only if the transitive closure $<_u^*$ of relation $<_u$ is an order relation. We called Ord(TS) the set of prefixes of behaviours satisfying this last property.
Then, the following result shows that Q_{TS} controls exactly the sequences of operations over A which are prefixes of correct behaviours.
Let FS be the set of firing sequences of Q_{TS}, then we have:

<u>Theorem 3.1</u> (*maximal serializability of Q_{TS}*):
$proj_A(FS) = Ord(TS)$. □

<u>Proof</u>:
The assertion $proj_A(FS) \subseteq Ord(TS)$ comes from the following lemma:

<u>Lemma 3.1</u>: $\forall h, k \in \mathbb{N}$, $\forall i,j \in [1,n]$, $\forall u \in FS$ $(T_i,h) <_v (T_j,k)$ and $proj_A(u) = v$ implies $(c_i,h) \to_u (c_j,k)$. □

<u>Proof of Lemma 3.1</u>: Relation $(T_i,h) <_v (T_j,k)$ means (definition 3.5):

(1) there exists two conflicting operations a and b such that $(a,b) \in A_i \times A_j$,

(2) the hth occurrence of a precedes in v the kth occurrence of b.

According to the construction of Q_{TS} (definition 3.3), (1) implies that an input queue $F_{\{a,b\}}$ is shared by transitions a and b and receives symbols c_i and c_j from the controllers. According to the firing rules of a FIFO-net (definition 3.2), point (2) implies that the hth deposit of symbol c_i in $F_{\{a,b\}}$ must have preceded the kth deposit of symbol c_j. Then, we can easily conclude, from the construction of Q_{TS}, that the hth occurrence of symbol c_i precedes in u the kth occurrence of symbol c_j. □
Obviously, the transitive closure of relation $\to_u$ is an order one; then, due to lemma 3.1, $<_u^*$ is an order relation for every firing sequence u. On the other hand, the fact that the projection over A of every firing sequence is a prefix of a behaviour is straightforward from the definition of Q_{TS}. So, $proj_A(FS) \subseteq Ord(TS)$.

In order to prove the other inclusion, we build a word c by catenating symbols c_i in an order compatible with the relation $<_u^*$, for some word u of Ord(TS). Due to the definition of $<_u$, this means that for every $(a,b) \in R \cap A_i \times A_j$, if the hth occurrence of a precedes in cu the kth occurrence of b, then the hth occurrence of symbol c_i precedes in cu the kth occurrence of symbol c_j. According to the construction of Q_{TS} and the firing rules of a FIFO-net, this allows transition a to be fired h times before the kth firing of transition b. This shows that cu is in FS, and consequently that u is in $proj_A(FS)$.

3.2.2 <u>Fairness</u>
First we define the notion of finite delay property.

<u>Definition 3.6</u> (*finite delay property*):

Let $N = < P, T, Pre, Post, Q, M_o >$ be a FIFO-net, and F be the set of firing sequences of N; let x be in T^ω; x satisfies the *finite delay property* if and only if:

- every prefix of x is in F;
- for every transition a in T and every prefix u of x, if for every v in T^* such that uv is a prefix of x, uva is in F (a is always enabled after u in x), then uwa is a prefix of x for some w in T^* (a is fired after u in x), i.e.,

$\forall a \in T, \forall u \leq x, (\forall v \in T^*, uv \leq x \Rightarrow uva \in F) \Rightarrow \exists w \in T^*, uwa \leq x.$ □

In the sequel, we shall note FDB the set of infinite words over $A \cup C$ which satisfy the finite delay property.

In this section, we prove (theorem 3.2), that Q_{TS} is fair i.e. every firing sequence can be extended into an infinite behaviour satisfying the finite delay property and every infinite word satisfying the finite delay property is fair.

The basic reason for which fairness of Q_{TS} is achieved comes from the persistency property verified by our construction combined together with the fact that we restrict ourselves to consider only infinite words satisfying the finite delay property.

First, we prove the following lemmas:

<u>Lemma 3.2</u> (*persistency of Q_{TS}*)

Q_{TS} is persistent, i.e.,

$\forall a,b \in A \cup C, \forall u \in FS, ua \in FS, ub \in FS \Rightarrow uab \in FS, uba \in FS.$ □

<u>Proof of Lemma 3.2:</u> In Q_{TS}, every place has only one output edge and the output edges of every queue is labelled by different symbols. So, the firing of any transition cannot disable the firing of other transitions.

<u>Lemma 3.3:</u> $\forall u \in FS, \forall i \in [1,n], \forall p \leq m_i$, if $M_u(P_{a_{i,p}}) = 1$ then $Muv(a_{i,p}) >$ for some v in $(A \cup C)^*$. □

<u>Sketch of proof of Lemma 3.3:</u> Since $M_u(P_{a_{i,p}}) = 1$, then, due to the definition of Q_{TS}, we must prove that, for some v in $(A \cup C)^*$, $c_i \leq M_{uv}(f)$ for every input queue f of $a_{i,p}$.

Since transition c_i can be always fired, then:

for some v, symbol c_i occurs in $M_{uv}(f)$ for every input queue f of $a_{i,p}$ (1).

So, Lemma 3.3 is obviously obtained by showing that:

for every input queue f of $a_{i,p}$ for which $c_j \leq M_{uv}(f)$, $i \neq j$, symbol c_j is removed from f in some extension of uv, $P_{a_{i,p}}$ still being marked (i.e., f is the input queue of some transition t, uvwt is a firing sequence for some w in $(A \cup C)^*$, and $M_{uvwt}(P_{a_{i,p}}) = 1$) (2).

We suppose (2) is not true and we show that, due to the persistency property of Q_{TS}, this allows to build sequences of transitions for which (1) is true and (2) is false.

By using the fact that the number of transitions is finite, we show that this leads to a contradiction.

Lemma 3.4: $\forall x \in FDB$, $\forall u < x$, $\forall i \in [1,n]$, $\forall p \leq m_i$,

(i) if $M_u(a_{i,p}>$ then $uva_{i,p} \leq x$ for some v in $(A \cup C)^*$,

(ii) if $M_u(P_{a_{i,p}}) = 1$ then $M_{uv}(a_{i,p}>$ for some v in $(A \cup C)^*$ such that $uv \leq x$. □

Sketch of proof of Lemma 3.4:

(i) comes from the finite delay property of x and the persistency property of Q_{TS} (Lemma 3.2).

Proof of (ii): Since c_i can be always fired and due to the finite delay property of x, then, for some v such that $uv \leq x$, symbol c_i occurs in every input queue of $a_{i,p}$ for the marking M_{uv}. So, the proof is the same as the proof of Lemma 3.3 except that, due to the finite delay property of x, we show that symbol c_j is removed from f after uv in x, $P_{a_{i,p}}$ still being marked (i.e., f is the input queue of some transition t, $uvwt \leq x$ for some w in $(A \cup C)^*$, and $M_{uvwt}(P_{a_{i,p}}) = 1$).

Now, we can state:

Theorem 3.2 (*fairness of Q_{TS}*):

1) FS = Pref (FDB),

2) $\forall x \in FDB$, $\forall i \in [1,n]$, $proj_{A_i}(x) = T_i^{\omega}$. □

Proof of theorem 3.2:

Proof of 1): Let u be in FS; due to Lemma 3.3 and the definition of Q_{TS}, it is possible to extend u by ending all the transactions yet started but not finished in u, and, by catenating the infinite word: $(c_1 T_1 c_2 T_2 \ldots c_n T_n)^{\omega}$ to the resulting word, we obviously obtain a word of FDB.

Proof of 2): It is obtained by showing that, for every prefix u of a word of FDB, the following property is satisfied: for every $i \in [1,n]$, if $a_{i,p}$ is the last operation of transaction T_i performed in u (i.e., $proj_{A_i}(u) = va_{i,p}$ for some v in A_i^*), then its successor will be fired after u in x (i.e., $uwa_{i,p(\mathrm{mod}\ m_i)+1} \leq x$ for some w in $(A \cup C)^*$).

This obviously comes from Lemma 3.4 and the definition of Q_{TS}. □

3.2.3 Application to the "dining philosophers" problem

Let n be the number of philosophers and let us assume that the individual behaviour of one philosopher i is:

$(\mathrm{think})_i$; $(\mathrm{take\ fork}_i)_i$; $(\mathrm{take\ fork}_{i(\mathrm{mod}\ n)+1})_i$; $(\mathrm{eat})_i$; $(\mathrm{release\ fork}_i)_i$; $(\mathrm{release\ fork}_{i(\mathrm{mod}\ n)+1})_i$.

where operations $(\mathrm{take\ fork}_{i(\mathrm{mod}\ n)+1})_i$ and $(\mathrm{release\ fork}_{i(\mathrm{mod}\ n)+1})_i$ conflict both with the corresponding operations of philosopher i(mod n)+1. (In fact, it is enough to suppose that (take $\text{fork}_{i(\text{mod } n)+1})_i$ conflicts with

(release $\text{fork}_{i(\text{mod } n)+1})_{i(\text{mod } n)+1}$ and (release $\text{fork}_{i(\text{mod } n)+1})_i$ conflicts with

(take $\text{fork}_{i(\text{mod } n)+1})_{i(\text{mod } n)+1}$).

Then applying the synchronization algorithm we have given, it is possible to show:
- two neighbours cannot eat concurrently (comes from the choice of the conflict relation and the correctness of Q_{TS}),
- there is no starvation (theorem 3.2).

(This solution is very similar to the one described in [11]).

3.3 A bounded synchronization algorithm

As we can see in example 3.2, queues are unbounded. We are going to define a particular conflict relation which we call pseudo-transitive relation and we will show that for every transaction system for which the conflict relation is a pseudo-transitive one, it is possible to build a fair bounded synchronization algorithm allowing maximal serializability.

Definition 3.2 (*pseudo-transitive conflict relation*):
A conflict relation (definition 2.1) is pseudo-transitive if and only if:
$\forall i, j, k \in [1,n],\ p \in [1,m_i],\ q,\ r \in [1,m_j],\ s \in [1,m_k],$

$a_{i,p}\ R\ a_{j,q}$ and $a_{j,r}\ R\ a_{k,s}$ then there exists $q \leq p$ and $h \in [1,m_k]$ such that $a_{i,1}\ R\ a_{k,h}$.

Remark: It can be shown that if for every behaviour u of a transaction system, $<_v$ is transitive for every prefix v of u, then R is pseudo-transitive.

Let $TS=\langle T, R\rangle$ be a transaction system such that R is a pseudo-transitive conflict relation. We define a synchronization algorithm B_{TS} where the behaviour of the controllers depends on the behaviour of the transactions.

B_{TS} is defined as Q_{TS} except that:

$\forall i \in [1,n],\ \text{Post}(P_{c_i}, a_{i,m_i}) = 1$ and $\text{Post}(P_{c_i}, c_i)$ is undefined.

This means that c_i is fireable each time that transaction T_i is performed (Figure 3.4)

In the sequel, FS will denote the set of firing sequences of B_{TS}.

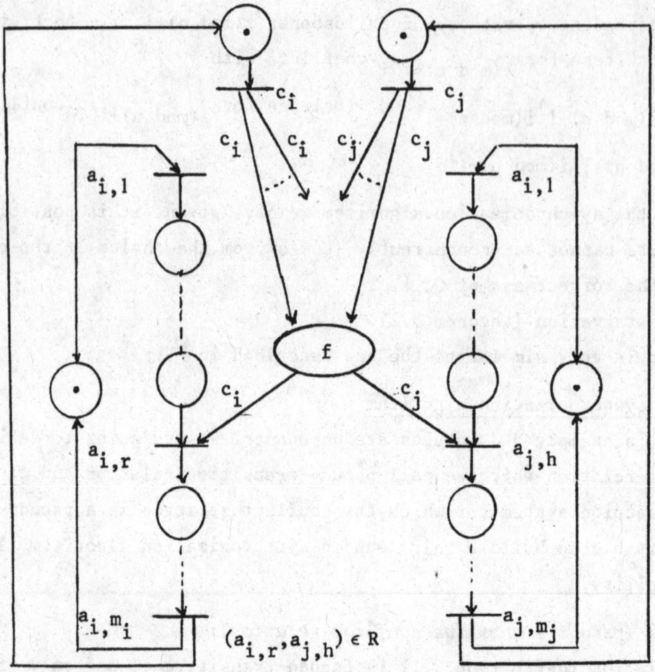

- Figure 3.4 -

Now, let us prove the correctness of B_{TS}.

3.3.1 Boundedness

Proposition 3.1 proves that all the input queues of B_{TS} are bounded.

Proposition 3.1 : $\forall f \in F$, $|M(f)|_{c_i} \leq 1$ for every marking M.

Proof:

The proof is obvious by choosing a proper place-invariant in the underlying Petri-net i.e. a net whose places counts the number of occurrences of symbols in the marking of a queue [4].

3.3.2 Maximal serializability

Theorem 3.3 proves that B_{TS} allows maximal serializability.

Theorem 3.3: $Proj_A(FS) = Ord(TS)$.

Proof:

1) $Proj_A(FS) \subseteq Ord(TS)$ comes from the fact that Lemma 3.1 is true in B_{TS}.

2) Let us prove that $Ord(TS) \subseteq Proj_A(FS)$.

We shall note $first_i(b)$ the fact that some operation b is the first operation of transaction T_i conflicting with some operation of another transaction.

Let u be in Ord(TS); we define:

$Z : \mathrm{Pref}(u) \to (A \cup C)^*$ by induction on the length of the prefixes of u in the following way:

$Z(e) = e$;

let $v \in A^*$, $b \in A$ such that $vb \leq x$;

$Z(vb) = Z(v)c_i b$ if first_i (b), $Z(v)b$ otherwise.

Let us show that Z(v) is in FS for every $v \leq u$.

For v=e, it is obvious. Let v be such that $Z(v) \in FS$; let $i \leq n$, $h \leq m_i$ such that $va_{i,h} \leq u$; let us show that $Z(va_{i,h}) \in FS$.

Let $w = Z(v)c_i$ if first_i $(a_{i,h})$, Z(v) otherwise.

If first_i $(a_{i,h})$ then, from the definition of B_{TS}, c_i is fireable after Z(v) $(M_{Z(v)}(c_i>)$. Let us suppose that $a_{i,h}$ is not fireable after $w(\neg M_w(a_{i,h}>)$; then due to the definition of B_{TS} and the firing rules, symbol c_j is the head symbol of the queue $F_{\{a_{i,h}, a_{j,m}\}}$, for some $j \leq n$ and $m \leq m_j$. Then, from the definition of Z and B_{TS}, this allows to show that the following relations are satisfied:

$(a_{i,h}, s) \to_{wa_{i,h}} (a_{j,m}, t)$ (1), $(a_{i,h}, a_{j,m}) \in R$ (2), $(a_{j,p}, a_{k,q}) \in R$ (3),

first_j $(a_{j,p})$ (4), $(c_j, t) \to_w (c_i, s)$ (5),

$s = |w|c_i$ and $t = |w|c_j$, for some $k \leq n$, $q \leq m_k$ and $p \leq m$.

Due to the pseudo-transitivity of R, we can deduce from (2), (3) and (4) that $(a_{j,p}, a_{i,r}) \in R$ for some $r \leq m_i$. Then due to (5), $(a_{j,p}, t) \to_w (a_{i,r}, s)$ (6).

From (1), (6) and definition 3.5, we conclude that $<^*_{va_{i,h}}$ is not an order relation. This contradicts the fact that u is in Ord(TS).

3.3.3 Fairness

The fairness of B_{TS} is shown in the following:

Theorem 3.4:

1) FS = Pref(FDB).

2) $\forall x \in FDB$, $\forall i \in [1,n]$, $\mathrm{proj}_{A_i}(x) = T_i^\omega$.

Proof: We use the following lemma:

Lemma 3.5: $\forall u \in FS$, $\forall i \in [1,n]$, $\forall p \leq m_i$,

if $M_u(a_{i,p}) = 1$, then either $|M_u(f)|_{c_i} > 0$ for every input queue f of $a_{i,p}$,

or $M_u(c_i>$. □

Lemma 3.5 is obvious from the definition of B_{TS}.

Due to lemma 3.5, lemmas 3.3 and 3.4 are true in B_{TS}. On the other hand, B_{TS} is obviously persistent. Then proof of theorem 3.4 is the same as the proof of theorem 3.2.

3.3.4 Application to the problem of updating multiple copies of a Data Base

Let $T_1,\dots,T_n$ be n transactions and $c_1,\dots,c_n$ be n copies of a Data Base such that each T_i consists first in reading the copy c_i and then in writing the n copies i.e.: T_i: read (c_i); write (c_1); ...; write (c_n)

Let $R = \{(\text{read}(c_i), (\text{write}(c_i)), (\text{write}(c_i)), \text{read}(c_i)), (\text{write}(c_i), \text{write}(c_i)), i \leq n\}$

One can verify that R is pseudo-transitive. So, this transaction system can be controlled by a bounded FIFO-net which allows maximal and fair serializability.

REFERENCES

[1] Bernstein P.A.; Goodman N.:
Concurrency Control and Distributed Database Systems.
Computing Surveys 13, N°2, 185-221 (1981).

[2] Dijskstra E.W.:
Hierarchical ordering of sequential process.
Acta Inf. 1, N°2, 115-138 (1971).

[3] Eswaran K.P.; Gray J.N.; Lorie R.A.; Traiger J.L.:
The Notions of Consistency and Predicate Locks in Database Systems.
Commun. ACM 19, N°11, 624-633 (1976).

[4] Finkel A.; Memmi G.:
FIFO-nets: a new model of parallel computation.
Proc. of the 6th G.I. Conf. on Theoretical Computer Science, Dortmund, Pays-Bas, Lect. Notes Comput. Sci. 150 (1983).

[5] Flé M.P.; Roucairol G.:
On Serializability of Iterated Transactions.
ACM SIGACT-SIGOPS Symp. on Princ. of Distributed Computing, Ottawa, Canada, 194-200 (1982).

[6] Karp R.M.; Miller R.E.:
Parallel Program Schemata.
J. Comput. System Sci. 3, 147-195 (1969).

[7] Keller R.M.:
Parallel Program Schemata and Maximal Parallelism.
J. Assoc. Comp. Mach. 20, N°3, 514-537 (1973).

[8] Kwong Y.:
On the absence of Livelocks in Parallel Programs.
Semantics of Concurrent Computations. Proceedings, Evian, France, Lect. Notes Comput. Sci. 70, 172-190 (1979).

[9] Mazurkiewicz A.:
Concurrent Program Schemes and their Interpretation.
Proceedings, Aarhus Workshop on Verification of Parallel Processes (1977).

[10] Papadimitriou C.H.; Bernstein P.A.; Rothnie J.B.:
Some computational problems related to Database Concurrency Control.
Proc. Conf. Theoretical Computer Science, Waterloo, Canada, 275-282 (1977).

[11] Roucairol G.:
Mots de synchronisation.
RAIRO, Informatique/Computer 12, N°4, 277-290 (1978).

CSP-PROGRAMS AS
NETS WITH INDIVIDUAL TOKENS

Ursula Goltz
Lehrstuhl für Informatik II
RWTH Aachen
Büchel 29 - 31
D-5100 Aachen
West - Germany

Wolfgang Reisig
Gesellschaft für Mathematik
und Datenverarbeitung - F1
Postfach 1240
5205 St. Augustin 1
West - Germany

Abstract

We define a subclass of predicate/transition-nets and show how to translate CSP-programs into such nets. We consider a subset of CSP for which Hennessy, Li and Plotkin have given an operational semantics in [HLP]. We show that the firing sequences of our net translation correspond to this operational semantics. Additionally, we also give a non-interleaving semantics to CSP by considering unfoldings and processes of the net translation.

This enables us to analyse CSP-programs applying net theoretic methods.

1. Introduction

CSP was introduced by Hoare [Ho] as a language for describing communicating sequential processes. It has become a standard model for programming languages using synchronised communication (Ada). Recently, the programming language occam was proposed which is strongly based on CSP [Ma].

We suggest a translation method which gives nets with individual tokens for CSP-programs. For this purpose, we define a subclass of predicate/transition-nets [GL]. We describe the dynamic behaviour of these nets by defining processes, similar to [GV], and unfoldings. Unfoldings have been introduced by Winskel [NPW,Wi]. They are further investigated in [GM2], and we generalise a definition given there to nets with individual tokens.

We consider the subset of CSP considered in [HLP]. It turns out that our net translation is equivalent to the operational semantics given in [HLP]. Transition firings in the net translation of a CSP-program correspond exactly to derivation steps in this operational semantics. Hence we can prove that the behaviour of our net translation corresponds closely to the conventional semantics of CSP.

What do we gain by giving this translation?

In terms of firing sequences, we represent the same behaviour as by an operational semantics. However, considering processes and unfoldings of the nets, we get more information. We are able to represent which actions are causally dependent on each other, and which are independent and may occur concurrently. This has interesting applications to fairness as shown in [Re2], where a partially ordered operational semantics for CSP is introduced. Furthermore, we are able to use net methods to analyse CSP-programs. We give some examples showing how net invariants and liveness criteria for nets can be applied to prove program properties.

2. Syntax and semantics of a CSP subset

As we want to compare our net translation of CSP with a more conventional semantics, we use the language CSP.1 of [HLP] and the operational semantics given there. In this section we shortly recall the definitions of [HLP].

2.1 Syntax

We assume the following domains:

Var - a set of variables, ranged over by x .

Exp - a set of expressions, ranged over by e , $V \subseteq Exp$ a set of values, ranged over by v ,

BExp - a set of boolean expressions, ranged over by b , $T \subseteq BExp$, $T = \{tt, ff\}$ truthvalues.

Lab - a set of process labels, ranged over by P, Q, R .

In addition it is assumed that substitution of expressions e' for variables x in expressions, e, b , makes sense, giving expressions $[e'/x]e$, $[e'/x]b$.

The syntactic categories are given using these domains:

Guards $G ::= b \mid b; P?x \mid b; P!e$

Commands $C ::= x := e \mid C_1; C_2 \mid \underline{skip} \mid \underline{abort} \mid P?x \mid P!e \mid \underline{if}\ G_1 \rightarrow C_1 [] \ldots [] G_n \rightarrow C_n\ \underline{fi}\ (n \geq 1) \mid$
$\underline{do}\ G_1 \rightarrow C_1 [] \ldots [] G_n \rightarrow C_n\ \underline{od}\ (n \geq 1)$

Let Lab(C) be the set of process labels occurring in C , Var(C) the set of variables in C .

Programs $Pr ::= P_1 :: C_1 \| \ldots \| P_n :: C_n$, where the P_i are all different,
$Lab(C_i) \subseteq \{P_j \mid 1 \leq j \leq n,\ j \neq i\}$, $i \neq j \Rightarrow Var(C_i) \cap Var(C_j) = \emptyset$.

Hence, as in [HLP] we do not allow nesting of parallel commands. It is not obvious how to generalise our translation approach to nested parallelism, that is to generalise finite marked nets immediately. However, it is possible to translate into finite nets using a similar method as shown in [GM], starting from infinite unfoldings. All other restrictions imposed in [HLP] could easily be removed.

As an example

$Pr_1 = P_1 :: x_1 := 1 ; \underline{do}\ odd(x_1) \rightarrow P_2?x_1\ \underline{od}\ \|$
$P_2 :: x_2 := 0 ; \underline{do}\ even(x_2) ; P_1!x_2 + 1 \rightarrow x_2 := x_2 + 2\ \underline{od}$

is a CSP-program.

2.2 Semantics

The operational semantics given in [HLP] considers a finite set $R = \{x_1,\ldots,x_r\}$ of variables, and registrates changes of States $\sigma : R \to V$. As usual, $\sigma[v/x_i]$ denotes the state identical to σ except at x_i where its value is v. For expressions e,b let $e\sigma, b\sigma$ be the result of substituting $\sigma(x_i)$ for each x_i in e,b respectively.

The operational semantics is given in terms of a relation from Programs × States to Programs × States. It shows the state change and the remaining program to be executed.

Let the set of Actions, ranged over by a, be

$\{P?v \mid P \in \mathrm{Lab},\ v \in V\} \cup \{P!v \mid P \in \mathrm{Lab},\ v \in V\} \cup \{\varepsilon\}$.

We assume that closed expressions e,b have values $[\![e]\!]$, $[\![b]\!]$ in V,T respectively.

We define the relations we need as the least ones satisfying the following implications.

Guards

I $[\![b\sigma]\!] = tt \Rightarrow <b,\sigma> \xrightarrow{\varepsilon} \sigma$

$<b;P?x,\sigma> \xrightarrow{P?v} \sigma[v/x] \quad (v \in V)$,

$<b;P!e,\sigma> \xrightarrow{P![\![e\sigma]\!]} \sigma$

II $[\![b\sigma]\!] = ff \Rightarrow <b,\sigma> \xrightarrow{\varepsilon} \underline{fail}$,

$<b;P?x,\sigma> \xrightarrow{\varepsilon} \underline{fail}$,

$<b;P!e,\sigma> \xrightarrow{\varepsilon} \underline{fail}$.

Commands

I 1. $<C_1,\sigma> \xrightarrow{a} <C_1',\sigma'> \Rightarrow <C_1;C_2,\sigma> \xrightarrow{a} <C_1';C_2,\sigma'>$

2. $<\underline{skip};C,\sigma> \xrightarrow{\varepsilon} <C,\sigma>$

II $<x := e,\sigma> \xrightarrow{\varepsilon} <\underline{skip},\sigma[[\![e\sigma]\!]/x]>$

III $<\underline{abort},\sigma> \xrightarrow{\varepsilon} <\underline{abort},\sigma>$

IV $<P?x,\sigma> \xrightarrow{P?v} <\underline{skip},\sigma[v/x]> \quad (v \in V)$

V $<P!e,\sigma> \xrightarrow{P![\![e\sigma]\!]} <\underline{skip},\sigma>$

VI 1. $<G_i,\sigma> \xrightarrow{a} \sigma' \Rightarrow <\underline{if}\ldots G_i \to C_i \ldots \underline{fi},\sigma> \xrightarrow{a} <C_i,\sigma'>$

2. $<G_i,\sigma> \xrightarrow{\varepsilon} \underline{fail}\ (i = 1,\ldots,n)$

$\Rightarrow <\underline{if}\ G_1 \to C_1 [\!] \ldots [\!] G_n \to C_n\ \underline{fi},\sigma> \xrightarrow{\varepsilon} <\underline{abort},\sigma>$

VII 1. $<G_i,\sigma> \xrightarrow{a} \sigma'$

$\Rightarrow <\underline{do}\ldots G_i \to C_i \ldots \underline{od},\sigma> \xrightarrow{a} <C_i;\underline{do}\ldots\underline{od},\sigma'>$

2. $<G_i,\sigma> \xrightarrow{\varepsilon} \underline{fail}\ (i = 1,\ldots,n)$

$\Rightarrow <\underline{do}\ldots\underline{od},\sigma> \xrightarrow{\varepsilon} <\underline{skip},\sigma>$.

Programs

I $\quad <C_i,\sigma> \xrightarrow{\varepsilon} <C_i',\sigma'>$

$\Rightarrow <\ldots\| P_i :: C_i \| \ldots,\sigma> \xrightarrow{\varepsilon} <\ldots\| P_i :: C_i' \| \ldots,\sigma'>$

II $\quad <C_i,\sigma> \xrightarrow{P_j?v} <C_i',\sigma'>, <C_j,\sigma> \xrightarrow{P_i!v} <C_j',\sigma>$

$\Rightarrow <\ldots\| P_i :: C_i \| \ldots \| P_j :: C_j \| \ldots,\sigma>$

$\xrightarrow{\varepsilon} <\ldots\| P_i :: C_i' \| \ldots \| P_j :: C_j' \| \ldots>,\sigma'>$

III $\quad <C_i,\sigma> \xrightarrow{P_j!v} <C_i',\sigma>, <C_j,\sigma> \xrightarrow{P_i?v} <C_j',\sigma'>$

$\Rightarrow <\ldots\| P_i :: C_i \| \ldots \| P_j :: C_j \| \ldots,\sigma>$

$\xrightarrow{\varepsilon} <\ldots\| P_i :: C_i' \| \ldots \| P_j :: C_j' \| \ldots,\sigma'>$.

Note that distributed termination is not observed here. Furthermore, abortion is modelled by unending computation.

A CSP-computation is

(i) a finite sequence $<Pr_1,\sigma_1> \xrightarrow{\varepsilon} <Pr_2,\sigma_2> \xrightarrow{\varepsilon} \ldots \xrightarrow{\varepsilon} <Pr_n,\sigma_n>$ or

(ii) an infinite sequence $<Pr_1,\sigma_1> \xrightarrow{\varepsilon} \ldots$.

It terminates if it is finite and $Pr_n = P_1 :: \underline{skip} \| \ldots \| P_n :: \underline{skip}$.
It deadlocks if it is finite but does not terminate.

The behaviour functions of programs, $\mathcal{R}$ and $\mathcal{T}$, are now defined by:

(i) $\mathcal{R}[\![Pr]\!](\sigma,\sigma')$ if there is a terminating computation from $<Pr,\sigma>$ to $<Pr',\sigma'>$ for some Pr' .

(ii) $\mathcal{T}[\![Pr]\!](\sigma)$ if every computation from $<Pr,\sigma>$ terminates.

As an example, for the program Pr_1 of section 2.1 we obtain only infinite computations with continuous growth of the values of x_1 and of x_2 .

3. A subclass of predicate/transition-nets

CSP programs will be translated to a special class of predicate/transition-nets [GL], which we will call CSP-nets. These will be nets marked by individual tokens representing program states. The nets will carry inscriptions refering to these states.

We start by giving the usual definition of the basic net structure. Note that we do not allow empty pre- or postsets of transitions.

Definition $\quad N = (S,T;F)$ is called a net iff

(i) S and T are disjoint sets (of places and transitions, respectively),

(ii) $F \subseteq (S \times T) \cup (T \times S)$, for all $t \in T$ there exist $s,s' \in S$ with sFt and tFs'

For $x \in S \cup T$, let $^\bullet x := \{y | yFx\}$ and $x^\bullet := \{y | xFy\}$. Let $^\circ N := \{x \in S \cup T | {}^\bullet x = \emptyset\}$.

We denote the components of a net N by S_N, T_N, F_N. Graphically, they are represented as usual by circles, boxes and arcs, respectively. We denote $S \cup T$ by N if no confusion is possible. If $^{\bullet}x$ or $x^{\bullet}$ have only one element y, we will sometimes denote y by $^{\bullet}x$ or $x^{\bullet}$, respectively.

For the translation of CSP-programs we will use net inscriptions using the domains Var, Exp, V, BExp, T and Lab as defined in section 2.1. Furthermore we need

Y - a new set of state variables, ranged over by y,
Subst ::= $y_1[ey_2/x]$, the substitution expressions,
Comm ::= P?x|P!e, the communication expressions.

We will represent intermediate states of CSP-programs by allowing states $\sigma : Var \to V$ as tokens in places.

To represent CSP-programs, we will need the following kinds of transitions:

1) Assignments x := e are translated as

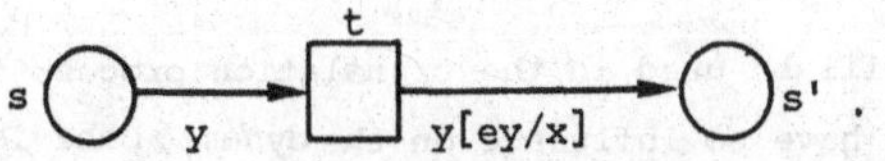

If s carries a token σ then t is enabled and may fire. The firing of t yields a new marking of the net, σ is removed from s and the state $\sigma[[\![e\sigma]\!]/x]$ appears as a token on s'.

2) Boolean guards are translated as

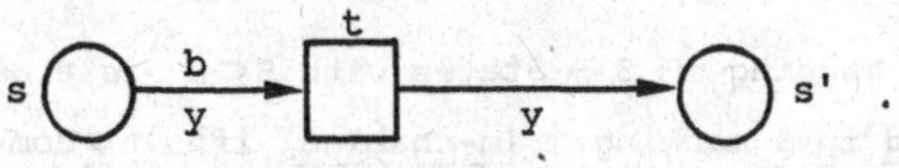

The transition t is enabled iff s carries a token σ satisfying the boolean expression b. In this case, t may fire moving σ from s to s'.

3) Communication caused by a command $P_2?x$ in process P_1 and a command $P_1!e$ in process P_2 is translated as

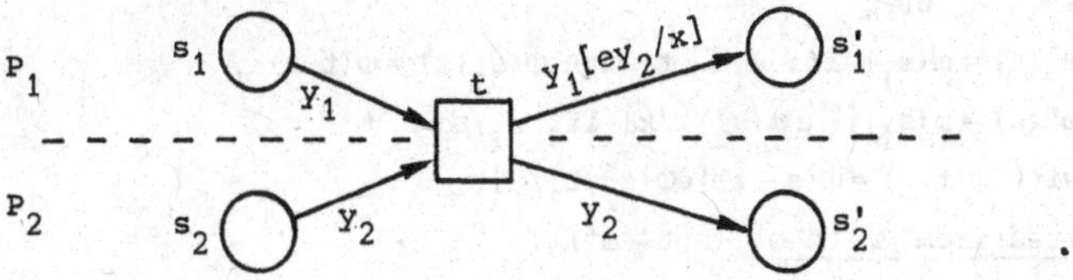

t is enabled if s_1 and s_2 carry arbitrary tokens σ_1, σ_2, respectively, and the firing of t moves σ_2 from s_2 to s_2', removes σ_1 from s_1 and adds $\sigma_1[[\![e\sigma_2]\!]/x]$ to s_1'.
If we have communication requests in guards, the arcs of this form of transition

may additionally be labelled by boolean expressions. Then t is only enabled if the tokens on the respective preplaces satisfy these boolean expressions.

We now give the formal definition of the class of nets we consider and of the firing rule.

<u>Definition</u> Let $N = (S,T;F)$ be a net, $\tau : T \dashrightarrow \text{Comm}$, $\beta : F \cap (S \times T) \dashrightarrow \text{BExp}$, $\varphi : F \longrightarrow Y \cup \text{Subst}$ with $\varphi(s,t) \in Y$ for all $(s,t) \in F \cap (S \times T)$ ($\dashrightarrow$ denotes partial functions).
$(S,T;F,\tau,\beta,\varphi)$ is called a <u>CSP-net</u> if $T = T_1 \cup T_g$ with

(i) $\forall t \in T_1 \; |{}^{\bullet}t| = |t^{\bullet}| = 1$ and $\varphi(t,t^{\bullet}) = y$ or $\varphi(t,t^{\bullet}) = y[ey/x]$ with $y := \varphi({}^{\bullet}t,t)$ (<u>local transitions</u>),

(ii) $\forall t \in T_g$ ${}^{\bullet}t$ and $t^{\bullet}$ can be written as ${}^{\bullet}t = \{s_1,s_2\}$ and $t^{\bullet} = \{s_1',s_2'\}$, and with $y_i := \varphi(s_i,t)$ we have $y_1 \neq y_2$ and $\varphi(t,s_1') = y_1[ey_2/x]$ and $\varphi(t,s_2') = y_2$ (<u>global transitions</u>).

The labellings τ of transitions will be used in the translation process to specify possible communications, but they have no influence on the dynamic behaviour of the net.

As before, we index the components of a CSP-net N by N. We distinguish certain places in the net which will carry the initial marking. (N,I), $I \subseteq S_N$, denotes a CSP-net with initial places I. Graphically, initial places will be denoted by black tokens.

Now, we define the dynamic behaviour of CSP-nets by stating the <u>firing rule</u>.

<u>Definition</u> For a CSP-net N, a mapping $m : S \dashrightarrow \text{States}$ with $S \subseteq S_N$ is a <u>marking</u> of N.
A transition $t \in T_N$ is <u>enabled</u> in a marking m (<u>m-enabled</u>) iff ${}^{\bullet}t \subseteq \text{dom}(m)$, $(t^{\bullet} \setminus {}^{\bullet}t) \cap \text{dom}(m) = \emptyset$ and $\forall s \in S_N \; \beta(s,t) = b \Rightarrow [\![b\, m(s)]\!] = tt$.
Let t be m-enabled.
Let m' be defined by

(i) $\text{dom}(m') = (\text{dom}(m) \setminus {}^{\bullet}t) \cup t^{\bullet}$,

(ii) for $s \notin t^{\bullet}$, let $m'(s) = m(s)$,

(iii) for $s \in t^{\bullet}$, let

$m'(s) = m(s_1)$ iff $s_1 \in {}^{\bullet}t$ with $\varphi(s_1,t) = \varphi(t,s)$,

$m'(s) = m(s_1)[[\![e\, m(s_2)]\!]/x]$ iff $s_1,s_2 \in {}^{\bullet}t$ with $\varphi(t,s) = \varphi(s_1,t)[e\varphi(s_2,t)/x]$.

Then <u>t fires from m to m'</u> $(m[t>m')$.
Let $[m>$ be the smallest set such that $m \in [m>$ and $m' \in [m>, m'[t>m'' \Rightarrow m'' \in [m>$.
$[m>$ is called the set of <u>reachable markings</u> (of m).

The definition of the follower marking m' above is unique because of the restriction imposed on φ-inscriptions in CSP-nets.

As examples, consider the types of transitions given above.

We consider CSP-nets with initial markings; (N,m) denotes a CSP-net N with initial marking m .

The firing rule gives the semantics for a single transition firing. To represent the whole behaviour of a net, we introduce the notion of unfolding (as a generalisation of a definition given in [GM2]). Unfoldings are based on cycle-free nets with places which can only be forwardly branched (representing non-deterministic choices). They were introduced in [NPW].

Definition We say a net N is cycle-free iff $\forall x \in N, \neg(x F_N^+ x)$ (where F_N^+ denotes the transitive closure of F_N). In such cases we define

(i) $x < y$ iff $x F_N^+ y$,

(ii) $x \# y$ iff $\exists t,t' \in T_N, t \neq t', {}^{\bullet}t \cap {}^{\bullet}t' \neq \emptyset, t \leq x, t' \leq y$
(x and y are in conflict),

(iii) x co y iff $x = y \vee \neg(x \leq y \vee y \leq x \vee x \# y)$
(x and y are concurrent),

(iv) $S \subseteq S_N$ is called a slice iff S is finite and
$\forall s_1, s_2 \in S, s_1$ co $s_2, \forall s \in N \setminus S\ \exists s' \in S$ with $\neg$(s co s') .

In the literature, slices are usually allowed to be infinite. Since we will only be interested in finite slices for our purposes, we have put this restriction into the definition.

Definition A cycle-free net K is called an occurrence net iff

(i) $\forall s \in S_K\ |{}^{\bullet}s| \leq 1$,

(ii) # is irreflexive,

(iii) K is founded, i.e. $\forall x \in K\ \{y | y \leq x\}$ is finite.

K is called a causal net iff K is an occurrence net with $\forall s \in S_K\ |s^{\bullet}| \leq 1$.

The foundedness restriction means that we only consider such behaviours of systems which may be generated by finite approximations. Now we can give the definition of unfolding as a mapping from an occurrence net into a CSP-net which satisfies certain requirements.

As processes for C/E-systems (one-safe nets) [Re1], unfoldings will only be defined for contact-free nets. All nets resulting from our CSP-translation will be contact-free.

Definition A CSP-net (N,m) is called contact-free iff, for each $t \in T_N$ and for each $m' \in [m>$, ${}^{\bullet}t \subseteq dom(m') \Rightarrow (t^{\bullet} \setminus {}^{\bullet}t) \cap dom(m') = \emptyset$.

Definition Let (N,m) be a CSP-net with initial marking m , and let K be an occurrence net.

Let $f_1 : K \to N$ with $f_1(S_K) \subseteq S_N$, $f_1(T_K) \subseteq T_N$, $f_1 \upharpoonright S$ injective for all slices S of K.
Let $f_2 : S_K \to$ States.
For a slices S of K, let m_S, the <u>marking associated with S</u>, be defined by
$\mathrm{dom}(m_S) = f_1(S)$, $m_S(f_1(s)) = f_2(s)\ \forall s \in S$.
$f = (K, f_1, f_2)$ is called an <u>unfolding</u> of N iff

$m_{\circ_K} = m$,

$\forall s \in S_N\ \forall t \in T_K : |f_1^{-1}(s) \cap {}^{\bullet}t| = sF_N f_1(t)$,

$|f_1^{-1}(s) \cap t^{\bullet}| = f_1(t) F_N s$

(interpreting $xF_N y$ as 0 or 1 according to $xF_N y$ holding or not).

For all slices S of K, all $t \in T_N$,

$$|f_1^{-1}(t) \cap \{t' \in T_K \mid {}^{\bullet}t' \subseteq S\}| = \begin{cases} 1 & \text{iff } t \text{ is } m_S\text{-enabled}, \\ 0 & \text{otherwise}. \end{cases}$$

For all slices S of K, all $t \in T_K$ with $f_1(t)$ m_S-enabled,
$S' := S \setminus {}^{\bullet}t \cup t^{\bullet} \Rightarrow m_S[f_1(t) > m_{S'}$.
(Note that S' is again a slice.)

<u>Example</u>

Consider the following small marked net.

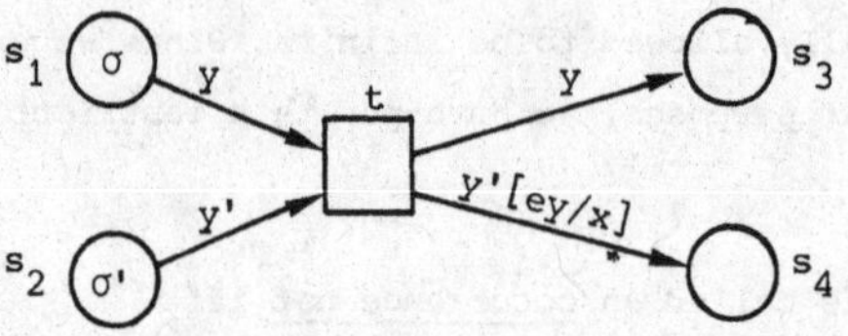

The unfolding of this net is

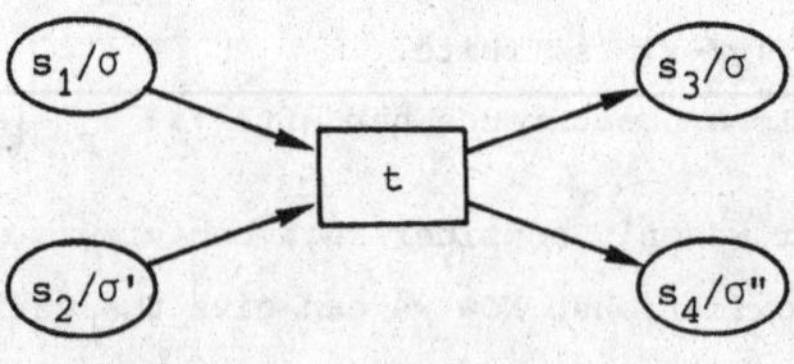

$\sigma'' := \sigma'[[\![e\sigma]\!]/x]$

<u>Lemma</u> Unfoldings of nets are unique up to isomorphism (see [GM2]).

Hence we will speak of 'the' unfolding of a net.

Next, we will characterise the possible computations of CSP-nets as <u>processes</u>, similar to the notion of process defined for relation nets in [GV]. We use a strict generalisation of the process notions for condition/event-systems [GLT] and place/transition-nets [GR], but use a result of [GM2] and define them as special left-closed subsets of the unfolding.

Definition Let K be an occurrence net, $K' \subseteq K$.

K' is an initial subnet of K ($K' \leq K$) iff

(i) ${}^{\circ}K' = {}^{\circ}K$,

(ii) $\forall x,y \in K: x \leq y \wedge y \in K' \Rightarrow x \in K'$ (K' is left closed in K),

(iii) $\forall t \in T_{K'}: t^{\bullet} \subseteq K'$ ($t^{\bullet}$ refers to F_K).

Let $f = (K, f_1, f_2)$ be unfolding of a marked CSP-net (N,m). Then $p = (K', p_1, p_2)$ is called a process of (N,m) iff K' is maximal such that $K' \leq K$, K' is a causal net and $p_i = f_i \upharpoonright K'$, $i = 1,2$.

Finally, we show that slices in the unfolding and in processes correspond to reachable markings of the marked CSP-net.

For this, we generalise two theorems of [BG].

Theorem Let K be an occurrence net and let $S \subseteq S_K$ be a slice of K, $S \neq {}^{\circ}K$. Then $\exists t \in T_K$ with $t^{\bullet} \subseteq S$.

Proof

We first show the following proposition.

(1): Let $t \in T_K$, $s \in S_K$ and $s_1, s_2 \in t^{\bullet}$. $s_1 \text{ co } s \Rightarrow \neg(s_2 \# s) \wedge \neg(s_2 \geq s)$.

$s_2 \# s \Leftrightarrow s_1 \# s$, since $\forall t' \in T_K\ t' \leq s_1 \Leftrightarrow t' \leq s_2$, $s_2 \geq s \Leftrightarrow s_1 \geq s$, since $s_2 \geq s \Leftrightarrow t \geq s$ (since $|{}^{\bullet}s| \leq 1$) and hence $s_2 \geq s \Leftrightarrow s_1 \geq s$.

Now, we prove the lemma indirectly assuming

(2): $\forall t \in T_K: t^{\bullet} \not\subseteq S$.

We construct for every $n \geq 0$ three sets as follows:

$\{t_0, \ldots, t_n\} \subseteq T_K$, $\{s_0, \ldots, s_n\} \subseteq S_K$, $\{s'_0, \ldots, s'_{n-1}\} \subseteq S_K$ with $s_i \neq s_j$ for $i \neq j$ and the following properties:

(i) $s_i \in S \cap t_i^{\bullet}$ for $0 \leq i \leq n$, $s'_i \in t_i^{\bullet} \setminus S$ for $0 \leq i < n$;

(ii) $s'_i \leq t_{i+1}$ for $0 \leq i < n$.

This yields the desired contradiction since S is finite.

$n = 0$: Pick $s_0 \in S$ such that ${}^{\bullet}s_0 \neq \emptyset$ (such an s_0 exists since $S \neq {}^{\circ}K$); put t_0 such that $\{t_0\} = {}^{\bullet}s_0$. Properties (i) and (ii) are trivially true for this choice. Now assume $\{t_0, \ldots, t_n\}$, $\{s_0, \ldots, s_n\}$, $\{s'_0, \ldots, s'_{n-1}\}$ already constructed.

By (2), $t_n^{\bullet} \not\subseteq S$; hence $\exists s'_n \in t_n^{\bullet} \setminus S$. Since S is a slice and $s'_n \notin S$, $\exists s \in S$ with $s'_n \leq s \vee s \leq s'_n \vee s \# s'_n$. Since $s_n \in S$, we have $s_n \text{ co } s$ and $s_n, s'_n \in t_n^{\bullet}$. Hence, by (1), $\neg(s'_n \# s) \wedge \neg(s'_n \geq s) \Rightarrow s'_n \leq s$. We show that $s \notin \{s_0, \ldots, s_n\}$. For suppose otherwise, i.e. $\exists i$, $0 \leq i \leq n$, with $s'_n \leq s_i$, hence $s'_n < t_i$ (since $|{}^{\bullet}s_i| \leq 1$). Then applying (ii) n-i times:

$$s'_n < t_i < s'_i < t_{i+1} < \ldots < t_n < s'_n$$

which contradicts cycle-freeness.

Hence $s \notin \{s_o,\ldots,s_n\}$ and we can define $s_{n+1} := s$, t_{n+1} such that $\{t_{n+1}\} = {}^{\bullet}s_{n+1}$ (the latter exists because of $s'_n < s_{n+1}$).

This completes the construction, (i) and (ii) are easily verfied for the new sets. □

<u>Theorem</u> Let (N,m) be a marked CSP-net.

$[m> = \{m_S | S$ is a slice of the unfolding of $(N,m)\}$.

<u>Proof</u>

Let $f = (K,f_1,f_2)$ be the unfolding of (N,m) . "$\subseteq$" Let $m' \in [m>$. We prove, by induction on the structure of $[m>$, that there exists a slice S of K with $m' = m_S$.

$m' = m : m = m_{\circ K}$ by definition of unfolding. Let $m'' \in [m>$ with $m''\ [t>m'$. By the induction hypothesis, there exists a slice S of K with $m'' = m_S$. Since t is m_S-enabled, there exists $t' \in T_K$ with ${}^{\bullet}t' \subseteq S$ and $f_1(t') = t$. Let $S' := S \setminus {}^{\bullet}t' \cup t'^{\bullet}$. Then $m''\ [t>m_{S'}$, and since the follower marking of m'', when firing t, is unique, $m_{S'} = m'$.

"$\supseteq$" For any slice S of K, let $T_S := \{t \in T_K | \exists s \in S$ with $t < s\}$. T_S is finite since S is finite and K is founded. Let S be a slice of K. We prove $m_S \in [m>$ by induction on $|T_S|$.

$|T_S| = 0 \Rightarrow S = {}^{\circ}K \Rightarrow m_S = m$.

Let $|T_S| = n+1$. Since S is a finite slice, there exists a transition $t \in T_K$ with $t^{\bullet} \subseteq S$ (using the above theorem). Clearly, $S' := S \setminus t^{\bullet} \cup {}^{\bullet}t$ is a slice of K and $|T_{S'}| = n$. By the induction hypothesis, $m_{S'} \in [m>$, and since $m_{S'}[f_1(t)>m_S$ by the definition of unfolding, we find $m_S \in [m>$. □

To establish the relationship between slices of processes and reachable markings, we need the following lemma.

<u>Lemma</u> Let K,K' be occurrence nets, $K \leq K'$.

Let $X \subseteq K$.

X is a slice of K $\Leftrightarrow$ X is a slice of K' .

<u>Proof</u>

We first prove, for $x,y \in K$, x <u>co</u> y in K $\Leftrightarrow$ x <u>co</u> y in K'. Let x <u>co</u> y in K. $x \leq y$ in K' $\Rightarrow$ $x \leq y$ in K. Similar for $y \leq x$ in K'. $x \# y$ in K' $\Rightarrow$ $\exists t,t' \in K'$ with $t \neq t'$, $t \leq x$, $t' \leq y$ and ${}^{\bullet}t \cap {}^{\bullet}t' \neq \emptyset$. $K \leq K' \Rightarrow t,t' \in K \Rightarrow x \# y$ in K.

Let x <u>co</u> y in K' $\Rightarrow$ x <u>co</u> y in K since $K \leq K'$.

Let X be a slice of K' $\Rightarrow \forall x,y \in X$ x <u>co</u> y and $\forall x \in K' \setminus X\ \exists y \in X$ with $\neg$(x <u>co</u> y) in K' $\Rightarrow \forall x,y \in X$ x <u>co</u> y and $\forall x \in K \setminus X\ \exists y \in X$ with $\neg$(x <u>co</u> y) in K $\Rightarrow$ X is a slice of K.

Let X be a slice of K $\Rightarrow \forall x,y \in X$: x <u>co</u> y in K $\Rightarrow \forall x,y \in X$: x <u>co</u> y in K' .

Let $x \in K' \setminus X$. If $x \in K$ then $\exists y \in K$ with $\neg$(x <u>co</u> y). If $x \notin K$, we wish to show $\exists y \in X$ with

$x \# y \vee y \leq x$. $x \notin K \Rightarrow x \notin {}^{\circ}K' \Rightarrow \exists x_o \in {}^{\circ}K'$ with $x_o < x$ and there exists $n \in \mathbb{N}$ and elements x_i , $1 \leq i \leq n$ with $x_o \leq x_1 \leq \ldots \leq x_n = x$ and $x_{i+1} \in x_i^{\bullet}$.

Let $s := \max\{x_i \mid 1 \leq i \leq n , x_i \in K\}$. $s \in S_K$ (since for $t \in T_K$, $t^{\bullet} \subseteq K$). If $s \in X$, then we have found $y := s \in X$ with $y \leq x$. If $s \notin X$, then $\exists y \in X$ with $s \leq y \vee y \leq s \vee s \# y$.

For $y \leq s$, we have found $y \in X$ with $y \leq s \leq x$. For $s \leq y$, we have $\exists t \in s^{\bullet}$, $t \in K$ with $t \leq y$ and $\exists t' \in s^{\bullet}$, $t' \notin K$ with $t \leq x$. Hence we have found $y \in X$ with $x \# y$.
For $s \# y$, $\exists t,t' \in T_K$, $t \neq t'$, $t \leq s$, $t' \leq y$ and ${}^{\bullet}t \cap {}^{\bullet}t' \neq \emptyset$. $t' \leq s \leq x \Rightarrow x \# y$. □

Hence, every slice of a process is also a slice of the unfolding and corresponds to a reachable marking.

4. Translation of CSP into CSP-nets

We start by defining some operations on nets which we will use in the translation process.

4.1 Composition operations for sequential nets

Our translation process will consist of two steps. First we translate the sequential components of the CSP program, then we combine these by a parallel composition. In this section we define two operations for sequential nets occurring in the first part of the translation.

Definition A CSP-net (N,I) is called sequential iff all transitions $t \in T_N$ are local and $|I| = 1$. (We abbreviate $(N,\{s\})$ by (N,s) .)

Then binary operation $\circ$ will describe sequential composition of two sequential nets.

Definition Let (N_1,s_1) , (N_2,s_2) be sequential CSP-nets, without loss of generality $N_1 \cap N_2 = \emptyset$.
If $s_1^{\bullet} = \emptyset$ then N_1 consists only of plase s_1 and we define $(N_1,s_1)\circ(N_2,s_2) := (N_2,s_2)$.
Otherwise, let $N_i = (S_i,T_i;F_i,\tau_i,\beta_i,\varphi_i)$, $i = 1,2$.
Then $(N_1,s_1)\circ(N_2,s_2) := (N,s_1)$ where $N := (S,T;F,\tau,\beta,\varphi)$,
$S := (S_1 \setminus N_1^{\circ}) \cup S_2$, $T := T_1 \cup T_2$, $\tau := \tau_1 \cup \tau_2$,
$F := ((F_1 \cup F_2) \cap (S \cup T)^2) \cup ({}^{\bullet}N_1^{\circ} \times \{s_2\})$, $\beta := \beta_1 \cup \beta_2$,

$$\varphi(x,y) := \begin{cases} \varphi_i(x,y) & \text{if} \quad x,y \in N_i \ (i=1,2) , \\ \varphi_1(x,s) & \text{if} \quad x \in {}^{\bullet}s , s \in N_1^{\circ} . \end{cases}$$

Hence $N_1 \circ N_2$ is obtained by identifying the end-elements of N_1 with the initial element of N_2 .

Example

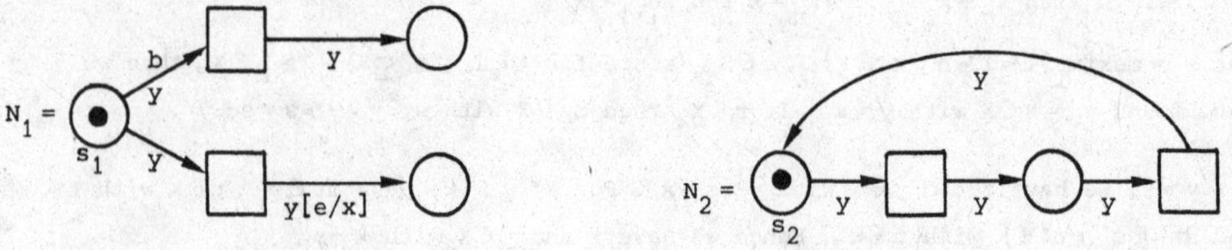

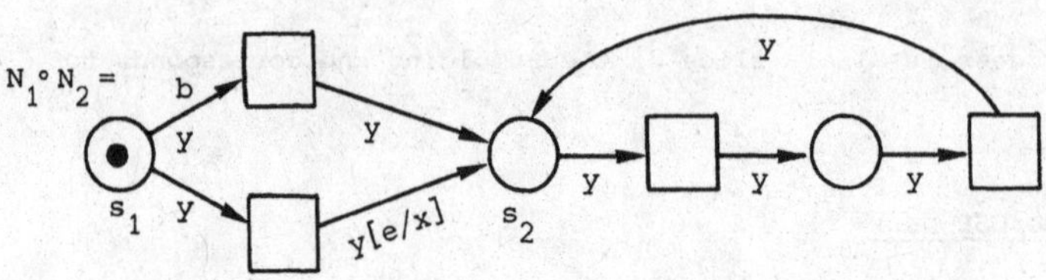

The binary operation + will describe the non-deterministic combination of two sequential nets.

Definition Let (N_1,s_1) , (N_2,s_2) be sequential CSP-nets, w.l.o.g.

$N_1 \cap N_2 = \emptyset$, $N_i = (S_i,T_i;F_i,\tau_i,\beta_i,\varphi_i)$, $i = 1,2$.

Then $(N_1,s_1) + (N_2,s_2) := (N,s_1)$ where $N := (S,T;F,\tau,\beta,\varphi)$,

$S := ((S_1 \cup S_2) \setminus \{s_1,s_2\}) \dot{\cup} \{s_o\}$, $T := T_1 \cup T_2$, $\tau := \tau_1 \cup \tau_2$,

$F := ((F_1 \cup F_2) \cap (S \cup T)^2) \cup \{s_o\} \times (s_1{}^{\bullet} \cup s_2{}^{\bullet}) \cup ({}^{\bullet}s_1 \cup {}^{\bullet}s_2) \times \{s_o\}$,

$\beta(s,t) := \beta_i({}^{\bullet}t,t)$ for $t \in T_i$ $(i = 1,2)$, $s \in S$,

$$\varphi(x,y) := \begin{cases} \varphi_i({}^{\bullet}y,y) & \text{if } y \in T_i \ (i=1,2) , \\ \varphi_i(x,x^{\bullet}) & \text{if } x \in T_i \ (i=1,2) . \end{cases}$$

Hence we obtain $N_1 + N_2$ by identifying the initial elements of N_1 and N_2 .

Note that this definition of a non-deterministic combinator is not always sensible. Consider the following example:

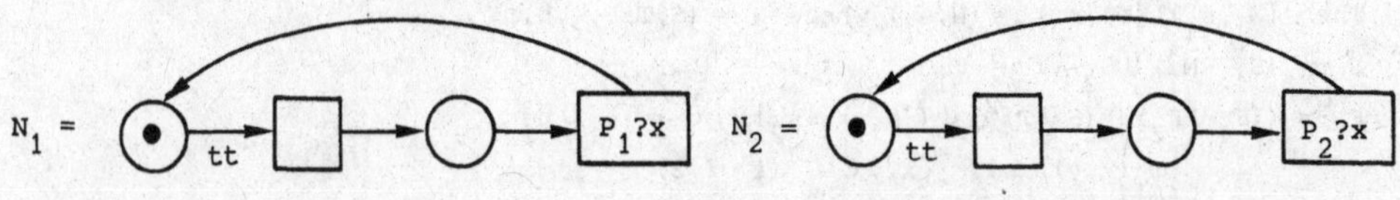

For the non-deterministic combination of both, we expect a possible choice between the two behaviours represented by N_1 and N_2 . This choice should be taken once in a certain situation, corresponding to the semantics of CCS and CSP. The wanted behaviour can be described by the following occurrence net:

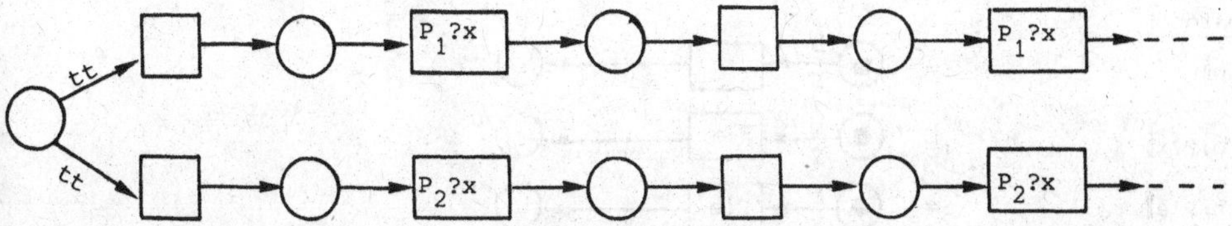

Unfortunately, the + -operator defined above yields

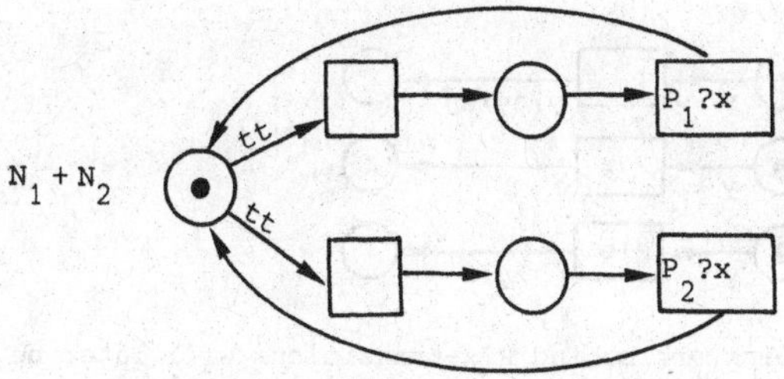

which has not the wanted behaviour.

However, for our CSP-translation such problems will not occur. The reason is that CSP does not allow non-determinism without introducing guards. It follows that our operands to + will always have initial places with empty presets.

This definition of + on nets given here corresponds exactly to Winskel's coproduct introduced in [Wi]. The problem pointed out above corresponds to the fact that coproducts are not always preserved by unfolding. However they are preserved for those nets whose initially marked places have empty presets, as stated in [Wi].

4.2 The translation functions N and N_p

We now define a translation function $N[\![\ldots]\!] : \mathrm{CSP} \rightarrow \mathrm{Nets}$, where Nets is the class of CSP-nets as defined in section 3. Actually, the translation of a CSP-program will yield an arbitrary representative of an equivalence class of isomorphic nets, only distinguished by choices for the sets of places and transitions. These sets have no significance, and representatives are only used when defining operations (independently from the chosen representative). Later we will no longer distinguish isomorphic nets.

We define the translation function by induction on the syntactic structure of (finite) CSP-programs. We use sequential CSP-nets until we perform the parallel composition in the last step. There we obtain a net with an initial element for each sequential component. These initial elements will later carry tokens representing the initial state of the program execution.

Let $y \in Y$ be some state variable.

<u>Guards</u>

$\mathcal{M}[\![b]\!]$:= 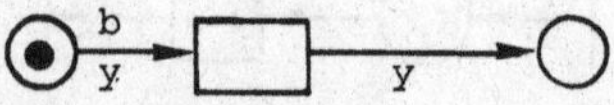

$\mathcal{M}[\![b;P?x]\!]$:= 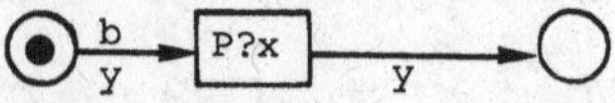

$\mathcal{M}[\![b;P!e]\!]$:= 

It is obvious how to define these three nets formally, using arbitrary sets S_N, T_N. The same holds for the next three cases.

<u>Commands</u>

$\mathcal{M}[\![x := e]\!]$:= 

$\mathcal{M}[\![P?x]\!]$:= 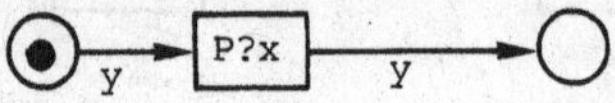

$\mathcal{M}[\![P!e]\!]$:= 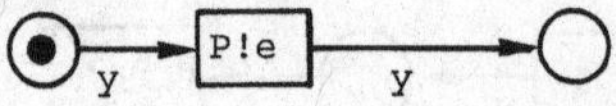

The inscription of the outgoing arc behind P?x-transitions will later be changed to represent the state change caused by the communication (if possible).

$\mathcal{M}[\![$<u>skip</u>$]\!]$:= 

For the translation of <u>abort</u>, we have to consider what the semantics of <u>abort</u> should be. In [HLP], it is modelled by non-ending computation, as shown in section 2. We persue an alternative approach here, modelling <u>abort</u> by deadlock, since this seems more natural to us. Later we show how to change the translation to correspond exactly to the semantics of [HLP].

$\mathcal{M}[\![$<u>abort</u>$]\!]$:= 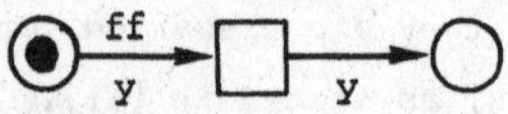

$\mathcal{M}[\![C_1;C_2]\!] := \mathcal{M}[\![C_1]\!] \circ \mathcal{M}[\![C_2]\!]$

$\mathcal{M}[\![$<u>if</u> $G_1 \to C_1 [\!] \ldots [\!] G_n \to C_n$ <u>fi</u>$]\!]$:= $(\mathcal{M}[\![G_1]\!] \circ \mathcal{M}[\![C_1]\!]) + \ldots + (\mathcal{M}[\![G_n]\!] \circ \mathcal{M}[\![C_n]\!])$

$\mathcal{M}[\![$<u>do</u> $G_1 \to C_1 [\!] \ldots [\!] G_n \to C_n$ <u>od</u>$]\!]$ is defined as follows:

Let $N := (\mathcal{M}[\![G_1]\!] \circ \mathcal{M}[\![C_1]\!]) + \ldots + (\mathcal{M}[\![G_n]\!] \circ \mathcal{M}[\![C_n]\!])$, ${}^{\circ}N = \{s_o\}$.

Let $\bigcup_{t \in T_N} \beta(s_o,t) = \{b_1,\ldots,b_n\}$.

We define N_e as 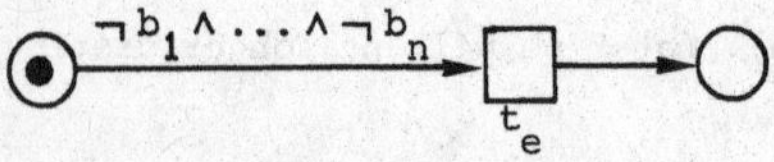 .

Let $N' = (S,T;F,\tau,\beta,\varphi)$ be defined by

$S := S_N \setminus N^{\circ}$, $T := T_N$, $\tau := \tau_N$,

$F := (F_N \cap (S \cup T)^2) \cup {}^{\cdot}N^{\circ} \times \{s_o\}$, $\beta := \beta_N$,

$$\varphi(x,y) = \begin{cases} \varphi_N(x,x^{\cdot}) & \text{if} \quad x \in T, \\ \varphi_N(x,y) & \text{if} \quad x \in S. \end{cases}$$

Then $\mathcal{M}[\![$<u>do</u> $G_1 \to C_1 [\!] \ldots [\!] G_n \to C_n$ <u>od</u>$]\!]$:= $(N',s_o) + N_e$.

N_e describes the exit of the loop when all conditions in the guards fail. In contrast to this, failure of all guards in an <u>if</u>-statement corresponds to <u>abort</u>, which we model by deadlock here. Failure of communication may cause deadlock both in <u>if</u>-statements and in loops.

<u>Example</u>

$\mathcal{M}[\![$ <u>if</u> $b;P?x \rightarrow x := e [\!] b' \rightarrow x := e'$ <u>fi</u> $]\!]$

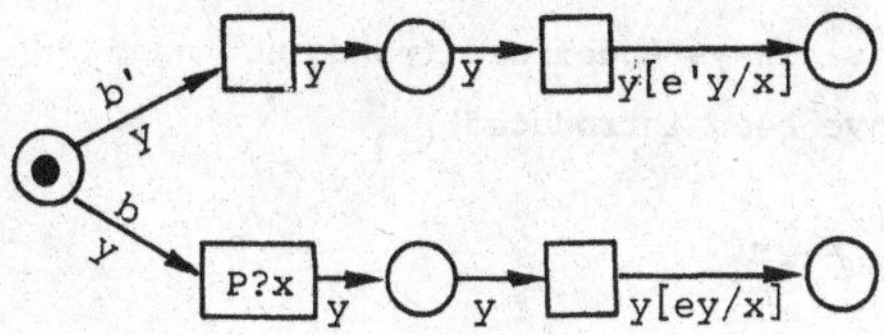

$\mathcal{M}[\![$ <u>do</u> $b;P?x \rightarrow x := e [\!] b' \rightarrow x := e'$ <u>od</u> $]\!]$

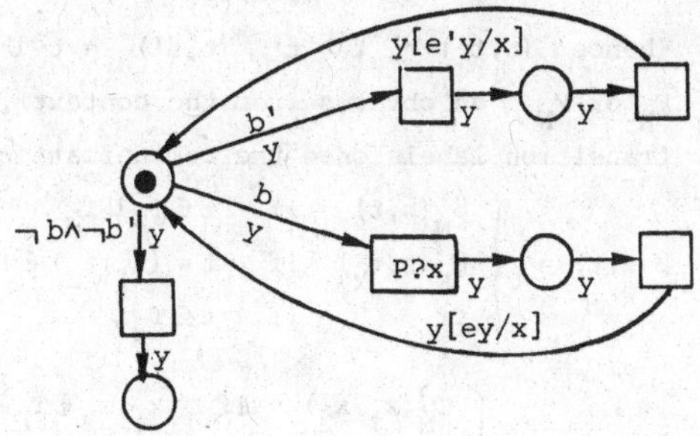

<u>Programs</u>

For the translation of programs, we first change the variables used in the arc inscription φ, to distinguish the sequential components.

Let $Pr = P_1 :: C_1 \| \ldots \| P_m :: C_m$.

Let $(N_i, I_i) = \mathcal{M}[\![C_i]\!]$ with $\varphi(x_1, x_2) \in \{y_i\} \cup \{y_i[ey_i/x] \mid e \in \mathrm{Exp}, x \in \mathrm{Var}\}$

for all $x_1, x_2 \in N_i$,

$N_i \cap N_j = \emptyset$ for $i \neq j$.

Let $N := \bigcup_{i=1}^{m} N_i$ (using set union for all components).

Now, we have to implement all possible communications, as indicated by transition labels τ. This is done by introducing a new transition for every pair of transitions with corresponding labels, and then omitting these transitions.

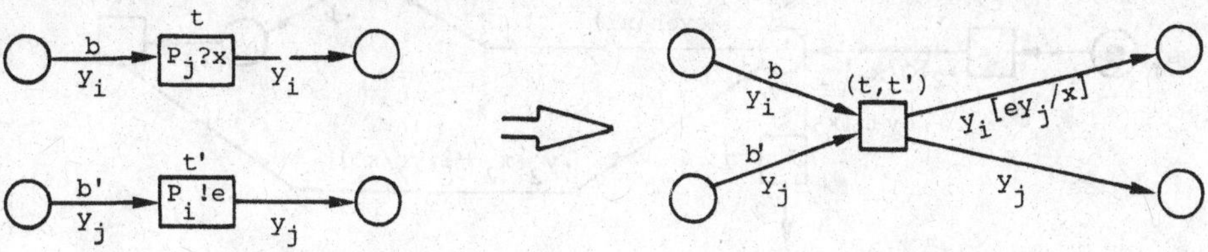

Furthermore, if there are any labelled transitions without any corresponding labelled transitions, these will not be allowed to fire (by adding an arc inscription ff).

Let $T_c := \{(t,t') \mid t \in N_i , t' \in N_j , \tau_N(t) = P_j?x , \tau_N(t') = P_i!e , x \in \mathrm{Var} , e \in \mathrm{Exp}\}$,

$T_d := \{t \in N \mid t$ carries a communication label, $(t,t') \notin T_c$ and

$(t',t) \notin T_c$ for all $t' \in N\}$.

We define $M[\![Pr]\!] := (N', I)$, where $N' = (S,T;F,\tau,\beta,\varphi)$ is defined as follows.

$$S := S_N,\ I := \bigcup_{i=1}^{m} I_i,$$

$$T := (T_N \setminus \{t \mid (t,t') \in T_c \vee (t',t) \in T_c\}) \,\dot{\cup}\, T_c,$$

$$F := (F_N \cap (S \cup T)^2) \cup \bigcup_{(t,t') \in T} \{{}^{\bullet}t \cup {}^{\bullet}t'\} \times \{(t,t')\}$$
$$\cup \bigcup_{(t,t') \in T} \{(t,t')\} \times \{t^{\bullet} \cup t'^{\bullet}\}$$

(hence ${}^{\bullet}(t,t') = {}^{\bullet}t \cup {}^{\bullet}t'$, $(t,t')^{\bullet} = t^{\bullet} \cup t'^{\bullet}$, the dots refer to the flow relation F_N or $F_{N'}$, as obvious from the context), τ is always undefined (we do not need transition labels once the communications have been introduced),

$$\beta(s,t) = \begin{cases} \beta_N(s,t) & \text{if } t \notin T_c \cup T_d, \\ \beta_N(s,t_k) & \text{if } t = (t_1,t_2) \in T_c,\ s \in {}^{\bullet}t_k, \\ ff & \text{if } t \in T_d, \end{cases}$$

$$\varphi(x_1,x_2) = \begin{cases} \varphi_N(x_1,x_2) & \text{if } x_1,x_2 \notin T_c, \\ \varphi_N(x_1,t_k) & \text{if } x_2 = (t_1,t_2) \in T_c,\ x_1 \in {}^{\bullet}t_k, \\ \varphi_N(t_2,x_2) & \text{if } x_1 = (t_1,t_2) \in T_c,\ x_2 \in t_2^{\bullet}, \\ y_i[ey_j/x] & \text{if } x_1 = (t_1,t_2) \in T_c,\ x_2 \in t_1^{\bullet}, \\ & \quad \tau(t_1) = P_j?x,\ \tau(t_2) = P_i!e. \end{cases}$$

As an example, the program P_1 of section 2.1 is translated as follows.

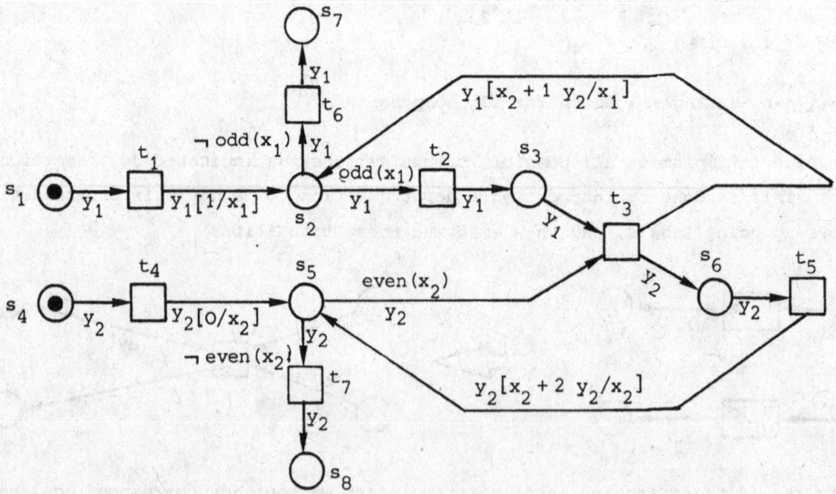

<u>An alternative version</u>

Even though this translation is convincing for us, we will give an alternative version. The reason is that we want to prove that the semantics of our net translation corresponds exactly in a very strong sense to the operational semantics given in [HLP].

Our translation satisfies nearly all requirements for that, with two exceptions. First, in the semantics of [HLP], as mentioned before, abortion is modelled by non-ending computation, whereas in our translation it is modelled as deadlock.

Secondly, [HLP] introduces a skip-action between the actions of C_1 and C_2 for $C_1;C_2$. It is stated that this was an arbitrary choice. Since we wanted to keep the nets as concise as possible, we have omitted them. We now reintroduce them to get our strong equivalence result stated in section 5.

We define $\mathcal{N}_p[\![\ldots]\!] : CSP \rightarrow Nets$ by changing $\mathcal{M}[\![\ldots]\!]$ as follows:

$\mathcal{N}_p[\![\underline{abort}]\!] :=$ 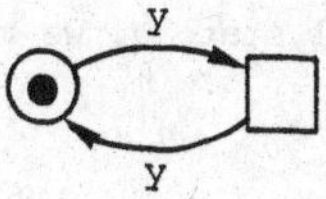

$\mathcal{N}_p[\![\underline{if}\ G_1 \rightarrow C_1 [\!] \ldots [\!] G_n \rightarrow C_n\ \underline{fi}]\!]$ is defined as follows:

Let $N := (\mathcal{N}_p[\![G_1]\!] \circ \mathcal{N}_p[\![C_1]\!]) + \ldots + (\mathcal{N}_p[\![G_n]\!] \circ \mathcal{N}_p[\![C_n]\!])$,

$\quad {}^{\circ}N = \{s_o\}$.

Let $\bigcup_{t \in T_N} \beta(s_o,t) = \{b_1,\ldots,b_n\}$.

We define N_a as 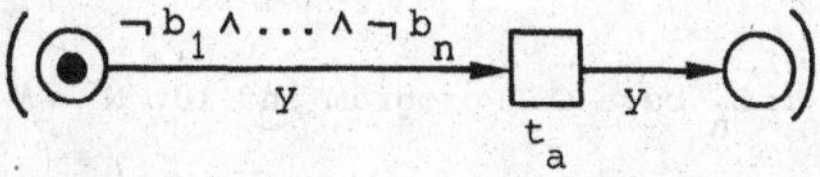 $\circ\, \mathcal{N}_p[\![\underline{abort}]\!]$.

Then $\mathcal{N}_p[\![\underline{if}\ G_1 \rightarrow C_1 [\!] \ldots [\!] G_n \rightarrow C_n\ \underline{fi}]\!] := (N,s_o) + N_a$.

This construction adds a self-loop for the case when all guards fail.

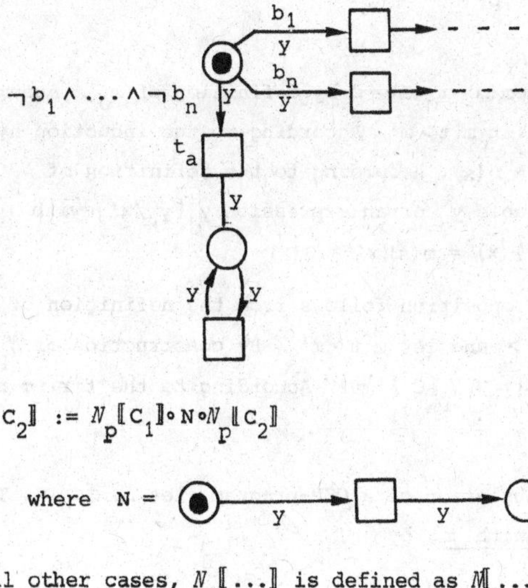

$\mathcal{N}_p[\![C_1;C_2]\!] := \mathcal{N}_p[\![C_1]\!] \circ N \circ \mathcal{N}_p[\![C_2]\!]$

where $N =$.

For all other cases, $\mathcal{N}_p[\![\ldots]\!]$ is defined as $\mathcal{M}[\![\ldots]\!]$.

4.3 Dynamic behaviour

Until now we have given a static translation of CSP-programs into nets. Using the net semantics in terms of processes or firing sequences, this yields a full description of the dynamic behaviour of CSP programs. It will turn out that firing sequences correspond to the usual interleaving semantics whereas processes give additional information about causal dependencies and independencies in a certain run of the program. For a detailed discussion of results obtained by discussing processes, see [Re2] where similar objects as processes are obtained directly by generalising the operational approach of [HLP].

To describe the behaviour of a program for a certain initial state σ, we mark all initial places of the net translation by σ.

Definition Let (N,I) be a CSP-net with initial places. For a state σ we define the initial marking m_σ by $\mathrm{dom}(m_\sigma) = I$, $m_\sigma(s) = \sigma$ for all $s \in I$.

We will sometimes abbreviate (N,m_σ) by N^σ.

For all follower markings m in our translation of CSP-programs, we can construct a corresponding global state σ_m. That this really gives a unique value for all variables is assured by the structure of the translation and the properties of CSP.

Proposition Let $Pr = P_1 :: C_1 \| \ldots \| P_n :: C_n$ be a CSP-program and let $N^\sigma = \mathcal{N}_p[\![Pr]\!]^\sigma$. Then, for all $m \in [m_\sigma>$:

(i) $\forall 1 \leq i \leq n \quad \forall x \in Var(C_i) \quad \forall s \in \mathcal{N}_p[\![Pr]\!] \setminus \mathcal{N}_p[\![C_i]\!] : m(s)(x) = \sigma(x)$

(ii) $|\mathrm{dom}(m) \cap \mathcal{N}_p[\![C_i]\!]| = 1$.

(This also holds using $\mathcal{N}$ instead of $\mathcal{N}_p$.)

Proof

(i) by induction: for $m = m_\sigma$, $\forall s \in \mathrm{dom}(m)$ $m_\sigma(s) = \sigma$ by definition of m_σ. Assume the proposition holds for $m \in [m_\sigma>$ and let $m[t>m'$. According to the induction hypothesis, for all $s \in {}^\cdot t \setminus \mathcal{N}_p[\![C_i]\!]$, $m(s)(x) = \sigma(x)$. According to the definition of $\mathcal{N}_p$, for all $s \in t^\cdot \setminus \mathcal{N}_p[\![C_i]\!]$, $\varphi(t,s)$ is a variable y_j or an expression $y_j[y_k/x']$ with $x' \neq x$. So, using the firing rule, $m'(s\ )(x) = m(s)(x) = \sigma(x)$

(ii) by induction: for $m = m_\sigma$, the proposition follows from the definition of N^σ. Assume the proposition holds for $m \in [m_\sigma>$ and let $m[t>m'$. By construction of $\mathcal{N}_p$, $|{}^\cdot t \cap \mathcal{N}_p[\![C_i]\!]| \leq 1$ and $|{}^\cdot t \cap \mathcal{N}_p[\![C_i]\!]| = 1 \Leftrightarrow |t^\cdot \cap \mathcal{N}_p[\![C_i]\!]| = 1$. According to the firing rule, the proposition holds for m'.

Definition Let (N,m_σ) be a marked translation of a CSP-program, let $m \in [m_\sigma>$. Then we define σ_m, the state associated with m, by

$$\sigma_m(x) = \begin{cases} m(s)(x) & \text{iff} \quad s \in \mathrm{dom}(m),\ m(s)(x) \neq \sigma(x), \\ \sigma(x) & \text{otherwise}. \end{cases}$$

Since slices of processes correspond to reachable markings we can define the final state σ_p of a process p.

<u>Definition</u> Let $p = (K, p_1, p_2)$ be a finite process of a marked translation (N, σ) of a CSP program. Then we define $\sigma_p := \sigma_{m_{K^\circ}}$, <u>p leads from σ to σ_p</u>.

Corresponding to the classification in [HLP] of CSP-computations, we call a process $p = (K, p_1, p_2)$ of (N, m)

- <u>terminating</u> iff p is finite and $\forall s \in K^\circ \; p_1(s) \in N^\circ$,
- <u>deadlocked</u> iff p is finite but not terminating.

As an example we consider the unfolding of $\mathcal{M}[\![Pr_1]\!]$:

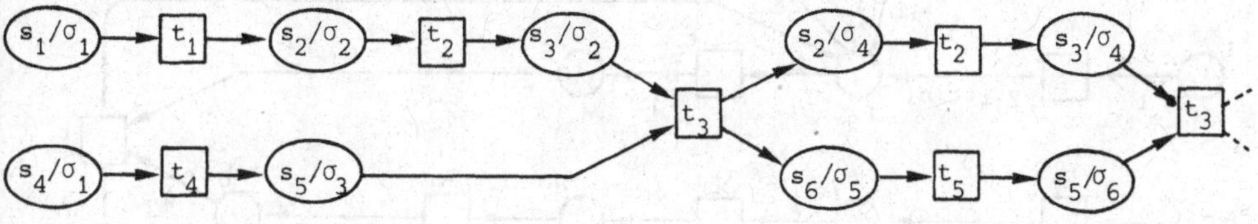

We will not specify the states σ_i explicitly here, as examples $\sigma_4(x_1) = 1$, $\sigma_6(x_2) = 2$.

Note that this unfolding is also an (infinite) process of $\mathcal{M}[\![Pr_1]\!]$, it represents the unique maximal process of the net. The reason is that this program is concurrent but deterministic, in the sense that there is no non-determinism introduced by $[\!]$. In this case, we get no branched places in the unfolding, and hence deterministic programs have exactly one process.

<u>Lemma</u> Let Pr be a CSP-program without $[\!]$-operators (containing only one command in <u>do</u>...<u>od</u> - and <u>if</u>...<u>fi</u> - commands). Then the unfolding of $(\mathcal{M}[\![Pr]\!], m_\sigma)$ $\sigma \in$ States, contains no branched places. (The same holds using $\mathcal{N}_p$ instead of $\mathcal{N}$).

<u>Proof</u>

Let (K, f_1, f_2) be the unfolding of $(\mathcal{M}[\![Pr]\!], m_\sigma)$. K contains a branched place $\Leftrightarrow$ there is a reachable marking m of $(\mathcal{M}[\![Pr]\!], m_\sigma)$ such that two transitions of $\mathcal{M}[\![Pr]\!]$ are m-enabled. This is only possible if there is a branched place in $\mathcal{M}[\![Pr]\!]$. By construction of $\mathcal{M}[\![Pr]\!]$ and since we have no $[\!]$-operators, branched places in $\mathcal{M}[\![Pr]\!]$ may only be generated for the exit-branch of <u>do</u>...<u>od</u> and when introducing communication.

For <u>do</u>...<u>od</u>, the arc inscriptions β ensure that there is exactly one enabled transition (the exit transition or the first transition of the only command inside <u>do</u>..<u>od</u>).

When introducing communication, we get a branched place iff there is a τ-labelled transition $t \in \mathcal{M}[\![C_{i_1}]\!]$ and two transitions $t_1, t_2 \in \mathcal{M}[\![C_{i_2}]\!]$, $i_1, i_2 \in \{1, \ldots, m\}$, $\tau(t_1)$ and $\tau(t_2)$ both complementary to $\tau(t)$, where $Pr = P_1 :: C_1 \| \ldots \| P_m :: C_m$. Then we get two new transitions $(t, t_1), (t, t_2) \in ({}^\bullet t)^\bullet$, but as we never have two transitions enabled in $\mathcal{M}[\![C_{i_2}]\!]$, they are never both enabled. □

The above program Pr_1 has no terminating processes. As a final example, consider the following program, Pr_2, which is non-deterministic and has terminating, deadlocking, and infinite processes:

$$Pr_2 = P_1 :: b := tt;\ \underline{do}\ b \rightarrow P_2!0 \,[\!]\, b \rightarrow b := ff\ \underline{od} \quad \|$$
$$P_2 :: x := 1;\ \underline{do}\ x > 0 \rightarrow x := x+1;\ P_1?x\ \underline{od}$$

$M[\![Pr_2]\!]$:

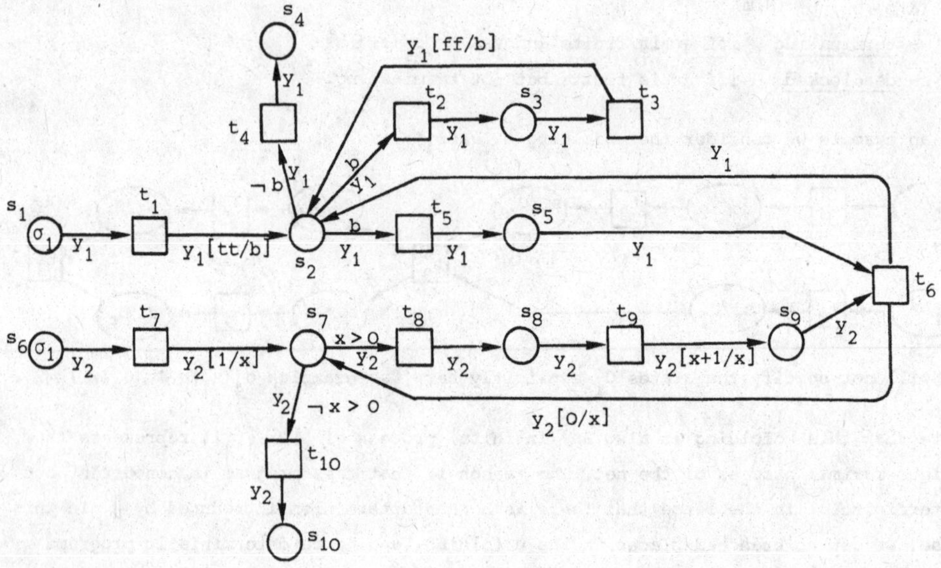

The following figure shows a terminating process of $M[\![Pr_2]\!]$, starting with $\sigma(b) = tt$, $\sigma_1(x) = 2$.

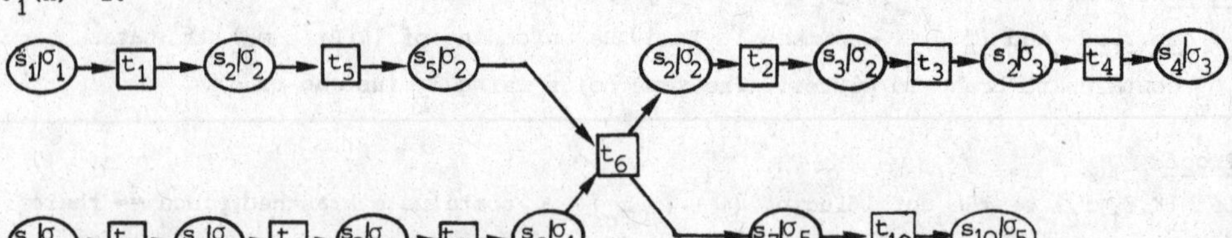

The process is terminating because $s_4^{\bullet} = \emptyset$ and $s_{10}^{\bullet} = \emptyset$ in $M[\![Pr_2]\!]$.

We obtain:

	σ_1	σ_2	σ_3	σ_4	σ_5
b	tt	tt	ff	tt	tt
x	2	2	2	1	0

The final state of the process is σ_p with $\sigma_p(b) = \sigma_3(b) = ff$ and $\sigma_p(x) = \sigma_5(x) = 0$.

5. Equivalence of the net translation to the operational semantics of CSP

In this section, we wish to show that the behaviour of our net translation of CSP-programs in terms of firing sequences corresponds exactly to the operational semantics given in [HLP]. We use a similar technique to the one used in [GM2], defining a derivation relation on unfoldings of marked CSP-nets.

Definition Let $N=(S,T;F)$ be a net, $X\subseteq N$. Then we define $N\restriction X := (S\cap X, T\cap X; F\cap X^2)$.

Definition Let $f=(K,f_1,f_2)$ be the unfolding of the marked CSP-net (N,m), let $G\subseteq T_K$, $G\neq\emptyset$, with $\forall t\in G: {}^{\bullet}t\subseteq {}^{\circ}K$ and $\forall t_1,t_2\in G: t_1\ \underline{co}\ t_2$.

Then $f \xrightarrow{G} f'$ iff $f'=(K',f_1',f_2')$ and $K' := K\restriction X$ where $X = K\setminus\{x\in K \mid \exists t\in G$ with $x\leqslant t \vee x\,\#\,t\}$, $f_i' := f_i\restriction K'$, $i=1,2$.

For $t\in T_K$, we abbreviate $f\xrightarrow{\{t\}} f'$ by $f\xrightarrow{t} f'$.

This derivation describes the firing of transitions in (N,m), the future behaviour of (N,m) after this step is given by the remaining piece of the unfolding.

Theorem Let Pr be a CSP-program, $\sigma\in$ States.

Let $f=(K,f_1,f_2)$ be the unfolding of $\mathcal{N}_p[\![Pr]\!]^{\sigma}$.

(i) $<Pr,\sigma> \xrightarrow{\varepsilon} <Pr',\sigma'> \Rightarrow$

$\exists t\in T_K$ with $f\xrightarrow{t} f'$, f' is unfolding of $(\mathcal{N}_p[\![Pr']\!], m)$ for some marking m with $\sigma_m=\sigma'$.

(ii) $f\xrightarrow{t} f'$, $t\in T_K \Rightarrow$ there exists a CSP program Pr' with f' unfolding of $(\mathcal{N}_p[\![Pr']\!], m)$, $\sigma_m=\sigma'$, and $<Pr,\sigma>\xrightarrow{\varepsilon}<Pr',\sigma'>$.

We shall prove the theorem inductively using the inductive definition of the derivation relation of [HLP] and of the translation function $\mathcal{N}_p$. We start by considering guards.

Definition For guards or commands X and markings m, let $f_X^m=(K,f_1,f_2)$ be the unfolding of $(\mathcal{N}_p[\![X]\!], m)$.

Lemma 1 For each guard G and each state σ

$$<G,\sigma>\xrightarrow{a}\sigma'\wedge\sigma'\neq \underline{fail} \Leftrightarrow f_G^{m_\sigma}\xrightarrow{t} \textcircled{\sigma}\ ,\ \text{where } f_G^{m_\sigma}=(K,f_1,f_2),\ T_K=\{t\} \text{ and}$$

$$\tau(f_1(t)) = \begin{cases} P?x & \text{iff } a=P?v,\ \sigma'=\sigma[v/x],\\ P!e & \text{iff } a=P![\![e\sigma]\!],\ \sigma'=\sigma,\\ \text{undefined otherwise}. & \end{cases}$$

Proof

By construction, $\mathcal{N}_p[\![G]\!]^{\sigma}$ =

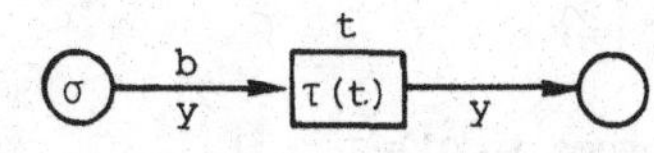

$f_G^{m_\sigma}$ = 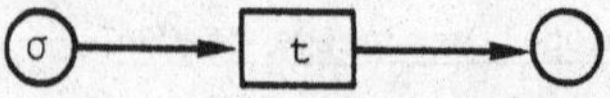

and

$$\tau(f_1(t)) = \begin{cases} P?x & \text{iff} \quad G = b\,;\, P?x \\ P!e & \text{iff} \quad G = b\,;\, P!e \\ \text{undefined otherwise} \end{cases}$$

The proposition follows by definition of $\xrightarrow{a}$ and $\xrightarrow{t}$. □

Lemma 2 For each guard G and each state σ

$<G,\sigma> \xrightarrow{\varepsilon}$ fail $\Leftrightarrow$ there exists no $f' = (K', f_1', f_2')$ such that $f_G^{m_\sigma} \xrightarrow{t} f'$ for $f_G^{m_\sigma} = (K, f_1, f_2)$, $t \in T_K$.

Proof

$<G,\sigma> \xrightarrow{\varepsilon}$ fail $\Leftrightarrow G = b \vee G = b\,;\, P?x \vee G = b\,;\, P!e$ and $[\![b\sigma]\!] = ff$.

$N_p[\![G]\!]^\sigma$ = 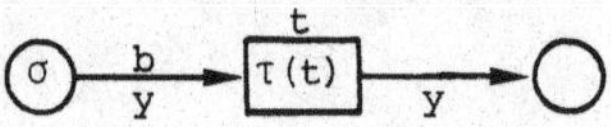

.

t is enabled $\Leftrightarrow [\![b\sigma]\!] = tt$ and the proposition follows. □

Lemma 3 For each command C , $<C,\sigma> \xrightarrow{\varepsilon} <C',\sigma'> \Leftrightarrow f_C^{m_\sigma} \xrightarrow{t} f_{C'}^{m_{\sigma'}}$, $f_C^{m_\sigma} = (K, f_1, f_2)$ and $\tau(f_1(t))$ undefined.

Proof

By induction on the structure of C . For C = x := e | skip | P?x | P!e the result follows by construction of $N_p[\![C]\!]$. Let $C = C_1 ; C_2$, $C_1 \neq$ skip.

$<C,\sigma> \xrightarrow{\varepsilon} <C',\sigma'> \Rightarrow \exists C_1'$ such that $C' = C_1' ; C_2$ and $<C_1,\sigma> \xrightarrow{\varepsilon} <C_1',\sigma'>$. By induction hypothesis, $f_{C_1}^{m_\sigma} \xrightarrow{t} f_{C_1'}^{m_{\sigma'}}$.

As $N_p[\![C]\!] = N[\![C_1]\!] \circ N \circ N[\![C_2]\!]$ with N = 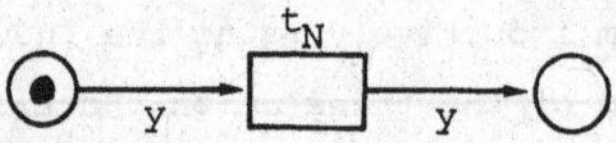

,

we have $t \in {}^\circ K^\cdot$ and $f_C^{m_\sigma} \xrightarrow{t} f_{C'}^{m_{\sigma'}}$.

Now assume $f_C^{m_\sigma} \xrightarrow{t} f_{C'}^{m_{\sigma'}} \Rightarrow f_{C_1}^{m_\sigma} \xrightarrow{t} f_{C_1'}^{m_{\sigma'}}$ (by construction of $N_p[\![C_1;C_2]\!]$) $\Rightarrow <C_1,\sigma> \xrightarrow{\varepsilon} <C_1',\sigma'>$ (by induction hypothesis) $\Rightarrow <C,\sigma> \xrightarrow{\varepsilon} <C',\sigma'>$ with $C' = C_1' ; C_2$.

Let C = skip; C_2 , then $N_p[\![C]\!] = N \circ N_p[\![C_2]\!]$, N as above.

$<C,\sigma> \xrightarrow{\varepsilon} <C',\sigma'> \Leftrightarrow C' = C_2$ and $\sigma' = \sigma \Leftrightarrow$ unfolding of $(N \circ N_p[\![C_2]\!])^\sigma \xrightarrow{t_N} f_{C'}^{\sigma'}$.

Let C = if $G_1 \to C_1 [\!] \ldots [\!] G_n \to C_n$ fi . Then ${}^\circ K^\cdot = \{t \mid f_1(t)$ enabled in $N_p[\![C]\!]^\sigma$ and $f_1(t) = t_a$ or $f_1(t) \in N_p[\![G_i]\!]$, $1 \leq i \leq n\}$.

$<C,\sigma> \xrightarrow{\varepsilon} <C',\sigma'>$

$\Leftrightarrow$ (i) $<G_i,\sigma> \xrightarrow{\varepsilon} \sigma$, $C' = C_i$ for some i , $\sigma' = \sigma$

or (ii) $<G_i,\sigma> \xrightarrow{\varepsilon} \underline{\text{fail}}$ for all i , $C' = \underline{\text{abort}}$, $\sigma' = \sigma$

(i) $\Leftrightarrow$ (Lemma 1) $f_{G_i}^{m_\sigma} \xrightarrow{t}$ (σ) ,

$\Leftrightarrow$ unfolding of $(N_p[\![G_i]\!] \circ N_p[\![C_i]\!])^\sigma \xrightarrow{t} f_{C_i}^{m_\sigma}$

$\Leftrightarrow f_C^{m_\sigma} \xrightarrow{t} f_{C_i}^{m_\sigma}$ (since for all $t' \in T_K$, $f_1(t') \notin N_p[\![C_i]\!] \Rightarrow t' \# t$) .

(ii) $\Leftrightarrow$ (Lemma 2) there exists no t,f' with $f_{G_i}^{m_\sigma} \xrightarrow{t} f'$, hence no $t \in T_K$ such that $f_1(t) \in N_p[\![G_i]\!]$, $1 \leq i \leq n$, is enabled in $N_p[\![C]\!]$

$\Leftrightarrow [\![b_i\sigma]\!] = ff$ for all $N_p[\![G_i]\!]$ =

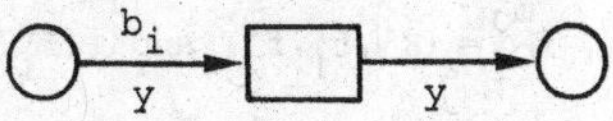

$\Leftrightarrow {}^\circ K^\bullet = \{f_1^{-1}(t_a)\}$ and $f_C^{m_\sigma} \xrightarrow{f_1^{-1}(t_a)} f_{\underline{\text{abort}}}^{m_\sigma}$.

Let $C = \underline{\text{do}}\ G_1 \to C_1 [\!]\ldots[\!] G_n \to C_n\ \underline{\text{od}}$, $<C,\sigma> \xrightarrow{\varepsilon} <C',\sigma'>$

$\Leftrightarrow$ (i) $<G_i,\sigma> \xrightarrow{\varepsilon} \sigma$, $C' = C_i;C$ for some i , $\sigma' = \sigma$

or (ii) $<G_i,\sigma> \xrightarrow{\varepsilon} \underline{\text{fail}}$ for all i , $C' = \underline{\text{skip}}$, $\sigma' = \sigma$.

$f_C^{m_\sigma}$ is of the following form:

For case (i):

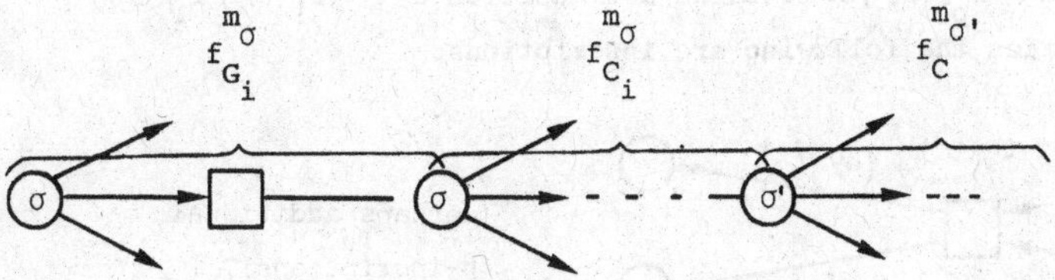

For case (ii):

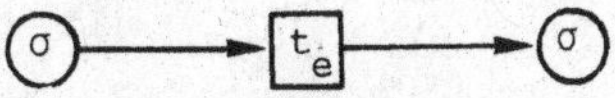

(since no transiton $t \neq t_e$ is enabled in $N_p[\![C]\!]$) .

Hence (i) $\Leftrightarrow f_C^{m_\sigma} \xrightarrow{t} f_{C_i;C}^{m_\sigma}$, $t \in M[\![G_i]\!]$ for some i ,

(ii) $\Leftrightarrow f_C^{m_\sigma} \xrightarrow{t_e} f_{\underline{\text{skip}}}^{m_\sigma}$ (using Lemma 1 and 2 analogously as for $\underline{\text{if}}\ldots\underline{\text{fi}}$) . □

Lemma 4 For each command C , $<C,\sigma> \xrightarrow{a} <C',\sigma'>$

and $a \neq \varepsilon \Leftrightarrow f_C^{m_\sigma} \xrightarrow{t} f_{C'}^{m_\sigma}$, $f_C^{m_\sigma} = (K,f_1,f_2)$

$$\text{and} \quad \tau(f_1(t)) = \begin{cases} P?x & \text{iff} \quad a = P?v \text{ , } \sigma' = \sigma[v/x] \text{ ,} \\ P!e & \text{iff} \quad a = P![\![e\sigma]\!] \text{ , } \sigma' = \sigma \end{cases}$$

Proof

Analogously to Lemma 3. □

Proof of the theorem

Let $Pr = P_1 :: C_1 \| \ldots \| P_n :: C_n$.

(i) $<Pr,\sigma> \xrightarrow{\varepsilon} <Pr',\sigma'> \Longleftrightarrow$

a) $<C_i,\sigma> \xrightarrow{\varepsilon} <C_i',\sigma'> \;\wedge\; Pr' = \ldots \| P_i :: C_i' \| \ldots$

or b) $<C_i,\sigma> \xrightarrow{P_j?v} <C_i',\sigma'>, <C_j,\sigma> \xrightarrow{P_j!v} <C_j',\sigma> \;\wedge\; Pr' = \ldots P_i :: C_i' \| \ldots \| P_j :: C_j' \ldots$

or c) $<C_i,\sigma> \xrightarrow{P_j!v} <C_i',\sigma>, <C_j,\sigma> \xrightarrow{P_i?v} <C_j',\sigma'> \;\wedge\; Pr' = \ldots P_i :: C_i' \| \ldots \| P_j :: C_j' \ldots$

a) $<C_i,\sigma> \xrightarrow{\varepsilon} <C_i',\sigma> \Rightarrow$ (Lemma 3)

$f_{C_i}^{m_\sigma} \xrightarrow{t} f_{C_i'}^{m_{\sigma'}}$, $f_{C_i}^{m_\sigma} = (K', f_1', f_2')$ and $\tau(f_1'(t))$ undefined.

$\Rightarrow$ (by construction of $N := \mathcal{N}_p[\![Pr]\!]$) $f_1'(t) \in T_N$

and ${}^{\bullet}t \subseteq {}^{\circ}K$. The result follows, since for all

$x \in K$ with $f_1(x) \in \mathcal{N}_p[\![C_j]\!]$, $j \neq i$, $\neg(x \leq t) \wedge \neg(x \# t)$.

b) $<C_i,\sigma> \xrightarrow{P_j?v} <C_i',\sigma'>, <C_j,\sigma> \xrightarrow{P_i!v} <C_j',\sigma>$ $\sigma' = \sigma[v/x]$, $v = [\![e\sigma]\!] \Rightarrow$ (Lemma 4)

$f_{C_i}^{m_\sigma} \xrightarrow{t} f_{C_i'}^{m_\sigma}$, $f_{C_i}^{m_\sigma} = (K^i, f_1^i, f_2^i)$ and $\tau(f_1^i(t)) = P?x$

$f_{C_j}^{m_\sigma} \xrightarrow{t'} f_{C_j'}^{m_\sigma}$, $f_{C_j}^{m_\sigma} = (K^j, f_1^j, f_2^j)$ and $\tau(f_1^j(t')) = P!e$

By construction of $N := \mathcal{N}_p[\![Pr]\!]$, N contains a transition $t'' := (f_1^i(t), f_1^j(t'))$, ${}^{\bullet}t'' \subseteq {}^{\circ}K$, $f_1(t'')$ carries the following arc inscriptions:

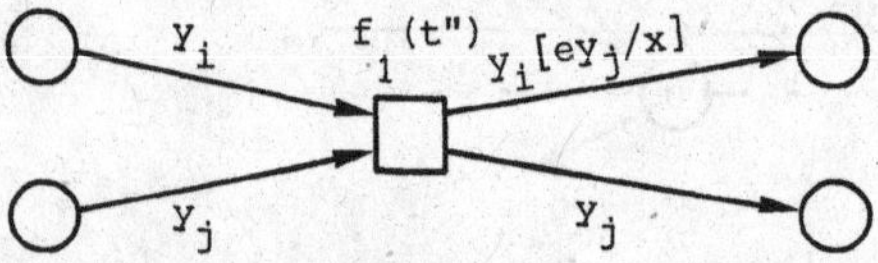

(perhaps additional β-incriptions),

hence the unfolding of $\mathcal{N}_p[\![Pr]\!]^\sigma$ is of the form

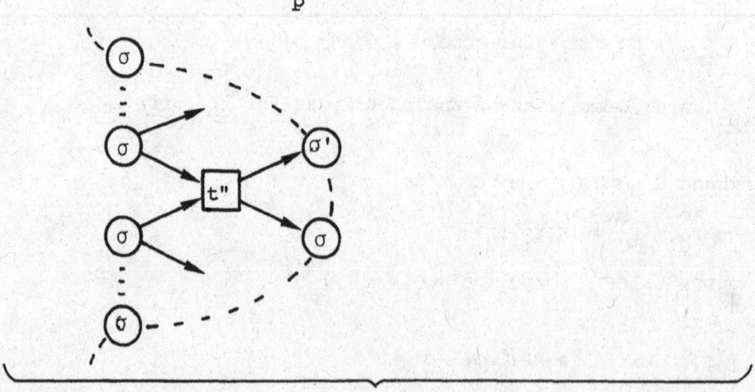

unfolding of $(\mathcal{N}_p[\![Pr' = \ldots P_i :: C_i' \| \ldots \| P_j :: C_j' \ldots]\!], m)$ with $\sigma_m = \sigma'$.

$\Rightarrow f \xrightarrow{t''} f'$, f' as required.

c) analogously to b).

(ii) $f \xrightarrow{t} f'$, $t \in \dot{T}_K \Rightarrow$ (by construction of $N_p[\![Pr]\!]$)

a) $f_1(t) \in N_p[\![C_i]\!]$ for some $i, \tau(f_1(t))$ undefined in $N_p[\![C_i]\!]$

or b) $f_1(t) = (t_i, t_j) \in T_c$, $t_i \in N_p[\![C_i]\!]$, $t_j \in N_p[\![C_j]\!]$, $\tau(t_i) = P?x$, $\tau(t_j) = P!e$,
$x \in Var$, $e \in Exp$.

a) $\Rightarrow f^{m_\sigma}_{C_i} \xrightarrow{t} f^{m_{\sigma'}}_{C'_i}$ and hence by Lemma 3 $\langle C_i, \sigma \rangle \xrightarrow{\varepsilon} \langle C'_i, \sigma' \rangle$

$\Rightarrow \langle Pr, \sigma \rangle \xrightarrow{\varepsilon} \langle Pr' = \ldots \| P_i :: C'_i \| \ldots, \sigma' \rangle$

and f' is unfolding of $(N_p[\![Pr']\!], m)$ with $\sigma_m = \sigma'$.

b) $\Rightarrow f^{m_\sigma}_{C_i} \xrightarrow{t_i} f^{m_\sigma}_{C'_i}$ and $f^{m_\sigma}_{C_j} \xrightarrow{t_j} f^{m_\sigma}_{C'_j}$ and by Lemma 4

$\langle C_i, \sigma \rangle \xrightarrow{P?v} \langle C'_i, \sigma' \rangle$, $\sigma' = \sigma[v/x]$ and $\langle C_j, \sigma \rangle \xrightarrow{P![\![e\sigma]\!]} \langle C'_j, \sigma \rangle$

$\Rightarrow \langle Pr, \sigma \rangle \xrightarrow{\varepsilon} \langle Pr' = \ldots \| P_i :: C'_i \| \ldots \| P_j :: C'_j \| \ldots, \sigma' \rangle$

and f' is unfolding of $(N_p[\![Pr']\!], m)$ with $\sigma_m = \sigma' = \sigma[v/x]$

(using the arc inscriptions of (t_i, t_j)). □

To establish the relationship between derivation sequences of the operational semantics of section 2 and processes of the net translation of CSP programs, we consider derivarion sequences of unfoldings and show how they generate processes.

A finite derivation sequence $f \xrightarrow{t_1} f^{(1)} \longrightarrow \ldots \xrightarrow{t_n} f^{(n)}$ of unfolding f is called maximal iff there exists no t, f' with $f^{(n)} \xrightarrow{t} f'$. (Infinite derivation sequences are always considered as maximal.)

<u>Lemma</u> Let $f \xrightarrow{t_1} f^{(1)} \xrightarrow{t_2} \ldots \xrightarrow{t_n} f^{(n)}$ $(\longrightarrow \ldots)$ be a finite (infinite) maximal derivation sequence of the unfolding $f = (K, f_1, f_2)$ of (N,m). Then $p = (K', p_1, p_2)$ with $T := \{t_i \mid \xrightarrow{t_i}$ is a step in the derivation sequence$\}$.
$K' = K \restriction ({}^\circ K \cup T \cup \{s \in S_K \mid \exists t \in T \text{ with } s \in {}^\bullet t \text{ or } s \in t^\bullet\})$, $p_i = f_i \restriction K'$, is a proccess of (N,m).

<u>Proof</u>
The result follows from the given construction, in particular we get only unbranched places in K' by definition of $\xrightarrow{t}$.

<u>Corollary</u> Let Pr be a CSP-Program.

(i) $\mathcal{R}[\![Pr]\!](\sigma, \sigma') \Longleftrightarrow$
there is a terminating process of $N_p[\![Pr]\!]$ from σ to σ'.

(ii) Pr has an infinite computation starting in a state $\sigma \Longleftrightarrow$
there is an infinite process of $N_p[\![Pr]\!]$ starting at σ.

(iii) Pr has a computation sequence which deadlocks, starting in a state $\sigma \Longleftrightarrow$
$N_p[\![Pr]\!]$ has a finite process starting at σ which deadlocks.

(iv) $\mathcal{T}[\![Pr]\!](\sigma) \Longleftrightarrow$ every process of $N_p[\![Pr]\!]$ starting with σ is a terminating process.

Proof

Using the theorem and the lemma above.

6. Analysing CSP programs in terms of nets

It is now worthwhile to ask what is gained by translating CSP to Petri nets. Besides a comparison of the power of the two concepts we saw already (with program Pr_1) that with processes we get a sharp distinction between non-deterministic and non-sequential behaviour. Furthermore, we can apply analysis techniques of net theory, e.g. S-invariants. As an example the following program Pr_3 implements mutual exclusion of the critical regions C_1 and C_2 in the CSP-processes P_1 and P_2, respectively. P_0 represents a semaphore.

$$\begin{aligned} Pr_3 = \; & P_1 :: \underline{do}\ tt;\ P_0?x_1 \rightarrow C_1;\ P_0!1;\ N_1\ \underline{od}\ \| \\ & P_0 :: \underline{do}\ tt;\ P_1!1 \rightarrow P_1?x_0 [\!] P_2!1 \rightarrow P_2?x_0\ \underline{od}\ \| \\ & P_2 :: \underline{do}\ tt;\ P_0?x_2 \rightarrow C_2;\ P_0!1;\ N_2\ \underline{od}\ . \end{aligned}$$

Then we get $\mathcal{M}[\![Pr_3]\!] =$

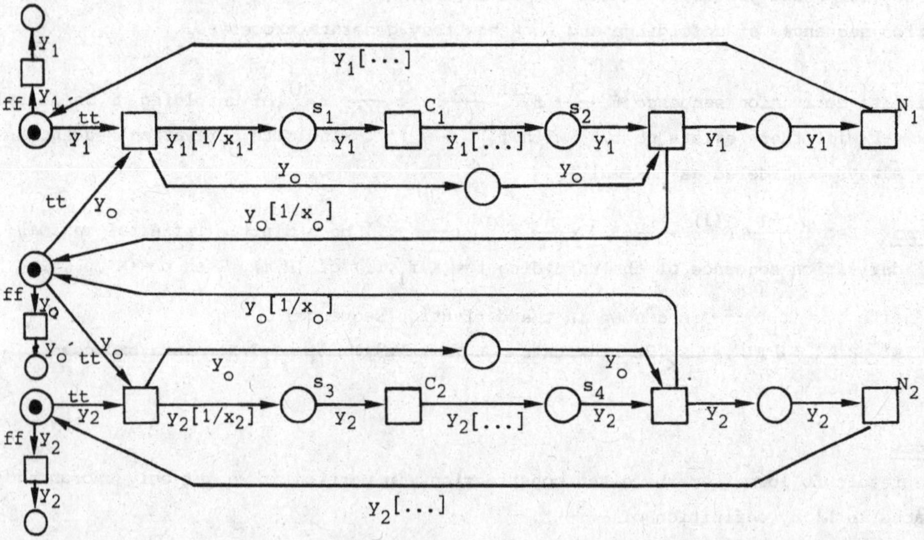

Obviously the places $s_0, \ldots, s_4$ constitute an S-invariant [Re1] with initially one token. Consequently there exists no reachable marking m such that s_1 and s_3 are both marked by m. Hence C_1 and C_2 are never both enabled under a reachable marking. This proves mutual exclusion of C_1 and C_2.

As a further example consider the following program Pr_4:

$$\begin{aligned} Pr_4 = \; & P_1 :: \underline{do}\ tt \rightarrow P_2!e_1 [\!] tt \rightarrow P_2?x_1\ \underline{od}\ \| \\ & P_2 :: \underline{do}\ tt \rightarrow P_1?x_2 [\!] tt \rightarrow P_1!e_2\ \underline{od} \end{aligned}$$

Then we get $\mathcal{M}[\![Pr_4]\!]$ =

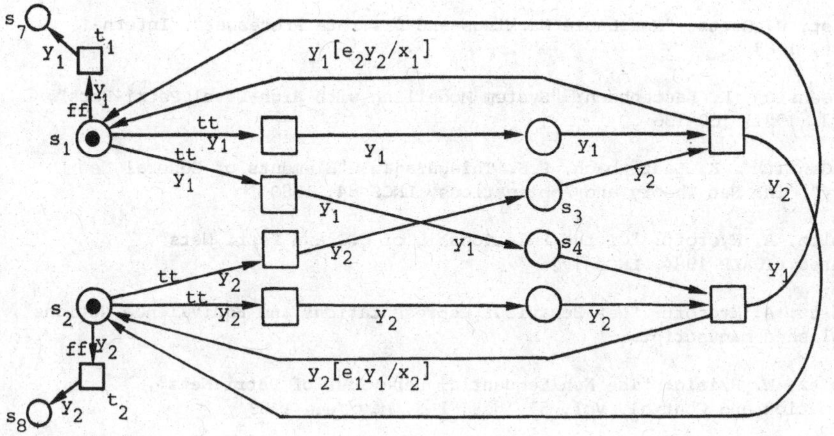

Obviously t_1, t_2, s_7, and s_8 can be skipped due to the arc condition ff. Then all arcs starting at the two branched places s_1 and s_2 have the condition tt. So the net is free choice, and s_1, s_2, s_3, s_4 are a deadlock. This deadlock contains no trap at all, hence no marked trap. Consequently, deadlock is possible in Pr_4 due to the well known deadlock/trap condition for liveness of free choice nets [Re1].

In general, we do not suggest to always translate CSP-programs into nets before analysing them, as we did for these examples. Rather we would like to use net analysis to derive proof rules for CSP.

For fairness considerations, we just refer to [Re2] since the unfoldings of the net translation correspond exactly to the operational semantics given there. Hence all the results can be transfered.

7. Conclusion

We have translated CSP-programs into a special class of predicate/transitions-nets, and we have shown that this yields nets with a behaviour which is strongly equivalent to an operational semantics of CSP. However, we have shown that this still gives interesting information since we obtain a partial order semantics. Furthermore, we are able to transfer net analysis methods. For future research, we hope to find by these investigations and similar work for CCS [GM1] an interesting subclass of nets, in particular of nets with individual tokens, which imposes some structure on the representation of concurrent systems and therefore allows for more powerful analysis tools.

A first step would be to consider net invariants and facts [GL,Re1] for the class of CSP-nets, and to try to prove more intricate program properties using these methods.

References

[BG] E. Best, U. Goltz: "Reachable Markings and Discrete Processes", Internal report, 1983

[GL] H.J. Genrich, K. Lautenbach: "System Modelling with High-Level Petri-Nets", TCS 13 (1981) 109-136

[GLT] H.J. Genrich , K. Lautenbach, P.S. Thiagarajan: "Elements of General Net Theory", in: Net Theory and Applications, LNCS 84, 1980

[GM1] U. Goltz, A. Mycroft: "On the Relationship of CCS and Petri Nets", in: proc. ICALP 1984, LNCS 172

[GM2] U. Goltz, A. Mycroft: "Net Behaviour Representations and Equivalence Notions", unpublished manuscript

[GR] U. Goltz, W. Reisig: "The Non-Sequential Behaviour of Petri Nets", Information and Control, Vol. 57, Nos. 2-3, May/June 1983

[GV] U. Goltz, U. Vogt: "Processes of Relation Nets", in: Petri Nets and Related Models, Newsletter No. 14, June 1983

[Ho] C.A.R. Hoare: "Communicating Sequential Processes", Communications of the ACM Vol. 21, No. 8, (1978), 666-677

[HLP] M. Hennessy, W. Li, G. Plotkin: "A first Attempt at Translating CSP into CCS", in: Proceedings of the 2nd International Conference on Distributed Computing, Paris 1981, IEEE, No. 81 CH 1591-7

[Ma] David May: "Occam", SIGPLAN Notices, Vol. 18, No. 4, April 1983

[NPW] M. Nielsen, G. Plotkin, G. Winskel: "Petri Nets, Event Structures and Domains", TCS 13, No. 1, Jan. 1981

[Re1] W. Reisig: A Petri Net Primer", Springer-Verlag 1984, to appear

[Re2] W. Reisig: "Partial Order Semantics for CSP-like Languages and its Impact on Fairness", in: proc. ICALP 1984, LNCS 172

[Wi] G. Winskel: "A New Definition of Morphism on Petri Nets", in: proc. STACS 1984, LNCS 166

DESIGN AND PROGRAMMING OF INTERFACES FOR MONETIC APPLICATIONS USING PETRI NETS

Theodor Hildebrand
Departement Techniques et Methodes, SLIGOS
20, rue des pavillons, F-92800 Puteaux, France

Abstract. The common methodology that SLIGOS applies to the implementation of communication systems relies on : multiprocessor architecture , formal specifications and direct implementation. The communication systems are composed of interfaces which interconnect point of sale terminals, department stores and banks with credit card applications.
This paper illustrates a design and programming technique of communication systems which makes extensive use of Petri Nets. Net representations at different levels of design are applied to the different stages of project realization: In the first stage Channel/Agency Nets are used for the design of a system configuration, which consists of several independent components. In the second stage specific Place/Transition Nets are used for the specification of protocols and services between the system components. In the third stage the interface components are specified by Place/Transition Nets and then directly implemented as net programs. We demonstrate this method through an example: the realization of an electronic authorization service for credit cards. This application had been developed in a short time and has operated sucessfully for several years. Advantages and shortcomings of the integration of Petri Nets on each level of the project realization are discussed.

Contents:

1. INTRODUCTION : AUTHORIZATION SERVICES

SLIGOS a French software service company, is the European leader in MONETIC applications. MONETIC is the French expression for payment systems using TELEMATIC and INFORMATIC. SLIGOS has implemented several distributed systems for smart cards, point of sale terminals, electronic authorization, videotext home banking etc... This paper is showing the electronic authorization service JADE /7/ to illustrate SLIGOS' software engineering methodology /10/ used for the implementation of network applications.

An authorization service establishes communications between the merchant and the authorization center for the customer's credit card, see figure 1 :

- the merchant asks for an authorization,
- then he gets a positive or negative reply from the authorization center.

The classical, non automated authorization service involves a rather complicated and lengthy sequence of operations :

- The merchant gets a credit card from a customer and dials - manually - the number of the authorization center for this particular card.
- He waits to be connected to an operator and answers the questions about the customer and the amount to be authorized.
- Then he waits again until he finally gets the authorization.

As a result the authorization centers have had to develop more efficient services.

SLIGOS offers a complete authorization service, called JADE, using a VIDEOTEXT terminal :

- An authorization terminal with a magnetic card reader is connected to the merchant's telephone.
- Part of the card reader unit is a microprocessor for automatic dialing and message exchange for the JADE routing system.

The merchant passes the credit card through the card reader and keys the amount into the terminal. The other operations are automatic. As a result there has been a significant reduction in authorization time (from more than 100 to less than 30 seconds).

In addition JADE offers several other advantages :

- It allows the merchant to have only one terminal for the different cards (VISA, AMERICAN EXPRESS, DINERS CLUB,...).

- It switches automatically to the classical oral mode if the authorization cannot be given electronically.

JADE has been in operation since 1982. 1500 merchants are expected by the end of 1984. The JADE routing service has been developed on a Petri Net based methodology which is presented in the next paragraph.

2. A NET BASED METHODOLOGY FOR PROJECT REALIZATION

2.1. Intercommunication System

SLIGOS choose a top down design and implementation method to realize in a very short time intercommunication systems /14,13/ such as the JADE routing service. The sequence of steps necessary for project realization can be resumed as follows :

(1) Design of system architecture (configurations of system components).
(2) Specification of the interaction between the components of the system.
(3) Specification of the components.
(4) Implementation and operational quality control of the components and the system.

SLIGOS decided to use net representation for stages (1), (2) and (3) of the realization of JADE (paragraph 4 presents advantages and shortcomings of this approach). In the following we recall the definition of Channel/Agency nets (C/A nets /2,18/) which had been applied in the first step of project realization : "C/A nets are the tool for the description of the static structure of systems at any appropriate level of detail. They abstract from concrete media for the representation of messages and from concrete actors transforming messages, but stress that both kinds of functional units have to be distinguished and that both are equally important. The components of a C/A net are interpreted as follows:

- ROUND (S element): CHANNEL = functional unit which contains messages
- SQUARE (T element): AGENCY = functional unit which processes messages
- ARCS (flow relation):
  . arc from channel C to agency A: A takes messages out of C.
  . arc from agency A to channel C: A puts messages into C."

(OBERQUELLE in /2/ pp 484,485)

The relation between the highest and lowest level of system configuration can be expressed by net morphisms. We will demonstrate this method in the following.

The general configuration of the system required is as follows /15/ :

- Two parties are to be connected by an INTERCOMMUNICATION SYSTEM.
- The REQUESTOR of the service (the LEFT PARTY) is for example a SLIGOS customer.
- The SERVER (or RIGHT PARTY) is for example SLIGOS.

This required architecture can be described by the simple C/A net in figure 2 :

- Two agencies represent the two PARTIES.
- A channel represents the INTERCOMMUNICATION SYSTEM.
- Two arcs connect the central channel to the LEFT and the RIGHT PARTY respectively.

The ITI methodology - for Intercommunication with Transport Interfaces /10/ - relies on the following steps of project realization, which can be applied to systems composed of communication interfaces :

(1) Design of the system architecture using channel agency nets : Agencies represent processes and channels interactions between them.

(2) Specification and validation of protocols (and services) between the active components (agencies) of the system. PAS nets (PAS = Protocole d'Acheminements SLIGOS, i.e. SLIGOS' routing protocol) had been designed for this particular purpose.

(3) Specification and validation of the interface components (agencies) of the system using PAS nets.

(4) Programming and operational control using adapted tools for the direct implementation of PAS nets. The resulting interface programs are written in a net based programming language.

The following paragraphs describe the steps of project realization in detail, paragraph 3 applies them to JADE as an example.

2.2. System Architecture

Channel/Agency nets are used to represent the system components and their interactions on the higher levels of system design. Especially for:

- logical and physical system configurations,
- functional and operational elements,
- details of system components (using net morphisms).

ITI architecture can be described by the C/A net in figure 3, which is a refinement of the intercommunication system in figure 2 :

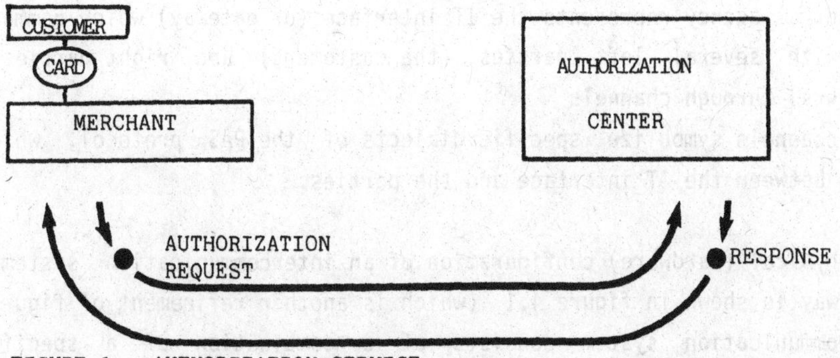

FIGURE 1 : AUTHORIZATION SERVICE
RESPONSE : Authorization or Defered Reply or Refusal

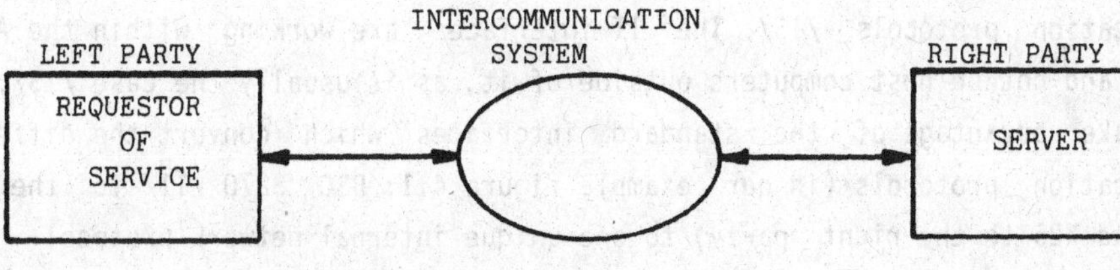

FIGURE 2 : INTERCOMMUNICATION SYSTEM

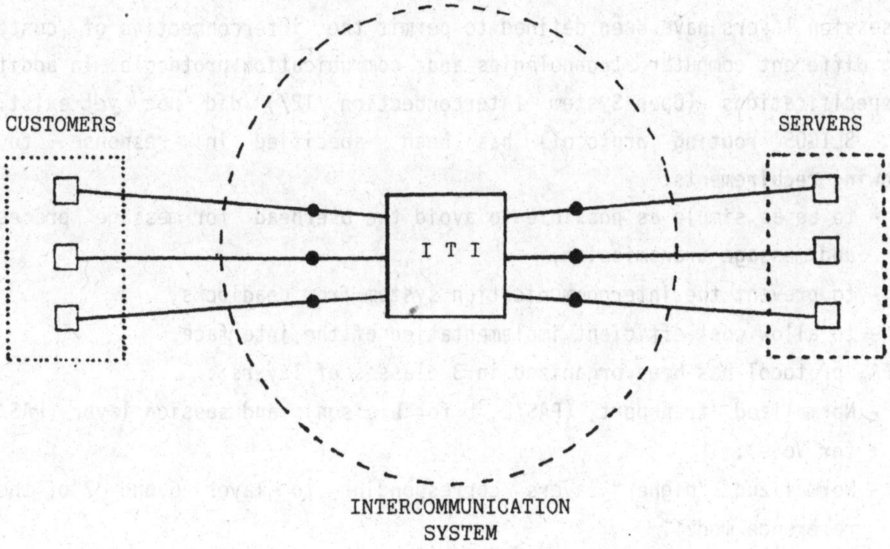

FIGURE 3 : INTERCOMMUNICATION TRANSPORT INTERFACE(ITI)
—●— PAS Protocol ..... Left Party ------- Right Party

- A central agency represents the IT interface (or gateway) which communicates with several left parties (the customers) and right parties (the servers) through channels.
- The channels symbolize specific dialects of the PAS protocol, which is used between the IT interface and the parties.

A typical physical (hardware) configuration of an intercommunication system with an ITI gateway is shown in figure 4.1. (which is another refinement of figure 2). The intercommunication system consists of a combination of a specific IT interface and standard interfaces (SI). These standard interfaces of SLIGOS' private packet switched network AVISO (i.e. the French acronym for "dynamic and intelligent routing for operational systems" /17/) exist for all common communication protocols /16/. The IT interfaces are working within the AVISO network and not on host computers outside of it, as is usually the case /13/. So they take advantage of the standard interfaces which convert the different communication protocols (in our example figure 4.1: BSC 3270 /11/ to the left party and X25 to the right party) to one unique internal network protocol. This modular architecture makes use of network technology for the implementation of a multiprocessor concept which is easily adaptable to growth.

For SLIGOS' first intercommunication system project in 1979 standard transport and session layers have been defined to permit the interconnection of customers using different computer technologies and communication protocols. In addition, OSI specifications (Open System Interconnection /12/) did not yet exist. PAS (i.e. SLIGOS' routing protocol) has been specified in response to the following requirements:

- to be as simple as possible to avoid the overhead for message processing and message transmission,
- to prevent the intercommunication system from deadlocks,
- to allow cost efficient implementation of the interface.

The PAS protocol has been organized in 3 classes of layers :

- Normalized transport (PAS/L, L for Liaison) and session layer (PAS/V, V for Voie).
- Normalized "higher" layers corresponding to layer 6 and 7 of the OSI reference model.
- Basic layers which can be either OSI conform (X25) or not (ASYNC, BSC 3270, SNA,...).

This flexible approach adapts both:classical (but existing) and modern protocols. Figure 4.2 represents the logical (protocol) configuration of the intercommunication system of figure 4.1; this C/A net is a refinement of the one

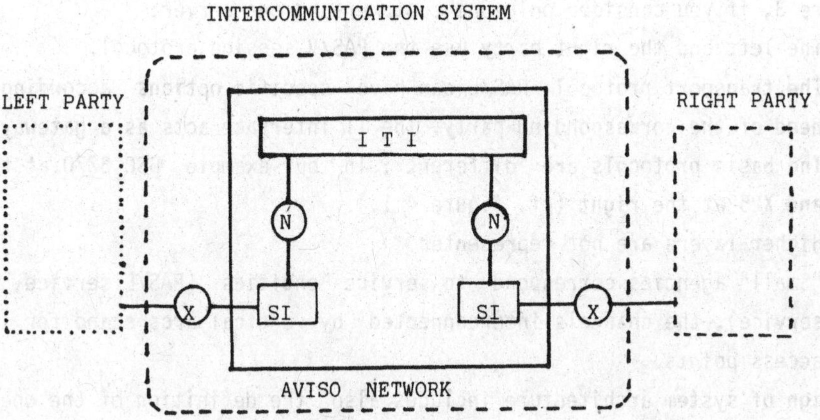

FIGURE 4.1. : NETWORK ARCHITECTURE (Physical Configuration)
SI = Standard AVISO Interface
N = Network Protocol
B = BSC 3270, X = X25

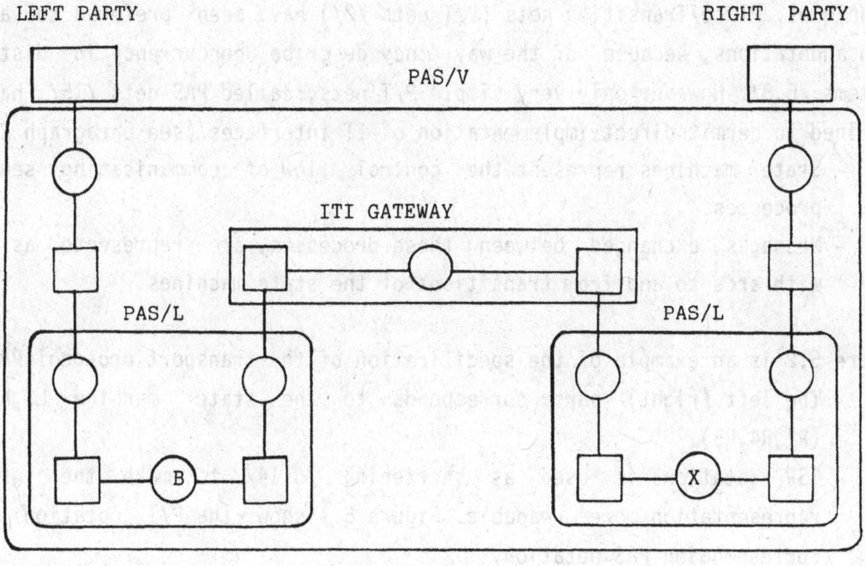

FIGURE 4.2. : PAS ARCHITECTURE (Logical Configuration)

in figure 3, if you consider only one customer and one server:

- The left and the right party use the PAS/V session protocol.
- The transport protocol PAS/L can have specific options according to the need of the corresponding party. The IT interface acts as a gateway.
- The basic protocols are different ; in our example BSC 3270 at the left and X25 at the right (cf. figure 4.1.).
- Higher layers are not represented.
- "Small" agencies correspond to service entities (PAS/L service, network service); the channels interconnected by vertical arcs stand for service access points.

The design of system architecture includes also the definition of the operations environment (automated control, back-up, alert signals...).

2.3. Protocol Specification

Given the requirements for the protocol PAS listed in the last paragraph, the protocol (and service) specification method should include verification techniques. Place/Transition nets (P/T nets /2/) have been prefered to automata with annotations, because of the way they describe concurrency in distributed systems /6,8/. However only very simple P/T nets, called PAS nets /15/, have been retained to permit direct implementation of IT interfaces (see paragraph 2.4):

- State machines represent the control flow of communicating sequential processes.
- Messages, exchanged between these processes, are represented as places with arcs to and from transitions of the state machines.

Figure 5.2 is an example of the specification of the transport protocol PAS/L:

- The left (right) party corresponds to the state machine L1,L2,L4,L5 (R1,R4,R5).
- CSP notation is used as shortening /6,14/ to make the graphical representation more readable. Figure 5.1 shows the P/T notation and the corresponding PAS notation.
- In addition, the network service used by the two parties to communicate with each other, can "transform" messages into errors (ER means "other message").

PAS nets are verified by the calculation of invariants of the underlying P/T nets. PAS/L and specific options for the adaptation to heterogeneous parties have been designed by the mean of PAS nets. The resulting transport protocol is very simple, but compatible with the OSI proposal /12,14/.

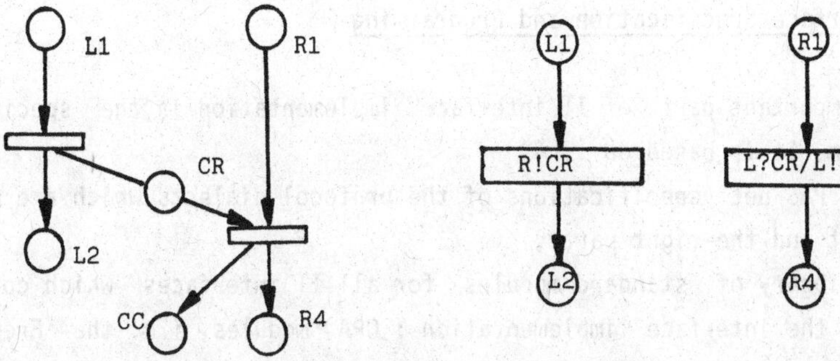

FIGURE 5.1. : PRINCIPE OF PAS NOTATION
at left : P/T Net at right : PAS Net

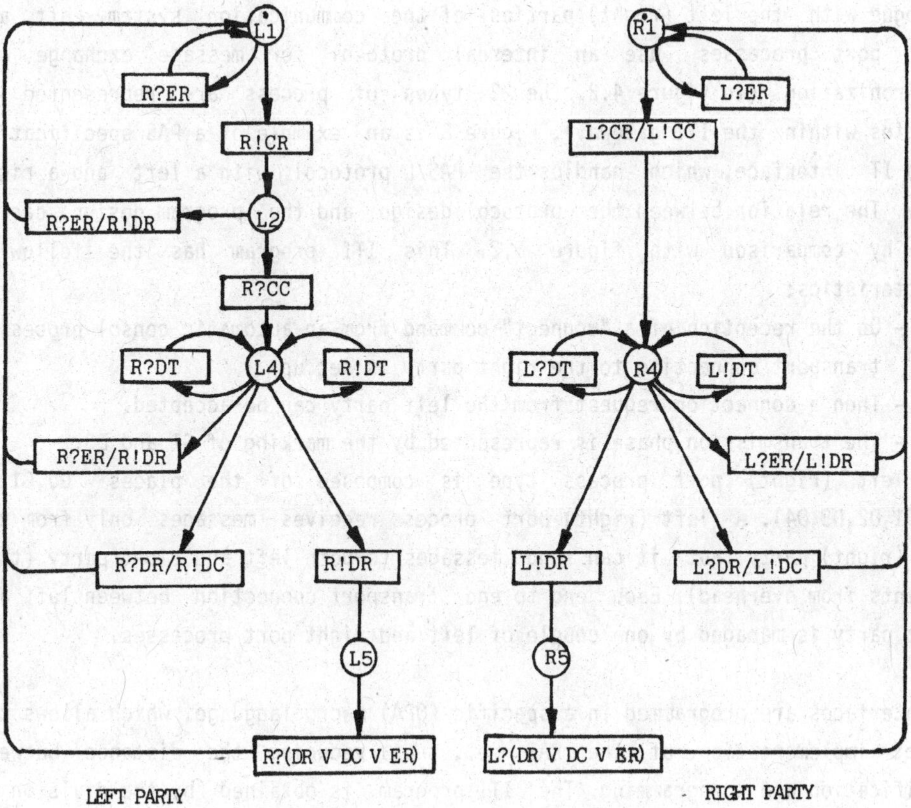

FIGURE 5.2. : PAS SPECIFICATION OF THE PAS/L TRANSPORT PROTOCOL

L : Left Party R : Right Party

MESSAGES :			
	CR = Connection request	CC =	C. Confirm
	DR = Disconnection request	DC =	D. Confirm
	DT = Data	ER =	Error

2.4. Interface Specification and Programming

The most important part of IT interface implementation is the specification of the program. It is based on :

- the PAS net specifications of the protocol dialects which are used by the left and the right party,
- a library of standard modules for all IT interfaces which contain tools for the interface implementation : OPA modules, i.e. the French acronym of "tools for PAS implementation" /1/.

The specification of the IT interface program is also written as a PAS net. An IT interface consists of two types of communication processes, called left port processes and right port processes. The left (right) port processes handle the dialogue with the left (right) parties of the communication system. Left and right port processes use an internal protocol for message exchange and synchronization. (In figure 4.2. the 2 types of process are represented by agencies within the ITI gateway). Figure 8 is an example of a PAS specification of an IT interface, which handles the PAS/L protocol with a left and a right party. The relation between the protocol design and the program design can be seen by comparison with figure 5.2. This ITI program has the following caracteristics:

- On the reception of a "connect" command from an automatic consol process a transport connection to the right party is set up.
- Then a connection request from the left party can be accepted.
- The transmission phase is represented by the marking of G1 and D3.

The left (right) port process type is composed of the places G0,G1,G2 (D0,D1,D2,D3,D4). A left (right) port process receives messages only from the left (right) party, but it can send messages to both left and right party (this prevents from overhead). Each end to end transport connection between left and right party is managed by one couple of left and right port processes.

IT interfaces are programmed in a specific (OPA) macro language, which allows the direct implementation of the PAS net, thus reducing the distance between specification and programming. The ITI program is obtained by the division of the PAS net into modules, called "ITI stars". An ITI star is the set of all transitions (T elements) on outgoing arcs around a given place. The star around D1 (figure 8) contains for example the transitions for the reception of messages CC and ER. Each star is coded separately with the help of OPA macro instructions. The left port process type of the IT interface (in figure 8) contains 3 stars, the right port process type 4 stars. An OPA dispatcher manages the firing of enabled transitions.

An ITI interface is compiled from two kinds of source code:

- OPA modules, containing a macro library and procedures for network services, internal communications, the OPA dispatcher, automatic control operations managers and other functions for easy maintenance and uniform operations of systems ITI.
- ITI modules which represent the higher programming level of the interface and which are composed of a sequence of stars according to the rules of ITI programming.

Each star is coded separately with standardised begin and end macro instructions. Within the star different "beams" corresponding to the transitions, can be distinguished. Each of them begins and ends with standardised OPA macros, the end macro indicates the next marked place of the port process. The beams are coded using OPA macros for message management, message translation (for example into a particular PAS/L dialect), alert signals etc. The firing of a transition of the PAS net is to compare to the execution of the code of the corresponding beam.

3. REALIZATION OF THE JADE SYSTEM

The multicard authorization service JADE is easy to use by the merchant. However the system JADE has been carried out as a rather complex routing system, see figure 6 (refinement of figure 2). It manages communications :

- between the authorization terminals of the merchants on one side,
- the authorization centers of the different cards on the other side.

The routing system JADE is composed of both :

- interpreter modules handling the communication protocols to the authorization terminals as well as to the authorization centers,
- application modules which control and route the authorization messages.

Dialects of the PAS protocol are used between the terminals, the modules and the authorization centers.

The system JADE had been built around the AVISO network, see figure 7 :

- standard interfaces (SI) translate the specific "basic" protocols into a network protocol,
- two types of ITI gateways (the products ITJAT and ITJAC) act as interpreter modules between the different dialects of the PAS protocol used within the system.

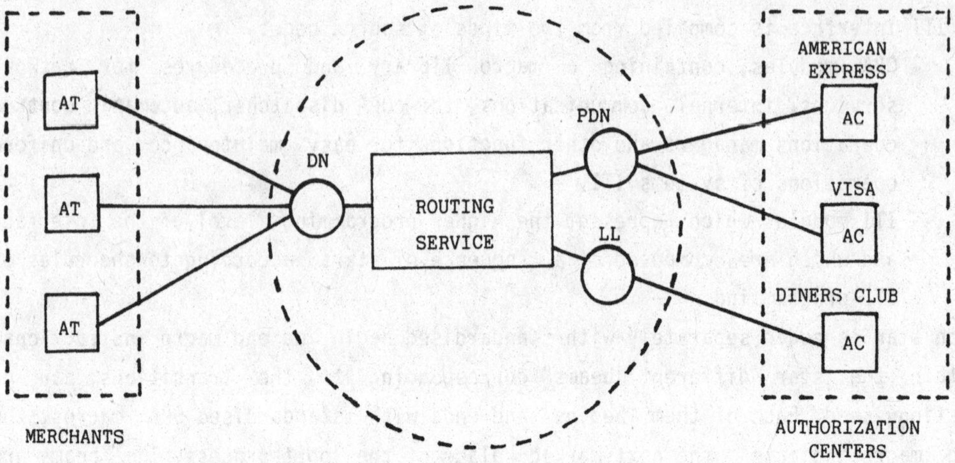

FIGURE 6 : CONFIGURATION OF THE JADE SYSTEM
AT = Authorization Terminal   AC = Authorization Center
DN = Dial Up Network   PDN = Public Data Network
LL = Leased Line

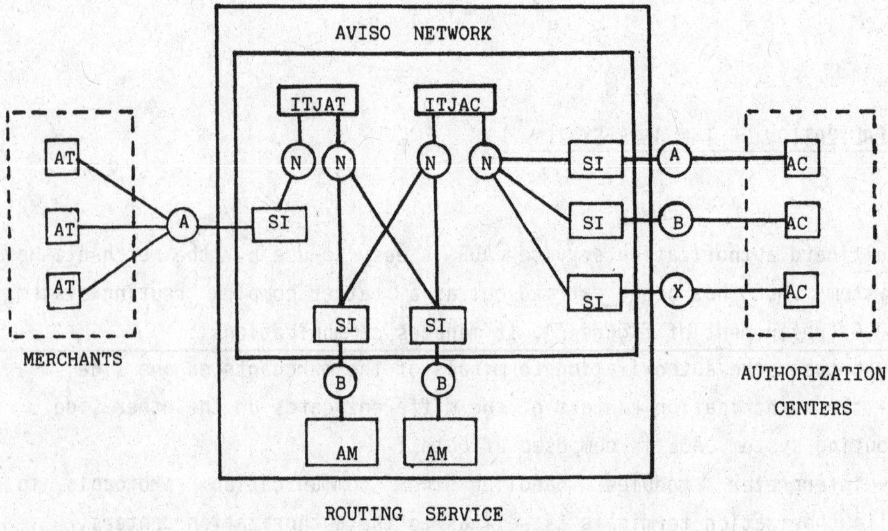

FIGURE 7 : PHYSICAL CONFIGURATION OF THE ROUTING SERVICE JADE
Basic Protocols : A = Asynchronous, B = BSC 3270, X = X25
N = Network Protocol, SI= Standard Aviso Interface
AM = Application Module, ITJAT and ITJAC = Interpreter Modules

The C/A net in figure 7 represents a refinement of figure 6 and a combination of two C/A nets like figure 4.1. ITJAT handles the communication protocol between the authorization terminals and the application modules (AM) ; ITJAC translates the communication protocol of the application module into the dialect of the authorization centers. A typical authorization traverses sequentially through a standard interface, ITJAT, another standard interface, the application module, a standard interface, ITJAC, a server specific standard interface to arrive at the authorization center.

Figure 9 is an example of the specification of the ITJAC program. The real net is more complicated because of the dialects of the particular centers. The flexibility and modularity of the JADE system are the result of the application of the ITI methodology.

4. COMMENTS ON NET BASED IMPLEMENTATIONS

For the development project of the authorization service JADE graphical net representation of systems and components have been chosen for all levels of design and implementation. In the following, we discuss the advantages and shortcomings of this approach.

4.1. System Architecture

C/A nets have been very helpful because of the rigorous semantic description rules for active and passive system components. This allowed the detection of design errors at an early stage of the project. This can be illustrated by the following example : A network can be represented either by a channel or by an agency, this depends up on the bordering network components connected to the outside : in the first case the network is considered passive and transparent to the users (like a leased line, cf. figure 6), in the second case standard interfaces (agencies) build the border (cf. figure 7). The confusion of these two aspects leads to errors (for example : the interconnection of two networks (channels) without description of a gateway between them). Unfortunately, we did not know of many theoretical results concerning C/A nets.

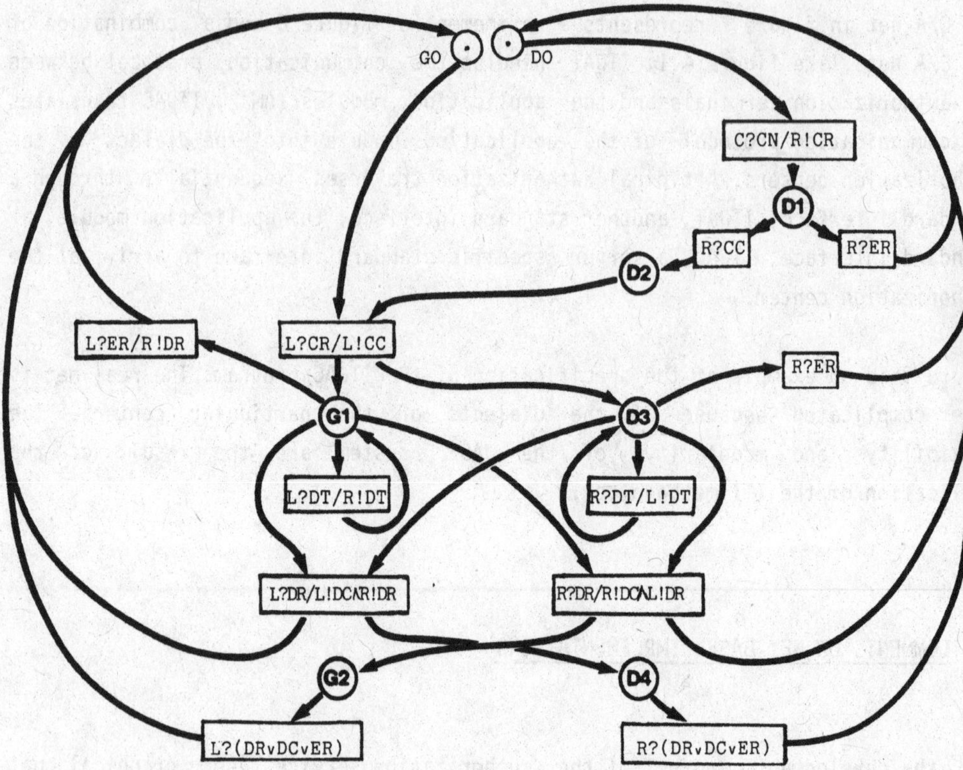

FIGURE 8 : PAS NET OF ITI PROGRAM (ITJAC)

C = Console Process, CN = Connect Command
(legend cf. figure 5.2.)

4.2 Protocol Design

he simplicity of PAS nets proved to be an advantage because of several reasons:

- The protocols were easy to explain to customers with the help of state machine terms; this was also accepted by engineers used to transaction processing. In addition, the token game created some further interest in Petri Nets.
- Implementation tools could be developed from earlier experiences with state machines.
- The readability was found to be acceptable when CSP terms had been introduced for the original P/T nets.

However we also experienced some problems:

- It was difficult to represent multilayer protocols (we are working on a solution).
- General protocol verification techniques (especially when considering timers) were not available. The existing publications were normally too far from implementation.
- We had no occasion to develop sufficient theoretical background for PAS nets.

Our objective has been a construction method of live and safe nets. Net theory has helped us guarantee the automatic resynchronization with our customers' programs and to handle error conditions. As a result PAS/L could have been kept simple. Nevertheless it contains an initial handshake for resynchronization and the case of imperfect functionning of "lower" service levels. (This is demonstrated in /14/ for a similar protocol.)

We started with a single net for the representation of all protocol layers. That allowed us to consider and implement only one net. But the lack of modularity became a problem when we had to add new options to the protocol. So we introduced equivalent subnets and a substitution technique, which we cannot present here. The subnet concept was also necessary to keep PAS programs maintainable. Better substitution methods are still needed. (Predicate / Transition nets had not been used because we were not familiar with verification techniques and implementation tools).

4.3. Program Specification

he use of PAS nets for the program specification presented several advantages:

- no transposition errors because of the similarity to the protocol specification,
- use of P/T net verification techniques,
- quick implementation with the help of OPA tools,
- simplicity of the implementation of protocol changes (5 days for a new server).

The shortcomings of this unusual appoach were:

- absence of a net programming language (we had to build "OPA" tools),
- lack of experience in programs functioning like P/T nets.

4.4. General Remarks

Our feeling is that net descriptions help to explain and to understand the functioning of complex systems. But they are only useful if they are clear and not confusing. Too much time was spent for designing and updating graphics in absence of a net editor. The uniformity of net representation for different levels of detail was convincing but we experienced initial reluctance of many customers and engineers:

- They were more used to pictures and computer symbols than to channels and agencies for the design of system configurations.
- Only few of them knew about net specifications (for protocols and programs), most had first to become familiar with net theory.
- The programming of PAS nets took up à great deal of time in the learning phase due to its difference from standard programming methods.

5. CONCLUSION

Petri Nets are known as an excellent tool for the verification of communication protocols. We have presented a design and implementation method for communication systems, this makes extensive use of nets on every stage of the project:

(1) The architecture of system components is designed at different levels of detail by means of C/A nets.

(2) The communication protocols (services) between components are specified as PAS nets, i.e. P/T nets adapted to communications.

Our experience during the development of the authorization service JADE has convinced us that net based design and programming is reasonable: (1) and (2) permit the parallel development of system components, reducing the delay of project realization; (3) reducing the risk of implementation errors and making program maintenance more flexible.

The ITI software engineering concept has been successfully applied to 6 projects. The important growth of electronic authorizations expected for 1985 will be easily handled by the modular and flexible ITI systems. We are now working on further enhancements of the methodology that will allow the substitution of subnet modules whithin net programs.

5. REFERENCES

/1/ C. BAGES :
"OPLINE : Sommaire des Releases des Produits OPA - Outils pour Protocoles d'Acheminement"
SLIGOS, Puteaux, France, 1983.

/2/ W. BRAUER (ed.) :
"Net theory and Applications"
Lecture Notes in Computer Science 84, SPRINGER, Berlin, 1980.

/3/ G. W. BRAMS :
"Reseaux de Petri : Theorie et Pratique"
MASSON, Paris, 1983.

/4/ G. DAUVERGNE :
"Produits ITBG - Création d'une version back-up"
Note DTM/TCOM/83/74, SLIGOS, Puteaux, France, 1983.

/5/ L. DEVINAST :
"ITISNA, Rapport de Stage DEA Systemes Informatiques"
Institut de Programmation, Université Pierre et Marie Curie (Paris VI), Paris, 1984.

/6/ M. DIAZ :
"Modelling and Analysis of Communications and Cooperation Protocols Using Petri Net Based Models"
Computer Networks, vol 6, 1982, pp 419-441.

/7/ P. DUPONT :
"VALITEL, les Commerçants et l'Autorisation de Paiement par VIDEOTEX"
Convention Informatique, Paris, 1982.

/8/ C. GIRAULT and P. ESTRAILLIER :
"Petri Nets Specification of Virtual Ring Protocols"
In : Applications and Theory of Petri Nets, Informatik Fachberichte 66, SPRINGER, Berlin, 1983.

/9/ O. HERZOG, W. REISIG and R. VALK :
"Petri Netze : Ein Abriss ihrer Grundlagen and Anwendungen"
Informatik - Spektrum 7, 1984, pp 20-27.

/10/ T. HILDEBRAND :
"Methodes de Réalisation d'Interfaces dans le Réseau Privé AVISO à SLIGOS"
Journées Internationales de l'Informatique et de l'Automatisme, Paris, 19-22 june 1984.

/11/ IBM :
"IBM 3270 Information Display System"
Component Description, GA27-2749-7.

/12/ ISO :
"Information Processing System - Open System Interconnection, Transport Protocol Specification"
ISO/TC - 97/SC - 16/WG6, TOKYO, june 1982.

/13/ R. JONES and T. HILDEBRAND :
"AVISO Operations and Future Developments of Interface Design Using Petri Nets"
In : Report of the 9th ISIS User Meeting, Italcable, Roma, 1984.

/14/ G. JUANOLE, B. ALGAYRES and J. DUFAU :
"Protocol Design and Modelling"
4th European Workshop on Applications and Theory of Petri Nets, Toulouse, 26-29 september 1983.

/15/ D. MOISSON and T. HILDEBRAND :
"PAS : Protocole d'Acheminement SLIGOS"
Note DTM/TCOM/83/05, SLIGOS, Puteaux, France, 1983.

/16/ JL. MORARD :
"Packet-switched data networks. An Introduction to TYMSHARE's Advanced Communications Technology"
TYMSHARE NETWORK SYSTEMS CONSULTING, St Cloud, France, 1982.

/17/ A. PIGAL :
"AVISO, Acheminements Variés et Intelligents pour Systèmes Opérationnels"
SLIGOS, Puteaux, France, 1982.

/18/ G. RICHTER :
"Netzmodelle für die Bürokommunikation"
Informatik - Spektrum 6, 1983, pp 210-220 and 7, 1984, pp 28-40.

TOWARDS REACHABILITY TREES FOR HIGH-LEVEL PETRI NETS

by
Peter Huber, Arne M. Jensen, Leif O. Jepsen, and Kurt Jensen
Computer Science Department, Aarhus University
Ny Munkegade, DK-8000 Aarhus C, Denmark

1. INTRODUCTION

High-level Petri nets [1, 4, 5, 6, 9] have been introduced as a powerful net type, by which it is possible to handle rather complex systems in a succinct and manageable way. The success of high-level Petri nets is undebatable when we speak about description, but there is still much work to be done to establish the necessary analysis methods. In [1,4,5] it is shown how to generalize the concept of place-invariants (s-invariants), from place/transition-nets (PT-nets) to high-level Petri nets (HL-nets). Analogously, [9] shows how to generalize transition-invariants (t-invariants). Our present paper constitutes the first steps towards a generalization of reachability trees, which is one of the other important analysis methods known for PT-nets [2, 7, 8].

The central idea in our paper is the observation, that HL-nets often possess classes of equivalent markings. As an example the HL-net describing the five dining philosophers in [4] has an equivalence-class consisting of those five markings in which exactly one philosopher is eating. These five markings are interchangeable, in the sense that their subtrees represent equivalent behaviours, where the only difference is the identity of the involved philosophers and forks. If we analyze one of these subtrees, we also understand the behaviour of the others.

This paper presents a proposal how to define reachability trees for HL-nets (HL-trees). For PT-nets the reachability trees in [2,7,8] are kept finite by means of <u>covering</u> markings (introducing ω-symbols) and by means of <u>duplicate</u> markings (cutting away their subtrees). For HL-trees we reduce by means of <u>covering</u> markings and by means of <u>equivalent</u> markings (for each equivalence-class we only develop the subtree of one node, while the other equivalent nodes become leaves of the tree). Reduction by equivalent markings is a generalization of reduction by duplicate markings. We describe an algorithm which constructs the HL-tree. The algorithm can easily be automated and we will soon start the work on an implementation. The constructed HL-trees turn out to be considerably smaller than the corresponding PT-trees (reachability trees for the equivalent PT-nets, obtained from the HL-nets by the method described in [4]).

The rest of the paper is organized as follows. Section 2 reviews the formal definition of HL-nets and ω-bags. In section 3 HL-trees are introduced by means of an example. Section 4 contains the formal definition of HL-trees and the algorithm to construct them. Section 5 discusses how to establish proof rules, by which properties of HL-nets can be derived from properties of the corresponding HL-trees. Section 6 contains two examples where HL-trees are constructed and compared with the corresponding PT-trees.

2. A BRIEF REVIEW OF HL-NETS AND DEFINITION OF ω-BAGS

In this section we review the basic concepts of HL-nets [6] and we generalize bags (allowing their elements to have multiplicity ω, representing an unlimited number of occurrences). Bags (multisets) are represented as formal sums as shown in [6]. By BAG(S) we denote the set of all finite bags over a non-empty set S. By $[A \to B]_L$ we denote the set of all linear functions with domain A and range B.

Definition An HL-net is a 6-tuple $H=(P,T,C,I_-,I_+,m_0)$ where

(1) P is a set of places
(2) T is a set of transitions
(3) $P \cap T = \emptyset$, $P \cup T \neq \emptyset$
(4) C is the colour-function defined from $P \cup T$ into non-empty sets
(5) I_- and I_+ are the negative and positive incidence-function defined on $P \times T$, such that $I_-(p,t), I_+(p,t) \in [BAG(C(t)) \to BAG(C(p))]_L$ for all $(p,t) \in P \times T$
(6) m_0, the initial marking, is a function defined on P, such that $m_0(p) \in BAG(C(p))$ for all $p \in P$. ■

Throughout this paper we assume P, T, C(p) and C(t) to be finite for all $p \in P$ and $t \in T$. A marking of H is a function m defined on P, such that $m(p) \in BAG(C(p))$ for all $p \in P$. A step of H is a function x defined on T, such that $x(t) \in BAG(C(t))$ for all $t \in T$. The step x has concession in the marking m iff $\forall p \in P: \sum_{t \in T} I_-(p,t)(x(t)) \leq m(p)$. A marking is dead iff only the empty step has concession in it.

When x has concession in m, it may fire and thus transform m into a directly reachable marking m', such that

$$\forall p \in P: m'(p) = m(p) - \sum_{t \in T} I_-(p,t)(x(t)) + \sum_{t \in T} I_+(p,t)(x(t)).$$

We indicate this by the notation $m[x>m'$. In this paper we will only consider steps which map a single transition $t \in T$ into a single firing-colour $c \in C(t)$, while all other transitions are mapped into the empty bag. Such a step is denoted by (t,c), where we sometimes omit the brackets. When for $n \geq 0$, $m[t_1,c_1>m_1[t_2,c_2>m_2 \dots m_{n-1}[t_n,c_n>m'$ the sequence $\sigma = (t_1,c_1)(t_2,c_2)\dots(t_n,c_n)$ is a <u>firing sequence</u> at m and m' is (forward) <u>reachable</u> from m, which we shall denote by $m[\sigma>m'$. By $R(m)$ we denote the set of all markings which are reachable from m. An HL-net is <u>bounded on place $p \in P$ and colour $c \in C(p)$</u> iff $\exists k \in \mathbb{N} \forall m \in R(m_0): m(p)(c) \leq k$, and it is <u>bounded</u> iff it is bounded on all places and all colours.

<u>Definition</u> An ω-bag over a non-empty set S is a function $b: S \to \mathbb{N} \cup \{\omega\}$ and it is represented as a formal sum $\sum_{s \in S} b(s)s$, where $b(s) \in \mathbb{N} \cup \{\omega\}$. ∎

$b(s)$ represents the number of occurrences of the element s. If $b(s) = \omega$ the exact value is unknown and may be arbitrarily large. An ω-bag b over the set S is <u>finite</u> iff its support $\{s \in S \mid b(s) \neq 0\}$ is finite. The set of all finite ω-bags over the non-empty set S will be denoted by ω-BAG(S). Summation, scalar-multiplication, comparison, and multiplicity of ω-bags are defined in the following way, where $b_1, b_2, b \in \omega\text{-BAG}(S)$, $n \in \mathbb{N}$ and $m \in \mathbb{N} \cup \{\omega\}$:

$$\omega + m = \omega \qquad \omega > n \qquad m\omega = \begin{cases} \omega \ \underline{\text{if}} \ m \neq 0 \\ 0 \ \underline{\text{if}} \ m = 0 \end{cases}$$

$$\omega - m = \omega \qquad \omega \geq m$$

$$b_1 + b_2 = \sum_{s \in S} (b_1(s) + b_2(s))s \qquad m \times b = \sum_{s \in S} (mb(s))s$$

$$b_1 \geq b_2 \Leftrightarrow \forall s \in S: b_1(s) \geq b_2(s)$$

$$b_1 > b_2 \Leftrightarrow (b_1 \geq b_2) \wedge (\exists s \in S: b_1(s) > b_2(s))$$

When $b_1 \geq b_2$ we also define subtraction: $b_1 - b_2 = \sum_{s \in S} (b_1(s) - b_2(s))s$.

A function $F \in [S \to BAG(R)]$, where S and R are non-empty sets, can be extended uniquely to a linear function $\hat{F} \in [BAG(S) \to BAG(R)]$, called the <u>bag-extension</u> of F: $\forall b \in BAG(S): \hat{F}(b) = \sum_{s \in S} b(s) \times F(s)$.

Analogously we define the <u>ω-bag-extension</u> of $F \in [S \to \omega\text{-BAG}(R)]$ to be $\bar{F} \in [\omega\text{-BAG}(S) \to \omega\text{-BAG}(R)]$, where $\forall b \in \omega\text{-BAG}(S): \bar{F}(b) = \sum_{s \in S} b(s) \times F(s)$.

An <u>ω-marking</u> of H is a function m defined on P, such that $m(p) \in \omega\text{-BAG}(C(p))$ for all $p \in P$. The concepts of step, concession and reachability are generalized from markings to ω-markings by replacing the word "marking" by "ω-marking". An ω-marking m_1 <u>covers</u> another ω-

marking m_2, $m_1 \geq m_2$, iff $\forall p \in P$: $m_1(p) \geq m_2(p)$, and it strictly covers, $m_1 > m_2$, iff $m_1 \geq m_2 \wedge m_1 \neq m_2$.

3. INFORMAL INTRODUCTION TO REACHABILITY TREES FOR HL-NETS

In this section we give, by means of an example, an informal introduction to our notion of reachability trees for HL-nets. The basic idea of a reachability tree is to organize all reachable markings in a tree-structure where each node has attached a reachable marking, while each arc has attached a transition and a firing-colour (which transforms the marking of its source-node into the marking of its destination-node). Such a tree contains all reachable markings and all possible sequences of transition-firings. By inspection of the tree it is possible to answer a large number of questions about the system. However, in general the reachability tree described above will be infinite. For practical use it is necessary to reduce it to finite size. This is done by covering markings and by equivalent markings which is a generalization of duplicate markings. Reduction by covering markings and duplicate markings are well known from PT-trees. Reduction by equivalent markings is, however, a new concept suitable for HL-trees and this idea is the primary result of our paper.

Covering markings. When a node has a marking m_2, which strictly covers the marking m_1 of a predecessor, the firing sequence transforming m_1 into m_2 can be repeated several times starting from m_2†. Thus it is possible to get an arbitrarily large value for each coefficient which has increased from m_1 to m_2. In the tree we indicate this by substituting in m_2, the ω-symbol for each such coefficient. The situation is analogous to the idea behind the "pumping lemma" of automata theory and it means that some of the places can obtain an arbitrarily large number of tokens of certain colours.

This kind of reduction results in a loss of information. In [8] it is shown, that if ω occurs in a PT-tree, it is not always possible to determine from the tree whether the net has a dead marking or not.

Duplicate markings. If there are several nodes with identical markings only one of them is developed further, while the others are marked as "duplicate". This reduction will not result in a loss of information

† If m_2 already contains ω the situation is more complicated, and it may be necessary to involve some extra firings, cf. the proof of lemma 3 in appendix 1 in [3].

because we can construct the missing subtrees from the one developed. Due to reduction by covering markings, two such subtrees may not be completely identical, but they will represent the same set of markings and firing sequences.

<u>Equivalent markings.</u> To introduce our notion of equivalent markings, we will now look at the HL-net for the five dining philosophers in [4]:

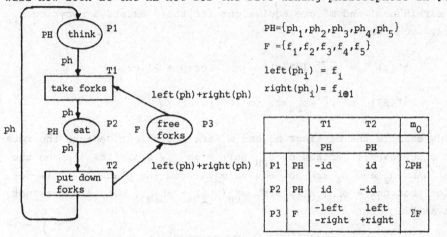

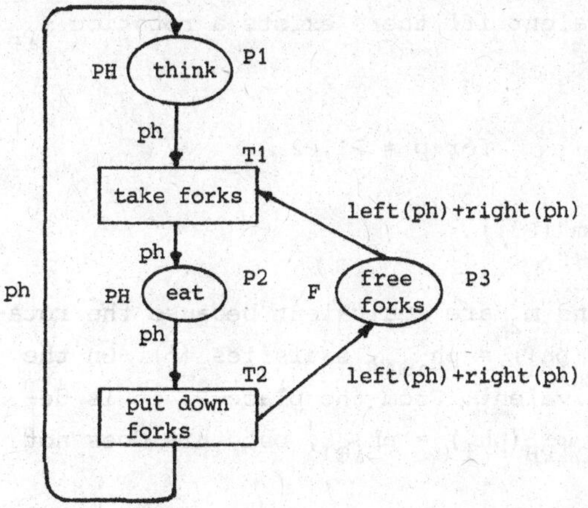

$PH=\{ph_1, ph_2, ph_3, ph_4, ph_5\}$

$F=\{f_1, f_2, f_3, f_4, f_5\}$

$left(ph_i) = f_i$

$right(ph_i) = f_{i\oplus 1}$

		T1	T2	m_0
		PH	PH	
P1	PH	-id	id	ΣPH
P2	PH	id	-id	
P3	F	-left -right	left +right	ΣF

<u>Fig. 1</u>: HL-net for the philosopher system.

We will now analyze the following markings:

$$m_1 = (ph_2+ph_3+ph_4+ph_5,\ ph_1,\ f_3+f_4+f_5)$$
$$m_2 = (ph_1+ph_3+ph_4+ph_5,\ ph_2,\ f_1+f_4+f_5)$$
$$m_3 = (ph_2+ph_4+ph_5,\ ph_1+ph_3,\ f_5)$$
$$m_4 = (ph_2+ph_3+ph_4+ph_5,\ ph_1,\ f_2+f_4+f_5)$$
$$m_5 = (ph_3+ph_4+ph_5,\ ph_1+ph_2,\ f_5).$$

By intuition we want m_1 and m_2 to be <u>equivalent</u>. The point is that we do not need to know the identity of eating philosophers, because all philosophers "behave in the same way". The marking m_3 contains a different number of eating philosophers and thus it is not equivalent to m_1 or m_2. However, two markings may be non-equivalent even though they have the same number of eating philosophers and the same number of free forks. In m_1 and m_2 the non-free forks are those belonging to the eating philosopher. This is not the case in m_4, and thus m_4 is not equivalent to m_1 or m_2. In m_5 the two eating philosophers are neighbours. This is not the case in m_3, and so these markings are not equivalent either.

To obtain equivalent markings we must demand that the identity of all philosophers and forks are changed by the same rotation. As an example, m_1 is obtained from m_2 by the rotation which adds 4 (in a cyclic way) to the index of each philosopher and fork.

To formalize the notion of equivalent markings we associate to the colour set PH the symmetry type "rotation" and we define a bijective correspondence between F and PH by a function $r \in [F \rightarrow PH]$, where $r(f_i) = ph_i$. Two markings m' and m" are equivalent iff there exists a rotation φ_{PH} of PH, such that

$$(*) \quad \begin{aligned} m'(p) &= \overline{\varphi_{PH}}\,(m''(p)) \qquad \text{for } p = P1, P2 \\ m'(P3) &= \overline{r^{-1} \circ \varphi_{PH} \circ r}\,(m''(P3)). \end{aligned}$$

In our example the markings m_1 and m_2 are equivalent because the rotation $\varphi_{PH} \in [PH \rightarrow PH]$, defined by $\varphi_{PH}(ph_i) = ph_{i \oplus 4}$, satisfies (*). On the other hand m_2 and m_4 are not equivalent. From the place P2 it is demanded that $ph_2 = \varphi_{PH}(ph_1)$, i.e. $\varphi_{PH}(ph_i) = ph_{i \oplus 1}$, but this does not work at P3:

$$m_2(P3) = f_1+f_4+f_5 \neq f_1+f_3+f_5 = \overline{r^{-1} \circ \varphi_{PH} \circ r}\,(m_4(P3)).$$

As a generalization of reduction by duplicate markings we will now reduce the reachability tree by equivalent markings: Only one element of each class of equivalent markings is developed further, and when a marking has several direct successors which are equivalent, only one of them are included in the tree.

Figure 2 shows an HL-tree obtained for the philosopher system. In the initial marking transition T1 can fire in all colours of PH producing five equivalent markings of which only one is included in the tree, while the existence of the others are indicated by the label attached to the corresponding arc. If we only reduced by covering markings and duplicate markings, the tree would have had 31 nodes (and exactly the same tree structure as the PT-tree corresponding to the equivalent PT-net).

The relation of equivalent markings is determined by the persons who analyze the system, and it must respect the inherent nature of the system. In the philosopher system, rotation is the suitable symmetry type. But in the telephone system of [6] arbitrary permutation would be the suitable symmetry type (since there is no special relation between a phone number and its nearest neighbours). In general, several symmetry types (rotation, permutation or identity-function) may be involved in the same system (for different colour sets).

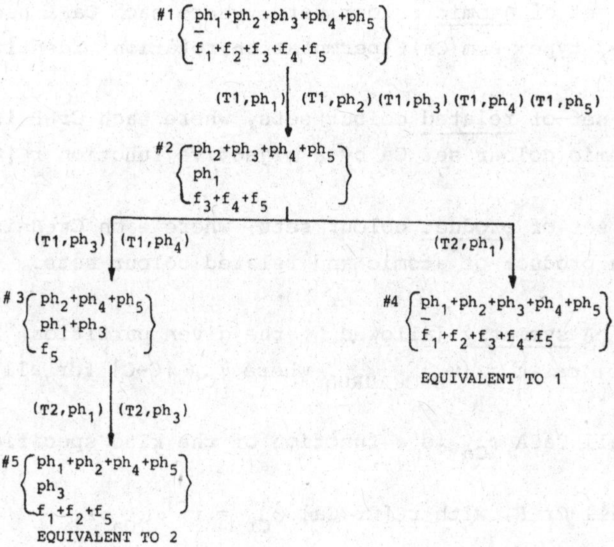

<u>Fig. 2</u>: HL-tree of the philosopher system. It is reduced by covering markings (none in this tree) and equivalent markings.

When the relation of equivalent markings is defined in a sound way (to be formalized in section 5), the reduction by means of covering markings and equivalent markings does not result in a loss of more information than reduction by covering markings and duplicate markings only. This means, that all net properties which can be proved by means of the PT-tree of the equivalent PT-net can also be proved by means of our (much smaller) HL-tree.

4. DEFINITION OF REACHABILITY TREES FOR HL-NETS

In this section we consider a fixed HL-net $H=(P,T,C,I_-,I_+,m_0)$.

<u>Definition</u> The set of colour sets $\{C(x) \mid x \in P \cup T\}$ is <u>partitioned</u> into three pairwise disjoint classes:

1) A is the set of atomic colour sets, where each $Ca \in A$ has attached a symmetry type: $sym(Ca) \in$ {permutation, rotation[†], identity}.

2) R is the set of related colour sets, where each $Cr \in R$ is related to an atomic colour set Ca by a bijective function $r \in [Cr \to Ca]$.

3) Π is the set of product colour sets, where each $C\pi \in \Pi$ is the cartesian product of atomic and related colour sets. ∎

Definition A symmetry (allowed by the given partition) is a set of bijective functions $\varphi = \{\varphi_C\}_{C \in A \cup R \cup \Pi}$ where $\varphi_C \in [C \to C]$ for all C and

(1) For all $Ca \in A$ φ_{Ca} is a function of the kind specified by sym(Ca).

(2) For all $Cr \in R$, with $r \in [Cr \to Ca]$ $\varphi_{Cr} = r^{-1} \circ \varphi_{Ca} \circ r$.

(3) For all $C\pi \in \Pi$, with $C\pi = C1 \times C2 \times \ldots \times Cn$

$$\varphi_{C\pi} = \varphi_{C1} \times \varphi_{C2} \times \ldots \times \varphi_{Cn}.$$

The set of symmetries (allowed by the given partition) is denoted by Φ. It is finite since P, T, C(p) and C(t) are assumed to be finite for all $p \in P$ and $t \in T$. ∎

The definition of φ_{Cr} can be visualized by the following commutative diagram:

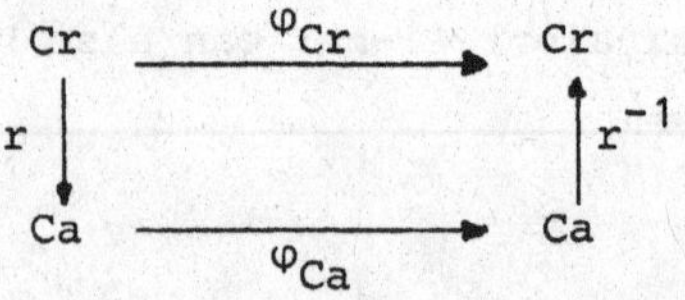

Since r is a bijection it follows that φ_{Cr} is a function of the kind specified by sym(Ca).

Technical remark: The definition of partition is here presented in its simplest form. In some cases (cf. the database example in section 6) it may be convenient/necessary to allow Π to contain subsets of cartesian products. If $C\pi = C^n \setminus \{(a,a,\ldots,a) \mid a \in C\}$ we define $\varphi_{C\pi} = (\varphi_C \times \varphi_C \times \ldots \times \varphi_C)|_{C}{}^{n}$, yielding a bijection on $C\pi$ as requested. Secondly, in special cases, there can be sets in use to construct products in Π

---

† When an atomic colour set has rotation as symmetry type it must be a finite set, indexed by 1,2,...,n where n is the cardinality.

which are not themselves ordinary colour sets in the HL-net. These sets have to be included as atomic or related sets.

Given an ω-marking m, a firing sequence $\sigma = (t_1,c_1)(t_2,c_2)\ldots(t_n,c_n)$ and a symmetry $\varphi\in\Phi$, we define an equivalent ω-marking $\varphi(m)$ by

$$\varphi(m)(p) = \overline{\varphi_{C(p)}}(m(p)) \text{ for all } p\in P$$

and an equivalent firing sequence $\varphi(\sigma)$ by

$$\varphi(\sigma) = (t_1,\varphi_{C(t_1)}(c_1))(t_2,\varphi_{C(t_2)}(c_2))\ldots(t_n,\varphi_{C(t_n)}(c_n)).$$

Definition Two ω-markings, m_1 and m_2, of H are equivalent, $m_1 \sim m_2$, iff there exists a symmetry $\varphi\in\Phi$ such that $m_1 = \varphi(m_2)$. It is easy to show that ~ is an equivalence relation. ■

We will draw attention to the fact, that given a net there are often several meaningful ways to define a partition. It is the user, who decides the partition and this choice determines the possible symmetries, and thus the relation of equivalent markings. In section 5 we define two soundness criteria for partitions and we establish four proof rules, which for sound partitions allow us to deduce properties of HL-nets from properties of the corresponding HL-trees.

Given the notions above we are now able to formalize the definition of reachability trees for HL-nets:

Definition The reachability tree, HL-tree, for an HL-net with an equivalence relation, ~, (specified by a partition) is the full reachability tree† reduced with respect to covering markings and equivalent markings:

(1) If a node y strictly covers a predecessor, z, then we assign $m_y(p)(c) := \omega$ for all $p\in P$ and $c\in C(p)$ satisfying $m_y(p)(c) > m_z(p)(c)$.

(2) Only one node in each (reachable) equivalence class of ~ is developed further. Only one node in a set of equivalent brothers is included in the tree. The other nodes are removed, but the arc to the included brother node contains information of their existence.

(3) Associated to each node is an ω-marking and a node-label. The node-label is a (possibly empty) sequence of status information, which may indicate that the marking is equivalent

† The full reachability tree contains all reachable markings and all firing sequences.

to the marking of an earlier processed node, covering the marking of a predecessor node, or dead.

(4) Associated to each arc from node n_1 to n_2 is an arc-label which is a list of firing information. Each element is a pair (t,c) where $t \in T$ and $c \in C(t)$. Each pair in the list has concession in the marking of n_1. Firing the first pair in the list results in the marking of n_2, whereas firing of the other pairs results in markings which are equivalent to the marking of n_2. ∎

Now we will describe our algorithm to produce the HL-trees. To create a new node we use the operation "NEWNODE(m,ℓ)", where m and ℓ are the ω-marking and node-label of the node. A new arc is created by "NEWARC(n_1,n_2,ℓ)" where n_1,n_2 and ℓ are the source-node, destination-node and arc-label. It is possible to append new information to an existing label, ℓ, by the operation "APPEND(ℓ,new-inf)". The ω-marking and the node-label of a node x is denoted by m_x and ℓ_x, respectively. The arc-label of the arc from node x to node y is denoted by ℓ_{xy}. By "NEXT(m,t,c)" we denote the ω-marking obtained by firing transition t with colour $c \in C(t)$ in the ω-marking m.

ALGORITHM TO PRODUCE HL-TREES

```
UNPROCESSED := {NEWNODE(m0,empty)}; PROCESSED := Ø
REPEAT
   SELECT some node x∈UNPROCESSED
   IF mx~my for some node y∈PROCESSED
   THEN APPEND(ℓx,"equivalent to y")
   ELSE IF no pair (t,c) has concession in mx
        THEN APPEND(ℓx,"dead")
        ELSE BEGIN {x is non-equivalent and non-dead}
                   FOR ALL (t,c) having concession in mx DO
                   BEGIN
                       m := NEXT(mx,t,c); ℓ:=empty
                       FOR ALL ancestors z with m>mz DO
                       BEGIN
                           FOR ALL p∈P,c∈C(p) where m(p)(c)>mz(p)(c) DO
                               m(p)(c) := ω
                           APPEND(ℓ,"covering of z")
                       END
                       IF m~mu for some node u being a son of x
                       THEN APPEND(ℓxu,"(t,c)")
                       ELSE BEGIN
                                v := NEWNODE(m,ℓ)
                                UNPROCESSED := UNPROCESSED ∪ {v}
                                NEWARC(x,v,"(t,c)")
                            END
                   END
             END
   UNPROCESSED := UNPROCESSED\{x}; PROCESSED := PROCESSED ∪ {x}
UNTIL UNPROCESSED = Ø
```

∎

The algorithm works in the following way: as long as there are more unprocessed nodes, one is selected and processed. The processing of a node starts with a check for equivalence with an already processed node, i.e. only the first processed node in each equivalence class of ~ is developed further. If no equivalent node is found, the node is checked for being dead. If it is not dead, for each pair (t,c) with concession a son is produced and included in the tree (unless it is an equivalent brother). Each HL-tree is a subtree of a PT-tree for the equivalent PT-net, obtained from the HL-net by the method described in [4]. In [2, 7, 8] it is shown that each PT-tree is finite. Thus each HL-tree is finite and our algorithm always halts.

Technical remark: The constructed HL-tree normally depends on the order in which the nodes are processed. This means that each HL-net may have several corresponding HL-trees. Normally an implementation enforces an ordering-rule for the processing of nodes, and this rule then determines the actual HL-tree, constructed for the HL-net by that implementation.

Technical remark: In an implementation of the algorithm it is crucial to minimize the time spent on testing for equivalence. In appendix 3 of [3] we describe a fairly effective algorithm to test two ω-markings for equivalence. Moreover our implementation will use hash coding to divide markings into subclasses in such a way, that equivalent markings always belong to the same subclass. This hash coding drastically decreases the number of pairs to be tested for equivalence.

5. WHAT CAN BE PROVED BY MEANS OF HL-TREES?

In this section we discuss how HL-trees can be used to prove properties of the corresponding HL-nets.

A proof rule is a theorem by which properties of HL-nets can be deduced from properties of HL-trees (or vice versa). For PT-trees [2,8] describe a number of such proof rules, from which it is possible to deduce information concerning: boundedness, coverability, reachability, liveness, etc. Some of the proof rules are total, in the sense that the question concerning presence or absence of the particular net property always can be answered by means of the proof rule. Other proof rules are partial, in the sense that the question only sometimes can be answered.

For HL-trees the situation is a bit more complicated, since the observed tree properties in a crucial way may depend on the chosen partition, which determines the relation of equivalent markings. Hence it is necessary to introduce the notion of a <u>sound</u> partition, which intuitively means that the partition respects the inherent symmetry properties of the HL-net. If for the philosopher system we allowed arbitrary permutation, instead of just rotation, this would be a typical example of a non-sound partition, since it neglects the fact that in this system there is another relationship between neighbours than between non-neighbours. Analogously, it would be non-sound to have both PH and F as atomic colour sets, since this would neglect the fact that there is another relationship between a philosopher and the two nearest forks than between the philosopher and the three remote forks.

<u>Definition</u> A partition is <u>sound</u> iff it satisfies the following criteria:

(SC1) $\forall p\in P \forall t\in T \forall \varphi\in \Phi\colon \widehat{\varphi_{C(p)}} \circ I_{\pm}(p,t) = I_{\pm}(p,t) \circ \widehat{\varphi_{C(t)}}$.

(SC2) $\forall \varphi\in \Phi\colon m_0 = \varphi(m_0)$. ■

SC1 can be visualized by the following commutative diagram:

$$\begin{array}{ccc} BAG(C(t)) & \xrightarrow{\widehat{\varphi_{C(t)}}} & BAG(C(t)) \\ {\scriptstyle I_{\pm}(p,t)}\downarrow & & \downarrow{\scriptstyle I_{\pm}(p,t)} \\ BAG(C(p)) & \xrightarrow{\widehat{\varphi_{C(p)}}} & BAG(C(p)) \end{array}$$

SC1 demands that the chosen partition for the HL-net and hence the set of allowed symmetries must agree with the firing of transitions in the sense that equivalent colours have to be treated in the "same" way. SC2 demands, that the initial marking has to be symmetric. In practice it is often nearly trivial to verify the soundness criteria by means of the following rules:

(R1) Due to the linearity of the functions, SC1 can be verified by checking only steps of the form (t,c).

(R2) If $I_{\pm}(p,t)$ is an identity-function or a zero-function SC1 is always satisfied.

(R3) When $I_{\pm}(p,t)$ is a sum of several functions, SC1 can be verified for each of them, separately.

(R4) When a function appears in $I_{\pm}(p,t)$ for several places/transitions it needs only to be considered once to verify SC1.

(R5) When the symmetry type of C(t) is identity, SC1 is always satisfied.

(R6) When the symmetry type of C(t) is rotation it is enough to consider the "one step forward" rotation to verify SC1.

(R7) When the symmetry type of C(t) is permutation it is enough to consider transpositions (interchanging of two elements) to verify SC1.

(R8) SC2 is satisfied iff
$\forall p\in P[\mathrm{sym}(C(p)) \neq \mathrm{identity} \Rightarrow \exists k\in \mathbb{N}_0 : m_0(p) = k\times \Sigma C(p))]$
where $\Sigma C(p)$ denotes the bag which contains exactly one occurrence of each colour in C(p).

As an example, soundness of the partition, chosen for the philosopher system in section 3, can easily be verified. We only have to prove the following properties, where r is the function relating F to PH, while φ_{PH} is the "one step forward" rotation on PH:

$$r^{-1}\bullet\varphi_{PH}\bullet r\bullet \mathrm{left} = \mathrm{left}\bullet\varphi_{PH}$$
$$r^{-1}\bullet\varphi_{PH}\bullet r\bullet \mathrm{right} = \mathrm{right}\bullet\varphi_{PH}\ .$$

To formulate our proof rules we need some notation. $R(m_0)$ is the set of markings which are reachable from m_0. $R(m_0)(p) = \{m(p)(c) \mid m\in R(m_0) \wedge c\in C(p)\}$ is the coefficients appearing at place p, while $R(m_0)(p)(c) = \{m(p)(c) \mid m\in R(m_0)\}$ is the coefficients appearing at place p for colour c. $T(m_0)$ is the set of nodes in the HL-tree having $\underline{m}_0$ as root. $T(m_0)(p)$ and $T(m_0)(p)(c)$ are defined analogous to $R(m_0)(p)$ and $R(m_0)(p)(c)$, respectively. Furthermore we define the function $\mathrm{map}_{C(p)} \in [C(P) \rightarrow \mathbb{P}(C(p))]$ as follows

$$\mathrm{map}_{C(p)}(c) = \{c'\in C(p) \mid \exists\varphi\in\Phi : \varphi_{C(p)}(c') = c\}.$$

<u>Observation</u>

(O1)

$$\mathrm{map}_{C(p)}(c) = \begin{cases} \{c\} \ \underline{\text{if}}\ \mathrm{sym}(C(p)) = \mathrm{identity} \\ C(p)\ \underline{\text{if}}\ \mathrm{sym}(C(p)) \in \{\mathrm{rotation},\mathrm{permutation}\} \end{cases}$$

We now formulate our four proof rules for HL-trees. They are generalizations of the proof rules for PT-trees given in [8].

PROOF RULES FOR HL-NETS

(PR1) H is bounded $\Leftrightarrow \forall p \in P: \omega \notin T(m_0)(p)$
prerequisite: SC1

(PR2)
$$\sup R(m_0)(p)(c)^{\dagger} = \max \bigcup_{c' \in map_{C(p)}(c)} T(m_0)(p)(c')$$
prerequisite: SC1, SC2

(PR3) $\exists \alpha \in T(m_0)$: "dead"$\in \ell_\alpha \Rightarrow \exists m \in R(m_0)$: m is dead
prerequisite: none

(PR4) $\exists m \in R(m_0)$: m is dead $\Rightarrow$
($\exists \alpha \in T(m_0)$: "dead"$\in \ell_\alpha$) $\vee$ ($\exists p \in P: \omega \in T(m_0)(p)$)
prerequisite: SC1

As an example on how the proof rules can be used, we again turn to the philosopher system with the HL-tree shown in figure 2. By applying PR1 we derive that the net is bounded, and from PR2 we see that 1 can be used as a uniform bound for all places and all colours. PR4 tells us that no reachable marking is dead.

To prove the correctness of our proof rules we need the following four lemmas:

Lemma 1 Assume SC1, then $\forall \varphi \in \Phi: m_1[\sigma>m_2 \Rightarrow \varphi(m_1)[\varphi(\sigma)>\varphi(m_2)$ for all ω-markings and all firing-sequences.

Proof See appendix 1 in [3].

Corollary Assume SC1 and SC2, then

a) $m_1 \sim m_2 \Rightarrow [m_1 \in R(m_0) \Leftrightarrow m_2 \in R(m_0)]$

b) $m_1 \sim m_2 \Rightarrow [m_1$ is dead $\Leftrightarrow m_2$ is dead$]$. ∎

Given an ω-marking m_ω and a marking m we define that m_ω agrees with m, $m_\omega \geq m$, iff

$$\forall p \in P \forall c \in C(p): m_\omega(p)(c) \neq \omega \Rightarrow m_\omega(p)(c) = m(p)(c)$$

i.e. for each pair p and c the coefficients in m_ω and m are identical or that of m_ω is ω. It is easy to prove the following:

† By convention $\sup A = \omega$, for $A \subseteq \mathbb{N}$, when $\forall k \in \mathbb{N} \exists a \in A: a \geq k$.

Observations

(O2) $m_\omega > m \Rightarrow \varphi(m_\omega) > \varphi(m)$ for all $\varphi \in \Phi$

(O3) $m_\omega > m \wedge m[\sigma > m' \Rightarrow \exists m'_\omega: m_\omega[\sigma > m'_\omega \wedge m'_\omega > m'$ for all firing sequences σ.

■

Lemma 2 Assume SC1, then $\forall m \in R(m_0) \exists \varphi \in \Phi \; \exists \alpha \in T(m_0): m_\alpha > \varphi(m)$.

Proof See appendix 1 in [3]. ■

Given an ω-marking m and $k \in \mathbb{N}$, then we define m^k as follows:

$$m^k(p)(c) = \begin{cases} k & \underline{\text{if}}\ m(p)(c) = \omega \\ m(p)(c) & \underline{\text{otherwise}} \end{cases}$$

for all $p \in P$ and $c \in C(p)$.

Lemma 3 $\forall \alpha \in T(m_0) \forall k \in \mathbb{N} \; \exists m \in R(m_0): m_\alpha > m \geq m_\alpha^k$.

Proof See appendix 1 in [3]. The proof of this lemma is by far the most complicated and it involves several induction arguments.

Corollary a) $\omega \in T(m_0)(p)(c) \Rightarrow \sup R(m_0)(p)(c) = \omega$

b) $k \in T(m_0)(p)(c) \Rightarrow k \in R(m_0)(p)(c)$. ■

Lemma 4 Assume SC1 and SC2, then

$$\sup R(m_0)(p)(c) = \max \bigcup_{c' \in map_{C(p)}(c)} T(m_0)(p)(c')$$

If only SC1 is assumed we get "≦" instead of "=".

Proof See appendix 1 in [3]. ■

Theorem The four proof rules PR1-PR4 are valid, under the given prerequisites.

Proof

PR1: The proof is by contradiction. Assume that H is bounded, and $\exists p \in P$: $\omega \in T(m_0)(p)$. Then $\omega \in T(m_0)(p)(c)$ for some colour $c \in C(p)$ and by the corollary of lemma 3 $R(m_0)(p)(c)$ is unbounded - contradiction with H being bounded.

Next assume that $\omega \notin T(m_0)(p)$, and H unbounded, i.e.

(1) $\exists p\in P\ \exists c\in C(p)\ \forall k\in\mathbb{N}\ \exists m\in R(m_0):\ m(p)(c)>k.$

For each of these m, by lemma 2,

(2) $\exists\alpha\in T(m_0)\ \exists\varphi^m\in\Phi:\ m_\alpha > \varphi^m(m).$

We then get

(3) $m_\alpha(p)(\varphi^m_{C(p)}(c)) \geq \varphi^m(m)(p)(\varphi^m_{C(p)}(c)) = m(p)(c)>k$

for each k in (1). "≥" follows from (2), "=" is an immediate consequence of the way $\varphi^m(m)$ is defined, while ">" follows from (1). Since $T(m_0)$ and Φ are finite it follows from (3) that $\exists\alpha'\in T(m_0):\ m_{\alpha'}(p)(\varphi^m(c)) = \omega$ - contradiction with $\omega\notin T(m_0)(p)$.

PR2: Identical to lemma 4.

PR3: Assume that $\exists\alpha\in T(m_0)$: "dead"$\in\ell_\alpha$. By lemma 3, $\exists m\in R(m_0): m_\alpha > m$. The marking m_α is dead, and since m is smaller it is dead too.

PR4: Assume that $\exists m\in R(m_0)$: m is dead, and $\forall\alpha\in T(m_0)$: "dead" $\notin\ell_\alpha$. By lemma 2, $\exists\varphi\in\Phi\ \exists\alpha\in T(m_0): m_\alpha > \varphi(m)$. The marking $\varphi(m)$ is dead, by the corollary of lemma 1. m_α is not dead and thus we conclude $m_\alpha > \varphi(m)$, which together with $m_\alpha > \varphi(m)$ yields $m_\alpha(p)(c) = \omega$ for some $p\in P$ and $c\in C(p)$. ∎

The following two lemmas are not necessary to establish the proof rules, but they provide useful insight in the structure of the reachability tree:

Lemma 5

$\forall\alpha 1,\alpha 2\in T(m_0)$ with $(t,c)\in\ell_{\alpha 1\ \alpha 2}$

$\exists m_1,m_2\in R(m_0)$ with $m_1[t,c>m_2$:

(i) $m_{\alpha 1} > m_1\ \wedge$

(ii) $m_{\alpha 2} > \begin{cases} m_2 & \text{\underline{if} } (t,c) = \text{head}(\ell_{\alpha 1\ \alpha 2}) \\ \varphi(m_2) \text{ for some } \varphi\in\Phi & \text{\underline{otherwise}}. \end{cases}$

Proof: See appendix 1 in [3]. ∎

Lemma 6 Assume SC1, then:

$\forall m_1, m_2 \in R(m_0)$ with $m_1[t,c\rangle m_2$

$\exists \varphi \in \Phi$

$\exists \alpha 1, \alpha 2 \in T(m_0)$ with $\varphi(t,c) \in \ell_{\alpha 1\ \alpha 2}$:

(i) $m_{\alpha 1} > \varphi(m_1) \quad \wedge$

(ii) $m_{\alpha 2} > \begin{cases} \varphi(m_2) \ \underline{\text{if}}\ \varphi(t,c) = \text{head}(\ell_{\alpha 1\ \alpha 2}) \\ \varphi' \circ \varphi(m_2) \text{ for some } \varphi' \in \Phi\ \underline{\text{otherwise}}. \end{cases}$

Proof: See appendix 1 in [3]. ∎

6. EXAMPLES OF THE USE OF HL-TREES

This section contains two examples which together with the system of the five dining philosophers, treated in section 3, illustrate a spectrum of the problems concerning the construction and analysis of HL-trees. The first example is a system, where the equivalence relation involves permutation, identity and products. The second example illustrates covering markings.

Data base system In [4] the system is described and analyzed by means of the invariant method. We define a partition by

atomic DBM:permutation; E:identity

product MB:subset of DBM×DBM.

An HL-tree for the data base system is shown in figure 3.
It is easy to verify that the chosen partition is sound (see appendix 2 in [3]). By applying PR1 we derive that the net is bounded, and from PR2 we see that 1 can be used as a uniform bound for all places and all colours. PR4 tells us that no reachable marking is dead.

The leaves of the tree are identical with #1 and #6, respectively. This is, however, a coincidence and it changes if the nodes are processed in another order. As mentioned earlier, an alternative to the HL-net is to construct the PT-tree for the equivalent PT-net. In the following table we compare the size of the HL-tree with the size of the PT-tree (for different sizes of DBM). Normally, the HL-trees are not just smaller than the corresponding PT-trees, but they also grow slower when the sizes of the involved colour sets increase.

number of elements in DBM	number of nodes in the HL-tree	number of nodes in the PT-tree
2	5	9
3	9	43
4	14	225
5	23	>1400

#1 $\left\{\begin{array}{ll} \Sigma DBM & \Sigma MB \\ - & - \\ - & - \\ \epsilon & - \end{array}\right\}$

(T1,a) | (T1,b) (T1,c)

#2 $\left\{\begin{array}{ll} \Sigma DBM-a & \Sigma MB-((a,b)+(a,c)) \\ a & (a,b)+(a,c) \\ - & - \\ - & - \end{array}\right\}$

(T3,(a,b)) | (T3,(a,c))

#3 $\left\{\begin{array}{ll} \Sigma DBM-a-b & \Sigma MB-((a,b)+(a,c)) \\ a & (a,c) \\ b & (a,b) \\ - & - \end{array}\right\}$

(T3,(a,c)) | (T4,(a,b))

#4 $\left\{\begin{array}{ll} - & \Sigma MB-((a,b)+(a,c)) \\ a & - \\ b+c & (a,b)+(a,c) \\ - & - \end{array}\right\}$ #5 $\left\{\begin{array}{ll} \Sigma DBM-a & \Sigma MB-((a,b)+(a,c)) \\ a & (a,c) \\ - & - \\ - & (a,b) \end{array}\right\}$

(T4,(a,b)) | (T4,(a,c))   (T3,(a,c)) |

#6 $\left\{\begin{array}{ll} \Sigma DBM-a-c & \Sigma MB-((a,b)+(a,c)) \\ a & - \\ c & (a,c) \\ - & (a,b) \end{array}\right\}$ #7 $\left\{\begin{array}{ll} \Sigma DBM-a-c & \Sigma MB-((a,b)+(a,c)) \\ a & - \\ c & (a,c) \\ - & (a,b) \end{array}\right\}$

EQUIVALENT TO 6

(T4,(a,c)) |

#8 $\left\{\begin{array}{ll} \Sigma DBM-a & \Sigma MB-((a,b)+(a,c)) \\ a & - \\ - & - \\ - & (a,b)+(a,c) \end{array}\right\}$

(T2,a) |

#9 $\left\{\begin{array}{ll} \Sigma DBM & \Sigma MB \\ - & - \\ - & - \\ \epsilon & - \end{array}\right\}$

EQUIVALENT TO 1

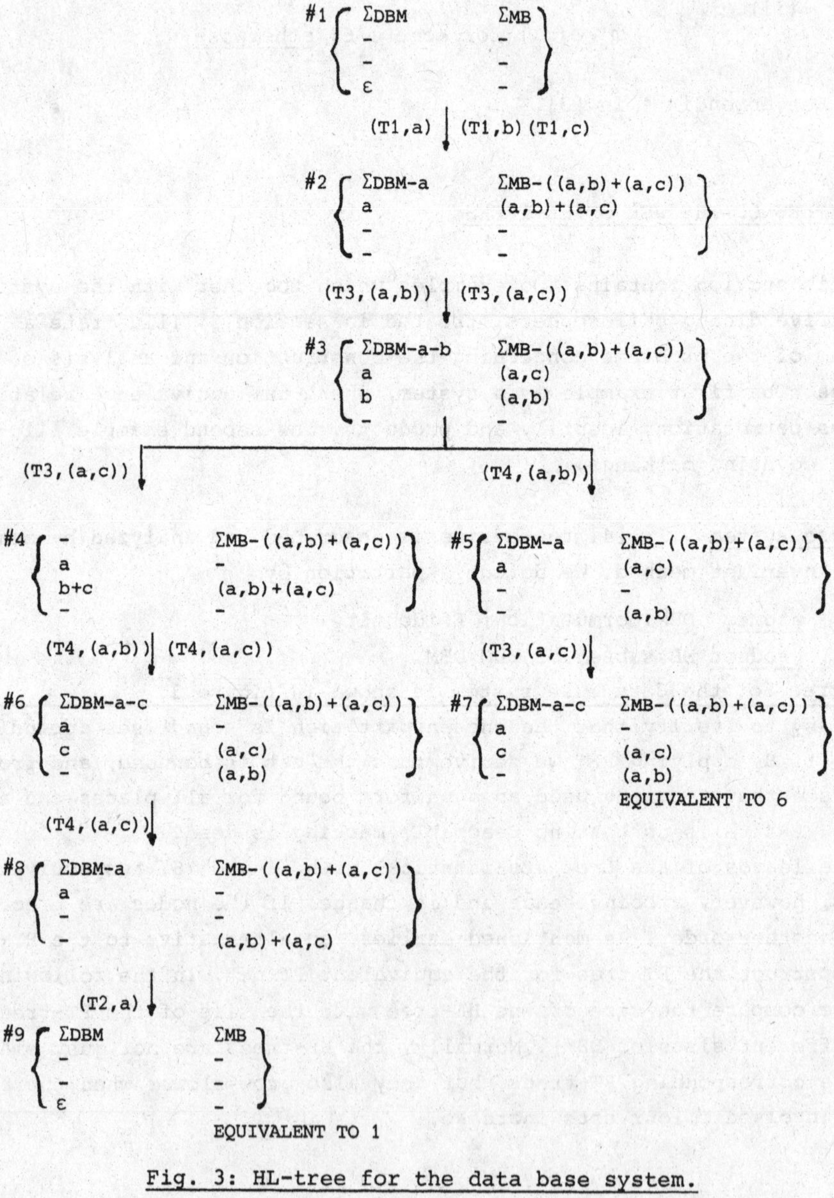

Fig. 3: HL-tree for the data base system.

Producer-consumer system   We have also constructed an HL-tree for a system, where two producers send two different kinds of messages to a consumer via an unbounded buffer. The HL-net and HL-tree for this system can be found in appendix 2 of [3]. Again, the chosen partition is sound, and the expected properties of the HL-net can be derived by means of the proof rules. The HL-tree has 30 nodes of which 17 are coverings (some of them even cover two other markings). As in the two other examples of this paper, the HL-tree for this system is remarkably smaller than the corresponding PT-tree, which has 93 nodes.

Acknowledgement   Some of the ideas in this paper are founded on a student project at Aarhus University with the following participants: Arne M. Jensen, Peter A. Nielsen, Erik Schjøtt, Kasper Østerbye and Kurt Jensen (Supervisor).

References

[1] H.J. Genrich and K. Lautenbach: System modelling with high-level Petri nets, Theoretical Computer Science 13 (1981), 109-136.

[2] M. Hack: Decidability questions for Petri Nets. TR 161, MIT, 1976.

[3] P. Huber, A.M. Jensen, L.O. Jepsen and K. Jensen: Towards reachability trees for high-level Petri nets. DAIMI PB-174, Computer Science Department, Aarhus University, 1984. Identical to the present paper, except for 3 appendices which contain the proof of lemmas 1-6, analysis of two examples, and our algorithm to test two ω-markings for equivalence.

[4] K. Jensen: Coloured Petri nets and the invariant-method. Theoretical Computer Science 14 (1981), 317-336.

[5] K. Jensen: How to find invariants for coloured Petri nets. In: J. Gruska, M. Chytill (eds.): Mathematical Foundations of Computer Science 1981, Lecture Notes in Computer Science, vol. 118, Springer-Verlag, 1981, 327-338.

[6] K. Jensen: High-level Petri nets. In: A. Pagnoni and G. Rozenberg (eds.): Applications and Theory of Petri Nets, Informatik-Fachberichte vol. 66, Springer-Verlag 1983, 166-180.

[7] R.M. Karp and R.E. Miller: Parallel program schemata. Journal of Computer and System Sciences, vol. 3 (1969), 147-195.

[8] J.L. Peterson: Petri net theory and the modellings of systems. Prentice-Hall 1981.

[9] W. Reisig: Petri nets with individual tokens. In: A. Pagnoni and G. Rozenberg (eds.): Applications and Theory of Petri Nets, Informatik-Fachberichte vol. 66, Springer-Verlag 1983, 229-249.

THE RESIDUE OF VECTOR SETS WITH APPLICATIONS TO DECIDABILITY PROBLEMS IN PETRI NETS

BY

RÜDIGER VALK and MATTHIAS JANTZEN

Fachbereich Informatik, Universität Hamburg
Rothenbaumchaussee 67, D-2000 Hamburg 13

Abstract

A set K of integer vectors is called right-closed, if for any element $\underline{m} \in K$ all vectors $\underline{m}' \geqslant \underline{m}$ are also contained in K. In such a case K is a semilinear set of vectors having a minimal generating set res(K), called the residue of K. A general method is given for computing the residue set of a right-closed set, provided it satisfies a certain decidability criterion.
Various right-closed sets which are important for analyzing, constructing, or controlling Petri nets are studied. One such set is the set CONTINUAL(T) of all such markings which have an infinite continuation using each transition infinitely many times. It is shown that the residue set of CONTINUAL(T) can be constructed effectively, solving an open problem of Schroff. The proof also solves problem 24 (iii) in the EATCS-Bulletin. The new methods developed in this paper can also be used to show that it is decidable, whether a signal net is prompt [Patil] and whether certain ω-languages of a Petri net are empty or not.

It is shown, how the behaviour of a given Petri net can be controlled in a simple way in order to realize its maximal central subbehaviour, thereby solving a problem of Nivat and Arnold, or its maximal live subbehaviour as well. This latter approach is used to give a new solution for the bankers problem described by Dijkstra.

Since the restriction imposed on a Petri net by a fact [GL] can be formulated as a right closed set, our method also gives a new general approach for „implementations" of facts.

1. Introduction

The basis of many decision procedures in vector addition systems or Petri nets is the so called "property of monotonicity". To give an example: if a sequence of transitions can fire in a given marking, this must also be possible in any marking that is (componentwise) not smaller. In particular, a marking is unbounded if for any integer n there is a place p and a firing sequence w, such that firing w in m brings more than n tokens to p. Consequently, unboundedness is a monotone property of markings.

A marking is called dead if any firing inevitably results in a total deadlock. Hence the property of a marking to be not dead is also monotone. This property can be rephrased as follows: $\underline{m}$ is not dead, if an infinite sequence of transitions can fire in $\underline{m}$. Being interested in some particular set $\hat{T} \subseteq T$ of transitions to be fired infinitely often we define: a marking $\underline{m}$ is $\hat{T}$-continual, if an infinite sequence of transitions can fire in $\underline{m}$ containing each $t \in \hat{T}$ infinitely often. $\hat{T}$-continuality is again a monotone property of markings.

To have control on the behaviour of a concurrent system, given by a Petri net, one may wish to know all markings having an undesired property, (e.g. to be unbounded, to be dead). The main purpose of this paper is to show, how finite representations of monotone marking sets can be effectively computed.

To give finite representations of infinite sets of integer vectors we will use the notions of regular and semilinear sets. It was proved in [CON] and [ES] that these two notions are equivalent.

According to [GRA], a subset $K \subseteq \mathbb{N}^k$ is called right-closed, if with $\underline{m} \in K$ each $\underline{m}' \geq \underline{m}$ is also contained in K. It is wellknown that the set of minimal elements of such a set is finite and is here called the residue res(K) of K. If $K \subseteq \mathbb{N}^k$ is right-closed and satisfies a particular decidable property, called RES, then res(K) can be effectively computed. In section 2 we give the algorithm and prove its correctness. The results of this section are very general and not specific for Petri nets or vector addition systems.

In section 3 we define place transition nets (P/T-nets) and the notions of bounded, dead, $\hat{T}$-blocked, and $\hat{T}$-continual markings.

The sets UNBOUNDED (NOTDEAD, NOTBLOCKED($\hat{T}$), CONTINUAL($\hat{T}$), resp.) of unbounded (not dead, not $\hat{T}$-blocked, $\hat{T}$-continual, resp.) markings are right-closed sets which satisfy property RES. Hence we can apply the results of section 2 to effectively compute the residue of these sets for a given P/T-net.

In section 4 we use residue sets res(K) to control the behaviour of a P/T-net $\mathcal{N}$ in such a way that all reachable markings are in K. The 'control' is completely integrated in the P/T-net and yields a new P/T-net N_K with the same number of places, but possibly additional transitions.

The construction of N_K is also a new method for the „implementation" of facts in P/T-nets in the sense of [GL].

In section 5 we then apply the construction to the right-closed sets K of not-dead and T-continual markings. Using the notion of transition system we show that N_K has the maximal subbehaviour with respect to well defined properties. Of particular interest is the net N_K where K is the set of $\hat{T}$-continual markings. N_K allows exactly the "live" firings of N and prevents from "non live" situations. These results give a solution to a problem of [NA] to realize the maximal "central" subbehaviour of processes. We also show how Dijkstra's wellknown banker's problem obtains a new solution.

In section 6 we show that the old problem of a transition to be "hot" is decidable and give applications of this result to the problem of promptness in P/T-nets. Also the emptyness problem for classes $\mathcal{B}_\omega^i$ and $\mathcal{K}_\omega^i$ of ω-behaviour of P/T-nets as introduced in [Va 83,Ca] is shown to be decidable.

We acknowledge the work of R. Schroff [Sch 1], who first gave an algorithm to compute the residue res(NOTDEAD). His algorithm was not published and is - compared with ours - very complicated. A result very similar to Theorem 2.13 is contained in [Gra, Lemma 3], however, the algorithm to compute res(K) for a right-closed set K given there is not mentioned explicitely and is perhaps not very practical. In [Sch 2] our result for effectively computing the set res(CONTINUAL(T)) is mentioned as an open problem. This result and applications to the set of unbounded markings, promptness, and the maximal live subbehaviour of a given P/T-net were first derived in [Va 76], but with again unnecessarily complicated proofs.

We thank the referees of the FOURTH EUROPEAN WORKSHOP ON APPLICATIONS AND THEORY OF PETRI NETS to have found some errors in a previous version.

For corrections and improvements we also thank H. Müller (especially for correcting Lemma 3.9) and D. Hauschild.

2. Finite representation of integer vector sets

We first recall some definitions on integer valued vector sets. Also the notions of regular and semilinear subsets of $\mathbb{Z}^k$ will be used. It is wellknown that both notions are equivalent [ES], [CON].

Definition 2.1

Let $\mathbb{N}_\omega := \{\omega\} \cup \mathbb{N}$, where ω is a new element satisfying :

$\forall n \in \mathbb{N} : n < \omega$, $\forall n \in \mathbb{N}_\omega : n + \omega := \omega - n := \omega$, $\min(n,\omega) := n$, $\max(n,\omega) := \omega$,

$(n+1)\cdot\omega := \omega$, $0\cdot\omega := \omega\cdot 0 := 0$.

The relations $\geq, \leq$, $=$ for vectors are understood componentwise and $x \lneq y$ is a shorthand for $(x \leq y$ and $x \neq y)$. the dyadic operations +,-,min, and max are evaluated componentwise too.

For sets $M, M' \subseteq \mathbb{N}_\omega^k$ define :

$\max(M,M') := \{ \max(\underline{m},\underline{m}') \mid \underline{m} \in M, \ \underline{m}' \in M' \}$,

$\max(M) := \max(M,M)$,

$\min(M,M') := \{ \min(\underline{m},\underline{m}') \mid \underline{m} \in M, \ \underline{m}' \in M' \}$

$\min(M) := \min(M,M)$.

Definition 2.2

For each $\underline{m} \in \mathbb{N}_\omega^k$ let $reg(\underline{m}) := \{ \underline{m}' \in \mathbb{N}^k \mid \underline{m}' \leq \underline{m} \}$ be the <u>region</u> specified by $\underline{m}$ and $hyp(\underline{m}) := \{ \underline{m}' \in \mathbb{N}^k \mid \underline{m}(i) \neq \omega$ implies $\underline{m}'(i) = \underline{m}(i) \}$ denotes the <u>hyperplane</u> specified by $\underline{m}$ and restricted to $\mathbb{N}^k$.

Lemma 2.3

For each $\underline{m} \in \mathbb{N}_\omega^k$ the sets $reg(\underline{m})$ and $hyp(\underline{m})$ are semilinear.

<u>Proof</u> trivial and omitted.

Definition 2.4

A set $K \subseteq \mathbb{N}^k$ is called <u>right-closed</u> iff $K = K + \mathbb{N}^k$.

Definition 2.5

Let K be a right-closed subset of $\mathbb{N}^k$ then the <u>residue set</u> of K, written res(K), is the smallest subset of K which satisfies $res(K) + \mathbb{N}^k = K$.

By this definition res(K) is a set of incomparable vectors with respect to the partial order $\leq$ and therefore by Dicksons lemma finite. Thus we obviously have :

Lemma 2.6

For each right-closed set $K \subseteq \mathbb{N}^k$ res(K) is finite and $K = res(K) + \mathbb{N}^k$ is a representation of K as a semilinear set.

<u>Lemma 2.7</u>

If K, K' are right-closed sets, then $K \cup K'$ and $K \cap K'$ are right closed, too.

<u>Proof</u> trivial and omitted.

If one knows the residue sets of the right-closed sets K and K', then it is easy to compute the sets $res(K \cup K')$ and $res(K \cap K')$.

<u>Lemma 2.8</u>

Let $K, K' \subseteq \mathbb{N}^k$ be right-closed sets.

(a) $res(K \cup K') = (res(K) \setminus K') \cup (res(K') \setminus K) \cup (res(K) \cap res(K'))$

(b) $res(K \cap K')$ can be computed by a simple algorithm (see [VJ]).

If a right-closed set K is given in the form $K = L + \mathbb{N}^k$, then it is not always possible to effectively compute $res(K)$ from a finite representation of L. The next result exhibits a necessary and sufficient condition, called property RES, to effectively construct the finite set $res(K)$.

<u>Definition 2.9</u>

For each set $K \subseteq \mathbb{N}^k$ define the predicate $p_K : \mathbb{N}_\omega^k \to \{true, false\}$ by $p_K(\underline{m}) := (\, reg(\underline{m}) \cap K \neq \emptyset \,)$. A set K is said to have <u>property RES</u> iff the predicate $p_K(\underline{m})$ is decidable for each $\underline{m} \in \mathbb{N}_\omega^k$.

The following theorem is a reformulation of Lemma 3 in [Gra]. But since we are interested in a more practical algorithm to compute $res(K)$ if this is possible, we present an algorithm to do so, and include a detailed proof for it's correctness.

<u>Theorem 2.10</u>

Let $K \subseteq \mathbb{N}^k$ be a right-closed set. Then $res(K)$ can be effectively constructed iff K has property RES.

<u>Proof</u>

Assume first that $res(K)$ can be computed. Then $K = res(K) + \mathbb{N}^k$ gives a semilinear representation of K. Since $reg(\underline{m})$ is a semilinear set, a representation of which can be found effectively, the question "$reg(\underline{m}) \cap K = \emptyset$?" is decidable.

Conversely assume that the question "$reg(\underline{m}) \cap K = \emptyset$?" is decidable for each $\underline{m} \in \mathbb{N}_\omega^k$. The following method can be used to effectively construct $res(K)$:

Let K be a right-closed subset of $\mathbb{N}^k$ for which property RES holds, i.e. $p_K(\underline{m}) := (reg(\underline{m}) \cap K \neq \emptyset)$ is decidable for each $\underline{m} \in \mathbb{N}^k$.

Algorithm to compute res(K)

(1) **begin** (* initialization *)

(2) $i := 0$; $M_o := \{(\omega, \ldots, \omega)\}$; $R_o := \emptyset$;

(3) **repeat**

(4) choose some $\underline{m} \in M_i$;

(5) **if** $p_K(\underline{m})$ = false **then** $M_i := M_i - \{\underline{m}\}$;

(6) **until**

(7) $p_K(\underline{m})$ = true **or** $M_i = \emptyset$

(8) **endrepeat** ;

(9) **if** $M_i = \emptyset$ **then** $\mathrm{res}(K) := R_i$ **and** **stop**

(10) **else**

(11) **begin** (* now $\mathrm{reg}(\underline{m}) \cap K \neq \emptyset$ and hence $\mathrm{reg}(\underline{m})$ contains at least one element of res(K); one such element will be found in the next repeat loop *)

(12) **repeat**

(13) choose some coordinate $\underline{m}(i)$ of $\underline{m}$ which in this loop has not been considered yet;

(14) replace $\underline{m}(i)$ in $\underline{m}$ by the smallest $n \in \mathbb{N}$ such that $p_K(\underline{m})$ for this new vector is still true;

(15) **until**

(16) all coordinates have been considered

(17) **endrepeat**; (* the new vector $\underline{m} \in \mathbb{N}^k$ found in this way will be an element of res(K) as will be shown in Lemma 2.15 below *)

(18) $R_{i+1} := R_i \cup \{\underline{m}\}$;
Let $\underline{m} = (x_1, \ldots, x_k)$ be the vector found in the preceding steps (lines (13) to (17)).

(19) $M_i' := \{(y_1, \ldots, y_k) \in N_\omega^k \mid \exists\, 1 \leq j \leq k : y_j := x_j - 1$ and $y_m = \omega$ for all $m \neq j\}$

(* M_i' is describing **all** the regions that do not contain the element $\underline{m}$, i.e. for $\mathrm{reg}(M_i') := \bigcup_{\underline{m}' \in M_i'} \mathrm{reg}(\underline{m}')$ one has $\mathbb{N}^k - \mathrm{reg}(M_i') = \{\underline{m}\} + \mathbb{N}^k$ *)

(20) $M_{i+1} := \min(M_i, M_i')$

(21) $i := i+1$;

(22) **endif**

(23) **goto** line (3)

(24) **end** (* algorithm *).

In [VJ] the total correctness of this algorithm is proved.

3. Computing certain right-closed sets in Petri nets

Let us first fix some notation for Petri nets or more precisely P/T-nets. For much more detail see [JV].

Definition 3.1

A P/T-net N = (P,T,F,B) is defined by

a finite set P of places,

a finite set T of transitions, disjoint from P, and

two mappings: $F : P \times T \to \mathbb{N}$

$B : P \times T \to \mathbb{N}$

called forward and backward incidence mapping. They can also be seen as (/P/,/T/)-matrices over $\mathbb{N}$, (where /S/ is the cardinality of a set S) . Let $\Delta := B - F$ be the incidence matrix of the P/T-net N .

F(t), B(t) and Δ(t) denote the t-column vector in $\mathbb{N}^{/P/}$ of F, B and Δ , respectively.

Definition 3.2

A marking $\underline{m} \in \mathbb{N}^{/P/}$ is a column vector giving a number $\underline{m}(p)$ of tokens for each place $p \in P$. A transition has concession in $\underline{m}$, written $\underline{m}(t>$, iff $F(t) \leq \underline{m}$. For $\underline{m} \in \mathbb{N}_\omega^{/P/}$ we also write $\underline{m}(t>$ iff $\exists\, \underline{m}' \in \mathrm{reg}(\underline{m}) : \underline{m}'(t>$.

For $\underline{m} \in \mathbb{N}_\omega^{/P/}$ we define $\underline{m}(t>\underline{m}'$ iff $m(t>$ and $m' = \underline{m} + B(t) - F(t) = \underline{m} + \Delta(t)$. We extend this notion to strings $w \in T^*$ by

(a) $\underline{m}(\lambda>\underline{m}$ for all $\underline{m} \in \mathbb{N}_\omega^{/P/}$ and

(b) $\underline{m}(wt> m''$ iff $\underline{m}' \in \mathbb{N}_\omega^{/P/} : \underline{m}(w>m'$ and $\underline{m}'(t>\underline{m}''$.

Again we say that w has concession in $\underline{m} \in \mathbb{N}_\omega^{/P/}$, written $\underline{m}(w>$, iff $\exists\, \underline{m}' \in \mathbb{N}_\omega^{/P/} : \underline{m}(w>\underline{m}'$.

For $\underline{m} \in \mathbb{N}_\omega^{/P/}$ we let $\Omega(\underline{m}) := \{p \in P \mid \underline{m}(p) = \omega\}$.

Definition 3.3

A P/T-net N = (P,T,F,B) together with an initial marking $\underline{m}_o \in \mathbb{N}^{/P/}$ and/or a labelling homomorphism $h : T^* \to X^*$ will be also called a P/T-net and is denoted by $(N,\underline{m}_o)$ and $(N,h,\underline{m}_o)$, respectively. For such a P/T-net $(N,\underline{m}_o)$ and a subset $K \subseteq \mathbb{N}^{/P/}$ we define the K-restricted set of firing sequences

$F_K(N,\underline{m}_o) := \{t_{i_1} t_{i_2} \dots t_{i_n} \in T^+ \mid \underline{m}_o(t_{i_1}> \underline{m}_1(t_{i_2}> \underline{m}_2 \dots \underline{m}_{n-1}(t_{i_n}> \underline{m}_n$ for markings $\underline{m}_i \in K \quad (0 \le i \le n) \}$

and the K-restricted reachability set

$R_K(N,\underline{m}_o) := \{ \underline{m} \in \mathbb{N}^{/P/} \mid \exists\, w \in F_K(N,\underline{m}_o) : \underline{m}_o(w>\underline{m} \}$.

For $K = \mathbb{N}^{/P/}$ these sets are the ordinary set of firing sequences $F(N,\underline{m}_o)$ and the reachabilty set $R(N,\underline{m}_o)$, respectively.
For a net $(N,h,\underline{m}_o)$ the language is defined by
$L(N,h,\underline{m}_o) := \{ h(w) \mid w \in F(N,\underline{m}_o) \}$. Until section 5 we assume $h(t) \neq \lambda \; \forall\, t \in T$.

Definition 3.4
Let $\Delta : T^* \to \mathbb{Z}^{/P/}$ be a homomorphism defined as follows :

$\Delta(\lambda) := \underline{0}$ (null-vector of suitable dimension)

$\Delta(t) := B(t) - F(t)$, and $\Delta(uv) := \Delta(u) + \Delta(v)$ for $u,v \in T^*$

We also use the Parikh image $\Psi : T^* \to \mathbb{N}^{/T/}$, where $\Psi(w)(t)$ gives the number of occurences of the transition t in the finite word $w \in T^*$.
We will also write $\Psi(w)(t) = \omega$ if w is an infinite sequence and this number is not finite. Δ and Ψ are related as follows

$$\Delta(w) = \Delta \underline{\Psi(w)}$$

which motivates the choice of the same symbol Δ for both notions (homomorphism and incidence matrix).

Modelling concurrent systems by Petri nets also the infinite behaviour is of importance. In this paper we also use the notion of infinite firing sequence of a P/T-net [Va 83].

Definition 3.5
X^ω denotes the set of infinite words $w = w(1)w(2)\dots$ over the alphabet X.
For $i \in \mathbb{N}$ $w(i)$ denotes the i-th element of w and $w[i] = w(1)w(2)\dots w(i)$ the prefix of length i of w.
For $w \in X^\omega$ the set $In(w) := \{ x \in X \mid x = w(i)$ for infinitely many $i \in \mathbb{N} \}$ is called infinity set of w .
An ω-word $w \in T^\omega$ of transitions in a net $N = (P,T,F,B)$ is said to have concession in a marking $\underline{m} \in \mathbb{N}^{/P/}$, again written $\underline{m}(w>$, if $\underline{m}(w[i]>$ for all $i \in \mathbb{N}$. $F_\omega(N,\underline{m}_o) := \{ w \in T^\omega \mid \underline{m}_o(w> \}$ is the set of all infinite firing sequences of N with initial marking $\underline{m}_o$.

For a motivated introduction to place/transition nets we refer to [JV] and [VV], where also the following construction of the coverability graph is used. It differs in some way from the original form in [KM]. The most important difference used here, is the possibility to start with an initial node containing ω-coordinates.

Definition 3.6

Let $N = (P,T,F,B)$ be a P/T-net and $\underline{m}_o \in \mathbb{N}_\omega^{/P/}$. A coverability graph $G(N,\underline{m}_o)$ of N will be a finite, directed, edge labelled graph consisting of a set of nodes $NODES \subseteq \mathbb{N}_\omega^{/P/}$, and a set $\rightarrow \subseteq NODES \times T \times NODES$ of labelled arcs. $G(N,\underline{m}_o)$ is defined **as given in [JV], but allowing ω-components in $\underline{m}_o$.**

Definition 3.7

Let $G := G(N,\underline{m}_o)$ be some coverability graph. For each node $\underline{m}' \in NODES$ of G define $L(G,\underline{m}') := \{ v \in T^* \mid \underline{m}' \overset{*}{\underset{v}{\rightarrow}} \underline{m}''$ is a path in G $\}$

$$\text{and} \quad L(G) := \bigcup_{\underline{m}' \in NODES} L(G,\underline{m}')$$

Lemma 3.8

Let $G(N,\underline{m}_o)$ be some coverability graph. Then $L(G)$ and $L(G,\underline{m}')$ for each $\underline{m}' \in NODES$ are regular subsets of T^* and effectively constructable from G. For each $\underline{m}'' \in reg(\underline{m}')$ the set $F(N,\underline{m}'')$ is a subset of $L(G,\underline{m}')$.

In addition, a set of places $P' \subseteq P$ is simultaneously unbounded in $R(N,\underline{m}_0)$ iff $\exists\, \underline{m} \in NODES: \Omega(\underline{m}) = P'$.

The last claim of Lemma 3.8 can be proved easily by using the construction of new ω-coordinates in line(11) of the coverability graph construction several times , and is omitted.

Lemma 3.9

Let $N = (P,T,F,B)$ and $G(N,\underline{m}_o)$ be some coverability graph of N with initial node $\underline{m}_o \in \mathbb{N}_\omega^{/P/}$. Then $v \in L(G)$ and $\Delta(v) \geq 0$ implies

$\exists\, u \in T^* \exists\, \underline{m}' \in reg(\underline{m}_o): uv \in F(N,\underline{m}')$.

Proof

One uses the characterization of unbounded places as given in Lemma 3.8 and the fact that there is always the possibility to choose such a v-path in $G(N,\underline{m}_o)$ with $\Delta(v) \geq 0$ of the form $\underline{m}_1 \overset{*}{\rightarrow} \underline{m}_2$ which satisfies $\Omega(\underline{m}_1) = \Omega(\underline{m}_2)$. The still missing details are again left for the reader.

Definition 3.10

Let N = (P,T,F,B) be a fixed P/T-net and $\underline{m} \in \mathbb{N}^{/P/}$ be an arbitrary marking of N.

(a) $\underline{m}$ is $\hat{T}$-blocked for a set $\hat{T} \subseteq T$ of transitions iff no transition $t \in \hat{T}$ has concession in a reachable marking $\underline{m}' \in R(N,\underline{m})$. When $\hat{T} = T$ then $\underline{m}$ is a total deadlock. (For T = {t} $\underline{m}$ is often called t-dead which we want to avoid because of possible confusion with the next definition.)

(b) $\underline{m}$ is called dead, iff $F(N,\underline{m})$ is finite.
Remark: If $\underline{m}$ is dead, then total deadlocks cannot be avoided. Such situations are sometimes called unsafe.

(c) $\underline{m}$ is called bounded, iff $R(N,\underline{m})$ if finite. Otherwise $\underline{m}$ is called unbounded.

(d) $\underline{m}$ is called $\hat{T}$-continual for some subset $\hat{T} \subseteq T$ of transitions, iff there is some infinite string $w \in T^{\omega}$ such that $\underline{m}(w>$ and $\hat{T} \subseteq In(w)$.
Remark: Every live marking $\underline{m}$ is $\hat{T}$-continual for $\hat{T} = T$, but the converse is usually not true. A marking $\underline{m}$ is $\hat{T}$-continual iff the predicate hot($\hat{T}$,$\underline{m}$) in (Ke) is true.

Now we define the following sets of markings according with (a) to (d) above :

(aa) NOTBLOCKED($\hat{T}$) := { $\underline{m} \in \mathbb{N}^{/P/}$ | $\underline{m}$ is not $\hat{T}$-blocked }
(bb) NOTDEAD := { $\underline{m} \in \mathbb{N}^{/P/}$ | $\underline{m}$ is not dead }
(cc) UNBOUNDED := { $\underline{m} \in \mathbb{N}^{/P/}$ | $\underline{m}$ is unbounded }
(dd) CONTINUAL($\hat{T}$) := { $\underline{m} \in \mathbb{N}^{/P/}$ | $\underline{m}$ is $\hat{T}$-continual }

From the monotonicity property of Petri nets it follows immediately that the four sets of markings defined by (aa) to (bb) are all right-closed. We shall now show that they also satisfy property RES.

Theorem 3.11

Let N = (P,T,F,B) be a fixed net and $\hat{T} \subseteq T$ be arbitrary. Then each set K $\in$ { NOTBLOCKED($\hat{T}$), NOTDEAD, UNBOUNDED, CONTINAL($\hat{T}$) } satisfies property RES.

Proof

Let be G := G(N,$\underline{m}$) for some $\underline{m} \in \mathbb{N}_{\omega}^{/P/}$.

case 1 : K = NOTBLOCKED($\hat{T}$)

From Lemma 3.8 one concludes that reg($\underline{m}$) $\cap$ K $\neq \emptyset$ iff for each $t \in \hat{T}$ there exists an arc in G which is labelled by t, i.e. $t \in L(G)$. This clearly is decidable, hence the set K has property RES.

<u>case 2</u> : K = NOTDEAD

Again from Lemma 3.8 one concludes that $reg(\underline{m}) \cap K \neq \emptyset$ iff there exists $v \in L(G)$ such that $\Delta(v) \geq \underline{0}$. Since L(G) is a regular subset of T^*, which can be constructed from G effectively, the set $\Delta(L(G)) := \{ \Delta(v) \mid v \in L(G)\}$ is a regular , hence semilinear, subset of $\mathbb{Z}^{/P/}$. Then $S := \Delta(L(G)) \cap \mathbb{N}^{/P/})$ is a semilinear subset of $\mathbb{N}^{/P/}$, a representation of which can be constructed effectively. Hence "$S \neq \emptyset$" is decidable and $S \neq \emptyset$ iff $\exists v \in L(G) : \Delta(v) \geq \underline{0}$. Thus K has property RES.

<u>case 3</u> : K := UNBOUNDED

Again we find : $reg(\underline{m}) \cap K \neq \emptyset$ iff $\exists\, v \in L(G) : \Delta(v) \gneq \underline{0}$. We construct the semilinear set $S := \Delta(L(G)) \cap \{ \underline{m}' \in \mathbb{N}^{/P/} \mid \underline{m}' \neq \emptyset \}$ and then $S \neq \emptyset$ iff $reg(\underline{m}) \cap K \neq \emptyset$, which is decidable using the finite representation of S. Hence, also in this case the set K has proprty RES.

<u>case 4</u> : $K = CONTINUAL(\hat{T})$

Let $\underline{e}_{\hat{T}} \in \mathbb{N}^{/T/}$ be defined by $\underline{e}_{\hat{T}}(t) :=$ <u>if</u> $t \in \hat{T}$ <u>then</u> 1 <u>else</u> 0 <u>fi</u>. We first show the following claim :

<u>claim</u> : $reg(\underline{m}) \cap K \neq \emptyset$ iff $\exists\, v \in L(G) : \Delta(v) \geq \underline{0}$ and $\Psi(v) \geq \Psi(\underline{e}_{\hat{T}})$.

To see this assume first, that there exists $v \in L(G)$ such that $\Delta(v) \geq \underline{0}$ and $\Psi(v) \geq \Psi(\underline{e}_{\hat{T}})$. Then by Lemma 3.9 there exists $\underline{m}' \in reg(\underline{m})$ and a string $u \in T^*$ such that $\underline{m}'(uv>$. Since $\Delta(v) \geq \underline{0}$ also $\underline{m}'(uv^n>$ for every $n \in \mathbb{N}$ and $\underline{m}'$ is $\hat{T}$-continual by $\hat{T} \subseteq In(v^\omega)$.

Conversely, if $m' \in reg(\underline{m})$ is $\hat{T}$-continual, then there exists an infinite sequence $w \in T^\omega$, such that $\underline{m}'(w>$ and $\hat{T} \subseteq In(w)$. Obviously w has a decomposition $w = w_1 w_2 w_3 \ldots$, where $w_i \in T^*$ and $\Psi(w_i) \geq \Psi(\underline{e}_{\hat{T}})$.

Now $\underline{m}'(w_1>\underline{m}_1$, $\underline{m}'(w_1w_2>\underline{m}_2$, $\underline{m}'(w_1w_2w_3>\underline{m}_3$, ... defines an infinite sequence of markings $\underline{m}', \underline{m}_1, \underline{m}_2, \ldots$. Therefore there must exist indices $i < j$ such that $\underline{m}_i \leq \underline{m}_j$.

Defining $v := w_{i+1} w_{i+2} \ldots w_j$ we then have $\underline{m}_i(v>\underline{m}_j$ with $\Delta(v) \geq \underline{0}$ and $\Psi(v) \geq \Psi(\underline{e}_{\hat{T}})$.

Since $\underline{m}_i \in R(N,\underline{m}')$ there exists $u \in T^*$ such that $\underline{m}'(u>\underline{m}''$ with $\underline{m}_i \in reg(\underline{m}'')$, hence $uv \in L(G,\underline{m})$ and $v \in L(G)$. This proves the claim.

Now, in order to decide whether there exists some $v \in L(G)$ with $\Delta(v) \geq \underline{0}$ and $\Psi(v) \geq \Psi(\underline{e}_{\hat{T}})$ we proceede as follows :

First, $R := L(G) \cap \{ w \in T^* \mid \Psi(w) \geq \Psi(\underline{e}_{\hat{T}}) \}$ is a regular set, since it is the intersection of two regular sets. A finite representation of R can be constructed from the coverability graph $G = G(N,\underline{m})$. Then $S := \Delta(R) \cap \mathbb{N}^k$ is a semilinear set, a finite representation of which can be effectively constructed.

The question "$S \neq \emptyset$?"is therefore decidable and equivalent to :

" $\exists v \in L(G) : \Delta(v) \geq \underline{0} \wedge \Psi(v) \geq \Psi(\underline{e}_{\hat{T}})$? "

Hence also in this case the set K has property RES.

The following result is a direct consequence of the proof of Theorem 3.11 and solves problem P24(iii) of the problem collection in [EATCS].

Theorem 3.12

Given a P/T-net $N = (P,T,F,B)$, a marking $\underline{m} \in \mathbb{N}^{/P/}$, and a set $\hat{T} \subseteq T$ of transitions, then

(a) It is decidable, whether $\underline{m}$ is $\hat{T}$-continual.

(b) It is decidable, whether $\underline{m}$ is $\hat{T}$-blocked.

(c) It is decidable, whether there exists an infinite firing sequence $w \in T^{\omega}$ such that $\underline{m}(w>$ and $In(w) = \hat{T}$.

Proof

The claim in case 4 of the proof for Theorem 3.11 says, that $\underline{m}$ is $\hat{T}$-continual iff some coverability graph $G(N,\underline{m})$ contains a path $\underline{m}' \overset{*}{\underset{v}{\rightarrow}} \underline{m}''$, labelled by $v \in T^*$, such that $\Delta(v) \geq \underline{O}$ and each $t \in \hat{T}$ occurs at least once in v. Hence we have (a).

Part (b) is even more simple, since case 1 of the preceding proof says, that $\underline{m}$ is $\hat{T}$-blocked iff $G(N,\underline{m})$ does not contain an arc $\underline{m}' \underset{t}{\rightarrow} \underline{m}''$ labelled by some $t \in \hat{T}$.

From the arguments given to verify the claim in case 4 of Theorem 3.11 one easily deduces that $\underline{m}$ has the desired property of (c) iff $G(N,\underline{m})$ contains a path $\underline{m}' \overset{*}{\underset{v}{\rightarrow}} \underline{m}''$ such that $v \in \hat{T}^*$, $\Delta(v) \geq \underline{O}$ and each $t \in \hat{T}$ occurs at least once within v.

The main result of this section can now be stated as follows :

Theorem 3.13

For each $K \in$ { NOTBLOCKED($\hat{T}$); NOTDEAD; UNBOUNDED; CONTINUAL($\hat{T}$) } the finite set res(K) can be constructed effectively.

Proof

Immediate consequence of Theorem 3.11 and Theorem 2.14.

An important application of Theorem 3.13 concerns the question, whether a given P/T-net is bounded for every initial marking.

Definition 3.14

A P/T-net $N = (P,T,F,B)$ is called bounded, iff $R(N,\underline{m})$ is finite for each marking $\underline{m} \in \mathbb{N}^{/P/}$.

Theorem 3.15

It is decidable, whether a given P/T-net $N = (P,T,F,B)$ is bounded.

Proof

N is bounded iff res(UNBOUNDED) $= \emptyset$, which is decidable by Theorem 3.13.

This Theorem has been proved in [Br] by a completely different method.

Known results on the boundedness problem allow to give a hint concerning the complexity of the algorithms considered here. A marking $\underline{m}$ of a P/T-net N is bounded iff there is no $\underline{m}' \in$ res(UNBOUNDED) with $\underline{m}' \leq \underline{m}$. On the other hand, there is a constant c such that boundedness of a marking $\underline{m}$ in a P/T-net N cannot be decided in space $2^{c\cdot\sqrt{size(N)}}$ [Li] [Ra]. The complexity of computing res(UNBOUNDED) cannot be smaller than this lower bound.

4. Controlling a P/T-net using residue sets.

Having computed a residue res(K) of a right-closed set K, it may be usefull to control a net in such a way that all reachable markings are lying in K. For the examples K = NOTDEAD and K = CONTINUAL(T) this is of particular importance, however, there will be other examples of interest too.

In the following we shall present a general construction for controlling the behaviour of an arbitrary P/T-net by some right-closed set K, just by changing its set of transitions and without adding new places

Properties of controlled nets using particular right-closed sets will be considered in section 5.

Construction 4.1

Let $(N,\underline{m}_o)$ with N = (P,T,F,B) be a P/T-net and $K \subseteq \mathbb{N}^{/P/}$ be a right-closed net satisfying property RES.

Then using the residue set res(K) we effectively construct the K-restriction $(N_K,h,\underline{m}_o)$, or $(N_K,\underline{m}_o)$ if h is not important, by a P/T-net N_K = (P,T',F',B') and λ-free homomorphism $h : T'^* \rightarrow T^*$ as follows:

a) $T' := T_1 \cup T_2$

where $T_1 := \{t \in T \mid \forall \underline{m}' \in res(K)\, \exists \underline{m} \in res(K):\ max(\underline{m}',F(t))+\Delta(t) \geq \underline{m}\}$

and $T_2 := \{t_{\underline{m}} \mid t \in T - T_1, \underline{m} \in res(K)\}$

b) for all $t \in T_1$ let $F'(t) := F(t)$ and $B'(t) := B(t)$

c) for all $t_{\underline{m}} \in T$ let

$$F'(t_{\underline{m}}) := max\,[F(t),\ \underline{m}-\Delta(t)] \quad \text{and} \quad B'(t_{\underline{m}}) := max\,[B(t),\ \underline{m}]$$

(Recall that by Def.2.5 max is evaluated for each place-component separetely).

Since $F(t,p) \geq \underline{m}(p)-\Delta(t,p) \iff$

$F(t,p) \geq \underline{m}(p)-B(t,p)+F(t,p) \iff$

$B(t,p) \geq \underline{m}(p)$

part c) can be equivalently formulated by

c') for all $t_{\underline{m}} \in T_2$, $p \in P$ let

$$(F'(t_{\underline{m}},p),\ B'(t_{\underline{m}},p)) := \underline{if}\ B(t,p) \geq \underline{m}(p)\ \underline{then}\ (F(t,p),\ B(t,p))\ \underline{else}\ (\underline{m}(p)-\Delta(t,p),\ \underline{m}(p))$$

d) h is defined by

$$h(t') := \begin{cases} t' & \text{if } t' \in T_1 \\ t & \text{if } t' = t_{\underline{m}} \in T_2 \end{cases}$$

If $(N,\underline{m}_o)$ is given together with initial marking $\underline{m}_o$, then the K-restriction $(N_K,h,\underline{m}_o)$ is defined only if $\underline{m}_o \in K$.

Remark

Note, that even if $t,t' \in T$ are such that

$F(t) \neq F(t')$ and $B(t) \neq B(t')$ and $\underline{m},\underline{m}' \in res(K)$

are all different, then $F'(t_{\underline{m}}) = F'(t'_{\underline{m}'})$ and $B'(t_{\underline{m}}) = B'(t'_{\underline{m}'})$ is possible and only one of $t_{\underline{m}}$ and $t'_{\underline{m}'}$ is actually needed.

Also for $\underline{m} \neq \underline{m}'$, $\underline{m},\underline{m}' \in res(K)$

it can happen that

$F'(t_{\underline{m}}) \leq F'(t_{\underline{m}'})$

which means, that whenever

$t_{\underline{m}'}$ is enabled in N_K so is $t_{\underline{m}}$ and

since $\Delta'(t_{\underline{m}}) = \Delta'(t_{\underline{m}'})$ we can omit the transition $t_{\underline{m}'}$ and use $T' - \{t_{\underline{m}'}\}$ instead of T' without affecting the result.

We will show that N_K behaves like N, when only markings in K are used. To be more precise, the reachable markings of N, starting in $\underline{m}_o \in K$ and never leaving K in between, are exactly those of N_K and a transition t in N can fire iff an equally labelled transition t' in N_K can do so.

Theorem 4.2

Let N be a P/T-net, K a right-closed set, and N_K the K-restricted P/T-net from Def. 4.1.

Then for all $m_1 \in K$, $t \in T$ we have:

(a) $m_1(t\rangle m_2$ in N and $m_2 \in K$ iff

$\exists\, t' \in T' : h(t') = t \wedge \underline{m}_1(t'\rangle \underline{m}_2$ in N_K.

In particular for all initial markings $\underline{m}_o \in K$ we have

(b) $R(N_K,\underline{m}_o) = R_K(N,\underline{m}_o)$

and (c) $L(N_K,h,\underline{m}_o) = F_K(N,\underline{m}_o)$

Proof: (see [VJ])

Remark

It is important to note that, even though $R(N_K,\underline{m}_o) = R_K(N,\underline{m}_o)$, it is often the case that $R(N_K,\underline{m}_o) \neq R(N,\underline{m}_o) \cap K$.

To illustrate the construction of the K-restriction N_K and Theorem 4.2 we give the following example.

Example 4.3

Consider the P/T-net N in Fig. 4.1. a) and $K:=res(K)+\mathbb{N}^4$ with $res(K) = \{\underline{m}_1,\underline{m}_2\}$ and $\underline{m}_1:=(2,0,0,0)$, $\underline{m}_2:=(0,0,0,1)$.

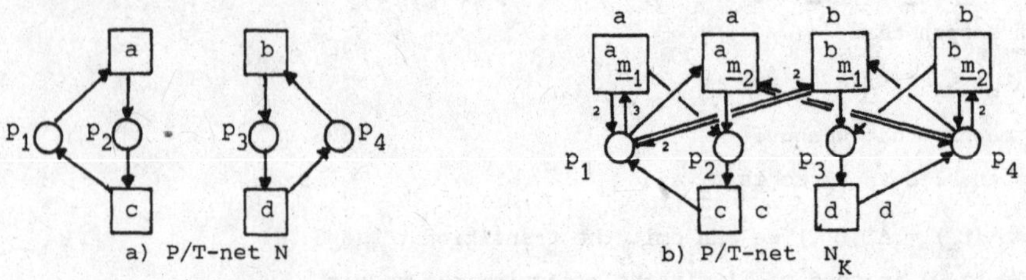

Fig. 4.1

By $\Delta(c)=(1,-1,0,0)$ and $\Delta(d)=(0,0,-1,1)$ and following the notation of Definition 4.1 we obtain:

$$T_1=\{c,d\},\ T_2=\{a_{\underline{m}_1}, a_{\underline{m}_2}, b_{\underline{m}_1}, b_{\underline{m}_2}\}$$

The construction of F and B results in the P/T-net N_K of Fig. 4.1 b). For each transition t the labelling h(t) is given outside the box of t .

To give an application of Theorem 4.2 we consider the initial marking $\underline{m}_o := \underline{m}_1+\underline{m}_2 \in K$.

Instead of looking at particular firing sequences we give an interpretation of N_K.

For the P/T-net $(N,\underline{m}_o)$ all reachable markings $\underline{m}\in R(N,\underline{m}_o)$ satisfy the following „invariant equations":

$$i_1 : \underline{m}(p_1)+\underline{m}(p_2) = 2$$

$$i_2 : \underline{m}(p_3)+\underline{m}(p_4) = 1$$

Together with the property $R(N_K,\underline{m}_o) \subseteq K$ of N_K it follows

$$(*): \forall\, \underline{m}\in R(N_K,\underline{m}_o) : (\underline{m}(p_2)=0 \vee \underline{m}(p_3)=0)$$

Hence, places p_2 and p_3 can be seen as „critical sections" of two „reader processes", represented by the two tokens in p_1 or p_2 and a „writer process" in the rigth hand side part of N_k. By Theorem 4.2 the labelled firing sequences $h(w) \in L(N_k,h,\underline{m}_o)$ are exactly those firing sequences $w\in F(N,\underline{m}_o)$ that respect the condition (*) of mutual exclusion. (How the net N_K can be systematically simplified will be shown later on).

Remark

In this example by the construction of the K-restriction we have found an "implementation" of the fact (*) in the sense of [GL]. This observation can be generalized as follows:

Every fact with bounded input places can be "implemented" by a K-restriction.

This is true, since facts can be equivalently formulated as

$$\forall\, \underline{m} \in R(N,\underline{m}_o) : \left(\underline{m}(p_1) \geq k_1\right) \vee \ldots \vee \left(\underline{m}(p_r) \geq k_r\right)$$

where $\{p_1, \ldots, p_r\}$ are the output places of the fact together with the complementary places of the input places.

The definition of N_K by Construction 4.1 is fairly general and independent from the initial marking $\underline{m}_o$. The only and obvious requirement is $\underline{m}_o \in K$, because $\underline{m}_o \notin K$ implies $R_K(N,\underline{m}_o) = F_K(N,\underline{m}_o) = \emptyset$ so that no construction would be needed.

This independence, however, usually leads to the construction of large P/T-nets N_K that could in many cases be simplified if there is just one fixed initial marking $\underline{m}_o$ for which the new P/T-net N_K has to be built.

For instance, the following case may occur: The initial marking $\underline{m}_o \in K$ is $\{t\}$-blocked in $(N,\underline{m}_o)$ for some $t\in T$. Then transition t is not needed for the construction of $(N_K,\underline{m}_o)$ and can (and should) therefore be removed from T before starting the construction of $(N_K,\underline{m}_o)$. Such a transition t is usually called dead in $\underline{m}_o$ (cf. Def. 6.1).

Moreover, even if t is not dead in $\underline{m}_o$ for N it may be dead for $\underline{m}_o$ in N_K. Since this property depends an K, we call such transitions K-dead for $\underline{m}_o$. K-dead transitions can be computed effectively from N and therefore removed before the construction of N_K. This is shown in [VJ], together with some further simplifications of the construction.

5 Maximal subbehaviour and liveness of P/T-nets

In this section we consider K-restricted P/T-nets $(N_K, \underline{m}_o)$ for some particular right-closed sets K. Their behaviour is characterized as the maximal subbehaviour of the original P/T-net $(N, \underline{m}_o)$ with respect to well-defined properties.

The behaviour of a system can be defined as the set all possible sequences of actions. For the definition of "maximal subbehaviour" we therefore use a formalism that is independent of the representation of states: a transition system. Since there is no partial ordering or operation defined on the state space, we cannot use the notion of closed nets etc. The connection to the previous sections will then be established by interpreting marking graphs of P/T-nets as transition systems. Therefore it is sufficient to consider only initially connected transition systems with finite sets of transitions.

Definition 5.1

A transition system $TS = (S, T, \rightarrow, s_o)$ is defined
by a set S of states
a set T of transitions
a transitional relation $\rightarrow \subseteq S \times T \times S$
and an initial state $s_o \in S$.

We write $s \xrightarrow{t} s'$ for $(s, t, s') \in \rightarrow$ and extend this notion to words $w \in T^*$
by $s \xrightarrow{\lambda} s$ for all $s \in S$,
$s \xrightarrow{wt} s'$ iff $\exists\, s'' \in S$: $s \xrightarrow{w} s'' \wedge s'' \xrightarrow{t} s'$
for all $s, s' \in S$, $w \in T^*$, $t \in T$.

$R(TS,s) := \{ s' \mid \exists\, w \in T^* : s \xrightarrow{w} s' \}$ is the set of states reachable from s and
$F(TS,s) := \{ w \in T^* \mid \exists\, s' \in S: s \xrightarrow{w} s' \}$ is the set of transition sequences from s.

$F_\omega(TS,s) := \{ w \in T^\omega \mid$ there is an infinite path $s \xrightarrow{w_1} s_1 \xrightarrow{w_2} s_2 \xrightarrow{w_3} \ldots$
and $w = w_1 w_2 w_3 \ldots \}$
is the set of infinite sequences of transitions from s.

$R(TS) := R(TS,s_o)$, $F(TS) := F(TS,s_o)$ and $F_\omega(TS) := F_\omega(TS,s_o)$ are the sets of reachable states in TS, finite and infinite transition sequences in TS, respectively. In this paper we assume S=R(TS) and T is finite for all transition systems TS.

Definition 5.2

A transition system $TS = (S,T,\rightarrow,s_o)$ is called

a) notblocked for $\hat{T} \subseteq T$, iff for every state $s \in R(TS)$ and some $t \in \hat{T}$ there is a $w \in T^*$ such that $wt \in F(TS,s)$.

b) notdead, iff for every state $s \in R(TS)$ the set $F(TS,s)$ is not finite

c) $\hat{T}$-continual for a subset $\hat{T} \subseteq T$ iff for every state $s \in R(TS)$ there is an infinite string $w \in F_\omega(TS,s)$ with $\hat{T} \subseteq In(w)$.

d) live, iff for every state $s \in R(TS)$ and every $t \in T$ there is a word $w \in T^*$ such that $wt \in F(TS,s)$.

These properties are not independent, as shown by the following simple theorem.

Theorem 5.3

A transition system $TS = (S,T,\rightarrow,s_o)$ is notblocked for $\hat{T}$ iff it is $\hat{T}$-continual. TS is T-continual iff TS is live.

Proof: Let be TS notblocked for $\hat{T} = \{t_1, \ldots, t_r\}$ and $s \in R(TS)$. Then there are words $w_1, \ldots, w_r \in T^*$ and states $s_1, \ldots, s_r \in S$ such that

$s \xrightarrow{w_1 t_1} s_1 \xrightarrow{w_2 t_2} s_2 \longrightarrow \ldots \xrightarrow{w_r t_r} s_r$. Repeating this construction we define inductively an infinite transition sequence w with $\hat{T} \subseteq In(w)$. Hence TS is $\hat{T}$-continual. The other statements of the theorem are now obvious.

Definition 5.4

Let $TS = (S,T,\rightarrow,s_o)$ be a transition system. A transition system $TS_i = (S_i,T,\rightarrow_i,s_o)$ is called a subsystem of TS iff $S_i \subseteq S$ and $\rightarrow_i \subseteq \rightarrow$.

If $\mathcal{C}(TS) = \{TS_i \mid i \in I\}$ is a set of such subsystems (with the same initial state), then

$$TS(\mathcal{C}) = \{S',T,\rightarrow',s_o\}$$

defined by $S' = \bigcup_{i \in I} S_i$ and $\rightarrow' = \bigcup_{i \in I} \rightarrow_i$ is the union of $\mathcal{C}(TS)$. It is the smallest subsystem containing all TS_i as a subsystem, and therefore called the $\mathcal{C}$-maximal subsystem of TS. (Recognize that in fact $R(TS(\mathcal{C})) = S'$.)

Definition 5.5

Let $TS = (S,T,\rightarrow,s_o)$ be a transition system. Then we define the following classes of subsystems:

a) notdead(TS) is the class of notdead subsystems of TS

b) if $\hat{T} \subseteq T$ then $\hat{T}$-continual(TS) is the class of all $\hat{T}$-continual subsystems of TS

c) live(TS) is the class of all live subsystems of TS.

Theorem 5.6

For given transition system $TS = (S,T,\rightarrow,s_o)$ and $\hat{T} \subseteq T$ the classes notdead(TS), $\hat{T}$-continual(TS) and live(TS) are closed under arbitrary union.

Hence the notdead-maximal subsystem TS(notdead),

the $\hat{T}$-continual-maximal subsystem TS($\hat{T}$-continual)

and the live-maximal subsystem TS(live) are uniquely defined and notdead, $\hat{T}$-continual, live, respectively.

Proof:

Let $TS_i = (S_i,T,\rightarrow_i,s_o)$, $i \in \{1,2\}$ be two $\hat{T}$-continual subsystems of $TS = (S,T,\rightarrow,s_o)$, $TS_3 = (S_3,T,\rightarrow_3,s_o)$ the union of TS_1 and TS_2, and $s \in R(TS_3)$. Then by $s \in S_3 = R(TS_1) \cup R(TS_2)$ we have $s \in R(TS_1)$ or $s \in R(TS_2)$. Assuming the first case, there is an infinite string $w \in T^\omega$ such that $w[n] \in F(TS_1,s)$ for all $n \in \mathbb{N}$ and $\hat{T} \subseteq In(w)$. All the states lying on the path corresponding to w are in $R(TS_1)$, hence by the definition of $\rightarrow_3$ we also have $w[n] \in F(TS_3,s)$ for all $n \in \mathbb{N}$ and $\hat{T} \subseteq In(w)$. Consequently, TS_3 is $\hat{T}$-continual too.

The case of the class notdead(TS) is similar but even simpler.

For the class live(TS) the Theorem follows from the first part the proof as special case $\hat{T} = T$, as stated in Theorem 5.3.

Definition 5.7

Let $(N,\underline{m}_o)$ be a P/T-net $N = (P,T,F,B)$ with initial marking $\underline{m}_o$. To $(N,\underline{m}_o)$ we associate the transition system $TS(N,\underline{m}_o) := (R(N,\underline{m}_o),T,\rightarrow,\underline{m}_o)$ where $(\underline{m}_1,t,\underline{m}_2) \in \rightarrow$ iff $\underline{m}_1,\underline{m}_2 \in R(N,\underline{m}_o)$ and $\underline{m}_1(t>\underline{m}_2$.

If $(N,h,\underline{m}_o)$ is a net with labelling homomorphism $h : T^* \rightarrow X^*$ then in $TS(N,\underline{m}_o)$ we replace T by X and t by h(t) in the definition of $\rightarrow$ and write $TS(N,h,\underline{m}_o)$.

If $(N,\underline{m}_o)$ is a P/T-net, then we say that a net $(N',\underline{m}_o)$ (resp. $(N',h,\underline{m}_o)$) has the $\mathcal{C}$-maximal subbehaviour of $(N,\underline{m}_o)$ (resp. of $(N,h,\underline{m}_o)$) iff the transition system $TS(N',\underline{m}_o)$ (resp. $TS(N',h,\underline{m}_o)$) is the $\mathcal{C}$-maximal subsystem of $TS(N,\underline{m}_o)$ (resp. of $TS(N,h,\underline{m}_o)$) with $\mathcal{C} \in \{$notdead, $\hat{T}$-continual, live$\}$.

We are now ready to formulate as a Theorem, that for a P/T-net $(N,\underline{m}_o)$ a P/T-net $(N',h,\underline{m}_o)$ with notdead-maximal, $\hat{T}$-continual-maximal or live-maximal subbehaviour can be effectively constructed.

Let us first recall the standard liveness definition for P/T-nets.

<u>Definition 5.8</u>

A P/T-net $(N,\underline{m}_o)$ or $(N,h,\underline{m}_o)$ with $N = (P,T,F,B)$ is <u>live</u>, if

$$\forall t \in T \ \forall \ \underline{m} \in R(N,\underline{m}_o) \ \exists \ \underline{m}' \in R(N,\underline{m}) : \underline{m}'(t\rangle.$$

<u>Theorem 5.9</u>

For every P/T-net $(N,\underline{m}_o)$ a P/T-net $(N',h,\underline{m}_o)$ can be effectively constructed such that anyone of the following properties holds:

a) $(N',h,\underline{m}_o)$ has the notdead-maximal subbehaviour of $(N,\underline{m}_o)$

b) $(N',h,\underline{m}_o)$ has the $\hat{T}$-continual-maximal " " "

c) $(N',h,\underline{m}_o)$ has the live-maximal " " "

<u>Proof:</u> see [VJ].

Let us mention that in case c) of the Theorem $R(N_K,\underline{m}_o)$ and $R(N,\underline{m}_o)$ are equal if $(N,\underline{m}_o)$ is live. By the result of Hack [Ha 76], however, it is undecidable whether two nets have the same reachability sets. Therefore our Theorem cannot be used as a decision procedure for liveness of $(N,\underline{m}_o)$.

<u>Example 5.10</u>

The right-closed set K = CONTINUAL(T) for the P/T-net N in Fig. 5.1 a) has the residue $res(K) = \{\underline{m}_1,\underline{m}_2,\underline{m}_3,\underline{m}_4\}$ with $\underline{m}_1 := (2,0,0)$, $\underline{m}_2 := (0,1,1)$, $\underline{m}_3 := (1,1,0)$, $\underline{m}_4 := (1,0,1)$.

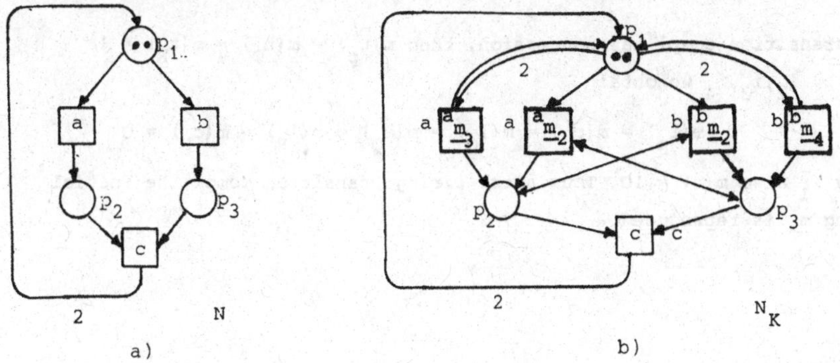

Fig. 5.1

The K-restriction $(N_K,h,\underline{m}_o)$ of $(N,\underline{m}_o)$ in Fig. 5.1 b) is constructed according to Construction 4.1 and simplifications, obtained by using the invariant equation: $\forall\ \underline{m} \in R(N,\underline{m}_o) : \underline{m}(p_1) + \underline{m}(p_2) + \underline{m}(p_3) = 2$.
$(N_k,h,\underline{m}_o)$ has the maximal live subbehaviour of $(N,\underline{m}_o)$.

Theorem 5.9 solves a problem of Nivat and Arnold [NA] for the case of P/T-nets. Using our terminology they call a behaviour $F(N,\underline{m}_o)$ central if $F(N,\underline{m}_o) \subseteq FG(F_\omega(N,\underline{m}_o))$ where $FG(L)$ is the set of finite prefixes of $L \subseteq X^\omega$. In [NA] the problem to realize the maximal central subbehaviour is solved for finite automata and stated as open problem for more powerful devices. Obviously the maximal central subbehaviour is the notdead-maximal subbehaviour in our terminology. Theorem 5.9 also gives a new solution to the older and celebrated banker's problem of Dijkstra [Di].

Example 5.11

We demonstrate our approach on the banker's problem,given by Dijkstra in 1965 as an example of a resource sharing problem. For the description of the problem we refer to [BH].

Fig. 5.2 shows the example in [BH] of the banker's problem as a P/T-net. The transition "compl" allows to restore the initial marking when all transactions of all customers are completed. The following invariant equations hold for all $\underline{m} \in R(N,\underline{m}_o)$:

$$i_1: m(c)+m(l_P)+m(l_Q)+m(l_R)=10$$
$$i_2: m(l_P)+m(c_P)+8\cdot m(t_P)=8$$
$$i_3: m(l_Q)+m(c_Q)+3\cdot m(t_Q)=3$$
$$i_4: m(l_R)+m(c_R)+9\cdot m(t_R)=9$$

When transition "compl" has concession, then $m(t_P) = m(t_Q) = m(t_R) = 1$ hence by i_2,i_3,i_4 we obtain

$$m(l_P) = m(c_P) = m(l_Q) = m(c_Q) = m(l_R) = m(c_R) = 0$$

and by i_1 also $m(c) = 10$. Thus after firing transition "compl" the initial marking $\underline{m}_o$ is reproduced.

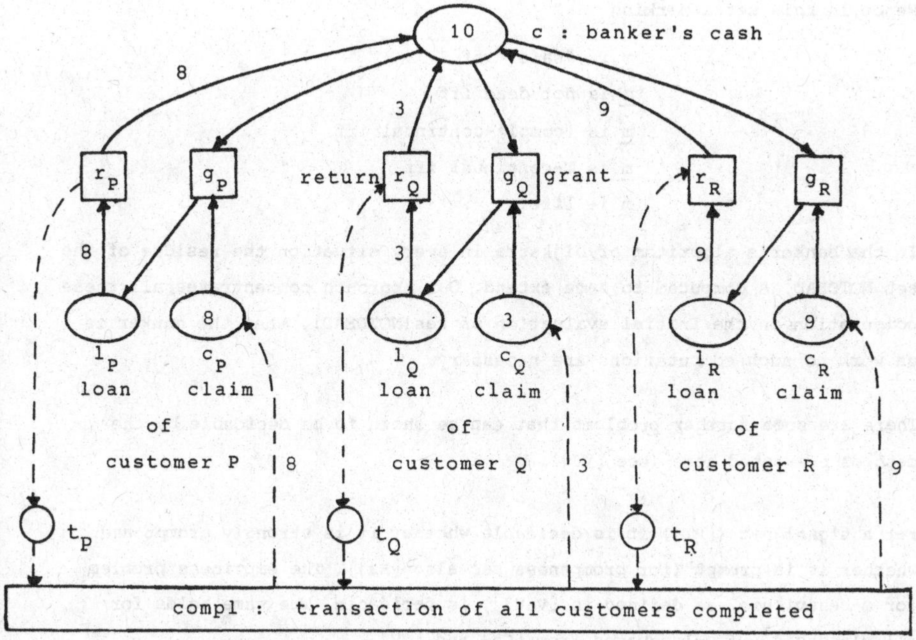

Fig. 5.2

Solving the banker's problem is equivalent to control the firing of transitions in such a way that total deadlocks are avoided. On the other hand the concurrent behaviour should be restricted as little as possible. Such a solution is given by the construction in Theorem 5.9 of a net $(N',h,\underline{m}_o)$ having the live-maximal subbehaviour of $(N,\underline{m}_o)$.

Let us compare this solution with Dijkstra's banker's algorithm. In this algorithm the banker uses a procedure to decide whether a state is "safe". A state is safe, iff it is possible for the banker to enable all present customers to complete their transactions within a finite time. The banker uses the procedure in a safe situation to decide whether a customer who wants to borrow another unit of money should be given one immediately, or be told to wait. The banker makes this decision by pretending to grant the money and then observing whether this leads to a safe situation or not.

Using the terminology of the P/T-net in Fig. 5.2 transition g_P, g_Q, or g_R is fired only if the resulting marking $\underline{m}$ is "safe", i.e.

$$\exists w \in T^*: \underline{m}(w>\underline{m}_o$$

Hence in this net a marking

$\underline{m}$ is "safe" iff

$\underline{m}$ is not dead iff

$\underline{m}$ is {compl}-continual iff

$\underline{m}$ is T-continual iff

$\underline{m}$ is life.

In the banker's algorithm of Dijkstra in every situation the residue of the set NOTDEAD is computed to some extend. Our approach concentrates all these computations in the initial evaluation of res(NOTDEAD). When the banker is on work no such computations are necessary.

There are some further problems that can be shown to be decidable by the methods presented here (see [VJ]).

For a signal net ([PT]) it is decidable whether it is strongly prompt and whether it is prompt (for promptness see also [Ha]). The emptiness problem for ω-behaviours, as defined in [Va83], is decidable. The same holds for all classes K_{ω}^{i} of ω-languages from [Ca] and [CV].

5 . References

[BH] P. Brinch Hansen: Operating System Principles, Prentice-Hall Inc, Englewood Cliffs (1973)

[Br] G. W. Brams Réseaux de Petri: Théorie et pratique Masson, Paris (1983)

[Bu] H. D. Burkhard: Two Pumping Lemmata for Petri nets, EIK, vol 17 (1981) 349-362

[By] H. W. Byrn: Sequential processes, deadlocks and semaphere primitives, Havard Univ., Tech. Rep. 7-75, Cambridge 1975

[Ca] H. Carstensen: Fairneß bei Petrinetzen mit unendlichem Verhalten. Univ. Hamburg, Fachbereich Informatik, Report B-93/82 (1982)

[Con] J. H. Conway: Regular Algebra and Finite Machines, Chapman and Hall (1971)

[CV] H. Carstensen, R. Valk: Infinite behaviour and fairness in Petri nets. Fourth European Workshop on Application and Theory of Petri Nets, Toulouse, France (1983)

[Di] E. W. Dijkstra: Co-operating sequential Processes; in F. Genuys (ed): Programming Languages Academic Press, London (1968), 43-112

[EATCS] E. Best/P. S. Thiagarajan, P24 (iii) in EATCS Bulletin 20 (1983) p 310

[ES] S. Eilenberg, M. P. Schützenberger: Rational sets in communicative monoids, J. Algebra 13 (1969), 173-191

[GL] H. J. Genrich, K. Lautenbach: Facts in place/transition-nets; Lecture Notes in Computer Science No 64, Springer-Verlag, Berlin (1978), 213-231

[Gra] J. Grabowski: Linear methods in the Theory of Vector addition systems I, EIK, vol 16 (1980) 207-236

[Ha] M. Hack: Petri net languages, MIT, Proj. MAC, Comp. Struct. Group Memo 124 (1975)

[Ha] M. Hack: The equality problem for vector addition systems is undecidable; Theoret. Computer Sci. 2 (1976), 77-95

[JV] M. Jantzen, R. Valk: Formal properties of place/transition nets, in: W. Brauer (ed), Net Theory and Applications, Lecture Notes in Computer Science No 84, Springer Verlag, Berlin (1979), 165-212

[Ke] R.M. Keller: Vector Replacement Systems: A Formalism for Modeling Asynchronous Systems, Comp. Sci. Lab., Princeton Univ., Techn. Rep. 117 (1972, revised 1974).

[KM] R.M. Karp, R.E. Miller: Parallel Program Schemata. Journ. Computer Systems Sci.; 3 (1969), 147-195

[La] L.H. Landweber: Decision problems for ω-automata, Math. Systems Theory 3 (1969), 376-384

[Li] R.J. Lipton: The Reachability Problem Requires Exponential Space. Yale Univ., Dept. of Comp. Sci., Research Report # 62 (1976)

[NA] M. Nivat, A. Arnold: Comportements de processur, Lab. Informatique Théor. et Programm., Univ. Paris 6 and 7, Paris (1982)

[PT] S.S. Patil, P.S. Thiagarajan: unpublished manuscript

[Ra] C. Rackoff: The Covering and Boundedness Problems for Vector Addition Systems, Theoretical Comp. Sci. 6 (1978), 223-231

[Sch] R. Schroff: Vermeidung von totalen Verklemmungen in bewerteten Petrinetzen, Ph.D. Theses, Techn. Univ. München (1974)

[Sch 2] R. Schroff: Vermeidung von Verklemmungen in bewerteten Petrinetzen, Lecture Notes in Computer Sci. No. 26, Springer-Verlag, Berlin (1975), 316-325

[Va 76] R. Valk: Prévention des bloquages aux systèmes paralleles, Lecture notes, Univ. Paris VI (1976)

[Va 83] R. Valk: Infinite behaviour of Petri nets. Theor. Computer Sci. 25 (1983) 3, 311-341

[VJ] R. Valk, M Jantzen: The Residue of Vector Sets with Applications to Decidability Problems in Petri Nets, Report IfI-HH-101/84, Fachbereich Informatik, Univ. Hamburg (1984)

[VV] R. Valk, G. Vidal-Naquet: Petri Nets and Regular Languages, Journ. of Computer and System Sciences 23 (1981) 3, 299-325

THE DESIGN OF A PROGRAM PACKAGE FOR AN INTRODUCTORY PETRI NET COURSE

Kurt Jensen
Computer Science Department
Aarhus University
Ny Munkegade
DK-8000 Aarhus C
Denmark

1. INTRODUCTION

This paper presents a program package which can be used to construct, edit, and analyse Petri nets. The programs have been designed with the main purpose of being of assistance in the teaching of Petri nets. The paper describes how the programs are used in an introductory Petri net course, at the Computer Science Department of Aarhus University.

The programs are written in Pascal and they are running at a PDP-10 installation at Aarhus University. Source code and documentation can be obtained, free of charge, by sending a dec-tape or floppy disc to the author at the address given above. This paper describes the general issues of our program package. For technical details the reader is referred to the user's manual [6].

The design of our programs has been governed by the following four objectives, but we do not claim that our programs fulfil all of them in an ideal way. We will return to this in section 3.

A) The programs shall provide a sufficient set of tools to construct, edit, and analyse place/transition nets and high-level Petri nets [5].

B) The programs shall illustrate, to the students, how to make a well-designed dialogue. By minimal efforts the user makes the maximal number of decisions, in a language which is natural to Petri net theory. Inconsistency in inputs is detected and reported. At all steps the user can examine the current progress, in a comprehensible form, and all detected errors can be corrected immediately with minimal retyping.

C) The programs shall illustrate, to the students, how to distribute tasks between man and machine. Decisions are made by man, while complicated calculations and bookkeeping are left to the computer.

D) The programs shall be usable at (at least) two different levels. A naive level requires basic knowledge of Petri net theory, but very little reading of the user's manual. An experienced level requires more reading in the user's manual, but then it also provides an efficient work situation with considerable freedom in the way matrices, reachability trees, etc. are handled (in particular with respect to the format in which these items can be output).

At an early stage of the design we decided that our programs should be used only for relatively small nets (containing less than sixty nodes). For this reason runtime-efficiency is not too important (except for the construction of reachability trees), and no structuring tools such as coarsening and refinement, defined in [2], are provided.

The programs have been implemented under the constraints of existing computer equipment and very limited programming resources. For most of them a prototype was made by students in an earlier Petri net course, and to diminish their programming efforts, a number of shortcuts were made; for example very little consideration was given to the runtime-efficiency of the prototypes. When the course finished, the programs were redesigned by me, and three of the students were employed to implement the improved versions. This required only ten months of manpower.

In section 2 we give a general overview of our programs; as for technical details the reader is referred to the user's manual [6]. In section 3 we compare our programs to some existing Petri net packages [1], [2] and [7], and we discuss, by means of the four design objectives, how our package can be improved. In section 4 we describe how our programs are used in an introductory Petri net course, and we evaluate the benefits of this.

2. GENERAL OVERVIEW OF THE PACKAGE

The package consists of four different programs, related as shown in the figure below, where transitions represent programs while places represent files.

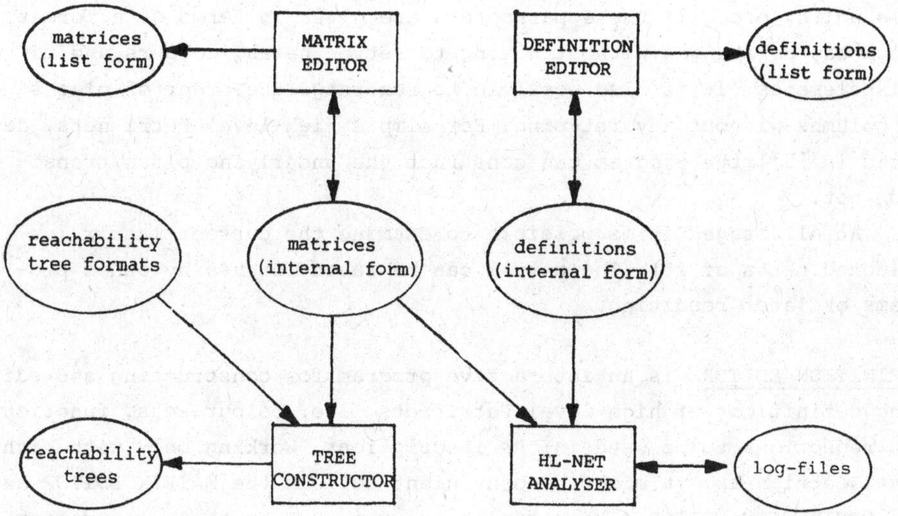

MATRIX EDITOR is an interactive program for constructing and editing all kinds of Petri net matrices. For places and transitions the names (together with additional information such as colour-sets) are entered one by one. Non-empty matrix-elements are entered by providing their contents and their coordinates (place number and transition number). No syntactic control of the matrix-elements is made (except for lenght) and this means that the program can be used to construct nearly all kinds of two-dimensional tables. Input errors may later be detected by the other programs, but they are usually few (at least those which violate syntax) and they can easily be corrected by a new run of the editor.

The constructed matrices are available in two different forms. A compressed internal form is suitable as input for the other programs, while a list form can be given immediately to a line printer. In this latter form the user can, to a large degree, determine the format by specifying the width of columns, the amount of space used for names and colours, the number of lines used to divide the matrix into suitable units, etc. All these parameters are given in terms of a format, which can be changed without having to retype names, colours and matrix-elements. It is also possible to rearrange the order of places or columns without any retyping. For simple high-level Petri nets, defined in [5], the program can construct the underlying place/transition net.

At all stages it is possible to examine the current matrix (or selected parts of it). The matrix can be saved for use by other programs or later reediting.

DEFINITION EDITOR is an interactive program for constructing and editing definitions of high-level Petri nets, i.e. colour-sets, functions and reductions to be used in the inscriptions. Working only with high-level Petri nets, it might be convenient to join the MATRIX EDITOR and the DEFINITION EDITOR into a single program, but by their separation the MATRIX EDITOR becomes a general tool, applicable for all kinds of Petri net matrices. The structure of the two programs is exactly the same. Commands are named in an analogous way, and as far as possible they take the same parameters.

TREE CONSTRUCTOR is a batch program for the construction of reachability trees for place/transition nets, using the algorithm described in [8]. The program constructs a list file containing the reachability tree, the maximal marking of each place and information about dead nodes. The format of the reachability tree can, to a large degree, be determined by the reachability tree format, but most users apply a standard format and do not have to learn about the format-parameters.

HL-NET ANALYSER is an interactive program for analysing high-level Petri nets, defined in [5], by means of place-invariants. It implements the transformation rules defined in [4]. These transformation rules, which are inspired by Gauss-elimination, allow the user to transform the incidence-matrix of a high-level Petri net without changing the set of place-invariants. For a number of systems it is possible to transform the incidence-matrix to a rather simple matrix, from which place-invariants can be found by simple inspection.

The user defines the transformations to be used. The program checks their validity and performs the detailed calculations. The transformations have been proved to be sound in the sense that all obtainable matrices have the original set of place-invariants. It may, however, for some systems be impossible to simplify the matrix in a significant way.

At all stages it is possible to examine the current matrix (or selected parts of it). The user can define place-invariants and ask the system to check whether they are consistent with the current matrix. All executed commands are recorded on a log-file, which later can be used as documentation or as a command-file allowing the user to rerun the session, possibly with minor changes. This is used, as a way to correct minor errors and shortcommings in earlier sessions, as backup in connection with system crashes, and as a very convenient way to demonstrate the facilities of the program by means of tutorial command-files.

3. HOW TO IMPROVE THE PACKAGE

In this section we describe, by means of the four design objectives, how our package can be improved.

Sufficient set of tools

Our package contains only a very limited set of tools to construct, edit and analyse Petri nets. To construct and edit nets it would be convenient also to be able to work directly with net diagrams, using a graphic workstation as described in [1] and [2]. We have installed [1] which is running on ICL Perq-systems. This allows us to create, modify and plot place/transition-nets. There are severe restrictions on the kind of net-diagrams which can be produced, but apart from that we are very impressed by the system. We have written a small program, which can convert net-files of [1] into matrix-files in the internal format of our own system.

To analyse place/transition nets it would be convenient to be able to calculate place-invariants and transition-invariants by solving matrix-equations as described in [7]. It would also be convenient to be able to perform the analysis of liveness, boundedness, reachability and net reductions, described in [7]. We have, however, no plans to develop such tools ourselves.

Instead we plan the following extensions to our package. First we have designed, but not yet implemented an interactive program to assist the user to analyse the reachability trees produced by the TREE CONSTRUCTOR. Secondly we have in [3] described how to define reachability trees for high-level Petri nets, in a way which exploits symmetry-relations and thus produces much smaller trees than for the corresponding place/transition nets. These ideas will be implemented in terms of a new TREE CONSTRUCTOR for high-level Petri nets, being complementary to the existing TREE CONSTRUCTOR for place/transition nets.

Dialogue

Our program package uses conventional text-screen terminals with limited local capabilities, and, remembering this as a prerequisite, we are quite satisfied with the dialogue. The package works with the concepts which are normally used for Petri nets, and there are rather good possibilities to change and reformat information without too much redundant typing. The package has a flat command-structure, in the sence that it is fast to move from one part of the package to another. Moreover the package is quite robust, in the sense that it is difficult to make serious irreversible errors, and in the sense that it allows minor variations of the official syntax.

The dialogue can, however, be improved if the programs are moved to our Perq-systems (or similar equipment). Then matrices can be defined by typing a text and pointing to those matrix-elements which shall contain the text (possibly with reversed sign). This will reduce the time necessary to enter a typical incidence-matrix. Analogously, the transformations can be invoked by pointing to the involved columns and rows instead of typing their numbers. It is not difficult to move our programs to the Perq-systems and this will be done, but probably not before we have changed from an older operating system to Unix.

Distribution between Man and Machine

In the HL-NET ANALYSER some of the work performed by the user can be implemented as part of the program. It will, in some situations, be possible for the program to detect and propose convenient transformations. This is the case for instance, when two columns are nearly identical, or when a column contains only two, or less, non-empty elements. For the other programs we see no way to substantially improve the distribution of work between man and machine.

Usable at Different Skill-levels

Our programs are usable at two different levels, as shown by the following examples. The unexperienced user will call a display command after each transformation, while the experienced user can save considerable time by demanding several transformations on the basis of the same display. The unexperienced user applies the standard formats, while the experienced user create private formats to obtain specialized layouts. The unexperienced user learns the systems by means of the extensive on-line help-information and the tutorial log-files, while the experienced user applies the brief form of help-information or only the constructive error-diagnostics.

As it can be seen from the discussion above, our programs are not an alternative, but a supplement to other Petri net packages such as [1], [2] and [7].

4. THE ROLE OF THE PACKAGE IN OUR INTRODUCTORY PETRI NET COURSE

Our introductory Petri net course is offered to the computer science students as an optional course in their third year. The purpose of the course is to show how Petri nets can be applied in system description and analysis. The more theoretical aspects of Petri nets (and other concurrency models) are provided by other courses. The course runs over 12 weeks, and the students are supposed to spend slightly less than 25% of their time on the course. An early version of the course is described in the cover picture story of the Petri net newsletter no. 11.

The course is divided into two parts. The first part lasts for seven weeks, with a 2-hour lecture and 2 hours of exercise each week (the students work in small groups under the supervision of older students). From the very beginning high-level Petri nets are introduced, and the students learn how to use them to describe different kinds of systems, such as distributed data bases, telephones, communication protocols, elevators, and resource allocation. Then the students are introduced to analysis methods such as reachability trees and place-invariants, and they use our program package to analyse some of the systems which they have already described.

The second part of the course lasts for five weeks and it is exclusively devoted to project work in groups of 3-5 students. The subjects are chosen by the students themselves, and they cover both application and theory. Last year five groups described and analysed selected systems, such as railway switches, elevators, traffic lights and gasoline pumps. Two groups designed programs, for the analysis of reachability trees and for the construction of high-level Petri net reachability trees (c.f. section 3). One group implemented a simple net-constructor and net-simulator on a graphic workstation, and another described the semantics of a concurrent programming language by means of Petri nets and denotational semantics. There is no examination at the end of the course, but the project work has to be approved.

It is our impression, from personal observation and interviews with students, that the program package is valuable to the course and most students find it easy to use. The package forces them to make precise and total descriptions of the considered systems. Compared with the early version of the course, more importance can now be attached to analysis of the systems. Previously, the students learned how to construct reachability trees, but the lack of a TREE CONSTRUCTOR made the method extremely cumbersome and errorprone. Analogously the HL-NET ANALYSER improves the students' understanding of the transformation rules, with which they earlier had great difficulties.

References

[1] M. Beaudouin-Lafon, Petripote: A graphic system for Petri net design and simulation, 4th European Workshop on Applications and Theory of Petri nets, Toulouse 1983.

[2] H.J. Genrich and R.M. Shapiro, A diagram editor for line drawings with inscriptions, in: Applications and Theory of Petri nets, A. Pagnoni and G. Rozenberg (eds.), Informatik-Fachberichte, vol. 66, Springer Berlin 1983, 112-131.

[3] P. Huber, A.M. Jensen, L.O. Jepsen and K. Jensen, Towards reachability trees for high-level Petri nets, Computer Science Department, Aarhus University, 5th European Workshop on Applications and Theory of Petri nets, Aarhus 1984 (also in this volume).

[4] K. Jensen, How to find invariants for coloured Petri nets, in: Mathematical Foundations of Computer Science 1981, J. Gruska and M. Chytil (eds.), Lecture Notes in Computer Science, vol. 118, Springer Berlin 1981, 327-338.

[5] K. Jensen, High-level Petri nets, in: Applications and Theory of Petri nets, A. Pagnoni and G. Rozenberg (eds.), Informatik-Fachberichte, vol. 66. Springer Berlin 1983, 166-180.

[6] K. Jensen, P. Huber, N.N. Larsen and I. Martinsen, Petri net package. User's manual, DAIMI MD-46, Computer Science Department, Aarhus University, version 3.1 1984.

[7] B. Montel et al., Ovide: A software package for the validation of systems represented by Petri net based models, 4th European Workshop on Applications and Theory of Petri nets, Toulouse 1983.

[8] J.L. Peterson, Petri net theory and the modelling of systems, Prentice-Hall, 1981.

ON COMMUNICATION PROTOCOL

MODELLING AND DESIGN

G. JUANOLE, B. ALGAYRES, J. DUFAU
Laboratoire d'Automatique
et d'Analyse des Systèmes du C.N.R.S.
7, avenue du Colonel Roche
31077 TOULOUSE CEDEX - France

ABSTRACT
The design of a protocol in a distributed computing system requires two successive modellings : the first one concerns the distributed system architecture modelling which must make clear what are the inputs and outputs of the remote communicating entities ; the second one concerns the formal modelling of the communication in the aim of a protocol verification.
The aim of this paper is to analyse the different architecture models which have been used in the different studies on protocols, to show their interest and their deficiency and finally to reach the one which allows to take into account all the environment of a protocol entity (we call, this model, the three level model). Petri nets are the formal tool which is used.

KEY-WORDS
Distributed systems ; system architecture ; modelling methodology ; protocol ; service ; Petri nets.

I. INTRODUCTION

The correct design of a protocol between distant entities in a distributed computing system requires two kinds of modelling :

- the first one concerns the modelling of the distributed system architecture : this modelling must make clear what are the inputs and outputs of each entity,
- the second one concerns the formal modelling of the protocol : this modelling must allow the protocol verification.

About the architecture model, we can, at first, refer to the ISO model i.e. a hierarchy of levels where a level (N) offers a service ((N) Service) to the level (N+1) by using the service of the level (N-1) i.e. the (N-1)Service. More precisely, in order to provide a (N) Service, two level (N) peer Entities (that we note (N)E) have a protocol to manage their cooperation ((N) protocol) : the (N) protocol is achieved by using the (N-1) service. When talking about a level (N), two kinds of exchanges have to be considered :

- the exchanges of Protocol Data Units (PDU) in the level (N) : that is a virtual communication,
- the exchanges of Service Primitives (Requests and Indications) with the adjacent levels (N+1) and (N-1) : theses ones are real exchanges.

When we want to focus on the study of a (N) protocol, it is essential to take into account, as architecture model, the simplest one to apply a formal modelling. Obviously, in the context of a (N) protocol analysis, it is impossible to take into account, for complexity reasons, the six other levels of ISO model.

The object of this paper is to describe the different architecture models which have been used along the different studies on the protocols, to show their capabilities as well as their limits and deficiencies and, from there, to reach the simplest model which must allow to perform a complete study.

We use, as formal modelling tool, the labelled Petri nets /KELL 76 - DIAZ 82/. The formal modelling is performed in two steps : first, we define the local model of an entity ; second, we interconnect the local models of the two entities (global model).

We will focus our analysis on the connection establishment (ce) phase and the connection termination (ct) phase in a level (N) /BREM 78 - SUNS 78 - ALGA 82 - JUAN 83/.

II. DIFFERENT ARCHITECTURE MODELS

II.1. One level model

This model only considers the virtual communication in a level (N). It is represented on Figure 1 : (N)EP is a (N)E which manages the PDU exchanges ; the virtual transmission medium which connects the two (N)EP's represents the virtual link in the level (N) where the PDU's are exchanged. The virtual transmission medium can be perfect or imperfect (i.e. we can have lost PDU, abnormally delayed PDU, duplicated PDU). This model has been used by /MERL 76/ for the alternating bit protocol modelling.

The use of this model has interest in order to design a protocol with what we call good intrinsic properties.

Definition : Protocol with good intrinsic properties.

1. Accounting for a perfect medium : it is a protocol such that the PDU exchange between the two peer entities lead them in coherent states (goal of the protocol). Furthermore the goal must be reached without pollution of the medium :
   - .by coherent states, in the ce phase, we want to say that each entity go in a state called "connected state" in such a way that the data transfer can normally begin i.e. : if data is sent from any entity, in the "connected state", this data will normally arrive in the remote entity itself in the "connected state",
   - .by coherent states, in the ct phase, we want to say that each entity go in a state called "disconnected state" only when it knows that it cannot receive more data from the remote entity.
   - .we call pollution of the medium the following fact : a PDU can indefinitely stay in the medium because it is not necessary to the evolution of an entity : then in order to not have medium pollution, each PDU must have an indispensable function.
2. Accounting for an imperfect medium : in addition to the properties expressed with a perfect medium, the protocol must have the recoverability property.

However, the one level model masks the relations between the (N) protocol and the (N) service (service obtained from level (N) by level (N+1)) : the different phases of a (N) protocol (connection establishment, connection termination, data transfer) are synchronised from level (N+1) which must then be necessary taken into account in order to effectuate a more complete analysis. Then we have to consider what we call a two level model (Figure 2).

II.2. Two level model

This model, used by /BOCH 78 - DANT 80 - JUAN 82/, is obtained from the one level model where we add a new part to the entity (N)EP : the new part (N)ES manages the transactions relative to the (N)Service i.e. the exchanges of (N)-Requests and (N)-Indications) between level (N+1) and level (N). The transmission medium is as with the one level model.

The introduction of the relations between level (N+1) and level (N) gives a more complete specification of the behaviour of an entity of the level (N). In addition to the capability of the one level model, the two level model allows :
- to view different scenarios relative to the couple (N)Service - (N)Protocol (they are masked in the one level model),
- to verify that a (N)Protocol provides a (N)Service.

However, in the aim of designing the level (N), the two level model, with the virtual transmission medium, presents an incomplete view of the distributed system behaviour : the PDU exchange between the peer entities in the level (N) is achieved through the use of the level (N-1) service (the level (N-1) is the transmission machine which is used by level (N) by means of real exchanges : the primitives of the (N-1)Service).

This machine can be in particular, a clever one and can take decisions on its own. For example, if the level (N-1) itself uses a connection - oriented protocol it can :
- decline to open a (N-1) connection because of a lack of resource,
- reset or clear a (N-1) connection, because of errors which appear in the level (N-1), and signal these situations to the level (N).

Then, we have to consider what we call a three level model (Figure 3).

II.3. Three level model

This model is obtained by adding to the two level model a new part to the entity (N)EP i.e. the part (N-1)ES which manages the exchange of (N-1)Service primitives. Then, we view that the virtual exchanges of PDU between two entities (N)EP is performed through the real exchanges of (N-1)Requests and (N-1)Indications between the parts (N-1)ES and the level (N-1).

This modelling obviously requires modelling the behaviour of the level (N-1) and then connecting the two peer entities in the level (N) by level (N-1) model.

The three level model is a generalization of the previous models as it includes, by completing them, all their specifications. It appears as the realistic reference model which must be considered for the steps of specification, validation and implementation of protocols in a distributed system.

III. USING THE ONE LEVEL MODEL

We use this model in order to show the design of a Protocol for the (ce) phase : (Pce).
The design is performed in three steps :
1) informal specification of the protocol (PDU exchange scheme, differents types of PDU, error control mechanisms),
2) modelling by Petri nets and looking at the general properties of the Petri net of the global model (boundedness, liveness) ; if the Petri net of the global model is bounded and live, we say that this net has good general properties,

3) interpretation of the Petri net model which has good general properties : is the (Pce) goal achieved ?

We will consider the following hypothesis : the conditions in the two entities (N)EP's for the connection establishment and in particular the use of the connection for data transfer (throughput, reliability,...), are identical. Therefore, as soon as one entity is called by the other one, it agrees to cooperate.

III.1. Protocol design

The design requires to take into account : the kind of relationship between the two entities (N)EP's (master-slave, i.e. the master (N)EP calls, and the slave (N)EP is called, or no master-slave) and the kind of transmission medium (perfect or imperfect).

III.1.1. Perfect medium

1. First specification of a protocol : (Pce)1

Accounting for the hypothesis above, we can define a (Pce)1 which uses a one way exchange scheme with the message CR (Connection Request) i.e. : the calling entity (N)EP considers itself, as connected, as soon as CR has been sent ; the called entity (N)EP considers itself, as connected, as soon as CR has been received. The labelled Petri-nets of the entities (N)EP are represented on the Figure 4 :

- state 1 represents the initial state or "disconnected state" ; state 2 represents the "connected state" ;
- the label ! X associated to a transition means the sending of X ; the label ? X associated to a transition means the reception of X.

2. Protocol modelling :

The protocol modelling (global model) requires to interconnect the nets of each (N)EP. Two ways of interconnection can be used /DEVY 79/: transition merging (i.e. a transition !, in an entity, merged with a transition ? in the remote entity) or shared place (i.e. a message is represented by a place in the medium, place which is an output place for a transition ! and an input place for a transition ?).

The transition merging is not realistic in a distributed context (on the other hand, it can be used in a local context of a computer where the message exchanges are effectuated by rendez-vous as in /ADA 80/ or CSP /HOAR 78/) ; note equally that the call crossing, which can occur when there is no master-slave relationship,is completely masked by the transition merging use (Figure 5). We then use the shared place method

We represent on Figures 6 and 7 the Petri nets which concern respectively the case of a master-slave relationship and the case of a no-master slave relationship (as in this section we are only concerned by the (ce) phase, we have introduced a transition T which abstracts the reinitialization procedure (connection termination) of the system after the two entities (N)EP have reached the "connected state").

We can see :

- on the Figure 6 : the Petri net has good general properties (boundedness, liveness) ; the (Pce) goal is equally achieved ; we then say that in the case of a master-slave relationship (Pce)1 has good intrinsic properties ;
- on the Figure 7 : in the hypothesis of a call crossing, if the two entities (N)EP go in the "connected state", on the other hand the shared places are unbounded what traducts a pollution of the medium. (Pce)1 is then, in this case, an incorrect protocol. To eliminate the medium pollution, we have to define a new protocol where : the calling entity (N)EP waits for a reply of the called entity before

considering the connection as established ; the called entity (N)EP considers the connection as established as soon as it has sent the reply. Then, we need a protocol with a two way handshake scheme.

3. <u>New specification of a protocol in the hypothesis of a no-master slave relationship</u> : (Pce)2

(Pce)2 is the simplest two way handshake scheme i.e. which only uses one type of PDU : CR(CR both represents a call and a reply to a call). The Petri net in the Figure 8 (l_1 (place after sending of a CR call) and l_2 (place after the reception of a CR call) are intermediate places) has good general properties (boundedness, liveness). Further we can see that the (Pce) goal is obtained.

III.1.2. <u>Imperfect medium which looses PDU's</u>

A. <u>Master-slave relationship</u>

1. <u>Analysis of protocol</u> (Pce)1

(Pce)1 is modelled in Figure 9 (CR loss is represented by the firing of the transition labelled "loss"). The net presents a deadlock : because of CR loss, the two entities are in inconsistent states (the calling entity, i.e. the master, is in the "connected state" ; the called entity, i.e. the slave, is in the "disconnected state"). This error occurs because the calling entity does not wait for a reply before considering the connection as established. Then we have to define a new protocol (Pce)1', with a two way handshake scheme. (Pce)1' : it uses the simplest two way handshake scheme (as (Pce)2) with, in addition, a Time-Out (TO) mechanism associated, in the calling entity (N)EP, to the CR sending.

2. <u>Analysis of protocol</u> (Pce)1'

We model it on Figure 10 :
- Time-Outs only happen when a CR is really lost ; that is why we have now represented the loss of a CR by a place which is an input place of the Time-Out transition /JUAN 82 - MOLL 82/ ; the label TO is asssociated to this transition ;
- when the called entity again receives CR, whereas it is already connected, it again replies CR and stays in the same place (that is represented by the transition labelled ?CR/!CR).

The net has good general properties (boundedness, liveness). However, we can see that, acounting for the loss of the CR replied by the called entity (N)EP , the (Pce) goal is not always obtained : if data is immediatly sent by the called entity (N)EP, a soon as it is in the "connected state", this data will not be taken into account by the calling entity (N)EP till the end of the recovery. <u>That shows that we have to define a new protocol accounting for the presence of a source function (i.e. data to send) in the called entity (N)EP</u> : before to consider itself as connected, the called entity (N)EP must, after the CR reply sending, still wait for the reception of a new PDU, from the calling entity (N)EP which indicates that this last one has received the CR reply (in the sequel, we call this new PDU "ACK"). Note however : if, in the called entity (N)EP, there is only a sink function (i.e. data reception), protocol (Pce)1', is enough.

This analysis is interesting because it emphasizes, in the hypothesis of a medium which looses PDU's that we have to precisely specify two levels of connection in an entity (N)EP :
- level 1 concerns the sink function ; it is reached as soon as the entity knows the wish of the remote entity to cooperate,
- level 2 concerns the source function ; it is reached as soon as the entity knows that the remote entity has the knowledge of its own wish to cooperate.

Note that the asymmetry in the two entities (N)EP (calling ; called) induces an asymmetry in the way where the levels 1 and 2 are reached :
- in a calling entity : levels 1 and 2 are simultaneously reached as soon as the CR reply, from the called entity, is received,
- in a called entity : level 1 is reached when the CR call, from the calling entity, is received (the called entity is said to be in the "partly connected state") ; level 2 is only reached when the PDU "ACK", from the calling entity, is received (the called entity is then in "the connected state").

Then, by considering a source function in the called entity (N)EP, we have the following assertion(1) on the behaviour of the protocol. Assertion (1) : the called entity N(EP) reaches the "connected state" if and only if the calling entity N(EP) has already reached its "connected state" (precedence relation).

Proof of Assertion (1) is carried out on the reachability graph. (The structural analysis of Petri nets is, on the other hand, useless in this case because we cannot express precedence relation with place invariants and transition invariants).

Actually formal technics such as temporal logic /LAMP 83/, which allow to describe the order in which things must happen, are under progress.

3. New specification : Protocol (Pce)1"
It uses a three way handshake scheme : a) CR call, from the calling entity, to the called entity ; b) CR reply, from the called entity to the calling entity ; c) ACK sending, from the calling entity, to the called entity, when the first one has received the CR reply.

In the calling entity, a Time-Out (TO) is associated to the sending of the CR call (TO is released when the CR reply is received). In the called entity, a TO is associated to the sending of the CR reply (TO is released when ACK is received).

If the called entity (N)EP receives again a CR call, after sending CR reply : it sends again CR reply and restarts the TO. In the calling entity (N)EP, after the reception of the CR reply : if it receives again CR reply, it sends again ACK.

The Petri net which represents protocol (Pce)1" is in Figure 11 :
- we call A,B,C,D (A',B',C',D') the places of the model of the calling (called) entity (N)EP ; C is the "connected state" of the calling (N)EP ; C' and D' are respectively the "partly connected state" and the "connected state" of the called (N)EP,
- about the places in the virtual medium : the places which represents the lost (N)PDU's appear with a L before the (N)PDU name ; two places are used to represent the (N)PDU $\overleftarrow{CR}$ because the called (N)EP can send it accounting for two different contexts in the calling (N)EP (the first context is when the TO is running ; the second one is when the TO is no more running).

The net has good general properties. This net gives the reachability graph which is on Figure 12 (the states are represented by concatenation of the names of the places, in the calling (N)EP and the called (N)EP, and the names of the places in the virtual medium ; the left part of the graph represents the occurrences of losses and the recovery) and which shows assertion (1) proof. Then the (Pce) goal is achieved.

B. No master-slave relationship

1. Analysis of protocol (Pce)2

We can see, in Figure 13, a severe deadlock situation occurs when, upon call crossing, one CR is lost : one entity (N)EP considers itself, as connected, (and then can send data) ; the other one is always waiting for CR reception (and then cannot take into account incoming data). This kind of error results from : 1) the loss of a CR and 2) because a CR has two meanings (i.e. it is both a call and a reply to a call).

It is then necessary the define Time-Out mechanisms to control the losses but, furthermore, to distinguish a reply to a call from a call (which is not necessary, when there is a master-slave relationship). We will call CC (Connection Confirm) the reply to CR. It is important to note that, taking into account this second point, has the following consequence : in the case of a call crossing, we will have the establishment of two connections i.e. the collision problem does not more exist (then on a connection, we always have the notion : calling ; called).

2. New specifications

From the previous consideration and by referring to the analysis made in section A, we can easily prove :

- accounting for only data transfer from the calling entity to the called entity : protocol (Pce)2', which is protocol (Pce)1', with CC instead of CR reply, is a correct protocol,
- accounting for data transfer from the called entity to the calling entity : protocol (Pce)2", which is protocol (Pce)1" with CC instead of CR reply, is a correct protocol.

III.2. Comment

The use of the one level architecture model, combined with the Petri net formal modelling and the assertion method, is then helpful in order to design protocols for the connection establishment i.e. : to define the PDU exchange scheme, the different types of PDU and the error control mechanisms. In the same way, we could show the design of protocols for the (ct) phase.

We still want to emphasize the interest of using Petri nets : looking at the general properties has shown medium pollution problems and deadlocks situations ; using the reachability graph has allowed to prove the achievement of the (Pce) goal.

IV. USING THE TWO LEVEL MODEL

IV.1. Hypothesis

* (N)Service : the primitives, i.e. Requests and Indications, of the (N)Service are :
  . (ce) phase : R-Co and I-Co for respectively the Connection Request and Connection Indication ; R-Ac and I-Ac for respectively the Acceptance Request and the Acceptance Indication ; (the specification of these last two primitives is enough because we suppose, in the example which is shown, that an entity (N)E, which receives a R-Co, or an entity (N+1)E, which receives a I-Co, agrees to cooperate ; in the contrary, we have to specify primitives of no-agreement).
  . (ct) phase : R-Di and I-Di for respectively the Disconnection Request and Disconnection Indication ; the disconnection is not a graceful one /SUNS 78/ ; any (N+1) entity can undertake the (ct) phase.

* Virtual transmission medium : it is perfect.

* (N)Protocol :
  . (ce) phase : (Pce)2', without TO ; it is the class 2 ECMA Transport Protocol /ECMA 80/.
  . (ct) phase : a protocol (Pct) which uses a two way handshake scheme with one type of message (DR, i.e. Disconnection Request used by the (N)E, which initiates the Disconnection, but equally by the other (N)E to reply).

IV.2. Modelling

We present in Figure 14.
1. The labelled Petri nets which represent the behaviour of the entities (N)E1 (calling entity) and (N)E2 (called entity) accounting for the (N)Protocol and (N)Service exchanges (the meaning of the different states appear from the transition labels ; the states 1_1 in (N)E1 and 2_1 in (N)E2, which are the "disconnected states", appear twice for clarity) :
- the transition labels have, in a general way, the form "Predicate/ Action" with, as Predicate, a reception (?X) and, as Action, consequences of this reception one emission (!Y) or two successive emissions (!Y, !Z) which represent the uninterruptible action undertaken by an entity after the reception (?X) ; X,Y,Z are a PDU and/or a (N)Service Primitive ; explain, for example, the transition from state 1_1 to state 1_2 in (N)E1 : after reception of R-Co from the local (N+1)Entity (Predicate : ? R-Co), (N)E1 sends the (N)PDU CR (Action : !CR) and now it is in the waiting state 1_2...
- some labels only have the particular form "Predicate" ; the explanation of these particular labels is the following :
  .(?DR) between states 1_4 and 1_1, in (N)E1, and 2_4 and 2_1, in (N)E2: because, for the Disconnection phase, the (N)Service has a one way exchange scheme whereas the (N)Protocol has a two way exchange scheme ; then (N)E1, in state 1_4, and (N)E2, in state 2_4, only need to receive a DR in order to return in the disconnected state ;
  .(?R-Di) between states 1_2 and 1_5 in (N)E1 : after the reception of R-Di (which represents what we call an incoherent behaviour of local user i.e. it comes to request the (ce) phase and, without waiting for the (ce) phase end, it immediatly requests for the (ct) phase), the entity (N)E1 must wait for the CC where the reference, choosen by (N)E2 to locally identify the connection, is included before sending a DR.

2. The places relative to each PDU in the virtual medium (the arrow indicates its direction).

The global model is then obtained by interconnecting the labelled Petri nets of the entities (N)E1 and (N)E2 by means of the places in the virtual medium which are the shared places. (Note that the transitions, where, in the associated label, the Predicate is (?PDU) and the Action includes (!PDU), a shared place is in their input places and in their output places).

IV.3. Information obtained from modelling

From the net transition invariants /BERT 79/, we obtain the firing sequences which represent the generated language. We give below two sequence examples :
- ?R-Co/!CR ; ?CR/!I-Co ; ?R-Ac/!CC ; ?CC/!I-Ac ; ?R-Di/!DR ; ?DR/!I-Di , !DR ; ?DR ; this sequence is a normal sequence which represents the normal (ce) phase and the normal (ct) phase, undertaken by (NE)E1 ; from this sequence which shows the (N)Service -

(N)Protocol synchronization, we can extract two parts :

.the (N)Service primitive sequence ?R-Co ; !I-Co ; ?R-Ac ; !I-Ac ; ?R-Di ; !I-Di ; which represents the provided (N)Service ; the (N)Service is represented in Figure 15 with numbers indicating the chronological order of the primitives,

.the PDU exchange sequence !CR ; ?CR ; !CC ; ?CC ; !DR ; ?DR ; !DR ; ?DR ; this sequence shows how the (N)Protocol works (that is the only aspect which can be examined with the one level model).

- ?R-Co/!CR ; ?R-Di ; ?CR/!I-Co ; ?R-Ac/!CC ; ?CC/!DR ; ?DR/!I-Di,!DR; ?DR ; this sequence represents the incoherent behaviour of the local user of (N)E1 and its consequences ; we represent on Figure 16 the (N)Service.

IV.4. Comments

The two level model, in addition to the one level model capabilities, allows to show the behaviour of the couple (N)Service - (N)Protocol i.e. how a (N)Service is provided by a (N)Protocol. In particular, it enables to view how the (N)Protocol reacts when there is a "vicious" behaviour of the user in the (N+1) level.

We here have to remark, in comparison with the Section III, that we have shown another interest of the use of Petri nets when designing protocols : their capability to give the generated language.

V. USING THE THREE LEVEL MODEL

V.1. Hypothesis

* <u>(N-1) level</u>

<u>Definition</u> : the (N-1) level uses a connection oriented protocol (we will suppose that the (N-1) connection is established). At any time, the (N-1) level can detect errors and send a Reset indication to each side of the (N) level (in the hypothesis where PDU's are in the (N-1) level, the PDU's are discarded before the Reset indication is sent).

* <u>(N-1) service</u>

The (N-1) service primitives, which are considered, then are :

.<u>R</u>equests to send <u>D</u>ata, the Data being a PDU (i.e. CR or CC or DR) : we note these Requests R'1-D(PDU) or R'2-D(PDU) according to the entity (N)E which sends the Request is the entity (N)E<u>1</u> or (N)E<u>2</u>,

.<u>I</u>ndications of <u>D</u>ata reception : we note these Indications I'1-D (PDU) or I'2-D(PDU) according to the entity (N)E which receives the Indication is the entity (N)E1 or (N)E2,

.<u>I</u>ndications of <u>Res</u>et : we note these Indications I'1-Res or I'2-Res.

* <u>(N-1) level architecture</u>

The architecture which is considered for the (N-1) level is the one indicated on the Figure 17 ; we represent it as a process with two queues in each direction (QD12 and QD21 are two <u>Q</u>ueues including the <u>D</u>ata for respectively the direction (N)E<u>1</u> to (N)E<u>2</u> and the direction (N)E<u>2</u> to (N)E<u>1</u> ; QRes1 and QRes2 are two <u>Q</u>ueues including the <u>Res</u>et Indication for respectively (N)E<u>1</u> and (N)E<u>2</u> ; each queue has only one buffer).

* <u>(N) protocol and (N) service</u>

They are identical to the ones of section IV. However, concerning the protocol, we have to add the following specification : after the reception of I'1-Res and I'2-Res by respectively the entity (N)E1 and the entity (N)E2, these last ones send I-Di to the entities of the (N+1) level and return to their "disconnected state" (i.e. we consider a (N)Protocol which does not recover after a Reset from the (N-1) level).

V.2. Modelling

V.2.1. Model elements

* Level (N-1) model
The different parts of the labelled Petri net (the four queues ; the purge mechanisms which represent the PDU discarding) are indicated in Figure 18 :
- the different queues are characterized by two places whose names have the sign e (for empty queue) or the sign f (for full queue) ; the initial marking of the net is equally given in Figure 18 ;
- the transition with the predicate E means the occurrence of an Error ((N-1) level internal condition) and then the (N-1)level decides to send a Reset to each side of the (N)level ; then, the queues QRes1 and QRes2 become full and the (N-1) level immediatly sends an I'1-Res to (N)E1 and an I'2-Res to (N)E2 if the queues QD12 and QD21 are empty ;
- the transitions, in the queues QD12 and QD21, labelled respectively with ?R'1-D(PDU) and ?R'2-D(PDU), represent the reception of Requests, from the (N) level, for the PDU transfer,
- the transitions, in the queues QD12 and QD21, labelled respectively with !I'2-D(PDU) and !I'1-D(PDU), represent the emission of Indications, from the (N-1) level, when the PDU transfer has been effectuated ; these transitions are fired if there are no Resets to send to the (N) level (Queues QRes1 and QRes2 are empty) ; in the other case, we first have the Purge actions of the Queues QD12 and QD21 and we then have the Indications of resets.

* Entities (N)E1 and (N)E2
The labelled Petri nets of (N)E1 and (N)E2 are indicated on Figure 19. They differ from the nets of the Figure 14 :
- at first, by labelling differently the transitions with !PDU and ?PDU : now these transitions are labelled with !R'1-D(PDU) ; !R'2-D(PDU) and ?I'1-D(PDU) ; ?I'2-D(PDU) ; that evidently shows the use of the (N-1) level service but equally that the level (N-1) is transparent to the PDU semantic) ;
- second, by adding the transitions with labels beginning by ?I'1-Res and ?I'2-Res which can start from any place in respectively (N)E1 and (N)E2 (at any time, the (N-1) level can send a Reset) ; these transitions are with dotted arcs.

V.2.2. Global modelling

We interconnect the models of the entities (N)E1 and (N)E2 and the (N-1) level model by the transition merging method. This method can now be used by considering that : first, each entity (N)E and its partner entity in the (N-1) level are in the same computer and second, the synchronization mechanism, in a computer, is by rendez-vous. if it is not the case, we have still to define and to model interface mechanisms in order to solve the problems of crossings in the interface between each entity (N)E and the level (N-1) /ALGA 82/. (Taking into account the interfaces with the three level model appears to be the most general and the most complete architecture model ; but we do deal with interface modelling in this paper).

Note that in order to effectuate the transition merging, we have to effectuate some modifications, on the design of nets given in Figures 18 and 19, which are not indicated in this paper /DUFA 83/.

V.3. Information obtained from the model

From the net transition invariants, we obtain all the firing sequences then the generated language which includes the language obtained by using the two level model (which itself includes the language obtained from the one level model) and, furthermore, all the scenarios resulting from Resets of the (N-1) level. (Then the influence of the asynchronym of (N-1) service is shown).

For example, we indicate below the sequence which represents the establishment of a connection and its termination due to the level (N-1) :
?R-Co/!R'1-D(CR) ; ?I'2-D(CR)/!I-Co ; ?R-Ac/!R'2-D(CC) ;
?I'1-D(CC)/!I-Ac ; ?I'1-Res/!I-Di ; ?I'2-Res/!I-Di.

We represent in Figure 20 the (N)Service extracted from this sequence.

IV.4. Comment

The example discussed in this section has shown how a couple (N)Service - (N)Protocol can be influenced by decisions taken on its own by the (N)Service.

CONCLUSION

At first, we want to emphasize the particular interest of the different architecture models and then we indicate what way to follow in order to make a complete design of a (N)Protocol.

The one level model is helpful in showing what we call the intrinsic properties of a (N)Protocol (different types of PDU ; PDU exchange scheme ; recoverability properties) ; we have, in particular related to the connection establishment phase, shown interesting results about the different protocols used in the existing systems.

However the one level model makes no reference to the (N)Service ; the two level model takes this aspect into account and then shows how a (N)Protocol works to provide a (N)Service. In particular, it is interesting to see how a (N)Protocol reacts when the user of the (N) level has a "vicious" behaviour.

The three level model allows to show in addition to the two level model properties, the influence of an asynchronous behaviour of the (N-1) level.

Then it appears that the three level architecture model is the most complete one in order to design and to analyse a (N)Protocol, which must provide a (N)Service (for an user which can have a "vicious" behaviour) and accounting for the use, as transmission machine, of a (N-1)Service which in addition to the normal work requested by the (N) level (transmission of (N)PDU's ; this transmission can be perfect or imperfect), can have an asynchronous behaviour (decisions taken of its own) which influences the couple (N)Service - (N)Protocol.

Finally, we say that a complete design of a (N)Protocol must be made by considering the triplet (N)Service - (N)Protocol - (N-1)Service : first, we have to specify the (N)Service ; second, we have to specify the (N-1)Service ; then we can specify the (N)Protocol which must fit to the constraints of both the (N)Service which is requested and the (N-1)Service which is used.

BIBLIOGRAPHY

/ADA 80/ "Reference manual for the ADA programming language", United States Department of Defence, Nov. 1980.

/ALGA 82/ B. Algayres, "Sur la modélisation, la validation et l'implémentation d'un protocole de transport", Thèse de Docteur-Ingénieur, INSA, ,n°84, Toulouse, Dec. 1982.

/BERT 79/ B. Berthomieu, "Analyse structurelle des réseaux de Petri" Thèse de Docteur-Ingénieur, UPS, Toulouse, Sept. 1979.

/BOCH 78/ G.V. BOCHMAN, "Finite state description of communication protocols", Computer Networks, vol.2, Oct. 1978.

/BREM 78/ J. Bremer, "Modèle formel pour la modélisation et la vérification des protocoles de réseaux d'ordinateurs", Thèse de Doctorat ès-Sciences Appliquées, Liège, 1978.

/DANT 78/ A. Danthine, J. Bremer, "Modelling and verification of end to end protocols", Computer Networks, vol.2, Oct. 1978.

/DANT 80/ A. Danthine, "Protocol representation with finite state models", IEEE Trans. on Comm., vol.COM-28, April 1980.

/DEVY 79/ M. Devy, M. Diaz, "Multi-level specification and validation of the control in communication systems", First Int. Conf. on Distributed Computing Systems, Huntsville, Alabama, Oct. 1979.

/DIA 82/ M. Diaz, "Modelling and analysis of communication and cooperation protocols using Petri net based models", Computer Networks, vol.6, n°6, Dec. 1982.

/DUFA 83/ J. Dufau, M. Diaz, P. Azema, B. Pradin, G. Juanole, "Conception et réalisation d'outils de spécification et de conception", Note Interne LAAS n°83.038, June 1983.

/ECMA 80/ ECMA/TC 24/80/67 Final Draft, Transport Protocol, July 1980.

/HOAR 78/ C.A.R. Hoare, "Communicating sequential processes", Comm. ACM, August 1978.

/JUAN 82/ G. Juanole, "Data transfer on a link : specification of a class of retransmission strategies for the error control. Formal modelling by Petri nets", Fifteenth Hawai International Conference on System Sciences, Jan. 1982.

/JUAN 83/ G. Juanole, B. Algayres, "Analysis for the design of a couple service-protocol : application to the transport connection establishment phase", Third Int. Workshop on Protocol Specification, Testing and Verification, Zurich, 1983.

/KELL 76/ R.M. Keller, "Formal verification of parallel programs", Comm. of the ACM, vol.19, n°7, July 1976.

/LAMP 83/ L. Lamport, "What good is temporal logic ?", IFIP 9th World Compuer Congress, Paris, Sept. 1983.

/MERL 76/ P.M. Merlin, D.J. Farber, "Recoverability of communication protocols. Implications of a theoretical study", IEEE Trans. on Comm., vol.COM-24, Sept. 1976.

/MOLL 82/ M.K. MOLLOY, "Performance analysis using stochastic Petri nets", IEEE Transactions on Computers, Sept. 1982.

/SUNS 78/ C. Sunshine, Y. Dalal, "Connection management in transport protocols", Computer Networks 2, 1978.

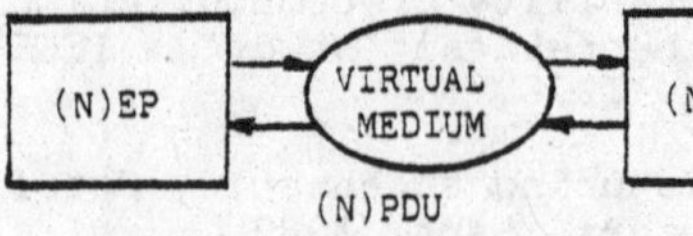

FIGURE 1. One level model

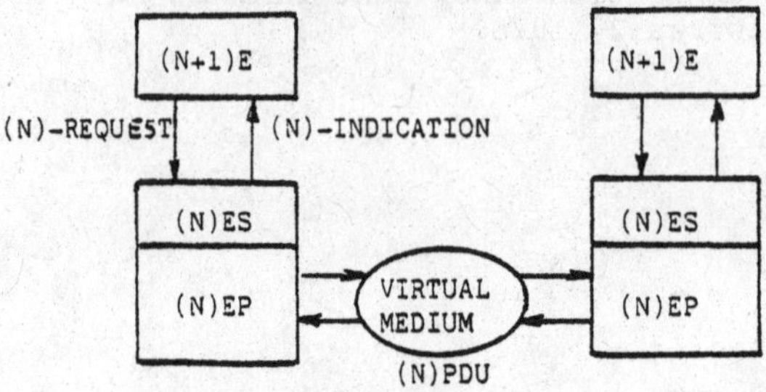

FIGURE 2. Two level model

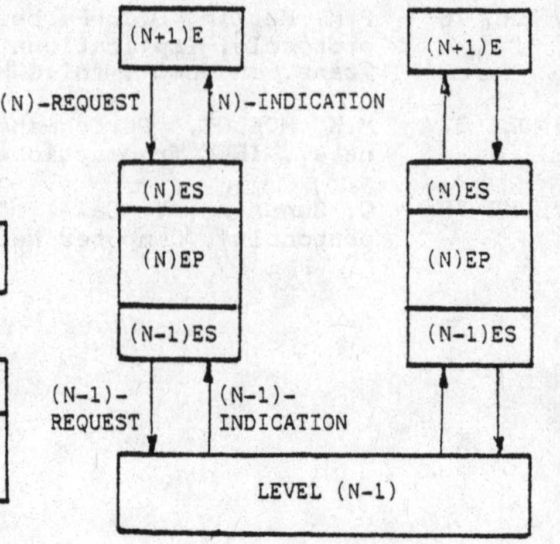

FIGURE 3. Three level model

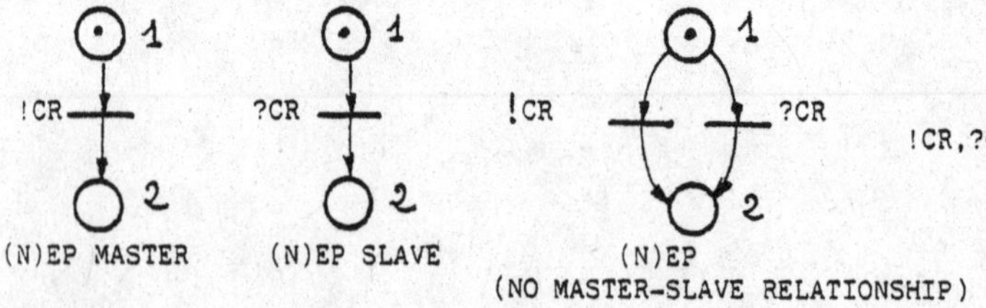

FIGURE 4. Entity models

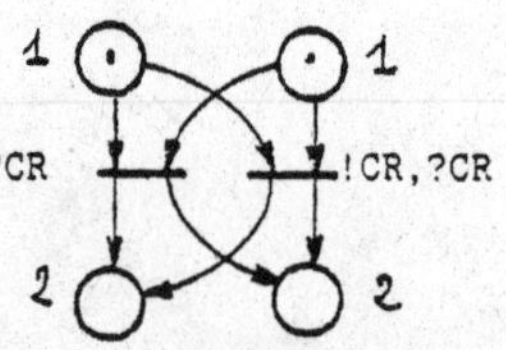

FIGURE 5. Call crossing is masked

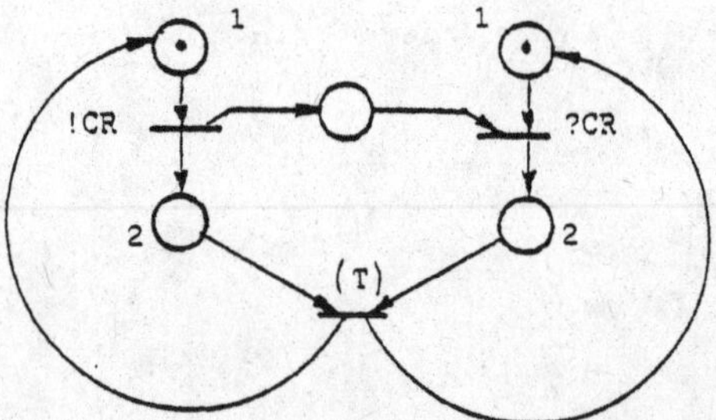

FIGURE 6. (Pce)1, when master slave relationship

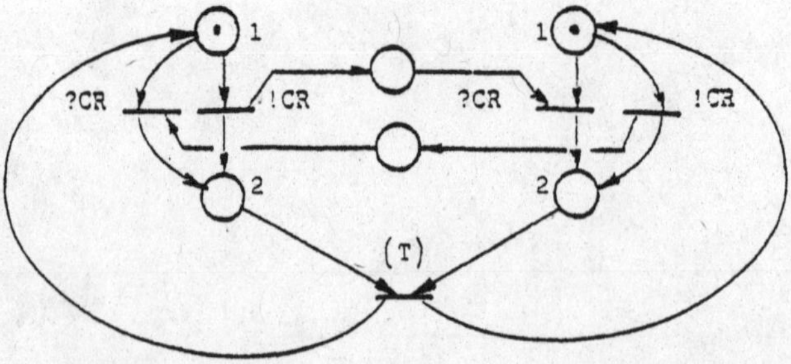

FIGURE 7. (Pce)1, when no master slave relationship

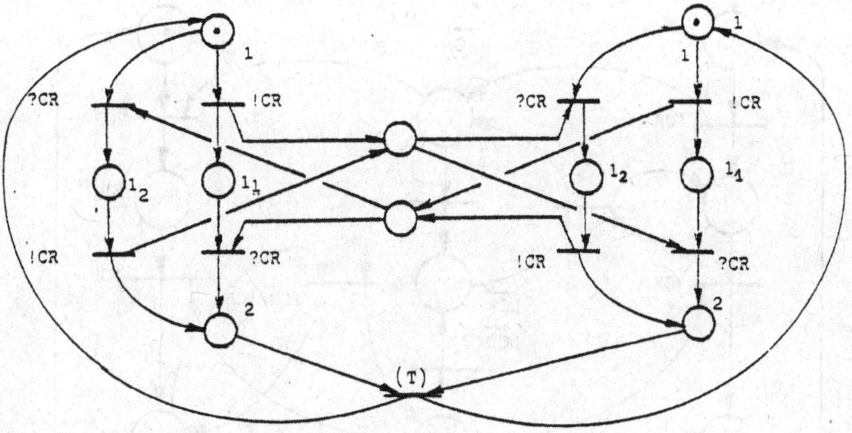

FIGURE 8. (Pce)2

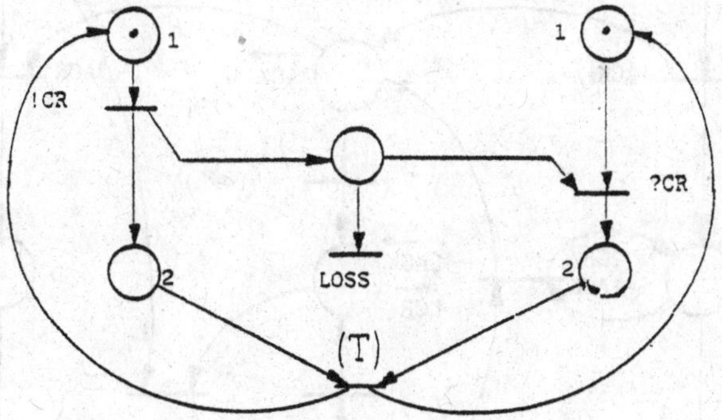

FIGURE 9. (Pce)1, when losses

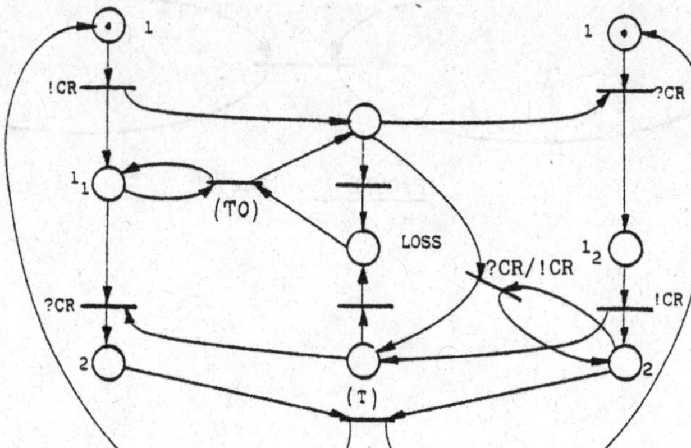

FIGURE 10. (Pce)1′

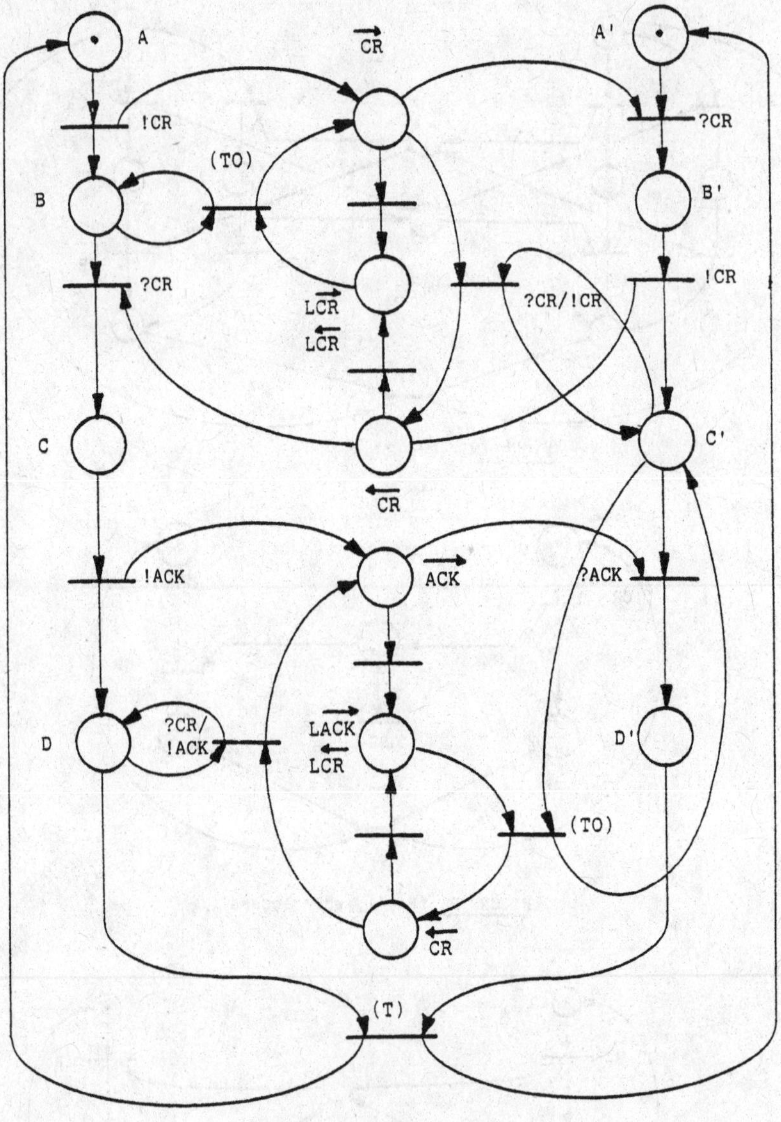

FIGURE 11. (Pce)1"

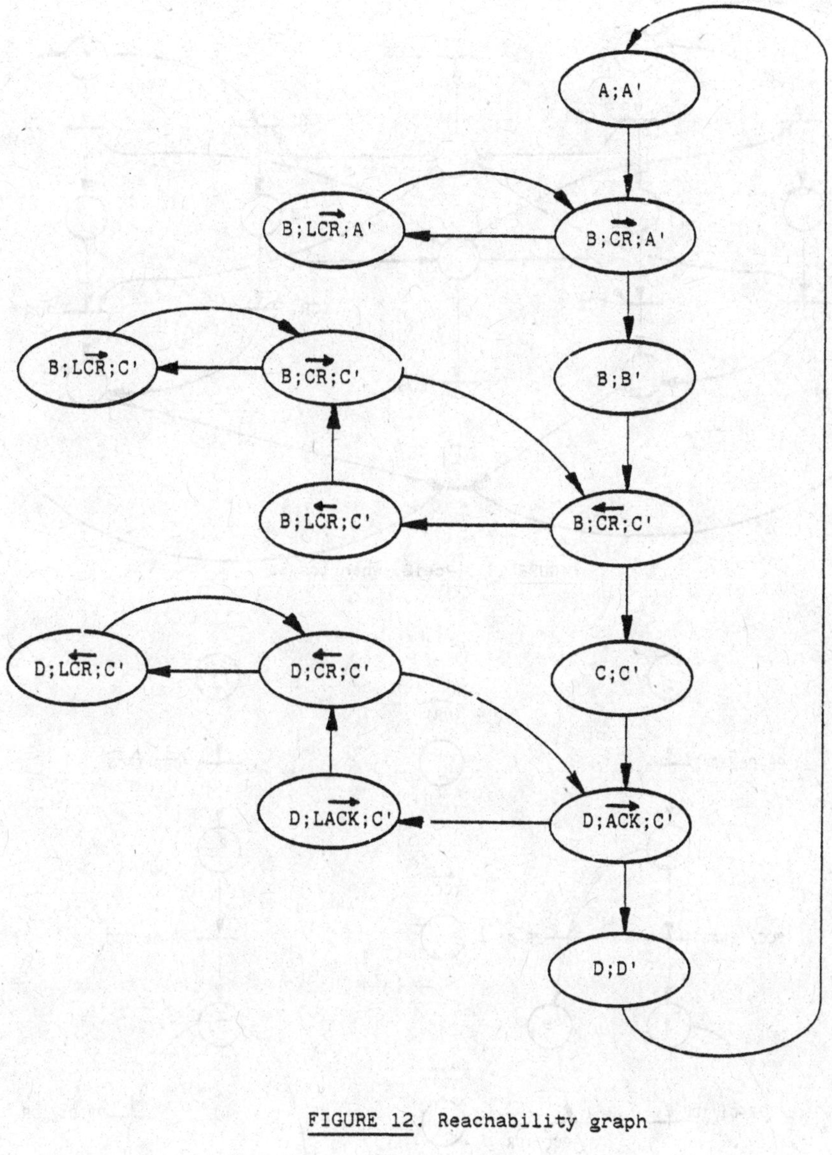

FIGURE 12. Reachability graph

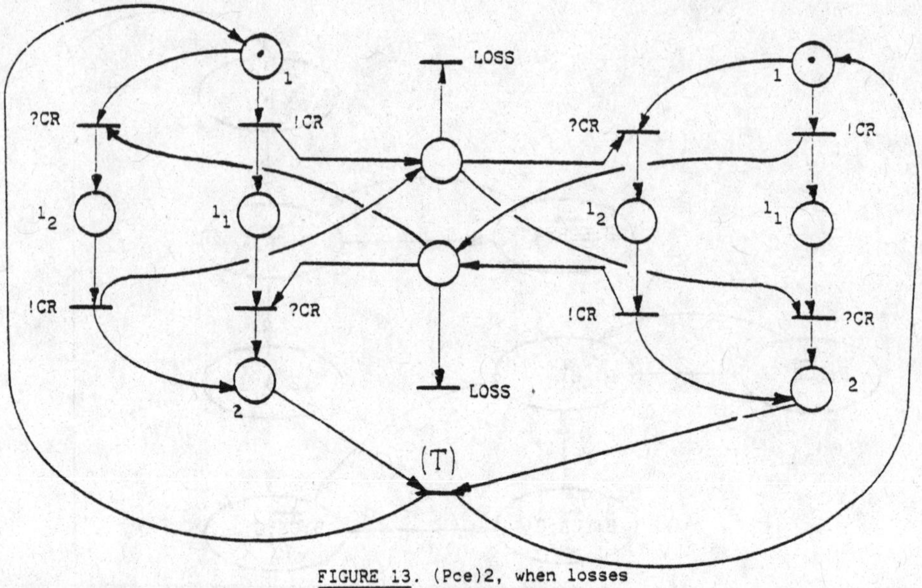

FIGURE 13. (Pce)2, when losses

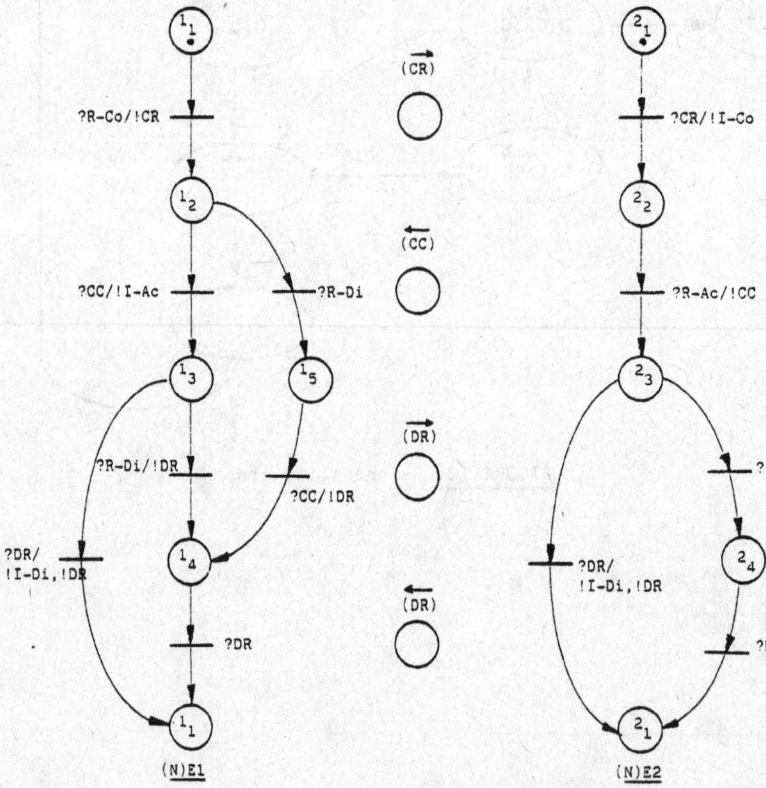

FIGURE 14. Elements of the two levels model

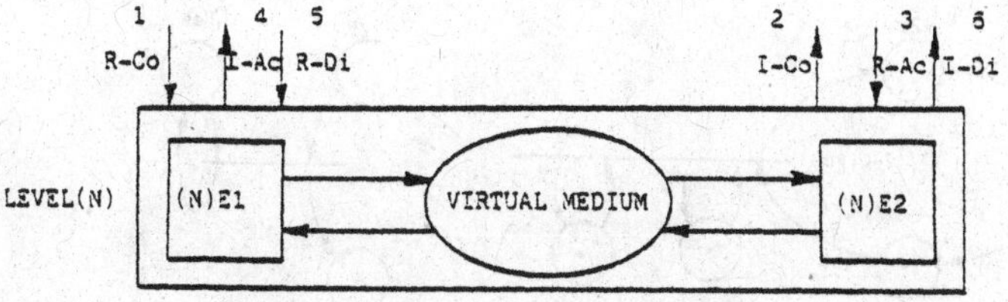

FIGURE 15. Normal (N)Service

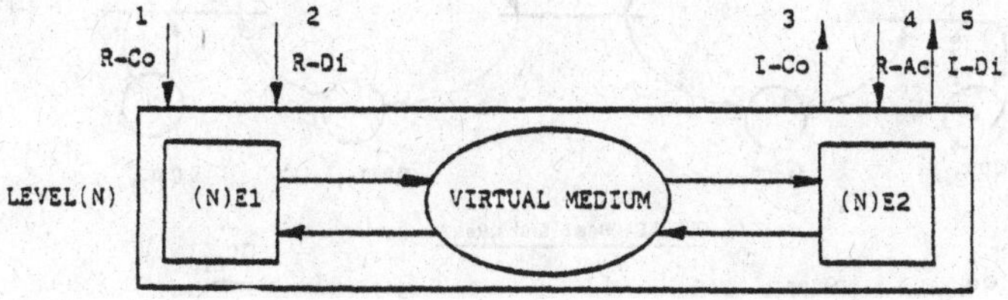

FIGURE 16. (N)Service, when user incoherent behaviour

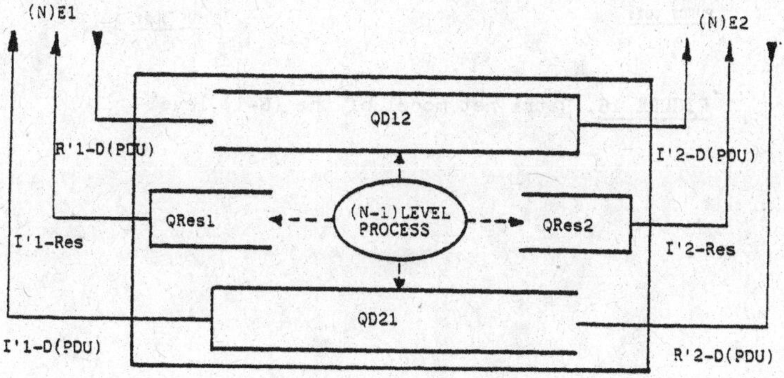

FIGURE 17. (N-1) level architecture

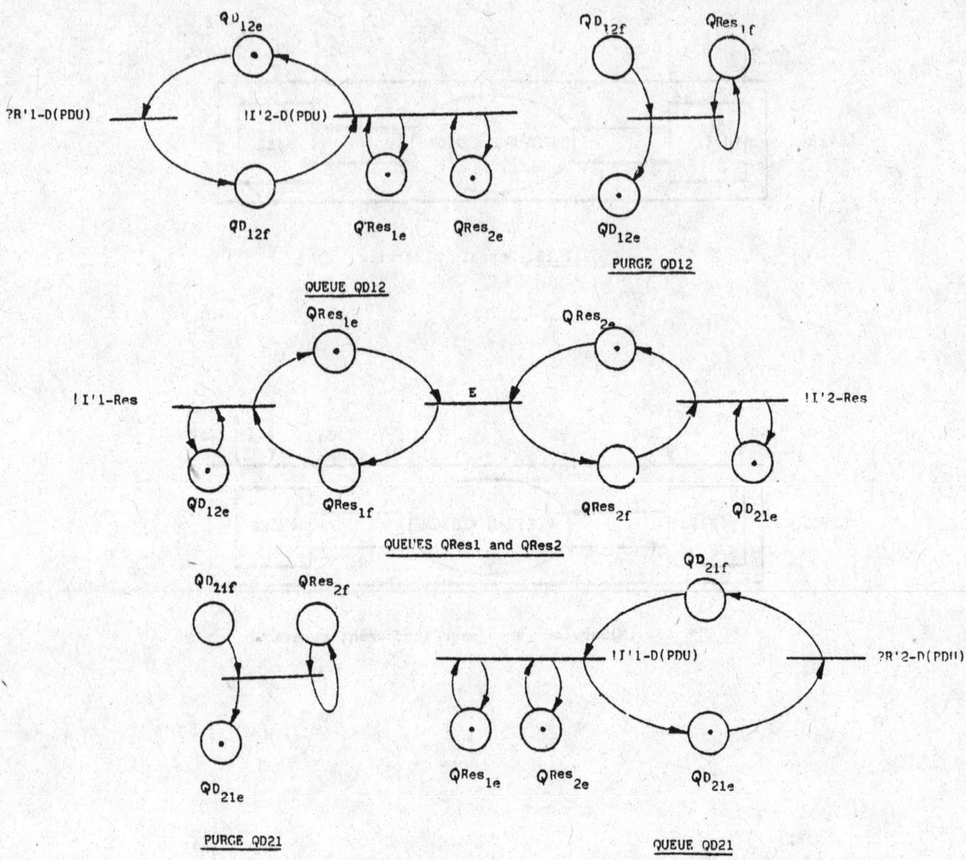

FIGURE 18. Petri net model of the (N-1) level

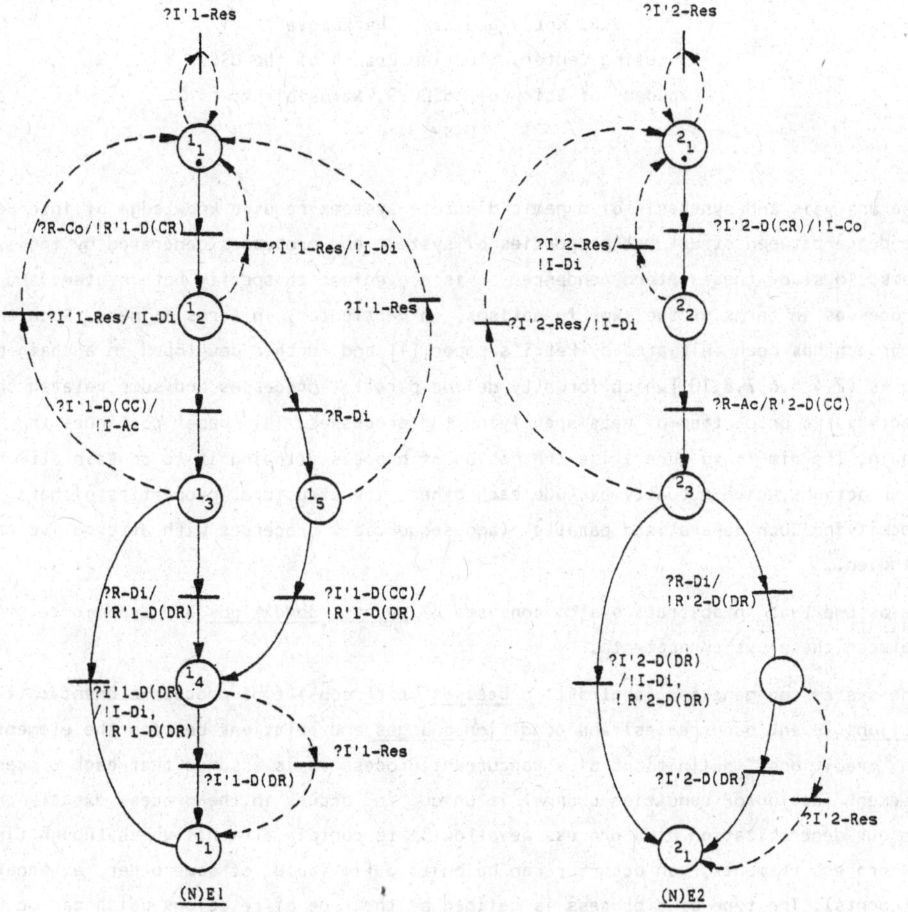

FIGURE 19. (N)E1 and (N)E2 in the three level model

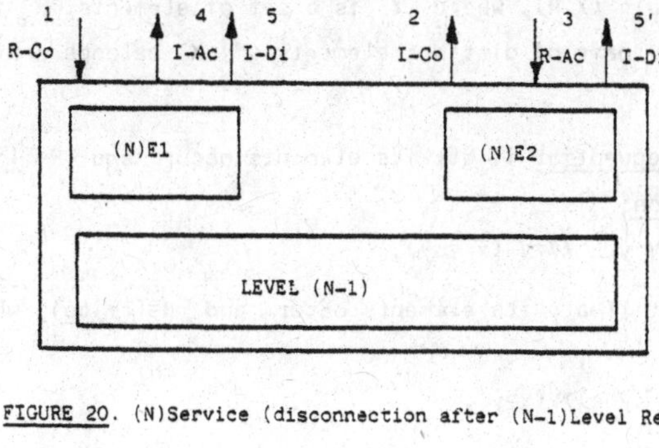

FIGURE 20. (N)Service (disconnection after (N-1)Level Reset)

ON STRUCTURAL PROPERTIES OF GENERALIZED PROCESSES

V.E. Kotov and L.A. Cherkasova
Computing Center, Siberian Branch of the USSR
Academy of Sciences, 630090, Novosibirsk,
USSR

The analysis and synthesis of dynamic discrete systems require knowledge of interdependence between structural properties of systems and processes generated by the systems. To study these interdependences it is convenient to specify both systems and processes in terms of the same formalisms, in particular, in terms of nets. Such an approach has been initiated by Petri's paper [1] and further developed in a chain of works [2,4,5,6,7,8,10]which formally define parallel processes and some related characteristic properties of nets specifying the processes. This paper continues the chain. Its aim is to generalize the notion of process allowing it to contain alternative actions which mutually exclude each other. The structural properties of nets specifying such generalized parallel (and sequential) processes with alternatives are studied.

We assume that an abstract system consists of <u>events</u>, <u>conditions</u> and dynamic relations between these system elements.

The system can generate (abstract) <u>processes</u> which consist of process element called <u>actions</u> (event occurrences) and <u>condition changes</u> and relations between the elements. In "traditional" definitions of a concurrent process it is assumed that each process element (action or condition change) is unique and occurs in the process exactly once. In our generalization of a process we allow it to contain elements which,though listed as process elements, can occur or can be omitted (in favour of some other, alternative elements). The type of a process is defined by the type of relations which can occur between the process elements. All these relations are derivatives of a basic relation $<$: $x < y$ can be interpreted as "if both x and y occurs in a process then x occurs earlier than y".

Thus, a process is a pair (X,R), where X is a set of elements, R is a finite set of relations in X. Any pair of distinct elements of X belongs precisely to one of the relations of R.

A process (X,R) is <u>sequential</u> if all its elements occur and $R=\{\underline{li}\}$, where <u>li</u> is a relation of <u>succession</u>:

$$x \ \underline{li}\ y \Leftrightarrow (x < y \vee y < x) \vee (x = y).$$

A process is <u>concurrent</u> if all its elements occur and $R=\{\underline{li},\underline{co}\}$, where <u>co</u> is a relation of <u>concurrency</u>:

$$x \ \underline{co}\ y \Leftrightarrow (\neg(x<y)\wedge\neg(y<x))\vee(x=y).$$

A process is sequential-alternative if $R=\{li, al\}$, where al is a relation of alternative:

$$x \; al \; y \Leftrightarrow (x \text{ occurs} \Rightarrow y \text{ is omitted}) \wedge (y \text{ occurs} \Rightarrow x \text{ is omitted}).$$

A process is concurrent-alternative if $R=\{li, co, al\}$, where the relations li, co, al are defined as above.

1. Definiton of classes of process nets.

A net is triple (P,T,F), where P is a non-empty set of places, T is a non-empty set of transitions, $F \subseteq P \times T \cup T \times P$ is an incidence relation. The following conditions are valid for the nets ($X = P \cup T$ is a set of all net elements: transitions and places):

A1. $P \cap T = \emptyset$

A2. $(F \neq \emptyset)$ $(\forall x \in X, \exists y \in X: xFy \vee yFx)$, i.e. every element is incident to at least one element of another type.

A3. $\forall p_1, p_2 \in P: (p_1^{\bullet} = p_2^{\bullet} \wedge {}^{\bullet}p_1 = {}^{\bullet}p_2) \Rightarrow p_1 = p_2$,

where ${}^{\bullet}x = \{y \mid yFx\}$ is a set of input elements for x,

$x^{\bullet} = \{y \mid xFy\}$ is a set of output elements for x.

A Petri net is $N=(P,T,F,M_o)$ where (P,T,F) is a finite net (X is finite) and $M_o: P \to \{0,1,2,\ldots\}$ is an initial marking.

We omit well-known definitions of transition firings, firing sequences, reachable markings, etc. One can find these definitions in [3] or other books and papers on Petri nets.

In a Petri net modelling a discrete system, transitions correspond to system events and places correspond to conditions.

In a Petri net, specifying a process, transitions correspond to process actions and places correspond to condition changes.

The following additional restrictions will be general for all considered below types of nets representing processes.

Let $H(N)=\{p \mid p \in P \wedge {}^{\bullet}p = \emptyset\}$ be a set of head places of the net N, $G(N)=\{p \mid p \in P \wedge p^{\bullet} = \emptyset\}$ be a set of tail places of N.

An ordered sequence of net elements $x_1, x_2, \ldots$ is called a path $D(x_1)$ from x_1, if $\forall i \geq 1: x_i F x_{i+1}$, and is called an inverse path $D^{-1}(x_1)$, if $\forall i \geq 1$, $x_i F^{-1} x_{i+1}$. A finite (inverse) path $(x, \ldots, y)$ is called an (inverse) segment and denoted by $D(x,y)$ ($D^{-1}(x,y)$).

A4. $\forall x, y \in X: (x \neq y \wedge xF^{+}y) \Rightarrow \neg(yF^{+}x)$, i.e. the net contains no loops.

A5. $(H(N) \neq \emptyset) \wedge (\forall x \in X, D^{-1}(x): D^{-1}(x)$ is finite).

This restriction demands that any net representing process should have non-empty set of head places and should not contain infinite inverse paths.

A6. $\forall t \in T: ({}^{\bullet}t \neq \emptyset \wedge t^{\bullet} \neq \emptyset)$, i.e. any transition has not less than one input and one output place.

A7. $\forall p \in P: M_0(P) = \begin{cases} 1, & \text{if } p \in H(N), \\ 0, & \text{otherwise.} \end{cases}$

The process nets have standard initial marking: each head place contains one token, other places have no tokens.

Axioms A5-A7 are non-traditional for the generally accepted definition of a process described by a net. They introduce on a base level some restrictions which pursue the main goal: 1) to any process net there must correspond some "real" process, 2) structural (syntactical) relations in a process net and semantical relations in the process generated by this net (i.e. corresponding to this net) must coincide.

Occurence nets [1] (or O-nets) representing concurrent processes are nets (with a standard marking) which in addition to the conditions A1-A7 will satisfy the following restriction.

A8. $\forall p \in P: (|{}^{\bullet}p| \leq 1 \wedge |p^{\bullet}| \leq 1)$, i.e every net place has only one input or output transition; all the places which do not belong to the set of head places or the set of tail places have one input and one output transition.

In the general case O-nets can be infinite. Any O-net is safe because of a standard initial marking and restrictions upon the net topology, assigned by the A4, A5, A8 conditions. An example of O-net is shown in Figure 1.

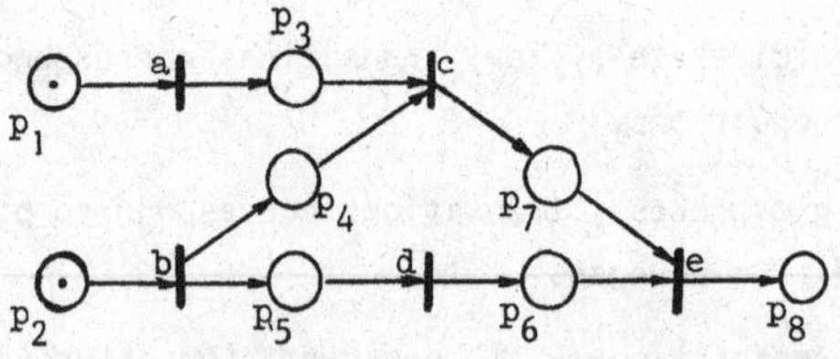

Figure 1.

This definition of occurrence net is a particular case of more general definition given in [1] because of restrictions A5, A6.

Now we introduce nets for describing processes with alternative. Sequential-alternative net (or S-net) satisfies in addition to the conditions A1-A7 the following restrictions:

A9. $|H(N)|=1$, i.e. the net has only one head place.

A10. $\forall t \in T: |{}^{\bullet}t|=1 \wedge |t^{\bullet}|=1$, i.e. any transition in the net has only one input and one output place.

It also follows from the conditions A9-A10 that S-nets are safe and they represent a connected graph. An example of S-net is shown in Figure 2.

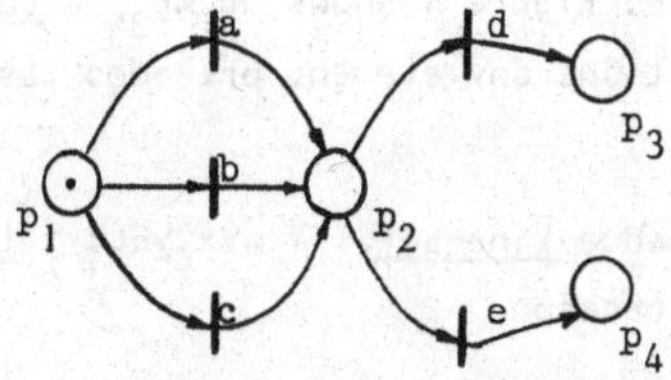

Figure 2.

We will present concurrent-alternative processes with the help of <u>acyclic nets</u>, or A-nets, which satisfy axioms A1-A7 and additional restriction A11 guaranteing the safeness of A-nets. Formal definition of the A11 condition will be given below. An A-net transition can have more than one input and output place and a place in its turn can be incidental to several transitions. An example of an A-net is shown in Figure 3a,b. Note that O-nets and S-nets form particular subclasses of A-nets.

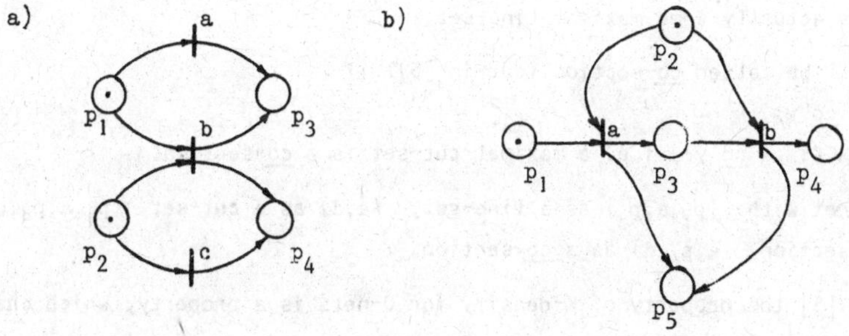

Figure 3.

2. O-nets and their properties.

All the relations defined here for process net elements are introduced with the help of the basic relation of <u>precedence</u> which is denoted by the symbol >. Let N=(P,T,F) be an arbitrary O-net.

$\forall x,y\in X:(x<y)\Leftrightarrow(x\neq y)\wedge xF^{+}y$,

i.e. element x is previous to the element y(x<y), if x differs from y and there is a segment D(x,y) in the net N. The relation of <u>succession</u> <u>li</u> in the O-net is defined as follows:

$\forall x,y\in X:x\ \underline{li}\ y\Leftrightarrow(x<y)\vee(x=y)\vee(y<x)$,

i.e. two elements x and y are in relation of succession if they are equal or one of them precedes the other.

T h e r e l a t i o n o f <u>c o n c u r r e n c y</u> <u>co</u> for the O-net elements is defined in the following way:

$x\ \underline{co}\ y\Leftrightarrow\neg(x\ \underline{li}\ y)\vee(x=y)$, i.e. two elements are concurrent, if they are equal or they are not bound by the relation of succession. For example, Figure 1 shows $p_1 < p_3$, a co b, c li p_2. Due to the reflexivity of li and co relations any element precedes itself and is concurrent to itself.

A non-empty subset $L \subseteq X$ is called a line-set, if $\forall x,y \in L$: x li y, i.e. two elements of L are in the relation of succession.

A non-empty subset $C \subseteq X$ is called a cut-set if $\forall x,y \in C$: x co y, i.e. any of its elements are concurrent.

Presented graphically, any of the O-net elements, belonging to some line, are on some path in a net graph, whereas, all the elements, forming a cut, are in no way connected by some path.

A set $L \subseteq X$ will be called li-section (line in [5]), if

(1) $\forall x,y \in L$: x li y;

(2) $\forall y \in X \setminus L$, $\exists x \in L$: $\neg$(x li y);

i.e. li-section is actually some maximal line-set.

A set of $C \subseteq X$ will be called co-section (cut in [5]) if

(1) $\forall x,y \in C$: x co y;

(2) $\forall y \in X \setminus C$, $\exists x \in C$: $\neg$(x co y), i.e. a maximal cut-set is a co-section.

Figure 1 shows a net with $\{p_1,a,p_3\}$ as a line-set, $\{a,d\}$ as a cut-set, $\{p_1,a,p_3,c,p_7,e,p_8\}$ as a li-section, $\{a,p_4,d\}$ as a co-section.

Proposed by Petri [1] the property of K-density for O-nets is a property, which characterizes their adequacy as net description of concurrent processes.

An O-net is called K-dense, if the intersection of any li-section and any co-section in the net contains only one element. The O-net shown in Figure 1 is K-dense; the O-net in Figure 4 is not K-dense, since the intersection of li-section $\{p_1,a,p_2,a_2,\dots\}$ and co-section $\{b_1,b_2,b_3,\dots\}$ is empty.

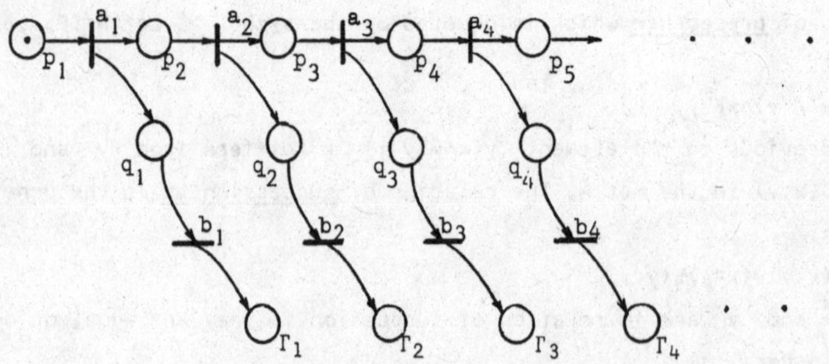

Figure 4.

The following theorems proved in [5] characterize the properties of K-dense and non-K-dense nets.

Theorem 1 (Best). A finite O-net is K-dense.

Theorem 2 (Best). In a non-K-dense O-net there exist an infinite li-section L and an infinite co-section C such that $L \cap C = \emptyset$.

Corollary 1 (Best). If any li-section in the O-net is finite then the net is K-dense.

Corollary 2 (Best). If any co-section in the O-net is finite, then the net is K-dense.

3. S-nets and their properties.

Sequential-alternative nets, or O-nets, are used when describing sequential-alternative processes. The precedence relation and the relation of succession li are defined in the same way as in the case of O-nets. The alternative relation al for S-net elements is defined in the following way:

$\forall x,y \in X,\ x \text{ al } y \Leftrightarrow \neg(x \text{ li } y) \vee (x=y)$

i.e. the x and y elements of an S-net are alternative if they are equal or are not successive.

The definition of li-section fully coincides with that of li-section for O-nets. We will call a set A of S-net elements an alternative cut-set if $\forall x,y \in A$: x al y, i.e. any two elements from A are alternative. Presented graphically all the S-net elements forming an altetrnative cut-set are in no way connected by a path.

The set $A \subseteq X$ is called an al-section if

(1) $\forall x,y \in A$: a al y;

(2) $\forall y \in X \setminus A,\ \exists x \in A: \neg(x \text{ al } y)$,

i.e. maximal alternative cut-set is called al-section. Figure 2 shows an example of an S-net in which the set $\{p_1,a,p_2,d,p_3\}$ is a li-section, $\{a,b,c\}$ is an al-section.

It follows immediately from the definitions of li- and al-sections that the intersection of any of the li- and al-sections of an S-net contains at most one element.

Similar to the case of O-nets there arises a problem of S-nets adequacy. If interpreted as descriptions of sequential-alternative processes they can be unacceptable as specifications of real "reasonable" processes. Among O-nets there exist K-dense O-nets which represent reasonable concurrent processes. For the same purposes the property of L-density is introduced for S-nets. The latter is defined in the following way: an S-net is L-dense, if the intersection of any pair of its li- and al-section contains one element. The S-net in Figure 2 is L-dense whereas the S-net in Figure 5 is not L-dense, because its infinite li-section $\{p_1,a_1,p_2,a_2,\dots\}$ does not intersect with the infinite al-section $\{b_1,b_2,b_3,\dots\}$.

According to the definition of a sequential-alternative process one and only one action must be realized in every complete alternative (al-section), on the other hand a token can pass in the given net along the infinite li-section $\{p_1, a_1, p_2, a_2, \dots\}$ and then no one of the actions $b_1, b_2, b_3, \dots$ will be realized.

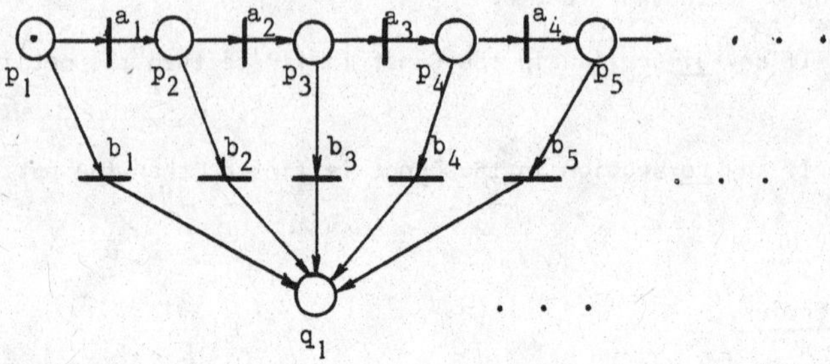

Figure 5.

Similar to O-nets the following theorems are valid for S-nets:

Theorem 3.1. Any of the finite S-nets is L-dense.

Theorem 3.2. In a non-L-dense S-net there exist an infinite li-section L and an infinite al-section A such that $L \cap A = \emptyset$.

Corollary 3.1. If any li-section in an S-net is finite, the net is L-dense.

Corollary 3.2. If any al-section in an S-net is finite, the net is L-dense.

4. A-nets and their properties.

From the computational point of view O-nets lack such important notions as branching or non-determinism while in Petri nets forward and backward conflicts are widely used constructions.

This lack may be motivated by the fact that Petri net semantics on the process level is defined as a class (a collection) of O-nets, and non-determinism in a Petri net corresponds to non-deterministic choice of process from this class. However, from the computational viewpoint it is preferable to deal with conflicts on semantical level and to express the behaviour of a system with conflicts as some unique integral semantic object. We will present concurrent-alternative processes by means of acyclic nets (or A-nets) introduced in Section 1.

The relations $>$ and li for nets elements are defined in the same way as in the case of O- and S-nets.

It is impossible to define the alternative relation for places and transitions in topologically uniform way since the nature of condition change and actions are different. The condition may be changed if at least one input action occurs, i.e. the place will get a token if at least one its input transition fires. The action occurs if all its input conditions have changed, i.e. the transition can fire if all its input places obtain tokens.

Two transitions t_1 and t_2 of A-net are weakly alternative in the following way

$$t_1 \,\underline{\tilde{al}}\, t_2 \Leftrightarrow (({}^{\bullet}t_1 \cap {}^{\bullet}t_2 \neq \emptyset) \vee (\exists p_1 \in {}^{\bullet}t_1 (\forall t_2' \in {}^{\bullet}p_1 : t_1' \,\underline{\tilde{al}}\, t_2) \vee (\exists p_2 \in {}^{\bullet}t_2 (\forall t_2' \in {}^{\bullet}p_2 : t_1 \,\underline{\tilde{al}}\, t_2')) \wedge$$

$$\wedge (t_1 \neq t_2),$$

i.e. different transitions are weakly alternative if they have one common input place or if an immediate predecessor of one of the transitions is weakly alternative to another.

Two transitions are alternative if

$$t_1 \,\underline{al}\, t_2 \Leftrightarrow (\neg (t_1 \,\underline{li}\, t_2) \wedge (t_1 \,\underline{\tilde{al}}\, t_2)) \vee (t_1 = t_2).$$

Two places p_1 and p_2 are weakly alternative if

$$p_1 \underline{al}\, p_2 \Leftrightarrow (\forall t_1 \in {}^{\bullet}p_1,\ \forall t_2 \in {}^{\bullet}p_2 : (t_1 \underline{al}\, t_2 \wedge t_1 \neq t_2)) \vee (p_1 \neq p_2)$$

The place p and the transition t are alternative if

$$p \,\underline{al}\, t \Leftrightarrow (\forall t' \in {}^{\bullet}p : t' \underline{al}\, t) \wedge \neg (t \,\underline{li}\, p).$$

For example, in the net shown in Figure 3b $a \,\underline{al}\, b$, $p_1 \,\underline{li}\, p_3$, $b \,\underline{li}\, p_5$, in Figure 3a $a \,\underline{al}\, b$, $b \,\underline{al}\, c$.

Two A-net elements x and y are concurrent if they are not connected by the relations of succession and alternative:

$$x \,\underline{co}\, y \Leftrightarrow (x=y) \vee \neg (x \,\underline{li}\, y \vee x \,\underline{al}\, y).$$

For example, in the net shown in Figure 3a $p_1 \,\underline{co}\, p_2$, $a \,\underline{co}\, c$, $p_3 \,\underline{co}\, p_4$.

The following table illustrates the properties of relations >, li, al, co

Properties \ Relations	<	li	al	co
Reflexvity	no	yes	yes	yes
Symmetry	no	yes	yes	yes
Transitivity	yes	no	no	no

The class of acyclic nets is defined by means of the above mentioned A1-A7 conditions and the following restriction

A11. $\forall p \in P,\ \forall t_1, t_2 \in T : (t_1, t_2 \in {}^{\circ}p \wedge t_1 \neq t_2) \Rightarrow t_1 \,\underline{\hat{al}}\, t_2.$

The definition of li- and co-sections cited above for O-nets are applied to the case of A-nets. An A-net al-section is defined in somewhat different way.

Lemma 4.1. Any acyclic net is safe.

Corollary 4.1. Let N be an acyclic net and t_1, t_2 - alternative transitions, i.e. t_1 al t_2. Then for any firing sequence τ of the net N is valid the following:

$$(t_1 \in \tau \Rightarrow \neg(t_2 \in \tau)) \wedge (t_2 \in \tau \Rightarrow \neg(t_1 \in \tau)).$$

If the relations li, co, al are considered as "coordinate axes" of some three-dimensional space, then O-nets are in a plane formed by the axes li and co (there are no alternative elements). Structural restrictions for O-nets, which guarantee an adequate net representation of processes were formulated by means of the notions li- and co-sections (all of them have to intersect pairwise). Similarly, to adequately represent sequential-alternative processes it was required that all the li- and al-sections should intersect pairwise. For A-nets adequately formalizing concurrent-alternative processes the following requirements should be satisfied. First, K-density and L-density of its subnets, introduced below, and, second another property, M-density, formulated in terms of the intersection of planes formed on the one hand, by li- and al-sections and, on the other hand, by li- and al-sections.

The net $N'=(P',T',F')$ is called a subnet of the net $N=(P,T,F)$ if $P' \subseteq P$, $T' \subseteq T$, $F' \subseteq F \cap (P' \times T' \cup T' \times P')$.

N o t e. While defining a subnet we do not require it to satisfy the condition A3; being different in the source net, places in a subnet may have the same set of incidental transitions. But it is important to remember that in the source net they were incidental to different transitions sets.

The net N' is called an O-subnet of the A-net N, if

1) N' is a subnet N,
2) N' is O-net,
3) $\forall t \in T': \{p \in P \mid pFt\} \subseteq P'$ and $\forall p \in P': F'(p,t)=F(p,t)$,

i.e. transition t in the O-subnet N' has the same set of input places and all the arcs connecting it with these places as in the A-net N.

We will call an O-subnet N' of the net N maximal if

1) for any O-subnet N" of the net N is valid that $N'' \subseteq N'$;
2) all the head places of N' are head places of N, i.e. $H(N') \subseteq H(N)$.

Figure 3a shows an example of the A-net N. Its set of maximal O-subnets is shown in Figure 6a,b.

Lemma 4.2. Let $N'=(P',T',F')$ be a maximal O-subnet of the A-net N. The following is valid:

$$\forall t_1, t_2 \in T': t_1 \neq t_2 \Rightarrow \neg(t_1 \text{ al } t_2) \text{ in N.}$$

The same relations are valid for places and arbitrary net elements.

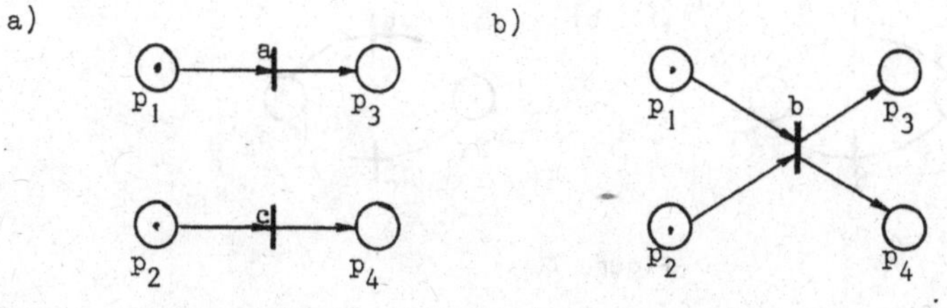

Figure 6.

Thus, the set of all maximal O-subnets of an A-net forms a projection of this A-net onto the plane (li, co).

Lemma 4.3. Let $N=(P,T,F)$ be an A-net, $N'=(P',T',F')$ be a maximal O-subnet. Then the following inclusion is valid:

$\forall t\in T':\{p\in P \mid tFp\}\subseteq P'$.

Theorem 4.1. Let N be an A-net, $\{N_i\}_{i\in I}$ be a set of all its maximal O-subnets. The free language of the net N coincides with the union of free languages of all its maximal O-subnets, i.e. $L(N)=\bigcup_{i\in I} L(N_i)$.

Thus, the set of maximal O-subnets forms the set of all possible concurrent processes, generated by A-net.

The N'-net is called an S-subnet of an A-net N, if

1) N' is a subnet of N;

2) N' is an S-net,

3) $\forall p\in P':\{t \mid tFp\}\subseteq T'$, $\forall t\in T':F'(t,p)=F(t,p)$,

i.e. the place p in N' has the same set of input transitions and all the arcs connecting it with these places as in the net N.

An S-subnet N' of an A-net N will be called a maximal S-subnet if

1) for any S-subnet N" of the net N, is true that $N''\subseteq N'$,

2) the head place $H(N')$ belongs to the set $H(N)$ of head places of N.

N o t e: This definition of an S-subnet is valid for A-nets which can be represented as superposition of S-nets, where the superposition operation "," is defined as follows:

Let $N_1=(P_1,T_1,F_1)$ be $N_2=(P_2,T_2,F_2)$, then $N=(N_1,N_2)=(P_1\cup P_2, T_1\cup T_2, F_1\cup F_2)$.

In the general case item 3 in the definition of S-subnets is recorded somewhat differently.

The set of maximal S-subnets of the A-net shown in Figure 3a consists of subnets shown in Figure 7a,b.

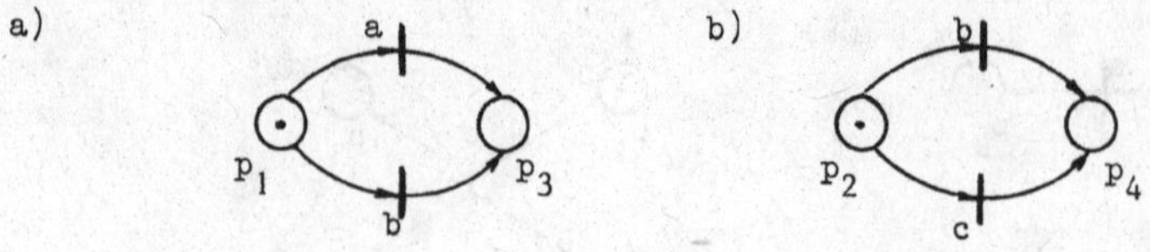

Figure 7.

Lemma 4.4. Let N be an A-net, N′ be its maximal S-subnet. Then

$\forall t_1, t_2 \in T' : (t_1 \neq t_2 \Rightarrow \neg(t_1 \ \underline{co}\ t_2)$ in N).

The similar assertions are valid for places and arbitrary net elements.

Thus, the set of all maximal S-subnets of an A-net N forms its projection onto the plane (li, al).

We will call a set A of A-net elements an alternative cut-set, if ∀x,y A: x al y in N and there exists a maximal S-subnet N′ in which the set A is an alternative cut-set. A-set A is called an al-section, if A is a maximal alternative cut-set in N, i.e. for any alternative cut-set A′ of N the condition $A' \supseteq A$ implies $A'=A$.

We will call an A-net K-dense, if all its maximal O-subnets are K-dense, and an A-net will be called L-dense if all its maximal S-subnets are L-dense.

We will call an A-net N M-dense if the intersection of any maximal S-subnet of N with any maximal O-subnet of net N results in some (unique) li-section of a net N. The uniqueness of the resultes li-section follows directly from the properties of maximal O- and S-subnets, formulated in Lemmas 4.2 and 4.4.

The A-net in Figure 3 is M-dense since the intersection of any of its maximal O-subnet (Figure 6a,b) with any maximal S-subnet (Figure 7a,b) is a li-section in the initial net. The A-net shown in Figure 3b is not M-dense for the intersection of its maximal O-subnet shown in Figure 8a with the maximal S-subnet in Figure 8b results in the line-set $L=\{p_1,a,p_3\}$ which is not a li-section (L is contained in the li-section $\{p_1,a,p_3,b,p_4\}$ of the net).

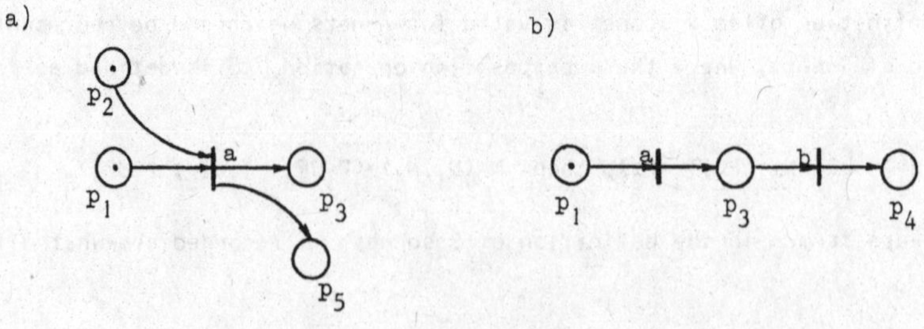

Figure 8.

We will call an A-net <u>dense</u> if it is K-dense, L-dense, M-dense. Figure 3a shows the example of a dense net. The A-net shown in Figure 9 is neither K-, or L-, nor M-dense.

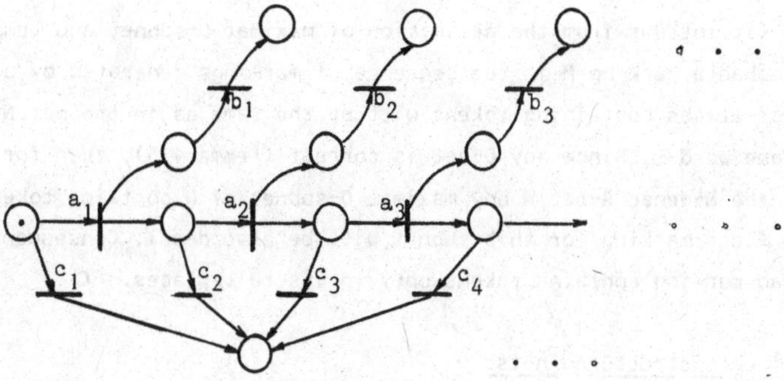

Figure 9.

Note that the finiteness of an O- or S-net guaranteed K- or L-density of this net. However the finite A-net may prove to be non-dense but only on account of being not M-dense.

The following assertions illustrate the adequacy of A-nets as net representations of concurrent-alternative processes.

We will call a net <u>correct</u> if for any reachable dead marking M (i.e. none of the net transitions can fire at M) and for any place p which doesn't belong to the set of tail places: M(p)=0. Note that in the general case there can be infinite A-nets without tail places and respectively without dead markings. In these cases they are considered to be correct.

<u>Lemma 4.5</u>. Any S-net and any O-net are correct.

The following lemmas characterize the properties of the M-dense nets.

<u>Lemma 4.6</u>. Let N be an M-dense A-net, N′ be a maximal S-subnet in N. Then any <u>li</u>-section L in N′ is a <u>li</u>-section in N as well.

<u>Lemma 4.7</u>. Let N be an M-dense A-net, N′ be a maximal O-subnet in N. Then a set of head places of N′ coincides with a set of head places of N, i.e. H(N′)=H(N).

<u>Lemma 4.8</u>. Let N be an M-dense A-net, N′ be a maximal S-subnet in N. Then any <u>li</u>-section L in N′ is also a <u>li</u>-section in N.

<u>Theorem 4.2</u>. An M-dense A-net is correct.

P r o o f. We will call a word of the net free language a dead one, if it leads to dead marking in the net. We have to show that any dead word leads to a dead marking containing tokens only in tail places of the net. As theorem 4.1 states for any (dead) word τ generating in the A-net N, there exists a maximal O-subnet N′, generating it. According to lemma 4.6 any <u>li</u>-section of the maximal O-subnet N′ is at the same time a *li*-section of the initial A-net N. Hence any tail place of N′ is also a tail place of N. Lemma 4.7 states that H(N′)=H(N) and that for any transition t from N′ a set of its input and output places in the net N′ is the same as in the net N (it follows from the definition of maximal O-subnet and lemma 4.3). Then for any reachable marking M in the sequence of markings generated by a dead word τ in N, a set of places containing tokens will be the same as in the net N′ when it generates the same word τ. Since any O-net is correct (lemma 4.5), then for any reachable marking in the M-dense A-net N any maximal O-subnet of N contains tokens only in its tail places (such marking for this subnet will be also dead). Consequently, the net N with a dead marking contains tokens only in its tail places. □

5. Subclasses of well-structured nets.

To apply the notions of K-, L-, M-density to the general class of Petri nets it is necessary to set up a correspondence between Petri nets and A-nets describing the process of their functioning.

Correspondence between Petri net and process net generated by Petri net will be considered as a result of some transformation called unfolding. Note first of all, that for finite Petri net satisfying the restrictions A1-A7 unfolding is trivial: the given Petri net and a process net generated by this net coincide.

Consider unfolding of the sequential nets as the first example.

A Petri net $N=(P,T,F,M_0)$ will be called sequential if

1) $\forall t\in T:(|{}^{\bullet}t|\leq 1 \wedge |t^{\bullet}|\leq 1)$,
2) $|H(N)|=1$.

We will call a cyclic component of sequential net its maximal cyclic subnet N′ such that $\forall y\in X\setminus X', \exists x\in X':\neg(xF^+y \wedge yF^+x)$.

A maximal subnet which contains no cyclic component forms an acyclic component.

It is clear that any sequential net N can be presented as a finite sequence of cyclic and acyclic components. A sequential net with an arbitrary initial marking is splitted into a set of sequentials with a standard marking. An unfolding of sequential nets with a standard marking consists of an unfolding of cyclic component and their "concatenation" with acyclic components.

Figure 5 shows an S-net which is a result of unfolding of the sequential net shown in Figure 10a.

In the general case, unfolding of a Petri net into a corresponding A-net consists of partitioning net into a collection of all sequential components. Each sequential component is unfolded by the above-mentioned method. Then we use a special indexing of each of the obtained unfolded nets and their "equalization". The latter is performed in such a way that maximal indices of transitions with the same labels in all unfolded nets are equal. At a final stage these nets are superposed in a special way.

The O-net shown in Figure 4 is a result of unfolding of the net in Figure 10 b, A-net in Figure 9 is a result of unfolding of Petri net shown in Figure 10 c.

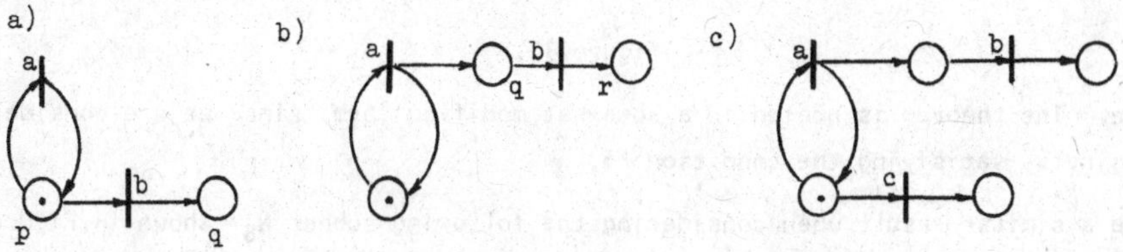

Figure 10.

A number of the following relations demonstrate the correspondence between a Petri net N and its unfolded process net $\hat{N}$.

1) Let pr^{-1} denote a mapping reverse to the unfolding transformation, i.e. $pr^{-1}: \hat{N} \to N$. Then for any transition $t \in T$; $pr^{-1}(t^\bullet) = (pr^{-1}(t))^\bullet$ and $pr^{-1}({}^\bullet t) = {}^\bullet(pr^{-1}(t))$.

2) if $x<y$ in $\hat{N}$, then $pr^{-1}(x) < pr^{-1}(y)$ in N.

3) $L(N)=L(\hat{N},\Sigma)$ where $L(N)$ is a free language of a Petri net N, $L(\hat{N},\Sigma)$ is a language of labelled net $\hat{N}$ in which $\forall t^{i,j} \in \hat{T}: \Sigma(t^{i,j})=t$, (i,j) are indices, obtained by the transition t from N with unfolding into A-net $\hat{N}$.

We will introduce now some additional notions and definitions.

Let a <u>simple path</u> in a net be a sequence of net elements $(x_1, x_2, \dots, x_n)$ such that $x_i F x_{i+1}$ for all i, $1 \le i \le n$, and $x_i \ne x_j$ for any two elements excluding maybe x_1 and x_n. A simple path is a <u>loop</u> if $x_1 = x_n$.

A place p is a <u>loop exit</u> if there is such transition in the loop that $p \in t^\bullet$ and there is no loop which contains both p and t. In the net shown in Figure 10 b place q is a loop exit.

When proving the following theorems some notions and results of Best [5] will be used.

An O-net $N'=(P',T',F')$ is called a <u>causal subnet</u> of an O-net $N=(P,T,F)$ if

1) $P' \subseteq P$, $T' \subseteq T$;

2) $\forall x,y \in P' \cup T' : x F'^{+} y \Leftrightarrow x F y$,

i.e. a set of relations (<u>al</u>, <u>li</u>, <u>co</u>) for the net N′ elements agrees with the same relations in the net N for similar elements.

Consider the O-net N_0 shown in Figure 11.

The following theorem gives topological characterization of non-K-density in O-nets.

<u>Theorem 3 (Best)</u>. An O-net is non-K-dense <=> O-net N_0 is a causal subnet of N.

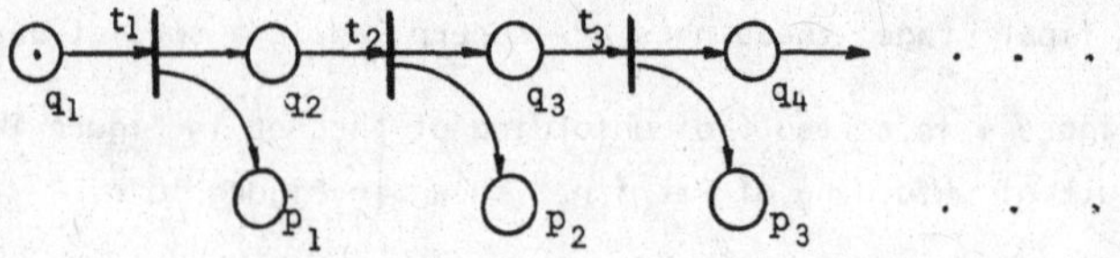

Figure 11.

N o t e. The theorem is quoted in a somewhat modified form, since we are considering process nets, satisfying the condition A5.

We have a similar result when considering the following subnet N_S shown in Figure 12, namely:

An S-net N is non-L-dense <=> N_S is a causal subnet of the net N.

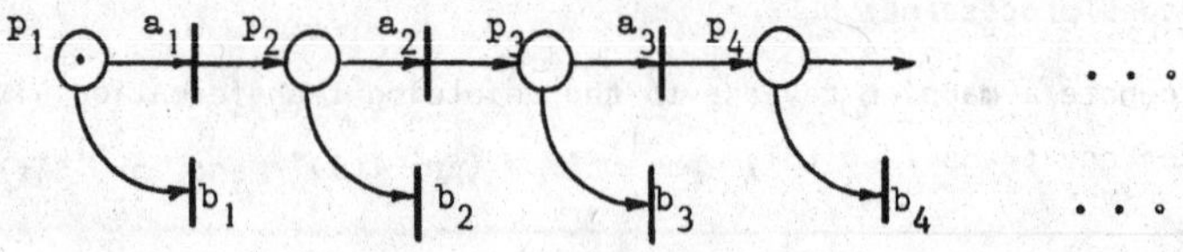

Figure 12.

<u>Theorem 5.1</u>. A Petri net N is non-K-dense <=> in a net N there exists an unbounded exit place p of a loop.

P r o o f. If a Petri net N is non-K-dense, then (by definition) the A-net $\hat{N}$ generated by the Petri net is non-K-dense. Then there is a non-K-dense maximal O-subnet $\hat{N}'$ in $\hat{N}$. Hence a net N_o is a causal subnet of the net $\hat{N}'$. Since in the net N a set of transitions T is finite, then in the infinite <u>li</u>-section $L=\{q_1,t_1,q_2,t_2,\ldots\}$ of the net N_o there exists an infinite sequence of transitions $\{a^1,a^2,a^3,\ldots\}$ generated by some transition a from the initial net N.

Properties of a maximal O-subnet imply that $\hat{x}<\hat{y}$ in $\hat{N}'$<=>$\hat{x}<\hat{y}$ in $\hat{N}$. Properties of unfolded net imply that $\hat{x}<\hat{y}$ in $\hat{N}$<=>xF^+y in N, where x ynd y are elements in N corresponding to $\hat{x}$ and $\hat{y}$ in $\hat{N}'$.

Since $\forall i\geq 1$ in $\hat{N}'$ holds $a^iF^+a^{i+1}$, then in the net N the following property is fulfilled: aF^+a, i.e. there exists a loop containing the transition a.

By lemma 4.3 the set of output places of the transition a^i, $\forall i\geq 1$ in the maximal O-subnet $\hat{N}'$ coincide with the set of output places of transition a^i, $\forall i\geq 1$, in the A-net $\hat{N}$, which in its turn corresponds to the set of output places of the transition a in a net N. Thus, there is correspondence between an output place p of transition a and the infinite <u>co</u>-section of places $p^1,p^2,p^3,\ldots$ in $\hat{N}'$, where $\forall i\geq 1: p^i\in(a^i)^{\bullet}$. Note,that p is not a part of cyclic component, containing transition a, i.e. $\neg(pF^+a)$. Otherwise, $\forall i\geq 1: p^iF^+p^{i+1}$, that is inconsistent with the initial condition $\forall i,j$: p^i <u>co</u> p^j.

Since the languages of the given Petri net and unfolded net coincide and the language of unfolded net coincides with the union of languages of its maximal O-subnets (Theorem 4.1) and in the maximal O-subnet there exists a firing sequence containing an infinite number of occurrences of transition a, then a loop of the net N containing transition a is functioning for an infinitely long time. Owing to that, the place p is not bounded.

The proof of sufficiency is similar to the proof of necessity.

By the condition of the theorem there exists in a net N such a loop L and transition a, belonging to the component L, that the place p is an output place of transition a, but p and a are not in any loop. Let q denote some input place of transition a in the loop L, (i.e. $qFa \wedge aF^{+}q$). Since place p is unbounded, the loop containing transition a is functioning for an infinitely long time. From the above cited relations between languages, input and output places of transitions in a Petri net, in a corresponding A-net and in its maximal subnet we have that there exists such a maximal O-subnet $\hat{N}'$, that contains infinite sequence of elements $q^1, q^2, q^3, \ldots, a^1, a^2, a^3, \ldots, p^1, p^2, p^3, \ldots$, corresponding to the elements q, a, p in the initial net N. Let find in $\hat{N}'$ the causal subnet $\hat{N}'_o$ containing these elements and show that a net $\hat{N}'_o$ is the net shown in Figure 11. Really, $\forall i \geq 1;\ q^i F a^i \wedge a^i F^{+} q^{i+1}$ in $\hat{N}'_o$, since $q\overset{+}{F}a \wedge a\ F^{+}q$ is in the net N. Thus, the sequence $\{q^1, a^1, q^2, a^2, \ldots\}$ generates an infinite <u>li</u>-section in $\hat{N}'_o$. It can be similarly shown that $\forall i,j \geq 1: p^i\ \underline{co}\ p^j$, for otherwise the place p would be a part of the loop, containing transition a. This contradicts the condition of the theorem. Therefore, using the theorem 3 (Best) we deduce that the maximal O-subnet $\hat{N}'$ is non-K-dense. Then the A-net $\hat{N}$ is also non-K-dense and the initial Petri net N is non-K-dense. □

The net shown in Figure 10 b is non-K-dense for the place q is an unbounded exit from a loop. For similar reason the net shown in Figure 10 c is also non-K-dense.

This result is similar to that of Reisig and Goltz [11], for the place p can be primarily unbounded for two reasons:

1) the place p is an output place of a transition which can be fire an infinitely long time because of initial marking (in [11] this is a transition without any input places) or

2) if the place p is an output place of a transition from some loop in which this transition can fire for an infinitely long time, and the place p not being a part of this loop.

Unboundness of the first type is not related to K-density, the second case remains as characterizing the connection of non-K-density with unboundness of a place.

<u>Theorem 5.2</u>. A sequential net N is non-L-dense<=>there exists a cyclic component in the net N with subsequent acyclic section.

The proof is similar to that of theorem 5.1. For example, the net N shown in Figure 10a is non-L-dense.

Let $\tau=t_1,t_2,\ldots,t_k,\ldots$ be the firing sequence of transitions in a net N such that $M_0[t_1>M_1[t_2>\ldots[t_k>M_k[t_{k+1}\ldots$ where M_0 is an initial marking in N. Denote by $\{M_0\}_\tau = \{M_0,M_1,M_2,\ldots\}$, i.e. $\{M_0\}_\tau$ is a set of reachable markings in the net N generated by a firing sequence τ. Let $t\in T$, M be some marking in N, let $M[t>$ denote the fact that a transition t will be able to fire with the marking M.

A net N is <u>non-fair</u> if there exists an infinite firing sequence τ and a transition t such that t enters the sequence τ finite number of times (possibly empty) and there exists an infinite sequence of markings $M_1,\ldots,M_k,\ldots$ from $\{M_0\}_\tau$ such that $\forall i\geq 1{:}M_i[t>$.

<u>Theorem 5.3.</u> A sequential net N is non-L-dense=>net N is non-fair.

P r o o f. Immediate corollary of theorem 5.2 since one can take as τ a firing sequence of transition from cyclic component and as t the first transition in the next acyclic component.

The class of free-choice nets is well-known in literature.

A Petri net $N=(P,T,F,M_0)$ is a <u>free-choice net</u> (FC-net) if $\forall p\in P, \forall t\in T{:}p\in{}^\bullet t \Rightarrow p^\bullet=\{t\}\vee {}^\bullet t=\{p\}$.

In a FC-net, if a place p has no more than one output transition then each of these transitions has a set of its input places which consists of exactly one place, namely, the place p.

For example, Figure 13 a,b shows nets which are free-choice nets, the nets shown in Figure 3 a,b do not belong to this class. We introduce transitive free-choice nets which form a more restrictive subclass of the class of FC-nets.

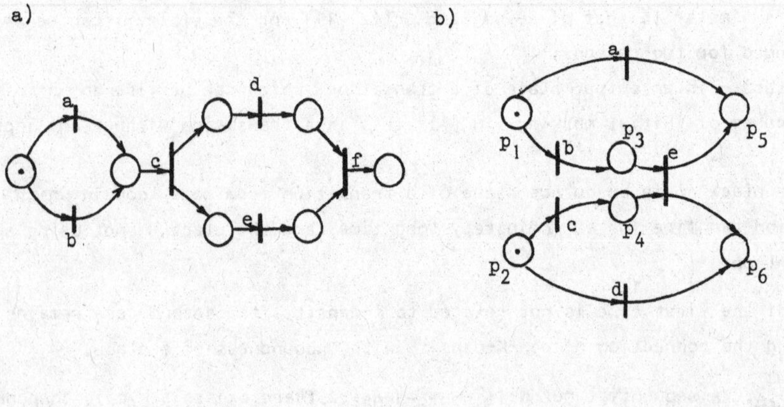

Figure 13.

The relation of weak alternative $\tilde{al}$, defined in Section 4 for elements of process nets, is similarly defined for Petri nets elements as well.

The net $N=(P,T,F,M_0)$ is called a transitive free-choice net (TFC-net) if

1) $\forall t_1,t_2 \in T: t_1 \tilde{al}\ t_2 \Rightarrow |{}^\bullet t_i| = |t_i^\bullet| = 1,\ i = 1,2;$

2) $\forall t \in T,\ \forall p_1,p_2 \in P: p_1,p_2 \in {}^\bullet t \Rightarrow \neg(p_1 \tilde{al}\ p_2).$

Thus, any transition being a part of a non-trivial alternative has unique input and unique output place and input places of any transition are concurrent.

For example, the net shown in Figure 13 a belongs to the class of TFC-nets, while the nets shown in Figure 3 a,b, 13 b are not TFC-nets.

The transitive free-choice net consists of alternating concurrent and sequential subnets; its unfolded process net also satisfies the conditions 1) and 2) in the definition of TFC-nets. We will denote process nets from this class by TFCP.

The relation of alternative al for process nets can be defined as follows.

$\forall x,y \in P \cup T:\ x\ al\ y \iff \exists p \in P(\forall D(p,x),\ \forall D(p,y): D(p,x) \cap D(p,y) = \{p\}).$

The following lemmas are valid:

Lemma 5.1. Let $N=(P,T,F)$ be a transitive free-choice process net, $N'=(P',T',F')$ be its maximal O-subnet. Then any li-section in N' is also a li-section of the net N.

Lemma 5.2. Let $N=(P,T,F)$ be a transitive free-choice process net, $N'=(P',T',F')$ be its maximal O-subnet. Then $H(N)=H(N')$.

Lemma 5.3. Let $N=(P,T,F)$ be a transitive free-choice process net, $N'=(P',T',F')$ its maximal S-subnet. Then any li-section in N' is a li-section of N.

Theorem 5.4. Let N be a transitive free-choice net. Then N is M-dense.

P r o o f. Immediately follows from the definition of M-density and lemmas 5.1, 5.2, 5.3. □

Conclusion.

The main aim of this paper has been to propose a next step in increasing the level of the presentation of non-sequential processes. Occurrence nets allow to specify and study asynchronous parallelism in processes. The propozed generalization (acyclic nets) gives the additional possibility to include in the specification non-determinism of conflict process elements. New notions arise such as al-sections, L-density, M-density which give topological characterization of distinction "good" and "bad" interrelation between intuitive concepts of sequential, parallel and alternative occurrences of events and conditions. The connection between K-, L-, M-density of process nets and, correspondingly, boundness, fairness and free-choice property of Petri nets has been indicated.

Proofs of the theorems and lemmas stated above will be presented elsewhere.

References

[1] Petri C.A. Non-sequential processes. ISP-Report 77.05. St.Augustin: Gesellschaft für Mathematik und Datenverarbeitung, 1971, 31 p.

[2] Petri C.A. Concurrency as a basis for system thinking. ISP-Report 78.06, St. Augustin: Gesellschaft für Mathematik und Datenverarbeitung, 1978, 20 p.

[3] Peterson J.G. Petri net theory and the modelling of systems. Prentice-Hall Inc., N.Y., 1981, 290 p.

[4] Petri C.A. Concurrency. Lecture Notes in Computer Science, vol.84, Springer-Verlag, Berlin, 1979, p.251-260.

[5] Best E. The relative strength of K-density. Lecture Notes in Computer Science, vol.84, Springer-Verlag, Berlin, 1979, p.261-276.

[6] Nielsen M., Plotkin G., Winskel G. Petri nets, event structures and domains. Lecture Notes in Computer Science, vol.70, Springer-Verlag, Berlin, 1979, p.266-284.

[7] Best E., Merceron-Brecht A. Some properties of non-sequential processes. ISF-Report 82.07, Gesellschaft für Mathematik und Datenverarbeitung, 1982, 23 p.

[8] Fernandez C., Thiagrajan P.S. D-Continuous Causal Nets: A Model of Non-Sequential Processes. ISF-Report 82.05, Gesellschaft für Mathematik und Datenverarbeitung, 1982, 40 p.

[9] Queille J.P., Sifakis J. Fairness and properties in transition systems - a time logic to deal with fairness. Research Report RR-292, IMAG, March, 1982, 30 p.

[10] Janicki R. On atomic nets and concurrency relations. Lecture Notes in Computer Science 88, Springer-Verlag, Berlin, 1980, p.320-333.

[11] Goltz V., Reisig W. Processes of place-transition nets. Lecture Notes in Computer Science, Springer-Verlag, Berlin, 1983, vol.154, p.264-277.

abstraction and for structuring systems in-the-large (i.e., for stepwise implementation, modularization and scoping) are underdeveloped.

Algebraic specification methods were taken because they give a precise interpretation of many useful high-level programming concepts, such as strong typing, generic operations and types, stepwise implementation and modularization. Classes of data objects can be specified independently from any representation of data and independently from any implementation of the operations of that class. A precise definition of correctness of implementation for abstract data types can be given [8,16], and writing modular specifications is supported by parameterization and combination mechanisms [9].

Non-sequential and distributed systems, however, consist of highly autonomous processing units that interact from time to time for exchanging information. This cannot be adequately specified in algebraic terms alone. These systems require an explicit description of externally observable behavior of their components in the sense of processes and interaction, and the designer must be able to clearly distinguish between concurrency, sequence and mutual exclusion of system operations. This distinction cannot be read into algebraic specifications because they rely on function application and thus entail a "natural sequentialization" [1].

A first approach to a unifying model, called *Decision-Action (DA) systems*, was described in [19]. But this description was mainly oriented towards net theoretic modeling concepts and did not yet fix a specific algebraic technique. The new idea, fully embodied in *SEGRAS*, is to use a variant of initial algebraic specification for specifying the invariant structure of DA systems. This variant is closely related to Horn logic.

SEGRAS may be contrasted with various other specification languages and methods, in particular with algebraic specification languages, such as Affirm [22], OBJ [15], and Clear [5]. Although Affirm has been used in combination with a state transition model to specify communication protocols, the authors themselves admit that their method is only able to "approximate the effect of concurrency" [27] by arbitrary interleaving of operations. Many approaches to distributed systems specifications are currently made with temporal logic (see, e.g., [20,28]). But these are not yet at the stage of a language — to be described in a reference manual and to be supported by tools. Various Petri net models have proven their use for specifying communication protocols in several practical applications [7]. However, these approaches emphasize control flow aspects and neglect data structuring aspects and stepwise implementation.

The following section reviews basic concepts of the specification method, while Section 3 introduces many language concepts along with small examples. In Section 4, a simple communication service is built upon the alternating bit protocol which models the service layer of a communication network. The protocol is synthesized from several separately developed system and data type abstractions; some properties of the protocol are analyzed by means of the invariance method.

2. Basic Concepts of the Method

2.1. Conditional Algebraic Specifications

Algebraic specifications define equivalence classes of values. Values, which we will call *data*, are time-invariant quantities. Hence, for data concepts of updating, sharing and instantiation have no meaning [21]. Constants in programming languages are examples for data, a fixed bitmap layout is an example for compound data.

An algebraic specification in our sense consists of a declaration of *type, function* and *test symbols* and of a set of universal Horn *rules* with positive conditions and one, possibly negative,

Stepwise Construction of Non-Sequential Software Systems Using a Net-Based Specification Language

Bernd Krämer
Institut für Systemtechnik, GMD Bonn
P.O. Box 1240
D-5205 St. Augustin 1

A specification language for non-sequential and distributed software systems is outlined by way of a series of examples. The language is based on an integration of initial algebra semantics and Predicate-Transition net semantics. Abstract system specifications are presented in terms of types, operations, conditional specifications and nets. The role of nets is to specify the behavior of a type of system in the sense of processes and their synchronisation. Domains, functions and relations, which make up the invariant structure of Predicate-Transition nets, are specified algebraically. The language supports modular and stepwise development of specifications applying and extending the algebraic concept of combination, parameterization and formal implementation to this kind of abstract systems specifications.

For illustration of the language features, we specify a simple communication service between two nodes of a computer network and partially implement it using the specification of three lower level types of systems that together comprise the alternating bit protocol.

1. Introduction

The aim of this paper is to illustrate the use of a net-based formal specification language, called *SEGRAS*, developed for the design and analysis of non-sequential and distributed software systems. The language relies on a careful integration of Predicate-Transition (PrT) nets [13,11] with place capacity one (called Predicate-Event nets, or PrE nets for short) and conditional algebraic specifications [9,29]. A syntax-directed editor for *SEGRAS* is already available [18]. It supports a convenient graphic notation of nets and a logic programming-like notation of conditional axioms and net constraints.

The reason why we took Net Theory [23,4] as one of the underpinning theories of *SEGRAS* is that it is particularly dedicated to modeling systems with decentralized control and shared components in a non-idealizing way. Communication and synchronization are described without reference to a global state and totally ordered time scale in the basic model of Condition-Event (CE) systems. For fundamental subtheories, useful formal notions and methods for verifying properties which concern the reliable coordination of operations in non-sequential systems have been developed. Partly, these methods are already implemented.

A weakness of conventional net models for a language approach is that concepts for data

I would like to thank the ADVANCES referee for helpful criticism of the preliminary version of this paper and my colleage H.W. Schmidt for his persevering collaboration in the development of the method presented and especially for his engagement in fixing the theoretical foundations; I am grateful to Frau Münch who prepared the excellent drawings.

conclusion. Type symbols name the carriers (i.e., the elements of an indexed family of sets) of a *typed* (many-sorted) *partial algebra*. Each function symbol names a total function, and each test symbol a partial function. It is beyond the scope of this paper to present the algebraic theory behind the language. Therefore, we only sketch the major differences to the basic algebraic specification and refer the interested reader to [26], where the algebraic background of *SEGRAS* is formalized.

2.1.1. Rules

Rules specify the mutual effects of operations. Their *normal form* is

$$\boxed{\langle lhs \rangle : \langle equ_1 \rangle, ..., \langle equ_n \rangle.} \text{ for } n \geq 0,$$

where the *premises* $\langle equ_i \rangle$ on the righthand side of a rule are equations and the *conclusion* $\langle lhs \rangle$ on the lefthand side is an equation $\boxed{e_l = e_r}$ or inequation $\boxed{e_l \neq e_r}$ between equally typed *expressions* e_l and e_r over function, test and variable symbols. Rules with the same conclusion $\boxed{e_l = e_r : \langle rhs_i \rangle.}$ or $\boxed{e_l \neq e_r : \langle rhs_j \rangle.}$ $(0 \leq i \leq m < j \leq n)$ can be abbreviated to[1]

$$\boxed{\begin{array}{ll} e_l = e_r: & \langle rhs_1 \rangle; ...; \\ & \langle rhs_m \rangle; \\ & \langle rhs_{m+1} \rangle, -; ...; \\ & \langle rhs_n \rangle, -. \end{array}}$$

The interpretation of a rule is similar to that of Horn logic except for the particularities of *weak equality* requiring that an equation $\boxed{e_l = e_r}$ is *satisfied* if and only if the expressions e_l and e_r are both defined and denote equal values in the algebra. Thus, the satisfaction of an inequation may be due to the undefinedness of either of its sides. The conclusion is satisfied if all premises $\langle equ_i \rangle$ of either alternative righthand side of a rule are satisfied. Because of inequality, inconsistencies, such as $e \neq e$, may arise. In such a case our specifications define no model at all. However, Schmidt and Kreowski have shown in [26] that if a specification is consistent its initial semantics is a data structure defined by the rules up to isomorphism.

Rules offer a convenient way for postulating definedness and undefinedness of some expression e because the rule $\boxed{e = e : \langle rhs \rangle.}$ ($\boxed{e = e : \langle rhs \rangle, -.}$) requires e to be defined (undefined) under the condition $\langle rhs \rangle$. As an abbreviation we write e – like a *literal* in a logical formula – instead of $e = e$.

2.1.2. Multiple-valued Operations and Product Types

We admit mutiple-valued operations viewing the cartesian product of types as a type automatically (i.e., without having to specify it separately). For this purpose we provide a standard tuple notation of product type values. As a special case of product formation the λ-ary product (or *unit type*) is allowed. A test with the unit result type is called a *predicate*. (Note that a test, generally, differs from a predicate because it may yield values if it is defined on the actual arguments.)

2.1.3. Parameterization and Abstract Implementation

SEGRAS offers three concepts for partitioning specifications into meaningful units and abstrac-

[1] Following the notation of the systems implementation langue CDL2 [2], we denote the logical "and" by ",", "or" by ";" and "not" (or better "fail") by "–"; the conclusion can be read like a procedure head and the logical combination of premises like a procedure body.

tion levels:

1. *Combination* and *separation* allow for incrementally putting together (or splitting up) specifications by forming the disjoint union of signatures (declarations) and rules. Constrained forms of these mechanisms, *extension* and *restriction*, guarantee that increments preserve the meaning of the incremented specification.
2. *Parameterization* allows for reducing a whole set of specifications to one schematic specification which is defined conditionally. The exact meaning of an actualized schema depends on the meaning of the actual parameter, i.e., of types, operations, and rules given elsewhere.
3. The separation of a unit into an *abstraction* and *implementation* serves the information hiding principle. The abstraction isolates the environment of use of an individual object from the environment of implementation of the whole class (type).

Parameterization and algebraic implementation as used in *SEGRAS* are not yet supported by a formal semantics. But we hope that the semantics of these concepts and the notion of correctness of implementation as defined by [8,29] can be carried over to our style of algebraic specification along the line taken in [26].

2.2. Behavior Specification

2.2.1. Systems

In contrast to the usual algebraic reading, we also consider mutable objects – more or less autonomous – that exist in time and space. They are called *systems* in *SEGRAS* and are the carriers of behavior. Examples for systems range from global variables in programs – understood as cells of variable contents with access primitives for defining and undefining that contents – up to complex distributed information systems, in which autonomous processors regularly check for data integrity.

A system has a *name* and a *state space.* In a given scope, the name allows one to identify uniquely a particular system and to examine and manipulate that system in different states. This is done by *actions* which are state changing operations with additional inputs (arguments) and outputs (results). The information in the system reached after certain executions is determined by *state tests* or *state functions.* These are mutable operations, i.e., they may yield different results when applied to the same argument – namely a system's name – at different "times". The definedness of a mutable operation and its actual result depend on the state of execution modelled by a net.

2.2.2. Informal Introduction to Decision-Action Systems

The behavior of these systems is specified by means of DA systems. DA systems are a variant of marked PrE nets (i.e., PrE systems) which offers additional syntactic concepts for modularization purposes and for specifying invariant assertions. (In [17] we give an example how to specify invariant assertions in *SEGRAS*.) Here, we can only sketch the conceptual differences of DA systems to the PrT net model introduced by Genrich and others in [11], and we refer the reader interested in theoretic issues to [25].

- Typed Nets. DA nets are a typed (many-sorted) version of PrT nets with capacity one, such that the syntax of net inscriptions and the specification of their meaning can be handled conveniently within the algebraic framework. For DA systems, algebras take over the role of the mathematical structure **U** associated with a PrT net in the original definition [13].

- **Named Event Schemes: Actions and Decisions.** In PrT nets, conditions of the underlying CE net are generated on the way of instantiating events, because only those conditions belong to the underlying system that are connected to events. For a schematic condition, different assignments to the same or to different event schemes may lead to the same condition (see below). The reason is that conditions are named by the instances of predicate symbols (e.g., P(2) or Q(1)); but these predicate symbols need not apply all those variable as arguments which are fixed by an assignment to some adjacent event scheme. For instance, P below does not apply variable *m*.

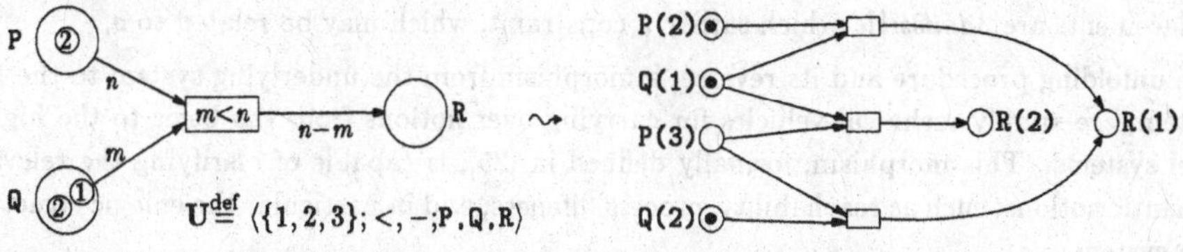

For events this is different. They are not named in PrT nets because the use of variable symbols is oriented towards an easy definition of the transition rule and thus towards the construction of synchronization graphs and processes. We also want an easy construction of high-level statemachine graphs [14] because statemachine decompositions play an important role with respect to modularity concepts in our method. Therefore, we name actions and decisions (event schemes) by tests and demand consistent replacement of variables only w.r.t. those variables occurring in such a test. Consequently, different assignments may lead to the same instance of an event. For example, if we wanted to name the action in the above system by test T, we could instantiate only a single event in the underlying net (cf. below left); if we named the action T(*m*) (or T(*n*)), two events in the above example were both named T(1) (T(2)) – and had to be identified, as illustrated by the net in the middle (right) below; if we named it T(*m*, *n*), we had get the same underlying net as above, where the events were named T(1,2), T(1,3) and T(2,3), from top to bottom.

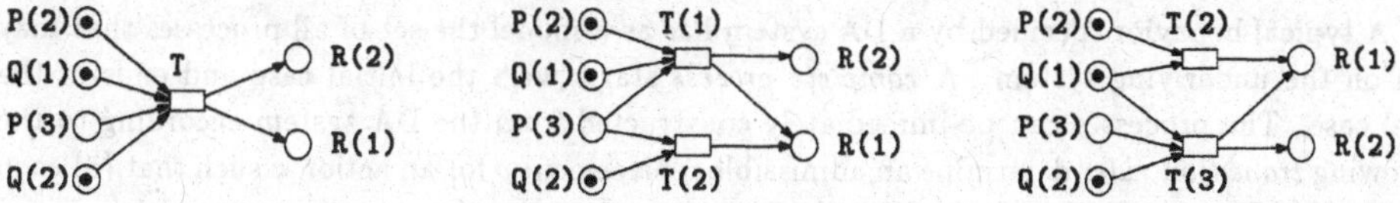

- **Syntax and Semantics.** For a specification language the separation of syntax and semantics is widely accepted. The reason is that one wants each syntactic scheme to induce a unique semantics, instead of enumerating the related mathematical structure or referring to well-known structures, such as sets, bags or strings.

The syntactic domain of a system specification is represented by a DA net, a specification of an initial case and some algebraic specification. Schematic conditions are inscribed with test or function symbols, actions and decisions with test symbols and arcs with *n*-tuples of expressions, where *n* is the number of different variables in the adjacent condition operation. The components of each tuple describe the replacement of the variables in the order of their first occurrence in the condition operation. Constraints related to actions and decisions are expressed by rules associated with the net. The result type of the test and function symbols inscribed to net symbols is always a distinguished *net type*[2] in the algebra. The flow relation

[2] This net type will, however, not appear on the syntactic level of *SEGRAS*. In the language, the distinction between functions and tests used in data type specifications and those used as net inscriptions is made by additional attributes in declarations, such as **test**, **state test**, **action**.

is algebraically conceived of as a binary relation on the carrier of this net type [25].

The meaning is determined by an algebra which uniquely defines a marked CE net, called the *underlying system*. The net can be constructed by instantiating all pairs (a_i, c_j) of adjacent actions a_i and condition schemes c_j in the following way: first, replace the variables in the selected c_j consistently by the components of the tuple on the arc — specifically the k-th variable by the k-th component, in the order of the first occurrence of some variable. Then, determine all flow relations of the underlying net by consistently replacing the remaining variables in the a_i and c_j by variable free expressions of appropriate type. Hereby, only those replacements are *admissible* which satisfy a constraint, which may be related to a_i.

The unfolding procedure and its reverse, a morphism from the underlying system to the DA system, are simply technical vehicles for carrying over notions from the basic to the higher level systems. This morphism, formally defined in [25], is capable of clarifying the relevant semantic notions, such as reachability, process, lifeness, and in particular the enlogic structure of a system.

- **Prelude and Postlude**. In DA systems, particular actions, called *prelude* and *postlude*, are used for specifying a marking class. All conditions of the underlying net that are flow related to an instance of a prelude belong to the initial case of a specific system of that type; all conditions connected to an instance of a postlude belong to its final case. All conditions of the final case are invalidated by an "occurrence" of a postlude such that none of the state changing actions of that system may occur afterwards. Actually, preludes and postludes are not actions in the usual net sense because they do not contribute to a system's behavior (see next section). For a uniform reading, however, they can be read like actions that have concession exactly once for a specific system. (In fig. 1 `init` denotes a prelude, and `annul` a postlude.)

2.2.3. Typical Behavior

A typical behavior specified by a DA system has as a model the set of all processes that may run on the underlying system. A *complete process* starts with the initial case and ends in the final case. The processes can be immediately constructed from the DA system according to the following *transition rule*: determine an admissible replacement ρ for an action a such that (a) each of the schematic preconditions pre_i of a carries a token for each instance of pre_i satisfying ρ, and (b) none of the schematic postconditions $post_j$ carries a token for each instance of $post_j$ satisfying ρ. Such an instance $\rho(a)$ has concession, and its occurrence removes all tokens determined from the pre_i and adds the tokens determined to the $post_j$. A process of the DA net in fig. 4, constructed in this way, is presented in fig. 5.

2.2.4. Typical Structure and Parts

The typical structure of a system is given by its composition of subsystems, terminating at the lowest level in *parts* (cf. [10] for net decomposition). Parts are particular high-level state-machine graphs with exactly one place which is inscribed with a *state function*, i.e., a totally defined mutable operation. The underlying system of a part is a state-machine graph [14]. Each instance of a prelude (or postlude) of a part must validate (invalidate) exactly one condition in the underlying system.

Fig. 1 gives an example for a part. c is a variable denoting the system type of interest; this variable is generally omitted in the arc inscritions because it colors the whole type of net and is, therefore, not relevant for the transition rule. n is a variable of data type **Nat'ural Numbers**.

∀ <u>Counter</u> c, <u>Nat</u> n:

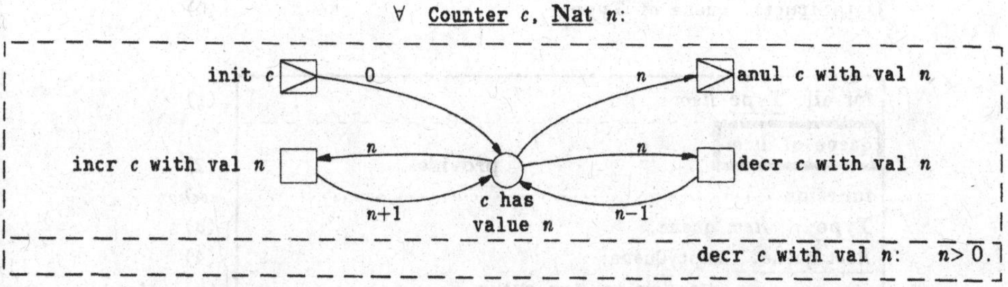

Figure 1: Decision-Action System for a Part of type Counter

The rule in the right lower corner constrains the set of events which can be instatiated from action decr c with val i by admissible replacements. So, the token (MyC,0) would describe an inadmissible replacement for this action because the associated constraint "$0 > 0$" is not satisfied. The underlying system is depicted in fig. 2. The net is infinite because the set of **Nat** expressions replacing variable n is infinite.

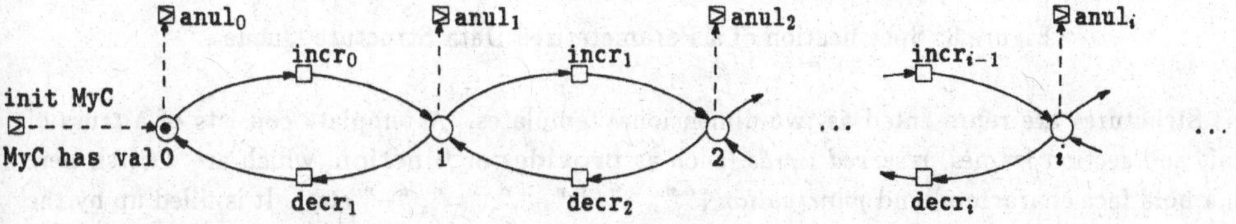

Legend: $\alpha_i \triangleq \alpha$ MyC with val i $\forall \alpha \in \{anul, decr, incr\}, 0 < i$

Figure 2: Underlying System of Fig. 1

Composition of parts a) based on shared resources (spatial congruence) leads to nondeterministic parts (coproduct of parts). Composition of parts b) based on interaction (temporal coincidence) leads to non-sequential systems (product of parts). The name of a non-sequential system determines the names of its coexisting subsystems by means of projection functions (see Section 3.2.3).

a) $c_1 \bigcirc \bullet \bigcirc c_2 \rightsquigarrow c_1 \bullet c_2 \bigcirc$ b) $a_1 \square \blacksquare \square a_2 \rightsquigarrow a_1 \blacksquare a_2 \square$

3. The Specification Language

This section describes the specification language $\mathcal{SEGRAS}$ in the form that is supported by our syntax-directed editor [18]. We refer to the examples in Fig. 3 and 4 when explaining the $\mathcal{SEGRAS}$ notation.

The basic device for structuring a $\mathcal{SEGRAS}$ description into a set of interrelated pieces is a *structure definition* – structure, for short. It is generally provided in two parts: an *abstraction* and, optionally, an *implementation*. The abstraction comprises a formal interface description. The implementation part hides details of how the interface is realized in terms of less abstract structures.

```
DataStruct:  queue of Type.                                  (0)
...
┌──────────────────────────────────────────────────────────┐
│ for all  Type Item                                       │ (1)
│           - - - - - - - - - - - - - - - - - - - - - - - -│
│ queue of Item                                            │
│                              provides                    │ (2)
│ ·function··························                      │  section
│ Type:    Item queue.                                     │ (3)
│ Item queue:  EmptyQueue;                                 │ (4)
│              enq Item to Item queue.                     │ (5)
│ ·test······························                      │  section
│ Item queue:  deq ↑Item from Item queue.                  │ (6)
│ ┌──────────────────────────────────────────────────────┐ │
│ │ for all  Item i, j, k    Item queue q, q'            │ │ ← leader
│ │ - - - - - - - - - - - - - - - - - - - - - - - - - - -│ │
│ │ (deq i from (enq i to EmptyQueue))= EmptyQueue:  .   │ │ (7)
│ │ (deq i from (enq j to q))= (enq j to (deq i from q)):│ │ (8)
│ │                                  q=enq k to q'.      │ │ ← unit
│ │ deq i from EmptyQueue:   -.                          │ │ (9)
│ └──────────────────────────────────────────────────────┘ │
└──────────────────────────────────────────────────────────┘
```

Figure 3: Specification of a Parameterized Data Structure Queue

Structures are represented as two-dimensional templates. A template consists of a truss of unit and section frames, *reserved words* (such as **provides** or **function**, which are written here in a bold face characters) and *punctuation* (":", ",", ";", ".", "=", "–" etc.). It is filled up by the designer with all the information constituting a specific structure.

3.1. Example

Fig. 3 presents a standard example for a data structure, namely a parameterized queue which simply specifies the FIFO property for any type of items. Variable *Item* ranges over the set of user-defined types (1). The variable represents a higher order argument of the structure specification that gets fixed when the structure is actualized.

3.2. Expression Syntax

The syntax of specification rules (7-9) has already been introduced in Section 2.1.1. Variables that are referred to in a unit or section must have been explicitly declared in a preceding *leader*. In this leader, the names of variables are enumerated and coupled with a specific type.

3.2.1. Declaration Rules

The declaration rules (3-6) determine the form of user-defined symbols to be used in specifications. Each application of a user-defined symbol must be preceded by a declaration. The lefthand side of such a rule (to the left of ":") denotes the result type, the righthand side introduces a particular symbol of that type. The unit result type is denoted by the empty tuple "()". As for specification rules, declarations with the same lefthand side can be abbreviated by use of ";".

Structure symbols are declared as particular functions the result type of which is either the predefined type DataStruct (0) or SystemStruct. An application of such a function identifies a particular specification, or scheme of specifications (2) if the structure symbol has arguments.

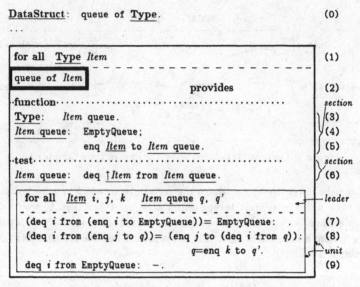

User-defined *type symbols* are introduced as particular functions the result type of which is the predefined data type Type (3) or System (cf. fig. 4). Among all types to be defined, system types form a subset. Systems are *instances* of system types. Type symbols may occur in infix or outfix *parameter positions* of symbols to denote a formal parameter (4-6) of that symbol. (Formal parameter positions are underscored here.)

3.2.2. Relational Notation and Derived Parameters

For the sake of syntactic flexibility, *SEGRAS* supports both a functional and a relational notation (as used in Prolog [6]). For the latter purpose, we allow for infix result parameters of operation symbols (6), called *derived parameters*, to In the declaration, derived parameter positions are preceded by "↑" to distinguish them from arguments. The user is free to view an operation with derived parameters as a many-to-one relation between its arguments and derived parameters without loosing the functionality of the operation symbol. For example, the indication of a derived parameter position for the test (6) in fig. 3 can be equivalently expressed by rule:

$$i=j: \quad (\texttt{deq}\ i\ \texttt{from}\ q)=(\texttt{deq}\ j\ \texttt{from}\ q).$$

3.2.3. Universal Type Constructions

In *SEGRAS* we offer some universal type constructions, namely cartesian product, disjoint union, and sequence. They are represented as specification units which apply the predefined operator ":=:". Such type constructions by convention stand for appropriate specifications. The following rule, taken from fig. 6, gives an example of a cartesian *product* of types (a record in Pascal), with user-defined *projection functions* sendq of_ and receiveq of_.

```
Node :=:  (Data queue:  sendq of_, Data queue:  receiveq of_).
```

This rule stands for the following specification:

```
function  Node:          (Data queue, Data queue).
function  Data queue:    sendq of Node;
                         receiveq of Node.

for all Node n,  Data queue q1, q2
        (sendq of n, receiveq of n)=n: .
        sendq of (q1, q2)=q1: .
        receiveq of (q1, q2)=q2: .
```

A *sequence* of equal subtypes can be declared by applying a projection function to a variable which ranges over some other type than the sequence type and its subtype. An example is given in fig. 4.

Disjoint *union* of types is simply declared by type *coercions*. An example is given in data structure Message in Appendix A, saying that the values of data type Msg are either of type MarkedData or of type NullMsg.

3.3. Actualization of Parameterized Structures

A parameterized structure is declared as structure symbol with inherited parameter positions. Syntactically,actualization can be understood as a kind of macro expansion uniformly replacing all occurrences of structure variables in the template by appropriate expressions. For instance, the consistent substitution of variable *Item* in our previous example by an actual parameter,

SystemStruct: queue of **Type**

...

for all **Type** *Item*

queue of *Item* — provides

function

System: *Item* queue; PotentialPair. (1)

Type: TwoItemsOrNil; *Item* in queue. (2)

TwoItemsOrNil: *Item* in queue/*Item* in queue; Nil. (3)

Item in queue: *Item*; Front; Tail. (4)

for all **Nat** *n*
Item queue :=: (**PotentialPair**: pair *n* in _). (5)

state function

PotentialPair <↑TwoItemsOrNil>. (6)

action

establish →*Item* queue;

enq *Item* to ↔*Item* queue [↑Nat, ↑*Item* in queue]; (7)

deq ↑*Item* from ↔*Item* queue [↑Nat, ↑*Item* in queue];

dissolve *Item* queue [↑Nat, ↑*Item* in queue].

for all *Item* in queue *l*, *s* *Item* *i* TwoItemsOrNil *t* *Item* queue *q* Nat *n*, *m*
such that 0 <*m*

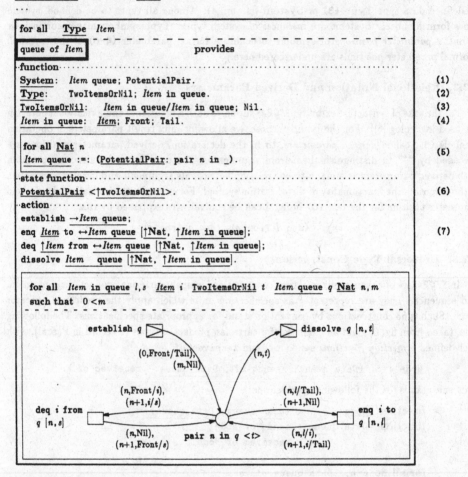

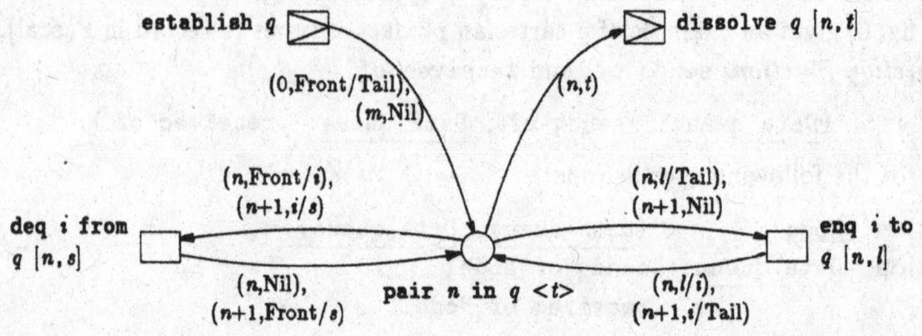

Figure 4: Specification of a Distributed Queue with Concurrent Enq- and Deq-Operations

say Msg[3], leads to the actualized specification queue of Msg. Such actualized specifications are again combinations in the sense of forming the disjoint union of types, operations and rules of the parameterized structure and the actual parameter type. This schematization mechanism also helps for avoiding naming conflicts, which may result from different actualization in the same scope, because the name of the parameter can be made part of type and operation symbols in the parameterized specification. (See, e.g., decisions `loose Msg` and `loose Bit` in of structure `TransportService` in Appendix A, which result from different actualizations of structure "*Package* `transmitter`".)

From the semantical point of view, it is yet unclear to what extend the standard parameter passing concept for algebraic specifications of abstract data types in [9] can be carried over here.

3.4. Example: A Queue with Concurrent Enq- and Deq-Operations

[3] See Appendix A for the specification of this type.

Fig. 4 is a respecification of our first example. From the rules in fig. 3 we could not conclude objectively whether the operations provided by the data structure may occur concurrently or not. However, the specification in fig. 4 clearly reveals that all instances of action **enq** may only occur in sequence; the same holds for all instances of **deq**. But each instance of **enq** is concurrent to any instance of **deq** for different items, provided that the actual queue contains more than one item. The FIFO property of the previous specification is kept herein, but additionally a distribution of the queue has been modelled, at the price of introducing a particular "representation" of the queue objects. Our second model also comes closer to our practical experience, from which we know that one may line up independently from another member at the front of that queue just leaving. The model embodied in our specification also reflects a specific way of queueing up by simply looking for ones predecessor, e.g., when entering a doctor's waiting room.

This specification requires some more types: two system types (1), namely *Item* **queue** – modeling the queue – and **PotentialPair** – modeling the type of parts which constitute a queue; further, we introduce two data types in (2) that serve for specifying the structure of tokens that may flow in the net. Function "_/_" in (3) relates two subsequently entered items to model the "direct successor-" relationship, and **Nil** represents an empty position beyond the true (i.e., occupied part of a) queue. Type *Item* **in queue** was introduced in (4) to require that all values of any actual parameter type, replacing *Item* in an actualization of the system structure, must be disjoint from the constant functions **Front** and **Tail**. These distinct values serve for selecting the appropriate item in case of an application of **enq** or **deq**. (5) schematically declares a system of type *Item* **queue** to consist of an infinite sequence[4] of parts of type **PotentialPair**. The state function in (6) refers to these parts only because we wanted to express any state change of some queue in terms of state changes of its parts.

The declaration section (7) introduces a prelude, two actions and a postlude. Here, we can see three additional kinds of parameter positions, indicating the establishment "→", the dissolution "←", or a change "↔" of an instance of the system type, which are caused by an occurrence of these actions. Some of the action symbols have a *hidden* part which is enclosed in square brackets. The hidden part of a symbol is not visible to the environment of use, and therefore declares no arguments for an outside application. So, it indicates that particular actions may appear identical to the observer but are considered different inside the system. This difference is based on additional variable bindings in the hidden part of an expression. Take, for example, action **deq** *i* **from** *q* [*n*,*s*] and the instances

deq (ThisItem) from (MyQ) [5,Tail], **deq (ThisItem) from (MyQ) [5,NextItem]**

Theses instances denote different events in the underlying system if **NextItem** and **Tail** denote different values in the algebra. The first were connected to conditions

pair 5 in (MyQ)<Front/ThisItem>, **pair 6 in (MyQ)<ThisItem/Tail>**[†]
pair 5 in (MyQ)<Nil>, **pair 6 in (MyQ)<Front/Tail>**

and the second to

pair 5 in (MyQ)<Front/ThisItem>, **pair 6 in (MyQ)<ThisItem/NextItem>**[‡]
pair 5 in (MyQ)<Nil>, **pair 6 in (MyQ)<Front/NextItem>**

When considering only the unbracketed part of **deq** only, we can instantiate exactly one event which is named **deq (ThisItem) from (MyQ)** and is connected to all of the above conditions. But there will never be a case containing both condition (†) and (‡), so that this event would never have concession.

[4] The unbounded size of queue systems causes no problems due to the axiomatic nature of our specifications, so that underlying system can be recursively enumerated.

3.4.1. Relating Data Structures to System Structures

Our favorite design style is to have a data structure as an abstraction of any system structure, such that the data structure isolates the essential structural properties and the system structure additionally provides for the essential behavioral properties. Furthermore, we aim at a standard implementation mechanism that ensures the correctness of implementation — as far as structural properties of a system specification are concerned. To give a flavor of how this is meant and what the basis of correctness considerations could be here, we discuss relevant notions along our previous examples of a queue and a distrubuted queue.

Proposition. The specification of system structure queue of *Item* in fig. 4 (Sq, for short) fulfils the FIFO property specified for data structure queue of *Item* (Dq) in fig. 3 — for all common actualizations.

To convince the reader of our observations, we first show that each expression which can be formed in Dq is represented by a case in Sq (completeness); then we demonstrate that all expressions which denote different values in Dq are represented by different cases in Sq (consistency)[5].

Completeness. It is easy to see that the expression EmptyQueue is represented by the initial case

$$c_0 = \{\texttt{pair(0)in(MyQ)<Front/Tail>},\ \texttt{pair}(i)\texttt{in(MyQ)<Nil>} \mid \forall i \geq 1\}.$$

In c_0 only an instance of enq may occur; this restriction corresponds to rule (9) in Dq. An occurrence of some enq in c_0 leads into some case c_1, in which both any instance of enq or deq may occur; this corresponds to rule (7) in Dq.

Now, assume a queue of length k. It is equivalent to an expression "$e = \texttt{enq}^k(i_k)\texttt{to(EmptyQueue)}$" – according to rules (7,8) in Dq – and is assumed to be represented by some case c. Then for $1 \leq k$, the following equation is satisfied:

$$\texttt{enq}(i_{k+1})\texttt{to}(e) = \texttt{enq}^{k+1}(i_{k+1})\texttt{to(EmptyQueue)}$$

This is represented by a case c' with

$$c' - c = \{\texttt{pair}(n+k)\texttt{in(MyQ)}< i_k/i_{k+1} >,\ \texttt{pair}(n+k+1)\texttt{in(MyQ)}< i_{k+1}/\texttt{Tail}>\}$$
$$c - c' = \{\texttt{pair}(n+k)\texttt{in(MyQ)}< i_k/\texttt{Tail}>,\ \texttt{pair}(n+k+1)\texttt{in(MyQ)<Nil>}\}$$

$\texttt{deq}(i_1)\texttt{from}(e) = \texttt{enq}^j(i_j)\texttt{to(EmptyQueue)}$, with $1 < j \leq k$, is represented by a case c'' with

$$c - c'' = \{\texttt{pair}(n)\texttt{in(MyQ)<Front/}i_1 >,\ \texttt{pair}(n+1)\texttt{in(MyQ)}< i_1/x >\}$$
$$c'' - c = \{\texttt{pair}(n)\texttt{in(MyQ)<Nil>},\ \texttt{pair}(n+1)\texttt{in(MyQ)<Front/}x >\}$$

and $x \in \{i_2,\texttt{Tail}\}$. For $k = 0$ (i.e., $e = $ EmptyQueue), e is represented by the initial case c_0 or one of the cases

$$c^n = \{\texttt{pair}(j)\texttt{in(MyQ)<Nil>},\ \texttt{pair}(n)\texttt{in(MyQ)<Front/Tail>} \mid \forall j \in (\mathrm{N} \cup 0)\backslash n\}\ \forall n \in \mathrm{N} \cup 0.$$

In c^n only an instance of enq may occur leading to an obvious case in which both kinds of actions of Sq may occur.

Consistency can be shown by constructing processes in Sq according to the structure of expressions in Dq, and to compare the resulting cases with these expressions. Because of steps, we consider each process as an equivalence class of lines, such that each line corresponds to a particular expression. Then, we have only to prove that equivalent lines leading to the same case correspond to equivalent expressions in Dq. We shall content ourselves with an illustration of one crucial situation of our example. The occurrence net in fig. 5, for instance, provides for two lines because of the step G= {deq *a* from MyQ, enq *c* to MyQ}. But these equivalent lines correspond to the expressions

[5] But we allow that different cases in Sq represent the same expression in Dq.

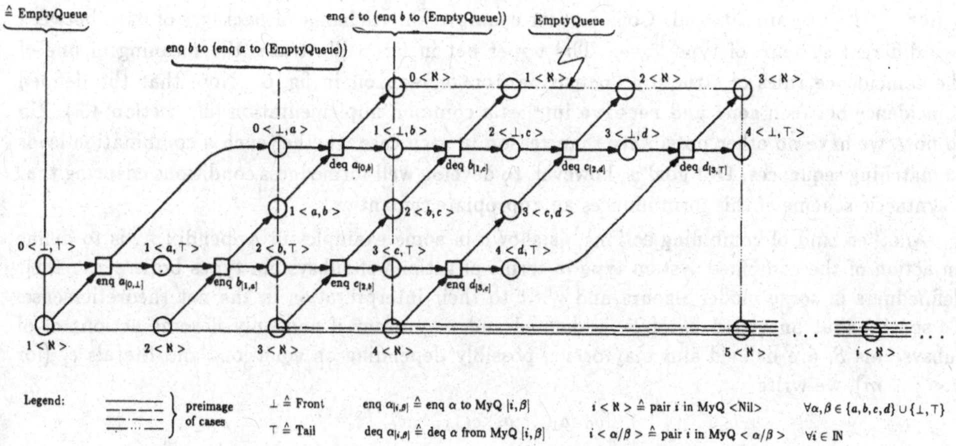

Figure 5: A Process of Fig. 4

enq *c* to (deq *a* from(enq *b* to(enq *a* to(EmptyQueue))))
deq *a* from(enq *c* to (enq *b* to(enq *a* to(EmptyQueue))))

which are equivalent according to rules (7) and (8) in Dq. A complete check can be performed by induction over the structure of expressions in Dq and of processes in Sq.

3.5. System Interaction and Combination of Nets

For data structures, it is clear from the work done by ADJ [29] and others what the notion of combination, extension or enrichment semantically mean; and these results hopefully apply to our specification technique for data structures under the condition that the specifications are consistent.

For system structures the situation is new because we have to deal with net specifications, too. The simplest case is a system structure S combined from system structures $S_1, \ldots, S_n$ by defining the system type of interest in S as the product or sequence of system types provided by the S_i and forming the union of operations, rules and nets inherited from the S_i's. However, if S provides for new actions, we have to decide how these can be expressed in terms of actions of the S_i to arrive at a useful notion of combination and correctness of implementation.

With regard to composition and decomposition of systems, we are mainly interested in the interaction of coexisting (sub-) systems. Interaction is semantically based on matching sequences of events occurring in the processes defined for the subsystems. This is to ensure that all proccesses that may run independently on the subsystems, are embedded in processes that may run on a system of the combined type.

Matching sequences can be schematically specified by making a set of actions of different types of subsystems coincide. Let a_i be actions of different types of subsystems S_i of S_0 and c_j equations or literals; then the rule

$$a_1 \blacksquare a_2 \blacksquare \ldots a_k\colon\ c_1,\ \ldots,\ c_m.$$

abbreviates from the following set of rules for $1 \leq i < k, 1 < j \leq k, i < j$

$$a_i = a_j\colon\ c_1,\ \ldots,\ c_m,\ a_i,\ a_j.$$

saying that every two events in the underlying system that can be instantiated from a_i and a_j are equal if both are defined and denote equal values in the model algebra and if the conditions

c_l (for $1 \leq l \leq m$) are satisfied. Consider, for example, the exchange of packages of data between two different systems of type Node. The upper net in fig. 8 illustrates the meaning of one of the coincidence rules of structure CommunicationConnection in fig. 6. Note that the defined coincidence between send and receive implies a common implementation (cf. section 4.3). Up to now, we have no other possibility than reason in each case whether such a combination leads to matching sequences. Our goal is, however, to develop well-formedness conditions ensuring that a syntactic scheme of this form induces an appropiate semantics.

Another kind of combining actions, as shown in some examples in Appendix A, is to define an action of the combined system type in terms of actions of subsystem types both w.r.t. their definedness in some model algebra and w.r.t to their interpretation in the net theoretic sense. To specify that an action a_0 of S_0 is defined and may occur if and only if some actions a_i of subsystems S_i are defined and may occur, possibly depending on equations and literals c_j (for $k < j \leq m$), we write

$$a_0\colon a_1, \ldots, a_k, c_{k+1}, \ldots, c_m.$$

4. Stepwise Specification of a Communication Service

4.1. Communication Layer

```
SystemStruct: Node; CommunicationConnection.

Node        provides queue of (Data)     and
function ........................................
System:   Node.

  Node :=: (Data queue: sendq of_,
            Data queue: receiveq of_).
action ..........................................
deliver Data to ↔Node;    take ↑Data from ↔Node;
↔Node send ↑Data;     ↔Node receive Data;
establish node →Node;    dissolve node ←Node.

  for all  Node n  Data  d
  - - - - - - - - - - - - - - - - - - - - - - -
  establish node n:  establish (sendq of n),
                     establish (receiveq of n).
  (deliver d to n) = (enq d to (sendq of n)):
                     enq d to (sendq of n).
  (n send d) = (deq d from (sendq of n)):
                     deq d from (sendq of n).
  (n receive d) = (enq d to (receiveq of n)):
                     enq d to (receiveq of n).
  (take d from n) = (deq d from (receiveq of n)):
                     deq d from (receiveq of n).
  dissolve n:    dissolve (sendq of n),
                 dissolve (receiveq of n).
```

```
CommunicationConnection   provides Node, Data
                          and
function ........................................
System:   ComCon.

  ComCon :=: (Node: n1 of_, Node: n2 of_).
action ..........................................
establish →ComCon;    dissolve ←ComCon.

  for all  ComCon cc  Data  d
  - - - - - - - - - - - - - - - - - - - - - - -
  establish cc: establish node (n1 of cc),
                establish node (n2 of cc).
  ((n1 of cc) send d)=((n2 of cc) receive d):.
  ((n1 of cc) receive d)=((n2 of cc) send d):.
  dissolve cc:  dissolve node (n1 of cc),
                dissolve node (n2 of cc).
.................................................
AB-Protocol    implemented on TransportService
state function ..................................
service of Comcon ready.
function ........................................
ComCon:  Service.
...
  for all  Service ab  Service ts  Msg m  Bit b
  - - - - - - - - - - - - - - - - - - - - - - -
  service of ab ready:
     (ab sendr)<Ready,m,b>,
       (ab receivr)<Wait,Nil,switch(b)>,
        (ab send-receive)<Empty>,
         (ab receive-send)<Empty>.
...
```

Figure 6: System Type Node composed of two independent Queues, and ComCon composed of two Interacting Nodes

Consider two nodes in a distributed network. They communicate with each other via a lower level transmission service. The user of a node is provided a deliver service for some data package to

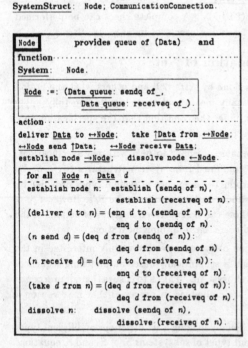

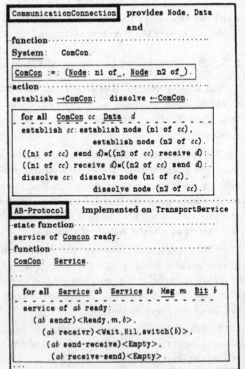

be transmitted to the other node, where the user is provided a service to take a data package sent. The other way round works analogously. In the specification of fig. 6 both sending and receiving part of a node are modelled by systems of type `Data queue`, resulting from an actualization of structure `queue of` *Item* in fig. 4. System structure `Node` in fig. 6 is an extension of the latter since it introduces a new type and several derived operations for renaming some actions of type `Data queue` and comprising the concurrent establishment and dissolution of the subsystems. A state of an instance of type Node is implied by a conjunction of the actual states of its two queue subsystems.

In a similar way, a communication connection can be specified as a combination of `Node`. But other than in the previous example, `CommunicationConnection` restricts the behavior defined by structure `Node` for systems of type `Node`. We require that action `send` of one node and action `receive` of the other node *coincide*, i.e., we disregard transmission slack or package loss on this level of abstraction.

4.2. Service Layer

The idealized communication described in the preceding section is now built on a transmission service taking into account that data packages may be lost, duplicated, or delayed. We assume that packages are transmitted from a sender to a remote receiver over an unreliable half-duplex transmission line and that these behave according to the the alternating bit protocol [3]. This protocol ensures reliable data transmission unless the connection is not completely interrupted. The protocol uses a single bit to represent the sequence number of a transmission cycle. Data and bit are formed to a message, which is repeatedly transmitted until it is acknowledged by the receiver in terms of a single bit. Only one message or acknowledgement is handled at a time.

The specification task has been decomposed into several steps of components' specifications from which the AB protocol is reconstructed by synthesis. All specifications are given in Appendix A. The combination graph in Appendix B shows the relationships between the structures induced by combination and actualization.

4.2.1. Stepwise Specification of the Alternating Bit Protocol

Sender. A system of type `Sender` is specified as a part referring to three values of the following data types: the `CntlState` component serves for distinguishing the intermediate states between the relevant actions of a sender; `Msg` is a union type, either being a pair of values of type `Data` and `Bit` or is a single value of type `NullMsg`; the acknowledgements received from a connected receiver are simply `Bit` values. The values referred to by this part have been used to distinguish three relevant states by inscribing them with different expressions over the state function. Because these expressions fix some of the derived values, they act as predicates, here, and can be considered as ***assertions*** about the behavior of this part. Such specified assertions can be used for consistency checking of the behavior specification.

Receiver. Structure and behavior of `Receiver` systems are similar to that of `Sender` systems. However, the actual sequence number is handled differently because the receiver runs after the sender in transmission cycles; this is reflected in the rules specifying constraints for action occurrences and in the initial case.

Message Loss. The conflict between the instances of actions `receive` and `lack` in the behavior of a `Sender` or `Receiver` system models the possibility that a message either may be received in time or is missing, which is usually recognized by a time-out mechanism in a concrete implementation. In our abstract specification, receiving an acknowledgement or message consists of the occurrence of one instance of action receive, while lack implies the definite omission [10] of all possible instances of receive.

Transmitter. A new aspect of *Package* transmitter is that the symbols transmit and loose *Package* are declared to be *decision* alternatives. We wanted to express that the choice, whether a package is transmitted or lost, depends on the transmitter and influences the behavior of the interacting sender or receiver. As explained in [19], decisions indicate conflict resolution depending on the environment of implementation, whereas actions express synchronization with the environment of use only. If two actions are in conflict, the initiative to resolve that conflict is assigned to the environment of use. By this distinction, the initiative to decide a conflict in a decomposed system is properly assigned to only one of several interacting systems, for each conflict situation.

4.2.2. Synthesizing the Protocol

A TransportService between two nodes can now be synthesized from four systems: one of type Sender, Receiver, Msg transmtr, and Bit transmtr. The rules of the combined system structure require certain actions of the four subsystems to coincide. The resulting protocol net is shown in fig. 8. It can be systematically reconstructed from the specifications of TransportService and the structures it is built upon. (The protocol net is similar to the net derived in [24], but our solution avoids confusion.)

4.2.3. Analyzing the Protocol

In a first step, let us isolate the relevant behavior in terms of an ordinary CE net by refraining from the algebraic specifications associated with the protocol net. This is useful because the interpretation of integer-valued S-invariants is much easier and suggestive; and it is appropriate because, for instance, the sender component in our protocol net unfolds into an underlying net which consists of $2n$ subnets formed by the conditions MyS<Ready,m,Nil>, MyS<Wait,m,Nil>, MyS<Receivd,m,b > and the events "MyS send m", "MyS lack ackn $[m]$", "MyS receive b $[m]$" and "MyS ignore previous ackn $[m,b]$", one for each Msg m, b either BitOn or BitOff, and n the number of different values for m in the model algebra. These subnets are spirally connected by the flows "(MyS<Received,m,b >,MyS accept ackn and take next d $[m,m',b]$)" and "(MyS accept ackn and take next d $[m,m',b]$, MyS<Ready,m,Nil>)".

For example we would like to prove that in any case

1. exactly one of the four protocol components is active, i.e., either
   (a) the sender is handling an acknowledgement received or a message to be sent,
   (b) the receiver is handling a message received or and acknowledgement to be sent, or
   (c) either of the transmission lines currently transmits a message or bit respectively;
2. Sender and receiver are in either of their states "Wait", "Receivd", or "Ready";
3. Each transmission direction is occupied by at most one package.

These properties can be proved using S-invariants:
let $M \in [M_0]$ an arbitrary follower marking of $M_0 = \{$S.Receivd[6], R.Wait, SR.Empty, RS.Empty$\}$, which results from the prelude;

1. The first property holds with
   $i_1 = M(\text{S.Wait})+M(\text{R.Wait})+M(\text{SR.Empty})+M(\text{RS.Empty})=3$

[6] S.Receivd stands for the condition (*TS* sendr)<Receivd,...> etc., m and b represent any value of type Msg or Bit respectively.

and with
i_2 = M(S.Receivd)+M(S.Ready)+M(R.Receivd)+M(R.Ready)+M(SR.m)+M(RS.b)=1
This invariant also ensures the alternating use of the half-duplex line by sender and receiver in either direction.

2. The second property follows from
i_3 = M(S.Wait)+M(S.Receivd)+M(S.Ready)=1 and
i_4 = M(R.Wait)+M(R.Receivd)+M(R.Ready)=1
3. The last property stated follows from
i_5 = M(SR.Empty)+M(SR.m)=1 and i_6 = M(RS.Empty)+M(RS.b)=1

S-invariants i_j ($j = 3,...,6$) generate four S-components [14] which correspond to the four subsystems of a Service system, while i_1 and i_2 correspond to two overlapping state machines: one comprising the passive states and one the active states of all subsystems. With the given initialization M_0, each S-component gets one token.

The T-invariants of the simplified protocol net generate a set of T-components and confirm the different transmission cycles which are carried by the net such as a) message or b) acknowledgement loss, c) loss of both, and d) a successful cycle without loss. The specified protocol is both life and safe. For instance, the support of T-invariant t_1

{s.send■sr.get, sr.loose Msg■r.lack msg, r.send■rs.get, rs.transmit■s.receive, s.accept or ignore[7]}

generates the subnet which describes a transmission cycle with message loss.

In a second analysis step, we forget about the Msg and Bit component in the algebraic structure, and only regard the subnet representing the Sender subsystem. We also draw the remaining constants of type CntlState from the state tests into the arc inscriptions, getting the following matrix representation of this subnet:

	send	lack	receive	accept	M_0	M_1	M_2	$\hat{f}$	$\hat{g}$
s<Ready>	− <Ry>	<Ry>		<Ry>	<Ry>			<Wg> · <Rd>	<Ry>
s<Wait>	<Wg>	− <Wg>	− <Wg>			<Wg>		<Ry> · <Rd>	<Wg>
s<Receivd>			<Rd>	− <Rd>			<Rd>	<Ry> · <Rd>	<Rd>

Figure 7: Incidence Matrix of the simplified Sender Net

The initial marking M_0 for some Service system protocol follows from an occurrence of prelude start (protocol) of structure TransportService.

According to [12] for $M \in [M_0\rangle \stackrel{\text{def}}{=} \{M_0, M_1, M_2\}$.
f(M) =<Ready> · <Wait> · <Receivd> is a linear type-1 S-invariant and
g(M)=1 is a linear type-2 S-invariant which corresponds to i_3 in the preceding discussion.

4.3. Using the AB Protocol to Implement the Communication Service

In fig. 8 we illustrate the implementation of structure CommunicationConnection by structure TransportService. Some declarations necessary for implementation are given in the implementation variant named AB protocol of CommunicationConnection in fig. 6. The implementation is graphically specified in fig. 8 by a net morphism. To keep the example easy to survey, only one communication direction – from Sender to Receiver – is shown. Furthermore, we have concentrated on the implementation of the higher level service action send ■ receive and implemented

[7] As the distinction between action accept and ignore only comes from the algebraic structure associated with the protocol net, these actions are folded to one action in the ordinary net to obey the requirement of simplicity.

it by a repetitive pattern of send, receive, and transmit actions on the lower level, obeying the AB protocol. The generic send and receive actions cause no problem since they can be uniquely distinguished by their parameter types Node, Sender and Receiver.

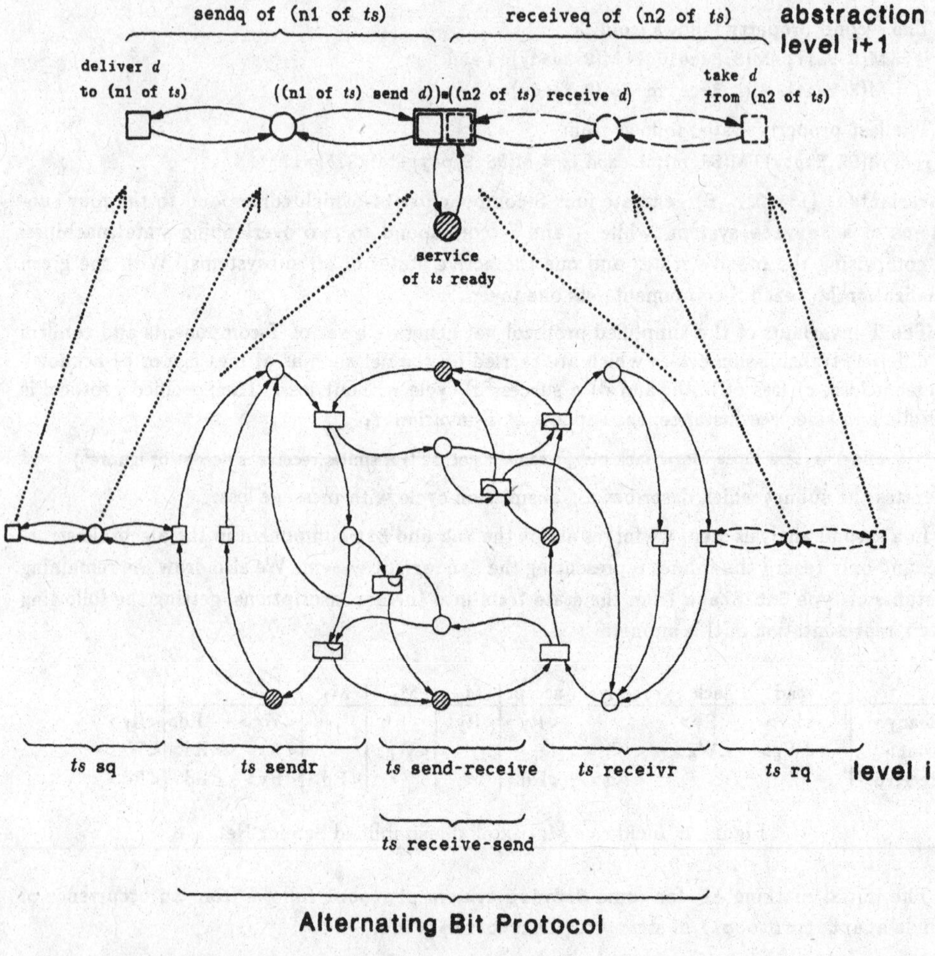

Figure 8: Implementing CommunicationConnection by TransportService

<u>Correctness</u>. The problem to find a formal notion of correctness system structure implementations is even more difficult than for pure algebraic implementations because behavior is involved. It requires to ensure that all processes that may run on the abstract specification are accomplished by processes that may run on the lower level specifications, taking into account all the implications established by the implementation. As far as the algebra of nets [25] is concerned, the results of [8], hopefully, apply. However, we lack appropriate correctness criteria w.r.t. behavior.

Therefore, we only perform a plausibility check that the processes running on TransportService (Ts) are embedded in (i.e., are preimages of) processes running on CommunicationConnection (Cc). We only discuss the implementation of the send ■ receive action.

It is easy to see that each initial case of Ts, which is graphically indicated by hatching, implies

an initial case of Cc with its queues being empty. In the initial case only an instance of **deliver** in Cc and of enq in Ts may occur. For non-empty send queues on both levels (which correspond one-to-one), we observe that an occurrence of send ▪ receive in Cc causes a change in Ts from some case $c1$ to case $c2$. This can be schematically described by (the relevant Bit and Data values are stressed by underscoring)

$$\begin{aligned} c1 - c2 = \{&\texttt{pair}(n-1)\texttt{in(Ts sq)<Front/}\underline{d_n}\texttt{>)},\ \texttt{pair}(n)\texttt{in(Ts sq)<}\underline{d_n}/d_{n+1}\texttt{>},\\ &\texttt{(Ts sendr)<Ready,}(d_{n-1},\underline{b})\texttt{,Nil>},\ \texttt{(Ts send-receive)<Empty>},\\ &\texttt{(Ts receivr)<Wait,Nil,}\underline{\texttt{switch}(b)}\texttt{>},\ \texttt{(Ts receive-send)<Empty>},\\ &\texttt{pair}(n-1)\texttt{in(Ts rq)<}\ d_{n-1}\texttt{/Tail>},\ \texttt{pair }(n)\texttt{in(Ts rq)<Nil>}\} \end{aligned}$$

$$\begin{aligned} c2 - c1 = \{&\texttt{pair}(n-1)\texttt{in(Ts sq)<Nil>)},\ \texttt{pair}(n)\texttt{in(Ts sq)<Front/}d_{n+1}\texttt{>},\\ &\texttt{(Ts sendr)<Ready,}(\underline{d_n},\underline{\texttt{switch}(b)})\texttt{,Nil>},\ \texttt{(Ts send-receive)<Empty>},\\ &\texttt{(Ts receivr)<Wait,Nil,}\underline{b}\texttt{>},\ \texttt{(Ts receive-send)<Empty>},\\ &\texttt{pair}(n-1)\texttt{in(Ts rq)<}\ d_{n-1}/\underline{d_n}\texttt{>},\ \texttt{pair}(n)\texttt{in(Ts rq)<}\underline{d_n}\texttt{/Tail>}\} \end{aligned}$$

$$\texttt{for } 0 < n,\ \underline{\texttt{Data in queue}}\ d_{n-1}, d_{n+1},\ \underline{\texttt{Data}}\ d_n,\ \underline{\texttt{Bit}}\ b$$

This change describes one successful transmission cycle with possible intermediate losses on the service level, and leads into a case $c2$ which allows for another transmission with an inverted sequence number, if the send queues are not empty.

Current Status and Future Work

We presented an elaborate specification language for designing and abstractly implementing non-seqential and distributed systems. The language offers a convenient surface including graphical representations. It is based on a well-engineered integration of two establish but complementary formalisms, namely Petri net theory and initial algebra. Although the formal semantics of the language is not as far developed as the syntax and informal semantics, it allows for useful experiments with designs of large systems.

Further work is required to secure the formal grounds of stepwise implementation of system structures, to delevelop testing and simulation concepts, and to find verification methods, particularly taking into account concepts for structuring systems in the large. We think of incremental analysis methods that may be applied to single system structures for local checks of necessary conditions and to postpone global analysis (of sufficient conditions) for the remaining problems. As to data structure specifications, formal proof methods for standard algebraic specifications apply to our method. As to system type specifications, similar techniques for verifying implementation correctness are not available yet. Although the implementation of a single action can be understood as a homomorphic mapping into a partial sequence of actions on a lower specification level, there are problems coming from the adjacent states and the possibility of cyclic behavior in the lower level net. A further problem is the systematic treatment of actions and states at the borderline of a refinement with respect to their correct embedding into both levels of behavior specification.

Many of the ideas on the formal specification and implementation of type abstractions and on graphical software specification have not been tested in practice, since their application to large systems requires an extensive level of interactive computer assistance. This was our motivation to implement a prototype version of an interactive syntax-directed editor for *SEGRAS*. The editor will be provided with useful analysis and simulation functions in later stages.

The described concepts and future tasks constitute a central part of the project GRASPIN that centers around formal and graphical specification of software systems and is going to develop the prototype of a workstation for the design and implementation of non-sequential systems. GRASPIN is supported in part by the Commission of the European Communities under the ESPRIT program.

REFERENCES

[1] Bauer, F.L. and Wössner, H., "Algorithmic language and program development", Springer-Verlag Berlin, Heidelberg, New York (1982)

[2] Bayer, M., Böhringer, B., Dehottay, J.P., Feuerhahn, H., Jasper, J., Koster, C.H.A. and Schmiedecke, U., *Software Development in the CDL2 Laboratory*, in "Software Engineering Environments", Hünke, H. (Ed.), North-Holland Publishing Company, ISBN 3-444-86133-5 (1981), 97–118

[3] Bochmann, G.v., "Architecture of Distributed Computer Systems", Lecture Notes in Computer Science **77**, Springer-Verlag Berlin, Heidelberg, New York, ISBN 3-540-09723-6 (1979)

[4] Brauer, W. (Ed.), "Net Theory and Applications", Lecture Notes in Computer Science **84**, Springer-Verlag Berlin, Heidelberg, New York, ISBN 3-540-10001-6 (1980)

[5] Burstall, R. and Goguen, J.R., *The semantics of Clear, a Specification Language*, in "1979 Copenhagen Winter School on Abstract Software Specification Proceedings", Lecture Notes in Computer Science **86**, Bjørner, D. (Ed.), Springer-Verlag Berlin, Heidelberg, New York, ISBN 3-540-10007-5 (1980), 292–332

[6] Clocksin, W.F. and Mellish, C.S., "Programming in Prolog", Springer-Verlag Berlin, Heidelberg, New York, ISBN 3-540-11046-1 (1981)

[7] Diaz, M., *Modelling and Analysis of Communication and Cooperation Protocols using Petri Net Based Models*, in "Protocol Specification, Testing and Verification", Sunshine, C. (Ed.), North-Holland Publishing Company, ISBN 0444-864814 (1982), 465–510

[8] Ehrig, H., Kreowski H.-J., Mahr, B. and Padawitz, P., *Algebraic Implementation of Abstract Data Types*, Theoretical Computer Science **20,3**, North-Holland Publishing Company (1982), 209–264

[9] Ehrig, H., Kreowski, H.-J., Thatcher, J.W., Wagner, E.G., and Wright, J.B., *Parameterized data types in algebraic languages*, in "Automata, Languages and Programming", Seventh Colloquium, Noordwijkerhout, the Netherlands, de Bakker J.W. and van Leeuwen, J. (Eds.), Lecture Notes in Computer Science **85**, Springer-Verlag Berlin, Heidelberg, New York, ISBN 3-540-10003-2 (1980), 157–168

[10] Genrich, H.J., *Extended simple regular expressions*, in Lecture Notes in Computer Science **32**, Bečvář, J. (Ed.), Springer-Verlag Berlin, Heidelberg, New York (1975)

[11] Genrich, H.J. and Lautenbach, K., *System modelling with high-level Petri nets*, Theoretical Computer Science **13,1**, North-Holland Publishing Company (1981), 109–136

[12] Genrich, H.J. and Lautenbach, K., *S-Invariance in Predicate-Transition Nets*, in "Applications and Theory of Petri Nets", Informatik-Fachberichte **66**, Pagnoni, A. and Rozenberg, G. (Eds.), Springer-Verlag Berlin, Heidelberg, New York, Tokyo, ISBN 3-540-12309-1 (1983), 98–111

[13] Genrich, H.J., Lautenbach, K. and Thiagarajan, P.S., *Elements of General Net Theory*, in [4], 21–38, 93–105

[14] Genrich, H.J. and Stankiewics-Wiechno, E., *A Dictionary of some Basic Notions of Net Theory*, in [4], 519–535

[15] Goguen, J. and Meseguer J., *Rapid Prototyping in the OBJ Executable Specification Language*, ACM SIGSOFT Software Engineering Notes **7, No 5** (December 1982), 75–84

[16] Goguen, J., Thatcher, J.W. and Wagner, E.G., *An Initial Algebra Approach to the Specification, Correctness, and Implementation of Abstract Data Types*, in "Current Trends in Programming Methodology", **Volume IV**, Data Structuring, Yeh, R.T. (Ed.), Prentice-Hall, Englewood Cliffs, New Jersey, ISBN 0-13-195735-X (1978), 80–149

[17] Krämer, B., *Formal and Semi-Graphic Specification of Non-Sequential Software Systems*, to appear in "Entwurf großer Software-Systeme", Berichte des German Chapter of the ACM, Remmele, W. (Ed.), B.G. Teubner, Stuttgart (1984)

[18] Krämer, B., Nieters, H.H., Schmidt, H.W., Bayer, M., Dehottay, J.P., and Singer, K., *A Syntax Directed Editor for a Semi-Graphic Language to Specifying Non-sequential Systems* in "Implementierung von Programmiersprachen", Tagungsunterlage zum GI-Fachgespräch, 7. März, Zürich, Ganzinger, H. (Ed.) (1984), 21–40

[19] Krämer, B. and Schmidt, H.W., *A High Level Net Language for Modeling Organisational Systems*, in "Adequate Modeling of Systems", Proceedings of the International Working Conference on Model Realism, Bad Honnef, FRG Wedde, H. (Ed.), Springer-Verlag Berlin, Heidelberg, New York, ISBN 3-540-12567-1 (1982), 156–170

[20] Lamport, L., *Specifying Concurrent Program Modules*, ACM Transactions on Programming Languages **5, 2** (April 1983), 190–222

[21] MacLennan, B.J., *Values and Objects in Programming Languages*, SIGPLAN Notices, **17,12** (December 1982), 70–79

[22] Musser, D.R., *Abstract Data Type Specification in the Affirm System*, in "Proceedings on Specifications of Reliable Software", IEEE Catalog **No 79** (1979), 47–57

[23] Petri, C.A., *General Net Theory*, in "Proceedings of the Joint IBM University of Newcastle upon Tyne Seminar", Shaw, B. (Ed.) (1976), 130–169

[24] Queille, J.P. and Sifakis, J., *Specification and Verification of Concurrent Systems in CESAR*, in "International Symposium on Programming", Fifth Colloquium, Turin, Italy, Dezani-Ciancaglini, M. and Montanari, U. (Eds.), Lecture Notes in Computer Science **137**, Springer-Verlag Berlin, Heidelberg, New York, ISBN 3-540-11494-7 (1982), 337–351

[25] Schmidt, H.W., *Towards a Net-Theoretic Notion of Type based on Predicate-Transition Nets*, in "Papers presented at the 5th European Workshop on Applications and Theory of Petri Nets", Aarhus, Denmark (1984), 330–345

[26] Schmidt, H.W. and Kreowski H.-J., *Conditional Specification in the Presence of Tests and Multi-Valued Symbols*, Arbeitsberichte der GMD **74** (1983)

[27] Sunshine, C.A., Thompson, D.H., Erickson, R.W., Gerhardt, S.L., and Schwabe, D., *Specification and Verification of Communication Protocols in AFFIRM Using State Transition Models*, in IEEE Transactions On Software Engineering, **SE-8,5** (1982), 460–489

[28] Schwartz, R.L. and Melliar-Smith, P.M., *Temporal Logic Specification of Distributed Systems*, in "Proceedings of The 2nd International Conference on Distributed Computing systems", Paris, France, IEEE Catalog No. 81CH1591-7 (1981), 446–454

[29] Thatcher, J.W., Wagner, E.G., and Wright, J.B., *Data Type Specification: Parameterization and the Power of Specification Techniques*, ACM Transactions on Programming Languages and Systems, **4,4** (1982), 711–732

A. Supplementary SEGRAS Specifications

SystemStruct: Sender; Receiver; Type transmitter; TransportService.
DataStruct: Message; Data; Bit; State.
...

```
Bit  provides
function
Type: Bit.
Bit:  BitOn; BitOff; Nil;
      switch Bit.
Bit:  BitOn; BitOff.
test
(): Bit unequals Bit.

for all  Bit b
- - - - - - - - - - -
switch BitOn=BitOff:.
switch(switch b)=b:.
b unequals (switch b):.
```

```
State  provides
function
Type: State.
State: Ready;
       Wait;
       Receivd.
```

```
TransportService  provides Sender, Receiver, Msg transmitter
                           Bit transmitter, queue of Data  and
function
System:  Service.

Service :=: (Sender: _sendr, Receiver: _receivr,
             Msg transmtr: _send-receive,
             Bit transmtr: _receive-send,
             Data queue: _sq, Data queue: _rq).
action
start →Service.

for all  Service ts  Msg  m  Bit  b  Data  d
- - - - - - - - - - - - - - - - - - - - - - - - -
start ts:
    start (ts sendr) with (BitOn),
     start (ts receivr) with (BitOff),
      passive start of (ts send-receive),
       passive start of (ts receive-send),
        establish (ts rq),  establish (ts sq).
((ts sendr) send m)■((ts send-receive) get m):.
((ts sendr) receive b)■((ts receive-send) transmit b):.
((ts sendr) lack ackn)■((ts receive-send) loose Bit):.
((ts receivr) send b)■((ts receive-send) get b):.
((ts receivr) receive m)■((ts send-receive) transmit m):.
((ts receivr) lack msg)■((ts send-receive) loose Msg):.
(deq d from (ts sq))■((ts sendr) accept ackn and take next d):.
(enq d to (ts rq))■((ts receivr) accept msg and deliver d):.
```

```
Sender          provides   Message, Stat
function
System:  Sender.
state function
Sender <↑CntlState, ↑Msg, ↑Bit>.
action
start →Sender with Bit;     ↔Sender send ↑Msg;
↔Sender receive Bit [↑Msg];   ↔Sender lack ackn [↑Msg];
↔Sender accept ackn and take next Data [↑Msg, ↑Msg, ↑Bit];
↔Sender ignore previous ackn [↑Msg, ↑Bit].

for all  Sender s  Msg m, m'  Bit b, b'  Data d, d'
- - - - - - - - - - - - - - - - - - - - - - - - - - -
```

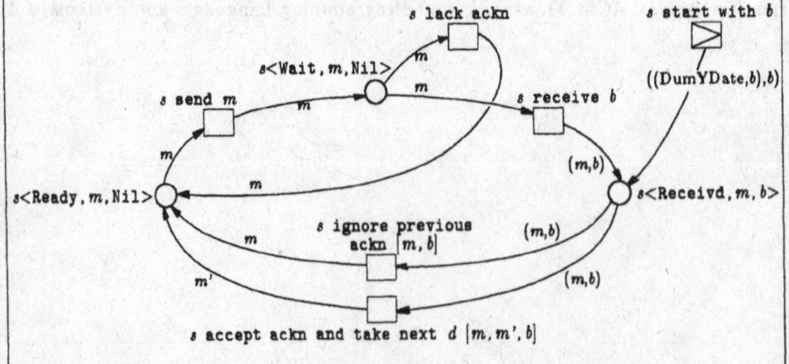

s accept ackn and take next d' [m, m', b]:   m=(d, b), m'=(d', switch(b)).
s ignore previous ackn [m, b]:   m= (d, b'), b unequals b'.

Data provides

function

Type: Data.

Data: DmYDate;

Message provides Data, Bit and

function

Type:Msg; MarkedData; NullMsg.

Msg: MarkedData; NullMsg.

NullMsg: Nil.

MarkedData :=: (Data, Bit).

for all Type *Package*

***Package* transmitter** provides

function

System: *Package* transmtr.

Type: EmptyChnl; Contents.

EmptyChnl: Empty.

Contents: EmptyChnl; *Package*.

state function

Package transmtr <↑Contents>.

action

active start of →*Package* transmtr with *Package*;

passive start of ⇥*Package* transmtr;

↔*Package* transmtr get *Package*.

decision

↔*Package* transmtr transmit ↑*Package*;

↔*Package* transmtr loose *Package*.

for all *Package* transmtr *t* *Package* *p*

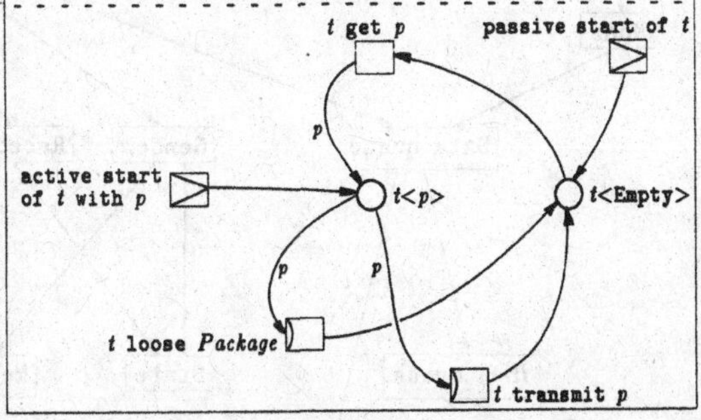

Receiver provides Message, Stat

function

System: Receiver.

state function

Receiver <↑CntlState, ↑Msg, ↑Bit>.

action

start →Receiver with Bit; ↔Receiver send ↑Bit;

↔Receiver receive Msg [↑Bit]; ↔Receiver lack msg [↑Bit];

↔Receiver accept msg and deliver ↑Data [↑Msg, ↑Bit, ↑Bit];

↔Receiver ignore previous msg [↑Msg, ↑Bit].

for all Receiver *r* Msg *m* Bit *b*, *b'* Data *d*

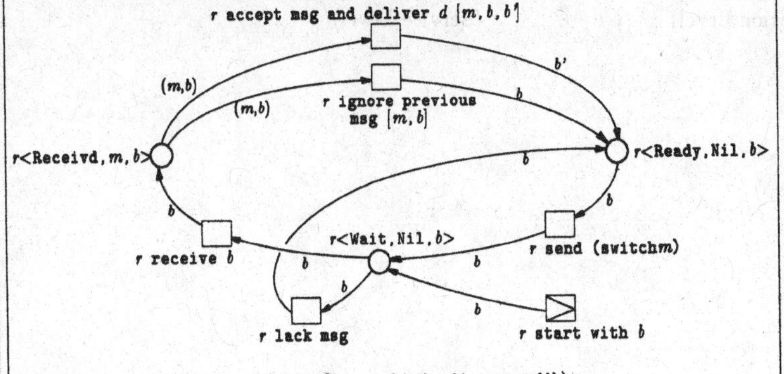

r accept msg and deliver *d* [*m*, *b*, *b'*]: *m*=(*d*, *b*), *b'*=switch(*b*)).

r ignore previous msg [*m*, *b*]: *m*= (*d*, *b'*), *b* unequals *b'*.

B. Structure Combination

The combination relations of a structured *SEGRAS* specification can always be represented by a finite directed acyclic graph. As an example, the graph below shows the interrelations between the data and system structures of our protocol example as they are established by their combination descriptions. Each arc represents a binary relation "_inherits from_" or "_is a combination with_" between a pair of structures (S_1, S_2), with S_1 on the arrowtail and S_2 on the arrowhead.

The combination graph also shows that structures can be used for combination on different levels of abstraction; e.g., `Data` or *Item* `queue` below.

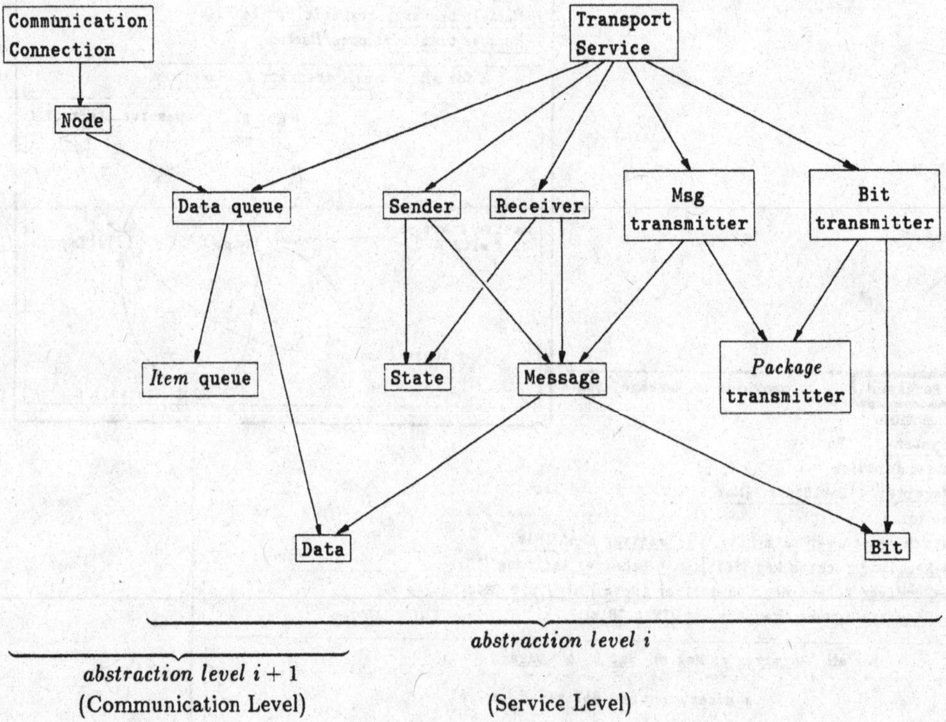

LIVENESS AND DUALITY IN MARKED-GRAPH-LIKE PREDICATE/TRANSITION NETS

Kurt Lautenbach
GMD - F1
Postfach 1240
D-5205 St. Augustin 1
West Germany

and

Anastasia Pagnoni
Università Luigi Bocconi
Istituto di Metodi Quantitativi
Via R. Sarfatti
I-20136 Milano
Italy

(o) Introduction

This paper has a twofold aim. First of all, a class of nets will be presented,which, even though originally introduced in order to represent certain phenomena related to communication protocols, has turned out to be of theoretical interest. This class of unary marked-graph-like predicate/transition nets allows interesting results because its elements are both simple and complex. The nets are simple w.r.t. their structure (marked graphs) and complex as pr/t nets. One interesting result, a necessary and sufficient criterion for liveness, will be presented.

Secondly, this class of nets has proved to be well suited for introducing and using a duality concept concerning not only the nets themselves but also their markings. This concept of duality will be presented and justified from several points of view. In particular, how the liveness criterion can be modified using the notion of the dual of a marked net will be shown.

The class of nets that we are dealing with in this paper is the extention of the one in [La 83] to the case in which the labels of different arcs incidenting with the same transition contain different variables.

(1) NOTIONS AND NOTATIONS

In this section first multisets and then a class of marked-graph-like predicate/transition nets are introduced.

Definition 1.1 Let $A = \{a_1,\dots,a_h\}$ be a finite set, $\mathbb{N} = 1,2,3;\dots$ the set of natural numbers, $\mathbb{Z}$ the set of integers;

we then call every mapping $m : A \rightarrow \mathbb{Z}$

a multiset on A

and every mapping $m_+ : A \rightarrow \mathbb{N} \cup \{o\}$

a non-negative multiset on A

As usual, we will represent multisets by formal sums writing

$$m = m(a_1)\, a_1 + m(a_2)\, a_2 + \dots + m(a_h)\, a_h.$$

By convention, we will omit coefficients equal to 1 and items with coefficients equal to 0. Consistently we set

$$0a_1 + 0a_2 + \dots + 0a_h := \emptyset \text{ (empty set)}$$

$MS(A)$ and $MS_+(A)$ denote the <u>set of all multisets</u> and the <u>set of all non-negative multisets</u> on A, respectively.

<u>Definition 1.2</u> Let $A = \{a_1, a_2, \dots, a_h\}$ be a finite set, m, m_1, m_2 multisets on A, $a \in A$ and $k \in \mathbb{Z}$. We define

$$-m := (-m(a_1))\, a_1 + (-m(a_2))\, a_2 + \dots + (-m(a_h))\, a_h$$

$$m = m_1 + m_2 \quad :\Longleftrightarrow \forall a \in A \quad [m(a) = m_1(a) + m_2(a)]$$

$$m = km_1 \quad :\Longleftrightarrow \forall a \in A \quad [m(a) = km_1(a)]$$

$$m_1 \leq m_2 \quad :\Longleftrightarrow \forall a \in A \quad [m_1(a) \leq m_2(a)]$$

$$a \in m \quad :\Longleftrightarrow m(a) \neq 0$$

where all signs on the righthand side denote the usual operations, equalities, inequalities in $\mathbb{Z}$.

For short, we will write

$$m_1 - m_2 := m_1 + (-m_2).$$

In the sequel we will use the following notions:

<u>Definition 1.3</u> Let $n \in \mathbb{N}$; and let

$$\langle h \rangle_n := \{ z \mid z \in \mathbb{Z} \wedge \exists\, k \in \mathbb{Z}\ [z - h = kn] \}$$

$$\langle N \rangle_n := \{ \langle 0 \rangle_n, \langle 1 \rangle_n, \dots, \langle n-1 \rangle_n \}.$$

We will call the elements of $\langle N \rangle_n$ <u>constant 1-tuples.</u>

$\langle N \rangle_n$ is the set of rest classes modulo n.

Notice that for $n = 1$ $\mathrm{card}(\langle N \rangle_1) = 1$. This single constant 1-tuple can be regarded as a token.

We will denote by $\oplus$ <u>the usual sum of rest classes (1-tuples)</u>, i.e:

$$\forall\, h_1, h_2 \in \mathbb{Z}\ [\langle h_1 \rangle_n \oplus \langle h_2 \rangle_n := \langle h_1 + h_2 \rangle_n]$$

<u>Definition 1.4</u> Let X be a non-empty, finite set of variables ranging over $\mathbb{Z}$. We will call every

$\langle x+h \rangle_n$ with $x \in X$, $h \in \mathbb{Z}$ <u>a variable 1-tuple</u> and denote by $\langle X+N \rangle_n$ the set of all variable 1-tuples. By convention, we assume X to be ordered alphabetically (or lexicographically) and we write, for instance, $i < j$.

As usual, we will omit the index n and write only $\langle h \rangle$ and $\langle N \rangle$, when the modulus n is known.

<u>Definition 1.5</u> Let $n \in \mathbb{N}$ and $v \in \mathbb{N}$. We define

$$\langle N \rangle_n^v := \langle N \rangle_n \times \langle N \rangle_n \times \dots \times \langle N \rangle_n \quad \text{(v times)}$$

and set $\langle h_1,h_2,\ldots,h_v\rangle_n := (\langle h_1\rangle_n, \langle h_2\rangle_n, \ldots, \langle h_v\rangle_n)$. The elements of $\langle N\rangle_n^v$ are called <u>constant (v-) tuples</u>.

$\oplus$ is extended to $\langle N\rangle_n^v$ in an obvious way:

$$\forall \langle h_1,h_2,\ldots,h_v\rangle_n, \langle k_1,k_2,\ldots,k_v\rangle_n \in \langle N\rangle_n^v$$

$$\langle h_1,h_2,\ldots,h_v\rangle_n \oplus \langle k_1,k_2,\ldots,k_v\rangle_n := \langle h_1+k_1,h_2+k_2,\ldots,h_v+k_v\rangle_n$$

Let X be a non-empty, finite set of variables ranging over $\mathbb{Z}$. We assume X to be ordered, e.g. alphabetically (<). We define

$$\langle X+N\rangle_n^v := \langle X+N\rangle_n \times \langle X+N\rangle_n \times\ldots\times \langle X+N\rangle_n \text{ (v times)}$$

and set $\langle x_1+h_1, x_2+h_2,\ldots, x_v+h_v\rangle := (\langle x_1+h_1\rangle, \langle x_2+h_2,\ldots, \langle x_v+h_v\rangle)$

The elements of $\langle X + N\rangle_n^v$ are called <u>variable v-tuples.</u> It is consistent to set $\langle N\rangle_n := \langle N\rangle_n^1$

and $\langle X+N\rangle_n := \langle X+N\rangle_n^1$.

Here too, we omit the index n, when the modulus is known.

<u>Definition 1.6</u> A quintuple G = (S,T,F,n,L) is called a <u>marked-graph-like unary predicate/transition net</u> (cf. [GL 81]) iff

- (S,T;F) is a finite directed net, where S is a set of unary predicates.
- $\forall p \in S\ [\text{card}(^\bullet p) = \text{card}(p^\bullet) = 1]$
  (i. e.: all predicates have exactly one input arc and one output arc)
- $\forall\ t_1,t_2 \in T\ [t_1\ F^*\ t_2]$
  (i. e.: the structure of the net is <u>strongly connected</u>)
- $n \in \mathbb{N}$ is the modulus of the tuples.
- $L : F \to \langle X + N\rangle_n$
  (i. e.: all arcs are labeled by <u>variable 1-tuples</u>)
- $\forall (a,b) \in S\times T \cup T\times S\ \ [(a,b) \in F \wedge (b,a) \in F \to L(a,b) \neq L(b,a)]$
  (i. e.: the net is <u>pure</u>).

By G_n we will denote the class of all marked-graph-like unary pr/t nets where n is the modulus of the tuples.

<u>Definition 1.7</u> Let $n \in \mathbb{N}$, $G = (S,T,F,n,L) \in G_n$, and $t \in T$. The set X_t of <u>variables concerning t</u> is defined by

$$X_t := \{ x \in X \mid \exists\ (a,b) \in F\ \ [t \in \{a,b\} \wedge L(a,b) = \langle x + k\rangle]\ \}$$

$$v_t := \text{card}(X_t)$$

Assume X_t to be ordered lexicographically.

<u>Definition 1.8</u>

Let $N = (S,T,F,n,L) \in G_n$. If $\forall t \in T\ [v_t = 1]$,

we call N <u>simple.</u>

(i) A net is defined to be simple when all labels of arcs incidenting with the same transition contain one and the same variable. As such, if a net is simple, we can always assume to have one single variable for the whole net. In fact we are allowed to consistently renaming the variables in each transition.

(ii) In the original definition of pr/t nets [GL 81] , the activation of transitions could be limited by conditions expressed in the form of transition-inscriptions. Here we renounce such inscriptions, since they are not essential to our formalism. Nevertheless, we will come back briefly to transition-inscriptions in the discussion of duality.

<u>Definition 1.9</u> Let $n \in \mathbb{N}$, $G \in G_n$, and $k \in X$. Assume both S and T to be ordered arbitrarily but fixedly. We call

$\mathcal{M} := \{M \mid M : S \rightarrow MS_+(\langle N \rangle)\}$ the set of <u>constant markings</u>

$\mathcal{M}_{\{k\}} := \{M \mid M : S \rightarrow MS_+(\langle \{k\} + N \rangle)\}$ the set of <u>markings parameterized by k</u>

$\mathcal{S} := \{Q \mid Q : S \rightarrow MS(\langle N \rangle)\}$ the set of <u>constant S-vectors</u>

$\mathcal{S}_{\{k\}} := \{Q \mid Q : S \rightarrow MS(\langle \{k\} + N \rangle)\}$ the set of <u>S-vectors parameterized by k</u>

$\mathcal{F} := \{V \mid \forall t \in T\, [t \xrightarrow{V} m_+ \in MS_+(\langle N \rangle^{\forall t})]\}$ the set of <u>constant forward firing vectors</u>

$\mathcal{F}_X := \{V \mid \forall t \in T\, [t \xrightarrow{V} m_+ \in MS_+(\langle X+N \rangle^{\forall t})]\}$ the set of <u>forward firing vectors parameterized by X</u>

$\mathcal{T} := \{W \mid \forall t \in T\, [t \xrightarrow{W} m \in MS(\langle N \rangle^{\forall t})]\}$ the set of <u>constant T-vectors</u>

$\mathcal{T}_X := \{W \mid \forall t \in T\, [t \xrightarrow{W} m \in MS(\langle X+N \rangle^{\forall t})]\}$ the set of <u>t-vectors parameterized by X</u>

Notice that $\mathcal{M} \subseteq \mathcal{S}$, $\mathcal{M}_{\{k\}} \subseteq \mathcal{S}_{\{k\}}$ $\mathcal{F} \subseteq \mathcal{T}$, $\mathcal{F}_X \subseteq \mathcal{T}_X$.- S and T-vectors will be written as column vectors.
S-vectors belonging to $\mathcal{M} \cup \mathcal{M}_{\{k\}}$ and t-vectors belonging to $\mathcal{F} \cup \mathcal{F}_X$ are called <u>non-negative</u>.

<u>Definition 1.10</u> Let be $G = (S,T,F,n,L) \in G_n$.
The incidence matrix $[G(p,t)]$ of G is defined by

$$G(p,t) := \begin{cases} L(t,p)-L(p,t) & \text{if } (p,t) \in F \cap (S\times T) \wedge (t,p) \in F \cap (F\times S) \\ -L(p,t) & \text{if } (p,t) \in F \cap (S\times T) \wedge (t,p) \notin F \\ L(t,p) & \text{if } (p,t) \notin F \qquad\qquad\quad \wedge (t,p) \in F \cap (T\times S) \\ \emptyset & \text{else} \end{cases}$$

The elements of $[G(p,t)]$ are elements of $MS(\langle X+N \rangle)$. In the sequel we will sometimes omit $\emptyset$-entries of S- and T-vectors.
With $G(p,-)$ and $G(-,t)$, respectively, we will denote rows and columns of $[G(p,t)]$.
If no ambiguity gets caused, we will write G instead $[G(p,t)]$.
With G^T and V^T, respectively, we will mark the transpose of a matrix G and of a

vector V.

The notions of an enabled transition, a transition firing, a reachable marking, etc. are defined as for general pr/t nets (cf. [GL 81]).

As usual, $[M_o\rangle$ denotes the class of markings reachable from M_o in forward direction,

$\langle M_o]$ denotes the class of markings reachable from M_o in backward direction,

$[M_o]$ denotes the class of markings reachable from M_o in forward and backward direction.

We assume $M_o \in [M_o\rangle$.

A simple but significant example is the following net $G_1 \in G_2$, which we will reconsider in the sequel several times.

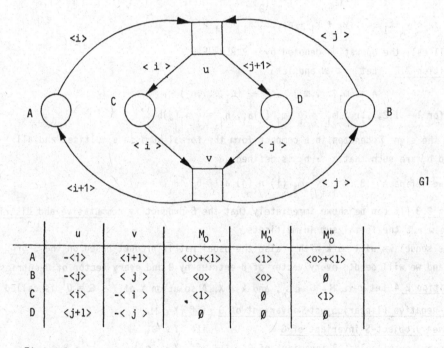

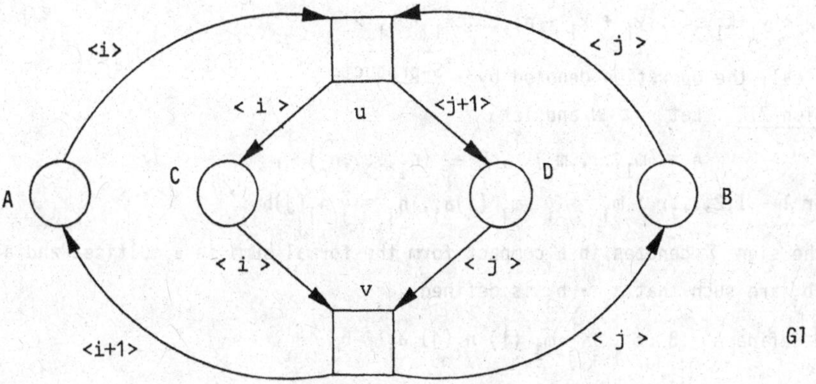

	u	v	M_o	M'_o	M''_o
A	-<i>	<i+1>	<o>+<1>	<1>	<o>+<1>
B	-<j>	< j >	<o>	<o>	Ø
C	<i>	-< i >	<1>	Ø	<1>
D	<j+1>	-< j >	Ø	Ø	Ø

Figure 1.1

(2) INVARIANCE

In this section object-S- and object -T-invariants will be defined for the nets of G_n on the basis of an S- and T-product, respectively. The S-product formalizes the intuitive idea of comparing tuples, whereas the T-product formalizes the substitution of variables in tuples.

Furthermore, a method for calculating object-S-and object-T-invariants will be presented.

The justification of both names object-S-invariant and object-T-invariant can be found in [LP84].

<u>Object-S-invariance</u>

<u>Definition 2.1</u> Let $n \in \mathbb{N}$, and $a \in \langle N\rangle_n^v \cup \langle X+N\rangle_n^v$, $b \in \langle N\rangle_n^w \cup \langle X+N\rangle_n^w$.

Let us denote with $\cdot$ the operation defined by

(i) $$a \cdot b := \begin{cases} 1 & \text{if } a = b \text{ identically} \\ 0 & \text{if } a = b \text{ has no solution} \end{cases}$$

(ii) $\emptyset \cdot a := a \cdot \emptyset := \emptyset \cdot \emptyset := 0$

(iii) for $l_1, l_2 \in \mathbb{N}$, $h_1,\ldots, h_{l_1}$, $k_1,\ldots, k_{l_2}$, $d \in \mathbb{Z}$, $x_1,\ldots, x_{l_1}$, $y_1,\ldots,y_{l_2} \in X$:

$$\langle x_1+h_1,\ldots, x_i+h_i,\ldots,x_{l_1}+h_{l_1}\rangle \cdot \langle y_1+k_1,\ldots, y_i+k_i,\ldots, y_{l_2}+k_{l_2}\rangle = \langle x_1+h_1,\ldots,x_i+h_i+d,\ldots, x_{l_1}+h_{l_1}\rangle \cdot \langle y_1+k_1,\ldots, y_i+k_i+d,\ldots, x_{l_2}+k_{l_2}\rangle$$

We will call the operation denoted by $\cdot$ <u>S-product.</u>

<u>Definition 2.2</u> Let $r \in \mathbb{N}$ and let

$$A = (m_1,\ldots,m_r)^T, \quad B = (n_1,\ldots,n_r)^T,$$

with for $l = 1,2,\ldots r$: $m_l = \sum_i m_l(i)a_i$, $n_l = \sum_j n_l(j)b_j$;

where the sign Σ denotes in a compact form the formal sums in a multiset and all a_i and b_j are such that $a_i \cdot b_j$ is defined.

Then we define $A^T \cdot B := \sum_{l,i,j} m_l(i)\, n_l(j)\, a_i \cdot b_j$

<u>Remark 2.3</u> It can be shown immediately that the S-product is <u>commutative</u> and <u>distributive</u> w.r.t. the formal sum in multisets.

In the sequel we will mark with $\cdot$ also the usual matrix product based on the S-product and we will denote every vector of $\emptyset$-entries by $\underline{\emptyset}$ and every vector of 0-entries by $\underline{0}$.

<u>Definition 2.4</u> Let $n \in \mathbb{N}$, $G \in G_n$, and $k \in X$. A solution Y of $Y^T \cdot G = \underline{0}^T$ is called

a <u>non-negative (linear) object-S-invariant of G</u> iff $Y \in M$,

a <u>(linear) object-S-invariant of G</u> iff $Y \in S$,

a <u>(linear) quasi-object-S-invariant of G</u> iff $Y \in S_{\{k\}}$.

<u>Definition 2.5</u> Let $n \in \mathbb{N}$, $G \in G_n$ and $I \neq \underline{\emptyset}$ a (quasi-) object-S-invariant of G. We call I <u>minimal</u> iff I is non-negative and there exists no non-negative (quasi-) object-S-invariant $\bar{I}$ of G s.t. $\bar{I} \leq I$ with $\bar{I} \neq I$, and $\bar{I} \neq \underline{\emptyset}$

<u>Remark 2.6</u> It can be proved that every non-negative (quasi-) object-S-invariant of a net $G \in G_n$ is a linear combination (with non-negative integer coefficients) of minimal (quasi-) object-S-invariants of G.

The following theorem provides for a characterization of (quasi-) object-S-invariants.

<u>Theorem 2.7</u> Let $n \in \mathbb{N}$, $G \in G_n$, $I \in S_{\{k\}}$. I is a (quasi-) object-S-invariant iff

$$\forall M_0, M \in \mathbb{M} \left[M \in [M_0] \longrightarrow I^T \cdot M = I^T \cdot M_0 \right]$$

<u>Proof</u> Observe that

$$I^T \cdot G = \underline{0}^T \quad \underline{\text{iff}} \quad \forall t \in T,\ \forall \alpha \in \langle N \rangle^{v_t} : \ I^T \cdot (G(-,t)^\circ \alpha) = 0,$$

where $G(-,t)\,^\circ\alpha$ denotes $G(-,t)$ after the consistent substitution of the elements of α in it.

<u>Suppose that</u> $I^T \cdot G = \underline{0}^T$. Let $M_0, M \in \mathbb{M}$, $M_0 \neq M$.

$M \in [M_0\rangle \longleftrightarrow \exists t_1, \ldots, t_j \in T : M = M_0 + \sum_{i=1}^{j} G(-,t_i) \circ \alpha_i$,

where $\alpha_i \in \langle N \rangle^{v_{t_i}}$.

Hence: $I^T \cdot M = I^T \cdot M_0 + \sum_{i=1}^{j} I^T \cdot (G(-,t_i) \circ \alpha_i) = I^T \cdot M_0$.

If $M \in \langle M_0]$, the proof is quite analogous.

<u>Suppose that</u> $\forall M_0, M \in \mathbb{M} : M \in M_0 \longrightarrow I^T \cdot M = I^T \cdot M_0$. For every $t \in T$ and every $\alpha \in \langle N \rangle^{v_t}$ one can find a marking M_0 s.t. t is enabled for α under M_0; e.g.

$$\forall p \in S : M_0(p) = \sum_{t \in T, \alpha \in \langle N \rangle^{v_t}} L(p,t)^\circ \alpha .$$

At M_0, every transition t is enabled for every constant v_t-tuple . Let M be the follower marking of M_0, after firing t for α. Then

$$I^T \cdot M = I^T \cdot (M_0 + G(-,t)^\circ \alpha) = I^T \cdot M_0.$$

Hence $\forall t \in T$, $\forall \alpha \in \langle N \rangle^{v_t} : I^T \cdot (G(-,t)^\circ \alpha) = 0$

and $\quad I^T \cdot G = \underline{0}^T$.

<u>Calculation of object-S-invariants</u>

Object-S-invariants of a net $G \in G_n$ can be calculated by solving a system of homogeneous linear difference equations. These equations can be directly deduced from the incidence matrix. Even though this method is a general one we will demonstrate it only by means of an example.

Let us again consider the net $G1 \in G_2$ (Fig. 1.1). The linear homogeneous equation system to be solved in order to obtain the quasi-object-S-invariants is $Y^T \cdot G1 = \underline{0}^T$. Since n = 2, the general form of a quasi-object-S-invariant of G1 is

$$I = \begin{bmatrix} x_A(o)\langle k\rangle + x_A(1)\langle k+1\rangle \\ x_B(o)\langle k\rangle + x_B(1)\langle k+1\rangle \\ x_C(o)\langle k\rangle + x_C(1)\langle k+1\rangle \\ x_D(o)\langle k\rangle + x_D(1)\langle k+1\rangle \end{bmatrix}$$

where $k \varepsilon X$ and $I^T \cdot G1 = \underline{0}^T$ is equivalent to

$$(2.8) \qquad \begin{cases} -x_A(i) \quad -x_B(j) + x_C(i) + x_D(j+1) = 0 \\ -x_A(i+1) + x_B(j) - x_C(i) - x_D(j) \quad = 0 \end{cases} \qquad \text{for } i,j \ \varepsilon \{0,1\}$$

($i+1$ and $j+1$ indicate the addition modulo 2.)

(2.8) has the following integer, minimal, semipositive solutions

$x_A(0)$	1	1	0	0
$x_A(1)$	1	1	0	0
$x_B(0)$	0	0	1	1
$x_B(1)$	0	0	1	1
$x_C(0)$	1	0	1	0
$x_C(1)$	1	0	1	0
$x_D(0)$	0	1	0	1
$x_D(1)$	0	1	0	1

The corresponding minimal quasi-object-S-invariants are

A	$\langle k\rangle + \langle k+1\rangle$	$\langle k\rangle + \langle k+1\rangle$	$\emptyset$	$\emptyset$
B	$\emptyset$	$\emptyset$	$\langle k\rangle + \langle k+1\rangle$	$\langle k\rangle + \langle k+1\rangle$
C	$\langle k\rangle + \langle k+1\rangle$	$\emptyset$	$\langle k\rangle + \langle k+1\rangle$	$\emptyset$
D	$\emptyset$	$\langle k\rangle + \langle k+1\rangle$	$\emptyset$	$\langle k\rangle + \langle k+1\rangle$

For k varying in $\mathbb{Z}$ we obtain the minimal object-S-invariants of G1:

	I_1	I_2	I_3	I_4
A	$\langle o\rangle + \langle 1\rangle$	$\langle o\rangle + \langle 1\rangle$	$\emptyset$	$\emptyset$
B	$\emptyset$	$\emptyset$	$\langle o\rangle + \langle 1\rangle$	$\langle o\rangle + \langle 1\rangle$
C	$\langle o\rangle + \langle 1\rangle$	$\emptyset$	$\langle o\rangle + \langle 1\rangle$	$\emptyset$
D	$\emptyset$	$\langle o\rangle + \langle 1\rangle$	$\emptyset$	$\langle o\rangle + \langle 1\rangle$

Remark 2.9 (i) The difference equation system (2.8) can be directly deduced from the incidence matrix G1 as follows:

- First, substitute in every row p of G1 $x_p(k)$ for $<k>$
- Second, set the column sums of the matrix thus obtained equal to zero.

(ii) Notice that in general (2.8) has to be solved for $i, j \in \{0,1,\dots,n-1\}$.

Object-T-invariance

Definition 2.10 With the former notations, for $a \in \langle N\rangle_n^{v_1}$ and $b \in \langle N\rangle_n^{v_2} \cup \langle X+N\rangle_n^{v_3}$ we set

(i) $a \circ b := a$

(ii) $\emptyset \circ b := b \circ \emptyset := \emptyset$

(iii) Let $X_t = \{x_1, x_2, \dots, x_w\}$ with $x_1 < x_2 < \dots < x_w$.

Let $\{x_{i_1}, x_{i_2}, \dots, x_{i_v}\} \subseteq X_t$, $h_1, h_2, \dots, h_v \in Z$

and $\langle a_1, \dots, a_w\rangle \in \langle X + N\rangle_n^w \cup \langle N\rangle_n^w$.

We set

$\langle x_1 + h_1, \dots, x_v + h_v\rangle \circ \langle a_1, \dots, a_w\rangle := \langle x_{i_1} + h_1, \dots, x_{i_v} + h_v\rangle$.

We will call the operation denoted by $\circ$ T-product.

This operation will be used in order to perform multiple substitutions, e.g. in connection with transition firings.

Definition 2.11 Let $s \in \mathbb{N}$ and let

$$A = (m_1, \dots, m_s)^T, \quad B = (n_1, \dots, n_s)^T,$$

with for $l = 1,\dots,s$: $m_l = \sum_i m_l(i) a_i$, $n_l = \sum_j n_l(j) b_j$ where the sign Σ denotes in a compact form the formal sums in a multiset and all a_i and b_j are such that $a_i \circ b_j$ is defined.

Then we define $A^T \circ B := \sum_{l,i,j} m_l(i)\, n_l(j)\; a_i \circ b_j$.

Remark 2.12 It can be shown that the T-product is distributive w.r.t. the formal sum in multisets. In contrast to the S-product the T-product is not commutative.

In the sequel we will mark with $\circ$ also the usual matrix product based on the T-product.

Definition 2.13 Let $n \in \mathbb{N}$, $G \in G_n$, and $k \in X$. A solution Y of $G \circ Y = \underline{\emptyset}$ is called

a non-negative (linear) object-T-invariant of G iff $Y \in F$,

a (linear) object-T-invariant of G iff $Y \in T$,

a (linear) quasi-object-T-invariant of G iff $Y \in T_{\{k\}}$

Definition 2.14 Let $n \in \mathbb{N}$, $G \in G_n$, and $J \neq \underline{\emptyset}$ a (quasi-) object-T-invariant of G.

We call minimal iff J is non-negative and there exists no non-negative (quasi-) object-T-invariant $\overline{J}$ of $\mathbb{G}$ s.t. $\overline{J} \leq J$ with $\overline{J} \neq J$ and $\overline{J} \neq \underline{\emptyset}$.

Calculation of object-T-invariants

The calculation of object-T-invariants of a net $G \in G_n$ is very similar to the one of object-S-invariants. Again a linear homogeneous difference equation system that can be deduced directly from the incidence matrix has to be solved.

As before, we will demonstrate the (general) method by means of the net $G1 \in G_2$. According to definition 2.13, the linear equation system to be solved is $G1 \circ Y = \underline{\emptyset}$. Since $G1 \in G_2$ and card (X) = 2, the general form of a quasi-object-T-invariant of G1 is

$$J = \begin{bmatrix} \sum\limits_{l,m \in \{0,1\}} x_u(l,m)\langle k+l,k+m\rangle \\ \sum\limits_{l,m \in \{0,1\}} x_v(l,m)\langle k+l,k+m\rangle \end{bmatrix}$$

$G1 \circ J = \underline{\emptyset}$ is equivalent to

$$(2.15) \quad \left\{ \begin{array}{lll} -\sum\limits_j x_u(i,j) & +\sum\limits_j x_v(i+1,j) & = 0 \\ -\sum\limits_i x_u(i,j) & +\sum\limits_i x_v(i,j) & = 0 \\ \sum\limits_j x_u(i,j) & -\sum\limits_j x_v(i,j) & = 0 \\ \sum\limits_i x_u(i,j+1) & -\sum\limits_i x_v(i,j) & = 0 \end{array} \right. \qquad \text{for } i,j \in \{0,1\}$$

Notice that in G1 for every transition t the ordered set X_t is $\{i,j\}$ with $i<j$. The difference equation system (2.15) has the following integer, minimal, semipositive solutions

$x_u(0,0)$	0	0	1	1
$x_u(0,1)$	1	1	0	0
$x_u(1,0)$	1	1	0	0
$x_u(1,1)$	0	0	1	1
$x_v(0,0)$	0	1	0	1
$x_v(0,1)$	1	0	1	0
$x_v(1,0)$	1	0	1	0
$x_v(1,1)$	0	1	0	1

The corresponding minimal quasi-object-T-invariants are

u	$\langle k,k+1\rangle + \langle k+1,k\rangle$	$\langle k,k+1\rangle + \langle k+1,k\rangle$	$\langle k,k\rangle + \langle k+1,k+1\rangle$	$\langle k,k\rangle + \langle k+1,k+1\rangle$
v	$\langle k,k+1\rangle + \langle k+1,k\rangle$	$\langle k,k\rangle + \langle k+1,k+1\rangle$	$\langle k,k+1\rangle + \langle k+1,k\rangle$	$\langle k,k\rangle + \langle k+1,k+1\rangle$

For k varying in $\mathbb{Z}$ we obtain the minimal object-T-invariants of G1:

u	<0,1> + <1,0>	<0,1> + <1,0>	<0,0> + <1,1>	<0,0> + <1,1>
v	<0,1> + <1,0>	<0,0> + <1,1>	<0,1> + <1,0>	<0,0> + <1,1>

Remark 2.16 (i) The difference equation system (2.15) can be directly deduced from the incidence matrix G1 as follows:

- First, in every column t of G1, $\sum_j x_t\,(i+h,j)$ and $\sum_i x_t\,(i,j+k)$ have to be substituted for <i+h> and <j+k>, respectively.
- Secondly, the row sums of the matrix thus obtained have to be set equal to zero.

(ii) In general (2.15) has to be solved for $i,j \in \{0,1,\dots,n-1\}$.

(3) LIVENESS

We will introduce a necessary and sufficient liveness condition for the nets of G_n that may be regarded as a fundamental property of marked-graph-like nets.
In connection with this liveness condition we will discuss a certain aspect of the relationship between net structure and net inscriptions.

Definition 3.1 Let $n \in \mathbb{N}$, $G \in G_n$, $M \in M$. M is called a live marking iff
$\forall M' \in [M> \forall t \in T \forall x \in X_t \forall k \in \{0,1,\dots,n-1\} \exists M'' \in [M'>$:
t is enabled for x = k under M".

Notice that we require for every transition t and every variable $x \in X_t$ that t can fire again and again for every value k which can be substituted for x. We do not require that t can fire again and again for all combinations of values which are conceivable for the variables of X_t.

Definition 3.2 Let $n \in \mathbb{N}$, $G \in G_n$, and $M \in M$. A non-negative object-S-invariant of G is said to be marked by M iff $I^T \cdot M > 0$

Now we can formulate the above-mentioned necessary and sufficient liveness condition.

Theorem 3.3 Let $n \in \mathbb{N}$, $G \in G_n$, and $M \in M$.
Let the net representation of each quasi-object-T-invariant of G be simple.
M is a live marking of G iff all minimal object-S-invariants are marked by M.

Proof Let M be live. Let I be a minimal object-S-invariant and $\bar{p} \in S$ such that $I(\bar{p}) > \emptyset$.
Then there is a(simple) object-T-invariant through $\bar{p}$, which is live for M.

Let $\langle h \rangle \in I(\bar{p})$. Moreover, let $\bar{p}\bullet = \{t\}$ and $L(\bar{p},t) = \langle i+k \rangle$.
Since M is live, $\forall M' \in [M> \exists M'' \in [M'>$:
$\forall p \in \bullet t \;\; M''(p) \geq L(p,t) \circ \langle h-k \rangle$
It follows that
$L(\bar{p},t) . \langle h-k \rangle = \langle h \rangle \in M''(\bar{p})$ and $I^T \cdot M'' > 0$. According to theorem 2.7

$I^T \cdot M = I^T \cdot M''$ and hence $I^T \cdot M > 0$.

Let M be non-live.

By definition, a transition t and a $k \in \{0,1,\dots,n-1\}$ exist s.t.under every marking $M' \in [M\rangle$, t is not activated for $x = k$.

Then at M a tuple α_1 is missing on a predicate $p_1 \in {}^\bullet t$.

Backtracing via ${}^\bullet p_1 = \{t_1\}$, a tuple α_2 is missing on a predicate $p_2 \in {}^\bullet t_1$ at M.

This backtracing procedure can be continued, but since the net and the tuple set as well are finite after a finite number of steps we will miss the same tuple α_i on the same predicate.

The former backtrace is obviously a backtrace even in <u>each</u> net GT, which is the net representation of a quasi-object-T-invariant.

Observe that in those simple nets firing t_s,so that α_2 is removed from the marking of p_2 and α_1 added to the marking of p_1, implies that

(3.4) $\alpha_2 \cdot L(p_2,t_1) = \alpha_1 \cdot L(t_1,p_1)$ holds.

Analogously for all steps of the backtrace.For each predicate p, let then m_p be the multiset of the tuples which we have missed on p in the backtracing procedure bet - ween the two times we have missed α_i.

Let I be the S-vector defined by $I(p) = m_p$.

When denoting by GT the incidence matrix of the generic simple net representing a quasi-object-T-invariant, then the equalities (3.4) ensure that for each transition t

$$I^T \cdot GT(-,t) = 0 \quad \text{holds}.$$

Since for a transition t, the vectors GT(-,t) are all vectors obtained from G(-,t) when expressing all variables around t by means of one and the same variable,it fol lows that $I^T . G(-,t) = 0$ holds identically.

So, I is an object-S-invariant of G which does not mark M.

<u>For example</u>, it is easy to see that the four quasi-object-T-invariants of G1 are simple (one is shown in Fig.3.1) and that the markings M_0 and M'_0(Fig.1.1) are live markings.

The minimal object-S-invariants $I_1,\dots,I_4$(cf.page 338) are marked by M_0 and M'_0.

This implies that all non-negative object-S-invariants are marked by M_0 and M'_0.

M''_0 is not live. A non-negative object-S-invariant not marked by M''_0 is I_4:

$$I_4^T \cdot M''_o = (\ \emptyset,\ \ \langle o\rangle + \langle 1\rangle,\ \ \emptyset,\ \ \langle o\rangle+\langle 1\rangle) \cdot (\langle o\rangle+\langle 1\rangle,\ \ \emptyset,\ \ \langle 1\rangle,\ \ \emptyset)^T = 0$$

Even though we have not admitted transition inscriptions for the nets of G_n,we now want to study net modifications which can be caused by adding inscriptions to tran sitions.

For example, adding the inscription <i>=<j> to both transitions of the net G1 has the same effect as transforming G1 into the following net G2

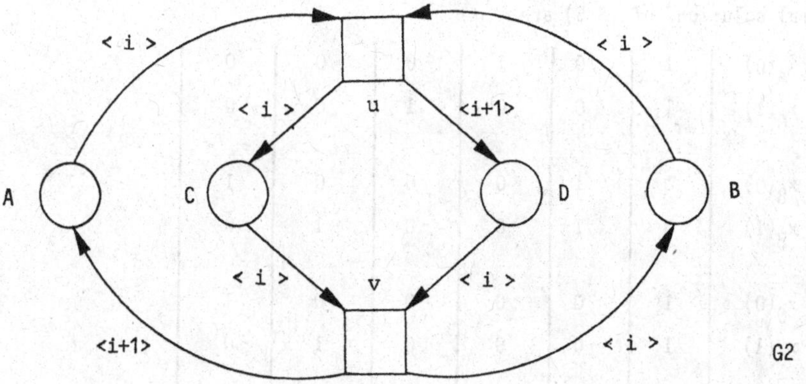

	u	v	M_0	M'_0	M''_0
A	-<i>	<i+1>	<0>+<1>	<1>	<0>+<1>
B	-<i>	<i>	<0>	<0>	Ø
C	<i>	-<i>	<1>	Ø	<1>
D	<i+1>	-<i>	Ø	Ø	Ø

Figure 3.1

We first want to compare G1 anf G2 w.r.t. liveness. Later on we will compare the respective dual nets.

Adding inscriptions to transitions means making it more difficult to enable these transitions. Consequently, it is more difficult to 'find' live markings. We want to investigate this difficulty, and so we start by calculating the minimal object-S-invariants of G2 ε G_2.

The general form of the quasi-object-S-invariants is

$$I = \begin{bmatrix} x_A(0)\langle k\rangle + x_A(1)\langle k+1\rangle \\ x_B(0)\langle k\rangle + x_B(1)\langle k+1\rangle \\ x_C(0)\langle k\rangle + x_C(1)\langle k+1\rangle \\ x_D(0)\langle k\rangle + x_D(1)\langle k+1\rangle \end{bmatrix} \text{ where } k \in X.$$

The linear homogeneous difference equation system to be solved in order to get the quasi-object-S-invariants is

$$(3.5)\quad \begin{cases} -x_A(i) - x_B(i) + x_C(i) + x_D(i+1) = 0 \\ x_A(i+1) + x_B(i) - x_C(i) - x_D(i) = 0 \end{cases} \quad \text{for } i \in \{0,1\}$$

(3.5) can be directly deduced from the incidence matrix G2. The integer, semipositi ve, minimal solutions of (3.5) are

$x_A(0)$	1	0	1	0	0	0
$x_A(1)$	1	0	0	1	0	0
$x_B(0)$	0	1	0	0	0	1
$x_B(1)$	0	1	0	0	1	0
$x_C(0)$	1	0	0	0	0	1
$x_C(1)$	1	0	0	0	1	0
$x_D(0)$	0	1	0	1	0	0
$x_D(1)$	0	1	1	0	0	0

The corresponding minimal quasi-object-S-invariants are

A	$\langle k \rangle + \langle k+1 \rangle$	$\emptyset$	$\langle k \rangle$	$\emptyset$
B	$\emptyset$	$\langle k \rangle + \langle k+1 \rangle$	$\emptyset$	$\langle k \rangle$
C	$\langle k \rangle + \langle k+1 \rangle$	$\emptyset$	$\emptyset$	$\langle k \rangle$
D	$\emptyset$	$\langle k \rangle + \langle k+1 \rangle$	$\langle k+1 \rangle$	$\emptyset$

and the minimal object-S-invariants of G2 are

A	$\langle 0 \rangle + \langle 1 \rangle$	$\emptyset$	$\langle 0 \rangle$	$\langle 1 \rangle$	$\emptyset$	$\emptyset$
B	$\emptyset$	$\langle 0 \rangle + \langle 1 \rangle$	$\emptyset$	$\emptyset$	$\langle 0 \rangle$	$\langle 1 \rangle$
C	$\langle 0 \rangle + \langle 1 \rangle$	$\emptyset$	$\emptyset$	$\emptyset$	$\langle 0 \rangle$	$\langle 1 \rangle$
D	$\emptyset$	$\langle 0 \rangle + \langle 1 \rangle$	$\langle 1 \rangle$	$\langle 0 \rangle$	$\emptyset$	$\emptyset$

Next, we want to calculate the object-T-invariants of G2. Since n = 2 and card (X) = 1 the general form of a quasi-object-T-invariant of G2 is

$$J = \begin{bmatrix} x_u(0) \langle k \rangle + x_u(1) \langle k+1 \rangle \\ x_v(0) \langle k \rangle + x_v(1) \langle k+1 \rangle \end{bmatrix} \quad \text{where } k \in X.$$

The difference equation system to be solved is

$$(3.6) \quad \begin{cases} - x_u(i) + x_v(i+1) = 0 \\ - x_u(j) + x_v(i) = 0 \end{cases} \quad \text{for } i \in \{0,1\}.$$

Again, (3.6) can be directly deduced from the incidence matrix G2.

The only integer, semipositive, minimal solution is

$$x_n(0) = x_n(1) = x_v(0) = x_v(1) = 1$$

The only minimal quasi-object-T-invariant and the only minimal object-T-invariant are respectively

$$
\begin{array}{c|cc}
u & <k> + <k+1> & \| \\
v & <k> + <k+1> & \|
\end{array}
\quad , \quad
\begin{array}{c|cc}
u & <0> + <1> & \| \\
v & <0> + <1> & \|
\end{array}
$$

A comparison between the minimal object -invariants of G1 and G2 shows that adding the inscription $<i> = <j>$ to both transitions of G1 increases the number of minimal object-S-invariants and decreases the number of minimal object-T-invariants. So, according to theorem 3.3, more minimal object-S-invariants have to be marked in order to get a live marking. This can be considered a reason for the greater difficulty in 'finding' a live marking in G2 (e.g. M_0' is no longer live). In addition, any reproduction in G2 is forced 'through' only one minimal object-T-invariant.

(4) DUALITY

In this section we want to introduce a duality concept for nets and their markings. This duality is based on the idea that backtraces in a net should be firing sequences in the dual net.

Even though this idea is obviously a very general one, we will restrict the duality concept to the nets of G_n (and their duals).

Furthermore, we will show that object-S-invariants (object-T-invariants) of a net are object-T-invariants (object-S-invariants) of its dual and vice versa.

__Definition 4.1__   Let $n \in \mathbb{N}$ and $G = (S,T,F,n,L) \in G_n$. The __dual net__ $G^D =$

(S^D, T^D, F^D, n, L^D) __of__ G is a pr/t net in which

(i) $\qquad S^D := T$ is the set of predicates of G^D

(ii) $\qquad T^D := S$ is the set of transitions of G^D

(iii) $\qquad F^D := F^{-1}$ is the flow relation of G^D

(iv) $\qquad$ n is the modulus of the tuples of G^D

(v) $\qquad L^D : \forall t \in S^D \, \forall p \in T^D \, \left[L^D(t,p) := <i-k> \longleftrightarrow L(p,t) = <i+k> \right]$
$\qquad\qquad$ where $i \in X$, $\quad k \in \mathbb{Z}$.

We will call the nets of $G_n^D := \{ G^D \mid G \in G_n \}$ __state-machine-like unary pr/t nets.__

__Definition 4.2__   Let $n \in \mathbb{N}$ and $G^D \in G_n^D$. The net $G \in G_n$ is called the __dual net of__ G^D. We will write $(G^D)^D := G$

__Definition 4.3__   Let $n \in \mathbb{N}$, $k \in X$, and $G^D = (S^D, T^D, F^D, n, L^D) \in G_n^D$. Suppose S^D and T^D to be ordered arbitrarily but fixedly.
Then we call

$$M^D := \{ M \mid \forall t \in S^D \left[t \xrightarrow{M} m_+ \in MS_+ (<N>^{v_t}) \right] \}$$
$\qquad$ the set of __constant markings of__ G^D

$$s^D := \{ Q \mid \forall t \in S^D \left[t \xrightarrow{Q} m \in MS(<N>^{v_t}) \right] \}$$
$\qquad$ the set of __constant S-vectors of__ G^D

$M_X^D := \{ M \mid \forall t \in S^D [t \xrightarrow{M} m_+ \in MS_+(\langle X+N \rangle^{Vt})] \}$ the set of <u>markings of G^D parameterized by X</u>

$S_X^D := \{ Q \mid \forall t \in S^D [t \xrightarrow{Q} m \in MS(\langle X+N \rangle^{Vt})] \}$ the set of <u>S-vectors of G^D parameterized by X</u>

$F^D := \{ V \mid V : T^D \longrightarrow MS_+(\langle N \rangle) \}$ the set of <u>constant forward firing vectors of G^D</u>

$F_{\{k\}}^D := \{ V \mid V : T^D \longrightarrow MS_+(\langle \{k\} + N \rangle) \}$ the set of <u>forward firing vectors of G^D parameterized by k</u>

$T^D := \{ W \mid W : T^D \longrightarrow MS(\langle N \rangle) \}$ the set of <u>constant T-vectors of G^D</u>

$T_{\{k\}}^D := \{ W \mid W : T^D \longrightarrow MS(\langle \{k\} + N \rangle) \}$ the set of <u>T-vectors of G^D parameterized by k</u>

Notice that $M^D \subseteq S^D$, $M_X^D \subseteq S_X^D$, $F^D \subseteq T^D$, $F_{\{k\}}^D \subseteq T_{\{k\}}^D$

S-vectors belonging to $M^D \cup M_{X_D}^D$ and

T-vectors belonging to $F^D \cup F_{\{k\}}$ are called non-negative

<u>Definition 4.6</u> Let $n \in \mathbb{N}$, $H \in G_n^D$, $k \in X$.

A solution Y of $Y^T \cdot H = \underline{0}^T$ is called

a <u>non-negative (linear) object-S-invariant of H</u> iff $Y \in M^D$,

a <u>(linear) object-S-invariant of H</u> iff $Y \in S^D$,

a <u>(linear) quasi-object-S-invariant of H</u> iff $Y \in S_{\{k\}}^D$

<u>Definition 4.7</u>

A solution Y of $H \circ Y = \underline{\emptyset}$ is called

a <u>non-negative (linear) object-T-invariant of H</u> iff $Y \in F^D$,

a <u>(linear) object-T-invariant of H</u> iff $Y \in T^D$,

a <u>(linear) quasi-object-T-invariant of H</u> iff $Y \in T_{\{k\}}^D$

<u>Definition 4.8</u> Let $I \neq \underline{\emptyset}$ a (quasi-) object-S-invariant of H.

We call I <u>minimal</u> iff I is non-negative and there exists no non-negative (quasi-) object-S-invariant $\bar{I}$ of H s.t. $\bar{I} \leq I$ with $\bar{I} \neq I$ and $\bar{I} \neq \underline{\emptyset}$

<u>Definition 4.9</u> Let $J \neq \underline{\emptyset}$ a (quasi-) object-T-invariant of H.

We call J <u>minimal</u> iff J is non-negative and there exists no non-negative (quasi-) object-T-invariant $\bar{J}$ of H s.t. $\bar{J} \leq J$ with $\bar{J} \neq J$ and $\bar{J} \neq \underline{\emptyset}$.

The following nets are the dual nets of G1 and G2

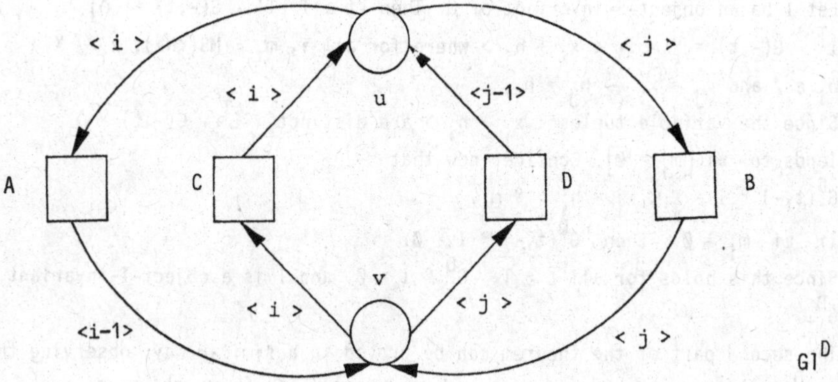

	A	B	C	D
u	- < i >	- < j >	< i >	< j-1 >
v	< i-1 >	< j >	- < i >	- < j >

Figure 4.1

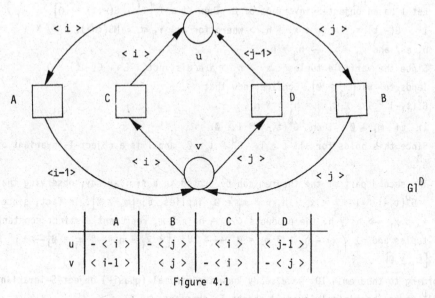

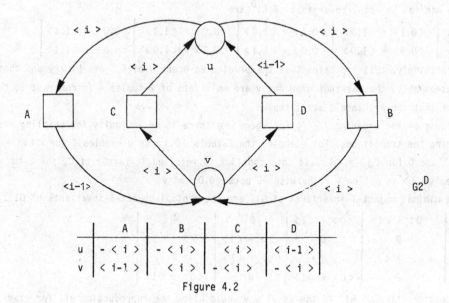

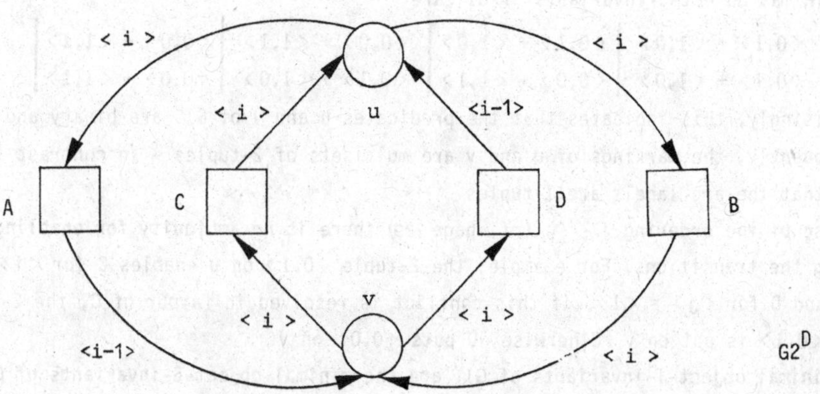

	A	B	C	D
u	- < i >	- < i >	< i >	< i-1 >
v	< i-1 >	< i >	- < i >	- < i >

Figure 4.2

The following theorem describes an important relationship between the object-invariants of a net and the object-invariants of its dual net.

Theorem 4.10 Let $n \in \mathbb{N}$ and $G \in G_n \cup G_n^D$.

Every object-S-invariant (object-T-invariant) of G is an object-T-invariant (object-S-invariant of G^D.

Proof:

Let I be an object-S-invariant of G. Then $\forall t \in T\ [I^T \cdot G(-,t) = 0]$.

$I^T \cdot G(-,t) = \sum_i m_i \cdot \langle x_i + h_i \rangle$ where for all i, $m_i \in MS(\langle N \rangle)$, $x_i \in X$, $h_i \in Z$ and $x_j = x_1 \Rightarrow h_j \neq h_1$.

Since the variable tuples $\langle x_i + h_i \rangle$ are distinct, $I^T \cdot G(-,t) = 0$ lends to $\forall i\ [m_i = \emptyset]$. Consider now that

$G^D(t,-) \circ I = \sum_i \langle x_i - h_i \rangle \circ m_i$.

If $\forall i\ \ m_i = \emptyset$ then $G^D(t,-) \circ I = \emptyset$.

Since this holds for all $t \in T$, $G^D \circ I = \underline{\emptyset}$ and I is a object-T-invariant of G^D.

The second part of the theorem can be proved in a similar way, observing that $G^D(t,-) \circ I = \sum_i \langle x_i - h_i \rangle \circ m_i = \emptyset$ implies $\forall i\ [m_i = \emptyset]$. In fact, since $x_j = x_1 \longrightarrow h_j \neq h_1$ the products $\langle x_i - h_i \rangle \circ m_i$ represent distinct constant tuples and $\sum_i \langle x_i - h_i \rangle \circ m_i = \emptyset \longrightarrow \forall i\ [\langle x_i - h_i \rangle \circ m_i = \emptyset] \rightarrow \forall i\ [m_i = \emptyset]$.

According to theorem 4.10, we already know the minimal (quasi-) object-S-invariants of $G1^D$ to be the minimal (quasi-) object-T-invariants of G1.

The minimal object-S-invariants of $G1^D$ are

u	<0,1> + <1,0>	<0,1> + <1,0>	<0,0> + <1,1>	<0,0> + <1,1>
v	<0,1> + <1,0>	<0,0> + <1,1>	<0,1> + <1,0>	<0,0> + <1,1>

Surprisingly, this indicates that the predicates u and v of $G1^D$ are binary and that, consequently, the markings of u and v are multisets of 2-tuples - in contrast to the fact that the arc labels are 1-tuples.

Because of the ordering i < j (cf. page 339) there is no ambiguity for enabling and firing the transitions. For example, the 2-tuple <0,1> on u enables C for <i> = <0> and D for <j> = <1>. If this conflict is resolved in favour of C, the 2-tuple <0,1> is put on v. Otherwise, D puts <0,0> on v.

The minimal object-T-invariants of $G1^D$ are the minimal object-S-invariants of G1 :

A	<0> + <1>	<0> + <1>	∅	∅
B	∅	∅	<0> + <1>	<0> + <1>
C	<0> + <1>	∅	<0> + <1>	∅
D	∅	<0> + <1>	∅	<0> + <1>

A consideration of $G1^D$ in the usual way would allow the reproduction of, for example, the 1-tuple <0> on u by firing D for <j> = <1> and A for <i> = <0>. This reproduction is not possible if $G1^D$ is considered as the dual net of G1. As the second object-T-invariant indicates, a reproduction by A and D is possible only if A and D both fire for both parameter values.

All this shows that the interpretation of $G1^D$ as a dual net is extremely different from the usual 'naive' one. But if we now add the restriction $\langle i \rangle = \langle j \rangle$ to both (binary) predicates, 2-tuples with different components are no longer possible. If we furthermore set $\langle k \rangle \sim \langle k,k \rangle$, both interpretations become isomorphic (cf. $G2^D$). Since the dynamic behaviour of the net G1 supplemented by the inscription $\langle i \rangle = \langle j \rangle$ to both transitions is equal to the one of G2, we may conclude that when a net is dualized transition inscriptions become predicate inscriptions without being altered.

So far, we have not dualized the markings. The underlying idea will be that in dual nets firing sequences and backtraces will correspond to each other.

<u>Definition 4.11</u> Let $n \in \mathbb{N}$, $G \in G_n$; let t_0 be a transition and M a marking of G; let α_0 be a constant v_{t_0}-tuple.

<u>set</u> i := 0;

(1) <u>if</u> t_i is enabled for α_i under M

<u>then</u> the backtrace is finished

<u>if</u> i = 0 <u>then</u> go to (2)

<u>else</u> go to (3).

<u>else</u> a 1-tuple β_{i+1} is missing on an input predicate p_{i+1} of t_i,

the input transition t_{i+1} of p_{i+1} puts a 1-tuple β_{i+1} on p_{i+1} if it fires for the v_t-tuple α_{i+1}

<u>set</u> i := i+1;

<u>for</u> j = 0,1...,i-1 <u>do</u>

<u>if</u> $t_j = t_i$ and $\alpha_j = \alpha_i$

<u>then</u> go to (4)

<u>else</u> go to (1);

(2) we say that the backtrace is empty; go to (5);

(3) we say that $(p_1, \beta_1),\dots, (p_i, \beta_i)$ is a backtrace of G; go to (5);

(4) we say that $(p_1, \beta_1),\dots, (p_i, \beta_i)$ is a cyclic backtrace of G; go to (5);

(5) end

<u>Remark 4.12</u> (i) The backtrace is empty if t_0 is enabled for α_0

(ii) The backtrace is cyclic if one meets one and the same transition t_j two times when it should be enabled for the same tuple α_j but is not.

If a transition t_i is (at least partly) enabled for α_i under M, then all 1-tuples on the input predicates of t_i, which contribute to that being (partly) enabled, form a barrier against the continuation of the backtrace.

If t_i is fully enabled this barrier is total.

In the dual net a backtrace can be interpreted as a firing sequence. If now an input predicate p_i of t_i carries a 1-tuple $\langle k \rangle$ which contributes to the enabling by α_i in the dual net p_i is a transition that is not allowed to fire for $\langle k \rangle$. In other words, the transition p_i is blocked for a parameter value $\langle k-h \rangle$ where h depends on the label of the input arc of p_i in the dual net.

Definition 4.12 (i) Let $n \in \mathbb{N}$, $G = (S,T,F,n,L) \in G_n$, $(p,t) \in F \cap (S \times T)$, $L(p,t) = \langle y+h \rangle$, where $y \in X$ and $h \in \mathbb{Z}$. Let M be a marking of G with $M(p) \geq \langle k \rangle$ where $k \in \mathbb{Z}$.

Then in G^D the transition p is not allowed to fire for $\langle y \rangle = \langle k \rangle$. We call p blocked for $\langle y \rangle = \langle k \rangle$.

(ii) So, every tuple of M corresponds to the blocking of a transition in G^D. We call the T-vector of these blockings a blocking of G^D and, for convenience, denote it also by M.

(iii) The blocking M of G^D is called the dual of the marking M of G, and vice versa.

(5) LIVENESS AND DUALITY

The aim of this section is to formulate two 'invariant-free' versions of the liveness criterion theorem 3.3.

According to theorem 3.3, the marking M_o of a net $G \in G_n$ whose quasi-object-T-invariants are all simple is live iff all minimal object-S-invariants are marked. This is equivalent to the fact that all minimal object-T-invariants of G^D contain blocked transitions (according to theorem 4.10), i,e, that no marking can be reproduced in G^D. We will show that this is equivalent to the fact that a certain homogeneous linear equation system is not semi-positively solvable under additional constraints depending on M_o.

Theorem 5.1 Let $N \in \mathbb{N}$, $G \in G_n$, and $M_o \in M$ and let the net representation of each quasi-object-T-invariant of G be simple. M_o is a live marking of G iff in G^D no marking can be reproduced under the blocking M_o.

Proof:

A marking M of G^D can be reproduced under M_o iff $\exists\, t_{i_1},\dots,t_{i_s} \in T^D$ (not necessarily all distinct) and $\exists\, \alpha_{i_1},\dots,\alpha_{i_s}$ with

$$\forall i_j \left[\alpha_{i_j} \in \langle N \rangle^{V_{t_{i_j}}} \wedge \alpha_{i_j} \not\leq M_o(t_{i_j})\right],$$

such that $M = M + \sum_{j=1}^{s} G^D(-,t_{i_j}) \circ \alpha_{i_j}$ where

$$\sum_{j=1}^{s} G^D(-,t_{i_j}) \circ \alpha_{i_j} = G^D \circ \left[\sum_{\{i_j | t_{i_j} = t_1\}} \alpha_{i_j}, \sum_{\{i_j | t_{i_j} = t_2\}} \alpha_{i_j}, \ldots, \sum_{\{i_j | t_{i_j} = t_{|T^D|}\}} \alpha_{i_j} \right]^T = \emptyset.$$

This is equivalent to stating that the object-T-invariant

$$Y = \left[\sum_{\{i_j | t_{i_j} = t_1\}} \alpha_{i_j}, \ldots, \sum_{\{i_j | t_{i_j} = t_{|T^D|}\}} \alpha_{i_j} \right]^T$$

does not match the blocking M_0.

Hence, Y is an object-S-invariant of G, which does not match the marking M_0 and by theorem 3.3 M_0 is not live.

<u>Corollary 5.2</u> Let $n \in \mathbb{N}$, $G \in G_n$ and $M_0 \in M$ and let the net representation of each quasi-object-T-invariant of G be simple. M_0 is a live marking of G iff $G^D \circ Y = \underline{\emptyset}$ has no solution $Y \in F^D$ with $Y \neq \underline{\emptyset}$ under the additional constraint

(5.3) $\forall k \in \mathbb{Z} \;\; \forall p \in T^D \left[M_0(p) \cdot \langle k \rangle \neq 0 \Rightarrow Y_p(k) = 0 \right]$.

<u>Proof:</u>

M_0 is live <u>iff</u> in G^D no marking can be reproduced under the blocking M_0.
This is true (cf. the proof of theorem 5.1) <u>iff</u>

$$\nexists\, t_{i_1}, \ldots, t_{i_s} \in T^D \text{ and } \exists\, \alpha_{i_1}, \ldots, \alpha_{i_s} \text{ with } \forall\, \alpha_{i_j} \in \langle N \rangle^{Vt_{i_j}},$$

such that

$$G^D \circ \left[\sum_{\{t_{i_j} | t_{i_j} = t_1\}} \alpha_{i_j}, \ldots, \sum_{\{t_{i_j} | t_{i_j} = t_{|T^D|}\}} \alpha_{i_j} \right]^T = \emptyset$$

and t_{i_j} is not blocked for α_{i_j} under M_0, i.e.

$$\forall k \in \mathbb{Z} \;\; \forall p \in T^D \left[M_0(p) \cdot \langle k \rangle \neq 0 \Rightarrow \forall i_j \left[t_{i_j} = t_p \Rightarrow \langle k \rangle \not\leq \alpha_{i_j} \right] \right]$$

This is equivalent to stating that

$$G^D \circ Y = \underline{\emptyset}$$

has no solution $Y \in F^D$ such that (5.3) holds.

This dual version of the liveness criterion does not need any invariant; the additional constraint depends on M_0 only.

Moreover, we are able to formulate another 'invariant-free' version of the liveness criterion, in which no duality concept is used.

<u>Corollary 5.4</u> Let $n \in \mathbb{N}$, $G \in G_n$, $M_0 \in M$ and let the net representation of each quasi-object-T-invariant of G be simple. M_0 is a live marking of G iff $Y^T \cdot G = \underline{0}^T$

has no solution Y with $Y \neq \underline{\emptyset}$ under the additional constraint $Y^T \cdot M_o = \emptyset$

Proof:

Follows immediately from corollary 5.2 and theorem 4.10. Observe that the constraint $Y^T \cdot M = 0$ is equivalent to the constraint (5.3).

Remark 5.5 If the equation systems of corollary 5.2 and 5.4 have a semipositive solution Y, then Y is a non-negative object-S-invariant that is not marked by M_o. So, if in these versions the criterion detects a non-live marking M_o, it also provides for the non-marked object-S-invariants, which is a hint for 'improving' the marking.

Let us again consider the net G1 (Fig.1.1). In order to solve the equation system $G1^D \circ Y = \underline{\emptyset}$ (cor. 5.2) or $Y^T \cdot G1 = \underline{0}^T$ (cor. 5.4) we have to solve the difference equation system (2.8) on page 338. The minimal integer semipositive solutions of (2.8) are also shown on page 338. The additional constraints in the corollaries are for M_o, M'_o, M''_o, respectively,

(5.6) $Y_A(0) = Y_A(1) = Y_B(0) = Y_C(1) = 0$

(5.7) $Y_A(1) = Y_B(0) = 0$

(5.8) $Y_A(0) = Y_A(1) = Y_C(1) = 0$

None of the solutions on page 338 satisfies (5.6) and (5.7). So, we have shown again that M_o and M'_o are live markings of G1.

The fourth solution on page 338 satisfies (5.8). So M''_o is not live, and the fourth object-S-invariant is not marked by M''_o.

References

[Bo 83] BOGEN M. : Berechnungen in einfachen synchronisationsgraphartigen Prädikat/Transitionsnetzen. Diplomarbeit, Universität Bonn, 1983

[GL 73] GENRICH H.J. and LAUTENBACH K. : Synchronisationsgraphen, Acta Informatica 2, 143-161, 1973

[GL 81] GENRICH H.J. and LAUTENBACH K. : System Modelling with High-Level Petri Nets, Theoretical Computer Science, 13, 109-136, 1981

[GL 83] GENRICH H.J. and LAUTENBACH K. : S-invariance in Predicate/Transition Nets, in: Application and Theory of Petri Nets, Informatik Fachberichte 66, Springer, 1983

[La 83] LAUTENBACH K. : Simple Marked-graph-like Predicate/Transition Nets, Arbeitspapiere der GMD Nr. 41, Juli 1983

[LP 84] LAUTENBACH K. and PAGNONI A. : Invariance and Duality in Predicate/Transition Nets and in Coloured Nets Arbeitspapiere der GMD, Dezember 1984

SEMANTICS OF CONCURRENT SYSTEMS: A MODULAR FIXED-POINT TRACE APPROACH*)

A.Mazurkiewicz
Institute of Computer Science
PAS,PKiN, P.O.Box 22
PL 00-901 Warszawa
Poland

ABSTRACT

A method for finding the set of processes generated by a concurrent system (the behaviour of a system) in modular way is presented. A system is decomposed into modules with behaviours assumed to be known and then the behaviours are successively put together giving finally the initial system behaviour. It is shown that there is much of freedom in choice of modules; in extreme case atoms of a system, i.e. subsystems containing only one resource, can be taken as modules; each atom has its behaviour defined a proiri. The basic operation used for composing behaviours is the synchronization operation defined in the paper. The fixed point method of describing sets of processes is extensively applied, with processes regarded as traces rather than strings of actions.

KEY WORDS AND PHRASES

Concurrent systems, concurrent processes, traces, modularity, fixed point method, synchronization, system composition, Petri nets.

1. INTRODUCTION

A system is modular, if it is composed of a number of subsystems (modules) ordered in a hierarchical way, such that behaviour of each of them can be determined by behaviour of its direct subsystems, independently of the rest of the system. Due to its obvious advantages, modularity is one of the main objectives of system designers.

*) This paper has been prepared during its author's stay at Institute for Foundations of Information Technology GMD MBH Bonn.

In the present paper it is shown that for systems based on Petri nets the modular approach to their behaviour description is always possible, even though nets have no explicit modular structure. Namely, it is shown that each net can be decomposed into a number of modules such that their behaviours can be put together giving in effect the initial net behaviour. This composition is made by means of an operation, called here the synchronization, with the property that the set of processes generated by a net composed from modules is the result of synchronization of sets of processes generated by the modules. The synchronization is a dyadic operation on sets of processes, idempotent, commutative, and associative. It turns out that there is much freedom in the choice of modules: every partition of the set of places of a net uniquely determines a decomposition of the net into modules.

Concurrent systems considered below are finite, (0,1)-marked Petri nets with transitions to be interpreted as actions concerning some objects; the net itself represents the control structure of the system. In this paper interpretations of transitions will be not dealt with and transitions will be regarded as some abstract actions. Processes are finite, partially ordered sets of such action occurrences; it has been found quite unnecessary to deal with infinite processes generated by a net, since all information about them can be inferred from the set of all finite processes of the net. Such a set will be called the activity of the net. Activities of nets will be expressed either by explicit (regular) expressions, or by some fixed point equations.Our main goal is to show how to construct an equation for the synchronized activities knowing equations for each of them separately.

To avoid combinatorial difficulties resulting from string representation of processes and caused by their interleaving, traces rather than strings will be used. Traces are equivalence classes of strings; strings are equivalent, if they differ from each other only in the ordering of mutually concurrent occurences of actions; such a difference is considered here as irrevalent.

Several concepts have influenced on the paper. The first one is the concept of a net to due to Petri [9],[2]; it gives theoretical foundations to the present approach. The second one is the notion of path expressions and the related theory developed by Newcastle group with Lauer, Shields and Best [5] and CSP language of Hoare [4]; their synchronization mechanism is very close to that presented here. The third one is the concept of projection as investigated by Györy et al.[3]; this notion has turned out to be of great importance for our paper. All these concepts, together with the notion of a trace [7] led to the present approach. It must be also pointed out that the importance of modularity in concurrent systems design has been early recognized by Milner [8]; he was the first to adopt modularity as a background of his CCS system. His approach, however, differs considerably from our approach.

The paper is organized as follows. First, some basic notions and facts concerning traces are given. Next, some operations on sets of traces are either recalled or defined; the notion of synchronization, crucial for the paper, is introduced in this section. In the following section a composition operation for nets is defined and it is shown that the activity of a net composed from modules can be expressed by synchronizing the activities of these modules. It is also shown that each net can be composed from its atoms, i.e. the simplest modules containing one place only and with activities explicitly given. The main theorem of this paper is contained in this section. Examples constitute the final part of the paper. It is shown how to deal with fixed point equations for activities and how to synchronize them. The first example has been elaborated in detail; in remaining ones some steps of solving procedures are omitted.

The standard mathematical notation is used through the paper. In addition, the following convention is adopted: whenever it causes no ambiguity, a symbol, a string composed of this symbol alone and a set of containing this string as the only element, will be denoted by the same symbol. In the notation used in this paper we will often identify a singleton set with its element.

2. DEPENDENCIES AND TRACES

Let A be a set of symbols fixed from now on, A* be the set of all finite sequences (strings) of elements from A, ε be the empty string, and let $\circ$ be the concatenation operation. Then $(A^*,\circ,\varepsilon)$ is a (free) monoid called the monoid of strings over A. Clearly, $(B^*,\circ,\varepsilon)$, for any $B \subseteq A$, is also a monoid of strings over B (with concatenation $\circ$ restricted to B).

Let D be a finite, symmetric relation contained in $A \times A$, with dom(D) = cod(D), reflexive in its domain, i.e. $x \in \mathrm{dom}(D) \Longrightarrow (x,x) \in D$. Every such relation will be called a <u>dependency</u> in A. Let A_D = dom(D) and let I_D be the complement of D in A_D, i.e. $I_D = A_D \times A_D - D$.

If $(a,b) \in D$ ($(a,b) \in I_D$), then we say that a,b, are <u>dependent</u> (<u>independent</u>, resp.) <u>in</u> D, or that a is <u>dependent on</u> (<u>independent from</u>, resp.) b <u>in</u> D. For each $a_1,\ldots,a_k \in A, k \geq 1$, let $D(a_1,a_2,\ldots,a_k)$ denote $\{a_1,a_2,\ldots,a_k\} \times \{a_1,a_2,\ldots,a_k\}$. Clearly, $D(a_1,a_2,\ldots,a_k)$ is a dependency in A. Observe that $\emptyset$, $A \times A$ are dependencies in A, and that if D',D" are dependencies in A, then so are $D' \cup D''$ and $D' \cap D''$.

Let $\equiv_D$ be the least congruence in $(A_D^*,\circ,\varepsilon)$ such that $(a,b) \in I_D \Longrightarrow ab \equiv_D ba$

(here and elsewhere we omit sign $\circ$ for concatenation). The quotient algebra $(A_D^*,\circ,\varepsilon)/\equiv_D$ is called the <u>trace algebra</u> generated by D, or over D. Equivalence classes of $\equiv_D$, i.e. elements of $A_D^*/\equiv_D$,are called <u>traces</u> generated by D, or traces over D. Observe that in case of $D = A_D \times A_D$ (or equivalently, $I_D = \emptyset$), traces are isomorphic to strings over A_D; thus, strings can be regarded as traces generated by a full dependency. Let $[w]_D$ denote the trace generated by a string $w \in A_D^*$. By known properties of quotient algebras we have, for each $w',w'' \in A_D^*, t,u,u',u'',v \in A_D^*/\equiv_D$:

$$[w']_D[w'']_D = [w'w'']_D ,$$
$$(tu)v = t(uv),$$
$$t[\varepsilon]_D = [\varepsilon]_D t = t,$$
$$tu'v = tu''v \iff u' = u''.$$

By its very definition the algebra of traces is similar to that of strings; any statement valid for traces is valid for strings, but clearly not vice versa. The difference is expressed by a generalization of Levi's Lemma for strings [6]; this generalization leads to the following property of traces. Let $t',t'' \in A_D^*/\equiv_D$,$e',e'' \in A_D^*/\equiv_D$; then

$$t'e' = t''e'' \iff \text{either } e' = e'' \text{ and } t' = t'', \text{ or } e'e'' = e''e' \text{ and } t' = te'', t'' = te' \text{ for some } t.$$

From this equivalence it follows that the equality $t'e' = t''e''$ implies equality or independency of e',e''.

More information about traces and sets of traces (trace languages) is contained in [1] and [7].

For a given dependency D, to each string w in A_D^* a labelled graph $\langle w\rangle_D$, called a <u>d-graph</u> for w over D, is assigned as follows:

1. $\langle\varepsilon\rangle_D$ is the empty graph (no nodes, no arcs);
2. For each $w \in A_D^*$, $a \in A_D$, $\langle wa\rangle_D$ results from $\langle w\rangle_D$ by the following procedure: (a) add to $\langle w\rangle_D$ a new node labelled by a; and (b) add to the obtained graph arcs leading to the new node from all nodes of $\langle w\rangle_D$ labelled by symbols dependent on a in D.

It can be proved that for each $u,w \in A_D^*$,

$$[w]_D = [u]_D \iff \langle w\rangle_D \cong \langle u\rangle_D ,$$

i.e. that the representation of traces by d-graphs is unique in both directions (up to an isomorphism). Thus, it is up to our choice what we mean when speaking about traces: classes of equivalent strings, or labelled graphs; both interpretations are equivalent.

Call a d-graph g the <u>composition</u> of d-graphs g',g", if g arises from the (disjoint) union of g', g" by adding to it new arcs leading from each node of g' to each node of g", provided they are labelled by dependent symbols. The algebra of d-graphs over D with composition defined as above and with the empty graph as a constant is a monoid isomorphic to the algebra of traces over D.

<u>Example</u> 1. Let D = D(a,b) ∪ D(b,c) ∪ D(b,d); then $[abc]_D$ is represented by the graph

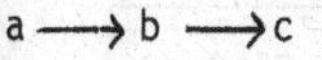

$[abcd]_D$ is represented by

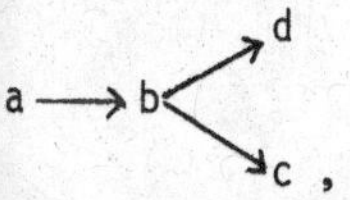

and their composition $[abc]_D[abcd]_D = [abcabcd]_D$ is represented by the graph

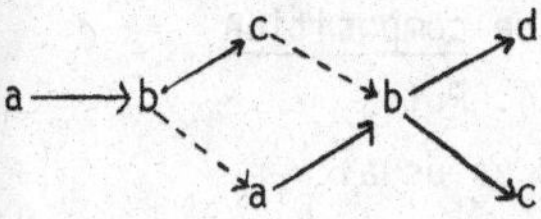

(here and elsewhere all arcs that follow by the transitive closure from other arcs are omitted; dotted lines indicate arcs added in the composition). □

Clearly, each d-graph is noncyclic and then its transitive closure represents a (partial) ordering of its nodes; treating nodes as occurrences of symbols they are labelled with, each d-graph determines a (partial) ordering of its symbol occurrences.

For a given trace t over D, we say that the symbol a is a <u>minimal</u> (<u>maximal</u>) symbol of t, if there is t' with $t = [a]_D t'$ ($t = t'[a]_D$, resp.). Observe that, in contrast to strings, traces may have more than one minimal (maximal) symbol; each two of them are independent in D. Clearly, minimal (maximal) symbols of a trace t are labels of minimal (maximal) nodes in the d-graph representing t, w.r.t. the above mentioned ordering.

Let in the sequel

$\underline{A}(D) = \{[a]_D: a \in A_D\}$,

$\underline{T}(D) = \{[w]_D: w \in A_D^*\}$, and

$\underline{P}(D) = 2^{\underline{T}(D)}$.

Having in mind our intended interpretation, elements of $\underline{A}(D)$ will be called <u>actions</u> over D, those of $\underline{T}(D)$ - <u>processes</u> over D, and those of $\underline{P}(D)$ - <u>activities</u> over D.

Let X be an activity over D and t be a process in X; we say that a trace u is a <u>continuation</u> of t in X, if $u \neq [\varepsilon]_D$ and $tu \in X$. A process t is said to have a continuation in X, if there is a continuation of t in X, otherwise t is said to have no continuation, or to be <u>complete</u> in X. Observe that if X, Y are activities and $X \subseteq Y$, then a process may be complete in X and not be such in Y. An activity containing some complete processes is said to have <u>deadlocks</u>; otherwise is said to be <u>live</u>, provided it is not empty.

Let t be a process over D; we say that actions a,b over D occur <u>concurrently</u> in t, if $(a,b) \notin D$ and, for some t' and t", t = t'abt"; clearly, in this case we have also t = t'bat". Actions a,b are said to be <u>concurrent</u> in an activity X, if X contains a process in which a,b, occur concurrently.

3. OPERATIONS ON ACTIVITIES

Let D be a dependency and $\sigma = [\varepsilon]_D$. For each $X,Y \in \underline{P}(D)$ the <u>composition</u> XY of X and Y is a set in $\underline{P}(D)$ defined by $XY = \{tu: t \in X, u \in Y\}$. Put $X^0 = \sigma$, $X^{n+1} = X^nX$, for each $n \geq 0$. The <u>iteration</u> X* is defined as usual:
$X^* = \bigcup_{n \in \omega} X^n$, $\omega = \{0,1,2,...\}$.

We have the following, easy to prove, properties of composition and iteration, for each $X,Y,Y',Y'',Z \in \underline{P}(D)$:

(a) $X\sigma = \sigma X = X$;

(b) $X\emptyset = \emptyset X = \emptyset$; $\emptyset^* = \sigma$;

(c) $X(YZ) = (XY)Z$;

(d) $X(Y' \cup Y'')Z = XY'Z \cup XY''Z$;

(e) if $XY'Z = XY''Z$, then $Y' = Y''$;

(f) $X^*Z = XX^*Z \cup Z$; $ZX^* = ZX^*X \cup Z$;

(g) $Y = XY \cup Z \Longrightarrow X^*Z \subseteq Y$; $Y = YX \cup Z \Longrightarrow ZX^* \subseteq Y$.

Conditions (f) and (g) state that X*Z (ZX*) is the least fixed point of a function f defined by $f(Y) = XY \cup Z$ ($f(Y) = YX \cup Z$, resp.).

Let D,D' be dependencies. For each $X \in \underline{P}(D)$ by the <u>projection</u> of X onto D' we mean an element $X|D'$ of $\underline{P}(D \cap D')$ defined as follows:

$$[\varepsilon]_D|D' = [\varepsilon]_{D \cap D'} ,$$
$$(t[a]_D)|D' = \begin{cases} (t|D')\,[a]_{D \cap D'}, \text{ if } a \in A_{D'} , \\ (t|D'), \text{ if } a \in A_D - A_{D'} , \end{cases}$$
$$X|D' = \{t|D' : t \in X\}.$$

Proposition 1. For any dependencies D,D',D", and each $X \in \underline{P}(D)$ the following conditions hold:

(a) $X|\emptyset = [\varepsilon]_\emptyset$;
(b) $\emptyset|D' = \emptyset$;
(c) $X|D' = X$, if $D = D'$;
(d) $(XY)|D' = (X|D')\,(Y|D')$;
(e) $(X \cup Y)|D' = (X|D') \cup (Y|D')$;
(f) $(X|D')|D'' = X|(D' \cap D'')$.

Proof. Follows directly from the definition. □

Example 2. Let $D = D(a,b,c,d)$, $D' = D(a,c,d) \cup D(b,c,d)$, $t = [abcd]_D$. Then $t|D' = [abcd]_{D'}$:

$t = a \longrightarrow b \longrightarrow c \longrightarrow d$,

t|D' = 

Let $D = D(a,c) \cup D(b,c)$, $D' = D(a,c,d)$, $t = [abcab]_D$. Then $t|D' = [aca]_{D(a,c)}$:

t = 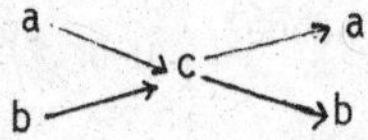 ,

$t|D' = a \longrightarrow c \longrightarrow a.$ □

By synchronization of $X \in \underline{P}(D')$ with $Y \in \underline{P}(D'')$ we shall mean a set of processes from $\underline{T}(D' \cup D'')$, i.e. an element of $\underline{P}(D' \cup D'')$, denoted here by $X \| Y$, and defined as follows: $X\|Y = \{t : t|D' \in X, t|D'' \in Y\}$. By this definition, if $t \in X\|Y$, then there are $t' \in X$, $t'' \in Y$ such that $t' = t|D'$, $t'' = t|D''$. In such a case we say that t is the synchronization of t' with t". Let us see what does it mean. By projection properties and by definition of orderings induced by dependencies, the following conditions hold: (a) each action occuring in t is an action of t' or of t", and no other action occurs in t; (b) action occurrences ordered in t' or in t" are ordered in the same way in t; (c) the number of occurrences of any action in t'(in t") is the same as in t.

The above conditions are exactly properties of what we would like to call the synchronization of t' with t". Observe that some action occurrences not ordered in t' or t" may become ordered in effect of synchronization. Since $X \| Y$ contains effects of synchronization of all processes from X and Y which are able to be synchronized, it is justified to call it the synchronized activity of X and Y.

Proposition 2. Let $t' \in \underline{T}(D')$, $t'' \in \underline{T}(D'')$. A synchronization of t' with t" exists if and only if $t'|D'' = t''|D'$.

Proof. Let $t'|D'' = t''|D' = [a_1 a_2 \ldots a_k]_{D' \cap D''}$, $k \geq 0$. Then, by the projection definition, there are strings $u_0, u_1, \ldots, u_k$ over $A_{D'} - A_{D''}$ and $w_0, w_1, \ldots, w_k$ over $A_{D''} - A_{D'}$ such that $t' = [u_0 a_1 u_1 a_2 \ldots u_{k-1} a_k u_k]_{D'}$ and $t'' = [w_0 a_1 w_1 a_2 \ldots w_{k-1} a_k w_k]_{D''}$. Put $t = [u_0 w_0 a_1 u_1 w_1 a_2 \ldots u_{k-1} w_{k-1} a_k u_k w_k]_{D' \cup D''}$; then $t|D' = t'$, $t|D'' = t''$, hence $t = t' \| t''$. Let now $t = t' \| t''$; then $t'|D'' = (t|D')|D'' = t|(D' \cap D'') = (t|D'')|D' = t''|D'$. □

Proposition 3. Let $X \in \underline{P}(D')$, $Y \in \underline{P}(D'')$. Then $X \| Y = \emptyset \iff X|D'' \cap Y|D' = \emptyset$.

Proof. Suppose $t \in X \| Y$; then there are $t' \in X$, $t'' \in Y$, such that $t = t' \| t''$; by the preceding proposition $t'|D'' = t''|D'$; since $t'|D'' \in X|D''$, $t''|D' \in Y|D'$, we have an element in $X|D'' \cap Y|D'$. Suppose $u \in X|D'' \cap Y|D'$; hence $u \in X|D''$ and $u \in Y|D'$; thus, there are $t' \in X$, $t'' \in Y$ such that $u = t'|D'' = t''|D'$; by the preceding proposition there is a t with $t = t' \| t''$, hence $t \in X \| Y$. □

The above criterion will serve for removing vanishing factors from synchronization equations in the sequel.

Synchronization can involve concurrency; e.g. let $[abc]_{D_1}$, $[dbe]_{D_2}$ be traces with $D_1 = D(a,b,c)$, $D_1 = D(d,b,e)$; then in the trace $[abc]_{D_1} \| [dbe]_{D_2} = [adbce]_{D_1 \cup D_2}$ concurrences of a,d and of c,e are concurrent:

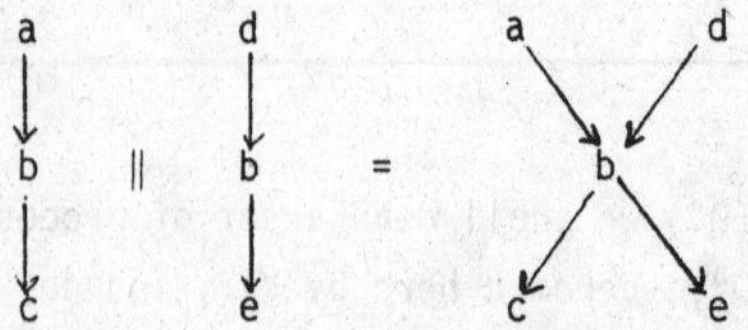

It can also reduce concurrency; e.g. let $[abcd]_{D_1}$, $[abcd]_{D_2}$ be traces with $D_1 = D(a,c,d) \cup D(b,c,d)$, $D_2 = D(a,b,c) \cup D(a,b,d)$; then in their synchronization $[abcd]_{D_1 \cup D_2}$ no action occurrences are concurrent:

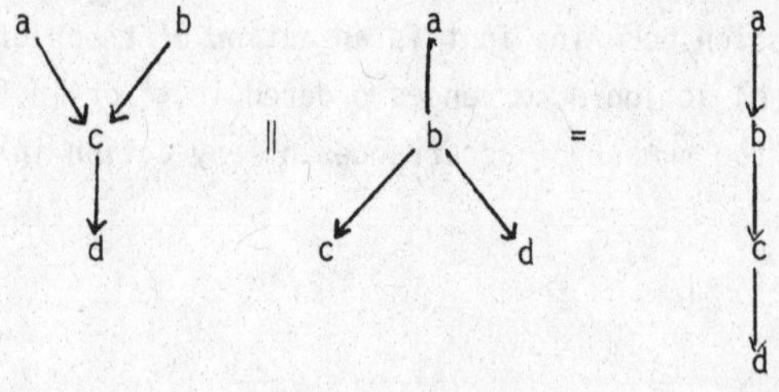

Let D,D',D" be dependencies, $\sigma' = [\varepsilon]_{D'}$, $\sigma" = [\varepsilon]_{D"}$, $\sigma = [\varepsilon]_{D' \cup D"}$.

Proposition 4. For each $X, X', X" \in \underline{P}(D')$, $Y \in \underline{P}(D")$, $Z \in \underline{P}(D)$, $V \in \underline{P}(D' \cup D")$, and $t \in \underline{T}(D' \cup D")$:

(a) $X \| X = X$;
(b) $X \| Y = Y \| X$;
(c) $X \| (Y \| Z) = (X \| Y) \| Z$;
(d) $X \| \emptyset = \emptyset$;
(e) $\sigma' \| \sigma" = \sigma$;
(f) $(X' \cup X") \| Y = (X' \| Y) \cup (X" \| Y)$;
(g) $X \| Y = X \cap Y$, if $D' = D"$;
(h) $((t|D')X) \| ((t|D")Y) = t(X \| Y)$;
(i) $(X(t|D')) \| (Y(t|D")) = (X \| Y)t$;
(j) $(t|D') \| (t|D") = t$;
(k) $V \subseteq (V|D') \| (V|D")$;
(l) $(X \| Y)|D' \subseteq X$, $(X \| Y)|D" \subseteq Y$.

Proof. (a) and (b) are obvious. Proof of (c): $t \in (X \| Y) \| Z \iff$
$\iff t|(D' \cup D") \in X \| Y,\ t|D \in Z \iff (t|(D' \cup D"))|D' \in X,\ (t|(D' \cup D"))|D" \in Y,\ t|D \in Z \iff$
$\iff t|D' \in X,\ t|D" \in Y,\ t|D \in Z$. The same result we get for $t \in X \| (Y \| Z)$. (d), (e), (f), (g) are obvious, (h), (i), (j) follow directly from the definition; to prove (k) observe first that the synchronization is monotonic w.r.t. both of its arguments, and projection, due to Proposition 1.(e) is also monotonic; thus, if $t \in V$, then $t|D' \in V|D'$ and $t|D" \in V|D"$, hence by (j) $t = (t|D') \| (t|D") \subseteq (V|D') \| (V|D")$. (l) follows directly from the definition. □

Observe that inclusions in (k) and (l) cannot be replaced by equalities. For, let $D' = D(a,b,e,f)$, $D" = D(c,d,e,f)$ and $D = D' \cup D"$, and let $V = [ac \cup bd]_D$; then $V|D' = [a \cup b]_{D'}$, $V|D" = [c \cup d]_{D"}$, but $(V|D') \| (V|D") = [ac \cup ad \cup bc \cup bd]_D \neq V$. Put $X = [ef]_{D'}$, $Y = [fe]_{D"}$; then $X \| Y = \emptyset$, hence $(X \| Y)|D' = \emptyset \neq X$, $(X \| Y)|D" = \emptyset \neq Y$.

Observe that by (b) and (c), i.e. from commutativity and associativity of the synchronization, it follows that the order of the synchronization evaluation for a number of activities is irrelevant. Observe also that from the proof of associativity we have for any dependencies $D_1, \ldots, D_k$, $k \geq 1$, and any $X_i \in \underline{P}(D_i)$, $1 \leq i \leq k$:
$t \in X_1 \| \ldots \| X_k \iff t|D_1 \in X_1, \ldots, t|D_k \in X_k$.

To simplify the notation, let us adopt the following hierarchy of operations on activities: composition, intersection, projection, synchronization, and union (thus the binding by composition is strongest).

Theorem 1. The synchronization operation $\|$ is the least function from $\underline{P}(D') \times \underline{P}(D")$ to $\underline{P}(D' \cup D")$ (w.r.t. the inclusion ordering of its values) meeting the following conditions:

(a) $(e|D')X\|(e|D")Y = e(X\|Y)$,

(b) $(X' \cup X")\|Y = X'\|Y \cup X"\|Y$,

(c) $X\|(Y' \cup Y") = X\|Y' \cup X\|Y"$,

(d) $\sigma'\|\sigma" = \sigma$,

for each $e \in \underline{A}(D' \cup D")$, $X,X',X" \in \underline{P}(D')$, $Y,Y',Y" \in \underline{P}(D")$.

Proof. Conditions (a)-(d) follow from Proposition 4. To prove minimality of $\|$, let $f: \underline{P}(D') \times \underline{P}(D") \to \underline{P}(D' \cup D")$ be an arbitrary function meeting conditions (a)-(d). We have to prove: $t \in X\|Y \Rightarrow t \in f(X,Y)$. (*)

Observe that due to (b) and (c) f is monotonic w.r.t. both its arguments. Let $\sigma \in X\|Y$; hence $\sigma' \in X$, $\sigma" \in Y$; by monotonicity of f we have $f(\sigma',\sigma") \subseteq f(X,Y)$; by (d) we get $\sigma \in f(X,Y)$. It means that (*) holds for $t = \sigma$. Assume (*) as introduction hypothesis and let $et \in X\|Y$ for $e \in \underline{A}(D' \cup D")$. Thus, $et|D' \in X$, $et|D" \in Y$. Since $t \in (t|D')\|(t|D")$ by induction hypothesis we get $t \in f(t|D', t|D")$, hence $et \in ef(t|D', t|D")$ and, by (a) and Proposition 1.(d) , $et \in f(et|D', et|D") \subseteq f(X,Y)$. Proof is completed by induction. □

Proposition 5. For each $Z \in \underline{P}(D' \cup D")$, if $Z|D" = \sigma"$, then $(Z|D')X\|Y = Z(X\|Y)$, and $X(Z|D')\|Y = (X\|Y)Z$.

Proof. $(Z|D')X\|Y = (\bigcup_{t \in Z} t|D')X\|Y = \bigcup_{t \in Z} ((t|D')X\|Y)$ (by additivity of $\|$) =

$= \bigcup_{t \in Z} ((t|D')X\|(t|D")Y)$ (by assumption) $= \bigcup_{t \in Z} t(X\|Y) = Z(X\|Y)$.

Proof of the second equality is similar. □

Proposition 6. For each $X,Y \in \underline{P}(D' \cup D")$, if $X|D" = \sigma"$, $Y|D' = \sigma'$, then $(X|D')\|(Y|D") = XY = YX$.

Proof. $(X|D')\|(Y|D") = X(\sigma'\|(Y|D"))$ (by Proposition 5) $= XY(\sigma'\|\sigma")$ (as above) $= XY\sigma = XY$.

The second equality follows from commutativity of the synchronization. □

Let D b a dependency. For each $X \in \underline{P}(D)$, $e \in \underline{A}(D)$, let $X/e = \{t: et \in X\}$. Thus, $e(X/e)$ is the set of all processes in X having e as (one of) their minimal action. For instance, let $D = D(a,b) \cup D(c,d)$, $X = [abcd \cup cad]_D$; then $X/[a]_D = [cbd \cup cd]_D$, $X/[b]_D = \emptyset$, $X/[c]_D = [abd \cup ad]_D$.

Since A_D is finite for each dependency D, for any $X \in \underline{P}(D)$ there is a finite number of actions $e_1,\dots,e_k \in \underline{A}(D)$, $k \geq 0$, such that $X - [\varepsilon]_D = e_1(X/e_1) \cup \dots \cup e_k(X/e_k)$.

For each $X \in \underline{P}(D)$ let $max(X) = \{t \in X$: t has no continuation in X$\}$. Thus, max(X) is the set of all complete processes in X.

Proposition 7. For each $X \in \underline{P}(D)$ and $e \in \underline{A}(D)$: $max(e(X/e)) = e\ max(X/e)$.

Proof. Let $t \in max(e(X/e))$; hence $t \in e(X/e)$; it means that there is $u \in X/e$ s.t. $t = eu$; since t has no continuation in e(X/e), u has no continuation in (X/e); therefore $u \in max(X/e)$, hence $t = eu \in e\ max(X/e)$. Let $t \in e\ max(X/e)$; hence $t = eu$ for some $u \in max(X/e)$; since u has no continuation in (X/e), eu cannot have a continuation in e(X/e); it means that $t \in max(e(X/e))$. □

Let D be a dependency, $\sigma = [\varepsilon]_D$.

Theorem 2. The max function is the least function from $\underline{P}(D)$ to $\underline{P}(D)$ (w.r.t. the inclusion ordering of its values) meeting the following conditions:

(a) $max(\bigcup e_i(X/e_i)) = \bigcup e_i max(X/e_i)$, $(1 \le i \le k,\ k \ge 0)$,

(b) $max(X \cup \sigma) = max(X)$, $(X \ne \emptyset)$,

(c) $max(\sigma) = \sigma$.

for each $e_1,\ldots,e_k \in \underline{A}(D)$, $X \in \underline{P}(D)$.

Proof. First prove that max meets the above conditions.

(a) Let $X = \bigcup e_i(X/e_i)$; then $t \in max(X)$ iff $t = e_i u$ and $u \in max(X/e_i)$ for some u,i; but it means that there is i with $t \in e_i max(X/e_i)$, i.e. $t \in \bigcup e_i max(X/e_i)$.

(b) Let $X \ne \emptyset$; if $X = \sigma$, then clearly $max(X \cup \sigma) = Max(X)$. If $X \ne \sigma$, then t has a continuation in X iff it has a continuation in $X \cup \sigma$; it means that (b) holds.

(c) For each t, $t \in max(\sigma) \iff t \in \sigma \iff t = \sigma$; it proves (c).

Now prove minimality of max. Let f be a function from $\underline{P}(D)$ to $\underline{P}(D)$ meeting conditions (a),(b),(c). We have to prove $t \in max(X) \Rightarrow t \in f(X)$, (*)

for each $t \in \underline{T}(D)$, $X \in \underline{P}(D)$. If $t = \sigma$, then $X = \sigma$, by definition of max; hence by (c) $f(X) = \sigma$, and $t \in f(X)$. Assume now (*) as induction hypothesis and let $et \in max(X)$ for some $e \in \underline{A}(D)$. By definition of max, $t \in max(X/e)$ and $X \ne \emptyset$; by induction hypothesis $t \in f(X/e)$, hence $et \in ef(X/e)$ and by (a) $et \in f(X)$, or $et \in f(X \cup \sigma)$; by (b) $et \in f(X)$. By induction,(*) holds generally.□

Proposition 8. For each $t \in \underline{T}(D)$, $X \in \underline{P}(D)$, $Y \in \underline{P}(D) - \{\emptyset,\sigma\}$: $Max(tX) = t\ max(X)$, and $max(Y^*) = \emptyset$.

Proof of both equalities is obvious. □

4. NETS AND THEIR COMPOSITIONS

By a net we shall understand here any ordered triple $N = (P,T,F)$, where P and T are finite,disjoint, nonempty sets (of places of N and of transitions of N, resp.), $F \subseteq P \times T \cup T \times P$ (the flow relation of N), with $dom(F) \cup cod(F) = P \cup T$. Let, for each $a \in T$, $p \in P$:

$pre(a) = \{p: (p,a) \in F\}$, (the precondition function),

$post(a) = \{p: (a,p) \in F\}$, (the postcondition function),

$prox(a) = pre(a) \cup post(a)$, (the proximity function),

$neighb(p) = \{a: (a,p) \in F \cup F^{-1}\}$,(the neighbourhood function).

Let D be a relation in $T \times T$ such that $(a,b) \in D \iff prox(a) \cap prox(b) \neq \emptyset$. Thus, D is a dependency relation, called the dependency in N.

Subsets of P are called configurations of N; the set 2^P of all configurations will be denoted by C.

The reachability of N is the least function R_N from $C \times C$ to $\underline{P}(D)$ (w.r.t. the inclusion ordering of its values), such that:

(a) $[\varepsilon]_D \in R_N(S',S'') \iff S' = S''$;

(b) $[a]_D \in R_N(S',S'') \iff pre(a) \subseteq S'$, $post(a) \subseteq S''$, $S' - pre(a) = S'' - post(a)$,for $a \in T$

(c) $st \in R_N(S',S'') \iff \exists S: s \in R_N(S',S)$, $t \in R_N(S,S'')$, for $s,t \in \underline{T}(D)$.

Traces in $R_N(S',S'')$ will be called processes in N from S' to S".

Let Q_N be a function from C to $\underline{P}(D)$ defined by the equality:$Q_N(S) = \bigcup_{S' \in C} R_N(S,S')$; the value of Q_N for a configuration S is the set of all processes in N from S to any of possible configurations of N; for this reason Q_N will be called the activity function of N.

Finally, let $U_N = \bigcup_{S \in C} Q_N(S)$; U_N will be called the total activity of N.

A configuration S of N such that $Q_N(S) = [\varepsilon]_D$ is called dead; let S_0 be a configuration of N; then it is clear that any process in N from S_0 to a dead configuration has no continuation in $Q_N(S_0)$. Therefore, by definition of max function, the set $max(Q_N(S_0))$ is the set of all processes in N from S_0 to dead configurations. If $max(Q_N(S)) = \emptyset$, $Q_N(S) \neq \emptyset$, then N is said to be live for S.

The set U_N and functions R_N,Q_N, describe the behaviour of N.

Let in the sequel indices i,j run always over the set $\{1,2,\ldots,k\}$ $(k \geq 1)$. Let $N_i = (P_i,T_i.F_i)$ be nets; we say that a net $N = (P,T,F)$ is P-composed, or simply composed of $N_1,N_2,\ldots,N_k$, if $P = \bigcup P_i$, $T = \bigcup T_i$, $F = \bigcup F_i$, and $P_i \cap P_j = \emptyset$ for $i \neq j$.

Let $N = (P,T,F)$ be a net composed of $N_1,\ldots,N_k$, $N_i = (P_i,T_i,F_i)$. Write R for R_N, and let symbols for all notions introduced above and concerning the net N_i be indexed with subscript i. We shall write also $[w]_i$ for $[w]_{D_i}$, for $w \in T^*$.

Proposition 9. $D = \bigcup D_i$.

Proof is obvious. □

Proposition 10. For all configuration S_i', S_i'' in C_i:

$$R(\bigcup S_i', \bigcup S_i'') = R_1(S_1', S_1'') \parallel \ldots \parallel R_k(S_k', S_k'').$$

Proof. Put $S' = \bigcup S_i', S'' = \bigcup S_i''$. We have to prove that for each $t \in \underline{T}(D)$

$t \in R(S', S'') \iff \forall i: t|D_i \in R_i(S_i', S_i'')$. (*)

We prove (*) by induction w.r.t. the inductive definition of the reachability function. There are three cases to be considered.

(a) $t = [\varepsilon]_D$.

$[\varepsilon]_D \in R(S', S'') \iff S' = S'' \iff \bigcup S_i' = \bigcup S_i'' \iff \forall i: S_i' = S_i''$ (by disjointness of P_i) $\iff$

$\iff \forall i: [\varepsilon]_i \in R_i(S_i', S_i'') \iff \forall i: [\varepsilon]_D|D_i \in R_i(S_i', S_i'')$.

(b) $t = [a]_D$, $a \in T$.

$[a]_D \in R(S', S'') \iff pre(a) \subseteq \bigcup S_i', post(a) \subseteq \bigcup S_i'', (\bigcup S_i') - pre(a) = (\bigcup S_i'') - post(a) \iff$

$\iff \forall i: a \notin T_i, S_i' = S_i''$, or $a \in T_i$, $pre_i(a) \subseteq S_i'$, $post_i(a) \subseteq S_i''$,

$S_i' - pre_i(a) = S_i'' - post_i(a) \iff \forall i: a \notin T_i, [\varepsilon]_i \in R_i(S_i', S_i'')$ or $a \in T_i$,

$[a]_i \in R_i(S_i', S_i'') \iff \forall i: [a]_D|D_i \in R_i(S_i', S_i'')$.

(c) $t = su$, $s, u \in \underline{T}(D)$, and let (*) hold for s, t.

$su \in R(S', S'') \iff \exists S: s \in R(S', S), t \in R(S, S'') \iff \forall i \exists S_i: s|D_i \in R_i(S_i', S_i)$,

$u|D_i \in R_i(S_i, S_i'') \iff \forall i: su|D_i \in R_i(S_i', S_i'')$.

Thus, by induction, (*) holds in general. □

For nets N, N_1, N_2 we write $N = N_1 \| N_2$, if N is composed of N_1, N_2.

Theorem 3. For all nets N, N_1, N_2, and all configurations S_1, S_1' of N_1, S_2, S_2' of N_2, if $N = N_1 \| N_2$, then:

$$R_N(S_1 \cup S_2, S_1' \cup S_2') = R_{N_1}(S_1, S_1') \parallel R_{N_2}(S_2, S_2'),$$
$$Q_N(S_1 \cup S_2) = Q_{N_1}(S_1) \parallel Q_{N_2}(S_2),$$
$$U_N = U_{N_1} \parallel U_{N_2}.$$

Proof. The first equality is a direct consequence of Proposition 10.

Let C, C_1, C_2 be sets of configurations of N, N_1, N_2, resp., and let $N = N_1 \| N_2$. Observe that the following equivalence holds: $S \in C \iff \exists S_1, S_2: S_1 \in C_1$, $S_2 \in C_2$, $S = S_1 \cup S_2$. Therefore $t \in Q_N(S_1 \cup S_2) \iff \exists S \in C: t \in R_N(S_1 \cup S_2, S) \iff$

$\iff \exists S_1' \in C_1, S_2' \in C_2: t \in R_N(S_1 \cup S_2, S_1' \cup S_2') \iff$

$\iff \exists S_1' \in C_1, S_2' \in C_2: t \in R_{N_1}(S_1, S_1') \| R_{N_2}(S_2, S_2') \iff t \in Q_{N_1}(S_1) \| Q_{N_2}(S_2)$.

Proof of the third equality is similar. □

This is the main result of the paper. Using it, the total net behaviour can be built up from the behaviour of its parts. Behaviour of parts can be expected to be easier to compute than that of the whole net; actually, there exists a "standard kit" of simple nets with behaviour already known, such that an arbitrary net can be composed from elements of this set. Such elements are defined below.

Call a net atomic, if its set of places is a one element set. Let $N = (P,T,F)$ be a net and put, for each $p \in P$, $N_p = (p,T_p,F_p)$, where $T_p = \text{neighb}(p)$ and $F_p = F \cap (T_p \times p \cup p \times T_p)$.

Obviously, N_p is an atomic net, called an atom of N, and N is composed of the set of its atoms. Put $A = \{a: (a,p) \in F, (p,a) \notin F\}$, $B = \{a: (a,p) \notin F, (p,a) \in F\}$, $C = \{a: (a,p) \in F, (p,a) \in F\}$. (In order not to obscure the notation we write A,B and C rather than A_p, B_p and C_p - however this should not lead to a confusion.)

Proposition 11. Let R denote the reachability of N_p. Then:

$$R(p,p) = [(C^*BA)^*C^*]_D ,$$
$$R(p,\emptyset) = [(C^*BA)^*C^*B]_D ,$$
$$R(\emptyset,p) = [(AC^*B)^*AC^*]_D ,$$
$$R(\emptyset,\emptyset) = [(AC^*B)^*]_D ,$$

where $D = (A \cup B \cup C) \times (A \cup B \cup C)$.

Proof can be formally carried on by simple induction (similar to that from the proof of Proposition 10); however, keeping in mind the reachability definition, validity of the assertion is obvious. □

Corollary 1. Let Q denotes the activity function of N_p. Then:

$$Q(p) = [(C^*BA)^*C^*(B \cup \varepsilon)]_D ,$$
$$Q(\emptyset) = [(AC^*B)^*(AC^* \cup \varepsilon)]_D ,$$

with the same dependency D as in Proposition 11. □

Corollary 2. The total activity function of N_p is $[(A \cup \varepsilon)(C^*BA)^*C^*(B \cup \varepsilon)]_D$, with D the same as above. □

The above proposition together with its corollaries gives us explicit regular expressions for the behaviour of atomic nets. Thus, we have a method for finding behaviour of an arbitrary net: first, decompose it into atomic nets; next, find their behaviour by the above proposition; and finally, by successive application of the synchronization operation, find the behaviour of the initial net.

Observe that every partition of the set of places of a net defines a decomposition of this net; thus, we have much of freedom in a choice of suitable components (moduls) of composition. Clearly, it is not necessary to start working with atoms; some bigger subnets can serve as initial ones, provided their behaviour has been already found on another occasion or is taken for granted.

5. EXAMPLES OF THE CALCULUS

In examples below we adopt the following notational conventions. First, we shall omit square brackets around trace representants; subscripts indicating dependencies will also be omitted. Instead, we shall give explicitly the corresponding dependency relations. Secondly, places of nets will be denoted by integers. Subnets and their behavioural functions will be subscripted with these integers; for instance, a subnet determined by places 2,5,7 will be denoted by N_{257}, its reachability by R_{257}, etc.

Example 3. (Fig.1). Let $N = (\{1,2,3,4\}, \{a,b,c,d\}, \{(1,a), (a,2), (2,b), (b,3), (3,c), (c,4), (4,d), (d,1)\})$. Find all processes in N from {1,3} to {1,3}.

1. Decomposition. Atoms of N are:

$N_1 = (1, \{a,d\}, \{(d,1), (1,a)\})$,
$N_2 = (2, \{a,b\}, \{(a,2), (2,b)\})$,
$N_3 = (3, \{b,c\}, \{(b,3), (3,c)\})$,
$N_4 = (4, \{c,d\}, \{(c,4), (4,d)\})$.

By Proposition 11 the reachability functions for atoms are:

$R_1 = R_1(1,1) = (ad)^*$, $D_1 = D(a,d)$,
$R_2 = R_2(\emptyset,\emptyset) = (ab)^*$, $D_2 = D(a,b)$,
$R_3 = R_3(3,3) = (cb)^*$, $D_3 = D(b,c)$,
$R_4 = R_4(\emptyset,\emptyset) = (cd)^*$, $D_4 = D(c,d)$.

2. Synchronization.

$R_{12} = R_1\|R_2 = (adR_1 \cup \varepsilon)\|(abR_2 \cup \varepsilon)$
$= adR_1\|abR_2 \cup adR_1\|\varepsilon \cup \varepsilon\|abR_2 \cup \varepsilon\|\varepsilon$ (by Proposition 4b,4f)
$= adR_1\|abR_2 \cup \varepsilon\|\varepsilon$ (by Proposition 3)
$= abd(R_1\|R_2) \cup \varepsilon$ (by Proposition 4e, 4h)
$= abdR_{12} \cup \varepsilon$.

Similarly $R_{34} = R_3\|R_4 = (cbR_3 \cup \varepsilon)\|(cdR_4 \cup \varepsilon) = cbdR_{34} \cup \varepsilon$.

Hence $R = R_{12}\|R_{34} = (abdR_{12} \cup \varepsilon)\|(cbdR_{34} \cup \varepsilon)$
$= abdR_{12}\|cbdR_{34} \cup \varepsilon\|\varepsilon$
$= acbdR \cup \varepsilon$.

By Theorem 1 we get $R = (acbd)^*$ with $D = D(a,b) \cup D(b,c) \cup D(c,d) \cup D(a,d)$; thus, actions (a,c) and (b,d) are concurrent in R. □

Example 4. Let $N = (\{1,2,3,4,5\}, \{a,b,c,d\}, \{(1,a), (a,4), (4,d), (d,5), (5,c), (c,1), (2,a), (a,3), (3,b), (b,2), (2,c), (c,3)\})$. Find all processes in N from {1,2} to {1,2} (Fig.2).

1. Decomposition. Atoms of N are:

$N_1 = (1, \{a,c\}, \{(c,1), (1,a)\})$,
$N_2 = (2, \{a,b,c\}, \{(b,2), (2,a), (2,c)\})$,
$N_3 = (3, \{a,b,c\}, \{(a,3), (c,3), (3,b)\})$,
$N_4 = (4, \{a,d\}, \{(a,4), (4,d)\})$,
$N_5 = (5, \{d,c\}, \{(d,5), (5,c)\})$.

Reachability of atoms (by Proposition 11):

$R_1(1,1) = (ac)^*, D_1 = D(a,c)$,
$R_2(2,2) = ((a \cup c)b)^*, D_2 = D(a,b,c)$,
$R_3(\emptyset,\emptyset) = ((a \cup c)b)^*, D_3 = D(a,b,c)$,
$R_4(\emptyset,\emptyset) = (ad)^*, D_4 = D(a,d)$,
$R_5(\emptyset,\emptyset) = (dc)^*, D_5 = D(d,c)$.

2. Synchronization.

$R_{23} = R_2 \| R_3 = ((a \cup c)b)^* \| ((a \cup c)b)^*$
$= ((a \cup c)b)^*$ (by Proposition 4a (idempotency));

thus, $R_{23} = abR_{23} \cup cbR_{23} \cup \varepsilon$.

$R_{123} = R_1 \| R_{23} = (acR_1 \cup \varepsilon) \| (abR_{23} \cup cbR_{23} \cup \varepsilon)$
$= acR_1 \| abR_{23} \cup \varepsilon \| \varepsilon$ (by Proposition 3)
$= ab(cR_1 \| R_{23}) \cup \varepsilon$ (by Proposition 4e, 4h)
$= ab(cR_1 \| (abR_{23} \cup cbR_{23} \cup \varepsilon)) \cup \varepsilon$ (R_{23} unfolding)
$= ab(cR_1 \| cbR_{23}) \cup \varepsilon$ (by Proposition 3)
$= abcbR_{123} \cup \varepsilon$,

$R_{1234} = R_4 \| R_{123} = (adR_4 \cup \varepsilon) \| (abcbR_{123} \cup \varepsilon)$
$= adR_4 \| abcbR_{123} \cup \varepsilon \| \varepsilon$
$= adbcbR_{1234} \cup \varepsilon$,

$R = R_{12345} = R_{1234} \| R_5 = (adbcbR_{1234} \cup \varepsilon) \| (dcR_5 \cup \varepsilon)$
$= adbcbR_{1234} \| dcR_5 \cup \varepsilon \| \varepsilon$
$= adbcbR \cup \varepsilon$.

Thus, by Theorem 1, $R = (adbcb)^*$ with $D = D(a,b,c) \cup D(a,d) \cup D(d,c)$; concurrent are (d,b) in R. □

Example 5. Let $N = (\{1,2,3,4,5,6\}, \{a,b,c,d,e,f\}, \{(1,a), (a,3), (3,e), (e,1), (1,b), (b,5), (5,f), (f,1), (2,c), (c,4), (4,e), (e,2), (2,d), (d,6), (6,f), (f,2)\})$. Find all complete processes in N from {1,2} (Fig. 3).

1. Decomposition. Take the following subnets as modules:

$N' = (\{1,3,5\}, \{a,b,e,f\}, \{(1,a), (a,3), (3,e), (e,1), (1,b), (b,5), (5,f), (f,1)\})$,
$N'' = (\{2,4,6\}, \{c,d,e,f\}, \{(2,c), (c,4), (4,e), (e,2), (2,d), (d,6), (6,f), (f,2)\})$.

Activities of modules:

$Q' = Q_{135}(1) = (ae \cup bf)^*(a \cup b \cup \varepsilon)$; $D_{135} = D(a,b,e,f)$,

$Q'' = Q_{246}(2) = (ce \cup df)^*(c \cup d \cup \varepsilon)$; $D_{246} = D(c,d,e,f)$.

Thus $Q' = aeQ' \cup bfQ' \cup a \cup b \cup \varepsilon$, and $Q'' = ceQ'' \cup dfQ'' \cup c \cup d \cup \varepsilon$.

2. Synchronization.

$Q = Q' \| Q'' = aceQ \cup bdfQ \cup ac \cup ad \cup bc \cup bd \cup a \cup b \cup c \cup d \cup \varepsilon$.

3. Finding complete processes in Q.

$max(Q) = max(aceQ \cup bdfQ \cup ac \cup ad \cup bc \cup bd \cup a \cup b \cup c \cup d \cup \varepsilon)$
$= a\ max(ceQ \cup c \cup d \cup \varepsilon) \cup b\ max(dfQ \cup c \cup d \cup \varepsilon)$
$\cup\ c\ max(aeQ \cup a \cup b \cup \varepsilon) \cup d\ max(bfQ \cup a \cup b \cup \varepsilon)$
$= ac\ max(eQ \cup \varepsilon) \cup ad\ max(\varepsilon) \cup bd\ max(fQ \cup \varepsilon) \cup bc\ max(\varepsilon)$
$\cup\ ca\ max(eQ \cup \varepsilon) \cup cb\ max(\varepsilon) \cup db\ max(fQ \cup \varepsilon) \cup da\ max(\varepsilon)$
$= ace\ max(Q) \cup bdf\ max(Q) \cup ad \cup bc$.

Hence by Theorem 2, $max(Q) = (ace \cup bdf)^*(ad \cup bc)$ with $D = D(a,b,e,f) \cup D(c,d,e,f)$. Actions (a,c), (a,d), (b,c), (b,d) are concurrent in max(Q). □

Example 6. Let N = ({1,2,3,4,5,6}, {a,b,c,d,e}, {(1,b), (b,2), (a,1), (2,a), (3,b), (b,4), (4,c), (c,3), (3,d), (d,4), (5,d), (d,6), (6,e), (e,5)}). Prove that N is live for {1,3,5} (a net is live, if its activity is not empty and contains no complete processes) (Fig. 4).

1. Decomposition. Take the following subnets as modules:

N_{12} = ({1,2}, {a,b}, {(1,b), (b,2), (2,a), (a,1)}),

N_{34} = ({3,4}, {b,c,d}, {(3,b), (b,4), (4,c), (c,3), (3,d), (d,4)}),

N_{56} = ({5,6}, {d,e}, {(5,d), (d,6), (6,e), (e,5)}).

Activities of modules:

$Q_{12} = Q_{12}(1) = (ba)^*(b \cup \varepsilon)$, $D_{12} = D(a,b)$;

$Q_{34} = Q_{34}(3) = ((b \cup d)c)^*(b \cup d \cup \varepsilon)$, $D_{34} = D(b,c,d)$;

$Q_{56} = Q_{56}(5) = (de)^*(d \cup \varepsilon)$, $D_{56} = D(d,e)$.

Thus $Q_{12} = baQ_{12} \cup b \cup \varepsilon$, $Q_{34} = bcQ_{34} \cup dcQ_{34} \cup b \cup d \cup \varepsilon$, and $Q_{56} = deQ_{56} \cup d \cup \varepsilon$.

2. Synchronization.

$Q_{1256} = Q_{12} \| Q_{56} = (ba)^*(b \cup \varepsilon)\ (de)^*(d \cup \varepsilon)$ (by Proposition 6)
$= (ba)^*(de)^*(bd \cup b \cup d \cup \varepsilon)$ (by independency a,b of d,e)
$= (de)^*(ba)^*(db \cup d \cup b \cup \varepsilon)$;

Thus, $Q_{1256} = (ba \cup de)Q_{1256} \cup bd \cup b \cup d \cup \varepsilon$.

$Q = Q_{1256} \| Q_{34} = Q_{1256} \| (bcQ_{34} \cup dcQ_{34} \cup b \cup d \cup \varepsilon)$
$= bacQ \cup ba \cup decQ \cup de \cup bcdc \cup dcbc \cup bcd \cup dcb \cup bc \cup dc \cup b \cup d \cup \varepsilon$
$= bacQ \cup decQ \cup S$,

where $S = bcdc \cup dcbc \cup bcd \cup dcb \cup bc \cup dc \cup ba \cup de \cup b \cup d \cup \varepsilon$.

3. Finding complete processes in Q.

$max(Q) = b\ max(acQ \cup cdc \cup cd \cup c \cup a \cup \varepsilon) \cup d\ max(ecQ \cup cbc \cup cb \cup c \cup e \cup \varepsilon)$;

$b\ \max(acQ \cup cdc \cup cd \cup c \cup a \cup \varepsilon)$

$= ba\ \max(cQ \cup \varepsilon) \cup bc\ \max(aQ \cup dc \cup d \cup \varepsilon)$

$= bac\ \max(Q) \cup bc\ \max(abacQ \cup adecQ \cup aS \cup dc \cup d \cup \varepsilon)$

$= bac\ \max(Q) \cup bca\ \max(bacQ \cup decQ \cup S) \cup bcd\ \max(aecQ \cup c \cup \varepsilon)$

$= bac\ \max(Q) \cup bca\ \max(Q) \cup bcd\ \max(aecQ \cup c \cup \varepsilon)$

$= bac\ \max(Q) \cup bcdc\ \max(aeQ \cup \varepsilon)$

$= bac\ \max(Q) \cup bcdcae\ \max(Q);$

Similarly (by symmetric arguments)

$d\ \max(ecQ \cup cbc \cup cb \cup c \cup e \cup \varepsilon) = dec\ \max(Q) \cup dcbcea\ \max(Q).$

Thus, $\max(Q) = (bac \cup dec \cup dcbcae \cup bcdcae)\ \max(Q)$, hence by Theorem,2 $\max(Q) = \emptyset$. It means that there are no complete processes in Q and since Q is not empty, the considered net is live. □

6. CONCLUDING REMARKS

A calculus for finding behavioural functions of concurrent schemata has been described above. Knowing sets of processes generated by such schemata it is possible, for a given interpretation of transitions, to find some properties of concrete systems. Interpretations and related issues will be considered in a separate paper.

Though the presented method is defined for Petri nets, it can be applied as well to other systems. Let a system have a number of resources(for instance, shared memory units); let a partition of resources be given; then each element of the partition, i.e. a subset of resources, together with all active system components attachted to it, constitutes a module with its own behaviour. The synchronization of these behaviours puts some constraints on them giving in effect the total system behaviour. The nature of synchronization is here the same as in case of Petri nets.

ACKNOWLEDGEMENTS

The paper has been prepared during its author's visit at GMD Bonn. The author thankfully acknowledges the conditions created by all staf of GMD F1 Institute for facilitate the preparing this paper. Special thanks are due to Prof. Dr. G. Rozenberg from Leiden University who encouraged and nearly forced the author to work on this paper.

REFERENCES

[1] Aalbersberg, IJ.J., Rozenberg, G.: Trace Theory - a Survey, Technical Report, Inst. of Appl. Math. and Comp. Sci., University of Leiden, 1984.

[2] Genrich, H.J., Lautenbach, K., Thiagarajan, P.S.: Elements of General Net Theory, LNCS 84, 1980.

[3] Györy, G., Knuth, E., Romai, L.: Grammatical Projections, Working Paper of Comp. and Automation Institute, Hungarian Academy of Sciences, 1979.

[4] Hoare, C.A.R.: Communicating Sequential Processes, CACM 21/8, 1978.

[5] Lauer, P.E., Shields, M.W., Best, E.: Design and Analysis of Highly Parallel and Distributed Systems, LNCS 86, 1979.

[6] Levi, F.W.: On semigroups,Bulletin of the Calcutta Mathematical Society, 36, pp.141 - 146, 1944.

[7] Mazurkiewicz, A.: Concurrent Program Schemes and Their Interpretations, DAIMI Report PB - 78, Aarhus University, 1977.

[8] Milner, R.: A Calculus of Communicating Systems, LNCS 92, 1980.

[9] Petri, C.A.: Nonsequential Processes, ISF Report 77.05, St.Augustin, GMD Bonn, 1975.

N:

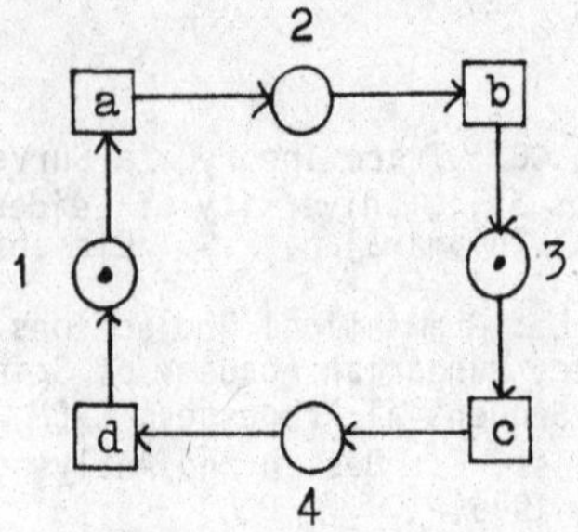

Decomposition:

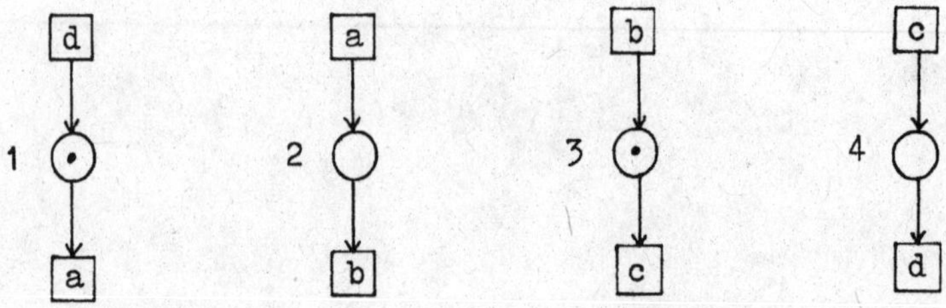

Example of a process in R:

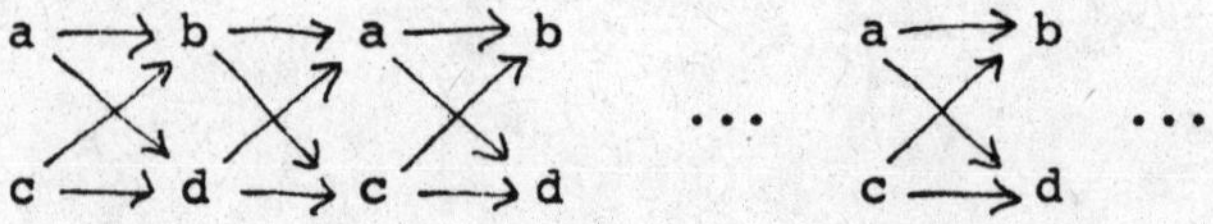

Fig. 1

N:

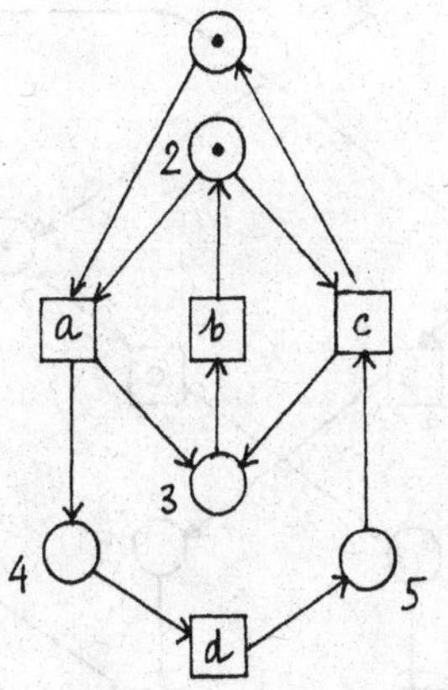

Decomposition:

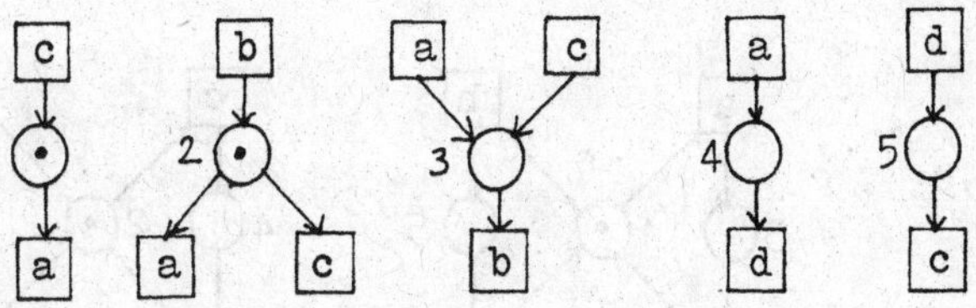

An example of a process in N:

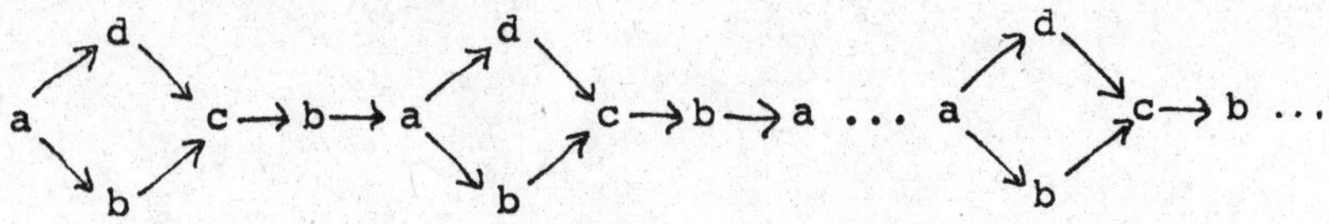

Fig. 2

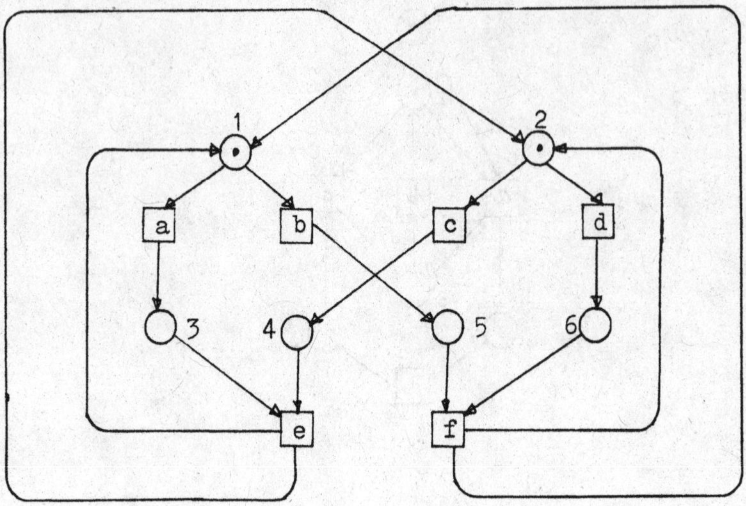

Decomposition:

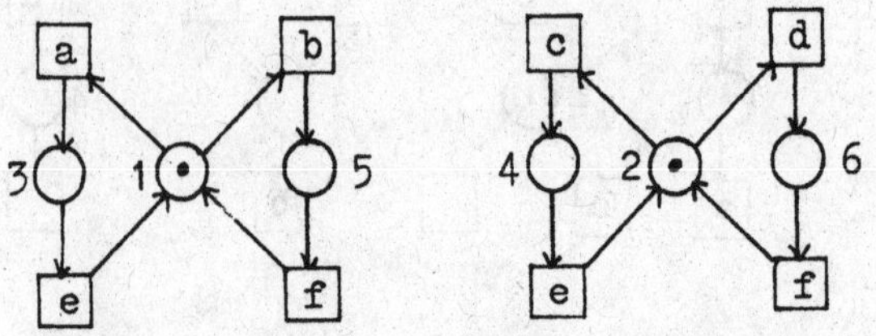

Fig. 3

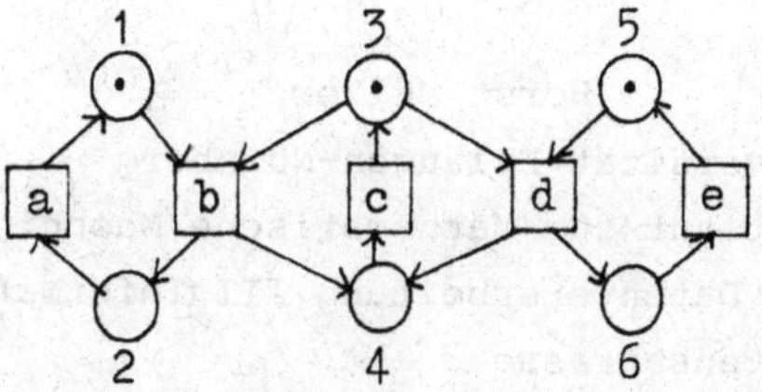

Decomposition:

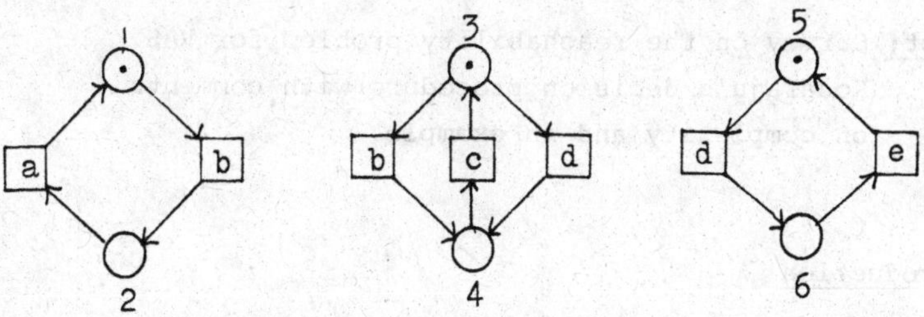

Fig. 4

THE REACHABILITY PROBLEM FOR VAS

Horst Müller
Universität Erlangen-Nürnberg
Institut für Mathematische Maschinen
und Datenverarbeitung III (Informatik)
Martensstrasse 3
D - 8520 Erlangen
West Germany

Abstract: Survey on the reachability problem for VAS. Kosaraju's decision procedure with comments on complexity and an example.

1. Introduction

I want to give a survey on the reachability problem for VAS. After some historical remarks I will speak about partial solutions and as a main part I will describe the general solution given by Kosaraju in 1982.

Let us begin with an informal definition of reachability questions. We can distinguish two types:

a) Reachability set problem:
Given a directed graph G and an initial node init.
Problem: Find a description of the set of all nodes reachable from init.

b) Reachability Problem:
Given a directed graph G, an initial node init and a final node fin.
Problem: Decide whether fin is reachable from init (on some path).

If G is a finite graph, then both problems may be solved using well know algorithms. If G is the graph of instantaneous descriptions of a Turing machine (arcs defined by the step function) then the halting problem car be considered as a special case of reachability. So in this case reachability is undecidable. In the case of VAS G has as nodes all markings (vectors) and arcs are given by the firing relation. Reachability in thi case is a well known hard problem. Lipton has shown in 1975 that it requires at least exponential space. Various slight modifications lead to undecidable problems. For a long time its decidability was an open question. As in similar cases of hard problems a lot of other problems were found being recursively equivalent or reducible to the reachability problem. The most important of them is the liveness problem which is of great practical interest.

The history of the problem up to its final solution may be compared with attempts of climbing to the top of some mountains (see Fig. 1). The first partial result was obtained by van Leeuwen in 1974 who solved the case of 3-dim. VAS. Next step was made in 1979 by Hopcroft and Pansiot extending to 5-dim. VAS with the help of a new concept of VASS. Another peak symbolizing reachability for the subset of persistent VAS was mastered independently by three persons in 1980: Grabowski, Mayr and the author.

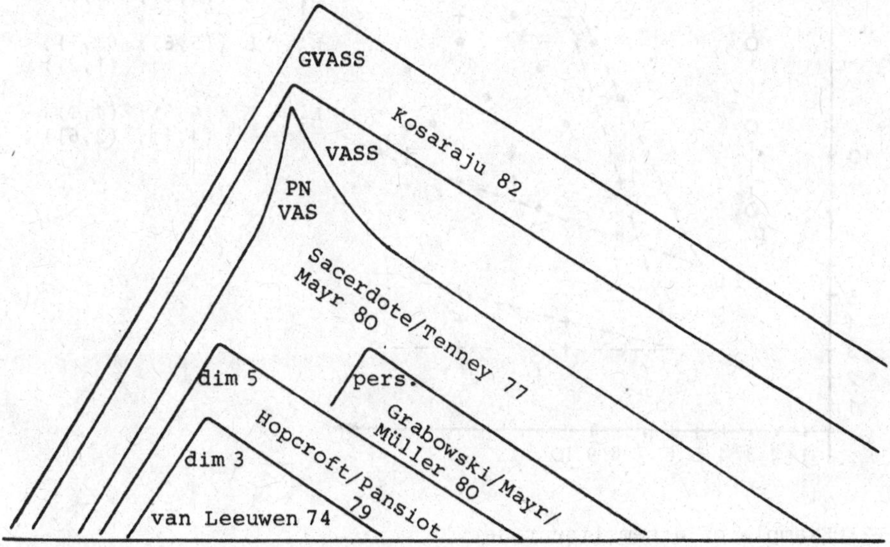

Fig. 1: Partial solutions of the reachability problem

Meanwhile - in 1977 - Sacerdote and Tenney claimed the solution of the general case. But there remained unfilled gaps in their proof. In 1980 Mayr as another clever climber found a steep way to the peak on which nobody was able to follow him - as far as I know. Finally in 1982 Kosaraju attacked the problem by making a round about tour first climbing to the higher mountain of GVASS and then coming back by specialization to the VASS and VAS peaks. This proof I checked during a research stay at the Technical University of Helsinki and found it nearly convincing. Only one gap remained which I was able to fill satisfactorily.

An important role in the field plays the concept of semilinear set. So let us shortly remember the definition.

A semilinear set SL is a finite union $SL = L_1 \cup L_2 \cup \ldots \cup L_\beta$ of linear sets L_i $(1 \le i \le \beta)$. A set $L \subseteq \mathbb{N}_o^n$ is linear iff there exist $c, p_1, \ldots, p_m \in \mathbb{N}_o^n$ so that $L = L(c; p_1, \ldots, p_m) = \{c + \sum_{j=1}^{m} x_j p_j \mid x_1, \ldots x_m \in \mathbb{N}_o\}$.
An example is shown in fig. 2.

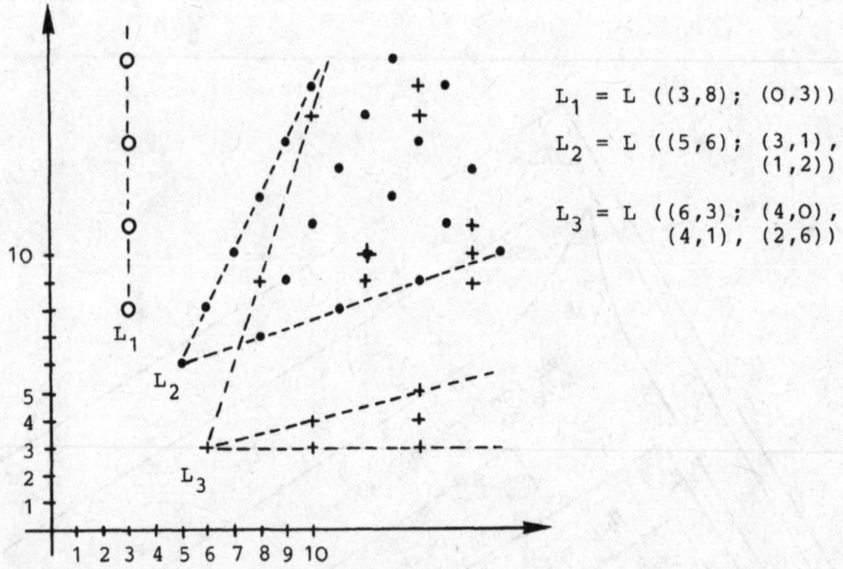

Fig. 2: Example of a semilinear set

We say that a set is effectively semilinear iff such a representation can be computed effectively. The sets L_i are called the linear parts of the semilinear set. The above mentioned partial solutions all solved the reachability set problem in showing effective semilinearity of the reach ability set.

Theorem: The reachability set of a VAS G is effectively semilinear, if

a) (Hopcroft/Pansiot; 79): Dim(G) ≤ 5,

b) (Grabowski/Mayr/Müller; 8o): G is persistent.

The element problem for effectively semilinear sets is decidable (Presburger arithmetic, solution of a system of linear equations). Many attempts to solve the general case were condemned to fail because they tried to show semilinearity of the reachability set. But any reasonable characterization of the reachability set would be in conflict with the undecidability of the equality problem for reachability sets.

Theorem (Hack 76): Equality of reachability sets of VAS is undecidable.

Hopcroft and Pansiot showed that their dimension 5 bound could not be improved by

Theorem (Hopcroft/Pansiot 79): There is a VAS of dimension 6 which has a non semilinear reachability set.

This VAS is constructed from a 3-dim. VASS by a general simulation procedure showing the equivalent power of VAS and VASS.

Theorem (Hopcroft/Pansiot 79):

a) Each VAS is a VASS

b) Each n-dim. VASS can be simulated by a (n+3)-dim. VAS.

This 3-dim. VASS with non semilinear reachability set is shown in Fig. 3. It is isomorphic to the Petri net in fig. 4. We will use it now to motivate the definition of a GVASS and some fundamental notions.

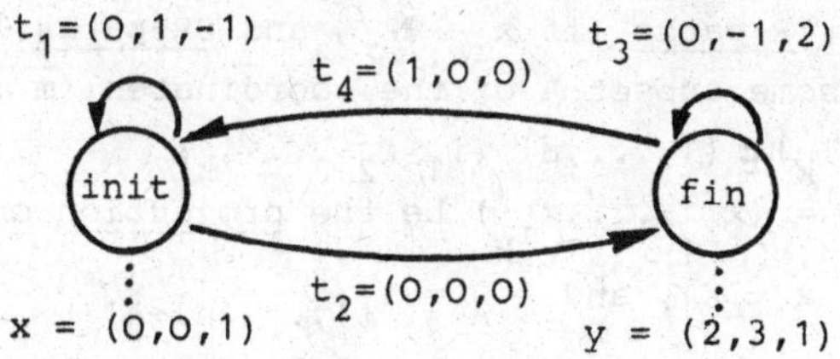

Fig. 3: Hopcroft/Pansiot - VASS G_1

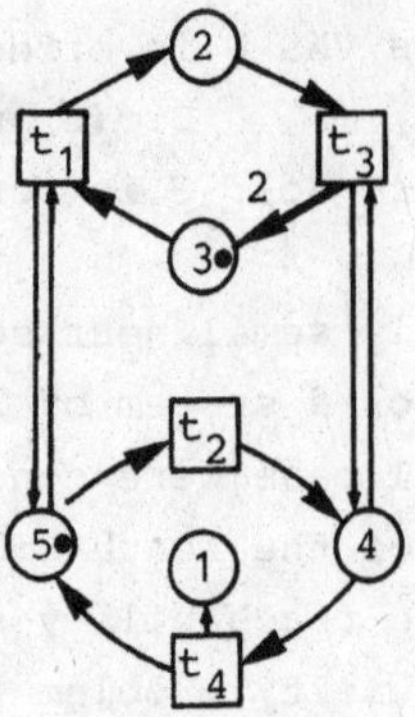

Fig. 4: Isomorphic Petri net with the non semilinear reachability set:

$$[oo1o1> = \{(x_1, x_2, x_3, o, 1) \mid o < x_2 + x_3 \leq 2^{x_1}\}$$

$$\cup \{(x_1, x_2, x_3, 1, o) \mid 0 < 2x_2 + x_3 \leq 2^{x_1+1}\}$$

2. Vector Addition Systems with states (VASS)

Fundamental for the proof is the concept of VASS introduced by Hopcroft/ Pansiot [Hop 79] which is equivalent to VAS and thus equivalent to pure Petri nets. A VASS can be defined as a product of a finite automaton and a VAS or as a finite directed graph whose edges are labeled by vectors of integers and has one initial and one final node. Furthermore an initial vector x and a final vector y are subjoined.

A step of the VASS leads from a configuration (q_i, x_i) to (q_{i+1}, x_{i+1}) if an arc labeled t goes from q_i to q_{i+1} (states of the automaton) and $x_{i+1} = x_i + t$ (vector addition). Sequences of steps define r-paths (with vectors $x_i \in \mathbb{Z}^n$), R-paths (if $x_i \in \mathbb{N}_o^n$) and SR-paths (if $\Pi_A(x_i) \geq \bar{0}$) with respect so some subset A of the coordinates ($\bar{m} := (m, m, \ldots, m)$).

For $A = \{i_1, \ldots, i_k\} \subseteq \{1, \ldots, n\}$ $(i_1 < i_2 < \ldots < i_k)$

let $\Pi_A(x, \ldots, x_n) = (x_{i_1}, \ldots, x_{i_k})$ be the projection on A,

$\Pi_A(X) = \{\Pi_A(x) \mid x \in X\}$, and $\Pi_{-A} = \Pi_{\{1,\ldots,n\}-A}$.

Example: $p = (\text{init}, o, o, 1)\ [t_1 t_1 t_2>\ (\text{fin}, o, 2, -1)$ is a r-path and a SR-path with resp. to A = {1,2} but no R-path.

Reachability problem for VASS: To decide:

$\exists \tau : (\text{init}, x)\ [\tau>\ (\text{fin}, y)$ is a R-path

The reachability set is $R(q,x) := \{(q', y) \mid \exists \tau : (q, x)[\tau>(q', y)\}$.

3. Generalized Vector Addition Systems with states (GVASS)

By inspection of G_1 one observes that an R-path from (init, x) to (fin, y) has to use t_4 exactly two times, because no other transition concerns the first component. By combining three copies of $G_1 - t_4$ we get the following VASS G_2 having an R-path iff G_1 has an R-path.
Furthermore we see that G_{21}, G_{22}, G_{23} cannot change the first component, so we know the first component of possible intermediate vectors y_1, x_2, y_2, x_3. Such components are called <u>rigid</u>. About the second and third component we suppose to know nothing, expressed by a don't care symbol ω in a <u>constraint vector</u> V_i resp. V_i'. This system G_2 is simpler

G_2:

$$G_{21} \qquad\qquad G_{22} \qquad\qquad G_{23}$$

$$x = V_1 = (0,0,1) \qquad V_2 = (1,\omega,\omega) \qquad V_3 = (2,\omega,\omega)$$

$$R_1 = \{1\} \qquad\qquad R_2 = \{1\} \qquad\qquad R_3 = \{1\}$$

$$V_1' = (0,\omega,\omega) \qquad V_2' = (1,\omega,\omega) \qquad y = V_3' = (2,3,1)$$

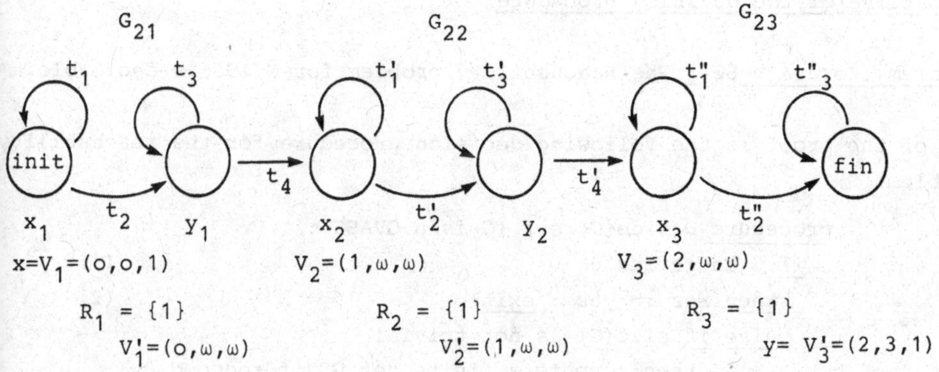

than G_1 in a sense defined later on and should motivate the <u>definition of a GVASS</u>, which is a finite chain of VASS G_i linked by edges from G_i to G_{i+1} and subjoined by constraint vectors V_i, V_i' and sets R_i of rigid coordinates satisfying the conditions

$$t_i \in \mathbf{Z}^n; \ V_i, \ V_i' \in (\mathbb{N}_0 \cup \{\omega\})^n; \ S_i := \{j \mid \Pi_j(V_i) \neq \omega\};$$

$$S_i' := \{j \mid \Pi_j(V_i') \neq \omega\}; \ R_i \subseteq S_i \cap S_i'; \ \forall t \text{ in } G_i : \Pi_{R_i}(t) = \bar{0}$$

$$x = V_1 \qquad\qquad V_i \ R_i \ V_i' \qquad V_{i+1} \ R_{i+1} \ V_{i+1}' \qquad\qquad V_s' = y$$

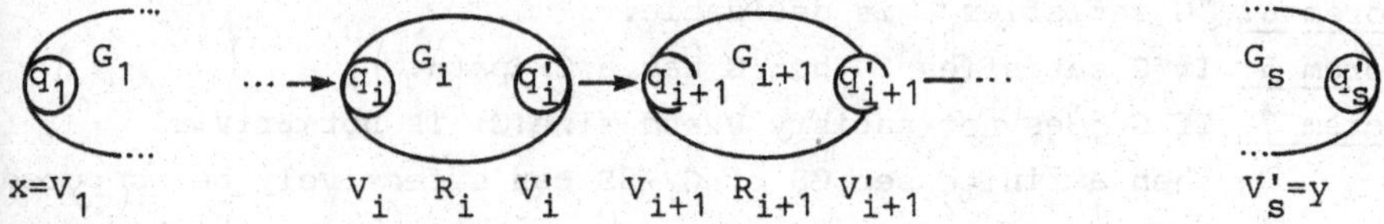

A <u>cr-path</u> p is a composition of r-paths p_i in G_i and connecting edges satisfying the given constraints:

$$p: (q_1,x_1)[p_1>_r(q_1',y_1)[t_1>(q_2,x_2) \ldots$$
$$(q_i,x_i)[p_i>r(q_i',y_i)[t_i>q_{i+1},x_{i+1}) \ldots \ [p_s>r(q_s',y_s)$$

$$\text{s.t. } x_i,y_i \geq \bar{o} \wedge \Pi_{S_i}(x_i) = \Pi_{S_i}(V_i) \wedge \Pi_{S_i'}(y_i) = \Pi_{S_i'}(V_i').$$

A <u>CR-path</u> p is a cr-path which is an R-path from (q_1,x_1) to (q_s',y_s).
<u>Reachability Problem for GVASS:</u> To decide the existence of a CR-path. If G has a CR-path we say shortly: 'G has a solution'.

4. Outline of the decision procedure

<u>Theorem (Kosaraju 82):</u> The Reachability problem for GVASS is decidable.

Aim of the proof is the following decision procedure for the reachability problem:

```
procedure Decide(G,res) {G is a GVASS}:
  if G satisfies θ                                          (1)
    then res := yes ; exit                                  (2)
    else if size(G) is not trivial
           then compute a finite set GS of reduced
                GVASS for G ;                               (3)
                for all G' ∈ GS do Decide (G',res)          od
           else res := no ; return                          (4)
         fi
  fi.
```

The correctness of this procedure follows from the following four theorems (numbering taken from Kosaraju):

(1) <u>Theorem 6:</u> "G satisfies θ" is decidable.

(2) <u>Theorem 5:</u> If G satisfies θ then G has a CR-path.

(3) <u>Theorem 7:</u> If G does not satisfy θ and size(G) is not trivial then a finite set GS of GVASS can effectively be computed such that

i) $\forall G' \in GS$: size(G') < size(G) and

ii) G has a CR-path iff $\exists G' \in GS$: G' has a CR-path.

(4) <u>Theorem 8:</u> If G does not satisfy θ and size(G) is trivial then G has no CR-path.

Termination is assured by the wellfounded multiset ordering for multisets of tripels of natural numbers ordered lexicographically. For a VASS G_i size is defined by

$$\text{size}(G_i) := (n - |R_i|, \text{ number of arcs in } G_i, \ 2n - (|S_i| + |S'_i|)).$$

For GVASS (composed as above):

$$\text{size}(G) := \text{multiset}(\text{size}(G_i) \mid i=1,\ldots,s)$$

5. Property Θ

The property Θ (for GVASS) is a crucial point of the story. It is a conjunction of Θ1, Θ2a and Θ2b given graphically by:

Θ1: $\forall m \geq 1: \exists$ cr-path p from (q_1, x) to (q'_s, y) :

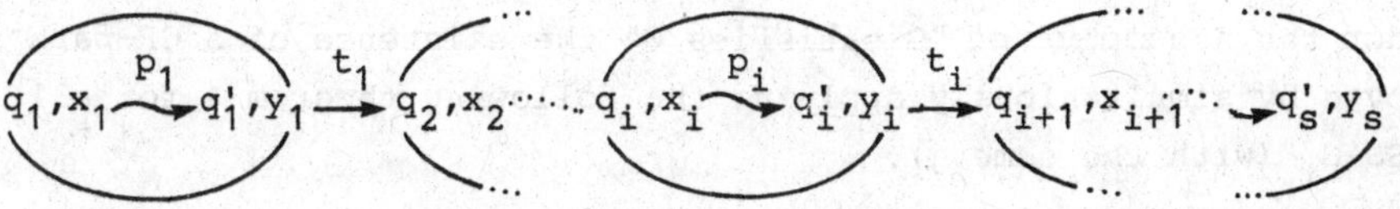

$$p = p_1 t_1 p_2 t_2 \ldots p_i t_i \ldots p_{s-1} t_{s-1} p_s$$

s.t. (a) $\forall i \ \text{fold}(p_i) \geq \bar{m}$ *)

and (b) $\forall i \ \Pi_{-S_i}(x_i) \geq \bar{m} \wedge \Pi_{-S'_i}(y_i) \geq \bar{m}$

Θ2a: $\forall i \ \exists \Delta_i \in \mathbf{Z}^n : \Pi_{S_i - R_i}(\Delta_i) \geq \bar{1} \wedge$

$$q_i, v_i \xrightarrow[\text{SR w.r.t. } S_i - R_i]{} q_1, v_i + \Delta_i \quad (\text{in } G_i)$$

Θ2b: $\forall i \ \exists \Delta'_i \in \mathbf{Z}^n : \Pi_{S'_i - R_i}(\Delta'_i) \geq \bar{1} \wedge$

$$q'_i, v'_i \xrightarrow[\text{SR w.r.t. } S'_i - R_i]{} q'_i, v'_i + \Delta'_i \quad (\text{in } G_i^{(\text{reverse})})$$

where $\Pi_j(v_j)$ = if $j \in S_i$ then $\Pi_j(V_i)$ else 0.

*) The folding (Parikh-Image) $z = \text{fold}(p)$ is a vector counting in $\Pi_j(z)$ the number of occurences of t_i in p.

To decide $\Theta 1$ one has to compute the (effectively computable) semilinear set $L_G = \{\text{efold}(p) \mid p \text{ cr-path}\}$, where for any cr-path p (composed as above)

$$\text{efold}(p) := (x_1, y_1, \ldots, x_i, y_i, \ldots, x_s, y_s, \text{fold}(p_1), \ldots, \text{fold}(p_s))$$

$$\in \mathbb{N}_o^{2ns+k} \quad \text{(where } k = \text{number of arcs in } G-\{t_1, \ldots, t_{s-1}\}$$

$\Theta 1$ holds iff at least one linear part of L_G satisfies:

Π_A(sum of all periods) $\geq \bar{1}$ for

A = {unconstraint components of $x_1, \ldots, y_s$, all edge comp.}

$\Theta 2a$ and $\Theta 2b$ are tested by constructing a coverability tree for each G_i and the reverse system $G_i^{(\text{reverse})}$.

6. Existence of a CR-path

Under the assumption of "G satisfies Θ" the existence of a CR-path is proved by simultaniously applying the following theorem 4 for all VASS G_i (with the same j).

Theorem 4: For any VASS G_i : If $\lfloor 1 \wedge \lfloor 2 \wedge \lfloor 3 \wedge \lfloor 4$, then $\exists j_o \forall j \geq j_o : \lfloor 5$.

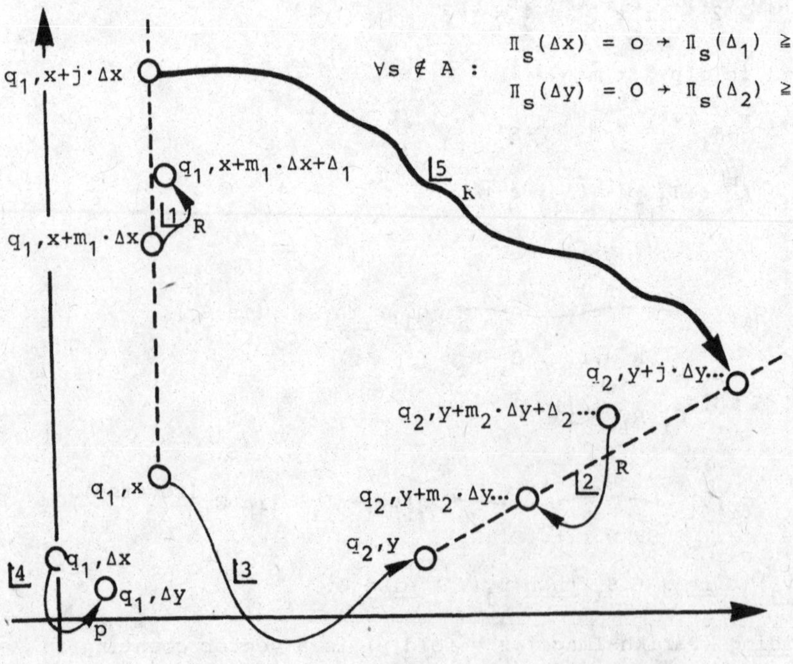

$\Delta x, \Delta y \geq \bar{0}$; $m_1, m_2 \geq 0$; $\forall t$ in G_i: $\Pi_A(t) = \bar{0}$; $\text{fold}(p) \geq \bar{1}$

Next main step is the reduction theorem. The correctness of the reduction depends on the following essential lemma 10.

7. The gap in lemma 10

Kosaraju states the following

Lemma 10: In any VASS, G, and for any initial configuration (q_1, x), the following hold:

(a) it can be effectively decided whether there exists a $\Delta \geq \bar{1}$ s.t. $(q_1, x+\Delta) \in R(q_1, x)$,

and

(b) if there does not exists any $\Delta \geq \bar{1}$ satisfying $(q_1, x+\Delta) \in R(q_1, x)$, then a constant c s.t. every point R-reachable from (q_1, x) has some coordinate value $\leq c$ can be effectively computed.

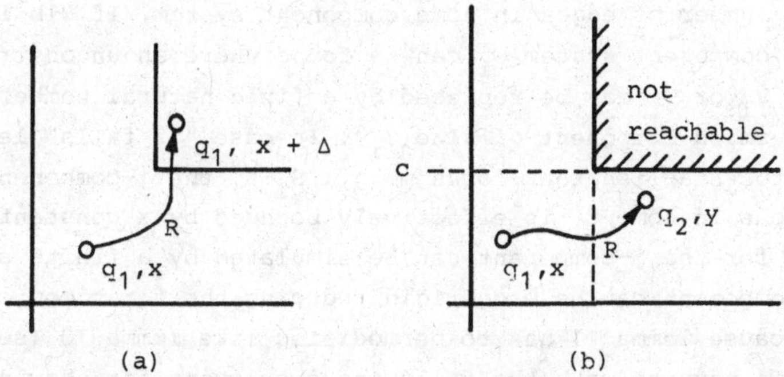

Fig. 5: To lemma 10

Lemma 10 (b) is not correct.

As a counterexample take the following VASS:

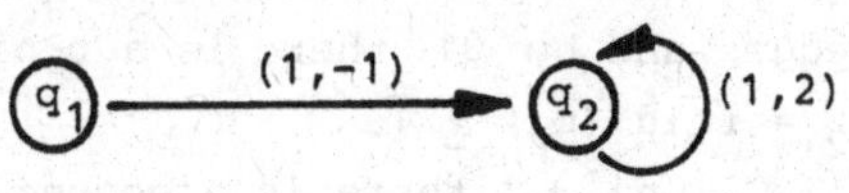

with initial configuration $(q_1, (o,1))$. Neither (a) nor (b) is satisfied because for any m $(q_2,(m+1,2m))) \in R(q_1,(o,1))$. Lemma 10 (a) is correct for any VASS. Lemma 10 (b) becomes correct if we make an additional assumption of strong connectedness:

(b') if there does not exist any $\Delta \geq \overline{1}$ satisfying $(q_1,x+\Delta) \in R(q_1,x)$ and G is (as a diagraph) strongly connected, then a constant c s.t. every configuration (q_2,y) R-reachable form (q_1,x) has some coordinate value $\leq c$ can be effectively computed.

Now we come back to the reduction.

8. Reduction

The proof of theorem 7 gives a reduction procedure. If size(G) is a multiset having no other elements than (o,o,o) and Θ is not satisfied then G has no CR-path (Theorem 8). For G with nontrivial size the reduction is dependent on the part of Θ not satisfied. If Θ1a is not satisfied, a reduction similar to the introductory example is made, reducing the number of edges in some component system. If Θ1b is not satisfied, a component system G_i can be found where an unconstraint component of V_i or V_i' may be replaced by a fixed natural number, thus reducing the third component of size(G_i). In case "Θ2 fails" lemma 11 (b) is used to establish that for some $j \in S_i - R_i$ the j-component in SR-computations in some G_i is effectively bounded by a constant c. The computations for the j-component can be simulated by a finite automaton. Then the j-component can be made rigid reducing the first component of size(G_i). Because lemma 11 has to be modified like lemma 10 (see section 7), we have to make the following supplement for showing that lemma 11 (b) is needed only for strongly connected VASS.

We may suppose that Θ1 is satisfied and that G has no isolated nodes (except in the case G has only one node; if there are isolated nodes $\neq q_\alpha, q_\alpha'$ in G_α, they can be eliminated without effecting the reachability question; if q_α or q_α' is isolated in G_α and $q_\alpha = q_\alpha'$, then there is no path from q_α to q_α' at all).
A one node G_α is strongly connected (trivial). If G has at least two nonisolated nodes, it has edges and by Θ1 there is a r-path p_2 from (q_α,x_α) to (q_α',y_α) s.t. $z_2 = \text{fold}(p_2) \geq \overline{1}$.
For $m_1 = \max\{\pi_j(z_2) \mid j \in \{1,\dots,n\}\} + 1$ there is a second path p_1 from (q_α,x_α) to (q_α',y_α) s.t. $z_1 = \text{fold}(p_1) \geq \overline{m}_1$. By lemma $\underline{6}$ $(z_1 - z_2 \geq \overline{1}$!)

there exists an unfolding of $z_1 - z_2$ from q_1 to q_1 showing strong connectedness of G_α. Now lemma 11 (b') is used. The rest of the proof remains unchanged.

9. Remarks on the complexity of the decision procedure

An essential part of the decision procedure is testing whether a GVASS satisfies property Θ. Testing $\Theta 2$ is done by 2s coverability tree constructions. This construction is of non primitive recursive complexity (cf. [Rac 78]) but in the following way it may be replaced by a better algorithm.

The property

"$\exists\Delta : \Pi_A(\Delta) \geq \overline{1} \wedge (q, v + \Delta) \in SR(q,v)$ w.r.t. A"

(essential for $\theta 2$) is a special case of the relativized coverability question

$\exists v' \, ((q,v') \in SR(q,v)$ w.r.t. $A \wedge \Pi_A(v') \geqq \Pi_A(v+\overline{1}))$

and this can be dedided in space $2^{cn \log n}$ ([RAC 78] Theorem 3.4. generalized to VASS).

Even if one replaces the coverability tree constructions by this more efficient algorithm the complexity remains unboundable by primitive recursive functions as a consequence of the following two theorems

Theorem (Mayr 8o): For any $n \in \mathbb{N}$ there exists a weak Petri net computer for the n-th Ackermann function, that is a VASS C_n such that the finite reachability set of C_n for a simple initial marking $\underline{x}_n$ has cardinality $Ack_n(2)$. For details and a simple proof see [MÜ 3].

Theorem For any $n \in \mathbb{N}$ there is a GVASS G_n which leads in one reduction step to a set GS_n of GVASS such that $|GS_n| \geqq Ack_n(2)$.

Proofoutline: Take as G_n the following system: (where C_n and $\underline{x}_n$ are from the above theorem)

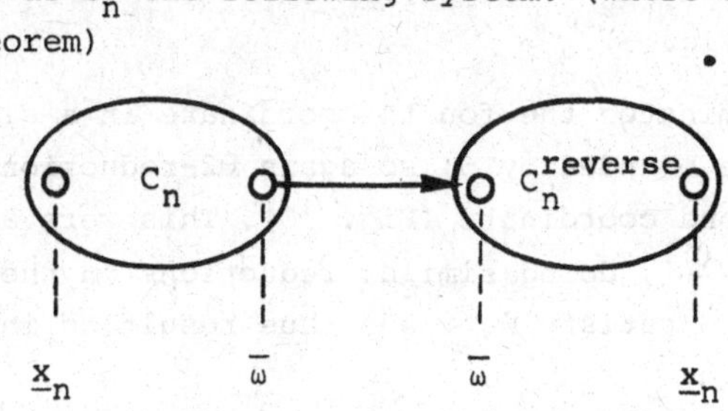

Fig. 6: GVASS G_n

10. Example, showing steps of Kosaraju's procedure

As a last part I shall give an example of an application of Kosaraju's decision procedure. Starting point is a given VAS (shown as a pure Petri Net in Fig. 7) an initial vector $\underline{x}$ = 12310 and a final vector $\underline{y}$ = 22001. By attaching a trivial one state automaton we get the initial GVASS $G^{(0)}$ consisting of only one VASS. The set $L^{(1)}$ of extended foldings of cr-paths in $G^{(0)}$ is the set of integer solutions of the equation $\underline{y} = \underline{x} + N \cdot \underline{z}$ where $N = (\underline{t}_1 \; \dots \; \underline{t}_6)$ is the net matrix and z = fold (p) for cr-paths p.

$L^{(1)}$ has two linear parts, one of them is of type

$L^{(1)}_1$: $(\underline{x}, \underline{y}, \omega\ \omega\ 1\ \omega\ \omega\ \omega)$ which means that t_3 is used exactly once in every cr-path p such that fold (p) $\in L^{(1)}_1$. By a Θ1-reduction this yields a doubling of $G^{(0)} - \{t_3\}$ as shown in Fig. 8.

Let $G^{(1)}$ be the resulting GVASS. The set $L^{(2)}$ of extended foldings in $G^{(1)}$ is computed by solving the system

$$\underline{y}_1 = \underline{x} + N^{(1)} \cdot \underline{z}_1,$$
$$\underline{x}_2 = \underline{y}_1 + \underline{t}_3$$
$$\underline{y} = \underline{x}_2 + N^{(2)} \cdot \underline{z}_2$$

(in twenty unkowns $\underline{y}_1, \underline{x}_2, \underline{z}_1, \underline{z}_2$). $L^{(2)}$ has 24 linear parts, one of them is of type

$$L^{(2)}_1 : \underline{x},\ \omega\ 2310,\ \omega\ 2001,\ \underline{y},\ \omega^{10}.$$

This gives by a Θ1-b reduction a GVASS $G^{(2)}$ with the same graph but sharper constraints V1', V2. Computing $L^{(3)}$ shows that $G^{(2)}$ satisfies Θ1 but not Θ2. Covering tree construction (or observing the invariant $\mathbf{u}_4 + \mathbf{u}_5 = 1$) gives a bound of 1 for the fifth coordinate. A Θ2-reduction 'replaces' the fifth coordinate by a finite automaton 'controlling' this coordinate (Fig. 9).

The next step eliminates the fourth coordinate in a similiar fashion. Now $\mathbf{u}_2$, $\mathbf{u}_3$, can be bounded by 6, so again Θ2-reductions 'eliminate' the third and second coordinate (Fig. 10). This were all reductions of the left half of $G^{(1)}$, doing similar reductions on the right half of $G^{(1)}$ yields a GVASS satisfying Θ and thus resulting in a 'reachable' answer.

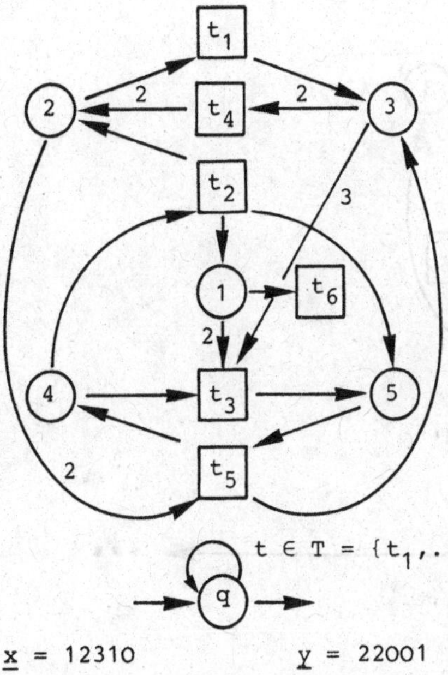

Fig. 7: Example, initial GVASS $G^{(o)}$

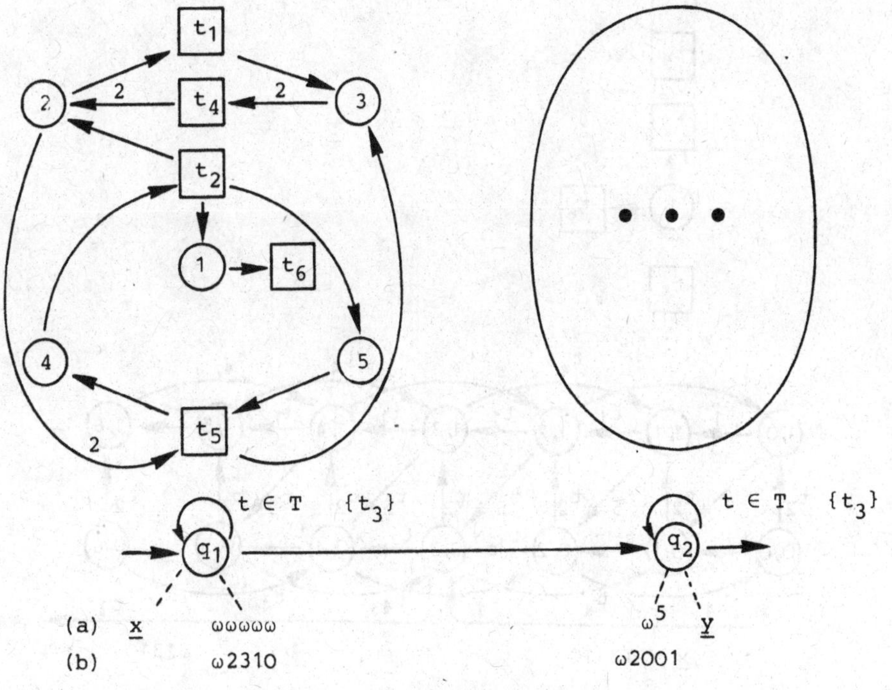

Fig. 8: Result of the first (a) and second (b) reduction

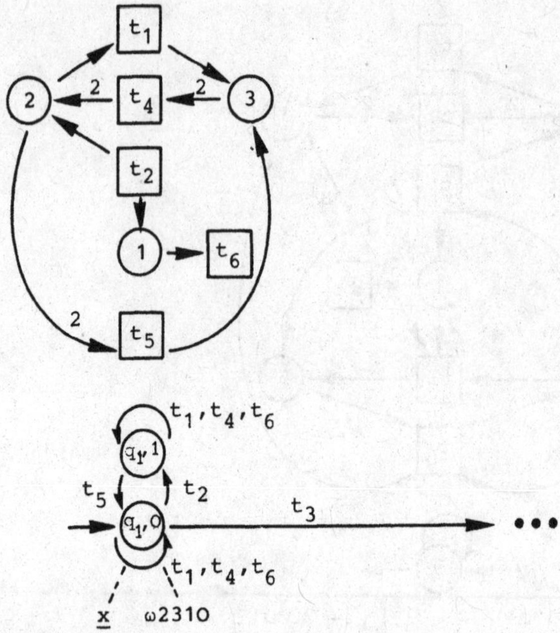

Fig. 9: Result of 4th reduction step

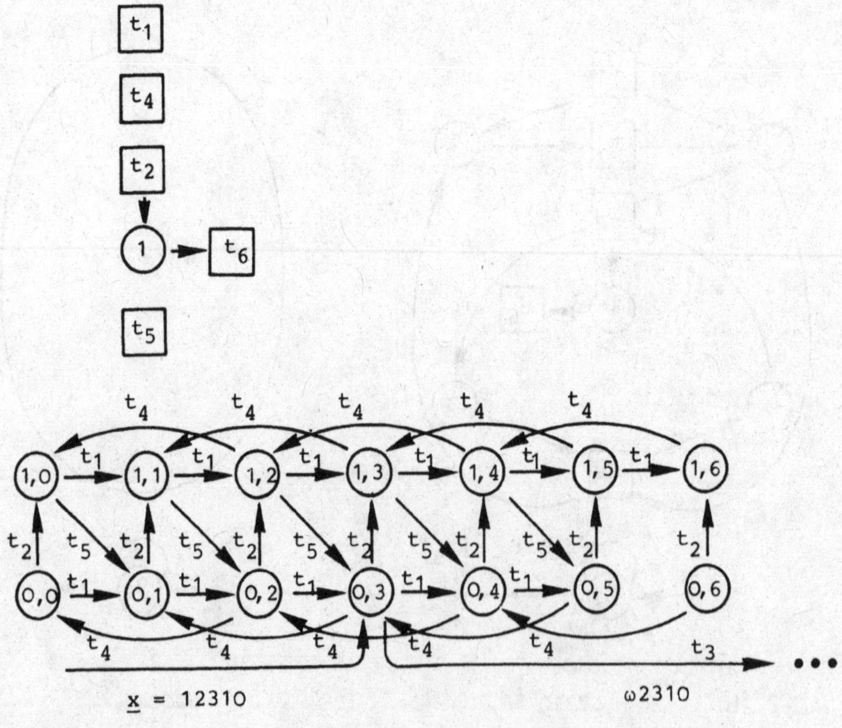

Fig. 10: Result of 6th reduction step

References

[Gra] Grabowski, J.: The decidability of Persistence for Vector Addition Systems. Information Processing Letters Vol. 11, No. 1 (1980)

[Hop] Hopcroft, J. and Pansiot, J.: On the reachability problem for 5-dimensional vector addition systems. Theor. Comp. Sc. 8, 135 - 159 (1979)

[Kos] Kosaraju, S.R.: Decidability of reachability in vector addition systems. Proc. 14th Ann. Symp. on Theory of computing, 267 - 281 (1982, prelim. version)

[Lee] van Leeuwen, J.: A partial solution to the reachability problem for vector addition systems. 6th Ann. ACM Symp. on Theory of Computing, 3o3 - 3o9 (1974)

[May1] Mayr, E.W.: An algorithm for the general Petri net reachability problem. Proc. 13th Ann. Symp. on Theory of Computing, 238 - 246 (1981)

[May2] Mayr. E.W.: Persistence of Vector Replacement Systems is Decidable. MIT LCS TM 189 (1980)

[Mü1] Müller, H.: On the reachability problem for persistent vector replacement systems. Computing Suppl. 3, 89 - 104 (1981)

[Mü 2] Müller, H.: On Kosaraju's Proof of the Decidability of the Reachability Problemfor VAS. Report on the 1st GTI-workshop (Ed. L. Priese) Uni-GH Paderborn, Reihe Theoretische Informatik Nr. 13 (1983)

[Mü3] Müller, H.: Weak Petri Net Computers for Ackermann functions, (EIK, forth coming)

[Rac] Rackoff, C.: The covering and boundedness problems for VAS. Theor. Comp. Sc. 6, 223 - 231 (1978)

[Sac] Sacerdote, G.S. and Tenney, R.L.: The decidability problem for VAS. 9th Ann. Symp. on Theory of Computing (1977)

K-DENSITY, N-DENSITY, AND FINITENESS PROPERTIES

Helmut Plünnecke

Gesellschaft für Mathematik und Datenverarbeitung
Institut für Methodische Grundlagen
Postfach 1240, Schloß Birlinghoven
D-5205 St. Augustin 1

Abstract

Modelling non-sequential processes by partially ordered sets (posets) leads to the concept of K-density which says that every cut and every line have (exactly) one point in common. The "simplest" example of non-K-density is given by a four-element poset the underlying graph of wich is "N-shaped"; a poset is called N-dense iff every (four-element) N-shaped subposet can be extended to an K-dense subposet by addition of *one* point. K-density implies N-density; for finite non-empty posets also the converse implication is true. It turns out that much weaker properties are sufficient; especially, it will be proved that an N-dense non-empty poset is K-dense if all cuts are finite.

Contents

1 Introduction

Partially ordered sets (posets) are a well-known tool for modelling non-sequential processes: The elements of the posets correspond to "local" states (conditions) and events, and the causal dependency between them is expressed by the order relation.

By definition, in a non-sequential process several things can happen at the same time; the corresponding structure in the modelling poset is a set of pairwise non-comparable elements. A maximal set with this property is called a *cut*; in a sense, a cut can be regarded as a special time reached during the progress of a process.

The most essential property of the (normal, sequential) time is that

(1) all things occur at a distinguished time, and

(2) every (maximal) sequential subprocess of a process is in a well-defined state at any time.

To make the set of cuts a reasonable concept of time one has to ensure that (1) and (2) are also valid in the non-sequential case. (1) can be easily derived from the axiom of choice, which allows to prove that every element of a poset is contained in at least one cut. Therefore we will restrict our attention to the question under which conditions the validity of (2) can be proved in the non-sequential case.

Maximal sequential subprocesses are represented by maximal totally ordered subsets of the modelling poset. Such subsets are called *lines*; hence (2) can be reformulated as follows:

(3) Every line intersects every cut at (exactly) one point.

Posets with the property (3) are called *K-dense* (cf. [3], [4]).

The "simplest" non-K-dense poset $N:=(N,\leq)$ is given by a four-element set $N:=\{a,b,c,d\}$ together with an order relation (cf. Fig. 1)

$$(\leq) := \mathrm{id}(N) \cup \{(a,b),(c,b),(c,d)\};$$

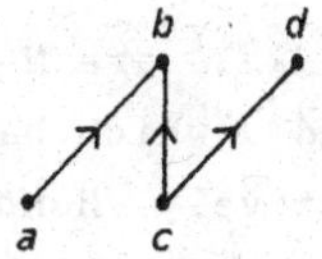

Fig. 1

obviously, $\{c,b\}$ is a line, and $\{a,d\}$, a cut with no common point. "N-shaped" posets like N can be used to define a weaker density requirement for arbitrary posets: A poset is called *N-dense* iff every (four-element) N-shaped subposet can be extended to an K-dense subposet by addition of *one* point. (Using the above notation for N this additional point must be properly between b and c).

It is clear that every K-dense poset is N-dense (using the axiom of choice the cuts and lines of an N-shaped subposet can be extended to cuts and lines of the (whole) poset); it is not difficult to show that *finite non-empty* N-dense posets are K-dense. But that is *not* true for all non-empty N-dense posets: We are now going to construct *infinite* N-dense posets I, J which are not K-dense.

<u>1.1 Example.</u> (Cf. Fig. 2.) Let

$I := \{1,2,3\}\times\mathbb{N}$,

$J := \{1,2\}\times\mathbb{N}$,

$$\leq \;:= \{((x,n),(y,m)) \mid (x,n),(y,m)\in I \wedge ((x=1 \wedge y\in\{1,2\} \wedge n\leq m) \vee (x=1 \wedge y=3) \vee (x\in\{2,3\} \wedge y=3 \wedge m\leq n))\};$$

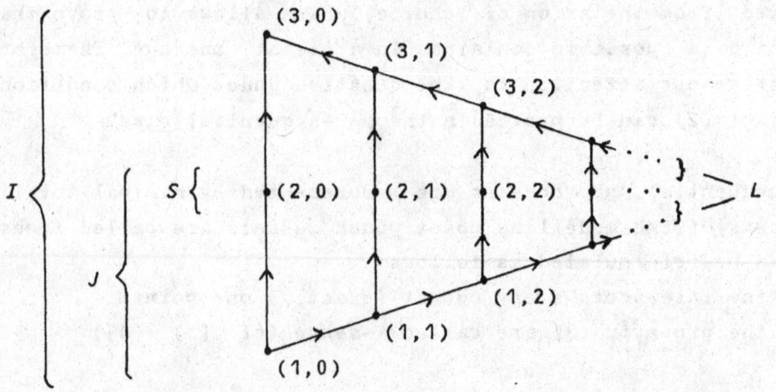

Fig. 2

$L := \{(x,n) \mid x\in\{1,3\}\wedge n\in\mathbb{N}\}$,

$S := \{(2,n) \mid n\in\mathbb{N}\}$.

Then[1)] $I:=(I,\leq)$ and $J:=(J,(\leq)\cap(J\times J))$ are N-dense non-empty posets; and S is an (infinite) cut in I and J which has no common point with the lines L and $L\cap J$ in I, J respectively. Hence I and J are not K-dense. Moreover, in I there are two points with an infinite chain between

[1)] In case confusion can be excluded we will use the same symbol for both a poset and its underlying set.

them (e.g. L between (1,0) and (3,0)). ■

There is an important difference between the violation of K-density by I and J: In I all lines "cross" all cuts ((1,0) and (3,0) are contained in all lines) but there are cuts and lines that do not meet, whereas in J there is a line which not even crosses a special cut ($L \cap J$ is completely below S). This suggests to split the concept of K-density: We say a poset has the *crossing property* iff every cut is crossed by every line, and we call a poset *K_0-dense* iff every cut is met by every crossing line. Then it is clear that a poset is K-dense iff it has the crossing property *and* is K_0-dense. By the above examples we see that the crossing property and the K_0-density are independent: The crossing property is true for I and not for J, and I is not K_0-dense whereas J is. (The K_0-density of J can be proved directly, or using the fact that all chains between any two points in J are finite, by the results stated below.)

This paper is aimed, firstly, at obtaining a number of general finiteness properties which are rather weak so that they are valid for a large class of infinite posets, but which are sufficient (together with N-density) to imply the crossing property and K_0-density, and hence K-density as a consequence. In particular, it will be proved that an N-dense non-empty poset is K-dense provided all of its cuts are finite, a result first published in [5]. We also generalize some of the theorems statet in [1] where special posets derived from occurrence nets are considered; such posets satisfy N-density and are "combinatorial" (which is another finiteness property to be considered below).

In the second part of this paper we apply the results obtained in sections 3 and 4: In section 5 we get necessary and sufficient conditions for the possibility of embedding an arbitrary poset into a K-dense combinatorial poset; in section 6 we introduce the concept of f[initely]-generable poset and show that an f-generable poset is K-dense iff it is N-dense *and* cut-finite. From the point of application this is the most interesting result, for there seem to be good reasons that in all practically interesting cases posets modelling real processes can be assumed to be f-generable.

This paper is organized as follows: In section 2 the basic definitions are introduced. Section 3 contains theorems about the relationship between different finiteness properties. In section 4 the main results about K-density are proved. These results are applied in sections 5 and 6. Section 7 contains some concluding remarks.

2 Basic Definitions

First, we give a survey of some well-known concepts related to partial orders.

2.1 Definition. Throughout the following let $P:=(P,\leq)$ be a partially ordered *non-empty*[2] set (poset), i.e. a non-empty set together with a reflexive, antisymmetric, and transitive relation $\leq$ on it. If $Q\subseteq P$, then $Q:=(Q,\leq)$ denotes the induced subposet $(Q,(\leq)\cap(Q\times Q))$; and we call an arbitrary poset Q' *embeddable* into P iff there is a subposet Q of P which is isomorphic to Q'.

$$x\simeq y \;:\Longleftrightarrow\; x,y\in P \wedge \neg x<y \wedge \neg y<x$$

defines the *co-relation* of P; and by $x<y$ and $x\sim y$ we denote $(x\leq y\wedge x\neq y)$ and $(x\simeq y\wedge x\neq y)$, respectively. ■

2.2 Definition. Let $L,S\subseteq P$. Then:

L chain $:\Longleftrightarrow (\forall a,b\in L)(a\leq b\vee b\leq a)$.
S antichain $:\Longleftrightarrow (\forall a,b\in S)a\simeq b$.
L line $:\Longleftrightarrow L$ maximal chain ; LI := Set of all lines.
S cut $:\Longleftrightarrow S$ maximal antichain ; C := Set of all cuts. ■

2.3 Definition. Let $A,B\subseteq P$. Then:

$\uparrow A := \{x\mid x\in P \wedge (\exists a\in A)a\leq x\}$, $\downarrow A := \{x\mid x\in P \wedge (\exists a\in A)x\leq a\}$.[3]
$\underline{\uparrow} A := \{x\mid x\in\uparrow A \wedge \neg(\exists a\in A)x<a\}$, $\overline{\downarrow} A := \{x\mid x\in\downarrow A \wedge \neg(\exists a\in A)a<x\}$.
$[A,B] := \underline{\uparrow} A\cap\overline{\downarrow} B$; Max$(A)$:= $A\cap\underline{\uparrow} A$, Min$(A)$:= $A\cap\overline{\downarrow} A$. ■

Obviously for antichains S we have $\underline{\uparrow} S = \uparrow S$ and $\overline{\downarrow} S = \downarrow S$. Hence $[\{a\},\{b\}]=\{x\mid a\leq x\leq b\}$; and therefore $[A,B]$ can be considered the "closed" interval consisting of all points "between" A and B; and we have

(4) $$(\forall S,T\in C)S,T\subseteq[S,T]\cup[T,S].$$

We call a poset *combinatorial* iff its order relation is the tran-

---

[2] This excludes only trivial cases: The empty poset has *not* the crossing property and is *not* K-dense, but N-dense, it has the strong crossing property (cf. below), and it is cut-finite, length-finite, ...

[3] $\uparrow A\cap\downarrow B := (\uparrow A)\cap(\downarrow B)$; etc.

sitive closure of the "neighbourhood relation" (e.g. I and J from 1.1 are combinatorial, the total order of the rational numbers $(\mathbb{Q},\leq)$ is not):

<u>2.4 Definition.</u> Let $x,y\in P$ and $A\subseteq P$. Then:

$x \triangleleft y \;:\Longleftrightarrow\; x,y$ are neighbours

$\quad :\Longleftrightarrow\; x<y \wedge (\forall z\in P)(x\leq z\leq y \Rightarrow x=z \vee z=y)$.

$A \;:=\; \{y \mid y\in P \wedge (\exists a\in A)\, y\triangleleft a\}$, [4]

$A^{\cdot} \;:=\; \{y \mid y\in P \wedge (\exists a\in A)\, a\triangleleft y\}$.

P combinatorial $:\Longleftrightarrow (\forall a,b\in P)(a<b \Rightarrow (\exists x_1,\ldots,x_n\in P)(a=x_1\triangleleft x_2\triangleleft\ldots\triangleleft x_n=b)$. ∎

The reason for calling combinatorialness a finiteness property is that a poset is combinatorial iff for any two points a, b the subposet $([\{a\},\{b\}],\leq)$ has at least one *finite* line. Hence assuming combinatorialness for a poset modelling reality means that general causal dependency results from "local" (irreducible) causal dependency between "neighbouring" states and events. In the next group of definitions we introduce additional finiteness properties which relate to the finiteness of special cuts or chains. (Some additional finiteness properties will be introduced in section 6.)

<u>2.5 Definition.</u>

P cut-finite $:\Longleftrightarrow$ All cuts are finite.

P length-finite $:\Longleftrightarrow$ All chains between any two points are finite

$\quad :\Longleftrightarrow (\forall a,b\in P)(\forall L)(L \text{ chain} \Rightarrow |[\{a\},\{b\}]\cap L|<\infty)$.

P s-length-finite $:\Longleftrightarrow$ P strongly length-finite

$\quad :\Longleftrightarrow$ All chains between any two subsets are finite

$\quad :\Longleftrightarrow (\forall A,B\subseteq P)(\forall L)(L \text{ chain} \Rightarrow |[A,B]\cap L|<\infty)$. ∎

<u>2.6 Definition.</u> Let S be an antichain in P. Then

$/S/ \;:=\; \{p \mid ([\{p\},S],\leq)$ and $([S,\{p\}],\leq)$ are length-finite$\}$

$\quad =:$ Finite surrounding of S;

and we call P *cut_0-finite* iff there is $F\in C$ such that the subposet $(/F/,\leq)$ is cut-finite. ∎

There is a cut_0-finite poset Q' which is *not* cut-finite: Let $Q:=\mathbb{N}\times\mathbb{N}$, $(n,m)\leq(r,s)$ iff $n=r\wedge m\leq s$, and let Q' be the poset consisting of Q and one additional element q such that q is greater than all elements of Q; then Q' has only one finite cut, namely $\{q\}$, and we have $/\{q\}/=\{q\}$. Obviously, Q' is not combinatorial; in the next section we

---

[4] $^{\cdot}A\cap B^{\cdot} := (^{\cdot}A)\cap(B^{\cdot})$; etc.

will show that for combinatorial posets cut_0-finiteness and cut-finiteness are equivalent.

The following definitions deal with density and crossing properties; except for the strong crossing property (which will be explained below) they are already mentioned in the introduction.

<u>2.7 Definition.</u>

P K-dense $:\Longleftrightarrow (\forall S\in C)(\forall L\in LI) S\cap L\neq\emptyset$.

P K_0-dense $:\Longleftrightarrow (\forall S\in C)(\forall L\in LI)(\downarrow S\cap L\neq\emptyset \wedge \uparrow S\cap L\neq\emptyset \Rightarrow S\cap L\neq\emptyset)$.

P N-dense $:\Longleftrightarrow (\forall a,b,c,d\in P)(a<b \wedge c<b \wedge c<d \wedge a\sim c \wedge a\sim d \wedge b\sim d$
$\Rightarrow (\exists e\in P)(c<e \wedge e<b \wedge a\sim e \wedge e\sim d))$.

P crossing $:\Longleftrightarrow$ P has the crossing property
$:\Longleftrightarrow (\forall S\in C)(\forall L\in LI)(\downarrow S\cap L\neq\emptyset \wedge \uparrow S\cap L\neq\emptyset)$.

P s-crossing $:\Longleftrightarrow$ P has the strong crossing property
$:\Longleftrightarrow (\forall A)(\forall L)(A$ antichain $\wedge A\neq\emptyset \wedge L$ chain $\Rightarrow$
$(L\subseteq\downarrow A \Rightarrow (\exists a\in A) L\subseteq\downarrow\{a\}) \wedge (L\subseteq\uparrow A \Rightarrow (\exists a\in A) L\subseteq\uparrow\{a\}))$. ■

Using the poset J from 1.1 and its dual J^{-1}, in the following proposition the strong crossing property is differently expressed by "embedding" conditions; similar embedding conditions are directly used in [1] to characterize K-density for occurrence nets. This means that for occurrence nets, the strong crossing property is equivalent to K-density, a result which will be generalized below.

<u>2.8 Proposition.</u> P has the strong crossing property iff neither J nor J^{-1} are embeddable into P.

<u>Proof.</u> If J is embeddable, then (cf.1.1) the antichain S and the line $L\cap J$ violate the strong crossing property. On the other hand, if S is a non-empty antichain and L is a line with $L\subseteq\downarrow S$ and if there is *no* $s\in S$ with $L\subseteq\downarrow\{s\}$, then there is no *finite* set $T\subseteq S$ with $L\subseteq\downarrow T$. Hence there are $x_1,x_2,\ldots\in L$ and $s_1,s_2,\ldots\in S$ with $x_1<x_2<\ldots$, $x_n<s_n$, and $s_n\sim x_m$ for $n<m$; and therefore J is embeddable into P. ■

The last definitions in this section concern some important subclasses of the set C of cuts.

<u>2.9 Definition.</u>

C-fin := Set of all *finite* cuts
:= $\{S \mid S\in C \wedge |S|<\infty\}$.

C-cross := Set of all cuts "*crossed*" by all lines

:= $\{S \mid S\in C \wedge (\forall L\in LI)(\downarrow S\cap L\neq\emptyset\wedge\uparrow S\cap L\neq\emptyset)\}$.

C-s-cross := Set of all cuts "*strongly crossed*" by all lines

:= $\{S \mid S\in C \wedge (\forall A)(\forall L)(A\subseteq S \wedge A\neq\emptyset \wedge L \text{ chain} \Rightarrow$

$(L\subseteq\downarrow A \Rightarrow (\exists a\in A)L\subseteq\downarrow\{a\}) \wedge (L\subseteq\uparrow A \Rightarrow (\exists a\in A)L\subseteq\uparrow\{a\}))\}$.

C-met := Set of all cuts *met* by all lines

:= $\{S \mid S\in C \wedge (\forall L\in LI)S\cap L\neq\emptyset\}$. ■

It is immediately clear, that C=C-fin, C=C-cross, C=C-s-cross, and C=C-met are equivalent to *P* cut-finite, *P* crossing, *P* s-crossing, and *P* K-dense, respectively.

3 Length-finiteness, Cut-finiteness, and Crossing Properties

We start with some basic relations between several finiteness and crossing properties.

3.1 Lemma. Let S be a *finite* non-empty antichain, and let L be a chain. Then

$$(L\subseteq\downarrow S \Rightarrow (\exists s\in S)L\subseteq\downarrow\{s\}) \wedge (L\subseteq\uparrow S \Rightarrow (\exists s\in S)L\subseteq\uparrow\{s\}).$$

Proof. Clear. ■

3.2 Proposition.

(5) C-fin $\subseteq$ C-s-cross $\subseteq$ C-cross.

(6) *P* length-finite $\Rightarrow$ C-s-cross = C-cross.

(7) *P* length-finite $\Rightarrow$ *P* combinatorial.

(8) *P* s-length-finite $\Rightarrow$ *P* length-finite $\wedge$ *P* s-crossing.

(9) *P* length-finite $\wedge$ *P* cut-finite $\Leftrightarrow$ $(\forall S,T\in C)|[S,T]|<\infty$.

Proof. The straightforward proofs of (8) and "(9),$\Leftarrow$" are left to the reader. (5) follows immediately using 3.1. If *P* is length-finite and $a<b$, then there is a *finite*, maximal chain $x_0,\ldots,x_r$ from a to b; hence $a=x_0\lessdot x_1\lessdot\ldots\lessdot=b$. This proves (7). To prove "(9),$\Rightarrow$" we assume that *P* is length-finite and cut-finite and that there are $S,T\in C$ with $|[S,T]|=\infty$. Repeatedly using the cut-finiteness we get the existence of $x_1\lessdot x_2\lessdot\ldots$ and $y\in T$ such that

$$|\uparrow\{x_n\}\cap[S,T]|=\infty \wedge x_n<y \quad \text{for } n=1,2,\ldots$$

contradicting the length-finiteness. To prove (6) we assume that *P* is length-finite and that there are $S\in$C-cross, a non-empty $A\subseteq S$ and a chain L such that $L\subseteq\downarrow A$. We can assume $L\neq\emptyset$. Then there is $l\in L$ and (because of $S \in$C-cross) $x \in \uparrow S$ such that $L \subseteq \downarrow\{x\}$; by the length-finiteness it follows that $|[\{l\},\{x\}] \cap L| < \infty$. Hence $\mathrm{Max}(L) \neq \emptyset$; and therefore $(\exists a \in A) L \subseteq \downarrow\{a\}$. Therefore C-cross$\subseteq$C-s-cross; together with (5) this implies (6). ■

The next example shows an extreme violation of the crossing property: There is a non-empty poset R with the property that for *all* cuts S of R there is a line L such that L is properly below S; therefore especially C-cross=$\emptyset$.

3.3 Example. For $l=1,2,\ldots$ let R_l be the set of all *finite* sequences $(n_1,\ldots,n_l)$ with elements in N, and we set $R := R_1 \cup R_2 \cup \ldots$; and for $x,y \in R$ with $x =: (x_1,\ldots,x_r)$ and $y =: (y_1,\ldots,y_s)$ we define $x \leq y$ iff $r \leq s$ *and* $y_u \leq x_u$ for $u=1,\ldots,r$. Then obviously $(R,\leq)$ is a poset. Next we are going to prove for $A \subseteq R$ by induction on l

(10) $$A \text{ antichain} \wedge A \subseteq R_l \Rightarrow |A| < \infty.$$

Clearly, this holds for $l=1$. We now assume (10) for $l=r$ and $A \subseteq R_{r+1}$. For arbitrary $a =: (n_1,\ldots,n_{r+1}) \in A$ let $a' := (n_1,\ldots,n_r)$ and $a'' := n_{r+1}$. We set $A' := \{a' \mid a \in A\}$. Then $\mathrm{Max}(A')$ is an antichain, hence by induction hypothesis $\mathrm{Max}(A')$ is finite. Therefore there are a finte set $B \subseteq A$ and $q \in$ N such that $\mathrm{Max}(A') = \{b' \mid b \in B\}$ and $(\forall b \in B) b'' \leq q$. We consider for $w \geq 0$ the sets $A_w := \{a \mid a \in A \wedge a'' = w\}$. We claim $A_w = \emptyset$ for $w > q$: Let $x \in A_w$ and $x'' = w > q$; we have $|\uparrow x' \cap R_r| < \infty$, hence there is $b \in B$ with $x' \leq b'$; therefore $x'' > q$ implies $x < b$, A no antichain, contradiction. For arbitrary w obviously $\{a' \mid a \in A_w\}$ is an antichain and therefore finite by induction hypotheses. Hence A_w is finite too; and because of $A = A_0 \cup A_1 \cup \ldots$ we get (10).

Let S be a cut in $(R,\leq)$. For arbitrary $y_1, y_2, \ldots \in$ N the set $S \cap \downarrow(y_1,\ldots,y_{m-1},0)$ is an antichain contained in $R_1 \cup \ldots \cup R_m$, hence because of (10) it is finite; and if $(y_1,\ldots,y_{m-1}) \notin \uparrow S$ therefore y_m exists such that $(y_1,\ldots,y_m) \notin \uparrow S$. Applying this result repeatedly and using the fact that $\uparrow S \cup \downarrow S = R$ yields the existence of a sequence $x_1, x_2, \ldots$ such that for all n

(11) $$z_n := (x_1,\ldots,x_n) \subseteq (\downarrow S \setminus S).$$

Obviously $z_1 < z_2 < \ldots$, and therefore there is a line L containing $z_1, z_2, \ldots$ Then $L \subseteq (\downarrow S \setminus S)$, for otherwise: $p \in L$ exists with $p \in \uparrow S$, $z_n < p$ for all n because of (11), $p \notin R_{n-1}$ for all $n > 1$, contradiction. Hence L is properly below S. ■

Our next aim is to prove for combinatorial posets the equivalence of cut_0-finiteness and cut-finiteness.

3.4 Lemma. Let S be a *finite* antichain in P. Then the subposet $(/S/,\leq)$ is length-finite.

Proof. Immediate using 3.1. ∎

3.5 Lemma. Let P be combinatorial, $S\in C$, and let the subposet $(/S/,\leq)$ be cut-finite. Then P is length-finite.

Proof. Suppose P is not length-finite. By 3.4 there is $p\in P\setminus(/S/)$; and we assume $p\in\downarrow S$. We set $G:=({}^{\cdot}/S/)\setminus(/S/)$. Then $\emptyset\neq G\subseteq\downarrow S$, and $\mathrm{Max}(G)=\emptyset$ (otherwise: $m\in\mathrm{Max}(G)$, hence $\{m\}^{\cdot}\subseteq/S/$; $|\{m\}^{\cdot}|<\infty$ because of the cut-finiteness of $(/S/,\leq)$; there are $s\in/S/$ and an infinite chain $I\subseteq[\{m\},\{s\}]$; hence due to 3.1 $i\in\{m\}^{\cdot}$ exists with $I\setminus\{m\}\subseteq[\{i\},\{s\}]$; then $I\setminus\{m\}$ is an infinite chain contradicting 3.4). Therefore an infinite chain $g_1<g_2<\dots$ exists in G, and there are also $h_1,h_2,\dots$ such that $g_l\lessdot h_l\in/S/\cap\downarrow S$ for $l=1,2,\dots$ We set $H:=\{h_1,h_2,\dots\}$. If $m<n$ then $\neg h_n\leq h_m$ (otherwise $g_m<g_n\lessdot h_n\leq h_m$ contradicting $g_m\lessdot h_m$); hence $|H|=\infty$, and $\downarrow\{h_l\}\cap H\subseteq\{h_1,\dots h_l\}$ is finite for all l. Let F be a cut in $(H,\leq)$. Then $|F|<\infty$, hence $\downarrow F\cap H$ is finite. We have $H\subseteq(\downarrow F\cap H)\cup[F,S]$; therefore $[F,S]$ is infinite contradicting (9) and 3.4. ∎

3.6 Theorem. Let P be combinatorial. Then

$$P \text{ cut-finite} \iff P \text{ cut}_0\text{-finite}.$$

Proof. Let P be cut_0-finite. Then there is $F\in C$ such that $(/F/,\leq)$ is cut-finite. By 3.5 P is length-finite. Hence $/F/=P$; and therefore P is cut-finite. The converse direction is trivial. ∎

The preceding theorem says that cut-finiteness for the whole (combinatorial) poset is equivalent to the cut-finiteness of the finite surrounding of at least one cut. The next theorem states an important property of cut-finite posets.

3.7 Theorem. Let P be cut-finite. Then

$$P \text{ length-finite} \iff P \text{ combinatorial}.$$

Proof. By applying (7) and 3.5. ∎

In the last theorem of this section a necessary and and sufficient condition for the strong crossing property is derived.

<u>3.8 Theorem.</u> Let P be combinatorial. Then

$$P \text{ s-crossing} \iff P \text{ crossing} \wedge P \text{ length-finite}.$$

<u>Proof.</u> "$\Leftarrow$" follows from (6). We now assume that P has the strong crossing property. Then P has the crossing property (cf. (5)). To prove the length-finiteness we use an indirect argument and assume that there are an *infinite* chain L and $a,b\in L$ with $L\subseteq\uparrow\{a\}\cap\downarrow\{b\}$. We set

$$X := \{x \mid x\in L \wedge |L\cap\downarrow\{x\}|<\infty\}, \quad Y := L\setminus X,$$

and get

$$a\in X \wedge b\in Y \wedge (\mathrm{Max}(X)=\emptyset \vee \mathrm{Min}(Y)=\emptyset)$$

(otherwise: $\mathrm{Max}(X)\neq\emptyset$, $m\in\mathrm{Min}(Y)$, $|L\cap\downarrow\{m\}|<\infty$, contradition). We restrict ourselves to the case $\mathrm{Max}(X)=\emptyset$, and are going to construct inductively three infinite sequences $x_0,x_1,\ldots$, $y_0,y_1,\ldots$, and $z_0,z_1,\ldots$ such that for $n=0,1,\ldots$ (12)-(15) hold:

(12) $$x_n\in X \wedge x_n\le y_n \wedge y_n \blacktriangleleft z_n,$$

(13) $$n\ge 1 \Rightarrow x_{n-1}<x_n \wedge z_n\le z_{n-1},$$

(14) $$\neg X\subseteq\downarrow\{y_n\} \wedge X\subseteq\downarrow\{z_n\},$$

(15) $$(\forall m\in\{0,\ldots,n-1\})(y_m\sim y_n \wedge y_m\sim x_n).$$

There is a finite sequence $e_1,\ldots,e_r$ with $a=e_1\blacktriangleleft e_2\blacktriangleleft\ldots\blacktriangleleft e_r=b$; hence s exists with $s\in\{1,\ldots,r-1\}$ and

(16) $$\neg X\subseteq\downarrow\{e_s\} \wedge X\subseteq\downarrow\{e_{s+1}\}.$$

We set $x_0:=a$, $y_0:=e_s$, and $z_0:=e_{s+1}$; then (12)-(15) are valid for $n=0$. We now assume that x_n, y_n, and z_n are already constructed for $n=0,\ldots,l$ such that (12)-(15) are valid. Because of (14) there is x with

(17) $$x\in X \wedge x_l<x \wedge x\notin\downarrow\{y_0,\ldots,y_l\},$$

hence there is a finite sequence $e_1,\ldots,e_v$ with

(18) $$x=e_1\blacktriangleleft e_2\blacktriangleleft\ldots\blacktriangleleft e_v=z_l.$$

Therefore s exists with $s\in\{1,\ldots,v-1\}$ such that (16) holds; and we set

$$x_{l+1}:=x, \quad y_{l+1}:=e_s, \quad z_{l+1}:=e_{s+1}.$$

Then (12)-(14) obviously hold for $n=l+1$. Let $m\in\{1,\ldots,l\}$. Because of (17) neither $y_{l+1}\le y_m$ nor $x_{l+1}\le y_m$; due to (12), (13), and (18) we get

(19) $$\neg y_m\le y_{l+1}$$

(otherwise: $y_m\le y_{l+1}\blacktriangleleft z_{l+1}\le z_m$, $y_m=y_{l+1}$ because of $y_m\blacktriangleleft z_m$, $x=x_{l+1}\le y_{l+1}=y_m$ contradicting (17)); and $\neg y_m\le x_{l+1}$ follows immediately from (19). Hence (15) holds for $n=l+1$ too. This completes the inductive construction.

We set $Y:=\{y_n \mid n\in\mathbb{N}\}$ and $L:=\{x_n \mid n\in\mathbb{N}\}$; then Y is an antichain, L is a chain, and $L\subseteq\downarrow Y$; but there is no $y\in Y$ with $L\subseteq\downarrow\{y\}$ contradicting the strong crossing property. ■

4 K-density and N-density

This section contains the main results concerning K-density and N-density. We will show that N-density together with certain additional finiteness properties implies K-density: In the first part of this section we take the strong crossing property and the cut-finiteness, respectively, as additional property; in the second part combinatorialness is assumed.

4.1 Proposition.

(20) P K_0-dense $\Rightarrow P$ N-dense.

(21) P K-dense $\Longleftrightarrow P$ crossing $\wedge$ P K_0-dense.

Proof. Clear. ∎

In a sense, the next theorem states the weakest finiteness condition kown so far which is sufficient to get, for N-dense posets, non-empty intersections between a given cut and arbitrary lines.

4.2 Theorem. Let P be N-dense. Then

$$\text{C-fin} \subseteq \text{C-s-cross} \subseteq \text{C-met};$$

especially, in an N-dense (non-empty) poset all *finite* cuts are met by all lines.

Proof. C-fin⊆C-s-cross was already proved in (5). Let $S\in$C-s-cross. First, we prove

(22) $$(\forall p\in\downarrow S)(\forall q\in\uparrow S)(p\leq q \Rightarrow (\exists y\in S)(p\leq y\leq q)).$$

We use an indirect argument and assume $p\in\downarrow S$, $q\in\uparrow S$, and

(23) $$p\leq q \wedge \uparrow\{p\}\cap\downarrow\{q\}\cap S=\emptyset.$$

We are going to construct inductively two sequences $x_0, x_1, \ldots$ and $y_0, y_1, \ldots$ such that for $n=0,1,\ldots$ (24)-(28) hold:

(24) $$x_n\in\uparrow\{p\}\cap\downarrow\{q\} \wedge y_n\in S,$$

(25) $$(\forall l\in\{0,\ldots n-1\})(x_l<x_n \vee x_n<x_l),$$

(26) $$(\forall l\in\{0,\ldots,n-1\})((x_l, x_n\in\downarrow S \Rightarrow x_l\leq x_n) \wedge (x_l, x_n\in\uparrow S \Rightarrow x_n\leq x_l)),$$

(27) $$x_n<y_n \vee y_n<x_n,$$

(28) $$(\forall l\in\{0,\ldots,n-1\})(\neg y_l\leq x_n \wedge \neg x_n\leq y_l).$$

There are $i,j\in S$ with $p\leq i$ and $j\leq q$; and we set

(29) $$x_0:=p,\ y_0:=i;\ x_1:=q,\ y_1:=j.$$

Then (24)-(28) are true for $n=0$ and $n=1$ because of (23). We now assume that x_n and y_n are constructed for $n=0,\ldots,r$ such that (24)-(28) are valid. Let

$$A:=\{l\mid l\in\{0,\ldots,r\} \wedge x_l\in\downarrow S\},\quad B:=\{l\mid l\in\{0,\ldots,r\} \wedge x_l\in\uparrow S\}.$$

Then $A\neq\emptyset$ and $B\neq\emptyset$ because of (29); hence $u\in\mathrm{Max}(A)$ and $v\in\mathrm{Max}(B)$ exist. Due to (26) we get for $l=1,\dots,r$

$$(x_l\in{\downarrow}S \Rightarrow x_l\leq x_u)\wedge(x_l\in{\uparrow}S \Rightarrow x_v\leq x_l).$$

From (24), (27), and (25) it follows that $x_u\leq y_u$, $y_v\leq x_v$, and $x_u<x_v$; and therefore and because of (23) we have

(30) $$y_v<x_v\wedge x_u<x_v\wedge x_u<y_u \;\wedge\; y_v\sim x_u\wedge y_v\sim y_u\wedge x_v\sim y_u\;.$$

Because of the N-density of P and (30) there are z, w with

(31) $$x_u<z\wedge z<x_v \;\wedge\; y_v\sim z\wedge z\sim y_u,$$

(32) $$w\in S\wedge(z\leq w\vee w\leq z).$$

We set

(33) $$x_{r+1}:=z,\quad y_{r+1}:=w;$$

then (24)-(27) are true for $n=r+1$. Let $s\in\{0,\dots,r\}$. First, we assume $x_s\in{\downarrow}S$ and get $x_s\leq y_s$,

(34) $$\neg y_s\leq x_{r+1}$$

(otherwise: $y_s\in{\uparrow}\{x_s\}\cap{\downarrow}\{x_{r+1}\}\wedge y_s\in S$ contradicting (23) and (24)),

(35) $$\neg x_{r+1}\leq y_s$$

(otherwise: $x_{r+1}\leq y_s$, $s\neq u$ because of (31) and (33), $s<u$, $x_u\leq x_{r+1}$, $x_u\leq y_s$, contradicting (28) for $n=u\leq r$). Analogously (34) and (35) are proved if $x_s\in{\uparrow}S$ is assumed instead of $x_s\in{\downarrow}S$. Hence (28) holds for $n=r+1$ too. This completes the inductive construction.

We set $X:=\{x_n\mid n\in\mathrm{N}\}$ and $Y:=\{y_n\mid n\in\mathrm{N}\}$, then $X\subseteq{\downarrow}Y\cup{\uparrow}Y$, and therefore (because of $S\in$C-s-cross) $r,s\in\mathrm{N}$ exist with $X\cap{\downarrow}Y\subseteq{\downarrow}\{y_r\}$ and $X\cap{\uparrow}Y\subseteq{\uparrow}\{y_s\}$ contradicting (28) for sufficiently large n. ■(22)

Let L be a line. $S\in$C-s-cross implies

(36) $${\downarrow}S\cap L\neq\emptyset\wedge{\uparrow}S\cap L\neq\emptyset.$$

If $p\in{\downarrow}S\cap L$, then because of (22) there is T with $\emptyset\neq T\subseteq{\uparrow}\{p\}\cap S$ and ${\uparrow}S\cap L\subseteq{\uparrow}T$; and due to $S\in$C-s-cross we get

(37) $$(\forall p\in{\downarrow}S\cap L)(\exists u\in S)(\forall q\in{\uparrow}S\cap L)p\leq u\leq q.$$

All "u's" the existence of which is guaranteed by (37) form a set U such that

(38) $$(\forall q\in{\uparrow}S\cap L)U\subseteq S\cap{\downarrow}\{q\}\wedge{\downarrow}S\cap L\subseteq{\downarrow}U.$$

Then $U\neq\emptyset$ because of (36); and therefore again using $S\in$C-s-cross yields the existence of a $z\in U$ with $z\in S$ and $(\forall p\in{\downarrow}S\cap L)(\forall q\in{\uparrow}S\cap L)(p\leq z\leq q)$. Then $u\in L$, hence $S\cap L\neq\emptyset$. Therefore C-s-cross$\subseteq$C-meet. ■

The following theorem is an immediate consequence of the preceding theorem and (20).

<u>4.3 Theorem.</u> If P has the strong crossing property, or if P is cut-finite [which implies the strong crossing property, cf. (5)], then

$$P \text{ K-dense} \iff P \text{ N-dense}. \qquad \blacksquare$$

For special *combinatorial* N-dense posets P derived from occurrence nets the preceding result was first shown by Best [1], where for these posets the equivalence of K-density and the strong crossing property was proved. (In [1], the latter property is expressed by embedding conditions, cf. above 2.8.)

This equivalence of K-density and the strong crossing property is *not* true for arbitrary posets: E.g. define J' as the poset consisting of the poset J from 1.1 and one additional point x such that $(1,n)<x$ for all n and x not comparable with all other points of J; then J' is K-dense but does not have the strong crossing property which can immediately be seen by using 2.8. In the remainder of this section, therefore we will restrict ourselves to *combinatorial* N-dense posets. For these posets we are going to show the equivalence of K-density and the strong crossing property; but our main concern will be to prove that K_0-density and K-density are equivalent to length-finiteness and strong length-finiteness, respectively.

<u>4.4 Lemma.</u> Let P be combinatorial and N-dense, let X be a chain with $\mathrm{Max}(X)=\emptyset$, and let $B\subseteq P$ such that $X\subseteq\updownarrow B$. Then there is an antichain S such that

(39) $$\neg(\exists s\in S)X\subseteq\downarrow\{s\},$$

(40) $$X\subseteq\downarrow S \wedge B\cap\uparrow X\subseteq\uparrow S.$$

<u>Proof.</u> We set

$$S := \{s\,|\,(\exists u\in\downarrow X)u\lessdot s\}\setminus\downarrow X;$$

and we will prove that S is an antichain with the properties (39) and (40). Suppose there are $a,b\in S$ with $a<b$. Then $d\in X$ and c exist such that $c\lessdot b$ and $c<d$ [here $\mathrm{Max}(X)=\emptyset$ is used]. Hence $a\sim c$ ($a\le c$ implies $a<d$ contradicting $a\notin\downarrow X$; $c<a$ contradicts $c\lessdot b$ because of $a<b$), $a\sim d$ ($a\le d$ contradicts $a\notin\downarrow X$; $d<a$ contradicts $c\lessdot b$ because of $c<d$ and $a<b$), $b\sim d$ ($b\le d$ contradicts $b\notin\downarrow X$, $d<b$ contradicts $c\lessdot b$ because of $c<d$). Because of the N-density four points a, b, c, d with these properties cannot exist; hence our supposition $a<b$ is wrong, and therefore S is an antichain. If there is $s\in S$ with $X\subseteq\downarrow\{s\}$, then there are u, v such that $u\lessdot s$ and $u<v\in X$; and it follows that $v<s$, $\neg u\lessdot s$, contradiction. This proves (39).

If $x\in X$, $b\in B$, and $x\le b$, then there is a finite sequence $x_0,x_1,\ldots,x_n$

such that $x=x_0 \lessdot x_1 \lessdot \ldots \lessdot x_n=b$. Hence $x_0 \in \downarrow X$ and $x_n \notin \downarrow X$ (otherwise: there are $x', x'' \in X$ with $b=x_n \leq x' < x''$, hence $x'' \notin \updownarrow B$, contradiction). There is $m \in \mathrm{Max}(\{l \mid x_l \in \downarrow X\})$, hence $0 \leq m < n$, $x_{m+1} \notin \downarrow X$, $x_{m+1} \in S$, $x \in \downarrow S$ and $b \in \uparrow S$. Applying this result twice we get (40): If $u \in X$, then there is $v \in B$ with $u \leq v$, hence $X \subseteq \downarrow S$; if $v \in B \cap \uparrow X$, then there is $u \in X$ with $u \leq v$, hence $B \cap \uparrow X \subseteq \uparrow S$. ■

<u>4.5 Theorem.</u>[5] Let P be combinatorial and N-dense. Then

(41) P K_0-dense $\Longleftrightarrow$ P length-finite,

(42) P K-dense $\Longleftrightarrow$ P s-crossing $\Longleftrightarrow$ P s-length-finite.

<u>Proof.</u> Let P be length-finite, $S \in C$, $L \in LI$, $p \in \downarrow S \cap L$ and $q \in \uparrow S \cap L$. Then $|[\{p\},\{q\}] \cap L| < \infty$; hence a, b, c, d exist such that

$$b \in \mathrm{Min}(\uparrow S \cap L) \wedge c \in \mathrm{Max}(\downarrow S \cap L) \wedge a,d \in S \wedge a \leq b \wedge c \leq d.$$

If $S \cap L = \emptyset$, then $b \notin S$, $c \notin S$, $a<b$, $c \lessdot b$, $c<d$, $a \sim c$, $a \sim d$, and $b \sim d$ contradicting the N-density of P. This proves "(41),$\Leftarrow$". To get the converse direction of (41) we use an indirect argumtent and assume that P is K_0-dense and that there are an *infinite* chain L and $a,b \in L$ with $L \subseteq \uparrow\{a\} \cap \downarrow\{b\}$. Then there is a line L' with $L \subseteq L'$; and we set $L'' := L' \cap [a,b]$,

$$X := \{x \mid x \in L'' \wedge |L'' \cap \downarrow\{x\}| < \infty\}, \quad B := L'' \setminus X,$$

and get

$$L \subseteq L'' \wedge a \in X \wedge b \in B \wedge (\mathrm{Max}(X)=\emptyset \vee \mathrm{Min}(B)=\emptyset)$$

(otherwise: $\mathrm{Max}(X) \neq \emptyset$, $m \in \mathrm{Min}(B)$, $|L'' \cap \downarrow\{m\}| < \infty$, contradition). We restrict ourselves to the case $\mathrm{Max}(X)=\emptyset$. We have $X \subseteq \updownarrow B$; applying 4.4 we get the existence of an antichain S such that (39) and (40) hold. There is a cut S' with $S \subseteq S'$. It follows that

(43) $$a \in X \subseteq \downarrow S' \cap L' \wedge b \in B \subseteq \uparrow S' \cap L';$$

Due to the K_0-density there is $s \in S' \cap L'$. Then because of (43) and (40)

(44) $$X \subseteq \downarrow\{s\}$$

and $s \in L'' = X \cup B \subseteq \downarrow S \cup \uparrow S$. Hence $z \in S \subseteq S'$ exists with $z \leq s$ or $s \leq z$, and we get $s=z \in S$. Therefore (44) contradicts (39). ■(41)

Next we are going to prove

(45) P s-crossing $\Rightarrow$ P s-length-finite.

We argue indirectly and assume that P is combinatorial, that it has the strong crossing property and that there are a chain L and $A,B \subseteq P$ with $L \subseteq [A,B]$ and $|L| = \infty$. Hence X exists with (cf. proof of 3.8) $X \neq \emptyset$, $X \subseteq L$, and $\mathrm{Max}(X) \neq \emptyset$ or $\mathrm{Min}(X) \neq \emptyset$. We restrict ourselves to the case $\mathrm{Max}(X) \neq \emptyset$. Due to 4.4 an antichain S exists with the properties (39) and (40); then $S \neq \emptyset$, and because of the strong crossing property there

[5] Cf. 3.8.

is $s \in S$ with $X \subseteq \downarrow\{s\}$ contradicting (39). ■(45)

If P K-dense, then: P crossing and P K_0-dense (by (21)), P length-finite (by (41)), P s-crossing (by 3.8); and if P s-length-finite, then: P length-finite and P crossing (by (8) and (5)), P K_0-dense (by (41)), P K-dense (by (21)). Together with (45) this yields (42). ■

The last theorem in this section is a useful tool for proving the N-density of combinatorial posets: It says that for these posets N-density is equivalent to a simple, "locally" verifiable condition.

4.6 Theorem. Let P be combinatorial. Then[6)]

(46) P N-dense $\iff \neg(\exists a,b,c,d \in P)(a \lessdot b \wedge c \lessdot b \wedge c \lessdot d \ \wedge\ a \ddagger c \wedge \neg a<d \wedge b \ddagger d)$.

Proof. "$\Rightarrow$" is clear. To prove "$\Leftarrow$" we assume the right-hand side of (46). Let $a,b,c,d \in P$ such that

$$a<b \wedge c \dot{<} b \wedge c<d \ \wedge\ a \sim c \wedge a \sim d \wedge b \sim d.$$

Then a sequence $p_1,\ldots,p_r$ exists with $c=p_1 \lessdot p_2 \lessdot \ldots \lessdot p_r=b$. Hence there are $u \in \mathrm{Min}(\{l \mid a \leq p_l\})$ and $v \in \mathrm{Max}(\{l \mid p_l \leq d\})$; then $v<u$ and $p_v<p_u$ because of $a \sim d$. If $v+1<u$ we are done; for then we set $e:=p_{v+1}$ and get $c<e \wedge e<b$ and $a \sim e \wedge e \sim d$. The proof is finished by inferring a contradiction from the assumption $v+1=u$: Then $c':=p_v \lessdot p_u=:b'$; using the combinatorialness of P we get the existence of a' and d' with $a \leq a' \lessdot b'$ and $c' \lessdot d' \leq d$; hence $a' \ddagger c'$, $\neg a'<d'$, $b' \ddagger d'$; and therefore a', b', c', d' "violate" the right-hand side of (46). ■

5 Embedding into K-dense Combinatorial Posets

Modelling a real process by a combinatorial poset P it may happen that P is *not* K-dense. But sometimes it is possible to embed P in a larger K-dense combinatorial poset P'; e.g. the N-shaped poset depicted in Fig. 1 can be enlarged to a K-dense poset by adding *one* point properly between b and c. As we will see later, in general such an embedding is *not* possible; this will especially turn out for the poset I from example 1.1.

In the following, the embedding problem will be dealt with in a more general fashion: We will show that every poset can be embedded into an N-dense combinatorial poset; and we will find necessary and

---

6) Cf. Fig. 1.

sufficient conditions for the possibility of embedding an arbitrary poset into a K-dense (resp. K_0-dense) combinatorial one.

5.1 Prerequisites. For arbitrary posets $P:=(P,\leq)$ we define $P_0:=(P_0,\leq_0)$ by

$$P_0:=(\leq),\quad (\leq_0):=\{((a,b),(c,d))\mid a\leq b\leq c\leq d \vee (a=c\leq b=d)\}.$$

Then P_0 is a poset. Let $\lessdot_0$ be the neighbourhood relation in P_0; and let $X\lessdot_0^\circ Y$ iff $X\lessdot_0 Y \vee X=Y$. For $a,b,c,d\in P$ we get

$$(a,b)\lessdot_0(c,d) \iff (a=b=c<d \vee a<b=c=d),$$

$$(a,b)\leq_0(c,d) \Rightarrow (a,b)\lessdot_0^\circ(b,b)\lessdot_0^\circ(b,c)\lessdot_0^\circ(c,c)\lessdot_0^\circ(c,d).$$

Hence P_0 is combinatorial, and due to 4.6, N-dense; and the injection $i: P \rhd\!\!\!\longrightarrow P_0$ defined by $p \longmapsto (p,p)$ for $p\in P$ yields an embedding of P into P_0. ∎

The preceding considerations imply the following theorem.

5.2 Theorem. Every poset P can be embedded into a N-dense combinatorial poset. ∎

5.3 Lemma.

(47) P_0 length-finite $\iff$ P length-finite.

(48) P_0 s-length-finite $\iff$ P s-length-finite.

Proof. "(47),$\Rightarrow$" and "(48),$\Rightarrow$" are clear. To prove "(48),$\Leftarrow$" let P be s-length-finite, let L be a chain in P_0 and $A,B\subseteq P_0$. We set

$$A':=\{a\mid(\exists y)(a,y)\in A\},\quad B':=\{b\mid(\exists x)(x,b)\in B\},$$

$$L' := \{l\mid(\exists y)(l,y)\in[A,B]\cap L\}.$$

Then L' is a chain in P, $L'\setminus \mathrm{Min}(L')\subseteq[A',B']$, and $|L'|<\infty$ because of the s-length-finiteness of P; hence we get the s-length-finiteness of P_0. The proof of "(47),$\Leftarrow$" is analogous. ∎

5.4 Theorem. A poset P can be embedded into a K_0-dense combinatorial poset if and only if P is length-finite.

Proof. If P is length-finite, the possibility of embedding follows from 5.1, 5.3 and 4.5. To prove "only if" let P be embedded into a K_0-dense combinatorial poset P'. Then due to 4.1 and 4.5 P' is length-finite, and therefore also P. ∎

5.5 Theorem. A poset P can be embedded into a K-dense combinatorial poset if and only if P is s-length-finite.

Proof. Analogous to the proof of 5.4. ∎

The preceding theorems imply that the total order of rational numbers (Q,≤) and the total order of real numbers (R,≤) cannot be embedded into K_0-dense combinatorial orders and therefore all the less into K-dense combinatorial ones. And there are also *combinatorial* posets that cannot be embedded into K_0-dense combinatorial posets: E.g. the poset *I* of example 1.1 has this property.

6 Finitely Generable Posets

Describing the asymptotic behaviour of systems by posets, the general restriction to cut-finiteness turns out to be too strong a restraint: E.g. in [2] the existence of *infinite* cuts is used to express special system properties. Obviously, cut-finiteness implies the finiteness of *all* antichains; and this remark suggests to replace cut-finiteness by a property which states the finiteness of special antichains only.

Looking at posets as models of real systems, in this connection two finiteness requests are quite natural (both of them implied by cut-finiteness): There is at least *one* finite cut and for all elements of the poset the set of (immediate) neighbours is finite. This is a rather weak property, which holds e.g. for the partial order of rational numbers (Q,≤): No rational number has an immediately neighbouring number, for between any two rational numbers there is an another one.

We restrict ourselves to combinatorial posets thus especially excluding all posets which trivially possess finite neighbourhoods only by having an empty neighbour relation. This leads us to the concept of f[initely]-generable poset which seems to be an acceptable compromise: It is strong enough to state a simple necessary and sufficient condition for K-density; on the other hand, it is so weak that posets modelling reality may be reasonably assumed to be f-generable.

6.1 Definition.

P degree-finite $:\Longleftrightarrow$ All (immediate) neighbourhoods are finite

$:\Longleftrightarrow (\forall p\in P)(|{}^{\cdot}\{p\}|<\infty \wedge |\{p\}^{\cdot}|<\infty)$.

P interval-finite $:\Longleftrightarrow$ All intervals between any two points are finite
$:\Longleftrightarrow (\forall a,b\in P)|[\{a\},\{b\}]|<\infty$. ■

6.2 Definition. P is called *f-generable* [finitely generable] iff (49)-(51) hold:

(49) P is non-empty and combinatorial;

(50) P has *at least* one finite cut [i.e. C-fin$\neq\emptyset$];

(51) P is degree-finite. ■

6.3 Lemma. Let P be combinatorial and degree-finite, let $X\subseteq P$, $\uparrow X\cap\downarrow X\subseteq X$, $F\subseteq X$, $|F|<\infty$, and $X\subseteq\uparrow F\cup\downarrow F$. Then

(52) $$|X|<\infty \Longleftrightarrow (\forall L)(L \text{ chain} \Rightarrow |X\cap L|<\infty.$$

Proof. Obviously "$\Rightarrow$". To prove the converse direction, we suppose the right-hand side of (52) and assume $|X\cap\uparrow F|=\infty$. Then there is $f_0\in F$ with $|X\cap\uparrow\{f_0\}|=\infty$. The degree-finiteness implies the existence of $f_1\in\{f_0\}^{\cdot}$ with $|X\cap\uparrow\{f_1\}|=\infty$. Continuing this construction we get an an infinte chain $f_0\lessdot f_1\lessdot\ldots$ contained in X contradicting our supposition. ■

6.4 Theorem. Let P be f-generable and length-finite. Then P is interval-finite,

(53) $$\text{C-fin} = \text{C-cross},$$

i.e. exactly the finite cuts are crossed by *all* lines, and

(54) $$(\forall S)(S \text{ antichain} \wedge |S|<\infty \Rightarrow (\exists S'\in\text{C-fin})S\subseteq S');$$

especially, the total poset P can be "covered" by *finite* cuts.

Proof. There is $F\in$C-fin. P is interval-finite due to 6.3. C-fin $\subseteq$ C-cross was already proved in (5). We now assume $S\in$C-cross and $|S|=\infty$. Then $|[S,F]\cup[F,S]|=\infty$ due to (4). We suppose $|[F,S]|=\infty$. Then by 6.3 we ge the existence of an infinite chain $L\subseteq[F,S]$. Due to 3.1 there is $f\in F$ with $L\subseteq\uparrow\{f\}$. Because $S\in$C-cross there is $q\in\uparrow S$ with $L\subseteq\downarrow\{q\}$. Hence $|[\{f\},\{q\}]\cap L|=|L|=\infty$ contradicting the length-finiteness. This proves (53).

To prove (54) let S be a finite antichain. Then due to the interval-finiteness we get $|[S,F]\cup[F,S]|=:m\in\mathbb{N}$. We set

$$F' := \{p \mid p\in\uparrow F\wedge(\forall L\in \text{LI})|[F,\{p\}]\cap L|\leq m\},$$
$$F'' := \{p \mid p\in\downarrow F\wedge(\forall L\in \text{LI})|[\{p\},F]\cap L|\leq m\}.$$

Then F' and F'' are finite because of 6.3. Obvoiusly $S\subseteq F'\cup F''$; and hence in the finite subposet $(F'\cup F'',\leq)$ there is a finite cut S' with $S\subseteq S'$. We will finish the proof by showing that S' is a cut in P. To this end suppose $p\notin\downarrow S'\cup\uparrow S'$; and we assume $p\in\uparrow F$. We have $F'\subseteq\downarrow S'\cup\uparrow S'$; therefore

$p \notin F'$. Due to the interval-finiteness there is a finite chain $p_1 \lessdot p_2 \lessdot \ldots \lessdot p_r = p$ in $[F,\{p\}]$ with maximal r and $p_1 \in F$. Hence there is s with $1 \leq s < r$, $p_s \in F_m$, and $p_{s+1} \notin F_m$. Therefore from the maximality of r it follows that $s+1 > m$, hence $s \geq m$. We have $p_s \notin \uparrow S'$ (otherwise $p \in \uparrow S'$). Hence there is $q \in S' \subseteq F' \cup F''$ with $p_s < q$. Because of $s \geq m$, the chain $p_1, \ldots, p_s, q$ has more than m elements, contradicting $q \in F' \cup F''$. ■

In the preceding theorem length-finiteness cannot be dispensed with: The poset I from 1.1 is f-generable and *not* interval-finite and C-fin≠C-cross=C; and define I' as the poset consisting of the poset I and the points $\{4\} \times \mathbb{N}$ such that $(1,m) < (4,n)$ for for all $m \leq n$ and $(4,n)$ not comparable with all other points of I; then I' is f-generable, but the only cut containing $(3,0)$ is the *infinite* cut $\{(3,0)\} \cup \{(4,n) \mid n \in \mathbb{N}\}$.

<u>6.5 Theorem.</u> Let P be f-generable. Then

P cut-finite $\iff$ P s-crossing $\iff$ P crossing $\wedge$ P length-finite.

<u>Proof.</u> By (5), 3.8, and (53). ■

<u>6.6 Theorem.</u> Let P be f-generable. Then:

(55) P cut-finite $\wedge$ P N-dense $\iff$ P K-dense.

(56) P length-finite $\Rightarrow$ (P N-dense $\iff$ C-fin = C-met).

<u>Proof.</u> (55) follows from 4.3, 4.1, (42), and 6.5. If P length-finite and N-dense, then we get C-fin=C-met using 4.2, C-met⊆C-cross, and (53). Finally, we assume P length-finite and C-fin=C-met, and let $a,b,c,d \in P$ form an N-shaped subposet according to Fig. 1; then by (54) there is $S \in$C-fin with $a,d \in S$, and $S \in$C-met yields the existence of $e \in S$ properly between b and c. ■

For applications the preceding theorem states the most interesting result; it turns out that in f-generable posets cut-finiteness is the only "global" condition necessary to ensure K-density. (Note that C-fin⊆C-met for *all* N-dense posets, cf. 4.2.) Similar results for causal nets were proved by Winskel [6]. The following theorem generalizing a result on occurrence nets due to Goltz and Reisig [2] says that in an f-generable poset with infinite cuts the violation of cut-finiteness takes place in the "proximity" of *every* finite cut.

<u>6.7 Theorem.</u> Let P be f-generable and *not* cut-finite, and let F be a *finite* cut. Then there is an *infinite* antichain S such that the subposet $([S,F] \cup [F,S], \leq)$ is interval-finite.

Proof. By 3.4, 3.6, and 6.4 $(/F/,\leq)$ is interval-finite and *not* cut-finite. Hence there is an infinite cut S in $/F/$; and this S has the required properties. ■

7 Conclusion

In this paper we studied the relationship between K-density and N-density for posets with different kinds of finiteness properties; in particular we introduced the concept of f[initely]-generable poset motivated by restrictions found in "real" processes. We proved that an N-dense non-empty poset is K-dense if all cuts are finite [cf. 4.3], and that for f-generable posets also the other direction holds: All cuts of an f-generable K-dense poset are finite [cf. 6.6].

Modelling the behaviour of real systems by non-empty posets, cut-finiteness may be considered a reasonable restriction, for in "reality" only a finite number of things can happen at the same time. Hence we can summarize our results as follows: If all cuts of a "modelling" poset can be interpreted in reality then N-density and K-density are equivalent.

Nevertheless, sometimes it is useful to admit models with infinite cuts too (e.g. in order to describe the asymptotic behaviour of a system). But in this case we get a similar result: In any "modelling" N-dense poset all "interpretable" cuts (and that are only the finite ones) are met by all lines [cf. 4.2].

8 References

[1] Best, E.: The Relative Strength of K-Density. In: Lecture Notes in Computer Science Bd. 84 : Net Theory and Applications, pp. 261-276. - Berlin : Springer-Verlag (1980)

[2] Goltz, U.; Reisig, W.: The Non-sequential Behaviour of Petri Nets. In: Information and Control 57 (1983), pp. 125-147

[3] Petri, C. A.: Nicht-sequentielle Prozesse. In: Universität Erlangen-Nürnberg, Arbeitsberichte des IIMD, Bd. 9, Nr.8, S. 57-82 (1976)

[4] Petri, C. A.: Concurrency. In: Lecture Notes in Computer Science Bd. 84 : Net Theory and Applications, pp. 251-260. - Berlin : Springer-Verlag (1980)

[5] Plünnecke, H.: Schnitte in Halbordnungen. - St. Augustin : Gesellschaft für Mathematik und Datenverarbeitung Bonn, ISF-Report 81.09 (1981)

[6] Winskel, G.: Events in Computation. - University of Edinburgh, Thesis (December, 1980)

A NET MODEL OF A LOCAL AREA NETWORK PROTOCOL

Klaus Voss
Institut für Methodische Grundlagen
Gesellschaft für Mathematik und Datenverarbeitung
D-5205 St. Augustin, Germany

Abstract

Predicate/Transition-Nets, a class of higher level Petri nets, are used to model the second protocol layer of the Local Area Network REDPUC. The model describes the protocol layer precisely and completely, including an essential part of its environment. Particularly, the switch-on and switch-off procedures for user stations are considered. In establishing the protocol net, some standard sub-models and the concept of modelling by macro transitional forms are presented, which both may be useful in a more general setting.

0. Introduction

At Pontifícia Universidade Católica do Rio de Janeiro (PUC/RJ), a Local Area Network (REDPUC) has been designed and implemented in a prototype version during the last two years by its departments of Informatics and of Electrical Engineering. The host computers of the network cooperate by exchanging messages via a communication medium. The correct operation of the network mainly depends on the protocol which governs this cooperation. This kind of a protocol is so complex that imagination alone is unable to cope with all conceivable behaviour of the system. Therefore, intuition and mere reasoning do not help very much to describe the system precisely and in its entirety and to make sure that it really possesses all the properties which have been envisaged by its designers and implementors.

The task of specifying and verifying distributed systems is particularly difficult because of the inherent concurrent, asynchronous, and non-deterministic nature of most of these systems. Moreover, for geographically distributed systems, the use of a central control mechanism is not adequate and the assumption of a global clock is not realistic. However, a number of suitable approaches to tackle this problem have been reported in the last years. Of course they have been applied also to the field of communication protocols [RW83]. In this area, the combination of state machine and programming language concepts as described in [BG77], [NHS83], or, based on the SARAH methodology, in [Sc81], has attracted much interest. Also timed Petri nets have been widely used (e.g., see [CR83]). However, we are not convinced that treating time as a separate concept as opposed to causality, will yield substantial advantages. On the contrary, if time is used to influence the occurrences of events, one has to be very careful not to leave the solid ground on which the results of net theory apply. Therefore, like us, a number of authors stick to the original idea of net theory [Pe73], [Br80], even when modelling protocols which normally include timing considerations [BT82], [EP80].

This report describes the use of Predicate/Transition-Nets (PrT-nets) to model the second layer of the REDPUC protocol. The protocol deals with the rules how stations communicate with each other, but not with the contents of the transmitted messages and their use. The protocol is modelled completely and "as it is", i.e., no omissions and no simplifications have been made in order to get a smoother model. Moreover, the model considers also the procedures for a station to become active or passive. An analysis of the net model is far beyond the scope of this report and shall be subject of a forthcoming paper.

The plan of this paper is as follows. The next section shall describe briefly the principles of the REDPUC protocol in an introductory form. This part has been contributed by D. Schwabe, one of the authors of the protocol. In section 2, some principles for modelling the protocol as a PrT-net are explained. The third section then presents the models for the bus, for the ring lists, and finally for the protocol itself. In section 4, we will discuss the limitations of the models as constructed so far, and we shall present a model for the stations switch-on and switch-off procedures. The last section is devoted to some concluding remarks.

1. The Local Area Network protocol

The Local Area Network REDPUC, developed at PUC/RJ, allows the interconnection of multi-purpose stations (host computers) via a coaxial cable. The stations interface the cable through a special piece of hardware called the bus interface, which executes the protocols necessary to regulate access to the transmission medium.

The bus access protocol is organized in a layered fashion, following the principle of the Reference Model for Open Systems Interconnection of ISO. The first layer is responsible for electrical interface with the cable, including coding and decoding of signals. The second layer, which is the object of this report, is responsible for enforcing an access discipline to the transmission medium. It is also in charge of detecting transmission errors, which is done by blocking the data to be transmitted into frames and calculating a cyclic redundancy code, called frame checking sequence (FCS), with the data. The FCS is sent together with the frame and recalculated, upon reception, directly from the data. The two values are then compared, any difference indicating an error.

When two or more stations transmit at the same time, a collision will occur and will cause an error to be detected by the receiving stations. It should be noted that the hardware of the bus interface is such that a station that transmits cannot hear its own transmission. Therefore, it will not be able to detect any errors or collisions.

Although the transmission medium is shared by all stations, the access protocol does not allow a station to transmit at any time. Instead, a round-robin discipline is imposed, thus forming a virtual ring among the stations. The basic mechanism used to achieve this is the notion of a token, which is understood as a permission to transmit. In other words, a station will transmit only if it is in possession of the token. Upon transmitting a message, a station will pass the token to the next station. In order to determine which is the next station, the transmitting station will consult a list, called cycle control list or ring list, which contains the transmitting station's view of the currently active stations in the network.

The operation of the network then follows a cycle, in which successive stations transmit data together with the token, which is in fact the address of the next station allowed to transmit (see Figure 1.1.).

```
transmitting stations:
   1       2       3       6       4                    1
 |2|    | |3|    | |6|    | |4|    | |FF|1|    | |      |  |2|    |
 ↑       ↑  ..tokens..  ↑       ↑  ↑                  ↑
<-----> <----->  ..intervals..  <--------> <-----> <----->
                                            ↑      ↑
                                     contention interval
<--------------- cycle -------------------------->
```

Figure 1.1. The transmission cycle

The station which is the last one in the ring list sends a hexadecimal FF as its token and additionally the address of the first station in its ring list. The reason for this will be explained below. If a station does not have any data to send, it must send an empty message together with the token. Since the medium is of broadcast type, all stations are able to follow the cycle by keeping track of the values of tokens being passed around, even when the message itself is not addressed to the particular station.

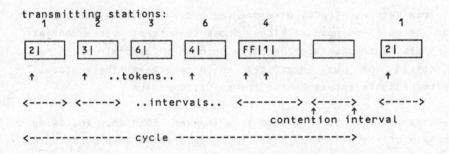

During normal operation each station knows what is the address of the station which is transmitting, given by the value of the last transmitted token. If the station which is supposed to be currently transmitting became inactive (for whatever reasons), the other stations will notice that there was an omission in the current transmission interval. If a station omits transmission or sends erroneous messages for three consecutive times, the other stations of the network will consider it inactive and remove it from their ring lists, thus removing the station from the cycle. When an omission or error is detected, each station must examine its ring list, and one of them will determine that it was supposed to be the next station in the cycle, i.e., it is the successor of the station that omitted transmission. This station then sends the message and the token to its successor.

Let us suppose now that a station that was inactive (i.e., was not in the cycle) wishes to become active and be able to send messages to other stations. It must somehow inform the other stations of its presence. In order to do that, there is a special interval, at the end of each cycle, when a station outside the cycle may announce its presence and request its insertion in the cycle. This interval is identified by the token value FF (hexadecimal) and is called <u>contention interval</u> for reasons that will become clear shortly. In the usual case, all stations will detect the occurrence of the contention interval and listen for insertion requests. If there is one request, all stations insert the requesting station at the end of their ring lists. Therefore, the successor of a newly inserted station is always FF. When a station has just been inserted in the cycle, it will spend the following cycle building its own new ring list.

A moment's reflection on the procedures described above will immediately raise the question of what happens when two (or more) stations wish to be inserted in the cycle at the same time. During the contention interval, both stations will transmit their requests at the same time, and a collision will occur. All the stations will detect this by receiving an incorrect frame; as mentioned previously, the transmitting stations will not detect this error.

When a collision is detected in the contention interval, all the stations in the network will go through a <u>reinitialization cycle</u>. Before actually entering this cycle, all stations will go through a long time-out period without transmitting (this period should be longer than the longest possible cycle), which ensures that all stations will actually enter the reinitialization cycle. In the reinitialization cycle, all stations physically connected to the network (a maximum of 255) are considered to be active, and all ring lists of all stations will be initialized to include all stations. The cycle then proceeds as usual, except that stations which do not transmit are immediately removed from the ring lists (instead of after three consecutive times). In this manner, after one cycle, the ring lists of all stations actually present will be reduced to reflect the real configuration of the network. After the reinitialization cycle, the network will return to the normal mode of functioning.

The protocol described thus far is such that it does not rely on any centralized form of control. A careful study will show that it is possible that a station is removed from the cycle without knowing it (since it cannot hear its own transmission). In order to detect this situation, each station must keep track of the occurrence of the contention interval. If it detects that two contention intervals occur without the station receiving the token, the station can deduce that it has been excluded from the cycle, and it must request its reinsertion.

Another exceptional situation that must be detected is the formation of sub-cycles. To prevent this, a station must also monitor the occurrence of two consecutive receptions of the token without an intervening contention interval. If this happens, the station must not transmit then, and therefore it will be excluded from the ring lists of the remaining stations after three times.

2. The use of Predicate/Transition-Nets for modelling

Predicate/Transition-nets (PrT-nets) are a first-order extension of ordinary Petri nets [GL81]. They allow to model even large concurrent distributed systems in a concise way without loosing the preciseness and formal background of Petri nets. Examples how this can be done are presented in [Vo80], [Vo82]. The reader is assumed to be familiar with the definition of this net type [GL81].

What has to be done first when modelling a system by PrT-nets is to define the sets of individuals to be dealt with, and the operators and relations which may be applied to these sets (in the transition formulas). In case of the REDPUC protocol, we obviously have to do with the set S of the nodes of the network, i.e., up to 255 stations connected to the bus. Their individual names shall be the natural numbers 0,1,2,...,254, and the variables used to denote the stations are a,b,c,... . The "token" that a station sends to determine the next transmitting station may be one of these station numbers or the number 255, which we always write in its hexadecimal form FF for ease of distinction. The relations to be applied to this set T={0,1,2,...,254,FF} are simply '=' and '≠', and the variable names used to describe a token are usually t and u. In order to be complete, we should mention that we sometimes use the value '?', when a station which is building up a new ring list, does not know the identity of the current sender due to a previous error.

At this point we would like to introduce some conventions used to improve the readability of the paper and of the net models. Firstly, for ease of reference, we give names to the nodes of the nets. These names are written inside the circles resp. in the lower right-hand corner of the boxes. Secondly, lower case letters are used to denote variables, whereas upper case letters and numerals denote individual values. Thirdly, double-headed arcs mean side-conditions (or non-destructive reading of a storage place) and have to be expanded in the obvious way (see [PS82]) to respect the usual definition of PrT-nets.

The fourth and most important convention has been influenced by the observation that the network protocol includes, at different locations, operations which perform the same kind of access to the same storage or transmission unit. It therefore seemed to be useful to define such an operation in general terms ("macro body") and then to use a special call of it ("macro call") at any location where it occurs in the net. To be more precise, a <u>macro body</u> is a net substructure with exactly one input transition (identified by a free, dangling input arc) and one not necessarily different output transition (identified by a free output arc). It has a name and a parameter list of variables, called parameter variables. A <u>macro call</u> is a transitional form which is inscribed by the name of the called macro and a parameter list of variables and/or constant values, called parameter values. A macro call in a net is interpreted as an abbreviation of, i.e., has to be replaced by a net sub-structure derived from the macro body according to the following <u>substitution rule</u>. Firstly, all parameter variables wherever they occur in the macro body, have to be replaced by the corresponding parameter values of the macro call. (Correspondence is by the respective positions in the parameter lists.) As a convention, nodes whose names in the macro body consist of a letter and a number, have to be attributed new names which are unique in the composite net. Secondly, the macro call has to be substituted by the above modified macro body such that the input resp. output arc of the macro call replaces the free input resp. output arc of the macro body. Finally, having replaced all macro calls, nodes with identical names have to be identified (in our case BUS, PH, EC, and RL). As an example, we look at Figure 3.4. Transition 15R must be replaced by a sub-net derived from the macro body of INSB defined in the upper left hand corner of the figure. Having changed every e to d and every f to FF there, this sub-net consists of (re-named) instances of the transitions 2R and 3R, connected with each other via a (re-named) instance of place R1, and also connected, as indicated, to the place RL which is a unique node in the composite protocol net.

The introduction of macros is motivated by three purposes. Firstly, it shall enhance the readability of the composite net by selecting macros and naming them in accordance to the language of the application area. Secondly, the composite net can be drawn in a quite dense and pretty fashion because many of the arcs pointing to the "central" nodes (like BUS e.g.) are not shown explicitly. The fact that the central nodes and their connections are hidden behind the macro calls is, on the other hand, a disadvantage because essential synchronization points can no more discovered at a glance. Finally, the use of macros facilitates the tasks of modifying the operations expressed by macros, because then only the macro bodies have to be changed.

3. The net models

The way how a station of the Local Area Network is connected to the transmission medium and how it is supposed to behave in certain cases is essentially the same for all stations, at least as far as the protocol level in question is concerned. Therefore we can use the same net structure to model each of the stations. This of course does not imply that, when taking a snapshot of the system's state, all stations are always in the same states and performing the same operations. Rather, we have 255 identically structured net models, but possibly with different markings of their places (which describe their respective states). To be able to distinguish the stations and their states from each other, we "qualify" each tuple of the net by the individual identification of the station to which it belongs. Thus all tuples of station 7, e.g., are of the form <7,...>. We then fold all these 255 nets into one by replacing the individual station numbers in the arc labels and transition inscriptions by a variable, say a. Doing this we obtain a net where each transition resp. place stands for a class of 255 ordinary transitions resp. places, a PrT-net. The only connection between the different layers of the net, i.e. the connection between different stations, is the communication medium. Thus the bus model is a basic building block of the protocol net.

3.1. The bus model

The basic component of this net is the place BUS, the medium for transmitting messages between the stations and for synchronizing these write and read operations. BUS is the only place of the whole net model whose class elements cannot be attributed one to one to the stations. Rather, it consists of 255•255 individual elements, one for each pair of stations.

There are two kinds of possible accesses to the bus, sending/transmitting and receiving/listening, which we describe by sub-nets called WRITE and LISTEN (see Figure 3.1). Both are used by macro calls in other nets. What has to be modelled is a synchronization mechanism which guarantees that each station writes or listens to the bus exactly once during any one interval, with listening occurring after writing of course. This means that we have to make sure that the following interval can only be started after all stations have accessed the bus once during the preceding interval. And by the same mechanism the actual token values have to be transmitted and multiple transmisssions during the same interval have to be detected. In the following, one possibility to model this mechanism is presented. We have reduced its complexity as much as possible. In fact, we do not know of any simpler model which meets the requirements stated above.

A marking of BUS consists of 6-tuples $\langle a,b,y,t_a,u_a,x_a\rangle$, which should be interpreted in the following way. The first element, a, denotes the sender, and the second element, b, the addressee of the tuple. The value of y may be W or R, which is the permission (given by a to b) to write or read the bus. The values of t_a and u_a are the <u>tokens</u> which are part of the message written by a, and x_a is 0 or 1, as discussed afterwards.

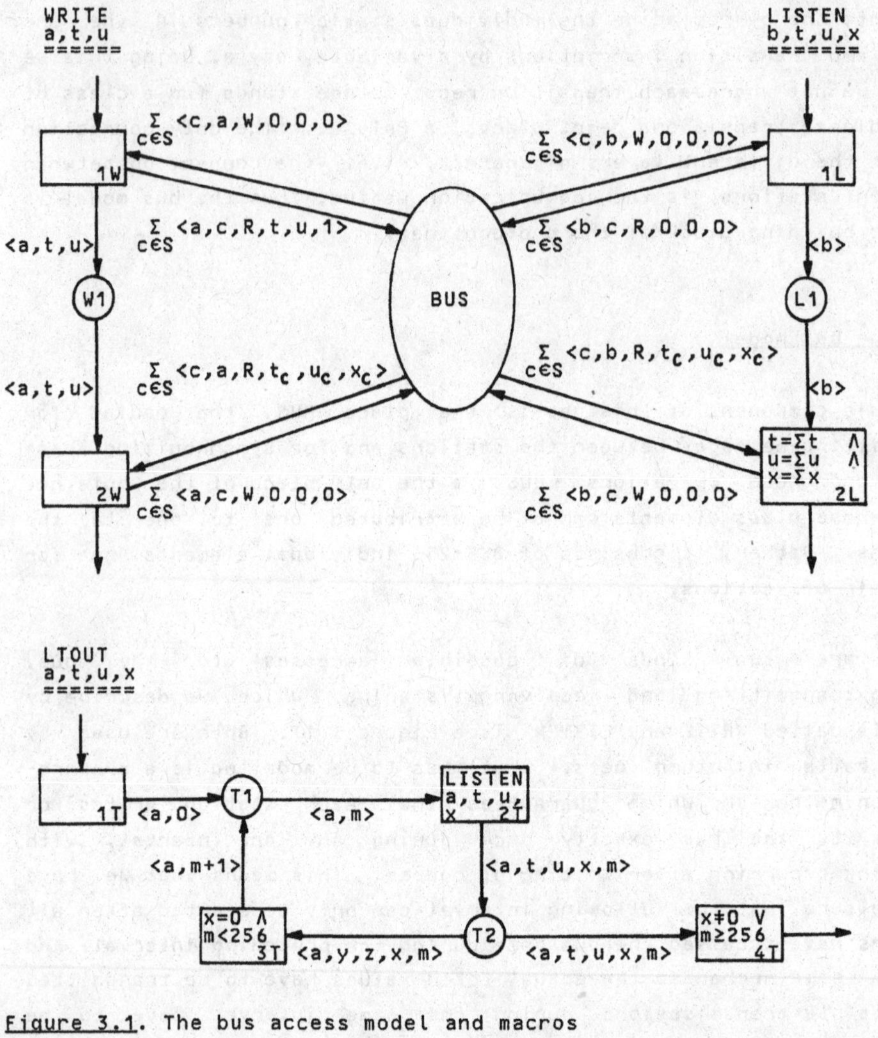

Figure 3.1. The bus access model and macros

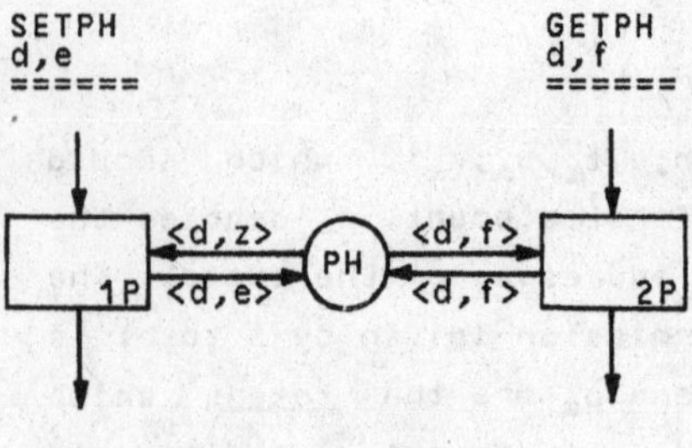

Figure 3.2. The phase macros

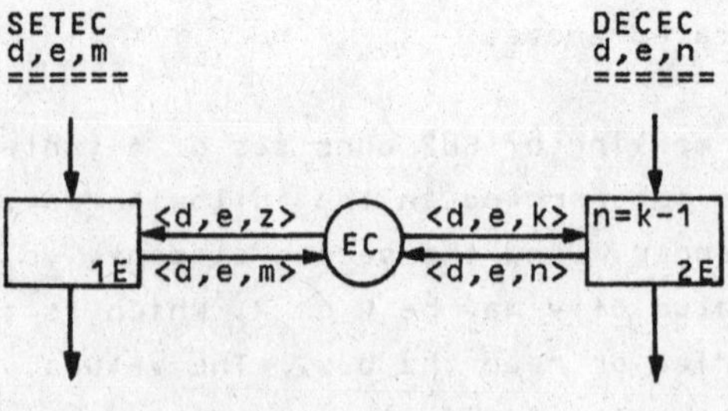

Figure 3.3. The error count macros

In modelling the bus we pursue the idea that each interval is divided into two steps, the first one for writing and the second one for reading. We assume that, at the begin of an interval, the marking of BUS is

$$M_0(BUS) = \sum_{a\in S} \sum_{b\in S} \langle a,b,W,0,0,0\rangle .$$

This means that transition 1W for each writing station a, and transition 1L for each listening station b is enabled, i.e., can remove $\Sigma\langle c,a,W,0,0,0\rangle$, resp. $\Sigma\langle c,b,W,0,0,0\rangle$ from BUS. (In this context, the formal sums Σ are always taken for $c\in S$.) A writing station a will simultaneously add $\Sigma\langle a,c,R,t,u,1\rangle$ to M(BUS), permitting each c to read the tokens t,u written by a. Concurrently, each listening station, by transition 1L, adds $\Sigma\langle b,c,R,0,0,0\rangle$ to M(BUS), such that M(BUS) at the end of the first step again consists of 255•255 tuples, but now with R as value of their third elements. Only after all stations have fired either transition 1W or transition 1L (first step), they can proceed to the second step. By transition 2W, any writer just replaces its input tuples $\Sigma\langle c,a,R,t_c,u_c,x_c\rangle$ by the output tuples $\Sigma\langle a,c,W,0,0,0\rangle$, whereby it gives his permission to start the next interval. It does not consider the values t_c, u_c, x_c, which represents the fact that a writer cannot read during the same interval. The listening stations b however, by transition 2L, read all tuples $\Sigma\langle c,b,R,t_c,u_c,x_c\rangle$ addressed to b, and form the sums (over all $c\in S$) $t=\Sigma t_c$, $u=\Sigma u_c$, $x=\Sigma x_c$, which constitute the result of the listening action. The first step of the next interval can start only if, for each of the 255 stations, transition 2W or 2L has been fired, thus restoring their part $\Sigma\langle a,c,W,0,0,0\rangle$ or $\Sigma\langle b,c,W,0,0,0\rangle$ of the initial marking of BUS. Consequently, during a step, all stations may work concurrently. But the next step can be started only if all stations have finished the preceding one. By this mechanism, the accesses to the bus are strictly synchronized.

We present an example to demonstrate that any station having performed its first step (1W or 1L) in an interval, cannot proceed immediately to the second step (2W or 2L). Assume $S = \{s_1, s_2\}$, and $a=s_1$ to be a transmitting station. (For convenience, in the following we omit always the last 3 elements of the 6-tuples on BUS.) By firing 1W for s_1, the initial marking $M_0(BUS) = \langle s_1,s_1,W\rangle + \langle s_2,s_1,W\rangle + \langle s_1,s_2,W\rangle + \langle s_2,s_2,W\rangle$ is transformed into $M(BUS) = \langle s_1,s_1,R\rangle + \langle s_1,s_2,R\rangle + \langle s_1,s_2,W\rangle + \langle s_2,s_2,W\rangle$. But to enable transition 2W for s_1, the precondition $\langle s_1,s_1,R\rangle + \langle s_2,s_1,R\rangle \le M(BUS)$ must hold. The missing tuple $\langle s_2,s_1,R\rangle$, however, can only be supplied by firing 1W or 1L for station s_2. Thus s_1 has to wait until s_2 has performed its first step as well before leaving the interval by 2W.

Finally, we would like to say a few words concerning the variable x mentioned above. As can be observed, any reader delivers a tuple with x=1 (by transition 1W) and any listener a tuple with x=0 (by transition 1L) to the bus. When a reader has read the contents of the bus by transition 2L, the sum $x=\Sigma x_c$ therefore contains the number of stations that have been transmitting during the current interval. In reality however, this number cannot be determined by any station. By inspecting the Frame Checking Sequence, it only knows when there were more than one. In our model, this is respected by the fact that, in case x>1, we never make use of the exact value of x. Rather, x will be examined by the receivers only in the following way:

x=0: no station has transmitted, interpreted as a time-out.

x=1: one sending station; t and u should be correct tokens.

x>1: more than one sender; collision and/or error. (In this case, the addition of the t_c- and u_c-values, in transition 2L, may be interpreted as a superposition of electrical pulses on the bus viewed as an electrical medium.)

One can easily verify that this model works even in the extreme cases in which the stations are either all transmitting or all receiving. In the latter case, all stations would read a message with x=0, which would cause a time-out to occur.

Subsequent to each contention interval, the stations listen to the bus if there is a <u>long time-out</u>, in order to determine whether a reinitialization cycle will follow or not. This long time-out is supposed to be longer than the longest possible cycle. Thus it is modelled as a sequence of 256 ordinary intervals without transmissions. The macro LTOUT in Figure 3.1 counts the number of consecutive silent intervals and renders as output the tuple <a,t,u,x> to station a. If x=0, then indeed 256 silent ordinary intervals have occurred, and the values of t,u are of no interest. If however x>0, then a station has transmitted a message before this "long" time has elapsed, and t,u will be the tokens contained in this first message.

3.2. The phase, the error counter, and the ring list macros

The kind of operation of a station depends on its actual "phase", i.e., it depends on whether the station is currently building up a new ring list (after having requested its re-insertion in the cycle during the last contention interval), whether the actual cycle is a reinitialization cycle, or whether none of both is true (which we call the "normal" phase). The actual phase of a station is reflected, for each station d, by the value of the variable p of the tuple <d,p> in the marking of place PH ("phase") of Figure 3.2. This value may be B ("building ring list"), R ("reinitialization") or N ("normal"). For accessing PH we define two macros, SETPH d,e which sets the phase value of station d from whatever it is ("z") to e, and GETPH d,f which merely determines the actual value f of the phase of d (Figure 3.2).

For each station d, place EC ("error counter") contains a set of 255 tuples <d,e,n>, one for each station e, in which the number n says how many consecutive errors of station e will still be tolerated by station d, before d will extinguish e in its ring list. In Figure 3.3, two macros are defined for performing the access to EC. SETEC d,e,m sets the error count for e (in the list of station d) unconditionally to m. DECEC d,e,n decreases that error count by 1, updates EC accordingly and delivers the resulting value also by the variable n.

Finally, we know that each station has a ring list which reflects its current knowledge about the sequence in which the stations transmit. This concept is similar but not identical to the notion of "virtual ring" as defined in [Le78]. Our approach to model these ring lists is to provide a place RL ("ring lists") which contains the ring lists of all stations. For each station d, its ring list consists of a number of tuples whose first element is the identity of the station to which it belongs (Figure 3.4). Besides that, every tuple contains the name r of a station which is actually a member of the ring list of d and the names of the predecessor and the successor of r in this ring list. Thus the ordering within a ring list is modelled by forward and backward pointers, which obviously is just one of several possible solutions. More precisely, if station r is contained in the ring list of station d, this is modelled by a tuple <d,q,r,s> in the marking of RL, whose first element d determines the owner of the ring list, the third element r is the station in question, and the second and fourth elements denote the predecessor q and the successor s of r in the ring list, respectively. A "complete" ring list of d, as established at the begin of each reinitialization cycle, contains the elements <d,FF,0,1>, <d,0,1,2>, <d,1,2,3>, ..., <d,253,254,FF>, <d,254,FF,0>. The "empty" ring list of station d is represented by marking RL with exactly one tuple <d,FF,FF,FF>. Figure 3.4 defines the macros concerning inspection and manipulation of the ring lists. They are,

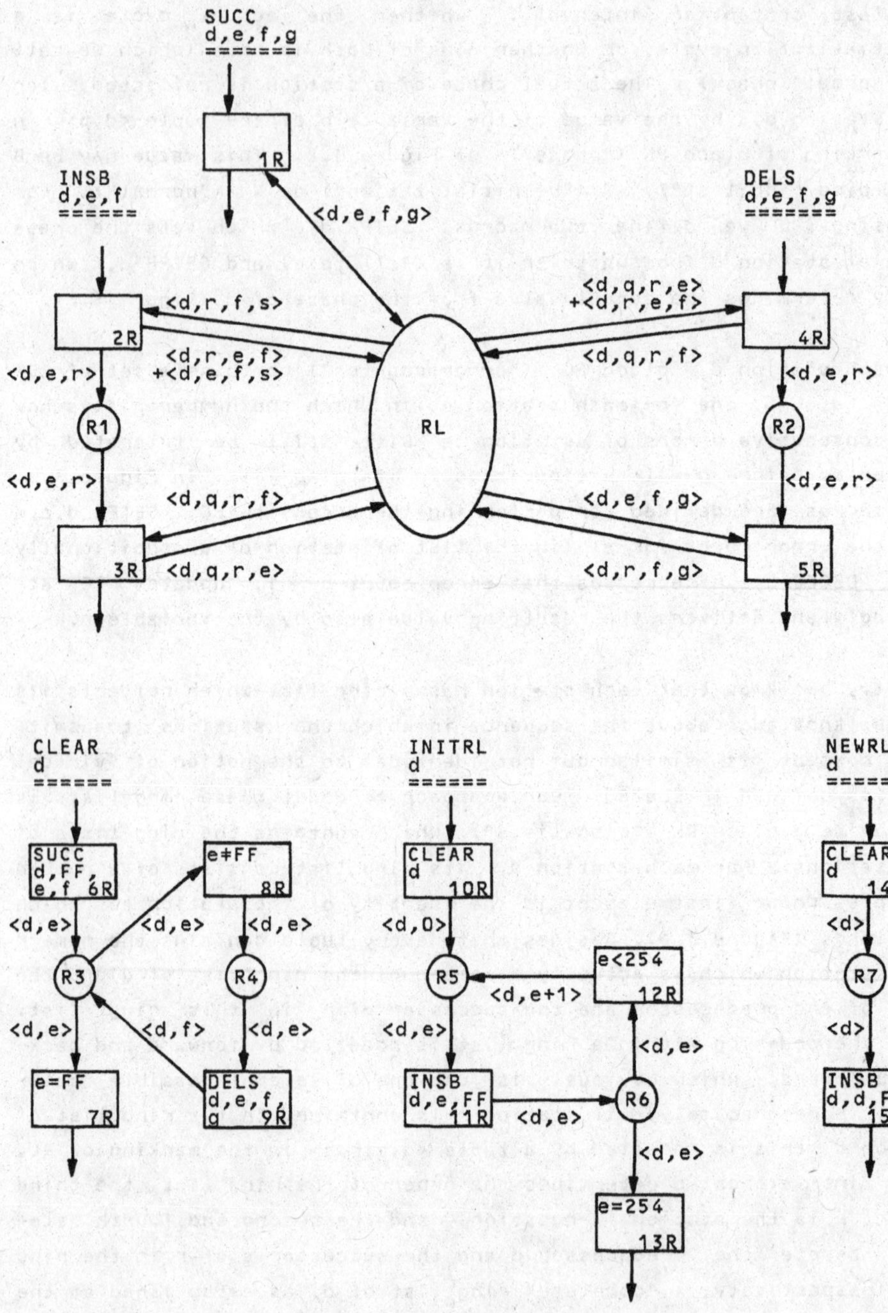

Figure 3.4. The ring list model and macros

always refering to the ring list of station d,

SUCC d,e,f,g: determine the (two) successors f and g of e,

INSB d,e,f: insert e before f,

DELS d,e,f,g: delete e and determine its successors f and g,

CLEAR d: set to "empty" ring list,

INITRL d: build up the "complete" ring list,

NEWRL d: build a new ring list with the elements d and FF.

3.3. The protocol model

Figure 3.5 contains the PrT-net model (first version) of the whole REDPUC protocol. It describes the behaviour of an arbitrary station a. In other words, the net can be interpreted as consisting of 255 nets, one for each station, where a layer is defined by substituting the variable a by the individual station number. These layers are connected with each other through the places PH, EC, and the global place BUS, as discussed before.

Note that due to space limitations, all arc labels in Figure 3.5 are written without the opening "<" and the closing ">". And to improve readability, place A has been drawn twice, at the top and at the bottom of the picture.

We begin the discussion of Figure 3.5 with the place SIC. The marking of SIC ("station-in-cycle indicator") contains, for every station a, a tuple <a,YES> resp. <a,NO>, indicating that a was included in the current cycle of transmitting stations resp. was not (yet).

For the first version of the protocol net we assume the following initial marking M_0:

$$M_0(PH) = \sum_{a\in S} \langle a,N\rangle, \quad M_0(SIC) = \sum_{a\in S} \langle a,NO\rangle, \quad M_0(A) = \sum_{a\in S} \langle a,0,0\rangle,$$

$$M_0(EC) = \sum_{a\in S} \sum_{c\in S} \langle a,c,3\rangle, \quad M_0(BUS) = \sum_{a\in S} \sum_{c\in S} \langle a,c,W,0,0,0\rangle,$$

$$M_0(RL) = \sum_{a\in S} (\langle a,FF,0,1\rangle+\langle a,0,1,2\rangle+\ldots+\langle a,254,FF,0\rangle),$$

$M_0(X) = 0$ for all remaining places X.

The assumption that the above initial marking is chosen will be dropped in section 4 where the switch-on and switch-off procedures are introduced. At that point we shall see that and how this marking can be produced during the switch-on process.

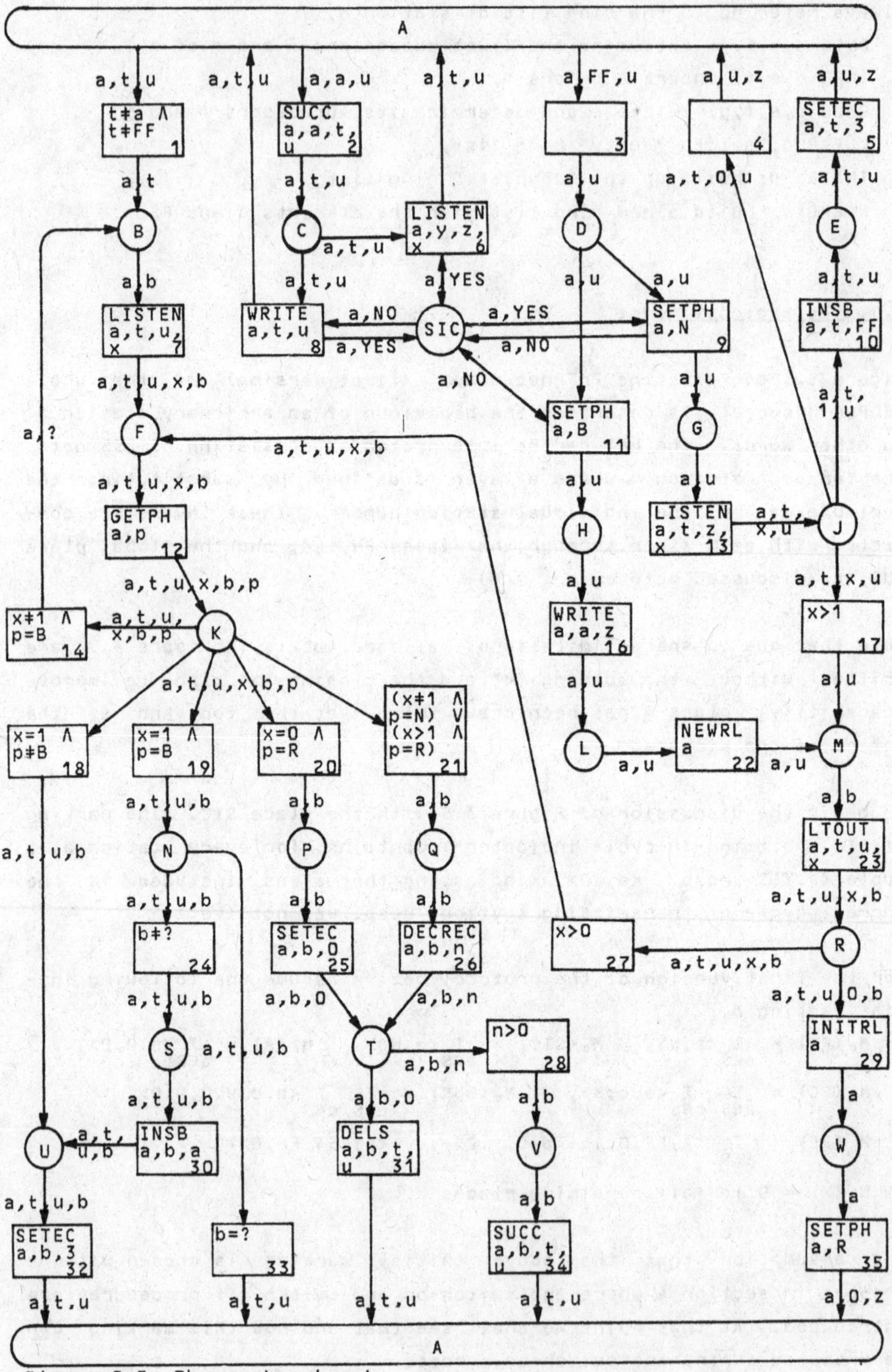

Figure 3.5. The protocol net

We would like to jump now right into a typical process of a station, describing the different states and branches through which it may run. We start with a state in which a new interval just begins, e.g. M_0. Place A is assumed to contain, for each station a, a tuple <a,t,u>. The value of t in this tuple is the "token" which was specified in the last message received by a. There are three possibilities for proceeding from this state depending on the value of the token t. One branch, starting with transition 1 (case A/1) if t≠a and t≠FF, is taken if station a is supposed to listen to the message on the bus during that interval. This branch consists of the left hand part of Figure 3.5 and includes the 5 alternative sub-branches at place K. The second branch starts with transition 2 (case A/2) and is chosen if t=a, i.e., if station a is supposed to transmit during that interval. It consists of transitions 2, 6, 8 and place C and is drawn in the upper central part of Figure 3.5. The third branch, starting with transition 3 (case A/3), describes the actions to be performed if the transmitted token t is equal to FF. This determines the last interval of a cycle, the subsequent contention interval and a possibly following long time-out. This branch is modelled at the right hand side of Figure 3.5. Only in this last case the second transmitted token, u, is of interest because it names the station which is supposed to transmit in the first interval of the next cycle.

<u>Case A/1</u>: If the value of t is neither station a itself nor equal to FF (transition 1), then a shall listen to the transmission of station t next. On place B, the variable denoting the sending station is renamed from t to b, in order not to be confused with the token t which will be received, together with new values of u and x, as part of the message of b (macro LISTEN in transition 7). As said before, u is of no interest if t≠FF. Having read the current phase p of a from PH (by macro GETPH in transition 12), the full information <a,t,u,x,b,p> is delivered to place K. Now it depends on the values of x and p which one of the five possibilities to continue is taken. Cases K/14, K/19, K/20, K/21 will be dealt with at the end of this section. In the normal case K/18, when x=1 (message reception okay) and p≠B (normal or reinitialization phase), transition 18 fires and enables transition 32, which in turn sets the error count of the sending station b to the maximum number of 3 tolerable errors. Then <a,t,u> is passed to A which means that the next interval may begin.

<u>Case A/2</u>: If the last token t read by station a was the number a itself, a is allowed to transmit next. In this case, transition 2 is

enabled which determines the successors t and u of a in the ring list of a. If <a,NO>≤M(SIC), i.e. this is the first time during the cycle that a gets the token, transition 8 updates SIC replacing <a,NO> by <a,YES>, and writes a message containing the tokens t,u on the bus, and it returns <a,t,u> to A in order to start a new interval. If however <a,YES>≤M(SIC), i.e. station a has already appeared in the cycle, this must be due to erroneous ring lists of other stations. In this case, a does not write, but instead is silent (transition 6), thus causing a time-out at the site of the listening stations.

<u>Case A/3</u>: If the last token t was FF, the value of u is the number of the station which is supposed to transmit in the first interval of the subsequent cycle. But before that, the contention interval of the current cycle is encountered. This contention interval starts with transition 3 which marks place D with <a,u>. Now, there are two possibilities to continue. If station a has sent during the current cycle it has to observe whether a stations wants its re-insertion in the cycle (case D/9). If however, a was not active during the current cycle it may claim for its re-insertion by sending its identity number in the contention interval (case D/11).

Case D/9: If a was included in the current cycle, <a,YES>≤M(SIC), then SIC is updated to contain <a,NO> and the phase is set to normal by transition 9. Subsequently, station a listens to the transmissions during the contention interval (transition 13). If x=0 (no request for insertion), nothing special has to be done and <a,u,z>, with arbitrary z, is returned immediately to A by transition 4. If x=1 (exactly one request for insertion in the ring list), transition 10 inserts the requesting station t as the last element before FF into the ring list of a. Then transition 5 sets the error count for this t to 3 and proceeds to the next cycle, where the first element u of the ring list is now the station to transmit next (z may have an arbitrary value). Finally, if x>1 (a collision has occurred), transition 17 puts <a,u> onto M, where u is re-named into b. Then transition 23 checks whether a long time-out follows. This can be decided by inspecting the output value x of LTOUT. In case x>0 (no long time-out) transition 27 will lead to a normal continuation of the procedure. In case x=0 (long time-out) transitions 29 and 35 will take provision for a reinitialization cycle to follow. During this cycle, which is characterized by the value R of the phase (transition 35), all stations construct a new ring list with all currently active stations. Starting with a complete ring list (macro INITRL of transition 29), they behave like in the normal phase, except that a station is removed from the ring list the first time it has the token but does not transmit (see below).

Case D/11: If <a,NO>≤M(SIC), i.e. a did not appear in the last cycle, transition 11 may occur, leaving SIC unchanged, updating the phase of a to B ("build new ring list") and passing <a,u> from D to H. This marks the first step of station a to request its insertion in the cycle. The next steps are to transmit a message with its identity a (and, only for reasons of having two "tokens" for WRITE, an arbitrary z) by transition 16 (transmission during the contention interval), and to establish a fresh and almost empty ring list (with the elements a and FF only) by the macro NEWRL of transition 22. After that, station a is interested to know whether it was the only station to transmit during the preceding contention interval. As it, as a writer, cannot read during this interval, it observes whether a long time-out follows next or not (transition 23). From now on, the further procedure follows the same pattern as has been discussed in the last part of case D/9 above.

Cases K/14 and K/19: After station a has requested its re-insertion successfully, it uses the succeeding cycle to build up a new ring list. If p=B ("building new ring list") and x≠1 (error or collision occurred), transition 14 delivers <a,?> to E, because it does not know the identity of the next sender. If however p=B and x=1 (transmission okay), transition 19 puts <a,t,u,b> on N. If it does not know the last sender, transition 33 passes the actual tokens t,u to A. If it knows the identity of the sender, the occurrence of transition 24 enables transition 30 which inserts, in the ring list of a, the name b of the sender before a, which in turn had already been inserted by transition 22. Thus the actual ring list is filled with the names of the currently active stations step by step. Finally, transition 32 sets the error count for b to 3 and proceeds to the next interval.

Cases K/20 and K/21: If the value of x reported by the last LISTEN is not equal to 1, an error/collision or a time-out has occurred. If this happens in the normal phase (x≠1 ∧ p=N), transition 21 passes control to transition 26, which decreases the error count of b by 1. The same procedure is taken in case of a collision/error during the reinitialization phase (x>1 ∧ p=R). If however, during the reinitialization phase, the station which is in turn does not transmit (x=0 ∧ p=R), transition 20 leads to transition 25 which sets the actual error count of b unconditionally to 0, because in this case the silent station shall be removed immediately from the ring list. All three possibilities end up with putting <a,b,n> on place T, where n is the actual error count of b as maintained by station a. At this stage, if n is still positive (transition 28), then transition 34 determines the successors t and u of b in the ring list, because t is supposed to be the next sender. If the error count has come down to 0, transition 31 with macro call DELS a,b,t,u determines b's successors t and u (assumed to be the next "tokens") and extinguishes b in a's ring list. Anyway, control is finally passed to A in order to start a new interval.

4. Completion of the model

When looking at the model established so far, one observes that two assumptions have been made which do not reflect the real behaviour of the network in a precise and complete way:

(a) all 255 stations start to work at the same time under well-known and identical conditions and they are active all the time,

(b) no errors occur in listening and writing to the bus.

Condition (a) seems to prevent that a station disappears from any ring lists and that a reinitialization cycle ever occurs. Thus, some quite challenging situations will never be encountered. Therefore it is advisable to drop at least assumption (a) and to model a mechanism by which the stations can be switched on and off. This shall be done next. There exist different possibilities for cancelling assumption (b) as well, but due to space limitations this point shall not be pursued further in this paper.

The synchronization mechanism as presented in section 3.1, is crucially dependent on the activity of all 255 stations and would be blocked by any passive node. This can be avoided by the following modification. Starting with

$$M_0(BUS) = \sum_{a \in S} \sum_{b \in S} \langle a,b,W,0,0,0 \rangle$$

as usual, for every passive station a, a dummy operation is introduced which performs the actions as indicated in the lower right hand corner of Figure 4.1 (DUMMY). This macro body consists of transitions 1D and 2D, connected via place D1, which shuffle sums of tuples to and from BUS in a way that keeps the synchronization mechanism running. These tuples do not contain any messages, but merely take provision that the next step of any interval is not blocked by inactive stations. (All

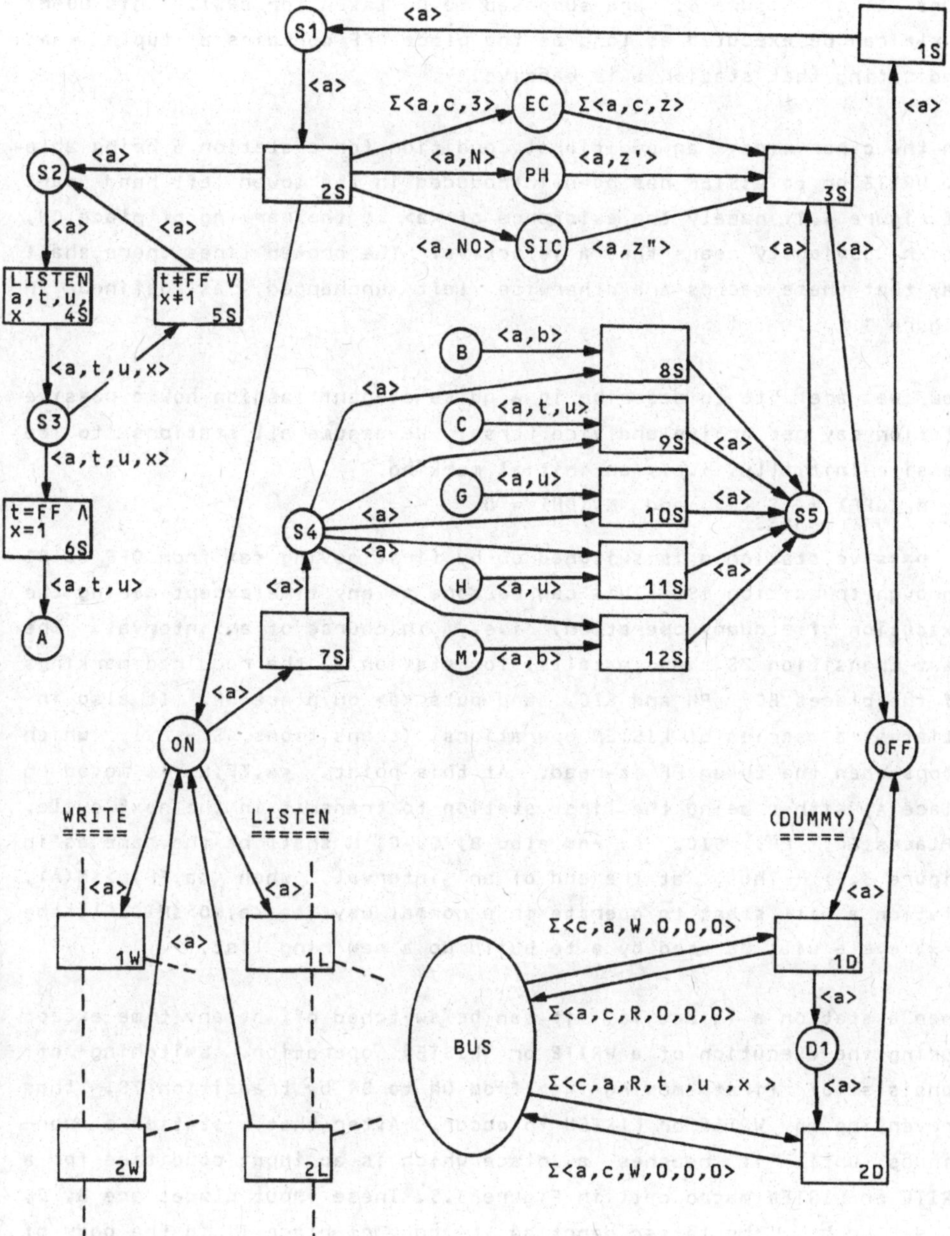

Figure 4.1. Switch-on and switch-off

sums Σ of Figure 4.1 are supposed to be taken for $c \in S$). This DUMMY cycle can be executed as long as the place OFF contains a tuple <a>, indicating that station a is passive.

On the other side, an additional condition for a station a being able to WRITE or to LISTEN has been introduced in the lower left hand part of Figure 4.1, namely the existence of <a> in the marking of place ON, which obviously means that a is active. The broken lines there shall say that these macros are otherwise left unchanged, as defined in Figure 3.1.

Now we are able to describe in a quite elegant fashion how a passive station may get active and vice versa. We assume all stations to be passive initially, i.e., an initial marking

$$M_0(OFF) = \sum_{a \in S} \langle a \rangle \quad \text{and} \quad M_0(ON) = 0.$$

A passive station a is switched on by first moving <a> from OFF to S1 through transition 1S. This can be done at any time except during the execution of a dummy operation, i.e., in course of an interval. The next transition 2S then installs, for station a, the required markings of the places EC, PH and SIC, and puts <a> on place ON. It also initiates a series of LISTEN operations (transitions 4S - 6S), which stops when the token FF is read. At this point, <a,FF,u> is moved on place A, with u being the first station to transmit in the next cycle. (Places EC, PH, SIC, A, and also B, C, G, H shall be the same as in Figure 3.5). Thus, at the end of an interval, when <a,FF,u>≤M(A), station a will start to operate in a normal way. As <a,NO>≤M(SIC), the next cycle will be used by a to build up a new ring list.

When a station a is active, it can be switched off at any time except during the execution of a WRITE or LISTEN operation. Switching off consists of first moving <a> from ON to S4 by transition 7S, thus preventing any WRITE or LISTEN to occur. After that, station a continues until it reaches a place which is an input condition for a WRITE or LISTEN macro call in Figure 3.5. These input places are B, C, G, H, or M', the latter denoting the copy of place T1 in the body of LTOUT obtained when substituting the LTOUT call in transition 23 of Figure 3.5. When one of these places is marked, the corresponding tuple is removed by one of the transitions 8S to 12S. (The assumption to continue operation of the switched-off station unto then is made only in order not to overload the net of Figure 4.1, which otherwise would have to contain <u>all</u> places of Figure 3.5 as input conditions for possible continuations in case of <a>≤M(S4).) Finally, transition 3S clears the places EC, PH and SIC and marks OFF by <a>, thus indicating that station a is passive now.

The entire model of the REDPUC protocol, consisting of the nets and macro definitions of Figures 3.1 - 3.5 and 4.1, shall have the following initial marking:

$M_0(OFF) = \sum_{a \in S} <a>$, $M_0(RL) = \sum_{a \in S} <a,FF,FF,FF>$,

$M_0(BUS) = \sum_{a \in S} \sum_{b \in S} <a,b,W,0,0,0>$,

$M_0(X) = 0$ for all remaining places X.

The markings of places A, EC, PH, and SIC are then initiated during the switch-on procedure as mentioned above.

5. Concluding remarks

In this report we have used Predicate/Transition-Nets to model the second protocol layer of the Local Area Network REDPUC. The net model which has been constructed covers the entire protocol including an essential part of its environment, the switch-on and switch-off procedures of the stations. The protocol has been modelled "as it is" and no attempt has been made to simplify it in order to achieve a smoother model. Thus, the model should be a true image of the real system which could be used as a common reliable reference for the designers, implementors and users of the network.

In the process of establishing the model, some results were gained which seem to be useful not only in the context of the REDPUC protocol, but which may be of more general value. Particularly the sub-models for ring lists, for the communication bus and for station switch-on and switch-off can be integrated as standard components in other system models as well. In addition, the concept of macro transitional forms is considered to be an effective means to describe a system in an application-oriented language and to reduce the size of models for large systems.

An evaluation of the applied modelling method and a comparison with other methods is far beyond the scope of this paper. However, a lot of interesting statements on this can be found in the literature which is given below. We feel that being able to describe precisely and completely such a complex and highly concurrent distributed system on three or four pages, is one of the great advantages of higher level Petri nets. The analytic power of net theory could not be demonstrated here. The analysis of the REDPUC protocol should be the topic of a forthcoming paper. The concepts to be applied for this purpose and some examples have been described in [GL81] and [Vo80].

Acknowledgements

This report was written while the author was as a guest researcher at Pontifícia Universidade Católica (PUC) do Rio de Janeiro. This visit was supported both by PUC and by GMD. The author is greatly indebted to Daniel Menascé and to Daniel Schwabe who assisted him, by several discussions and by reviewing earlier versions of this report, to understand and to model the REDPUC protocol correctly.

References

[BT82] Berthelot, G., Terrat, R.: Petri Nets Theory for the Correctness of Protocols. IEEE Trans. Comm., Vol. 30, No. 12, 1982, pp. 2497-2505.

[BG77] Bochman, G.V., Gecsei, J.: A Unified Method for the Specification and Verification of Protocols. Information Processing 77, B. Gilchrist (ed.), IFIP, North-Holland Publ. Comp., 1977, pp. 229-234.

[Br80] Brauer, W. (ed.): Net Theory and Applications. LNCS 84, New York, Springer-Verlag, 1980.

[CR83] Coolahan, J.E., Rossopoulos, N.: Timing Requirements for Time-Driven Systems Using Augmented Petri Nets. IEEE Trans. Software Eng., Vol. SE-9, No. 5, Sept. 1983, pp. 603-616.

[EP80] Eckert, H., Prinoth, R.: A Method for Analyzing Communication Protocols. GMD-IFV Internal Report, Darmstadt, Dec. 1980.

[GL81] Genrich, H.J., Lautenbach, K.: System Modelling with High-Level Petri Nets. Theoretical Computer Science 13, North-Holland Publ. Comp., 1981, pp. 109-136.

[Le78] LeLann, G.: Algorithms for Distributed Data Sharing Systems which Use Tickets. Proc. 3rd Berkeley Workshop on Distr. Data Management and Computer Networks, Aug. 1978.

[NHS83] Nelson, R.A., Haibt, L.M., Sheridan, P.B.: Casting Petri Nets into Programs. IEEE Trans. Software Eng., Vol. SE-9, No. 5, Sept. 1983, pp. 590-602.

[Pe73] Petri, C.A.: Concepts of Net Theory. Math. Found. of Computer Science: Proc. Symp. and Summer School, High Tatras. Math. Inst. Slovak. Acad. of Sciences, 1973, pp. 137-146.

[PS82] Projektgruppe Schnittstellen: Modellierung existierender Schnittstellen mit Netzen. GMD-Studien Nr. 69, GMD, St. Augustin, Sept. 1982.

[RW83] Rudin, H., West, C.H. (eds.): Protocol Specification, Testing and Verification, III. Proc. IFIP WG6.1 3rd Int. Workshop Protocol Specification, Testing and Verification. Armonk, NY, 1983.

[Sc81] Schwabe, D.: Formal Techniques for the Specification and Verification of Protocols. UCLA, Los Angeles, Report No. CSD-810401, Apr. 1981.

[Vo80] Voss, K.: Using Predicate/Transition-Nets to Model and Analyze Distributed Database Systems. IEEE Trans. Software Eng., Vol. SE-6, Nov. 1980, pp. 539-544.

[Vo82] Voss, K.: Nets as a Consistent Formal Tool for the Stepwise Design and Verification of a Distributed System. In Hawgood, J. (ed.): Evolutionary Information Systems. North-Holland Publ. Comp., IFIP, 1982, pp. 173-191.

IN PRAISE OF FREE CHOICE NETS

P.S. Thiagarajan, K. Voss
Institut für Methodische Grundlagen
Gesellschaft für Mathematik und Datenverarbeitung
D-5205 St. Augustin, Germany

Abstract

Live and safe free choice nets constitute an attractive class of Petri nets. This is evidenced by the fundamental results worked out by Hack. There are some essential additional properties which make them even more appealing. In this paper we bring out these additional structural and behavioural properties. We shall also argue that these properties are what makes live and safe free choice nets fly. We show through examples that each such property breaks down for a "next" larger class of nets called simple nets.

0. Introduction

We think that live and safe free choice nets (LSFC nets, for short) constitute a very attractive sub-class of Petri nets. Their primary appeal, of course is an aesthetic one. Free choice nets represent a lovely combination of the notion of a state machine (conflicts yes, concurrency no) and the dual notion of a marked graph (concurrency yes, conflicts no). This is amply and elegantly brought out in the decomposition theory of LSFC nets developed by M. Hack [Ha72]. From the point of view of modelling real systems, these systems containing concurrency, but only freely decidable conflicts and no confusion at all, are particularly attractive because they exclude certain "undesired" kinds of behaviour.

In this paper, we want to point out some additional properties of LSFC nets. Each property seems to admit a sensible interpretation. And it breaks down when we go over to larger sub-classes of live and safe Petri nets. We then draw the conclusion that the class of systems modelled by LSFC nets is a very privileged class of distributed systems.

The construction of this paper is as follows. The next section is devoted to developing the required notations. In chapter 2 we present some results concerning the structural components of a LSFC net. In particular we show that the behaviour of a state-machine-like component of a LSFC net is not constrained in any way, except for "delays", by the composite net. A marked-graph-like component can be exercised in its own right as a live and safe marked graph.

In section 3 we deal with behavioural aspects of a LSFC net. First we show that in such a net either all forward and backward reachable markings are good (i.e. live and safe) or all of them are bad. Thus one cannot choose between good and bad "futures" of the system. We then prove that in any infinite stretch of behaviour, fair local choices are not only necessary but also sufficient to ensure a kind of global fairness. Finally we cite a result from [TV83] which deals with subsets of transitions viewed as interfaces of the system to its environment. It gives a characterisation of the "promptness" of a LSFC net with respect to an interface, a property which demands that the system should not run indefinitely without communicating with its environment.

After stating each result, we shall present an example to make the point that the property in question does not hold for the class of live and safe simple nets. In the concluding chapter of the paper, we shall look at related recent literature on free choice nets.

Most of the observations reported here have been collected over a period of years. No stunning originality is claimed for any one of the results, but we felt it would be useful to collect them together in one document. We do claim though ignorance. We are not aware of any of these results being reported elsewhere.

1. Preliminaries

For reading this paper, familiarity with the work of Hack [Ha72] would be helpful though it is not absolutely necessary (see also [JV80]). We shall adopt the standard terminology (see [GS80]) concerning nets, markings, and the firing rule for Petri nets.

Every net considered here, unless otherwise stated, is assumed to be finite and connected. We often refer to S-elements as places and T-elements as transitions. The object of study will be a marked net $\Sigma = (S,T;F,M^0)$ in which $N_\Sigma = (S,T;F)$ is the underlying (directed) net of Σ and M^0 is the initial marking of N_Σ. Where Σ is clear from the context, N_Σ will be written as N.

Let M and M' be markings of the net N=(S,T;F) and $t \in T$. Then M[t>M' denotes the fact that t can fire at M to lead to the marking M'. This notation is extended to sequences of transitions in the obvious way. For most parts, it is sufficient to work with firing sequences and we shall do so. However, for formulating the concept of fairness we need the notion of a step. Let N=(S,T;F) be a net, M a marking of N and $T' \subseteq T$. Then T' is enabled at M and may occur in one step iff for each $s \in S$: $M(s) \geq |T' \cap s^\bullet|$.
If T'={t} is a singleton, we say that t rather than {t} is enabled at M. For $S' \subseteq S$, we often write $M(S')$ instead of $\sum_{s \in S'} M(s)$.

A non-empty set of places $S_1 \subseteq S$ of a net N is a deadlock iff ${}^\bullet S_1 \subseteq S_1{}^\bullet$. It is a trap iff $S_1{}^\bullet \subseteq {}^\bullet S_1$. A deadlock <trap> is minimal iff no proper subset of it is also a deadlock <trap>.

A <u>free choice net</u> is a net $N=(S,T;F)$ in which $\bigwedge s\in S$: $|s^\bullet|>1 \Longrightarrow {}^\bullet(s^\bullet)=\{s\}$. A <u>simple net</u> is a net $N=(S,T;F)$ in which $\bigwedge s_1,s_2\in S$: $s_1{}^\bullet\cap s_2{}^\bullet\neq\emptyset \Longrightarrow s_1{}^\bullet\subseteq s_2{}^\bullet \vee s_2{}^\bullet\subseteq s_1{}^\bullet$. Among the nets which have been investigated, the simple nets constitute the smallest class which properly includes the class of free choice nets and the largest class of nets about which some results on liveness and related properties are available [Co72], [BS83].

For convenience, we deviate from the conventions used in [Ha72] and [GS80] in the following way: A <u>S-graph</u> is a net $N=(S,T;F)$, where for every $t\in T$: $|t^\bullet|,|{}^\bullet t|\leq 1$. A <u>T-graph</u> is a net $N=(S,T;F)$ in which for every $s\in S$: $|s^\bullet|,|{}^\bullet s|\leq 1$.

Let $\Sigma=(S,T;F,M^0)$ be a marked net. If N is a free choice net <simple net, S-graph, T-graph> then we call Σ a <u>marked</u> free choice net <simple net, S-graph, T-graph>. In a marked net, $[M^0\rangle$ shall denote the <u>forward marking class</u> defined by M^0, and $[M^0]$ the <u>full marking class</u> defined by M^0.

The net $N=(S,T;F)$ is said to be <u>live</u> at the marking M iff $\bigwedge M'\in[M\rangle$ $\bigwedge t\in T$ $\bigvee M''\in[M'\rangle$ such that t is enabled at M''. N is said to be <u>safe</u> at M iff $\bigwedge M'\in[M\rangle$ $\bigwedge s\in S$: $M'(s)\leq 1$. The marked net $\Sigma=(S,T;F,M^0)$ is live <safe> iff N_Σ is live <safe> at M^0. We abbreviate live and safe free choice nets as LSFC nets.

The two important structural entities of a marked net will be called S-components and T-components. Let $\Sigma=(S,T;F,M^0)$ be a marked net, $N=(S,T;F)$ the underlying net of Σ.
A sub-net $N_1=(S_1,T_1;F_1)$ is called a <u>S-component</u> of Σ iff

a) N_1 is a strongly connected S-graph,

b) N_1 is the sub-net generated by S_1, (cf. [GS80]).

N_1 is called a <u>SM-component</u> of Σ iff, moreover,

c) $M^0(S_1)=1$.

A sub-net $N_2=(S_2,T_2;F_2)$ is called a <u>T-component</u> of Σ iff

a) N_2 is a strongly connected T-graph,

b) N_2 is the sub-net generated by T_2.

Whenever we talk about a net N and a sub-net N_1 of N then the $\bullet$-notation will refer to the incidence structure of N. Thus, if $N_1=(S_1,T_1;F_1)$ is a S-component of $\Sigma=(S,T;F,M^0)$ then $\bigwedge t\in T_1$: $|{}^\bullet t\cap S|=1=|t^\bullet\cap S|$. If N_1 is also a SM-component then $\bigwedge M\in[M^0]$: $M(S_1)=1$. And similarly, if $N_2=(S_2,T_2;F_2)$ is a T-component of Σ, then $\bigwedge s\in S_2$: $|{}^\bullet s\cap T|=1=|s^\bullet\cap T|$.

Hack calls a SM-component a "1-token strongly connected state machine" and a T-component a "strongly connected marked graph" [Ha72]. A "marked graph" in the sense of [CHEP71] may be viewed as - and we shall do so in this paper - a marked T-graph if one takes the nodes as transitions and the arcs as 1-in 1-out places. Notice that for a T-component one does not - and in some sense cannot - say anything about the submarking induced on it by the marked net containing that T-component.

The rest of the required terminology shall be developed as and when needed. To conclude this section, we recall two fundamental results about LSFC nets from [Ha72]:

Theorem 1.1. Let $\Sigma=(S,T;F,M^0)$ be a LSFC net and $x \in S \cup T$. Then there is a SM-component $N_1=(S_1,T_1;F_1)$ and a T-component $N_2=(S_2,T_2;F_2)$ of Σ such that $x \in S_1 \cup T_1$ and $x \in S_2 \cup T_2$. In other words, Σ is covered by its SM-components (and hence by its S-components) as also by its T-components. □

Theorem 1.2. Let $\Sigma=(S,T;F,M^0)$ be a marked free choice net. Then the following conditions are equivalent:

a) Σ is live and safe,

b) Σ is covered by its SM-components and every sub-net generated by a minimal deadlock is a strongly connected S-graph which is marked at M^0. □

2. Structural properties of live and safe free choice nets

In stating and proving the results of this section we will make use of the following notations and conventions:

Let $\Sigma=(S,T;F,M)$ be a marked net, $t \in T$, and $\pi \in T^*$ a firing sequence at M with $M[\pi>M'$. Then π is said to be a t-enabling sequence at M iff t is enabled at M'. Let $|\pi|$ denote the length of the sequence π. Then π is called a minimal t-enabling sequence at M iff π is a t-enabling sequence at M and for every other t-enabling sequence π' at M: $|\pi| \leq |\pi'|$.

If X is a set of symbols, $\beta \in X^*$ a sequence of symbols and $x \in X$, then $\#(\beta/x)$ shall denote the number of times x appears in β. If $X' \subseteq X$, we write $\#(\beta/X')$ to mean $\sum_{x \in X'} \#(\beta/x)$.

This notation will not only be applied to firing sequences but also to (directed) paths and (directed) circuits which can and shall be viewed as sequences of net elements.
If $X' \subseteq X$, then $PROJ(\beta|X')$ is the sequence obtained by deleting all symbols from β that are not in X'. Finally, let $N_1=(S_1,T_1;F_1)$ be a sub-net of $N=(S,T;F)$. Then we define
$Tin(N_1) = \{t \in T \setminus T_1 \mid t^\bullet \cap S_1 \neq \emptyset\}$ and $Tout(N_1) = \{t \in T \setminus T_1 \mid {}^\bullet t \cap S_1 \neq \emptyset\}$.

For the theorems 2.2 and 2.3 we make use of the following observation:

<u>Lemma 2.1</u>. Let $\Sigma=(S,T;F,M^0)$ be a marked net and $N_1=(S_1,T_1;F_1)$ a sub-net of N_Σ. For a firing sequence π of Σ with $M^0[\pi>M$ suppose that $\#(\pi/Tin(N_1)) = 0 = \#(\pi/Tout(N_1))$. Then in the marked net $(S_1,T_1;F_1,M^0{}_1)$, $PROJ(\pi|T_1)=\pi_1$ is a firing sequence at $M^0{}_1$ with $M^0{}_1[\pi_1>M_1$, where $M^0{}_1$ and M_1 are M^0 and M restricted to S_1, respectively. □

Our first result states that in a LSFC net, the behaviour of a SM-component is not constrained in any way, except possibly for "delays", by the composite net.

<u>Theorem 2.2</u>. Let $\Sigma=(S,T;F,M^0)$ be a LSFC net, $N_1=(S_1,T_1;F_1)$ a SM-component of Σ, and $\Sigma_1=(S_1,T_1;F_1,M^0{}_1)$ where $M^0{}_1$ is M^0 restricted to S_1. Let $FS[\Sigma]$ and $FS[\Sigma_1]$ denote the set of firing sequences of Σ and Σ_1, respectively. Then, $FS[\Sigma_1] = \{PROJ(\pi|T_1) \mid \pi \in FS[\Sigma]\}$.

<u>Proof</u>: a) $\{PROJ(\pi|T_1)|\pi \in FS[\Sigma]\} \subseteq FS[\Sigma_1]$, follows from Lemma 2.1 because N_1 is a sub-net of Σ with $T_1={}^\bullet S_1 \cup S_1{}^\bullet$. Hence $Tin(N_1)=\emptyset=Tout(N_1)$.
b) The inclusion in the other direction is shown by induction on the length of firing sequences. Let $\pi \in FS[\Sigma_1]$ with $|\pi|=k$.
1) $k=0$, trivial.
2) $k>0$. Let $\pi=\pi_1 t$ with $|\pi_1|=k-1 \geq 0$ and $t \in T_1$. Let $M^0{}_1[\pi_1>M_1$ (in Σ_1). By the induction hypothesis there exists $\pi' \in FS[\Sigma]$ such that $PROJ(\pi'|T_1)=\pi_1$. Let $M^0[\pi'>M$ (in Σ). Once again because ${}^\bullet S_1 \cup S_1{}^\bullet=T_1$, it follows from Lemma 2.1 that M_1 is M restricted to S_1. Let $\{s\}={}^\bullet t \cap S_1$. Since t is fireable at M_1 (in Σ_1), $M_1(s)=M(s)=1$.

If $|{}^\bullet t|=1$, then t is fireable at M in Σ, and obviously $\pi' t \in FS[\Sigma]$ and $PROJ(\pi' t|T_1)=\pi$.

So assume $|{}^\bullet t|>1$. Then because N is a free choice net we have $s^\bullet=\{t\}$. Since Σ is live we can find a minimal t-enabling sequence β at M. Now every place in S_1 other than s is unmarked at M because N_1 is a

SM-component. And $s\bullet=\{t\}$. Hence $\#(\beta/T_1)=0$. Clearly then $\pi'\beta t\in FS[\Sigma]$, and moreover $PROJ(\pi'\beta t|T_1)=\pi$. □

This result is not true for live and safe simple nets as the following example shows (Fig. 2.1). The marked net corresponding to the SM-component generated by {a,d} allows all firing sequences defined by ((1+2)3)*. But $\{PROJ(\pi|\{1,2,3\}) \mid \pi\in FS[\Sigma]\}$ is given by (1323)* where $FS[\Sigma]$ is the set of firing sequences of the composite system. Thus the behaviour of the SM-component in the composite net is more restricted than its behaviour as an autonomous system.

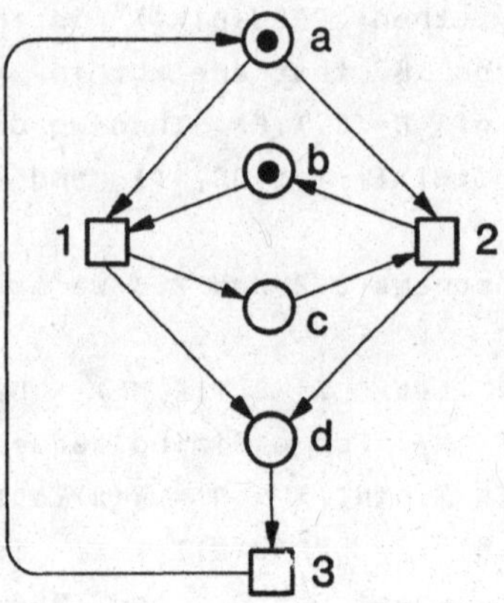

Figure 2.1.

The next result states that a T-component of a LSFC net can be exercised in its own right as a live and safe marked T-graph. First we note a simple observation concerning marked graphs, stating it - for sake of uniformity - in terms of marked T-graphs.

Lemma 2.3. Let $\Sigma=(S,T;F,M^0)$ be a marked T-graph which is strongly connected. Suppose that Σ is not live. Then there exists an integer k such that every firing sequence of Σ is of length at most k.

Proof: Follows easily from the theory of marked graphs, cf. [GL73]. □

Next we show that we can "monotonically increase" the liveness of a T-component by suitably exercising the composite net. In going through this result, it is convenient to recall that a marked T-graph is live iff every elementary circuit carries a token at the initial marking [GL73]. We shall also adopt the convention of denoting the submarking of a T-component of a LSFC net by attaching the subscript "2" to the marking of the composite net.

Lemma 2.4. Let $\Sigma=(S,T;F,M^0)$ be a LSFC net, $N_2=(S_2,T_2;F_2)$ a T-component of Σ and $\{\Pi_1,\Pi_2,\ldots,\Pi_n\}$ the set of elementary circuits of N_2. Suppose $\Sigma_2=(S_2,T_2;F_2,M^0{}_2)$ is not live. Then there exists $M\in[M^0>$ (in Σ) such that

$$\sum_{i=1}^{n} M(\Pi_i) > \sum_{i=1}^{n} M^0(\Pi_i).$$

(By $M(\Pi_i)$ we mean of course $M(S_i)$ where S_i is the set of places that Π_i passes through.)

Proof: Set $Tin(N_2)=T'$ and $Tout(N_2)=T''$. Since Σ_2 is not live, some elementary circuit of N_2 is not marked at M^0. But as Σ is live, it follows $T'\neq\emptyset$. Let $t\in T'$ and π a minimal t-enabling sequence at M^0 such that $\#(\pi/T')=0$. Set $M^0[\pi t>M'$.

Suppose that $\#(\pi t/T'')=0$. (Note that in general, $T'\cap T''\neq\emptyset$.) Then it is easy to verify that $M'=M$ satisfies the required conditions, and we are done.

So assume that $\#(\pi t/T'')\neq 0$. Then πt can be expressed as $\pi t=\pi_{11}t'\pi_{12}$ where $t'\in T''$ and $\#(\pi_{11}/T'')=0$. Since $t'\in T''$, for some $s'\in S_2$ we must have $|s'\bullet|\geq 2$ and $s'\bullet\cap T_2\neq\emptyset$; after all N_2 is strongly connected. Now by the free choice net property we know that for some $t_1\in T_2$, $\bullet t_1=\{s'\}$ so that $\pi_{11}t_1$ is also a firing sequence at M^0 (in Σ). Let $M^0[\pi_{11}t_1>M^1$ and $PROJ(\pi_{11}t_1|T_2)=\pi_1$. Then it is easy to verify that:

1) $|\pi_1|>0$ and π_1 is a firing sequence at $M^0{}_2$ (in Σ_2) with $M^0{}_2[\pi_1>M^1{}_2$,
2) $\#(\pi_1/T'')=0$,
3) $\sum_{i=1}^{n} M^1(\Pi_i) = \sum_{i=1}^{n} M^0(\Pi_i)$.

The third fact is a consequence of the observation that in a marked T-graph, the number of tokens on an elementary circuit remains invariant through transition firings. Clearly, N_2 is not live at $M^1{}_2$ because it is not live at $M^0{}_2$.

So we can apply the argument presented above for M^0, to the marking M^1. Then either we will find the required marking M or we can construct a firing sequence π_{21} (in Σ) at M^1, $t_2\in T_2$ and $M^2\in[M^1>$ which together satisfy:

1) $M^1[\pi_{21}t_2>M^2$, $\#(\pi_{21}/T'')=0$,
2) $PROJ(\pi_{21}t_2|T_2)=\pi_2$ is a firing sequence at $M^1{}_2$ (in N_2) with $M^1{}_2[\pi_2>M^2{}_2$,
3) $\sum_{i=1}^{n} M^2(\Pi_i) = \sum_{i=1}^{n} M^1(\Pi_i)$.

At this stage, we have derived for the strongly connected T-graph N_2: N_2 is not live at $M^0{}_2$; $M^0{}_2[\pi_1>M^1{}_2$; $M^1{}_2[\pi_2>M^2{}_2$; $|\pi_1|,|\pi_2|>0$. From the previous lemma it follows at once that the sequence of markings $M^1,M^2,\ldots$ generated in this fashion will eventually terminate by yielding the required marking M. □

<u>Theorem 2.5</u>. Let $\Sigma=(S,T;F,M^0)$ be a LSFC net and $N_2=(S_2,T_2;F_2)$ a T-component of Σ. Then there exists $M\in[M^0>$ such that N_2 is live and safe at M_2.

<u>Proof</u>: Since Σ is safe and N_2 is the sub-net generated by T_2, it follows easily that for every marking $M'\in[M^0>$, N_2 is safe at M'_2. Thus it is sufficient to find a $M\in[M^0>$ such that N_2 is live at M_2.
To this end, let $\{\Pi_1,\Pi_2,\ldots,\Pi_n\}$ be the set of elementary circuits of N_2. If N_2 is live at $M^0{}_2$ we are done. If not, we can find, according to the previous lemma, $M^1\in[M^0>$ such that $\sum_{i=1}^{n} M^1(\Pi_i) > \sum_{i=1}^{n} M^0(\Pi_i)$.
Indeed, by repeated application of the previous lemma we can generate a sequence of markings in $[M^0>$ of the form $M^0, M^1, M^2, \ldots$ which
1) either terminates with the required marking M, or
2) is of infinite length such that for every positive integer j, $\sum_{i=1}^{n} M^j(\Pi_i) > \sum_{i=1}^{n} M^{j-1}(\Pi_i)$.
The second possibility is ruled out because the safety of Σ guarantees that for any arbitrary marking $M'\in[M^0>$, $\sum_{i=1}^{n} M'(\Pi_i) \leq n \times |S_2|$. □

We note that the marking M demanded in the above theorem can be systematically constructed via the proofs of Lemma 2.4 and Theorem 2.5. We also observe that this result can be made to sound more impressive as follows:

<u>Corollary 2.6</u>. Let $\Sigma=(S,T;F,M^0)$ be a LSFC net and N_2 a T-component of Σ. Then for every $M'\in[M^0>$ there exists $M\in[M'>$ such that N_2 is live and safe at M_2. □

Once again the result mentioned above does not hold for simple nets. In the live and safe simple net of Fig. 2.2, there exists no marking which is forward reachable from the one indicated and at which the T-component generated by the three outer transitions is live.

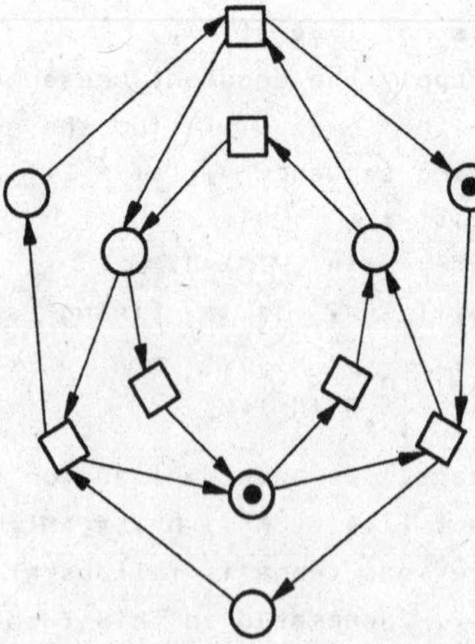

<u>Figure 2.2</u>.

The next result deals with elementary circuits

in LSFC nets. We know already that every S- component and every T-component of a LSFC net contains at least one elementary circuit, and that the intersection of a S-component and a T-component is a set of elementary circuits. Moreover we have:

Theorem 2.7. In a LSFC net $\Sigma=(S,T;F,M^0)$ every elementary circuit of N_Σ is contained in a S-component and in a T-component of Σ. □

The proof of the above theorem has been omitted due to space limitations. A detailed proof can be found in [TV83] where the following stronger maximality result is proved:
Let Σ be a LSFC net and N_1 be a sub-net of N_Σ. Suppose N_1 is a strongly connected T-graph <S-graph>. Then there is a T-component <S-component> N_2 of Σ such that N_1 is a sub-net of N_2. On the other hand, for any T-component <S-component> N_1 of Σ there is no strongly connected T-graph <S-graph> in Σ which strictly contains N_1.
Theorem 2.7 then is an easy corollary of the above result.

The fact that the above theorem does not hold for live and safe simple nets, can be illustrated by use of the net in Fig. 2.1. In this net, the elementary circuit a 1 c 2 d 3 a is contained neither in a S-component nor in a T-component.

3. Behavioural properties of marked free choice nets

The first result of this section states that a free choice net is live and safe with respect to its initial marking M^0 if and only if it is live and safe with respect to every marking which is forward or backward reachable from M^0. Stated differently, this means that going backward from M^0 cannot lead to a marking at which there exists a choice between a good, i.e. live and safe continuation and a bad one.

Theorem 3.1. Let $N=(S,T;F)$ be a free choice net and M a marking of N. Then N is live and safe at M iff for all $M'\in[M]$, N is live and safe at M'.

Proof: Suppose that N is live and safe at M, and for some $t\in T$ and some marking M' of N, we have that $M'[t>M$. Let $\Sigma=(S,T;F,M)$ and $\Sigma'=(S,T;F,M')$. Every SM-component of Σ is also a SM-component of Σ'. Consequently, Σ' is also covered by its SM-components.

Every minimal deadlock of Σ is also a minimal deadlock of Σ'. But then by Theorem 1.2, every minimal deadlock of Σ is a strongly connected S-graph which is marked at M. Clearly then every minimal deadlock of Σ' is also a strongly connected S-graph which is marked at M'. Therefore, Σ' is live and safe according to Theorem 1.2. The result now follows from the definition of [M]. □

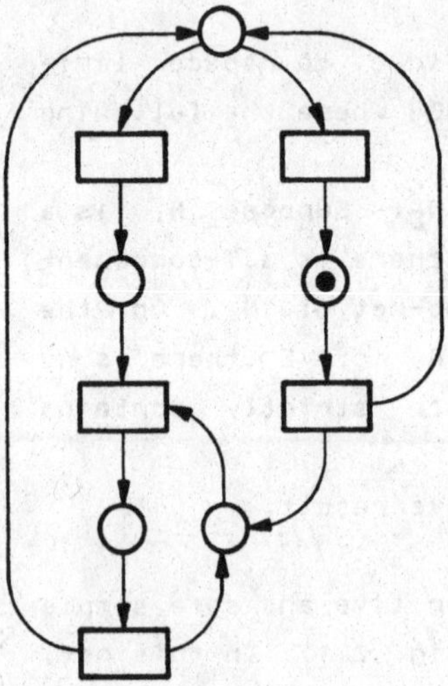

Figure 3.1.

Figure 3.2.

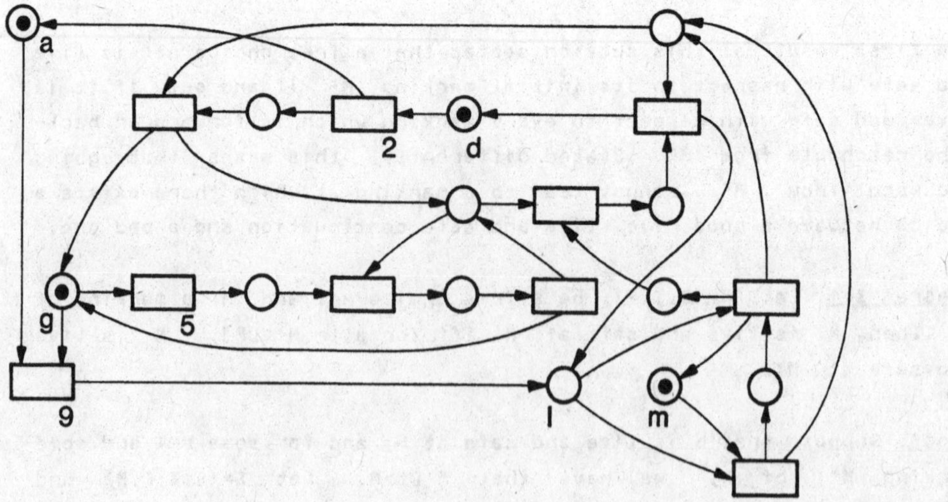

Figure 3.3.

This result is not true if we drop either safety (Fig. 3.1) or liveness (Fig. 3.2). And the property fails as well if we move beyond the class of free choice nets. This is shown for a simple net in Fig. 3.3 where at the marking shown, the net is neither safe (fire transition 2) nor live (fire transition 5). But firing transition 9 yields a marking at which the net is both live and safe.

The next result deals with fairness. It turns out that in a LSFC net there is a straightforward way of guaranteeing that, in any infinite stretch of behaviour, no part of the net will be starved. We simply have to ensure that the local (free) choices when they are made, they are made in a "fair" fashion. Consequently, in our interleaved mode of behavioural description (i.e. through firing sequences), we wish to concentrate on the decisions which have to do with resolving conflicts. And we want to separate this notion from the more conventional idea of ensuring "that a transition which <u>can</u> occur <u>will</u> occur sooner or later". Although this distinction is somewhat delicate we believe that it is worthwhile keeping these two ideas separate, even at the cost of working with a fairly complicated formalism.

Let $\Sigma=(S,T;F,M^0)$ be a marked net. We first introduce the binary relation $CF \subseteq [M^0> \times \mathcal{P}(T)\backslash\{\emptyset\}$ through the definition:
$(M,T')\in CF$ iff $|T'|>1$, each t in T' is enabled at M, and for each $t,t'\in T'$ with $t\neq t'$: $\{t,t'\}$ is <u>not</u> enabled at M. For a given $T'\subseteq T$ and $M\in[M^0>$, we say that M is a <u>conflict-marking</u> for T' iff $(M,T')\in CF$.

Now for the main definition. Let $\pi=t^0t^1t^2\ldots$ be an infinite firing sequence at M^0 and $\pi'=M^0t^0M^1t^1M^2t^2\ldots$ the corresponding <u>augmented firing sequence</u>, i.e. with $M^i[t^i>M^{i+1}$ for $i\geq 0$.
Then π is said to be <u>locally fair</u> iff it satisfies:
If for some $T'\subseteq T$ there is an infinite sub-sequence of π' of the form $M^{i_1}t^{i_1}M^{i_2}t^{i_2}\ldots$ such that for every $k>0$: $(M^{i_k},T')\in CF$ and $t^{i_k}\in T'$, then
for each $t\in T'$ there is an infinite sub-sequence of π' of the form $M^{j_1}t^{j_1}M^{j_2}t^{j_2}\ldots$ such that for every $k>0$: $(M^{j_k},T')\in CF$ and $t^{j_k}=t$.
Finally, π is said to be <u>globally fair</u> iff every element of T appears infinitely often in π.

To prove the desired result for free choice nets we make use of the following lemma:

Lemma 3.2. Let $\Sigma=(S,T;F,M^0)$ be a marked free choice net. For $T'\subseteq T$ with $|T'|>1$ and $M\in[M^0>$: $(M,T')\in CF$, iff there exists $s\in S$ such that $\{s\}={}^\bullet T'$ and $M(s)=1$.

Proof: Follows easily from the definitions. □

Theorem 3.3. Let $\Sigma=(S,T;F,M^0)$ be a LSFC net and π an infinite firing sequence of Σ at M^0. Then, π is locally fair iff it is globally fair.

Proof: From Theorem 1.1 we conclude that N_Σ is strongly connected. Now assume that π is locally fair. As π is infinite and T is finite, at least one transition t must appear infinitely often in π. Consider some transition $t'\neq t$. Let $t=t_0,s_0,t_1,s_1,\ldots t_n,s_n,t_{n+1}=t'$ be a directed path from t to t' in N_Σ. We can now show, by induction on n, that t' also appears infinitely often in π.

1) n=0. t_0 appears infinitely often in π, $s_0\in t_0{}^\bullet$, and Σ is safe. Hence some output transition of s_0, say t_1', must also appear infinitely often in π. That t_1 must also appear infinitely often follows from Lemma 3.2 and the definition of local fairness.

2) n>0. Follows immediately from the induction hypothesis and the basis step.

The second half of the result follows easily from the definitions and Lemma 3.2. □

In the live and safe simple net of Fig. 3.4, firing alternatingly the

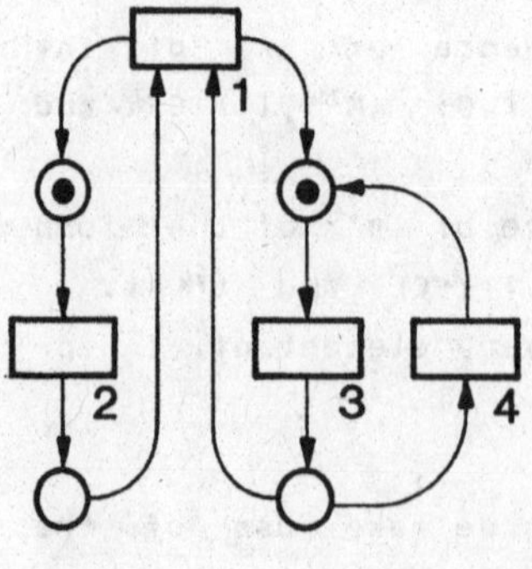

Figure 3.4.

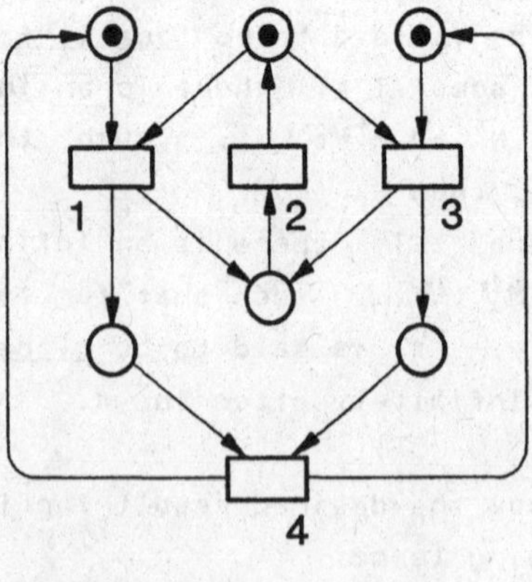

Figure 3.5.

transitions 3 and 4 (at the indicated marking) is locally fair because transition 1 is never enabled in that firing sequence. But obviously it is not globally fair. We should like to acknowledge that this example is due to E. Best.

In Fig. 3.5 we show a live and safe simple net in which the firing sequence 1232412324... is globally fair but not locally fair.

Finally, we would like to define a behavioural property called promptness and to characterise it for LSFC nets. Due to space limitations, the proof of the main result is omitted; a detailed proof is given in [TV83].

For a marked net $\Sigma=(S,T;F,M^0)$, we may view a non-empty subset Te of its transitions as representing the interface to its environment. This set Te of <u>external transitions</u> is assumed to be observable from the outside, whereas occurrences in the set $Ti=T\setminus Te$ of <u>internal transitions</u> are hidden. Viewed differently, Te constitutes the actions through which the system communicates with its environment and Ti consists of merely internal operations. From a system and its subsystems, we normally demand that they should not keep performing internal operations indefinitely without any communication with the outside. This property shall be called promptness. Stated formally, a marked net $\Sigma=(S,T;F,M^0)$ with $\emptyset\neq Te\subseteq T$ and $Ti=T\setminus Te$ is called <u>prompt relative to</u> Te iff there exists an integer k such that for every $M\in[M^0>$ and every firing sequence $\pi\in Ti^*$ at M, $|\pi|\leq k$.

LSFC nets admit the following characterisation of promptness:

<u>Theorem 3.4</u>. Let $\Sigma=(S,T;F,M^0)$ be a LSFC net and $\emptyset\neq Te\subseteq T$. Then Σ is prompt relative to Te iff for every T-component $N_1=(S_1,T_1;F_1)$ of Σ, $Te\cap T_1\neq\emptyset$. □

To prove this result, we had to generalise slightly the notion of T-allocation as introduced by Hack [Ha72]. A T-allocation of a marked net now shall be a function which, for each place, selects not just one output transition, but a non-empty subset of its output transitions. The notion of T-reduction, yielding a non-empty sub-net, is modified accordingly. Then the main idea of the proof is to show that for an infinite firing sequence of T-allocated transitions that reproduces a marking $M\in[M^0>$, any transition appearing in the sequence is contained in the T-reduction defined by the T-allocation.

The condition for promptness in Theorem 3.4 can be shown to be sufficient for larger classes of nets under fairly mild restrictions. However, it is not necessary for the class of live and safe simple nets, as can be demonstrated by means of the net of Fig. 2.2. We choose Te to consist of the three inner transitions, and we observe that none of them is contained in the T-component generated by the three outer transitions of the net figure.

4. Conclusions

The aim of this paper has been to argue that LSFC nets are an attractive class of Petri nets. To do so we have established a number of properties which hold for this class but not for the larger class of live and safe simple nets.

The first property (Theorem 2.2) states that a LSFC net may be viewed as a composition of a number of <u>autonomous</u> live and safe state machines. The SM-components do not interfere with each other apart from having to wait on each other sometimes for synchronising.

The second part (Theorem 2.5) deals with the dual notion of a T-component. It states that a T-component of a LSFC net is a periodic, potentially infinite, non-sequential process that can be run without interrupt. In essence, the result says that the T-component represents the basic building block out of which the behaviour of the LSFC net is composed. A much tighter result has been obtained by M.W. Shields in [Sh81], which is presented in a more succinct and - we think - lucid fashion in [BS83]. This nice result, however, applies only to a proper sub-class of LSFC net and at present it is not clear to us what the corresponding result is for the whole class of LSFC nets.

The last structural result we have shown states that the T-components <S-components> of a LSFC net are its maximal T-graphs <S-graphs>. As a consequence (Theorem 2.7), each of the elementary circuits which in some sense constitute the intersection of state machines and marked graphs, can be embedded as a whole into a S-component and into a T-component. It will be interesting to understand the relationship between a S-component and a T-component which share a given elementary circuit.

The result concerning the marking class (Theorem 3.1) follows at once from Hack's characterisation of LSFC nets. As a consequence, we know that we can obtain a LSFC net from a given LSFC net by "backtracking", by firing the transitions backwards and forwards. This comes in handy when we wish to synthesise LSFC nets whose initial markings are not reproducible. Indeed this result and the next one were observed in working out the synthesis theory of a sub-class of LSFC nets called well-behaved bipolar schemes [GT83].

The fairness result (Theorem 3.3) needs no additional explanation. The concept we are trying to delineate is best brought out in the example of Figure 3.5. We have not spent any effort in trying to relate this concept of fairness to a wide variety of possibly similar approaches that can be found in the literature (see for example [QS82]).

The last result is a characterisation of prompt LSFC nets. It could be very useful in the phases of system specification and design, because normally one is interested in such systems and modules which definitely communicate with their environment from time to time.

To conclude, the distributed systems modelled by LSFC nets constitute an important class because they are particularly easy to implement. One is guaranteed that no arbitration - and hence no arbiters - are needed. In the jargon, LSFC nets, and hence the systems modelled by them are confusion-free. Here we have tried to show that there are other attractive dividents to be gained by sticking to LSFC nets if the problem at hand permits this. In addition, through our various examples, we have tried to issue a warning: simple nets are not simple, they are going to be messy and difficult objects to deal with. Avoid them if possible!

References

[BS83] Best, E.; Shields, M.W.: Some Equivalence Results for Free Choice and Simple Nets and on the Periodicity of Live Free Choice Nets. Proc. CAAP 83, 8th Colloquium on Trees in Algebra and Programming, L'Aquila, March 9-11, 1983, 14 pp.

[Br80] Brauer, W. (ed.): Net Theory and Applications. Lecture Notes in Computer Science 84. Springer-Verlag, Berlin Heidelberg New York, 1980

[Co72] Commoner, F.: Deadlocks in Petri Nets. Wakefield, Applied Data Research Inc., CA-7206-2311, 1972

[CHEP71] Commoner, F.; Holt, A.W.; Even, S.; Pnueli, A.: Marked Directed Graphs. J. Computer and System Science 5, 1971, pp. 511-523

[GL73] Genrich, H.J.; Lautenbach, K.: Synchronisationsgraphen. Acta Informatica 2, 1973, pp. 143-161

[GS80] Genrich, H.J.; Stankiewicz-Wiechno, E.: A Dictionary of some Basic Notions of Net Theory. In [Br80], pp. 519-535

[GT83] Genrich, H.J.; Thiagarajan, P.S.: A Theory of Bipolar Synchronisation Schemes. Report DAIMI PB-158, Aarhus University, March 1983, 130 pp. Also to appear in TCS.

[Ha72] Hack, M.H.T.: Analysis of Production Schemata by Petri Nets. Project MAC, Massachusetts Institute of Technology. Cambridge, Massachusetts, Feb. 1972, 119 pp.

[Ho74] Holt, A.W.: Final Report for the Project 'Development of the Theoretical Foundations for Description and Analysis of Discrete Information Systems'. Wakefield, Mass., Massachusetts Computer Associates Inc., 20.5.1974

[JV80] Jantzen, M.; Valk, R.: Formal Properties of Place/Transition Nets. In [Br80], pp. 165-212

[QS82] Queille, J.P.; Sifakis, J.: A Temporal Logic to Deal with Fairness in Transition Systems. Proc. of 23. FoCS, 1982, pp. 217-225. Also to appear in Acta Informatica.

[Sh81] Shields, M.W.: On the Non-Sequential Behaviour of Systems Possessing a Generalised Free Choice Property. Internal Report CRS-92-81, Edinburgh University, Sept. 1981.

[TV83] Thiagarajan, P.S.; Voss, K.: A Fresh Look at Free Choice Nets. Arbeitspapiere der GMD, Nr. 58, St. Augustin, Oct. 1983, 42 pp. Also to appear in Information and Control.

abbreviation of an ordinary Petri-net: the underlying ordinary Petri-net (UOP-net for short). We shall see in section II-2 that the flows of an UP/T-net correspond to those of its UOP-net. Thus, given an UP/T-net, a solution for computing its flows is to unfold it, i.e., to construct its UOP-net. This was the solution used in [Mm83].

However, such a solution is expensive in time and space, and provides invariants whose meaning is not always clear. Furthermore when the number of colors is infinite - in which case UP/T-nets have the computational power of Turing's machines - it is no longer possible to unfold the nets.

In section II-3, we shall define three classes of flows which can be systematically calculated, directly on the folded net, even when the number of colors is infinite. In addition they provide invariants which can be easily interpreted.

Though these classes do not cover all the flows, it seems that they contain the most usual ones.

I UNARY-PREDICATES/TRANSITIONS-NETS

I-1 Mathematical notations

When individual-tokens are used in a Petri-net, the marking of a place becomes a multiset (ie. a set which may contain multiple occurrences of elements). The algebra of finite multisets over a set E is isomorph to the algebra of functions from E to N with a finite support. For example, the multiset {a,b,a,c} over the set E = {a,b,c,d} corresponds to the function f: a→2,b→1,c→1,d→0. In the following, we shall use the algebra of functions.

Let E be a set, we denote by [E] the set of functions from E to Z which have a finite support. It is a free Z-module generated by E (cf. e.g. [CH56] ch.III). For all e in E, we denote by d_e or merely e the function null for every element of E except for e where it takes the value 1. d_e is an element of [E] and,

$$\forall f \in [E],\quad f = \sum_{e\in E} f(e)d_e = \sum_{e\in E} f(e)e$$

Thus, instead of f: a→2,b→1,c→1,d→0, we shall write f = 2a+b+c. The function |.| defined from [E] to N by

$$|f| = \sum_{e\in E} f(e) \quad \forall f\in[E]$$

is a linear function. |f| is called the length of f. For example, the length of 2a+b+c is 4. [E] is ordered by the relation ≤ defined by

$$\forall f,f'\in[E],\quad f \leq f' \iff (\forall e\in E,\ f(e) \leq f'(e))$$

We denote by $[E]_+$ the set of elements f of [E] such that $0 \leq f$. Let W and M be two vectors of functions and let C be a matrix of functions, we denote by ${}^tW.M$ the generalized scalar product of W and M and by ${}^tW.C$ the generalized matrix product of ${}^tW$ and C, when they can be defined. Thus,

$${}^tW.M = \sum_j W_j \circ M_j$$

$$({}^tW.C)_i = \sum_j W_j \circ C_i^j$$

COMPUTATION OF FLOWS
FOR UNARY-PREDICATES/TRANSITIONS-NETS

Jacques VAUTHERIN
-Ecole Polytechnique
91128 Palaiseau CEDEX. FRANCE
-L.R.I. (bat. 490). Université Paris-Sud
F-91405 Orsay CEDEX. FRANCE

Gerard MEMMI
E.N.S.T.
46, rue Barrault
75634 Paris CEDEX 13
FRANCE

INTRODUCTION

As far as Petri-nets analysis is concerned, the possibility of deriving invariant assertions from vectors of integers - called flows ([LS74]) and computable directly on the net - has proved to be very useful. In the last few years, this method has been successfully extended to models derived from Petri-nets which have been developed to enable the study of ever more complex systems. (Colored and High-level Petri-nets [Je79], [Je82], Predicates/ Transitions-nets [GL79], [GL82], Relational-nets [Re82], FIFO-nets [Mm83]). As far as we know, no other model for parallel computation can provide such analysis results, especially when the description of the system under consideration uses parameters.

However to be effective, this method must be associated with algorithms that generate all, or at least some, classes of flows.

Although the notion of quasi-invariants used in [GL82] for Predicates/Transitions-nets (Pr/Tr-nets), lends itself to systematic computations ([Mv81]), it doesn't really fulfill our expectations. Indeed, quasi-invariants contain free variables which have to be bound to give invariant assertions over markings. But not every way of binding the variables is valid, and so far, with the exception of some particular nets (marked-graph-like Pr/Tr-nets [LP82]), no general and systematic method to find the correct ways of binding has been published.

The notion of weight-function used in [Je82] for High-level Petri-nets seems more practical since it allows to find invariant assertions over markings in a straightforward way. But no general algorithm has been provided for this model.

In this paper, we present some classes of flows which can be systematically computed. We use a model which stands between Pr/Tr-nets and colored Petri-nets as defined in [Br83]. This model is called Unary-predicates/transitions-nets (UP/T-nets for short). Roughly speaking, an UP/T-net is a Pr/Tr-net where tokens are 1-uples. This model will be defined more precisely in the first part of this paper. The choice of this model results from the following considerations:

- among the models already developed, the Pr/Tr-nets model seems to be one of the most "expressive", from a graphical representation point of view.
- each FIFO-net ([Mm83]) can be associated with an UP/T-net in a natural way (forgetting the order of tokens).

In section II-1, we shall give a definition of flows for UP/T-nets, using this notion of weight-functions.

As long as the number of types of tokens - or colors - is finite, UP/T-nets and ordinary Petri-nets have the same computational power. In fact, each UP/T-net can be viewed as an where the sign o denotes the composition of functions (i.e. $f \circ g(x) = f(g(x))$). When C is a matrix of elements of [E], we denote by |C| the matrix obtained from C by replacing each element by its length.

I-2 Definitions

Now, we can give the definition of an UP/T-net.

Definition. An Unary-Predicates/Transitions-net is a 7-uple R = <P,T;A,X;PRE,POST;DOM> where
- P and T are two disjoint finite sets of places and transitions respectively.
- A and X are two disjoint non empty sets. X is supposed to be finite. We shall call respectively color an element of A, variable an element of X, label an element of $[A+X]_+$ and interpretation a function from X to A. S will denote the set of all interpretations.
- PRE and POST are two functions from PxT to $[A+X]_+$, respectively called forward incidence function and backward incidence function.
- DOM is a function defined on T such that, for each transition t, DOM(t) is a set of interpretations called the domain of the transition t and denoted by D_t.

The incidence matrix of the net is the matrix $C = (C_p^t)$ defined by

$$C_p^t = \text{POST}(p,t) - \text{PRE}(p,t)$$

The UP/T-nets model can be viewed as the result of the application of simple transformations rules on the original model of Petri-nets. Intuitively, by using individual-tokens and variables, we can fold respectively several places into a single one and several transitions into a single one. An example is given on fig.1. The net shown on fig.1a will be called the underlying ordinary Petri-net of the UP/T-net shown on fig.1c (this notion will be precised in section II-2).

Example 1. Associated with the sets A = {a,b}, X = {x} and D_t = S = {(σ1: x→a), (σ2: x→b)} fig.1c defines an UP/T-net R_0. Its incidence matrix is

C	T
P_1	$-a$
P_2	$-x$
P_3	$2x$

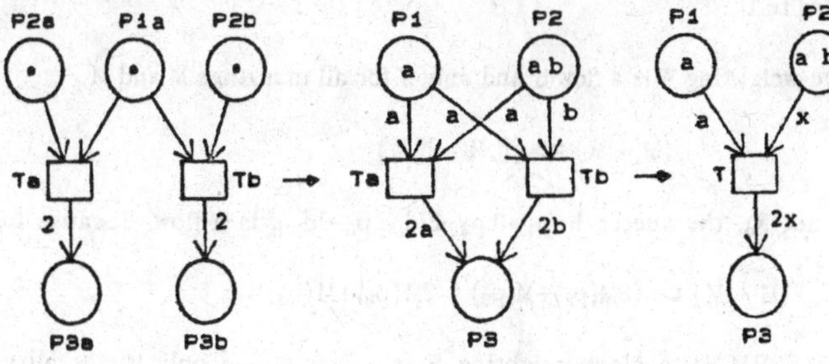

fig.1a fig.1b fig.1c

fig. 1

We have defined the structure of an UP/T-net. Now let us see how it is running.

Let σ be an interpretation, we define an extension of σ from A+X to A, still denoted by σ, such that $\sigma|_A = Id_A$. Then, there is one and only one linear extension of σ from [A+X] to [A]. When no mistake is possible, this linear extension will also be denoted by σ. Then,

$$\forall f \in [A+X], \quad \sigma(f) = \sum_{a \in A} (f(a) + \sum_{x \in \sigma^{-1}(a)} f(x))a \quad (1)$$

Definition. A marking is a function M from P to $[A]_+$. We shall say that a marking M' is directly reachable from an other marking M when there is a transition t and an interpretation σ of D_t such that

- $\forall p \in P, \quad \sigma(PRE(p,t)) \leq M(p)$ (t is firable from M)
- $\forall p \in P, \quad M'(p) = M(p) + \sigma(C_p^t)$

This property will be denoted by $M \rightarrow M'$

A particular marking M_o called initial marking is associated with the net. Then, we define the set of reachable markings by

$$R(M_o) = \{ M \,/\, M_o \rightarrow^* M \}$$

where $\rightarrow$ denotes the transitive closure of $\rightarrow$.

In the net R_o, the marking M: $p1 \rightarrow 0, p2 \rightarrow b, p3 \rightarrow 2a$, is directly reachable from the initial marking M_o: $p1 \rightarrow a, p2 \rightarrow a+b, p3 \rightarrow 0$ shown on fig.1c. Indeed, the conditions of the preceding definition are satisfied by the transition t and the interpretation $\sigma 1$.

II FLOWS

II-1 Definitions

Let U be a free finite type Z-module, we call place-weighting on U, a vector $W=(Wp)_{p \in P}$ of linear functions from [A] to U.

Definition. A place-weighting W is a flow if and only if for all markings M and M',

$$(M \rightarrow^* M') \Rightarrow (W.M = W.M')$$

For example, for the net R_o, the vector W: $p_1 \rightarrow 0, p_2 \rightarrow 2Id_{[A]}, p_3 \rightarrow Id_{[A]}$, is a flow, because for all markings M and M',

$$(M \rightarrow^* M') \Rightarrow (2M(p_2)+M(p_3) = 2M'(p_2)+M'(p_3))$$

Theorem 1. [LAUTENBACH]. A place-weighting W is a flow if and only if, for all t member of T and for all σ member of D_t,

$$\sum_{p \in P} Wp(\sigma(C_p^t)) = 0 \quad (2)$$

Proof. It is the usual theorem on the flows and it results from the linearity of the functions W_p.

II-2 The underlying ordinary Petri-net

At the beginning of this paper, we introduced (briefly) a notion of underlying ordinary Petri-net. When A is finite, it can be precised and will provide a first procedure for the computation of flows.

Let suppose that A is finite. For each UP/T-net R, we shall define the underlying ordinary Petri-net by $\underline{R} = \langle \underline{P}, \underline{T}, \underline{PRE}, \underline{POST} \rangle$ with

$$\underline{P} = P \times A$$
$$\underline{T} = \{(t,\sigma),\ t \in T,\ \sigma \in D_t\}$$
$$\underline{PRE}((p,a),(t,\sigma)) = \sigma(PRE(p,t))(a)$$
$$\underline{POST}((p,a),(t,\sigma)) = \sigma(POST(p,t))(a)$$

Let $\underline{C}$ be the incidence matrix of $\underline{R}$ the flows w of $\underline{R}$ are defined by the equation

$$^t w.\underline{C} = 0$$

On the other hand, one can check that condition (2) can be rewritten as

$$^t \underline{W}.\underline{C} = 0$$

where $\underline{W}$ is obtained from the vector W by replacing each element W_p by the vector $(W_p(a)), a \in A$. So, if we take U = Z, the flows of R correspond with those of $\underline{R}$. Moreover, it can be proved that for all U, there is an injection from the set of the flows on U of R to the set of the flows of $\underline{R}$.

Thus, given an UP/T-net R, we associate with its incidence matrix $\underline{C}$ the "unfolded" matrix C, and we denote by F_0 the set of vectors $w = (w_{p,a})$ of integers such as

$$^t w.\underline{C} = 0$$

It is known that the set of flows of an ordinary Petri-net is a free finite type Z-module, and we have algorithms to compute a base of this set. Clearly these results can be applied to F_0.

In the case of R_o, F_0 admit the following base

(0,1,0,0,0,0)
(-1,-1,1,1,0,0)
(0,0,2,0,1,0)
(2,2,0,0,1,1)

C	T_a	T_b
P_{1a}	−1	−1
P_{1b}		
P_{2a}	−1	
P_{2b}		−1
P_{3a}	2	
P_{3b}		2

II-3 Type-1,2 and 3-flows

Our purpose is now to define classes of flows which can be systematically computed, as it is for F_0, but directly on the folded net, even if A is infinite or if A is defined with the help of parameters (in this cases, it is not possible to unfold the matrix).

We will introduce three classes: the elements of the first one express invariant assertions on the number of tokens in the places of the net. The second class is related to general invariant assertions satisfied by all the colors ($W_p(a)$ independent of 'a'). The third one deals with invariants on a particular color 'a' ($W_p(a')=0\ \forall a'\neq a$).

Remark. From now on, in order to simplify the notations, we shall write $\sum$ instead of $\sum_{p\in P}$.

Type-1-flows

In a marking M, the number of tokens on a place p is $|M_p|$ (with the notation $M_p = M(p)$). Then, we are going to look for invariant assertions of the following type:

$$(M \to^* M') \Rightarrow (\sum w_p|M_p| = \sum w_p|M'^p|) \quad \text{with } w_p \in Z$$

Before that, we have to notice that an interpretation does not change the length of a label. This can easily be checked, using (1):

$$\forall f\in[A+X],\ \forall\sigma\in D_t,\quad |\sigma(f)| = \sum_{a\in A} f(a) + \sum_{x\in X} f(x) = |f|$$

Now, let us take U = Z and $Wp = w_p|.|$ with $w_p\in Z$. Then,

$$(2) \Leftrightarrow (\ \forall t\in T,\ \forall\sigma\in D_t,\ \ \sum w_p|\sigma(C_p^t)| = \sum w_p|C_p^t| = 0 \quad (3)\ )$$

This leads to the following definition:

Definition. Let F_1 be the set of solutions of

$$^t w.|C| = 0$$

where $w = (w_p)$ is a vector of integers, we call type-1-flows the vectors of functions $W = (w_p|.|)$ with $w = (w_p)$ in F_1. It results from theorem 1 that for all w member of F_1 and for all markings M and M',

$$(M \to^* M') \Rightarrow (\ ^t w.|M| = {}^t w.|M'|)$$

For example, in the net R_0, w = (−1,1,0) is a type-1-flow. The invariant assertion associated is

$$\forall M\in R(M_0),\quad |M_{p2}| - |M_{p1}| = 1$$

|C|	T
P_1	−1
P_2	−1
P_3	2

Type-2-flows

Now, we are going to look for invariants satisfied by all the colors. That is to say invariant assertions of the following type:

$$(M \to^* M') \Rightarrow (\ \forall a\in A,\ \ \sum w_pM_p(a) = \sum w_pM'_p(a) \quad (6)\ )$$

which can also be written

$$(M \to^* M') \Rightarrow (\ \sum w_pM_p = \sum w_pM'_p)$$

So, we take $U = [A]$ and $Wp = w_p Id_{[A]}$, $w_p \in Z$. Then,

$$(2) <=> (\forall t \in T, \forall \sigma \in D_t, \ \sum w_p \sigma(C_p^t) = \sigma(\sum w_p C_p^t) = 0 \quad (4))$$

(4) is difficultly manageable because it depends on σ. But,

$$((4') \ \forall t \in T, \ \sum w_p C_p^t = 0) => (4)$$

This leads to the definition

Definition. Let F_2 be the set of solutions of

$$^t w.C = 0$$

where $w = (w_p)$ is a vector of integers, we call type-2-flows the vectors of functions $W = (w_p Id)$ with $w = (w_p)$ in F_2. According to theorem 1, for all w member of F_2 and for all markings M and M',

$$(M \to^* M') => (^t w.M = {}^t w.M')$$

In the net R_o, $w = (0,2,1)$ is a type-2-flow. The invariant assertion associated is

C	T
P_1	$-a$
P_2	$-x$
P_3	$2x$

$$\forall M \in R(M_o), \quad 2 M_{p2} + M_{p3} = 2a+2b$$

Remark. In general, (4) does not imply (4'), therefore F_2 does not provide all the flows that we were looking for at the beginning of the paragraph (cf (6)). However, one can prove that the following condition is sufficient to have an equivalence between (4) and (4'): for all t member of T,

1/ $\forall a \in L, \exists \sigma \in D_t, \ \sigma^{-1}(a) = \phi$

2/ $\forall x \in X, \exists a \in A, \exists \sigma \in D_t, \ \sigma^{-1}(a) = \{x\}$

where L denotes the set of colors effectively present in the matrix C. In particular, this condition is satisfied by colored Petri-nets (as defined in [Br83]).

Type-3-flows

Let 'a' be a color, the number of tokens in a place p, colored by 'a', in a marking M, is $M_p(a)$. We shall denote by δ_a the function defined from [A] to Z by

$$\forall f \in [A], \quad \delta_a(f) = f(a)$$

Then, invariant assertions related to the color 'a' can be written

$$(M \to^* M') => (\sum w_p \delta_a(M_p) = \sum w_p \delta_a(M'_p))$$

Let f be a label, we define the projection of f on the color 'a' by $\Pi_a f \in [A+X]$ such that

$$\Pi_a f(a) = f(a)$$
$$\Pi_a f(a') = 0 \quad \forall a' \in A, \ a' \neq a$$
$$\Pi_a f(x) = f(x) \quad \forall x \in X$$

Then it is easy to prove (using (1)) that for all interpretation σ and for all label f,

$$\delta_a \circ \sigma(f) = \delta_a \circ \sigma[\Pi_a(f)]$$

Now, we take $U = Z$ and $Wp = w_p\delta_a$, $w_p \in Z$. Then, (2) is equivalent to

$$(5) \quad \forall t \in T, \forall \sigma \in D_t, \quad \sum w_p\delta_a \circ \sigma(C_p^t) = \delta_a \circ \sigma[\sum w_p \Pi_a(C_p^t)] = 0$$

And we have

$$((5') \quad \forall t \in T, \quad \sum w_p \Pi_a(C_p^t) = 0) \Rightarrow (5)$$

Definition. Let F_3 be the set of solutions of

$$^t w.\Pi_a(C) = 0$$

where $w = (w_p)$ is a vector of integers, we call type-3-flows on the color 'a' the vectors of functions $W = (w_p\delta_a)$ with $w = (w_p)$ in F_3. According to theorem 1, for all w member of F_3^a and for all markings M and M',

$$(M \to^* M') \Rightarrow (\,^t w.\delta_a(M) = \,^t w.\delta_a(M'))$$

For example, in the net R_o, $w = (1,0,0)$ is a type-3-flow on the color b. The invariant assertion associated is

$$\forall M \in R(M_o), \quad M_{p1}(b) = 0$$

$\Pi_b(C)$	T
P_1	
P_2	$-x$
P_3	$2x$

Remark. As for type-2-flows, we give a sufficient condition to have an equivalence between (5) and (5'): for all t member of T,

$$1/ \ \exists \sigma \in D_t, \quad \sigma^{-1}(a) = \phi$$

$$2/ \ \forall x \in X, \exists \sigma \in D_t, \quad \sigma^{-1}(a) = \{x\}$$

Systematic computation

Theorem 2. F_1, F_2 and F_3^a (for all color 'a') are free finite type modules. For each one, a base can be computed, respectively from the matrix $|C|$, C, $\Pi_a(C)$ by using Hermite's reduction method [FC69],[KB78] (it gives polynomial algorithms).

Proof. Each set can be considered as the kernel of a linear function from the free finite type Z-module Z^P to the free finite type Z-module $[L+X]^T$.

As far as R_o is concerned, F_1, F_2, F_3^a and F_3^b respectively have

$$B_1 = \{(-1,1,0),(2,0,1)\}, \quad B_2 = \{(0,2,1)\}$$

$$B_3^a = \{(0,2,1)\}, \quad B_3^b = \{(1,0,0),(0,2,1)\}$$

for bases and we have seen that F_0 have for base

$$B_0 = \{(0,1,0,0,0,0),(-1,-1,1,1,0,0),(0,0,2,0,1,0),(2,2,0,0,1,1)\}$$

$$B_0 = \{(0,1,0,0,0,0),(-1,-1,1,1,0,0),(0,0,2,0,1,0),(2,2,0,0,1,1)\}$$

As a general property, it is easy to check that we have the following diagrams (where the arrows represent injections)

For A infinite:

For A finite:

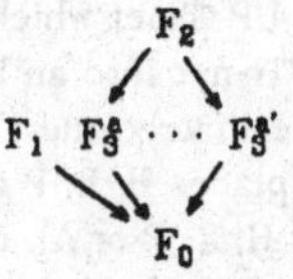

Indeed, $F_2 = \bigcap_{a \in L} F_3^a$, and when A is finite,

- each vector w of F_3^a can be associated with a vector $\underline{w}$ of F_0 by

$$(\underline{w}_{p,a} = w_p \ \forall p \in P) \wedge (\underline{w}_{p,a'} = 0 \ \forall p \in P, \forall a' \neq a)$$

- each vector w of F_1 can be associated with a vector $\underline{w}$ of F_0 by

$$\underline{w}_{p,a} = w_p \ \forall p \in P, \forall a \in A$$

In the case of R_o, F_0 is covered by F_1, F_3^a and F_3^b. The following example shows that it doesn't hold in general.

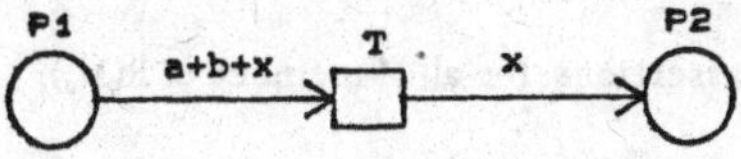

fig.2

Example 2. In the net shown on fig.2, with A = {a,b,c}, X = {x} and D_t = S, we obtain the respective bases

$$B_1 = \{(1,3)\}$$

$$B_2 = B_3^a = B_3^b = \phi$$

$$B_3^c = \{(1,1)\}$$

$$B_0 = \{(1,1,1,3,3,3),\ (0,0,1,0,0,1),\ (0,1,0,1,2,1)\}$$

The first vector of B_0 corresponds to the vector of B_1, the second one corresponds to those of B_3^c, but the third one cannot be generated.

III EXAMPLE

Finally, let us examine the example of a network of databases described in [GL79] and [Je79]. Since the places H, R, P and A are marked with 2-uples, the Pr/Tr-net given in [GL79] is not an UP/T-net. However, it is possible to replace each 2-uple <i,j> by a single color '$c_{i,j}$'. Then the resulting net is an UP/T-net which is equivalent to the initial net. This technique allows to transform every Pr/Tr-net into an UP/T-net. Unfortunately, it is followed by a loss of information in the incidence matrix and thus a loss of computable flows. In order to avoid that, we shall duplicate the places H, R, P and A in the following way: whenever the color '$c_{i,j}$' is added to the place X (X = H, R, P or A), or substracted from X, the color 'a_i' is added to Xg or substracted from Xg and the color 'a_j' is added to Xd or substracted from Xd. We have to notice that such a duplication is different from the unfolding procedure described in section II-2 since it is independent of the number of colors (here, each place is duplicated twice; more generally, a place marked with t-uples would be duplicated t times). The resulting net, its initial marking and its incidence matrix are given on fig.3.

Let n be the number of database managers. The manager 'i' is associated with the color 'a_i', and a message from the manager 'i' to the manager 'j' is represented by the color '$c_{i,j}$'. So,

$$A = A_1 \cup A_2 \cup \{\not c\}, \text{ with } A_1 = \{a_i \,,\ 1 \leq i \leq n\} \text{ and } A_2 = \{c_{i,j} \,,\ 1 \leq i,j \leq n \,,\ i \neq j\}$$

$$X = \{s,r,q,x\} \cup \{m_i \,,\ u_i \,,\ 1 \leq i \leq n-1\}$$

The domains associated to each transition are

$$D_{T1} = D_{T2} = \{\sigma \,/\, \sigma(s) \in A_1 \wedge ((s=a_j) \Rightarrow (\forall i,\ m_i = c_{j,k} \wedge u_i = a_k,\ k=i+j \bmod n))\}$$

$$D_{T3} = D_{T4} = \{\sigma \,/\, \sigma(x) \in A_2 \wedge ((x=c_{i,j}) \Rightarrow (q=a_i \wedge r=a_j))\}$$

Type-1-flows give the following assertions: for all M member of $R(M_o)$,

$$|M(H)|=|M(Hg)|=|M(Hd)|,\ |M(R)|=|M(Rg)|=|M(Rd)|$$
$$|M(P)|=|M(Pg)|=|M(Pd)|,\ |M(A)|=|M(Ag)|=|M(Ad)|$$

$$|M(a)|+|M(b)|+|M(c)|=n$$
$$|M(c)|=|M(P)|$$
$$|M(H)|+M(R)|+|M(P)|+|M(A)|=n(n-1)$$
$$|M(R)|+|M(P)|+|M(A)|=(n-1)|M(b)|$$

$$|M(b)|+|M(d)|=1 \quad (i_3)$$

and type-2-flows give the assertions: for all M member of $R(M_o)$,

$$M(a)+M(b)+M(c) = \textstyle\sum a_i \quad (i_1)$$
$$M(H)+M(R)+M(P)+M(A) = \textstyle\sum c_{i,j} \quad (i_2) \qquad [i]$$
$$M(c)=M(Pd) \quad (i_4)$$
$$M(Hg)+M(Rg)+M(Pg)+M(Ag) = (n-1)\textstyle\sum a_i \qquad [ii]$$
$$M(Hd)+M(Rd)+M(Pd)+M(Ad) = (n-1)\textstyle\sum a_i$$
$$M(Rg)+M(Pg)+M(Ag) = (n-1)M(b) \qquad [iii]$$

The indications in brackets refer to invariants given in [Je79].

It is clear that the way we used to unfold the places H, R, P, A leads to the following assertions:

$$a_i \leq M(Xg) \iff \exists j \,/\, c_{i,j} \leq M(X)$$

$$a_j \leq M(Xd) \iff \exists i \,/\, c_{i,j} \leq M(X)$$

for X = H, R, P or A. Then, one can prove, from invariants [i], [ii], [iii], that: for all M member of $R(M_o)$

$$a_i \leq M(b) \Rightarrow \forall j,\ c_{i,j} \leq M(R)+M(P)+M(A)$$

$$c_{i,j} \leq M(R)+M(P)+M(A) \Rightarrow a_i \leq M(b)$$

Proof: $a_i \leq M(b) \Rightarrow^{[iii]} (n-1)a_i \leq M(Rg)+M(Pg)+M(Ag) \Rightarrow^{[ii]} a_i \nleq M(Hg)$

$\Rightarrow (\forall j,\ c_{i,j} \nleq M(H)) \Rightarrow^{[i]} (\forall j,\ c_{i,j} \leq M(R)+M(P)+M(A))$.

$c_{i,j} \leq M(R)+M(P)+M(A) \Rightarrow^{[i]} c_{i,j} \nleq M(H) \Rightarrow a_i \nleq M(Hg)$

$\Rightarrow^{[ii]} a_i \leq M(Rg)+M(Pg)+M(Ag) \Rightarrow^{[iii]} a_i \leq M(b)$.

These assertions are equivalent to the invariant (i_5) of [Je79].

CONCLUSION

We have seen that F_1, F_2, F_3^a can be computed with the help of polynomial algorithms, without unfolding the net. This allows A not to be given in extension, what is often useful or even necessary in the modelling of systems. We are building a tool which uses these algorithms.

The example 2 shows that it would be useful to look for other classes of flows, or, at least, for refinement of the classes already presented. An other interesting question would be to know the cases where F_0 is covered by F_1, F_3^a.

At last, we think that it will be possible to extend our calculus to all Pr/Tr-nets. Meanwhile, one can transform Pr/Tr-nets into UP/T-nets as it is shown by the last example.

ACKNOWLEDGEMENT

We would like to thank G. Roucairol whose remarks and criticism were helpful.

REFERENCES

[Br83] Brams G.W.:
Réseaux de Petri: Théorie et pratique.
Masson editeur, Paris (1983).

[CH56] Chevalley C.:
Fundamental concepts of algebra.
Academic press inc - Publishers - New York (1956).

[FC69] Fiorot J.C.; Gondran M.:
Résolution des systèmes linéaires en nombres entiers.
Bulletin de la direction des Etudes et Recherches EDF, Série C, N°2 (1969).

[GL79] Genrich H.J.; Lautenbach K.:
Predicate/Transition-nets.
Net Theory and Application, Lect. Notes Comput. Sci. 84 (1980).

[GL82] Genrich H.J.; Lautenbach K.:
S-invariance in Predicate/Transition-nets.
Applications and Theory of Petri-nets, Informatik Fachberichte 66 (1983).

[KB78] Kannan R.; Bachem A.:
Polynomial algorithm for computing the Smith and Hermite normal forms of an integer matrix.
Report 7895-OR, Institut fur Okonometrie und Operations Research, Univ. Bonn (1978).

[Je79] Jensen K.:
Coloured Petri-nets and the invariant-method.
DAIMI PB-104, Aarhus University (1979).

[Je82] Jensen K.:
High-level Petri-nets.
Applications and Theory of Petri-nets, Informatik Fachberichte 66 (1983).

[LP82] Lautenbach K.; Pagnoni A.:
Liveness and duality in marked-graph-like Pr/Tr-nets.
Proc. of the 4th European Workshop on Application and Theory of Petri-nets, Toulouse, France (1983).

[LS74] Lautenbach K.; Schmid H.:
Use of Petri-nets for proving correctness of concurrent process systems.
Information Processing 1974, North-Holland Pub. Co. (1974).

[Mm83] G. MEMMI
Methodes d'analyse de réseaux de Petri, réseaux a files et applications aux systèmes temps réel.
Thèse de doctorat d'Etat, Université P. et M. Curie, Paris (1983).

[Mv81] Mevissen H.:
Algebraische bestimmung von S-invarianten in Pr/Tr-netzen.

ISF-Report 81.01, 12 Oktober 1981 (1981).

[Re82] Reisig W.:
Petri-nets with individual tokens.
Applications and Theory of Petri-nets, Informatik Fachberichte 66 (1983).

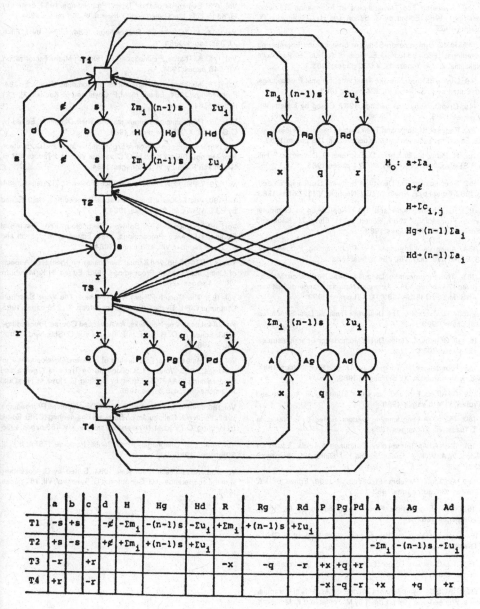

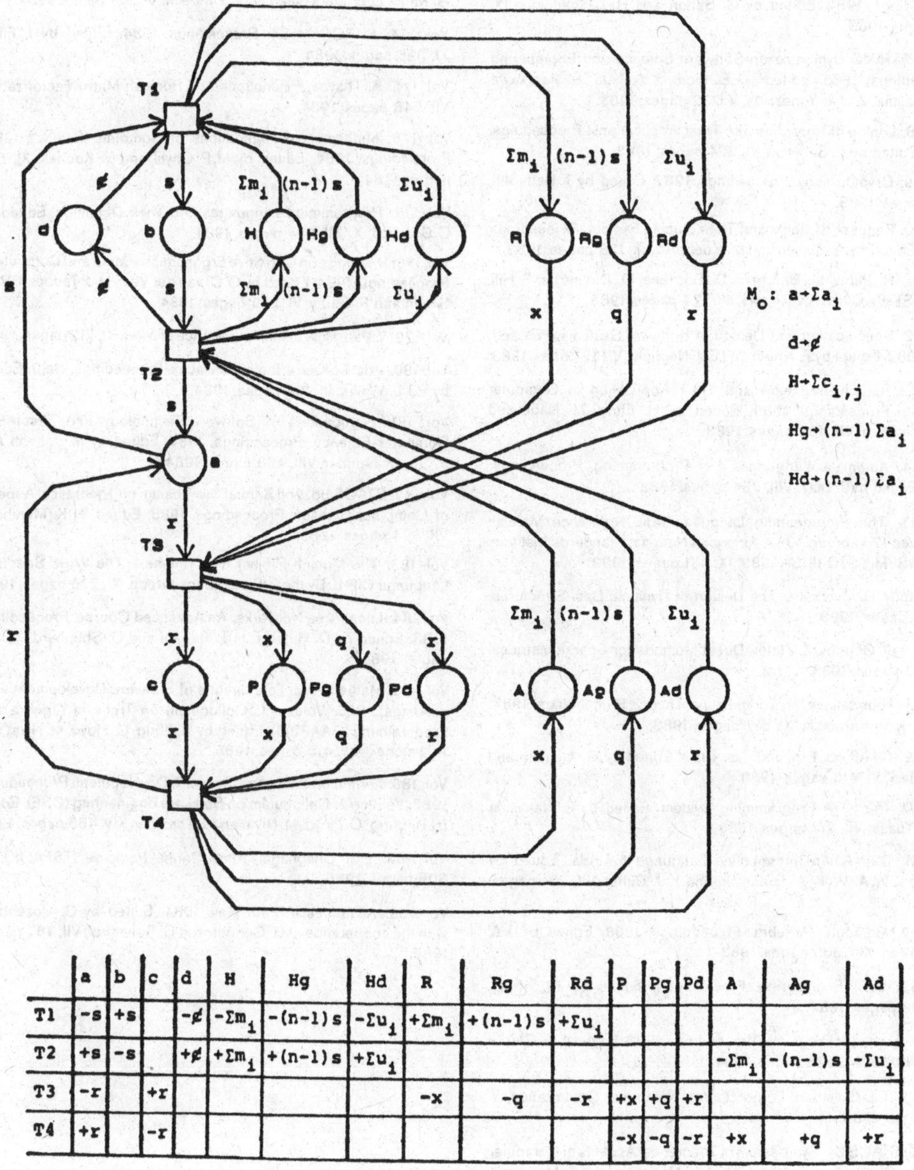

	a	b	c	d	H	Hg	Hd	R	Rg	Rd	P	Pg	Pd	A	Ag	Ad
T1	-s	+s		$-\emptyset$	$-\Sigma m_i$	-(n-1)s	$-\Sigma u_i$	$+\Sigma m_i$	+(n-1)s	$+\Sigma u_i$						
T2	+s	-s		$+\emptyset$	$+\Sigma m_i$	+(n-1)s	$+\Sigma u_i$							$-\Sigma m_i$	-(n-1)s	$-\Sigma u_i$
T3	-r		+r					-x	-q	-r	+x	+q	+r			
T4	+r		-r								-x	-q	-r	+x	+q	+r

fig.3

Vol. 142: Problems and Methodologies in Mathematical Software Production. Proceedings, 1980. Edited by P.C. Messina and A. Murli. VII, 271 pages. 1982.

Vol. 143: Operating Systems Engineering. Proceedings, 1980. Edited by M. Maekawa and L.A. Belady. VII, 465 pages. 1982.

Vol. 144: Computer Algebra. Proceedings, 1982. Edited by J. Calmet. XIV, 301 pages. 1982.

Vol. 145: Theoretical Computer Science. Proceedings, 1983. Edited by A.B. Cremers and H.P. Kriegel. X, 367 pages. 1982.

Vol. 146: Research and Development in Information Retrieval. Proceedings, 1982. Edited by G. Salton and H.-J. Schneider. IX, 311 pages. 1983.

Vol. 147: RIMS Symposia on Software Science and Engineering. Proceedings, 1982. Edited by E. Goto, I. Nakata, K. Furukawa, R. Nakajima, and A. Yonezawa. V. 232 pages. 1983.

Vol. 148: Logics of Programs and Their Applications. Proceedings, 1980. Edited by A. Salwicki. VI, 324 pages. 1983.

Vol. 149: Cryptography. Proceedings, 1982. Edited by T. Beth. VIII, 402 pages. 1983.

Vol. 150: Enduser Systems and Their Human Factors. Proceedings, 1983. Edited by A. Blaser and M. Zoeppritz. III, 138 pages. 1983.

Vol. 151: R. Piloty, M. Barbacci, D. Borrione, D. Dietmeyer, F. Hill, and P. Skelly, CONLAN Report. XII, 174 pages. 1983.

Vol. 152: Specification and Design of Software Systems. Proceedings, 1982. Edited by E. Knuth and E. J. Neuhold. V, 152 pages. 1983.

Vol. 153: Graph-Grammars and Their Application to Computer Science. Proceedings, 1982. Edited by H. Ehrig, M. Nagl, and G. Rozenberg. VII, 452 pages. 1983.

Vol. 154: Automata, Languages and Programming. Proceedings, 1983. Edited by J. Díaz. VIII, 734 pages. 1983.

Vol. 155: The Programming Language Ada. Reference Manual. Approved 17 February 1983. American National Standards Institute, Inc. ANSI/MIL-STD-1815A-1983. IX, 331 pages. 1983.

Vol. 156: M.H. Overmars, The Design of Dynamic Data Structures. VII, 181 pages. 1983.

Vol. 157: O. Østerby, Z. Zlatev, Direct Methods for Sparse Matrices. VIII, 127 pages. 1983.

Vol. 158: Foundations of Computation Theory. Proceedings, 1983. Edited by M. Karpinski, XI, 517 pages. 1983.

Vol. 159: CAAP'83. Proceedings, 1983. Edited by G. Ausiello and M. Protasi. VI, 416 pages. 1983.

Vol. 160: The IOTA Programming System. Edited by R. Nakajima and T. Yuasa. VII, 217 pages. 1983.

Vol. 161: DIANA, An Intermediate Language for Ada. Edited by G. Goos, W.A. Wulf, A. Evans, Jr. and K.J. Butler. VII, 201 pages. 1983.

Vol. 162: Computer Algebra. Proceedings, 1983. Edited by J.A. van Hulzen. XIII, 305 pages. 1983.

Vol. 163: VLSI Engineering. Proceedings. Edited by T.L. Kunii. VIII, 308 pages. 1984.

Vol. 164: Logics of Programs. Proceedings, 1983. Edited by E. Clarke and D. Kozen. VI, 528 pages. 1984.

Vol. 165: T.F. Coleman, Large Sparse Numerical Optimization. V, 105 pages. 1984.

Vol. 166: STACS 84. Symposium of Theoretical Aspects of Computer Science. Proceedings, 1984. Edited by M. Fontet and K. Mehlhorn. VI, 338 pages. 1984.

Vol. 167: International Symposium on Programming. Proceedings, 1984. Edited by C. Girault and M. Paul. VI, 262 pages. 1984.

Vol. 168: Methods and Tools for Computer Integrated Manufacturing. Edited by R. Dillmann and U. Rembold. XVI, 528 pages. 1984.

Vol. 169: Ch. Ronse, Feedback Shift Registers. II, 1-2, 145 pages. 1984.

Vol. 171: Logic and Machines: Decision Problems and Complexity. Proceedings, 1983. Edited by E. Börger, G. Hasenjaeger and D. Rödding. VI, 456 pages. 1984.

Vol. 172: Automata, Languages and Programming. Proceedings, 1984. Edited by J. Paredaens. VIII, 527 pages. 1984.

Vol. 173: Semantics of Data Types. Proceedings, 1984. Edited by G. Kahn, D.B. MacQueen and G. Plotkin. VI, 391 pages. 1984.

Vol. 174: EUROSAM 84. Proceedings, 1984. Edited by J. Fitch. XI, 396 pages. 1984.

Vol. 175: A. Thayse, P-Functions and Boolean Matrix Factorization, VII, 248 pages. 1984.

Vol. 176: Mathematical Foundations of Computer Science 1984. Proceedings, 1984. Edited by M.P. Chytil and V. Koubek. XI, 581 pages. 1984.

Vol. 177: Programming Languages and Their Definition. Edited by C.B. Jones. XXXII, 254 pages. 1984.

Vol. 178: Readings on Cognitive Ergonomics – Mind and Computers. Proceedings, 1984. Edited by G.C. van der Veer, M.J. Tauber, T.R.G. Green and P. Gorny. VI, 269 pages. 1984.

Vol. 179: V. Pan, How to Multiply Matrices Faster. XI, 212 pages. 1984.

Vol. 180: Ada Software Tools Interfaces. Proceedings, 1983. Edited by P.J.L. Wallis. III, 164 pages. 1984.

Vol. 181: Foundations of Software Technology and Theoretical Computer Science. Proceedings, 1984. Edited by M. Joseph and R. Shyamasundar. VIII, 468 pages. 1984.

Vol. 182: STACS 85. 2nd Annual Symposium on Theoretical Aspects of Computer Science. Proceedings, 1985. Edited by K. Mehlhorn. VII, 374 pages. 1985.

Vol. 183: The Munich Project CIP. Volume I: The Wide Spectrum Language CIP-L. By the CIP Language Group. XI, 275 pages. 1985.

Vol. 184: Local Area Networks: An Advanced Course. Proceedings, 1983. Edited by D. Hutchison, J. Mariani and D. Shepherd. X, 497 pages. 1985.

Vol. 185: Mathematical Foundations of Software Development. Proceedings, 1985. Volume 1: Colloquium on Trees in Algebra and Programming (CAAP'85). Edited by H. Ehrig, C. Floyd, M. Nivat and J. Thatcher. XIV, 418 pages. 1985.

Vol. 186: Formal Methods and Software Development. Proceedings, 1985. Volume 2: Colloquium on Software Engineering (CSE). Edited by H. Ehrig, C. Floyd, M. Nivat and J. Thatcher. XIV, 455 pages. 1985.

Vol. 187: F.S. Chaghaghi, Time Series Package (TSPACK). III, 305 pages. 1985.

Vol. 188: Advances in Petri Nets 1984. Edited by G. Rozenberg with the cooperation of H. Genrich and G. Roucairol. VII, 467 pages. 1985.